CIM

STUDY TEXT

Stage 1
New Syllabus

Customer Communications

In this August 2002 edition

- Updated for the new syllabus examinable in December 2002
- Practical guidance on e-marketing
- Material supporting integrative assessment

BPP Publishing
August 2002

First edition August 2002

ISBN 0 7517 4126 4

British Library Cataloguing-in-Publication Data
A catalogue record for this book
is available from the British Library

Published by

BPP Publishing Limited
Aldine House, Aldine Place
London W12 8AW

www.bpp.com

Printed in Great Britain by W M Print
45-47 Frederick Street
Walsall, West Midlands
WS2 9NE

We are grateful to the Chartered Institute of Marketing for permission to reproduce in this text the syllabus and past examination questions. We are also grateful to Karen Beamish of Stone Consulting for preparing the integrative assessment material.

	Page
How to use this study text	(v)
Syllabus and guidance notes	(xi)
List of websites	(xvii)
The exam paper	(xx)
Continuous assessment	(xxi)

■ Introduction ■ Structure and process ■ Preparing for Assignments ■ Presentation of the Assignment ■ Time management for Assignments ■ Tips for writing Assignments ■ Writing reports ■ Core and Optional Assignments.

Unit summary	(xxxv)

Part A: Customers and stakeholders

1	Who is the customer?	3
2	Focus on the customer	27

Part B: Buying behaviour

3	Buying behaviour	55

Part C: Implementing elements of the promotional mix

4	Marketing communications	85
5	The promotional mix	106
6	Advertising and sales promotion	130
7	PR and corporate communication	161
8	New technologies and media	188

Part D: Face-to-face communication

9	Communication skills	225
10	Planning effective messages	249
11	Oral and face-to-face communication	269
12	Written communication	303
13	Statistical and graphic information	345

Part E: Customer service and customer care

14	Customer care	377
15	ICT and customer service	409

Question bank 431

Pilot paper 441

Answer bank 451

Answers to pilot paper 479

Objective testing bank questions and answers 493

List of key concepts 505

Index 506

Order form

Review form & free prize draw

How to use this Study Text

Aims of this Study Text

To provide you with the knowledge and understanding, skills and applied techniques required for passing the exam

The Study Text has been written around the new CIM Stage 1 Syllabus (reproduced below, and cross-referenced to where in the text each topic is covered).

- It is **comprehensive**. We do not omit sections of the syllabus as the examiner is liable to examine any angle of any part of the syllabus - and you do not want to be left high and dry.
- It is **on-target** - we do not include any material which is not examinable. You can therefore rely on the BPP Study Text as the stand-alone source of all your information for the exam.

To allow you to study in the way that best suits your learning style and the time you have available, by following your personal Study Plan (see below)

You may be studying at home on your own until the date of the exam, or you may be attending a full-time course. You may like to (and have time to) read every word, or you may prefer to (or only have time to) skim-read and devote the remainder of your time to question practice. Wherever you fall in the spectrum, you will find the BPP Study Text meets your needs in designing and following your personal Study Plan.

To tie in with the other components of the BPP Effective Study Package to ensure you have the best possible chance of passing the exam

Recommended period of use	Elements of BPP Effective Study Package
3-12 months before exam	**Study Text** Acquisition of knowledge, understanding, skills and applied techniques
1-6 months before exam	**Practice and Revision Kit (9/2002)** There are numerous examination questions to try, graded by topic area, along with realistic suggested solutions prepared by marketing professionals in the light of the Examiner's Reports. The new Stage 1 syllabus kits include a bank of short-form interactive questions. The September 2002 edition will include the December 2001 and June 2002 papers, where relevant to the new syllabus.
1 –6 months before exam	**Success Tapes** Audio cassettes covering the vital elements of your syllabus in less than 90 minutes per subject. Each tape also contains exam hints to help you fine tune your strategy.

Settling down to study

By this stage in your career you may be a very experienced learner and taker of exams. But have you ever thought about *how* you learn? Let's have a quick look at the key elements required for effective learning. You can then identify your learning style and go on to design your own approach to how you are going to study this text - your personal Study Plan.

Key element of learning	Using the BPP Study Text
Motivation	You can rely on the comprehensiveness and technical quality of BPP. You've chosen the right Study Text - so you're in pole position to pass your exam!
Clear objectives and standards	Do you want to be a prizewinner or simply achieve a moderate pass? Decide.
Feedback	Follow through the examples in this text and do the Action Programme and the Quick Quizzes. Evaluate your efforts critically - how are you doing?
Study Plan	You need to be honest about your progress to yourself - do not be over-confident, but don't be negative either. Make your Study Plan (see below) and try to stick to it. Focus on the short-term objectives – completing two chapters a night, say - but beware of losing sight of your study objectives
Practice	Use the Quick Quizzes and Chapter Roundups to refresh your memory regularly after you have completed your initial study of each chapter

These introductory pages let you see exactly what you are up against. However you study, you should:

- **Read through the syllabus and teaching guide** - this will help you to identify areas you have already covered, perhaps at a lower level of detail, and areas that are totally new to you
- **Study the examination paper section**, where we show you the format of the exam (how many and what kind of questions etc).

Key study steps

The following steps are, in our experience, the ideal way to study for professional exams. You can of course adapt it for your particular learning style (see below).

Tackle the chapters in the order you find them in the Study Text. Taking into account your individual learning style, follow these key study steps for each chapter.

Key study steps	Activity
Step 1 *Chapter Topic List*	Study the list. Each numbered topic denotes a **numbered section** in the chapter.
Step 2 *Setting the Scene*	Read it through. It is designed to show you **why the topics in the chapter need to be studied** - how they lead on from previous topics, and how they lead into subsequent ones.
Step 3 *Explanations*	Proceed **methodically** through the chapter, reading each section thoroughly and making sure you understand.
Step 4 Key *Concepts*	**Key concepts** can often earn you **easy marks** if you state them clearly and correctly in an appropriate exam.
Step 5 *Exam Tips*	These give you a good idea of how the examiner tends to examine certain topics – pinpointing **easy marks** and highlighting **pitfalls**.
Step 6 *Note Taking*	Take **brief notes** if you wish, avoiding the temptation to copy out too much.
Step 7 *Marketing at Work*	Study each one, and try if you can to add flesh to them from your **own experience** - they are designed to show how the topics you are studying come alive (and often come unstuck) in the **real world**.
Step 8 *Action Programme*	Make a very good attempt at each one in each chapter. These are designed to put your **knowledge into practice** in much the same way as you will be required to do in the exam. Check the answer at the end of the chapter in the **Action Programme review**, and make sure you understand the reasons why yours may be different.
Step 9 *Chapter Roundup*	Check through it very carefully, to make sure you have grasped the **major points** it is highlighting
Step 10 *Quick Quiz*	When you are happy that you have covered the chapter, use the **Quick quiz** to check your recall of the topics covered. The answers are in the paragraphs in the chapter that we refer you to.

Developing your personal Study Plan

Preparing a Study Plan (and sticking closely to it) is one of the key elements in learning success.

First you need to be aware of your style of learning. There are four typical learning styles. Consider yourself in the light of the following descriptions. and work out which you fit most closely. You can then plan to follow the key study steps in the sequence suggested.

Learning styles	Characteristics	Sequence of key study steps in the BPP Study Text
Theorist	Seeks to understand principles before applying them in practice	1, 2, 3, 7, 4, 5, 8, 9, 10 (6 continuous)
Reflector	Seeks to observe phenomena, thinks about them and then chooses to act	
Activist	Prefers to deal with practical, active problems; does not have much patience with theory	1, 2, 8 (read through), 7, 4, 5, 9, 3, 8 (full attempt), 10 (6 continuous)
Pragmatist	Prefers to study only if a direct link to practical problems can be seen; not interested in theory for its own sake	8 (read through), 2, 4, 5, 7, 9, 1, 3, 8 (full attempt), 10 (6 continuous)

Next you should complete the following checklist.

Am I motivated? (a) ☐

Do I have an objective and a standard that I want to achieve? (b) ☐

Am I a theorist, a reflector, an activist or a pragmatist? (c) ☐

How much time do I have available per week, given: (d) ☐

- the standard I have set myself
- the time I need to set aside later for work on the Practice and Revision Kit
- the other exam(s) I am sitting, and (of course)
- practical matters such as work, travel, exercise, sleep and social life?

Now:

- take the time you have available per week for this Study Text (d), and multiply it by the number of weeks available to give (e). (e) ☐
- divide (e) by the number of chapters to give (f) (f) ☐
- set about studying each chapter in the time represented by (f), following the key study steps in the order suggested by your particular learning style.

This is your personal **Study Plan**.

Short of time?

Whatever your objectives, standards or style, you may find you simply do not have the time available to follow all the key study steps for each chapter, however you adapt them for your particular learning style. If this is the case, follow the Skim Study technique below (the icons in the Study Text will help you to do this).

Skim Study technique

Study the chapters in the order you find them in the Study Text. For each chapter, follow the key study steps 1-2, and then skim-read through step 3. Jump to step 9, and then go back to steps 4-5. Follow through step 7, and prepare outline Answers to the Action Programme (step 8). Try the Quick Quiz (step 10), following up any items you can't answer. You should probably still follow step 6 (note-taking).

Moving on...

However you study, when you are ready to embark on the practice and revision phase of the BPP Effective Study Package, you should still refer back to this Study Text:

- As a source of **reference** (you should find the list of Key Concepts and the index particularly helpful for this)
- As a **refresher** (the Chapter Roundups and Quick Quizzes help you here).

Important note: The *Customer Communications* Study Text

The *Customer Comunications* syllabus is designed to be highly practical, drawing together and applying the key skills and background knowledge obtained from the other Stage 1 modules. It is not really a new or discrete subject in its own right. Rather, it aims to develop and assess the student's ability to:

- Draw on information from a variety of sources, and learning from all Stage 1 areas
- Apply that information and learning in an integrated fashion, to workplace and/or simulated (case study) marketing projects

So, for example, when 'Market Research' appears in this Syllabus, it is assumed that you will have covered market research theory and techniques as part of your other studies.

This BPP Study Text for *Customer Communications* therefore relates to the syllabus in a practically integrative way. It is designed specifically to help you apply your learning from the other modules, whether to workplace tasks and assessments or to an examination Case Study.

Key Concepts

In order to help you transfer your learning to the real world, we use this feature to introduce you to some of the technical terms, abbreviations and 'buzzwords' used by marketing professionals. (These also appear in list form at the back of the text.)

Marketing at Work

The syllabus specifically requires students to develop an awareness of what marketers are actually doing 'out there': what new initiatives are being attempted; what is working and what is not; how different organisations tackle the same tasks. We encourage you to collect cuttings of ads, examples of

promotions, articles on marketing campaigns (for example in *Campaign, PR Week, Marketing Week* and other relevant journals and newspaper Media sections). We also encourage you whenever possible (and when professional discretion allows) to swap stories of successes, failures and house styles with other students and practitioners. Our 'Marketing at Work' section will help - but it should only be a prompter to the kind of insatiable curiosity about other people's efforts that makes a good marketing professional.

Action Programme

Customer communications may be assessed through workplace tasks, skills audits and/or an integrated Case Study approach. You must get used to attempting a wide variety of marketing tasks and analysing your performance according to relevant criteria. Our Action Programme exercises take you step by step through this active learning process.

Pilot paper and marking guide

We have included the CIM Pilot Paper, suggested answers and marking guide at the back of the text as an indication of the kind of questions you could expect in the exam.

A note on pronouns

On occasions in this Study Text, 'he' is used for 'he or she', 'him' for 'him or her' and so forth. Whilst we try to avoid this practice it is sometimes necessary for reasons of style. No prejudice or stereotyping according to sex is intended or assumed.

Syllabus and guidance notes

Aim

The Customer Communications module provides the entry level skills and application in the development and use of communications for Stage 1. It aims to provide participants with a working knowledge of customers' buying behaviour and the promotional mix as well as communications techniques.

Participants will not be expected to have any prior qualifications or experience in a marketing role. They will be expected to be conversant with the content of the Marketing Fundamentals module before undertaking this module.

Related statements of practice

Cb.1 Develop direct or indirect communications
Cb.2 Deliver direct or indirect communications
Gb.1 Support the management of customer relationships
Gb.2 Deliver effective customer service

Learning outcomes

Participants will be able to:

- Recognise organisations as open systems and explain the importance of relationships between the organisation and its suppliers, intermediaries, customers and other key stakeholders in a changing environment.
- Explain why it is important for marketers to understand consumer and industrial buying behaviour for marketing decisions.
- Explain the elements of the promotional mix and its fit with the marketing planning process.
- Explain the advantages and disadvantages of the range of communications tools available to an organisation.
- Develop internal and external communications using appropriate tools to suit a variety of target audiences and using an understanding of customer behaviour and customer information.
- Select appropriate verbal and non-verbal communications with people inside and outside the organisation.
- Demonstrate the importance of customers and customer service and apply customer care principles to create positive relationships with customers in a variety of contexts.

Knowledge and skill requirements

Element 1: Customers and stakeholders (20%)	
1.1	Explain what is meant by the terms 'customer', 'stakeholder' and 'user'
1.2	Demonstrate the fundamental importance of 'customers' to all forms of organisations, including services and the need to clearly identify them
1.3	Describe the link between the marketing concept, a customer focus and relationship marketing.
1.4	Appreciate the need for effective internal and external customer communications and their link to and role in maintaining customer focus, developing and sustaining good customer relations and relationship marketing in creating loyalty and customer retention.
1.5	List the factors that cause change in customers and the subsequent impact on marketing programmes.

Element 2: Buying behaviour (10%)	
2.1	Explain the difference between consumer buyer behaviour and organisational buyer behaviour.
2.2	Explain the importance of understanding buyer behaviour.
2.3	Describe the decision-making unit (DMU) and the roles of its constituents.
2.4	The decision making process (DMP) for consumers and organisations.
2.5	The impact and effect of the DMU and the DMP on the communications mix.

Element 3: Implementing elements of the promotional mix (50%)	
3.1	Explain the concept of, and need for, an integrated marketing communications approach and the links between communications and marketing planning.
3.2	Explain the role and importance of promotion in marketing.
3.3	Explain the structure and function of the communication process.
3.4	Describe the tools of promotion (the promotion mix).
3.5	Explain the planning process for developing and implementing promotional strategies and individual elements of the promotional mix.
3.6	Explain how above-the-line and below-the-line activities are used.
3.7	Explain the key stages and considerations when developing and designing advertisements.
3.8	Describe the role and scope of PR and its contribution to the promotional mix.
3.9	Explain the role of corporate identity, brand image and logos in corporate communication with customers
3.10	Distinguish between the different forms of integrated mail media, such as direct mail leaflets and mail order advertising.
3.11	Explain the role of point of sale (POS) material and how it is developing in response to changing customer needs.

3.12	Explain the role of packaging in the promotions mix.
3.13	Describe the role of exhibitions as a communications tool and their role in promotions.
3.14	Explain the role of information and communications technology (ICT) in communications, including digital TV and interactive marketing.
3.15	Describe current trends and developments in promotions and their impact on organisations.

Element 4: Face-to-face communication (10%)	
4.1	Describe the communication process and explain the importance and the advantages and disadvantages of different types of communication in a variety of face-to-face situations.
4.2	Identify barriers to communication and explain how they can be avoided and overcome.
4.3	Explain the communications planning process to produce effective strategies for improving alternative communications formats
4.4	Explain the importance of effective body language, tone, verbal and listening skills in communication and strategies for developing and improving verbal, non-verbal and listening skills.
4.5	Interpret, summarise and present oral, written and graphical information.
4.6	Explain key communication factors to consider in meetings, including arranging and convening a meeting, documentation involved and strategies for conducting a meeting.
4.7	Plan, prepare and deliver a presentation using appropriate and effective visual aids and media.
4.8	Use a variety of formats to communicate with internal and external customers including telephone, letters, memoranda, notices, reports and emails.

Element 5: Customer service and customer care (10%)	
5.1	Explain the concept of customer care and its importance in consumer, business-to-business, not-for-profit and public sector organisations.
5.2	Explain the importance of quality and customer care and methods of achieving quality.
5.3	Explain the relationship between customer care, customer focus and relationship marketing.
5.4	Explain the importance of obtaining customer feedback and devising contingencies for dealing with customer complaints.
5.5	Describe how to plan and establish a customer care programme.
5.6	Demonstrate an understanding of how ICT is used in customer service, for example through the use of databases.

Assessment

CIM will offer two forms of assessment for this module from which centres or participants may choose: written examination and continuous assessment. CIM may also recognise, or make joint awards for, modules at an equivalent level undertaken with other professional marketing bodies and educational institutions.

Overview and rationale

Approach

The ultimate importance of Customer Communications is based on the importance of both customers and communications to the success of organisations. Without identifying who customers are and their buying habits, we cannot begin to understand them. Without this fundamental understanding, we cannot develop appropriate and effective communications.

Therefore, the rationale for the module is that it provides marketers with a comprehensive range of communication tools aimed at establishing and maintaining relationships with our customers, both internal and external. In addition, it emphasises the role that we have to play in nurturing and developing our relationships.

The syllabus has now been greatly refined, ensuring both horizontal and vertical separation and integration.

- *Horizontally* the module includes customer behaviour and customer care moved from the Marketing Fundamentals module of the current Certificate syllabus. The use of marketing research, previously included in this module, has been moved to Marketing Environment to avoid overlap. The practical application of communications skills is reinforced in Marketing in Practice.
- *Vertically* this module provides a foundation for Marketing Relationships at Stage 2, which builds on this module by developing higher level of knowledge and understanding for communicating.

Syllabus content

This module, like the other modules across all levels of the CIM Syllabus, has been modified and improved. These modifications have tried to take into account the changes to The Marketing Customer Interface, to be renamed Marketing Relationships, the Stage 2 module which is a logical follow-on and progression from Customer Communications.

With this in mind, the percentages for indicative weightings are:

- Customers and stakeholders (20%)
- Buying behaviour (10%)
- Implementing elements of the promotional mix (50%)
- Face-to-face communication (10%)
- Customer service and customer care (10%)

Those tutors already familiar with the previous Customer Communications syllabus will be able to identify key changes to the content, particularly the inclusion of and greater emphasis on buying behaviour and customer care, previously covered in Marketing Fundamentals although both areas were covered in the previous syllabus to an extent, and building relationships with stakeholders.

Element 1 – Customers and stakeholders

The key message that needs to be communicated to participants of the importance of customer centred organisations. Tutors need to differentiate between the different types of 'customers' that marketing participants will communicate with. The difference between internal and external customers should be reinforced and the differences between customer and consumers should be emphasised. The link and the importance between good communications and maintaining and nurturing good relationships with customers should be discussed along with the many factors which cause changes in customers and the subsequent impact on marketing programmes. Tutors should introduce the concept of relationship marketing and its importance, although this will be covered in greater depth in Element 5. The key message here is the role of communication in managing this relationship, to guiding and supporting customers through changing circumstances and situations, including for example, the need to develop new products in response to changing consumer attitudes.

Element 2 – Buying behaviour

The concepts of the decision-making units and the role of stakeholders should be introduced in relation to the communication process. At a basic level, participants should be able to understand and identify the needs of different target audiences in both not for profit organisations and a variety of business sectors. Participants need to have a good understanding of understanding buying behaviour within decision making units and the impact of the DMU on both the decision making process and ultimately on the communications mix.

Element 3 – Implementing elements of the promotional mix

The key point here is that participants should be aware of basic theories about the communication process and customer behaviour so that participants can design effective customer communications at a basic level.

Consequently it would be appropriate to introduce the encoding/decoding process of communication. In addition, it would be appropriate to introduce participants to a simplified black box model of consumer behaviour and combine it with the various influences on consumer behaviour.

Participants should develop a comprehensive understanding of the range of promotion tools available to them and be able to develop and implement promotional activities and individual elements of the promotional mix. Therefore, practical exercises around developing advertisements, planning exhibitions, developing effective sales promotion and devising PR campaigns would all be useful practical measures to deepen understanding and assist in application.

The role of ICT should be discussed, including digital TV and interactive marketing. Participants are not expected to have technological expertise in this area. Tutors should impress upon candidates that they need to be aware of developments in this area and their dynamic nature and impact by reading appropriate marketing magazines and the quality press. Key points for discussion will include how digital technology will impact upon media decisions and how developments in digital technology (for example interactive catalogues, newsletters and video conferencing) will influence media decisions and improve communication.

A basic knowledge of consumer behaviour can be applied so that participants are capable of drafting a variety of communications, bearing in mind their target audience, and the use of appropriate tone and language.

The concept of and need for an integrated marketing communications approach should be introduced as a way of pulling together this element. It will introduce participants to the strategic role of communications however, more importantly, it will encourage participants to view and consider each element of the promotional mix as part of a cohesive whole, whose individual elements go towards creating an overall picture.

Finally, participants should look beyond current practice and give consideration to trends and developments in promotions and their impact on organisations.

Element 4 - Face-to-face communication

Tutors will again describe the communications process and explain the importance and the advantages and disadvantages of different types of communication in a variety of face-to-face situations. Tutors will explain the importance of effective body language, tone, verbal and listening skills in communication and strategies for developing and improving verbal, non-verbal and listening skills. Participants must also develop the skill of interpreting, summarising and presenting oral, written and graphical information. Good practice for participants would be to write reports that interpret customer data, market trends and issues relating to electronic methods of communication.

Participants should be able to identify barriers to communication and be able to explain how they can be avoided and overcome.

Key communication factors to be considered in planning key communications events must be given due consideration, for example, the key communication factors involved in planning and conducting meetings or planning and preparing a presentation. This could involve approaches to pitching for work from clients or dealing with presentations from suppliers. Tutors should also encourage participants to look at the importance of effective listening.

Tutors should also highlight the variety of formats used to communicate with internal and external customers, including telephone, letters, memoranda, notices, reports and emails.

Element 5 - Customer service and customer care

Customer Relationship Marketing is important in marketing today. As such, it is critical that participants understand the concept of customer service and customer care and its importance in consumer, business-to-business, not-for-profit and public sector organisations.

Tutors should explain the importance of quality and customer care and methods of achieving quality of service. Tutors should also explain the relationship between customer care, customer focus and relationship marketing.

Participants should be able to devise contingency plans for dealing with customer complaints in the context of a well-planned customer care programme. As a result of this, participants will be better informed at to how to develop and establish a customer care programme.

Finally, participants should demonstrate an understanding of how ICT is used as part of the delivery of customer service, for example building customer databases and using Customer Relationship Management (CRM) software programmes as part of automated customer handling processes.

List of Websites

The Chartered Institute of Marketing	
www.cim.co.uk www.cim.virtualinstiture.com www.cimtutors.com (Tutors only)	The CIM site with information and access to learning support for participants. Full details of all that's new in CIM's Educational offer including their
www.marketing portal.cim.co.uk	newsletter – Education Express.

Publications on line	
www.ft.com	Extensive research resources across all industry sectors, with links to more specialist reports.
www.the times.co.uk	One of the best online versions of a quality newspaper.
www.theeconomist.com	Useful links, and easily-searched archives of articles from back issues of the magazine.
www.mad.co.uk	Marketing Week magazine online.
www.marketing.haynet.com	Marketing magazine online.
www.stir.ac.uk/marketing/academy	Journal of Marketing Management online, the official Journal of the Academy of Marketing
http://mitsloan.mit.edu/smr/index.html	Free abstracts from Sloan Management Review articles
www.hbsp.harvard.edu	Free abstracts from Harvard Business Review articles
www.ebusiness.uk.com	Allows subscription to a new monthly paper-based magazine containing up to date case studies and updates on ebusiness trends
www.ecommercetimes.com	Daily enews on the latest ebusiness developments

Sources of useful information	
www.1to1.com	The Peppers and Rogers One-to-One Marketing site which contains useful information about the tools and techniques of relationship marketing
www.balancetime.com	The Productivity Institute provides free articles, a time management email newsletter, and other resources to improve personal productivity
www.bbc.co.uk/edu	The Learning Zone at BBC Education contains extensive educational resources, including the video, CD Rom, ability to watch TV programmes such as the News online, at your convenience, after they have been screened
www.busreslab.com	Useful specimen online questionnaires to measure customer satisfaction levels and tips on effective Internet marketing research
www.lifelonglearning.co.uk	Encourages and promotes Lifelong Learning through press releases, free articles, useful links and progress reports on the development of the University for Industry (UFI)
www.marketresearch.org.uk	The Market Research Society. Contains useful material on the nature of research, choosing an agency, ethical standards and codes of conduct for research practice
www.nielson-netratings.com	Details the current levels of banner advertising activity, including the creative content of the ten most popular banners each week
www.open.ac.uk	Some good Open University videos available for a broad range of subjects
www.open.gov.uk	Gateway to a wide range of UK government information
www.srg.co.uk	The Self Renewal Group – provides useful tips on managing your time, leading others, managing human resources, motivating others etc

www.statistics.gov.uk	Detailed information on a variety of consumer demographics from the Government Statistics Office
www.durlacher.com	The latest research on business use of the Internet, often with extensive free reports
www.cyberatlas.com	Regular updates on the latest Internet developments from a business perspective
www.nua.ie	Regular updates on the latest Internet developments from a business perspective
http://ecommerce.vanderbilt.edu	eLab is a corporate sponsored research centre at the Owen Graduate School of Management, Vanderbilt University
www.kpmg.co.uk www.eyuk.com www.pwcglobal.com	The major consultancy company websites contain useful research reports, often free of charge
http://web.mit.edu	Massachusetts Institute of Technology site has extensive research resources
www.adasoc.org.uk	Advertising Association
www.dma.org.uk	The Direct Marketing Association
www.theidm.co,uk	Institute of Direct Marketing
www.export.org.uk	Institute of Export
www.bl.uk	The British Library, with one of the most extensive book collections in the world
www.inst-mgt.org.uk	Institute of Management
www.ipd.co.uk	Institute of Personnel and Development
www.emerald-library.com	Full text journal articles on a range of business topics
www.whatis.com	Directory of Internet terminology
www.isi.gov.uk	The Information Society site with details of government projects, white papers and pending legislation
www.w3.org	An organisation responsible for defining worldwide standards for the Internet

Case studies

www.1800flowers.com	Flower and gift delivery service that allows customers to specify key dates when they request the firm to send them a reminder, together with an invitation to send a gift
www.amazon.co.uk	Classic example of how Internet technology can be harnessed to provide innovative customer service
www.broadvision.com	Broadvision specialises in customer 'personalisation' software. The site contains many useful case studies showing how communicating through the Internet allow you to find out more about your customers
www.doubleclick.net	DoubleClick offers advertisers the ability to target their advertisements on the web through sourcing of specific interest groups, ad display only at certain times of the day, or at particular geographic locations, or on certain types of hardware
www.facetime.com	Good example of a site that overcomes the impersonal nature of the Internet by allowing the establishment of real time links with a customer service representative
www.streamwave.co.uk	Online demonstrations of the latest technological developments which will form the basis of the next generation of Internet Marketing communication applications
ww.hotcoupons.com	Site visitors can key in their postcode to receive local promotions, and advertisers can post their offers on the site using a specially designed software package
www.streamwave.co.uk	Online demonstrations of the latest technological developments which will form the basis of the next generation of Internet Marketing communication applications

Overseas bodies

www.nikkeibp.asiabiztech.com	AsiaBizTech is a source of business and technology information focused upon Japan and Asia.
www.asiasource.org	Asia Source is a resource developed by the Asia Society to provide information on events across Asia
www.ecasa.org.za	The Electronic Commerce Association of South Africa promotes the use of electronic commerce to improve South Africa's commercial, industrial and government business efficiency
www.emc.be	The European Marketing Confederation aims are: To apply a common set of standards in marketing education and training across Europe, and align professional qualifications. To be recognised within the European Institutions as the body to accredit professional marketing qualifications and build links between professional training institutions and industry.
www.worldmarketing.org	The World Marketing Association was established for the purpose of bringing together the leadership of the marketing associations from around the world.
www.internet2.edu	Internet2, is a project to bring focus, energy and resources to a new development of standards of teaching, research and learning. It involves over 170 United States of America (USA) Universities working in partnership with industry and government. It is developing and deploying advanced network applications and technologies to accelerate the creation of tomorrow's Internet.
www.ec-europe.org	Electronic Commerce Europe is an association that promotes, co-ordinates and assists the development of electronic commerce in Europe
www.ansi.org	American National Standards Institute – represents US business interests with respect to the Internet
www.ama.org	American Marketing Association – US group dedicated to serving the educational and professional needs of marketing executives.
www.redherring.com	Red Herring is a business strategy magazine site, with a USA focus, providing information and articles on cutting-edge business and marketing strategy

The Exam Paper

Format of the paper

'Case study' format

Part A	Marks
Compulsory question relating to the case study	40
Part B	
Three questions from a choice of six relating to the case study (20 marks each)	60
	100

The new syllabus Pilot Paper, BPP's suggested answers and marking guide are reproduced at the back of the Study Text.

Analysis of Pilot Paper

Part A (compulsory question worth 40 marks)

1 Information given relating to the *Ford Fiesta*. As a product manager analyse data and recommend future marketing strategy in a formal report using graphs.

Part B (three questions, 20 marks each)

2 Presentations, agendas, memoranda
3 Sponsorship
4 Recruitment advertisement
5 Customer care and relationship marketing
6 Promotion tools
7 Presentations, visual presentations, ICT

GUIDE TO CONTINUOUS ASSESSMENT: CUSTOMER COMMUNICATIONS

- Aims and objectives of this guide
- Introduction
- Continuous assessment structure and process
- Preparing for assignments: general guide
- Presentation
- Time management
- Tips for writing assignments
- Writing reports

Aims and objectives of this *Guide to Continuous Assessment*

- To understand the scope and structure of the Continuous Assessment process
- To consider the benefits of learning through Continuous Assessment
- To assist students in preparation of their assignments
- To consider the range of communication options available to students
- To look at the range of potential assessment areas that assignments may challenge
- To examine the purpose and benefits of reflective practice
- To assist with time-management within the assessment process

Introduction

It is now over six years since the Chartered Institute of Marketing (CIM) introduced Continuous Assessment (ie assignment based assessment) as an alternative to the examination process.

At time of writing, there are over 80 CIM Approved Study Centres that offer the Continuous Assessment option as an alternative to examinations. This change in direction and flexibility in assessment was externally driven by industry, students and tutors alike, all of whom wanted a test of practical skills as well as a knowledge-based approach to learning.

At Stage 1, all modules are available via this Continuous Assessment route. Continuous Assessment is however optional, and examinations are still available. This will of course depend upon the nature of delivery within your chosen Study Centre.

Clearly, all of the Stage 1 subject areas lend themselves to assignment-based learning, due to their practical nature. The assignments that you will undertake provide you with an opportunity to be **creative in approach and in presentation.** They enable you to give a true demonstration of your marketing ability in a way that perhaps might be inhibited in a traditional examination situation.

Continuous assessment offers you considerable scope to produce work that provides existing and future **employers** with **evidence** of your **ability.** It offers you a **portfolio** of evidence which demonstrates your abilities and your willingness to develop continually your knowledge and skills. It will also, ultimately, help you frame your continuing professional development in the future.

It does not matter what type of organisation you are from, large or small, as you will find substantial benefit in this approach to learning. In some cases, students have made their own organisation central to their assessment and produced work to support their organisation's activities, resulting in subsequent recognition and promotion: a success story for this approach.

So, using your own organisation can be beneficial (especially if your employer sponsors you). However, it is equally valid to use a different organisation, as long as you are familiar enough with it to base your assignments on it. This is particularly useful if you are between jobs, taking time out, returning to employment or studying at university or college.

To take the Continuous Assessment option, you are required to register with a CIM Accredited Study Centre (ie a college, university, or distance learning provider). **Currently you would be unable to take the Continuous Assessment option as an independent learner**. If in doubt you should contact the CIM Education Division, the awarding body, who will provide you with a list of local Accredited Centres offering Continuous Assessment.

Structure and process

The **assignments** that you will undertake during your studies are normally set **by CIM centrally** and not usually by the study centre. All assignments are validated to ensure a structured, consistent, approach. This standardised approach to assessment enables external organisations to interpret the results on a consistent basis.

Each module at Stage 1 has one assignment, with four separate elements within it. This is broken down as follows.

- The **Core Section** is compulsory and worth 40% of your total mark.
- The **Elective Section** has four options, from which you must complete **two**. Each of these options is worth 25% of your total mark. Please note here that it is likely that in some Study Centres the option may be chosen for you. This is common practice and is done in order to maximise resources and support provided to students.
- The **Reflective Statement** is also compulsory. It is worth 10%. It should reflect what you feel about your learning experience during the module and how that learning has helped you in your career both now and in the future.

The purpose of each assignment is to enable you to demonstrate your ability to research, analyse and problem-solve in a range of different situations. You will be expected to approach your assignment work from a professional marketer's perspective, addressing the assignment brief directly, and undertaking the tasks required. Each assignment will relate directly to the syllabus module and will be applied against the content of the syllabus.

All of the Assignments clearly indicate the links with the syllabus and the assignment weighting (ie the contribution each assignment makes to your overall marks).

Once your Assignments have been completed, they will be marked by your accredited centre, and then **moderated** by a CIM External Moderator. When all the assignments have been marked, they are sent to CIM for further moderation. After this, all marks are forwarded to you by CIM (not your centre) in the form of an examination result. Your **centre** will be able to you provide you with some written feedback on overall performance, but **will not** provide you with any detailed mark breakdown.

Preparing for Assignments

The whole purpose of this guide is to assist you in presenting your assessment professionally, both in terms of presentation skills and overall content. In many of the assignments, marks are awarded for presentation and coherence. It might therefore be helpful to consider how best to present your assignment. Here you should consider issues of detail, protocol and the range of communications that could be called upon within the assignment.

Presentation of the Assignment

You should always ensure that you prepare two copies of your Assignment, keeping a soft copy on disc. On occasions assignments go missing, or second copies are required by CIM.

- Each Assignment should be clearly marked up with your name, your study centre, your CIM Student registration number and ultimately at the end of the assignment a word count. The assignment should also be word-processed.
- The assignment presentation format should directly meet the requirements of the assignment brief, (ie reports and presentations are the most called for communication formats). You **must** ensure that you assignment does not appear to be an extended essay. If it does, you will lose marks.
- The word limit will be included in the assignment brief. These are specified by CIM and must be adhered to.
- **Appendices** should clearly link to the assignment and can be attached as supporting documentation at the end of the report. However failure to reference them by number (eg Appendix 1) within the report and also marked up on the Appendix itself will lose you marks. Only use an Appendix if it is **essential** and clearly adds value to the overall Assignment. The Appendix is not a waste bin for all the materials you have come across in your research, or a way of making your assignment seem somewhat heavier and more impressive than it is.

Time management for Assignments

One of the biggest challenges we all seem to face day-to-day is that of managing time. When studying, that challenge seems to grow increasingly difficult, requiring a balance between work, home, family, social life and study life. It is therefore of pivotal importance to your own success for you to plan wisely the limited amount of time you have available.

Step 1: Find out how much time you have

Ensure that you are fully aware of how long your module lasts, and the final deadline (eg 10 weeks, 12 weeks, 14 weeks etc). If you are studying a module from September to December, it is likely that you will have only 10-12 weeks in which to complete your assignments. This means that you will be preparing assignment work continously throughout the course.

Step 2: Plan your time

Essentially you need to **work backwards** from the final deadline, submission date, and schedule your work around the possible time lines. Clearly if you have only 10-12 weeks available to complete three assignments, you will need to allocate a block of hours in the final stages of the module to ensure that all of your assignments are in on time. This will be critical as all assignments will be sent to CIM by a set day. Late submissions will not be accepted and no extensions will be awarded. Students who do not submit will be treated as a 'no show' and will have to resubmit for the next period and undertake an alternative assessment.

Step 3: Set priorities

You should set priorities on a daily and weekly basis (not just for study, but for your life). There is no doubt that this mode of study needs commitment (and some sacrifices in the short term). When your achievements are recognised by colleagues, peers, friends and family, it will all feel worthwhile.

Step 4: Analyse activities and allocate time to them

Consider the **range** of activities that you will need to undertake in order to complete the assignment and the **time** each might take. Remember, too, there will be a delay in asking for information and receiving it.

- Preparing terms of reference for the assignment, to include the following.

1	A short title
2	A brief outline of the assignment purpose and outcome
3	Methodology – what methods you intend to use to carry out the required tasks
4	Indication of any difficulties that have arisen in the duration of the assignment
5	Time schedule
6	Confidentiality – if the assignment includes confidential information ensure that this is clearly marked up and indicated on the assignment
7	Literature and desk research undertaken

  This should be achieved in one side of A4

- A literature search in order to undertake the necessary background reading and underpinning information that might support your assignment
- Writing letters and memos asking for information either internally or externally
- Designing questionnaires
- Undertaking surveys
- Analysis of data from questionnaires
- Secondary data search
- Preparation of first draft report

Always build in time to spare, to deal with the unexpected. This may reduce the pressure that you are faced in meeting significant deadlines.

Warning!

The same principles apply to a student with 30 weeks to do the work. However, a word of warning is needed. Do not fall into the trap of leaving all of your work to the last minute. If you miss out important information or fail to reflect upon your work adequately or successfully you will be penalised for both. Therefore, time management is important whatever the duration of the course.

Tips for writing Assignments

Everybody has a personal style, flair and tone when it comes to writing. However, no matter what your approach, you must ensure your assignment meets the **requirements of the brief** and so is comprehensible, coherent and cohesive in approach.

Think of preparing an assignment as preparing for an examination. Ultimately, the work you are undertaking results in an examination grade. Successful achievement of all four modules in a level results in a qualification.

There are a number of positive steps that you can undertake in order to ensure that you make the best of your assignment presentation in order to maximise the marks available.

Step 1 – Work to the Brief

Ensure that you identify **exactly what the assignment asks you to do**.

- If it asks you to be a marketing manager, then immediately assume that role.
- If it asks you to prepare a report, then present a report, not an essay or a letter.
- Furthermore, if it asks for 2,500 words, then do not present 1,000 or 4,000 unless in both instances it is clearly justified, agreed with your tutor and a valid piece of work.

Identify if the report should be **formal or informal**, who it should be **addressed to**, its **overall purpose** and its **potential use** and outcome. Understanding this will ensure that your assignment meets fully the requirements of the brief and addresses the key issues included within it.

Step 2 – Addressing the Tasks

It is of pivotal importance that you address **each** of the tasks within the assignment. **Many students fail to do this** and often overlook one of the tasks or indeed part of the tasks.

Many of the assignments will have two or three tasks, some will have even more. You should establish quite early on, which of the tasks:

- Requires you to collect information
- Provides you with the framework of the assignment, ie the communication method.

Possible tasks will include the following.

- *Compare and contrast.* Take two different organisations and compare them side by side and consider the differences ie the **contrasts** between the two.
- *Carry out primary or secondary research.* Collect information to support your assignment and your subsequent decisions
- *Prepare a plan.* Some assignments will ask you to prepare a plan for an event or for a marketing activity – if so provide a step by step approach, a a rationale, a time-line, make sure it is measurable and achievable. Make sure your actions are very specific and clearly explained. (Make sure your plan is SMART.)
- *Analyse a situation.* This will require you to collect information, consider its content and present an overall understanding of the actual situation that exists. This might include looking at internal and external factors and how the current situation evolved.
- *Make recommendations.* The more advanced your get in your studies, the more likely it is that you will be required to make recommendations. Firstly **considering and evaluating your options** and then making justifiable **recommendations**, based on them.
- *Justify decisions.* You may be required to justify your decision or recommendations. This will require you to explain fully how you have arrived at this decision and to show why, supported by relevant information, this is the right way forward. In other words, you should not make decisions in a vacuum; as a marketer your decisions should always be informed by context.

- *Prepare a presentation.* This speaks for itself. If you are required to prepare a presentation, ensure that you do so, preparing clearly defined PowerPoint or overhead slides that are not too crowded and that clearly express the points you are required to make.
- *Evaluate performance.* It is very likely that you will be asked to evaluate a campaign, a plan or even an event. You will therefore need to consider its strengths and weaknesses, why it succeeded or failed, the issues that have affected it, what can you learn from it and, importantly, how can you improve performance or sustain it in the future.

All of these points are likely requests included within a task. Ensure that you identify them clearly and address them as required.

Step 3 – Information Search

Many students fail to realise the importance of collecting information to **support** and **underpin** their assignment work. However, it is vital that you demonstrate to your centre and to the CIM your ability to **establish information needs**, obtain **relevant information** and **utilise it sensibly** in order to arrive at appropriate decisions.

You should establish the nature of the information required, follow up possible sources, time involved in obtaining the information, gaps in information and the need for information.

Consider these factors very carefully. CIM are very keen that students are **seen** to collect information, **expand** their mind and consider the **breadth** and **depth** of the situation. In your *Personal Development Portfolio*, you have the opportunity to complete a **Resource Log**, to illustrate how you have expanded your knowledge to aid your personal development. You can record your additional reading and research in that log, and show how it has helped you with your portfolio and assignment work.

Step 4 – Develop an Assignment Plan

Your **assignment** needs to be structured and coherent, addressing the brief and presenting the facts as required by the tasks. The only way you can successfully achieve this is by **planning the structure** your Assignment in advance.

Earlier on in this unit, we looked at identifying your tasks and, working backwards from the release date, in order to manage time successfully. The structure and coherence of your assignment needs to be planned with similar signs.

In planning out the Assignment, you should plan to include **all the relevant information as requested** and also you should plan for the use of models, diagrams and appendices where necessary.
Your plan should cover your:

- Introduction
- Content
- Main body of the assignment
- Summary
- Conclusions and recommendations where appropriate

Step 5 – Prepare Draft Assignment

It is good practice to always produce a **first draft** of a report. You should use it to ensure that you have met the aims and objectives, assignment brief and tasks related to the actual assignment. A draft document provides you with scope for improvements, and enables you to check for accuracy, spelling, punctuation and use of English.

Step 6 – Prepare Final Document

In the section headed 'Presentation of the Assignment' in this unit, there are a number of components that should always be in place at the beginning of the assignment documentation, including **labelling** of the assignment, **word counts**, **appendices** numbering and presentation method. Ensure that you **adhere to the guidelines presented**, or alternatively those suggested by your study centre.

Writing reports

Students often ask 'what do they mean by a report?' or 'what should the report format include?'.

There are a number of approaches to reports, formal or informal: some report formats are company specific and designed for internal use, rather than external reporting.

For Continuous Assessment process, you should stay with traditional formats.

Below is a suggested layout of a Management Report Document that might assist you when presenting your assignments.

- ***A Title Page*** – includes the title of the report, the author of the report and the receiver of the report
- ***Acknowledgements*** – this should highlight any help, support, or external information received and any extraordinary co-operation of individuals or organisations
- ***Contents Page*** – providing a clearly structured pathway of the contents of the report – page by page
- ***Executive Summary*** – a brief insight into purpose, nature and outcome of the report, in order that the outcome of the report can be quickly established
- ***Main body of the report divided into sections, which are clearly labelled***. Suggested labelling would be on a numbered basis eg:
  - 1.0 Introduction
  - 1.1 Situation Analysis
  - 1.1.1 External Analysis
  - 1.1.2 Internal Analysis
- ***Conclusions*** – draw the report to a conclusion, highlighting key points of importance, that will impact upon any recommendations that might be made
- ***Recommendations*** – clearly outline potential options and then recommendations. Where appropriate justify recommendations in order to substantiate your decision
- ***Appendices*** – ensure that you only use appendices that add value to the report. Ensure that they are numbered and referenced on a numbered basis within the text. If you are not going to reference it within the text, then it should not be there
- ***Bibliography*** – whilst in a business environment a bibliography might not be necessary, for an **assignment-based report it is vital**. It provides an indication of the level of research, reading and collecting of relevant information that has taken place in order to fulfil the requirements of the assignment task. Where possible, and where relevant, you could provide academic references within the text, which should of course then provide the basis of your bibliography. References should realistically be listed alphabetically and in the following sequence

- Author's name and edition of the text
  - Date of publication
  - Title and sub-title (where relevant)
  - Edition 1st, 2nd etc
  - Place of publication
  - Publisher
  - Series and individual volume number where appropriate.

Resources to support Continuous Assessment

The aim of this guidance is to present you with a range of questions and issues that you should consider, based upon the assignment themes. The detail to support the questions can be found within your BPP Study Text and the 'Core Reading' recommended by CIM.
Additionally you will find useful support information within the CIM Student website www.cim.co.uk -: www.cimvirtualinstitute.com, where you can access a wide range of marketing information and case studies. You can also build your own workspace within the website so that you can quickly and easily access information specific to your professional study requirements. Other websites you might find useful for some of your assignment work include www.wnim.com - (What's New in Marketing) and also www.connectedinmarketing.com - another CIM website.
Other websites include: -

www.mad.com	-	Marketing Week
www.ft.com	-	Financial Times
www.thetimes.com	-	The Times newspaper
www.theeconomist.com	-	The Economist Magazine
www.marketing.haynet.com	-	The Marketing Magazine
www.ecommercetimes.com	-	Daily news on e-business developments
www.open.gov.uk	-	Gateway to a wide range of UK government information
www.adassoc.org.uk	-	The Advertising Association
www.marketresearch.org.uk	-	The Marketing Research Society

Core and Optional Assignments

We are not at liberty to give you specific guidance on the core or optional elements of the Customer Communications Assignment. However, it will be useful to consider the possible assignment themes, and how you might approach the subject areas in terms of research, a questioning approach and meeting the requirements of the brief. The format is usually predetermined by CIM, and generally takes the form of a report or presentation.

Possible Assignment Themes

Although we cannot publish the contents of the assignment, we can provide you with an indication of some **possible themes** that the assignment and its elements will focus upon. Assignment themes and weighting will change with each sitting every six months. The purpose of this section will therefore be, to provide you with key questions and issues that you should consider based around the subject areas. You must be clear that whilst these are valid points you may not need to use them all (or alternatively, you may be required to look much further afield.)

You will find your learning from Marketing Fundamentals particularly useful within this module. You might want to look back at key areas and remind yourself of its importance.

For the purpose of Customer Communications, the assignment themes include: -

Possible Core (40%)

Stakeholder Communications

Possible Electives (50% in total)

- Assessing Customer Care and Customer Service Provision
- Communication Skills – Meetings and Presentations relating to below-the line media
- Comparison of Consumer and Business-to-Business issues within Customer Communications
- Examining cost effective methods of below-the-line media

Reflective Statement

Reflecting upon your learning experience, what you did well, how you did it and how it might influence and direct your future.

Before moving on to the detail of the assignment, it might be useful to focus your mind on the **learning outcomes** of the Customer Communications module, as well as the **related skills** for marketers. Look back at page (9) to see this again.

(i) By considering what the learning outcomes are for the module, you will understand the scope of the task ahead of you in terms of completing the Continuous Assessment process.

(ii) Key skills are undoubtedly something that most students will have come across by now. They demonstrate the importance of not just **acquiring knowledge**, but being able to **apply it** through the use of a range of related key skills for marketers. In undertaking Continuous Assessment project work, you will find that the key skills are not only used, but also continually stretched and developed.

Possible Core - Stakeholder Audience

Stakeholder communications is concerned with understanding successful communication to a range of different audiences that directly impact upon the organisation. You would be advised to consider the **role of communication** and how to effectively communicate with stakeholders.

Below is a list of **key points**, **questions** and **considerations** that you will find worthwhile thinking about when the assignment is released to you by your Study Centre. Clearly you may not need to use all of this information, and there may be broader areas that you find you need to cover, but what follows is a starting point.

- What is a stakeholder – can you **define** it?
- Who are **your organisation's** stakeholders?
- How **important** are these stakeholders to your organisation?
- What **influence** do these stakeholders have upon your organisation?
- How often do you **communicate** with them?
- What **methods of communication** do you use for each group – are you able to describe them?
- What are the different **types of message** you send to your stakeholders?
- **Justify** your existing communication methods. What drives them - is it corporate style, budget restrictions, etc?
- What **impact** does your communication have – it is positive or negative?
- Could it be improved, streamlined and be more **effective**?
- What **other communication options** are available to you?
- What communication options are the most **appropriate** to each stakeholder group?
- How can you **evaluate** their success?
- Think about how communications could be **improved**, and justify your decisions. That means that once you have selected a route, you should:
  - Clearly explain why you think this is the most appropriate communication method
  - Why it will be effective
  - How it could further develop important stakeholder relationships.

Possible Elective Options

For the second and third element of your assignment you (or indeed your Study Centre) will choose two from a selection of four options. Again, we are not at liberty to disclose the assignment and can only provide you with potential issues, questions and considerations that you may want to incorporate in your assignment in the future.

Possible option: Assessing Customer Care and Customer Service Provision

Below is a list of **key points**, **questions** and **considerations** that you will find worthwhile thinking about when the assignment is released to you by your Study Centre. Clearly you may not need to use all of this information, and there may be broader areas that you find you need to cover, but what follows is a starting point.

- What is **customer care**?
- What are **customer services**?
- **Who** are your customers?
- How **important** are they?
- Why do organisations **lose** their customers?
- Why is **customer satisfaction** often so difficult to achieve?
- Where does **quality** fit into customer care?
- How does quality **enhance** customer relationships?
- What do you understand by **customer focus**?
- What is a **customer care system**?
- What are the **key processes** that organisations should implement to ensure high levels of customer care?
- Why is **relationship marketing** such a pivotal aspect of customer care?
- Do you feel that **ICT** can help to improve customer care?
- If you were setting up a **customer care programme**, what would the components of the programme be?
- What mechanisms can be used to measure customer care **effectiveness**, and **evaluate** its overall success?

Possible option - Communication Skills – Meetings and Presentations relating to below-the-line media

This particular element will focus on your skills in setting up meetings and developing professional presentations. There will be a scenario that underpins this particular element that will test your knowledge of other elements of the Customer Communications syllabus.

Below is a list of **key points**, **questions** and **considerations** that you will find worthwhile thinking about when the assignment is released to you by your Study Centre. Clearly you may not need to use all of this information, and there may be broader areas that you find you need to cover, but what follows is a starting point.

Promotional elements to consider:

- What is **below-the-line** media?
- What **forms** can it take?
- How does the **promotional mix** support the marketing mix?
- Why is **promotion** such an important aspect of marketing?
- What **elements** of the promotional mix are most relevant to below-the-line media?
- What are the key **advantages** of below-the-line media?
- How are **below-the-line activities** used in your organisation?
- How can below-the-line activities be used to underpin the **brand** and **corporate image** of he organisation?
- How can below-the-line activities be used **internally** within the organisation?

Meetings

- What are the **objectives** of meetings?
- What **types of meetings** can you hold or attend?
- What are the important components of **setting up** a meeting?
- What are the critical **resources** you might need to set up meetings?
- What **administrative processes** and meeting **documents** are required when setting up a meeting?
- What is an **agenda** and what should it contain?
- Why is it important to have a **chairperson** for the meeting, and a secretary?
- What are meeting **minutes** and why are they important?
- Why is it important to **close** a meeting properly?

Presentations

- Why is it important to have **objectives** for meetings and presentations?
- When **preparing** for presentations what are the key considerations?
- When preparing a **PowerPoint** presentation, what are the key issues?
- **Resources** for presentations (projector, support materials and other visual aids)

Possible option - Comparison of Consumer and Business-to-Business issues within Customer Communications

There are a wide number of issues relating to this particular option and it requires you to have a good understanding of the key differences between consumer and business-to-business marketing in the context of customer communications.

Below is a list of **key points**, **questions** and **considerations** that you will find worthwhile thinking about when the assignment is released to you by your Study Centre. Clearly you may not need to use all of this information, and there may be broader areas that you find you need to cover, but what follows is a starting point.

- Define what is meant by **business-to-business** marketing. Can you identify the **key characteristics** of business-to-business markets?
- What is **consumer-based marketing**? Can you identify the key characteristics of consumer-based marketing?
- Can you identify the **key differences** between the two?
- Why is it important to understand **buyer-behaviour** for both consumer-based and business-to-business marketing communications?
- Do you know what the **decision making process** (DMP) is for each of the two sectors?
- What is the **decision-making unit** (DMU) for each sector?
- How can decision-making units be influenced by the **communications mix**?
- Can you identify the most **effective communications** for consumer markets?
- Do you know the **preferred methods** for communicating with business-to-business markets?
- Why does the **marketing communications effort** need to be different for consumer and business-to-business markets?
- **Communication barriers** are quite significant in many markets, including internal markets. What are the typical barriers to communication that might exist and how might you overcome them?
- Can you think of any barriers that might exist that are **specific** to the business-to-business and consumer based markets?
- How might **marketing research** be used to help establish the best methods of communications for both sectors?
- What effect has **ICT** had on communications in both business-to-business and consumer sectors?

Possible option - Examining cost effective methods of below-the-line Media

This is the final elective option for Elements 2 and 3 of Customer Communications, and reflects very much upon the knowledge required for Elective Option 2. Of course, the context of the assignment will differ.

As with the other elective options, below is a list of **key points**, **questions** and **considerations** that you will find worthwhile thinking about when the assignment is released to you by your Study Centre. Clearly you may not need to use all of this information, and there may be broader areas that you find you need to cover, but what follows is a starting point.

The key questions and issues include:

- What is your understanding of **below-the-line media** and what are the key forms of media included within it?
- What is your understanding of **above-the-line media** and what are the key forms of media included within it?
- In the main, below-the-line media is a more **cost effective** method of communicating with customers – why is this so?
- When sending out customer communications it is important to **target** your market effectively. Segmentation and targeting are closely linked. How do you use segmentation in order to establish who your target market is?
- What are the most **effective methods** of below-the-line media within your own organisation?
- Are you able to **recommend** any suggestions for change – if so what would they be?
- How would you communicate change to the **stakeholders** you currently communicate to?
- How would you **measure the success** of below-the-line media campaigns?
- Has the way in which your organisation and its competitors undertake customer communications changed in the past few years? If so, how and why?
- What do you think are the current **trends** and developments in marketing communications?
- What are the key **drivers of change** in the way in which organisations communicate with their customers?
- What impact has **ICT** had on customer and stakeholder communications?

Reflective Statement

The final aspect of your assignment may ask you to prepare a 500 word reflective statement, where you will be required to reflect upon your **activities** and your **personal development** in the selected areas for the duration of your course. This is a very underestimated part of the assignment, and one many students fail to address effectively. It is this part of the assignment that actually brings all of your work together.

There are a number of **key components** that you should always include.

- Where did you start off at the very beginning of this course? What were your particular strengths, weaknesses and knowledge gaps within Customer Communications?
- What activities have you been involved in to achieve completion of your assignments?
- What did you do well?
- What could you have done better, and why?
- Do you feel that you have improved throughout the module?
- What value has this learning process added to your overall learning experience?
- Do you feel that the work undertaken will benefit you in your future personal development and organisational development?
- How will you continue to develop this area in the future? How do you anticipate you might use it?

One of the key considerations must be the 'future'. Many people see reflection as 'thinking about something that has happened in the past'. Whilst this is true, we must also reflect upon 'how this will help us in the future'.

You may find that as a result of this learning process your **career aspirations** have completely changed. You may find that you have become more confident and ambitious, and that through consolidating your learning in this way you have considerably more to offer. If this is the case do not be afraid to say so, and demonstrate how the whole learning process has influenced you and how it will drive you forward.

Earlier in this guide you were provided with a range of skills in relation to approaches to assignments, research and report formation. With the above information and the approaches describe you should be able to produce a professional assignment. Refer back to the earlier part of the unit on how to present assignments and research if necessary.

Where appropriate provide relevant **examples** so that you can show your tutor and CIM what your organisation does. This will help to back you up in your evaluation and justifications.

Unit Summary: Customer Communications

You may have come to the end of the unit feeling that this is going to be hard work. Well you would be right in thinking this. But, as we suggested in the early part of this unit, it is likely to be one of the most beneficial learning processes you will embark upon, as you take your CIM qualifications.

The process of development prepares you to be a marketing professional in the future. It provides you with practical experience and an opportunity to apply the theory in a practical situation. You will demonstrate to your existing or future employer that you have the ability to learn, develop, grow, progress and contribute significantly to the marketing activity within the organisation.

You have been provided with a range of hints and tips in presentation of assignments, development and approaches to your core and optional assignments.

Continuous Assessment, like examinations, is a serious business, and you should consider the level of ongoing commitment that this process requires. The more you put in the more you are likely to get out. It will not be enough to leave all of your work to the end of the course as it destroys the ethos and benefit of the assignment. Use it as a continuous development tool for the duration of the course. A structured approach to the learning process will maximise its benefits to you.

We have tried to give you some insight into how to approach the core and optional assignments that you will embark upon. However, please ensure that you read the assignment carefully when it arrives, and address it directly. We have aimed to show you the level of detail you should enter into in order to produce an effective and professional piece of work.

The CIM qualifications are professional qualifications and therefore, to be successful you must take a professional approach to your work

Part A

Gathering, analysing and presenting information

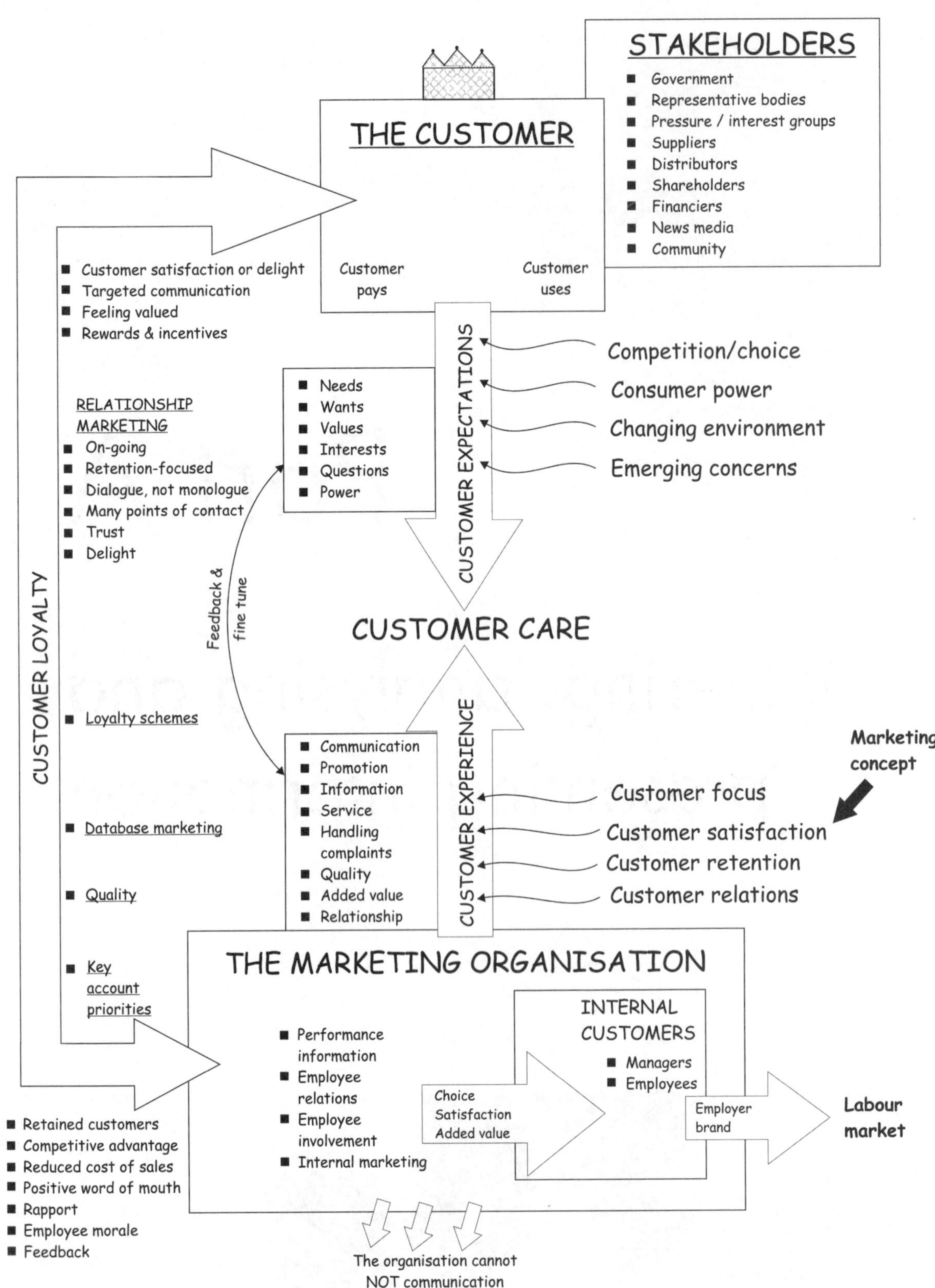
STAKEHOLDERS
Government
Representative bodies
Pressure / interest groups
Suppliers
Distributors
Shareholders
Financiers
News media
Community
THE CUSTOMER
Customer pays
Customer uses
Customer satisfaction or delight
Targeted communication
Feeling valued
Rewards & incentives
RELATIONSHIP MARKETING
On-going
Retention-focused
Dialogue, not monologue
Many points of contact
Trust
Delight
Needs
Wants
Values
Interests
Questions
Power
CUSTOMER EXPECTATIONS
Competition/choice
Consumer power
Changing environment
Emerging concerns
CUSTOMER LOYALTY
Feedback & fine tune
CUSTOMER CARE
Loyalty schemes
Database marketing
Quality
Key account priorities
Communication
Promotion
Information
Service
Handling complaints
Quality
Added value
Relationship
CUSTOMER EXPERIENCE
Marketing concept
Customer focus
Customer satisfaction
Customer retention
Customer relations
THE MARKETING ORGANISATION
Performance information
Employee relations
Employee involvement
Internal marketing
Choice
Satisfaction
Added value
INTERNAL CUSTOMERS
Managers
Employees
Employer brand
Labour market
Retained customers
Competitive advantage
Reduced cost of sales
Positive word of mouth
Rapport
Employee morale
Feedback
The organisation cannot NOT communication

Who is the customer?

1

Chapter Topic List	
1	Setting the scene
2	Customers
3	Stakeholders
4	Who *exactly* is the customer?

Learning Outcomes

- ☑ Distinguish customers from consumers or users, and external customers from internal customers.
- ☑ Understand the nature of the marketing organisation as an open system.
- ☑ Identify the various stakeholders and audiences of the organisation's marketing communications.
- ☑ Begin to appreciate the importance of customer communications.
- ☑ Begin to appreciate the need to identify and understand customers in order to communicate effectively and build relationships with them.

Syllabus References

- ☑ Explain what is meant by the terms 'customer', 'stakeholder' and 'user' (1.1)
- ☑ Demonstrate the fundamental importance of 'customers' to all forms of organisations, including services and the need to clearly identify them. (1.2)

Key Concepts Introduced

- Customer
- Internal customer
- User
- Stakeholder

1 Setting the scene

1.1 You may already realise that this is a very broad subject, given the scope of the words 'customer' and 'communications'! You should also, however, begin to see how intensely practical and widely relevant it is.

Focus on the customer

1.2 Customer Communications is important, first of all, because **the customer is important**. In Chapter 2 of this Text, we will discuss in detail the importance of the customer to organisations of all kinds, and the need to centre marketing communications on the customer in order to secure – not just product awareness and purchase – but, increasingly, loyalty and on-going relationship. '

1.3 The key point is: **the whole commercial process depends on the customer**. Without customers, there would be no economic activity; no marketing.

- The Chartered Institute of Marketing defines marketing as: 'the management process which identifies, anticipates and supplies **customer requirements** efficiently and profitably'.
- Marketing guru Philip Kotler asserts that: 'To succeed in today's marketplace companies must be **customer focused**, winning customers from competitors and keeping them by delivering greater value. (*Marketing: An Introduction*)
- Alison Baverstock *(Commonsense Marketing for Non-Marketers)* puts it even more bluntly, suggesting that the most important advice in business is the following sentence.

  'Marketing means **thinking about the customer**.'

1.4 The focus of Customer Communications is the customer. Does that sound obvious? Perhaps it should. But consider the following examples of marketing communications, the likes of which you probably encounter every day.

- A personalised letter from a real estate agent offering to sell your house. (You are a renter.)
- A brochure for a DVD player which describes in detail the technical specifications of the machine and the advanced science underlying them.
- An automated telephone system which invites callers to select from a long and complicated menu of available departments and types of call.
- A customer service person trying to explain to a disappointed customer how difficult and complex an operation it is to supply the service as advertised.
- A sales person in a retail outlet who is 'busy' talking to colleagues while someone is waiting to ask a question.

- A television advertisement that exploits sexual or racial stereotypes to attract viewers' attention.

What might the marketing organisation be putting first in each case? Its preferred selling strategy or excellence in product development; the requirements of its administrative structure and systems; the culture of its work force or its advertising agency, perhaps. But not the needs, wants, expectations and perceptions of its customers.

1.5 Throughout your studies for this subject, and for each example, exercise and assessment question you encounter, you will be invited to ask yourself the following questions.

- **Who is the customer** in this relationship or transaction?
- **What are the needs of the customer** in this relationship or transaction?
- **What are the communication needs of the customer**, as the target audience for this marketing message?

Focus on communications

1.6 Customer Communications is important, secondly, because **communications are important**.

1.7 Communication is at the heart of all transactions and relationships with customers.

(a) **Communications may be part of the product or service itself**: for example, in the case of media, information and communications technology (ICT) and Internet markets; education, training and consultancy; advice and information services.

(b) **Communications are central to the exchange or transaction process: they 'help people to buy'**.

- **Informing** and making potential customers aware of the organisation's offering
- **Persuading** current and potential customers of the desirability of entering into an exchange relationship
- **Reminding** customers of the benefits of past transactions with a view to encouraging repeat purchase
- **Differentiating** between competing offerings, helping consumers to decide which transactions to make and stimulating competition

(You might like to remember these aims by the acronym DRIP.)

(c) **Communications create and sustain brand identity**. A 'brand' is a name or term, symbol or design – and associated messages – which identify the maker or seller of a product and shape consumer's perceptions of that product. Branding helps marketers to segment markets; to gain name awareness; to build up associations and expectations in regard to the product; and to foster recognition of and loyalty to the brand. (Think about 'household name' brands such as Coca Cola, Nike sportswear or Sony entertainment systems.)

(d) **Communications define and create relationships with the customer**. Relationships depend on communication, and the quality of relationships depends on the quality of communication: it's as true in the marketplace as in our personal lives. Regular, appropriately targeted and personalised marketing communications – such as product updates, related product offers, special incentives and rewards, and opportunities to give feedback – look beyond one-off transactions to on-going association and involvement.

(e) **Communications are part of customer service and customer care**. Effective service requires willingness to give accurate, timely and relevant information to customers - and willingness to listen, in return, to customers' needs, wants and feedback. The manner of communication, particularly in front-line customer service roles handling transactions, queries and complaints, is a vital ingredient in customer perceptions of service.

(f) **Communications are key to competitive advantage**. Forsyth (*Communicating with Customers*) suggests that 'If products are essentially similar, then poor communication alone may be sufficient to aim a customer away from one supplier and towards another.' Effective customer-focused communications may be a way of differentiating the organisation and its offering from competitors – and a great opportunity to gain competitive advantage!

1.8 You may have thought of 'customer communications' primarily in the form of advertisements, press coverage, promotions, direct mail campaigns and so on. But the product or service itself represents communication to customers. In the case of a meal at a restaurant, for example, the appearance and taste of the food conveys a marketing message which will influence whether they return – and what messages they give to other people about their experience. The décor of the premises, the friendliness of the staff, the way that a complaint is dealt with or a telephone booking is taken are all part of the customer's experience – and a form of marketing communication.

1.9 An organisation cannot NOT communicate. Every aspect of the marketing mix – especially, but not only, the promotional mix – sends a message to customers and potential customers. It is vital to recognise the wide range of messages an organisation can give out and the various ways in which these messages can be communicated.

1.10 That's why **integration** is a key concept in modern marketing communications. As Forsyth notes, 'Good customer contact is not created through a few isolated incidents that achieve high impact. It must be created amongst an on-going multitude of contacts, in every way and at every level.'

The organisation as an open system

1.11 A system can be described simply as 'an entity which consists of interdependent parts'. Every system has a 'boundary' which defines what it is: what is 'inside' and what is 'outside' the system. Anything outside the system is said to be its 'environment'. In systems theory, it is possible to have a closed system, which is shut off from the environment and independent of it. An **open system**, however, is one which is **connected to** and **interacts with** its environment. It takes in influences from the environment and, in turn, influences the environment by its activities.

1.12 In the 1950s, the systems approach was applied to organisations, emphasising that:

- Organisations are not static structures (as suggested by conventional organisation charts): they **continually react and adapt** to internal and external changes.
- Organisations must be aware of their **relationship to their environment** – including other people (such as customers) and organisations (such as suppliers and distributors) who influence and are influenced by their activities.
- Organisations must **manage the interface** between themselves and the environment: the points at which other people and organisations 'meet' the organisation. This is a key role of marketing communications.

1.13 Organisations take in a wide variety of inputs from the environment and generate outputs *to* the environment in the course of their activities. (Figure 1.1)

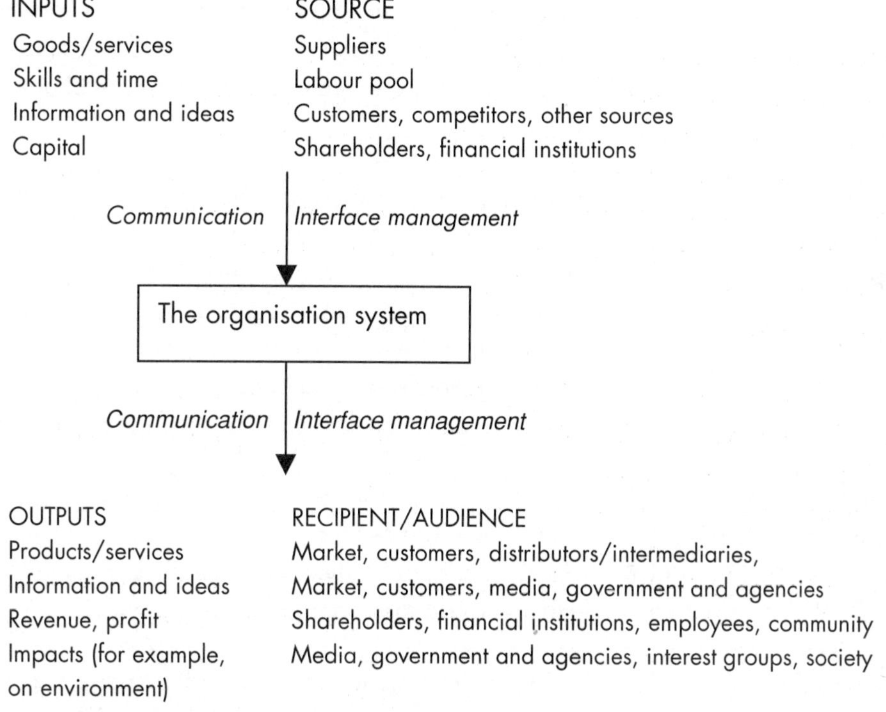

Figure 1.1: The organisation as an open system

Action Programme 1

Think about each of the outputs in our open system diagram. (If you wish, it may help to focus on a specific organisation that you know.)

- What kinds of communications to and from the organisation that would be involved in each?
- What kinds of activities would represent the 'interface' between the environment and the system in each case?
- Why might management of this interface be important?

1.14 We will now look at some of the key players in the environment of the marketing organisation system.

2 Customers

Target audiences of the marketing message

2.1 Who is the customer? There are a number of different audiences for the marketing message.

Customer/audience	Some purposes of communication
Purchasers of the product or service (current or past)	■ Inform of changes to the product/service, terms or conditions, to support continuing purchase ■ Maintain on-going contacts and offerings to encourage repeat purchase and customer loyalty ■ Acknowledge and/or reward long-term or repeat customers for their loyalty ■ Encourage past purchasers to try the product/service again (for example if it has changed in response to feedback) ■ Gather feedback to improve or fine-tune the offering and customer service
Consumers or **users** of the product or service (current or past)	■ Providing the product/service itself (for example giving advice or information) ■ Help them to use the product/service more effectively (for example customer support, instructions, after sales service) ■ Encourage or reward repeated use and recommendation to others ■ Encourage trial of related offerings ■ Gather feedback on their experience of use to improve or fine-tune
Potential purchasers and/or users of the product or service	■ Convey promotional messages: raising Awareness of the product, Interest in it, Desire to try it, Action to buy it (AIDA) ■ Gather feedback on their response to your offering/promotions so you can target them more effectively in future
Internal customers or consumers of marketing services and information within the organisation.	■ Give them information about marketing plans and customer needs so that they can co-ordinate their efforts in line with shared marketing objectives ■ Share customer feedback and customer care goals, to educate and motivate them towards organisation-wide customer focus
Other **stakeholders**: groups who have a legitimate interest in organisational activities.	■ Give and receive information necessary for them to fulfil their roles in relation to the organisation (for example as suppliers, distributors or employees) ■ Give and receive information necessary for the organisation to fulfil its responsibilities in relation to them (for example the community, interest groups, employees or government agencies) ■ Establish mutually-satisfying on-going working relationships.

Customers and users

2.2 Ted Johns (*Perfect Customer Care)* makes the distinction between **customers** and **users**.

Key Concept

A **customer**is the purchaser of goods and services.

A **user** is the recipient, consumer or end user of goods and services.

2.3 Not all organisations would find this distinction between the 'customer' (the person who pays) and the 'user' (the person who consumes) relevant. However, not-for-profit organisations, such as local authorities, charities, libraries and schools, for example, often have a diversity of people and groups interested in the products and services they supply. These may be variously described as 'clients', 'users' or 'customers', even through the products/services are paid for by other parties: taxpayers, government, donors and so on, who may or may not be recipients of the products or services themselves.

2.4 It is important that you should be able to distinguish, where appropriate, between the customer and the user from a marketing point of view. Users may or may not be the same people who have bought the product, and may or may not have had a direct say in the purchase decision – but they are the ones who experience the product or service, and their needs and wants may influence the purchase decision made by the customer.

2.5 **Customer satisfaction** with the experience of purchase – including product availability, cost, the convenience of the transaction and the quality of in-store service – will be an important factor in maintaining loyalty, repeat business and word-of-mouth promotion of the product/service and/or of the intermediary through which it is sold. However, **user satisfaction** is also important, as it is likely to motivate customers who have bought a product/service on their behalf to make repeat or related purchases – or not.

Action Programme 2

Cite some examples of products or services for which the distinction between customer and user may be significant.

2.6 Although it is often convenient to refer to 'the customer' as a single, identifiable unit at whom marketing communications can be directed, in practice things are not so simple: decisions of whether and what (and when and where) to buy may involve more than one person. In Chapter 3, we will examine further the role of the various stakeholders in a purchase decision, or the **decision making unit (DMU)**.

Internal customers

2.7 So far, we have defined a customer as someone who buys and/or uses a product or service from the marketing organisation. However, it may be argued that, within the marketing organisation, various departments or units are customers or consumers of the products and services of other departments and units.

Key Concept

The **internal customer**concept extends the principles of market forces to the internal processes of the organisation. Any unit of the organisation whose task contributes to the task of other units (whether as part of the process or in an advisory or service relationship) can be regarded as a supplier of products or services, the users or consumers of which are thus regarded as internal customers.

2.8 'Staff' functions in organisations (like Accounts, Administration, IT or Human Resources) are explicitly intended to provide services, advice and support to front-line functions such as Sales and Production. The HR function, for example, provides products and services (recruitment and selection advice, the design and delivery of training programmes, industrial relations negotiations and so on): the Marketing function (among others) may therefore be seen as an **internal customer** of HR.

2.9 However, it may be argued that any unit of the organisation whose task contributes to the task of other units (whether as part of business processes and information flows or in an advisory or support relationship) can be regarded as a **supplier of service** – like any other supplier used by the organisation. The users or consumers of this service are thus **customers** of the unit.

2.10 Suppose that a unit in an organisation focuses on an activity or process for its own sake, attaching to it no objective or purpose outside the department's job descriptions, rules and procedures. It may become inflexible and take for granted its relationship to other units, having a 'take it or leave it' attitude to the service it provides. (After all, it's 'only' an internal matter.) It may become complacent about the quality of its service and the maintenance of relationships within the organisation, because it appears to have an effective monopoly on that service or task: 'if we don't do it – who will?'

2.11 The internal customer concept aims to challenge such complacency.

(a) **Customer choice** operates within the organisation as well as in the external market environment. If an internal service unit fails to provide the right service at the right time and cost, it cannot expect customer loyalty: it is in **competition** with other internal – and external – providers of the service. The use of agency, consultancy and freelance labour and expertise is growing across many sectors. Think about marketing services: there are many providers to whom market research, advertising, PR and other projects could be contracted out, particularly where specialist expertise (Web site design, say, or advice on language and culture in international markets) is required.

(b) The unit's prime objective thus becomes the efficient and effective identification and satisfaction of the internal customer's needs, wants and expectations. This has the effect of **integrating the objectives** of service and front-line units throughout the organisation: **all** activity is effectively targeted at serving the customer – **or serving someone who does**. It also makes units look at the **added value** they are able to offer in fulfilling their functions.

(c) **Marketing** – the creating, building and maintaining of mutually beneficial exchanges and relationships – is important in the internal market of the organisation as well as the external market. The 'exchanges' sought may be co-operation in fulfilling shared objectives, or two-way flows of information.

Action Programme 3

Who might be the internal customers of the marketing function? What might be their key needs/expectations?

2.12 In terms of marketing communications, the internal customer concept means:

(a) Providing the **information** needed and **expected** by internal customers to enable them to fulfil their objectives and to serve external customers. Examples include supplying information about product launches, advertising and promotions to sales and customer service staff so that they can answer questions intelligently and correctly.

(b) Communicating and dealing with all individuals and groups in the organisation in a way that is compatible with building **positive customer relations**. The same dynamics apply as with external customers: courtesy, patience, mutual respect, consideration.

(c) **Internal marketing**: promoting the marketing concept to other functions in the organisation, in order to foster customer-focused values organisation-wide and to help people understand how their work roles relate to customer satisfaction. As we will see in Section E of this Text, effective customer care is **everyone's** responsibility – but it may be up to the marketing function to create this awareness and motivate the appropriate response.

Action Programme 4

What kind of (a) events and (b) communication vehicles might offer opportunities for the marketing function to promote and support customer focus in an organisation?

You may like to consider the kinds of communications released by your own organisation's marketing department. If there is a corporate Intranet or departmental Web page, this might be a good starting point.

[Key Skill for Marketers: Using ICT and the Internet]

---

3 Stakeholders

3.1 So far, we have identified customers and employees of the marketing organisation (including managers) as potential target audiences for external and internal marketing communications. However, there are other parties who have a relationship with the organisation, or who are affected by its activities – and who therefore have an interest or 'stake' in them. These parties, 'publics' or interested audiences are called **stakeholders**.

Key Concept

The **stakeholders** of an organisation (activity or decision) are individuals, groups or organisations that have a legitimate interest or 'stake' in it, by virtue of its potential to affect them.

3.2 The stakeholders of an organisation may include the following (Figure 1.2)

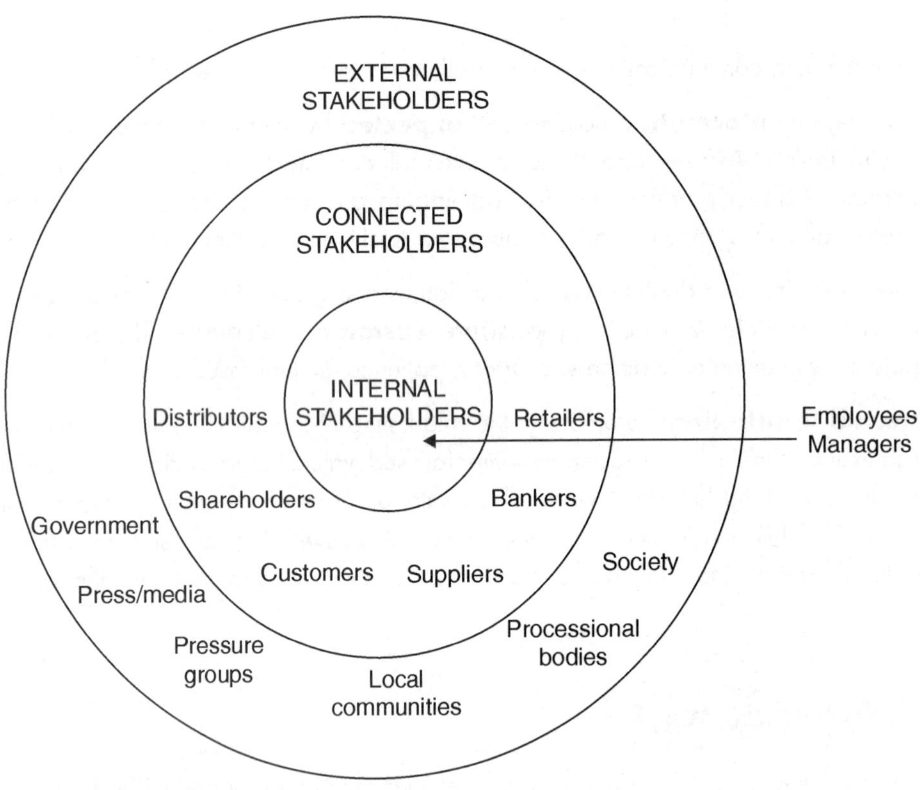

Figure 1.2 Stakeholders in the marketing organisation

Exam Tip

A question on communication with stakeholders was set in the December 2000 exam (under the previous syllabus). 6 marks were available merely for identifying the range of stakeholders, and the examiners were disappointed that candidates lost easy marks by neglecting to do so. Make sure that you have a good grasp of basic 'big picture' factors. Note also that you may be required to draft communications for stakeholder audiences: job advertisements (targeted at potential employees), media releases (targeted at the Press), marketing presentations (targeted at distributors or marketing agencies) and so on. In later chapters, we will cover communication planning and techniques that can be used for a variety of audiences: just bear in mind that there is a variety of audiences!

3.3 The **publics** and **stakeholders** of a marketing organisation are covered in detail in the *Marketing Environment* module, which should underpin your thinking on why and how marketing communication should be targeted to each stakeholder group. We will summarise some of the key issues here.

Stakeholders as target audiences

3.4 The targeting of marketing communication to different stakeholder groups will depend on:

- Their particular motives, interests and objectives in dealing with the organisation and
- The extent of their influence or power to affect the fulfilment of organisational objectives

3.5 The interests and influence of the various **internal stakeholder** groups can be summarised as follows.

Stakeholder	Interests	Influence
Managers	■ The organisation's survival and growth ■ Fulfilment of task goals and accountabilities ■ Fulfilment of personal goals (career advancement, security and so on)	■ Shape the strategy of the organisation ■ Plan, organise, co-ordinate, control and command all aspects of performance ■ Create corporate culture and image in the outside world
Employees and/or volunteer workers	■ The organisation's survival and growth (continued employment/prosperity) ■ Fulfilment of personal goals (security, income, responsibility, challenge) ■ Fulfilment of task goals	■ Key resource: ultimate source of all added value ■ Scarce resource: impact on bottom line, competitive edge ■ Negative power: threat of withdrawn or restricted labour
Trade union or other employee representative bodies	■ Protecting the interests and rights of members in the work place ■ Negotiation of favourable terms, conditions and grievance resolution ■ Wielding influence for socio-political goals	■ Rights enforced by employment legislation/regulation ■ Collective negotiating strength ■ Negative power to impose industrial action ■ Influence on attitudes of government, public and employees

3.6 The interests and influences of **connected stakeholders** can similarly be summarised as follows.

Stakeholder	Interests	Influence
Shareholders	■ Return on investment in the company ■ Involvement in decision-making through participation in shareholder meetings and election of officials	■ Owners of the company ■ Voting power at company meetings ■ Negative power to sell shares
Customers/ consumers	■ Satisfaction of a complex range of expectations and motives for purchase (value for money, quality, symbolic value, enjoyable purchase experience and so on) ■ Congruence with social concerns and values (for example environment and business ethics)	■ Target and ultimate *raison d'être* of all business activity ■ Source of current and future revenue ■ Source of feedback information for improvement/development ■ Negative power to withdraw custom, support competitors
Financial institutions	■ Security of loans made ■ Return on investment ■ Mutually beneficial on-going business relationship	■ Negative power to withhold, restrict or withdraw credit facilities
Suppliers	■ Timely and complete payment for services, as contracted ■ Mutually beneficial on-going business relationship	■ Meet supply needs, for efficient production and work flow ■ Part of total customer 'value delivery system': may offer competitive advantage ■ Negative power to restrict service or aid competitors
Marketing intermediaries (such as distributors, retailers, and marketing services agencies)	■ 'Push' and 'pull' support for sales: reliable supply, quality/added value, promotional and point-of-sale support ■ Earnings (for example through discount margins, fees or commissions) ■ Mutually beneficial on-going business relationship	■ Help to promote, sell and distribute goods/services ■ Promotional and point-of-sale support ■ Negative power to withhold payment or services, or aid competitors

Marketing at Work

Four Square

Four Square (suppliers of Klix drinks systems, among others) have strong quality principles, communicated from parent company Mars.

- The concept of the **'internal customer'** is highly developed and considerable time has been devoted to the 'Putting Customers First' campaign, involving both internal and external customers. Each associate in the company has to have a company service objective included in his/her annual standards of performance.
- There is a seven-step programme – including communication and training – to develop all **suppliers** to be 'suppliers of excellence'.
- On the customer side, drinks system **distributors'** staff are not only given technical training in servicing, fault finding and learning, but also a lot of sales and customer care training.

Personnel Management, September 1992

3.7 **External stakeholder** groups are likely to have quite diverse objectives and to have a varying ability to persuade the organisation to try and meet them. Strategies for communicating with them will therefore vary, according to their location (local, national or international), areas of interest (single issue or broad range of concerns) and so on.

Action Programme 5

See if you can draw up a similar table for a selection of external stakeholder groups, illustrating their interests (what they will want from the marketing organisation) and their influence (why the marketing organisation would want to take them into account).

If convenient, you may like to share this activity with other students and pool your ideas. *[Key Skill for Marketers: Presenting Information]*

3.8 The more influence a stakeholder group has in a given context, the more important it will be for the marketing organisation to consider its interests and objectives in order to gain the desired response. The ability to identify and analyse stakeholder groups will allow the marketer to determine:

- Appropriate **channels of communication** to target relevant groups, to gain efficient access for the message
- Appropriate **media of communication** to suit their needs and characteristics, to attract them to the message
- Appropriate **modes of communication** to express the message in a way that reflects their interests, motives and objectives – and in a way that establishes and maintains **constructive on-going professional relationships**

Action Programme 6

Identify the internal and external stakeholder groups of your own organisation, or one you know well (perhaps as a stakeholder yourself). How regularly – and in what circumstances – does the organisation communicate with each group? What means of communication are used? How does this shape the relationship between the organisation and each stakeholder?

3.9 Remember, customers are only one stakeholder in the marketing organisation – but they are arguably the most **important** – as we will see in Chapter 2. Remember, too, that:

- Members of **all** stakeholder groups (internal and external) are also **potential customers** for the organisation's products and services
- Members of **all** stakeholder groups (internal and external) are links in the chain that **delivers value to the organisation's customers**

Marketing at Work

Spennymoor School

Spennymoor School, a 740-pupil comprehensive school in the North East of England, defines its 'customers' as the students (the direct users of the educational services), their parents (who pay for them), local industry (as potential consumers of the employable labour produced by the school) and the community (as beneficiaries of the good citizenship produced by the school).

Action Programme 7

Consider the case of:

- A local council which provides services and amenities to the surrounding area.
- A charitable organisation which raises funds and volunteer support for environmental 'clean up' activities nationwide.

Who are the customers of these organisations? To what other stakeholder groups will they need to address marketing messages?

4 Who *exactly* is the customer?

Why is it important to identify the customer?

4.1 It should be self-evident that in order to identify, anticipate and satisfy customer requirements, marketers must have some idea of who the customer is!

- Whose needs and wants will you take into account when developing products and services?
- Whose needs and wants will you take into account when selecting product/service benefits to highlight in your promotional messages?
- Whose needs and wants will you take into account when designing incentives and rewards for product/service trial, repeat purchase or recommendation to others?
- To whom will you send marketing messages?

- How can you make efficient use of your marketing expenditure by **not** sending messages to people for whom they will not be relevant? (If you have ever received unsolicited advertising material – via mail or e-mail – you know what we mean...)
- From whom will you gather feedback on their response to your product/service and marketing messages?

In other words, who is your **target audience**?

4.2 As Kotler *(Marketing: An Introduction)* notes: 'Companies know that they cannot satisfy all consumers in a given market. At least, they cannot satisfy all consumers in the same way: there are too many different kinds of consumers with too many different kinds of needs. And some companies are in a better position to serve certain segments of the market than others.'

4.3 The organisation thus need to identify and focus in on its customers and potential customers, through **target marketing**, whereby it:

- Divides the total market into smaller segments according to relevant characteristics (**market segmentation**)
- Selects the most promising (potentially profitable) segments of the market (**market targeting**)
- Develops a marketing mix that will most profitably and competitively serve and satisfy the targeted segments (**market positioning**)

These concepts are covered in the *Marketing Fundamentals* module.

4.4 Customers may be segmented and targeted according to a range of factors, such as: **demographics** (age, gender, income/occupation, family size and so on); **social class or status** (socio-economic variables such as income, education, occupation, residential area); **family life cycle** (stages of the structure, membership and interests of the family over time); **psychographics** (lifestyle, or activities/interests/opinions).

4.5 Focusing in on customer characteristics enables the organisation to target its marketing communications. For example, widely different styles of products and promotional messages are used in youth markets than more mature markets – and different again in the emerging 'grey' market to older consumers (increasingly important in ageing societies, where over-50s are becoming the largest group with the highest disposable income).

Action Programme 8

What problems might emerge for a company that failed to communicate effectively with the 'grey' market (just as one example of ignoring the needs of a particular audience)?

How do you get to know your customers?

4.6 Traditionally, the main approach to identifying and describing market segments and target audiences has been market research. Market research (which is covered in detail in the *Marketing Environment* module) is intended to help organisations to identify potential sources of new customers; to find out what their existing customers think about them; and to anticipate their needs, wants and interests in order to target offerings and marketing messages appropriately.

4.7 Research information is used to model dynamics such as:

- Consumer expectations and experience of products and brands
- Consumer awareness of and responses to specific marketing messages and media
- Consumer needs, wants and interests
- Consumer buying preferences and habits

Action Programme 9

List five areas in which market research data might help you improve your marketing communications.

4.8 However, market research cannot be seen as a universal panacea, and certainly never as an end in itself. Some experts openly doubt the value of research, citing examples of successful companies who never engage in it, and of struggling companies who have invested a great deal in it.

4.9 Postma (*The New Marketing Era)* argues that the **stated preferences and intentions** of consumers are notoriously subjective and unreliable: there can be a considerable difference between the answers given and actual behaviour. Only **actual purchase behaviour** can be depended on to give the true picture of what customers perceive, want, and will buy and keep buying. Fortunately, as Postma argues: 'The technical components of the information revolution, in tandem with the associated media revolution, now make it increasingly possible to manage markets according to **actual behaviour on an individual level**.'

4.10 The new information and media technologies to which Postma refers facilitate:

(a) **Data capture** – for example, through point of sale transactions, hits on Web sites and responses to direct-response TV advertising – about consumers' media, browsing, response and buying patterns.

(b) **Database management**, allowing marketers to access and manipulate captured data so that they can:

- Target, customise and even personalise marketing communications
- Manage relationships with individual clients, as opposed to more or less defined 'target groups'

4.11 Organisations may gather large amounts of **data about customers** in the course of business.

Type of data	Examples	Communication uses
Customer contact details	Names, addresses, telephone/email/fax contacts	Mailing list marketing, direct customer contact
Professional details	Company, job title, responsibilities	Contact and message targeting in business to business (B2B) marketing
Personal details	Gender, age, marital status, number of people in household, interests, media consumed, shopping preferences etc	Targeting of messages and offers to interests and preferences of customer; use of relevant media
Transaction history	What products/services have been ordered from the firm, how often, how much spent	Target buying patterns and preferences; identify valuable customers for focused contact
Call/contact history	Sales or after sales service calls made, complaints/queries received, meetings at shows/exhibitions	Plan and integrate contacts to avoid overlap/confusion; ensure follow-up of initial contacts; ensure follow-up of complaints/queries
Current transaction details	Items currently on order, dates, prices, delivery arrangements	Ensure follow-up as promised; answer customer queries/complaints intelligently
Special account details (for example where customer loyalty or incentive schemes are used)	Membership number, loyalty or incentive points earned, discounts awarded	Maintain contact; reward and acknowledge; identify 'valued' customers

4.12 Customer data (and data about potential customers, prospects or leads) may come from the following sources.

- EPOS (Electronic Point of Sale) recorded data on all sales transactions and orders. Transaction details may be input manually, or by bar code reader or 'swiping' of magnetic-stripped customer cards.
- **Internet** contacts and transactions, recorded electronically as users visit, browse, register, respond to advertising, subscribe or purchase via the organisation's Web site.
- **Transaction documents**, such as order forms, invoices, credit applications and customer account records.
- Details gathered by telemarketers (in-coming and outgoing calls), sales and customer service staff on every **contact with customers**.
- Details provided by customers on **customer care, feedback and market research** forms and questionnaires; on on-pack coupons, entry forms or phone lines for **promotional competitions, prize draws or incentives**; or when applying for

credit accounts, discount schemes, valued customer cards and other **loyalty and incentive schemes**.

- **Enquiries** for further information or **sales 'leads'** in response to promotion: via telephone, mail, reply coupons, 'hits' on the Web site, details submitted at exhibitions or trade fairs and so on.

Marketing at Work

Vons Grocery Company (US)

The Vons Grocery Company of California is one of the foremost builders and users of databases in the US. Foodstore customers enter the database by filling out a cheque authorisation application, and are issued a Vons Value Plus Card. When swiped at checkout, this produces automatic discounts on selected items **of interest to that individual customer**. Each time the card is used, the store builds a profile of the purchases of that individual customer. As well as **customising communications with individual customers** (for example, sending out manufacturers' discount coupons on relevant products), the scheme is a powerful tool for building customer loyalty programs. In 1995, for example, Vons offered club members a free turkey for Thanksgiving if they purchased $300 worth of goods at Vons between September 27 and October 31: the EPOS database recorded total cumulative purchases by each customer during that period. The next generation of Value Plus Cards will store data such as the cardholder's birthday for **personal acknowledgement**: a powerful relationship-building tool.

Samsonite Corporation

Samsonite, the major luggage manufacturer, maintains three customer databases. One is built on product registration cards, which include purchase details, demographic and lifestyle questions – and an incentive to send the card in. The second is built on calls to the Samsonite Freecall enquiry number, which is featured on all advertising. The third is built around information request/response cards bound into magazines that carry their advertisements. Because Samsonite sells through retail outlets, it does not want to compete with its own distributors by direct marketing. However, it uses its databases to profile its customers, product by product, and to study their feedback so as to make design improvements. It uses answers to lifestyle questions to spot new product opportunities.

(Adapted from *Marketing Planning,* James W Taylor)

From 'the customer' to '*this* customer'

4.13 Hammer and Champy *(Re-engineering the Corporation,* 1993) suggest that 'the mass market has broken into pieces, some as small as a single customer'. They argue that the idea of the mass market – founded on the belief that consumers were more or less alike – has collapsed with the competitive shift of power to the customer. 'Now that they have choices...customers no longer behave as if they are all cast in the same mould. Customers – consumers and corporations alike – demand products and services designed for their unique and particular need. There is no longer any such notion as "the customer": there is only "**this customer**".

4.14 It is now possible to distinguish between:

- **Mass marketing**: one-to-all or one-to-many communications, **without specialisation** of the message or medium
- **Target marketing**: one-to-many or one-to-few communications **with specialisation** of the message and medium for each identified segment of the whole market
- **One-to-one marketing**: one-to-few or one-to-one communications with **individualised** message and medium for each highly targeted member or individual customer

4.15 Peppers and Rogers (*The One to One Future)* argue that: 'In the one-to-one future, it won't be how much you know about *all* of your customers that's important, but how much you know about *each* of your customers.' They emphasise the need for two-way communication vehicles and feedback mechanisms – interactive communication and dialogue – as a way of learning about customers and developing customer relationships.

4.16 We will follow up this discussion throughout the Text.

Chapter Roundup

- Organisations are open systems, taking inputs from their environment and creating outputs to their environment. This whole process depends on the communication of information.
- Organisations cannot NOT communicate. All actions, relationships and physical manifestations – as well as deliberately transmitted communications – convey a marketing message.
- A customer is the purchaser of goods and services: a user or consumer is the recipient or end-user of the goods and services.
- The internal customer concept suggests that units of the organisation whose task contributes to that of other units may be seen as suppliers of goods or services to internal customers. Customer choice and competition therefore influence internal as well as external market relationships.
- Many individuals and groups have an interest or 'stake' in the organisation's activities: they are stakeholders in the organisation.
- Each stakeholder has particular interests which are reflected in its communication needs. Each has more or less influence on the ability of the organisation to fulfil its objectives.
- Internal and external customers of the organisation have a high degree of influence, and consideration will have to be given to getting their needs met.
- Specific customer groups (market segments and 'target audiences') can be identified through market research. In addition, it is increasingly possible to identify actual customer groups and individual customers, through the use of data capture and database management.
- Marketing has moved from mass communication to targeted communication and now towards direct 'one-to-one' marketing.

Quick Quiz

1 Complete the following sentences, using the words in the box below.

- (1)......... may be defined as 'the management process which identifies, anticipates and (2)......... customer requirements efficiently and (3)..........' (CIM)
- 'To succeed in today's marketplace, companies must be (4)......... focused, winning customers from (5)......... and (6)......... them by delivering greater (7).........' (Kotler)

value	profitability	supplies	keeping	competitors
customer	marketing			

2 An open system is one which operates freely without reference to its environment.

☐ True ☐ False

3 The person who pays for or purchases goods and services may be called the:

A Consumer
B Internal customer
C User
D Customer

4 The marketing department's supplying data about price changes to sales and customer service staff would most clearly constitute which of the following activities?

Internal customer information	Internal customer relations
Internal marketing	Internal customer choice

5 Identify the following as internal (I), connected (C) or external (E) stakeholders.

(1) Employee association ☐ (2) Advertising agency ☐
(3) Advertising Standards Authority ☐ (4) Supplier ☐
(5) Board of directors ☐ (6) The CIM ☐

6 List three sources of suppliers' influence on the organisation.

7 The development of a marketing mix that will most profitably and competitively serve and satisfy a target segment of a market is called:

A Market segmentation
B Market targeting
C Market positioning
D Market research

8 The stated preferences and intentions of consumers, as elicited by market research, is the most reliable basis available for anticipating buyer behaviour.

☐ True ☐ False

9 Classify the following items of customer data under the appropriate headings in the box below.

(1) Sales calls made (2) Credit card number debited (3) Items on order
(4) Media consumed (5) Invitation to exhibition accepted (6) Age

Personal data	Call/contact history	Current transaction data

10 An individualised message and medium for each highly member or individual customer is called .... marketing.

Answers to Quick Quiz

1 (1) Marketing, (2) supplies, (3) profitably, (4) customer, (5) competitors, (6) keeping, (7) value

2 False

3 D

4 Internal customer information

5 (1) I, (2) C ,(3) E, (4) C, (5) I, (6) E

6
1. Meet supply needs for efficient production and work flow
2. Part of total customer value delivery system: competitive advantage
3. Negative power to restrict service or aid competitors

7 C

8 False

9 Personal data: 4, 6. Call/Contact: 1,5. Current transaction: 2, 3

10 One-to-one

Now try Question 1 from the Question Bank at the end of this Text

Action programme review

1 *Products/services.* Communications: promotional messages (for example advertisements, product packaging and point of sale display); briefing of distributors; transaction information (for example order confirmations, invoices). Interface: representatives of the organisation deal with distributors (for example through networking, negotiations, everyday activity) and – supremely – with customers (for example through customer service, answering the telephone).

Information/ideas. Communications: may be the product/service itself; part of promotion and corporate image (for example company news released to the media); part of customer service (for example answering queries, sales support). Interface: information delivery via Web site, personal contact, press releases, advertisements, exhibitions etc.

Revenue/profit. Communications: financial reports and returns to shareholders and government agencies (such as the Inland Revenue) – and also (perhaps) promotion of donations to community causes or employee profit-sharing (for example). Interface: how these messages are conveyed.

Impact. Communications: product warnings and instructions; public relations messages. Interface: how these messages are conveyed.

Effective communication at the interface will determine the image of the organisation and the satisfaction of the recipients – which will in turn determine the quality and duration of their continuing relationship with the organisation.

2 One example is the market for children's toys, where the 'customer' is (usually) the parent but the 'user' is (usually) the child. Some companies focus marketing on parents, stressing educational benefits, safety and so on. Others aim directly at children (focusing on fun, peer group acceptance and appealing themes and characters), because children exert psychological pressure on the buying decision.

3 Customers of marketing activity include:

- Senior management and shareholders, who expect the strategic objectives of the organisation to be met through effective and efficient marketing activity.
- The production function, who expect to be given (or consulted on) realistic product specifications and delivery schedules; to have their efforts justified by the success of the product in the market place (that is, that their output is effectively 'sold').
- The accounting and administrative functions, who expect clear and accurate budgets, forecasts and records of expenditure, sales and so on.
- The members of the organisation as a whole, who expect to be given information – and particularly 'good news'; to identify with a positive image; to participate in effective customer service, with the support of training and information; and to feel that the product is being effectively marketed, so that their own efforts are not wasted.

4 Events such as product launches or re-launches, new promotional initiatives, press coverage and other 'newsworthy' items (such as site visit by an important client, or the winning of a key customer account) may act as a prompt to some internal PR. Opportune vehicles for such internal marketing messages may include: a company newsletter, journal or e-bulletin; notice boards and their equivalent Intranet pages; departmental and other meetings; motivational events (such as sales conferences, award presentations); or the promotion/explanation of initiatives such as Customer Care Circles, feedback/suggestion schemes or training programmes.

5 Some of the ideas you may have come up with are as follows.

Stakeholder	Interests	Influence
Government (national and local) and government agencies	■ Corporate tax revenue ■ Healthy level of economic activity, balance of trade ■ Compliance with legislation ■ Reports and returns ■ Support for development and employment ■ Support of socially responsible cultural values by corporations	■ Power to enforce requirements through legislation, regulation, bureaucracy and sanctions ■ Control taxation, grants and other financial constraints and incentives ■ Power to send own marketing messages: mobilise public opinion on social responsibility issues

Professional bodies	■ Protect the interests of members ■ Promote professional standards and ethics	■ Ensure standards and ethics of professional staff ■ Influence on public/corporate policy through expertise
Pressure and interest groups	■ Promotion of a cause or issue ■ Protection of the rights or interest of the group (for example consumer protection)	■ May shape government policy ■ Mobilise public (consumer) opinion for or against organisation ■ Negative power to boycott
Press/media	■ Access to information of interest to relevant audiences ■ Competitive advantage over other news/entertainment providers ■ Revenue from the sale of advertising space	■ Shape public (consumer) opinion for or against organisation policies/practices ■ Control access to public through media coverage
The community and society at large	■ Access to products/services ■ Access to employment ■ Legal and socially responsible business and employment practices ■ Positive (or minimal negative) impact on social structures, the environment and so on	■ Represent potential consumers and employees: power to give or withhold support ■ Power to influence government policy and consumer opinion

6 This was a research and reflection exercise, requiring you to apply some of the principles discussed to your own experience. This is a useful learning technique: get used to reflecting on your own experience of marketing communications – both as a marketer and as a customer/recipient/stakeholder.

7 *Local authority.* The customers are the people who receive the services or use the amenities, especially if they also pay for them (for example through local tax charges). Other stakeholder audiences include the employees, local businesses and not-for-profit organisations (who may benefit from or compete with local government initiatives for funds), and the Press (especially local media).

Charity. The customers are, arguably, the beneficiaries of the services: in this case, local communities and environmental groups. However, key stakeholder audiences will include current and potential funders and volunteers (without whom the activities would cease). Others will include the Press and government, whom the organisation will attempt to persuade of the importance of local environment issues, and interest groups who may support them in this attempt.

8 Older consumers are a lucrative and growing target market which may simply go unreached (and certainly undeveloped in terms of customer relationships and loyalty) if communication is poor. A competitive opportunity will be missed. Older consumers may find pro-youth messages offensive, patronising or alienating: they may ignore advertising messages (undermining other promotional activity), and may even react against the product/brand or organisation. Their feedback may not be sought, perpetuating the problem.

9 Examples include:

- How different people (or market segments) respond to different communications and advertising media
- Factors influencing customers' responses to media and messages (repetition, presentation, timing, length and so on)
- Importance of various factors in eliciting responses (for example, words or tone of voice in customer service)
- Customer preferences for particular media, methods and themes
- Different approaches taken by other organisations/sectors: media used, policies etc.

Focus on the customer

2

Chapter Topic List	
1	Setting the scene
2	The importance of customer focus
3	Customer focus
4	Relationship marketing
5	Supporting customers through change
6	Internal customer focus

Learning Outcomes

- ☑ Appreciate the importance of the customer and the need for customer-focused organisations
- ☑ Outline how communications can be used to establish a customer focus and to establish and manage customer relations
- ☑ Appreciate the importance of customer retention and loyalty and the need for relationship marketing
- ☑ Explain changing customer needs and their impact on marketing programmes
- ☑ Explain how the concept of 'customer focus' can be applied to internal customers

Syllabus References

- ☑ Describe the link between the marketing concept, a customer focus and relationship marketing (1.3)

☑ Appreciate the need for effective internal and external customer communications and their link to and role in maintaining customer focus, developing and sustaining good customer relations and relationship marketing in creating loyalty and customer retention (1.4)

☑ List the factors that cause change in customers and the subsequent impact on marketing programmes (1.5)

Key Concepts Introduced

- Marketing concept
- Consumerism
- Customer relations

1 Setting the scene

1.1 In Chapter 1, we suggested that studying Customer Communications was important because the key to effective marketing is the belief that the **customer is important**. Keeping your eye on this fact, and acting out of that awareness, may be called **customer focus**: it underlies the whole module.

1.2 In this chapter, we discuss:

- Why customer satisfaction should be the focus of the organisation
- How customer focus manifests itself in marketing communications
- How marketing communications can be used to develop profitable on-going relationships with customers

1.3 The practical implications of these concepts for customer care, customer service and customer relationship management will be discussed in more detail in Part E of this Text.

The marketing concept

1.4 According to Kotler, the marketing concept:

- Starts with a well-defined market
- Focuses on customer needs
- Co-ordinates and integrates all marketing activities that might affect customers and
- Aims to make profits by creating long-term customer relationships based on customer value and satisfaction

Key Concept

The **marketing concept**holds that 'achieving organisational goals depends on determining the needs and wants of target markets and delivering the desired satisfactions more effectively and efficiently than competitors' (Kotler)

1.5 This concept can be contrasted with other concepts or orientations by which organisations conceive, conduct and co-ordinate their marketing activities.

Concept	Focus	Means	Aims
Marketing concept	Customer needs and wants; long-term customer relationships	Integrated marketing activities	Profitability through customer satisfaction
Selling concept	Existing products made by the firm; creating sales transactions	Energetic selling and promoting	Profitability through sales volume
Production concept	Assumed customer demand for product availability and affordability	Improving production and distribution efficiency	Profitability through efficiency
Product concept	Assumed customer demand for product quality, performance and features	Continuous product improvements	Profitability through product quality

1.6 The marketing concept can be stated in various ways. Peter Drucker defines it as 'Marketing is the whole business seen from the point of view of its final result, that is from the customer's point of view.' Malcolm HB McDonald (*The Marketing Plan)* puts it even more succinctly: 'marketing means finding out what people want and giving it to them'. You might like to start collecting your own examples of customer-focused mission statements and marketing messages.

Marketing at Work

LL Bean (US catalogue retailer)

'To inspire its employees to practise the marketing concept, LL Bean has for decades displayed posters around its offices that proclaim the following:

What is a customer? A customer is the most important person ever in this company, in person or by mail. A customer is not dependent on us, we are dependent on him. A customer is not an interruption of our work, he is the purpose of it. We are not doing a favour by serving him, he is doing us a favour by giving us the opportunity to do so. A customer is not someone to argue or match wits with, nobody ever won an argument with a customer. A customer is a person who brings us his wants, it is our job to handle them profitably to him and to ourselves.'

Kotler, *Marketing: An Introduction*

1.7 An organisation that practises the **marketing concept** will practise **customer focus**. It will pursue customer satisfaction, customer loyalty and on-going mutually profitable relationships with customers (**relationship marketing**). We will discuss some of the implications later in this chapter. First, we will look at **why** the customer is so important.

2 The importance of customer focus

Why is the customer important?

2.1 It has become a truism to say 'the customer is king'. But **why** is (s)he so important? At a basic level:

(a) Organisations need customers to buy their products and services in order to ensure the flow of revenue (and, for commercial concerns, profit): without them, the organisation would not survive.

(b) In many cases (especially for service organisations), organisational activities and processes would cease altogether without customers and consumers: you can't provide a service if there's no-one to provide it **to**!

(c) Customers provide organisations with essential information to enable them to develop and adjust their business and marketing strategies, programmes and practices, including:

- Information about their needs, wants, media consumption and buying preferences
- Feedback on the effectiveness of the organisation's activity: level of satisfaction with products/service and customer service; response to specific marketing messages and campaigns; awareness and perception of the brand; and so on.
- Changing requirements – which represent future marketing opportunities.

Why is customer satisfaction important?

2.2 The business environment is characterised by **increasing competition** (and therefore **customer choice**) through trends such as:

(a) The increasing **freedom of international trade** and globalisation: this can be seen both in the harmonisation of trade in blocs such as the EU and the Americas, and in the globalisation of trading through the Internet.

(b) **E-commerce and on-line marketing**, by which business of all sizes and types can reach an international audience with a 24-hour, 7-day marketing presence and service.

(c) **New technologies** (such as databases and the Internet in the field of communications) and **organisational methods** (such as flexible working and the empowerment of front-line staff) which allow a high degree of product (and message) differentiation, customisation and real-time responsiveness to customer demands.

(d) **Deregulation** (of sectors such as financial services) and **privatisation** (of utilities and public services), forcing former monopolies and bureaucracies to compete for customers and communicate in more flexible ways.

Action Programme 1

Reflect on your own experience as a customer. Has increasing competition changed the way you respond to poor service, lack of product availability, high prices and other negative experiences?

How easy would it be to 'take your business elsewhere' if you have an unsatisfactory experience:

- Getting access to Customer Communications study material in a public library?
- Rectifying a fault in your telephone, electricity or gas service?
- Reading an appeal from a charity organisation for funds and/or volunteers?
- Watching a television programme or channel?
- Ordering complex manufacturing components required by your business's production process?

2.3 Choice broadens consumers' perception and expectations of quality, value and service – and empowers them to demand these standards by having the option of taking their custom elsewhere.

Key Concept

Consumerismis a term used to describe the increased importance and power of consumers. It includes the increasing organisation of consumer groups, and the recognition by producers that consumer satisfaction is the key to long-term profitability.

2.4 **Consumerism** started as an attempt to even up the relationship between individual consumers and large, powerful corporations. The basis of consumerism is often taken to be former US President Kennedy's Consumer Bill of Rights, which highlighted four basic rights.

- The right to **safety** (when using products/services)
- The right **to be informed** (through responsible product labelling and instructions and labelling, clear terms and conditions of service, and accurate marketing claims)
- The right to **choose** (through availability of choice/competition and restraint of coercive marketing techniques)
- The right **to be heard** (through feedback, complaints and appeals)

2.5 Some organisations (especially service providers) have adopted **customer charters**, or statements of what types and levels of service the customer is entitled to expect. In the UK, they are used by organisations such as Consignia (the Post Office), the National Health Service, utilities and local government. (A full list can be viewed at Service First: www.servicefirst.gov.uk.) The idea of a charter is to manage customers' expectations: limiting the organisation's exposure to unreasonable demands and complaints. However, charters also have the effect of raising awareness that customers are entitled to hold the organisation **accountable** for service standards.

2.6 The legal environment also reinforces marketers' obligations and customer's rights in several areas.

(a) **Legislation** has increasingly protected consumer interests in regard to product labelling, promotional claims, safety, terms and conditions of sale and so on.

(b) **Independent regulatory bodies** (such as the Advertising Standards Authority in the UK: www.asa.org.uk) develop and enforce **codes of conduct**.

(c) **Decisions in the courts** have set common law precents awarding compensation for breach of contract, damaging effects arising from purchase or use and so on. It is generally recognised that consumer societies are becoming increasingly 'litigious': that is, prone to initiate legal proceedings in the event of dissatisfactions and negative consequences. Successful individual or class action lawsuits against organisations reinforce customer demands.

Marketing at Work

Accra Daily Mail (8/3/2002) recently reported the introduction of a Consumer Protection Act in Ghana, enabling consumers to return goods and foodstuffs of inferior quality and to form consumer associations and watchdog groups in order to help stamp out consumer fraud.

The article describes problems at both ends of the business scale.

- Large companies with little competition (such as Ghana Telecom) who tend to be complacent and impervious to customer criticism.
- Small entrepreneurs selling below-quality merchandise at inflated prices at street stalls and markets.

'[The Act's] primary purpose is to give extra power to ordinary citizens, so that they are able to push big business in particular to improve its service.'

'Ghana: Power to the consumer' (www.africaonline.com/site/Articles)

2.7 Just as importantly, customer satisfaction **creates a marketing message** – positive or negative. Friends and family members are valued, and therefore influential, sources of information for consumers making purchase decisions. Consider the following statistics.

- The average unhappy customer tells nine other people about the experience. (13% tell twenty or more people!)
- The average happy customer tells five other people – and many of those become customers of the business that was praised.

Why is it important to keep customers?

2.8 Successful marketing is not just about attracting customers, or making sales: there are increasing pressures to **retain customers** and foster **customer loyalty**.

(a) **Competition**

Customer loyalty helps to minimise the risk of customers switching brands or service providers, especially in consumer markets where:

- Inertia (a preference to stick with what you know) can easily be overcome by competitor offers or promotions
- Switching is relatively hassle-free (there is no relationship with the supplier)

(b) **Profitability/cost-effectiveness**

Estimates suggest that the cost of attracting a new customer may be between three and seven times that of keeping a current customer happy! Loyal customers may also, progressively, generate:

- Repeat purchases
- Related purchases (cross-selling)
- Purchases of increased value and complexity
- Word of mouth promotion/recommendation to other potential customers

(c) **Risk management**

Loyal customers provide relatively reliable revenue and turnover. They may also support the favoured supplier when market and economic conditions are bad.

(d) **Relationship**

Rapport and familiarity can be built up with repeat customers. This means that:

- Cost-effective communication channels can be established
- Information on customer needs and wants can be more effectively gathered
- The effects of problems (for example product recalls) can be minimised by trust
- Customers may be more open to offers of related products and incentives

(e) **Goodwill**

Positive word-of-mouth promotion and recommendation by loyal customers is a powerful and cost-effective marketing and public relations tool.

Action Programme 2

Thinking in terms of making a simple product sale, why do you think it would cost more to sell to a new customer than to an existing one?

How readily would you change: (a) the model of car you drive? (b) the bank or building society with which you have an account?

2.9 Customers are more likely to become repeat customers, loyal customers and perhaps even active advocates or recommenders of the product or service if they:

- Consistently **experience satisfaction** – or better!
- Are **acknowledged and rewarded** for their loyalty and
- Perceive that they **have a relationship** with the supplier

We will discuss each of these aspects, and the communications that facilitate them, below.

3 Customer focus

3.1 Customer focus means practising the marketing concept: seeing things **from the customer's point of view**.

3.2 Cathy Ace *(Successful Marketing Communications)* argues that the seven 'Ps' of the extended marketing mix (Product, Price, Place, Promotion, People, Processes and Physical evidence) have a producer or service provider focus. She suggests seven customer-focused 'C' alternatives.

Producer/provider focused activity	Customer/consumer focused activity
Product Plan product/service mix	**Choice** Consider how customers make choices: differentiate and inform to support the purchase decision
Price Consider all elements of the price mix	**Cost** Consider how customers perceive value for money
Place Manage distribution channels	**Convenience** Consider what customers find convenient: they may not like the channels (for example Internet) that are most 'efficient'
Promotion Persuade customers that the product meets their needs	**Communication** Enter into dialogue with customers; inform and support their decision-making: they are increasingly aware that promotion is being used to persuade or manipulate
People Select, train and manage staff in service delivery	**Care** Communicate and implement customer care values
Processes Organise, plan and control systems and operations	**Corporate Competence** Understand customer expectations and convey commitment to deliver: customers don't need to know **how** things are done (much less how difficult they are to do...)
Physical evidence Manage all physical factors (premises, logos etc)	**Consistency** Ensure that customer contacts and experiences are alike, to establish recognition and positive associations.

Marketing at Work

Postma (*The New Marketing Era)* suggests that Philips (electronics) advertising slogans over the years demonstrate a concern with product rather than with market: "From sand to client" (pointing out the silicon origin of the microchip), "Philips invents for you" and "Let's make things better". 'The last one,' comments Postma, 'may be excellent for an internal motivational campaign, but again it projects a production-oriented rather than market-oriented approach.

Contrast the slogans of Brand Power (a consumer guide) 'Helping you buy better', or Toyota cars 'O what a feeling!' Look out for advertising that sees things through the customer's eyes...

Focus on customer satisfaction

3.3 We discuss **customer care** (and related issues of customer service and quality) in Part E of this Text. To give you an overview, however, Lele and Sheth suggest '**four fundamentals of customer satisfaction**'.

(a) The **product** must meet customer needs, wants and expectations for quality and functionality. No amount of promotional support and sales service makes up for shoddy products that don't work, fall apart or otherwise disappoint.

(b) **Sales and promotion activities** must manage and fulfil customer expectations to create a positive experience of doing business with the supplier.

- **Promotional messages** should be clear and realistic, to avoid disappointment.
- The **attitudes** of all customer-contact people should be positive, professional and customer-focused.
- **Intermediaries** who sell on behalf of the organisation (retail outlets, call centres) should be trained and motivated to share this customer focus.

(c) **After-sales activities** must continue to create a positive experience for the customer, as well as building mutually supportive relationships.

- **Support services** (for example warranties, servicing, user training and help lines) facilitate the customer in using the product safely and satisfyingly.
- **Feedback and adjustment** (for example measuring customer satisfaction and addressing complaints) are crucial in minimising dissatisfaction and demonstrating commitment to customer satisfaction.

(d) Corporate culture must support and express the desire to maximise customer satisfaction. Cultural values about the customer are reflected in mission statements and slogans, but also in the criteria used for staff selection, performance appraisal and reward, and in the culture of management: whether or not managers allow, facilitate and empower staff to make customer needs their first priority.

3.4 Such an integrated approach to customer satisfaction requires **internal marketing** to stakeholders (such as managers, employees and intermediaries) as well as **external marketing** to customers and potential customers.

3.5 Consistent customer satisfaction is **essential** to keep customers. However, it is worth noting that it may not be **sufficient**! Torsten H Nilson (*Chaos Marketing)* suggests that:

'The reactive principles of the marketing textbooks, "fulfilling customer needs and wants", was perhaps a key to success in the 1950s and 1960s, but in today's marketplace there are too many companies who can supply what the customer wants. The reactive following of customer requests is just not good enough. To avoid any misunderstandings, this does not mean that you should not worry about the customer, rather the reverse: by being proactive, you can ensure that you **oversatisfy your customers**, even surprising them with the quality of the offer.'

Action Programme 3

Reflect on your own experience as a customer.

- How have you been dissatisfied by a product/service? What was the effect of this experience? How might more effective communication have satisfied your needs or expectations better?
- How have you been 'oversatisfied' or 'delighted' by an organisation's anticipating your needs or exceeding your expectations? What was the effect of this experience – and how long did it last?

Focus on customer relations

Key Concept

Customer relationsis the planned and sustained effort to establish and maintain goodwill and mutual understanding between an organisation and its customers.

3.6 Customer relations is the **interface between customers and the organisation** at any given point of contact. Since the organisation will inevitably project an image and create a potential relationship (positive or negative) in its dealings with customers – and since the competitive costs of creating a **negative** image can be high – it makes sense to **manage the messages** being projected.

3.7 Communication plays a vital role in customer relations, particularly in:

(a) **Establishing relationships** with customers: keeping in contact, showing that the customer is remembered and valued. (We discuss this further in the context of 'relationship marketing' below.)

(b) **Providing customer service**: transaction, query and complaint handling. One survey has suggested that the primary reason why customers switch their allegiance from one supplier to its competitors is not product quality but **poor customer relations**: lack of contact or apparent indifference on the part of staff.

(c) **Issues management**: addressing potential controversies or sensitive matters (such as product recalls, or – for internal customers – staff redundancies) before they become crises.

(d) **Spreading good news**: informing customers of the organisation's successes (market leadership, quality awards, employer awards and so on) in order to confirm customers' trust in, and identification with, the organisation or brand.

(e) **Gathering feedback** from customers, both for product/service improvement and to convey interest in the customer's views, experience, needs and wants.

Action Programme 4

The following is an extract from an article in *The Guardian* (13/4/2002), illustrating how poor customer communications can highlight, worsen or even create customer relations problems.

'Watch your plastic closely. A number of credit card companies have recently been changing their customer loyalty schemes – often making them less generous – or fiddling around with their fees... And what has really riled some cardholders is the way these changes are being communicated.

'[One holder of several cards issued by HBC Bank]... says he objects to what he claims is the "sneaky" way the fee is being introduced. As a result he says he will be cancelling his cards. In each case he was sent a letter headed, "Important changes to your terms and conditions", which alerted him to an increase in the handling fee on cash advances. The letter ends: "Please also see the enclosed leaflet for further changes to your terms and conditions". [The customer] says it would be all too easy to ignore this sentence, and the leaflet accompanying the letter. "But only if you read the small print do you find out about their new condition which imposes a £10 charge if the card is not used in each six-month period. This seems to me a really underhand way of imposing a new charge which many cardholders may not have any idea about until it's imposed."

'A spokesman for HBC Bank... says it costs money to run a credit card account and it believes that where people do not use their card, it is "only fair" to levy a £10 fee to offset some of these costs...'

'Meanwhile [another customer] couldn't believe his eyes when he received a letter from Alliance & Leicester relating to his MoneyBack credit card. The letter states: "At Alliance & Leicester, we are continually looking to improve the products and services that we provide for our customers" – then goes on to say, in a very oblique and easily overlooked way, that it is actually cutting the loyalty perks that some customers enjoy.'

Task: Draft point-form notes for a presentation to a banking industry meeting, highlighting the customer communication issues raised by this extract.

[Key Skill for Marketers: Presenting Information]

Focus on customer loyalty

3.8 Customer care, customer service and customer relations all contribute to customer loyalty. In addition, organisations may use **loyalty** or **customer reward** programmes, such as Air Miles, various retail discount/rebate/bonus/dividend cards and voucher schemes. These typically offer incentives for repeat business, in the hope that:

- A brand preference or 'habit' will develop from repeat purchase and familiarity, the inertia of which may create loyalty
- A sense of 'belonging' to a virtual community will reinforce the supplier-customer relationship (loyalty schemes are often expressed as 'clubs')
- The incentives and their accessories (VIP cards etc) will make customers feel valued and will add value to purchases

- Gather feedback data which can be used to fine-tune the marketing mix towards genuine (quality- and satisfaction-based) incentives to loyalty.

3.9 Some commentators define such programmes as relationship marketing (see below), while others see many of them as no more than heavily disguised sales promotions: they create customer retention (on-going transactions) – but not loyalty (emotional commitment to the organisation or brand). Postma *(The New Marketing Era)* notes wryly that:

'If you take a look at the stamps, points, air miles, and whatever else you collect in your wallet, it is hard to know where your loyalties lie. If I sleep in a hotel in a certain chain so often that I receive a regular customer card, do we then have a relationship? Or is it just a question of enjoying ever greater advantages if I limit myself to that chain? I even get extra air miles if I show a card from some frequent-flyer programme, and if I pay with my credit card I earn even more points. The piling up leads to confusion, and a limitation of the "relationship". Because who exactly am I having this relationship with?'

3.10 A more radical approach to customer loyalty is one which attempts to create a genuine **affinity** or **rapport** between the customer and the organisation, the brand and the 'community' of its customers. This approach may more properly be described as **relationship marketing**.

Marketing at Work

Tescos Clubcard (UK)

'As of 2000, Tesco claimed to have saved £500million by implementing what is now regarded by the industry as the worldwide benchmark in terms of successful loyalty programs... Clubcard has also been the nucleus for many other successful business initiatives.

'By incorporating the Clubcard data into its in-house Geographic Information System (GIS), Tesco has been able to identify gaps in the market where it could roll out new retail formats (Tesco Metro, Express etc) that would accommodate the needs of particular segments of the grocery shopping market. In addition to this, the data has been used to drive strategies in crucial areas such as product selection, pricing... and local area marketing.

'With the UK having the highest proportion of Internet grocery shopping in Europe, Tesco was able to leverage the detailed transaction history and geodemographic data that it held on Clubcard holders to identify customers with the highest propensity to be attracted to this channel. In 2000 Tesco Direct was not only positioned as the UK market leader, it also topped the list of global online grocery retail sales. Similar data mining techniques helped identify the best prospects as it diversified its business and rolled out Tesco Personal Finance and Tesco Net, an Internet service provider.

'With [results] like these, the loyalty card can be viewed as a tool that is much more than an expensive means for rewarding your best customers. It does, however, require taking a more holistic view of how the new-found market intelligence and in-depth insight into your customers' behaviour can unearth untapped potential within the market space you operate in.'

AdNews (Australia), 5/7/2002

4 Relationship marketing

Key Concept

Relationship marketing is a relatively new body of marketing theory which changes the focus from **getting** customers (although this is still seen as vital) to **keeping** customers. A sale transaction is only the start of an organisation's on-going relationship with a customer.

4.1 Relationship marketing (covered in more detail in Part E of this Text) is characterised by:

- Focus on long-term customer satisfaction and retention
- Development of two-way dialogue with customers rather than one-way promotion
- Seeking on-going relationship with customers rather than occasional transactions

4.2 There are five broad levels of customer relationship.

Basic	The organisation sells the product/service without initiating or inviting any further contact with the customer.
Reactive	The customer is invited to contact the organisation if there are any problems with the product/service.
Accountable	The organisation follows up the sale, asking the customer if there have been any problems, and inviting feedback for future product/service improvements.
Proactive	The organisation contacts the customer on a regular basis for a range of purposes (additional offerings, incentives, updates, loyalty rewards, feedback opportunities).
Partnership	Organisation and customer exchange information and work together to effect customer savings and added value. (Most appropriate for high-value 'key account' customers and business markets where firms have few high-profit customers.)

4.3 Many types of organisation have begun to move from basic or reactive to proactive relationships. Many car dealerships, for example, no longer just sell cars, but subsequently offer to service them and keep in touch with buyers (with service reminders or invitations to test drive new models). Some even offer high-value customers special benefits such as Owners Clubs for particular models, opportunities to undertake special advanced driving courses or drive on racing circuits and so on.

4.4 Relationship marketing tends to operate in three main ways.

(a) Borrow the idea of **customer/supplier partnerships** from industry. By sharing information and supporting each other's shared objectives, marketers and their customers can create real mutual benefits.

(b) Recreate the **personal feel** that characterised the old-fashioned corner store. Make customers feel **recognised and valued as individuals** and demonstrate that that their **individual needs** are being recognised and catered for. (This is particularly easy to do with new technologies such as the Internet, databases and computer-integrated telephone systems.)

(c) **Continually deepen and improve** the relationship. Make sure that every customer experience satisfies – and even **delights** – through reliable product quality, customer care and value-adding contacts.

4.5 Communications are essential to support relationship marketing in various ways.

(a) All aspects of **customer relations** – including all customer contacts with the brands, products, marketing messages and representatives of the organisation – need to be managed with a focus on customer care.

(b) The organisation should use extensive **interaction and feedback** mechanisms to learn about (and from) customers – with the stated aim of continually meeting their needs more effectively. 'In order to leverage relationship marketing, marketers need to move from monologue to dialogue with customers.' (Allen et al, *One to One Web Marketing*)

(c) The organisation should maintain **direct and regular customer communication**, through multiple points of contact and across a range of reasons for contact: information about products, special offers, special events, trade/market news updates, invitations, follow-up and service calls, feedback and care lines and so on.

(d) The organisation should maintain multiple exchanges with a number of stakeholders (**network relationships**) rather than a single focus on customers. Customer relationships are important – but so too are other links in the 'customer value delivery' chain such as financiers, suppliers, distributors and the media.

(e) Dialogue and developing trust provide a basis for the **customisation and personalisation of customer contacts**, which adds value to service. Databases can be used to record and store a memory of customer, prospect and commercial contacts, so that future contacts can be targeted and/or personalised to varying degrees. Examples include:

- Linking **telephony** to on-line databases, providing call centre staff with immediately accessible details of customers and their past purchases, and allowing them to 'recognise' callers and personalise the contact
- Using **individually addressable** marketing media and channels (such as direct mail and e-mail), to contact customers personally, rather than through mass media (such as advertising). Electronically stored data can be merged with standard document formats to provide apparently personal communications.
- **Customising** and **targeting** marketing messages on the basis of the known characteristics of the customer or prospect – from basic transaction-captured data (name, address, gender) to researched/gathered data (age, stated preferences, buying habits) to electronically gathered data (such as actual media consumption patterns and past purchase history).

(f) **Guiding and supporting** customers through changes in the organisation's offerings, and in their own circumstances, environment and requirements over time. We will explore this in some detail below.

Marketing at Work

Amazon.com (worldwide)

Amazon.com is a retail organisation specialising in books (and an increasingly diversified range of related leisure products). It has developed a world-leading relationship marketing strategy which utilises to the full the technological opportunities provided by on-line marketing and database management. Some of the relationship-building devices it uses include:

- Complete personalisation of the site for registered users
- The option to receive targeted e-mail recommendations, reminders and offers
- A virtual community of users through interactivity, notice boards and customer home pages
- Customer discretion as to communication/contact/privacy preferences
- Transparency about the sources and uses of personalised information
- Added-value site services such as free e-cards, gift certificates and out-of-print book searches
- Convenient and secure on-line purchase transactions, follow-up and order tracking
- A very friendly, up-beat personal tone

The best way to get a flavour of how this works is to get on-line! Check out www.amazon.com or www.amazon.co.uk.

5 Supporting customers through change

Changes by the marketing organisation

5.1 One of the key roles of communication in relationship marketing and customer retention is to guide and support customers through changes in the organisation's marketing mix. The aim of such communication is:

- To minimise uncertainty, concern or inconvenience which might act as 'push' factors to make customers turn elsewhere
- To demonstrate the organisation's commitment to an on-going business relationship with customers.

5.2 Situations requiring such communication include the following.

(a) **Problems** and **issues**, such as customer complaints, the need to make corrections to published details or modify advertising claims, or the need for product safety/health warnings or recalls. On-going customer and public relations may involve a range of communications: swift publication of apologies, corrections and reassurance; adjustment of individual customer complaints; the pro-active use of Helplines and Carelines to assure customers that support and information is available.

(b) **Changes to the product/service**. Customers may be accustomed – even loyal – to it in its current form. They may require advance notification (if changes will affect them significantly), revised instructions for use (if altered), and persuasion that the modifications are in their interests (more efficient or effective, easier to use etc).

(c) **Changes to charges, terms and conditions**. These must be clearly and openly communicated, particularly if they can be perceived to be detrimental to the customer: there is high potential for customer dissatisfaction if the organisation is perceived to be 'sneaky' about them, as in the credit card example in Action Programme 4 above.

(d) **Changes to delivery or access systems**. These may present positive marketing messages (for example introducing longer opening hours or 24hour/7day phone access to customer service) or persuasive challenges (for example replacing bank counter staff with Internet banking, marketed as more convenient access – but perceived as an erosion of service, particularly by older customers).

(e) **Changes to brand identity**. Changes must be made gradually and/or promoted repeatedly to customers, in order to minimise loss of recognition. This applies to product packaging, brand identity and, particularly, names: Accenture (formerly Andersen Consulting) and Consignia (formerly The Post Office) exemplify the difficulty of re-establishing brand awareness.

(f) **Changes to methods of payment**. Customers used to cash and cheque payments may have concerns about the introduction of cashless systems such as direct debit, credit card, phone and Internet payment. They will need to be reassured about security and persuaded of convenience.

(g) **New product introduction**. This presents a positive opportunity to extend the relationship with the customer, especially if the new product can be demonstrated to meet their known needs. A wide variety of communications will be required to introduce the product, establish the brand, encourage trial (where appropriate) and offer post-purchase instruction and support (where required).

5.3 **Internal** customers will also need to be kept informed about all the above changes, in order to maintain correct and consistent customer service and communication.

Changes affecting customers

5.4 The customer environment is covered in detail in the *Marketing Environment* module, and will in any case depend on the country and market in which you are operating. However, the following table highlights some of the many changes affecting internal and external customers, and suggests how these changes may impact on marketing activities.

	Change	Marketing response
Political/ legal factors	**Legislative and regulatory changes** Affect lifestyle (for example compulsory seatbelts or non-smoking environments), consumer rights (for example product safety and labelling) and employee rights (for example communication & consultation)	Adjust or develop products/systems to facilitate compliance (for example seat belts in all cars) and comply with consumer and employee rights. Emphasise social responsibility and self-regulation (for example by the tobacco industry on cigarette advertising)

<table>
<tr><td>Economic factors</td><td>Economic recession
■ Restricts disposable income and salary rise expectations. Alters spending patterns (by businesses and consumers), especially in lower income brackets.
■ Erodes job security. Encourages short contract and flexible working.</td><td>Develop priority-need and value-for-money offerings. Facilitate lower-value transactions and support credit purchase. Offer loyalty discounts. Target marketing to priority needs and value for money.

Communicate loyalty to employees. Promote flexibility values & benefits for employees and customers.</td></tr>
<tr><td></td><td>Globalisation of trade
Allows access to worldwide products and information (for example via Internet)</td><td>Focus on international awareness and competitiveness. Seize opportunity for global trade (for example via Internet).</td></tr>
<tr><td>Social/ cultural/ factors</td><td>Aging population
Falling birth rates in Western societies, creating a higher proportion of older consumers and workers.</td><td>Develop offerings to target emerging 'grey' market: eg retirement planning, leisure, travel. Promote positive images of mature people: avoid offensive stereotypes. Recruit mature customer-contact staff to build rapport. Empathise with needs and preferences (for example restricted access to electronic media, preference for face-to-face transaction, restricted income)</td></tr>
<tr><td></td><td>Changing family structures/lifestyle
▪ More multiple income households: less time for domestic activity; focus on maximising leisure time.
▪ More working women with independent income. Males assuming domestic functions for example shopping, childcare
▪ Increase in non-family households: single/divorced/widowed.</td><td>Develop offerings to target time-poor people (for example convenient meals, household services, leisure pursuits). Promote understanding of busy lifestyle: fast service, convenience, after hours or 24-7 trading/service. Adjust media mix to reach working audience.

Target new male/female roles: for example cars/financial services for women; food and domestic products for men. Challenge gender stereotypes.

Develop offerings to meet single household needs eg food packaged in single servings.</td></tr>
<tr><td></td><td>Racial diversity
Increase in career and cultural mobility, through migration, working abroad, exposure to other cultures through media, travel, education.</td><td>Develop offerings and messages to target culturally distinct segments (values, needs and wants of immigrants, expatriates) and culturally diverse markets (desire to experiment with international foods, culture, travel). Avoid racially discriminatory employment /business practices and offensive stereotypes in advertising.</td></tr>
</table>

	Improvements in education ▪ Wider take-up of higher secondary and tertiary education. ▪ Media and buying sophistication: awareness of promotional techniques and consumer rights	Develop offerings to meet rising demand for product/service quality, and eg travel and information products. Move from persuasion to communication. Avoid spurious 'experts', exaggerated claims. Comply with consumer rights and demands.
	Changing attitudes ▪ Demand for social responsibility: eg environmental concerns; issues of global economic equity ▪ Social attitudes; eg erosion of respect for authority/institutions; declining class consciousness; sensitivity to discrimination	Need to gather market information and feedback to monitor changes. Develop offerings and messages to reflect changing attitudes and concerns: for example environmentally friendly products and packaging; ethical and sustainable business practices in developing nations Less (satirical) use of authority figures in brand endorsement; sexually/racially inclusive language etc.
	Emerging concerns New information or pressure groups highlighting concerns: health risks of tobacco, obesity, food additives, mobile phone use etc.	Need to gather market information and feedback to monitor changes. Adjust product to minimise health/safety risks. Develop new products with health/safety benefits. Self-regulate responsible marketing (eg avoid targeting children with tobacco advertising). Communicate care for customer/employee health and safety.
	Environmental concerns ▪ Increasing cost of energy (non-renewable resources) ▪ Pollution and environmental impact of industrial processes and waste disposal	Develop 'green' offerings and messages: energy efficiency of products; absence of harmful substances (eg CFCs); product packaging lower-volume, higher-degradability; sustainable resource use (eg recycled materials)
Technology factors	**Constant technological development** ▪ New products/services (eg Internet services, home electronics, ICT and media) ▪ Accelerated obsolescence of old products ▪ New media: large volume of information, potential for direct/personalised contact, multi-media presentations	Inform and instruct customers about new products and media: reassure, minimise risk and insecurity. Depending on strategy, innovate or develop continuous product improvement to maintain competitive standing and customer service. Manage customer perceptions of constant obsolescence: emphasise improved satisfaction. Take advantage of new media and technologies for direct marketing, customer relationship management and promotion. Build an effective Web site for promotion and/or transaction. Use multi-media effectively. Reassure customers about privacy and security concerns.

Marketing at Work

Certain supermarket chains have bowed to the pressure exerted by parents in removing chocolates and sweets from low-level display at the checkouts. Parents pointed out that these items were available in-store for purchase by parental decision: to place them at checkouts appeared to be a cynical attempt at leading bored youngsters to force last-minute impulse purchases. The lesson? Effectively targeted marketing communication in one decade – overtaken by changes in customer sophistication and awareness in the next.

Changes in consumer lifestyles have had a radical effect on family restaurants such as Pizza Hut (in Australia) which have closed down most of their eat-in restaurants in city areas. Despite a traditional offering of hearty portions, value for money and child-friendly atmosphere and facilities, Pizza Hut has found that urban families no longer have time to sit down and eat together. The chain now focuses on take-away and delivery only outlets, which meet the need for fast service and home delivery. (Sydney Daily Telegraph, 29/7/02)

For another example, you might like to check out the 'Tescos Expansion (Certificate)' discussion in the **Hot Topics** pages of the CIM's Virtual Institute Web site (www.cim.virtualinstitute.com). Hot Topics is a great resource: we recommend that you explore it!

5.5 In the table above, we have discussed changes affecting customers in general. Of course, many of these changes will also be experienced over time by individual customers: we might call these **personal changes**. An organisation equipped for database marketing may be able to track and respond to these changes in a more personalised way: monitoring changes in individual customers' circumstances and attitudes and targeting offerings, incentives and contacts accordingly.

(a) As customers age, the organisation may be able to target them with appropriate products and services: retirement planning; leisure ideas; less expensive options and concessions. It may appoint older members of staff as their contact within the firm, and show empathy with mature needs and perspectives in all direct communications. (The Australian Pensioners and Insurance Agency has as its slogan: 'Understanding, not just insurance'.)

(b) As customers' family circumstances change, the organisation may target offerings and messages to the needs and wants of families with young children (for example family-friendly premises), older children (for example educational values) or the empty nest (for example new leisure time and interests). It may also wish to monitor separation, divorce or bereavement, avoiding offers that are no longer appropriate.

(c) As customers' career and financial circumstances change, the organisation may need to be alert to changing needs. During prime career years, for example, customers may be amenable to aspirational (income, status, professional, lifestyle) products and images. In the face of redundancy or retirement, however, they may require a focus on payment assistance, value-for-money, opportunities or new interests. In business-to-business markets, customer career changes may also be tracked to maintain and exploit established buyer contacts.

Action Programme 5

The State Government of New South Wales, Australia, is considering regulating food advertising to children, following survey findings that (a) there has been an alarming rise in childhood obesity and related health concerns and (b) food ads made up about half of all advertisements shown to child TV audiences, with confectionery and fast food restaurants prominent among an average seven food ads screened per hour during children's programmes. [*Sydney Daily Telegraph, 22/7/2002*)

If you were a marketer for a well-known fast-food chain in New South Wales, what kinds of messages would you plan to send:

(a) To consumers?

(b) To existing customers of your local outlet, to whom you exercise relationship marketing?

(c) To employees within your organisation?

(d) To state health authorities?

6 Internal customer focus

The importance of internal customer communications

6.1 People are arguably an organisation's most important marketing resource: ultimately, decision-making and communication by managers and employees are what shapes the interface with the customer and other stakeholders. Human Resource Management is outside the scope of this module, but you should be aware of the use of internal marketing communications in the following areas.

Employer branding	The organisation's image, mediated by communication, creates an employer brand: the organisation's **image or identity as an employer** in the market for which it competes for quality labour. **Recruitment communications** (job ads, application handling, interviews and so on) are public relations exercises. They must reflect the organisation's values and make an attractive offering to potential employees.
Employee communication and involvement	In many countries, there are **legal requirements** for formal communication and consultation with employees on matters that affect them. Sharing of marketing information encourages employees to **identify with the organisation**, its products/services and its customers ('selling' quality and customer care values). It also supports **task performance** (keeping employees informed about new products and marketing programmes) and **decision-making** (supplying market information to management). Internal communications (for example, meetings, presentations, newsletters, Intranet sites, suggestion schemes) can be used to improve **information flow** in all directions through the organisation. This may be particularly helpful where it encourages information- and ideas-sharing between management and front-line customer-facing staff.

Employee relations	Armstrong *(Strategic HRM)* describes the aims of employee relations as: ▪ Building **stable and co-operative relationships** with employees and minimising conflict ▪ Achieving **commitment** through employee involvement and communications processes ▪ Developing **mutuality**: a common interest in achieving the organisation's goals, through the development of a culture of shared values Co-operative employee relations depend on direct and open communication with employees, and giving employees a voice on matters that concern them (including customer care and quality).

Exam Tip

A question in the December 2000 exam (under the old syllabus) specifically tackled employee communications about a forthcoming product launch. According to the examiner, 'the key point here is that marketing is about communication': solutions which suggested the withholding of information from employees, while 'plausible', did not sit well with a marketing orientation!

Marketing at Work

United Biscuits (UK)

Consider how United Biscuits promotes itself as an employer in the following extract from an Annual Report. Note the recognition of the interests and rights of employees, and of their importance to the organisation – and how it is reflected in the **style** of this internal marketing message. Note also the awareness of other stakeholders.

'To achieve the dynamic morale and team spirit based on mutual confidence without which a business cannot be successful, people have to be cared for during their working lives and in retirement.

In return we expect from all our staff loyalty and commitment to the company. We respect the rights and innate worth of the individual. In addition to being financially rewarding, working life should provide as much job satisfaction as possible. The company encourages all employees to be trained and developed to achieve their full potential.

United Biscuits takes a responsible attitude towards employment legislation and codes of practice, union activities and communications with staff. We place the highest priority on promoting and preserving the health and safety of employees. Employees, for their part, have a clear duty to take every reasonable precaution to avoid injury to themselves, their colleagues and members of the public.'

Action Programme 6

Get hold of the Report and Accounts of your organisation and/or any other that interests you. What attitudes towards employees are expressed there? What are the internal and external marketing effects of these kinds of statements?

If relevant, draft some recommendations for how the report might be improved, as a marketing message to (a) employees and (b) potential employees of the organisation.

Chapter Roundup

- 'Marketing is the whole business seen from the point of view of its final result, that is from the 'customer's point of view.' (Drucker) This may be called customer focus.
- Customers are essential to organisational activity. Satisfying customers is important because of increasing competition and the potential for negative PR – as well as their rights under consumerism, customer charters and legislation/regulation.
- The fostering and maintenance of customer loyalty – or long-term customer satisfaction – has benefits for competitive advantage, customer retention, the cost-effectiveness of sales, risk management, information-gathering and goodwill promotion.
- Customer relations is the planned and sustained effort to establish and maintain goodwill and mutual understanding between an organisation and its customers.
- Relationship marketing involves engaging in two-way dialogue with customers and maintaining on-going contacts and relationships with them. Part of this process is guiding and supporting customers through changing circumstances.
- Internal marketing communication can create positive employer branding, employee involvement and satisfaction and positive employee relations.

Quick Quiz

1 Allocate the following phrases to the correct boxes below.

(1) Customer needs and wants
(2) Energetic selling and promoting
(3) Existing products made by the firm
(4) Integrated marketing activities
(5) Profit through business volume
(6) Profit through customer satisfaction

	Focus	Means	Aims
Marketing concept			
Selling concept			

2 The increasing organisation of groups to promote the rights of consumers is called:

A Competition
B Charter
C Consumerism
D Customisation

3 Fill in the blanks in the following sentence, using the words given in the box below.

The idea of a customer charter is to manage customers' (1)……… However, it also has the effect of raising (2) ……… that (3)……… are entitled to hold the organisation (4)……… for service(5)………

awareness	accountable	expectations	standards	customers

4 The average unhappy customer tells *how* many other people about the experience?

A 0
B 5
C 9
D 20

5 It is more cost-effective to attract a new customer than to keep an existing customer happy.

☐ True ☐ False

6 Supply the customer-focused alternatives to the Ps of the extended marketing mix.

Producer/provider focus	Customer/consumer focus
Product	
Price	
Place	
Promotion	
People	
Processes	
Physical evidence	

7 List Lele and Sheth's 'Four fundamentals of customer satisfaction'

8 'The planned and sustained effort to establish and maintain goodwill and mutual understanding between an organisation and its customers' is called:

A Customer service
B Customer loyalty
C Customer relations
D Customer focus

9 A relationship where the organisation contacts the customer on a regular basis for a range of purposes may be classified as:

Basic	Reactive	Accountable	Proactive	Partnership

10 List seven social factors affecting consumers.

Answers to Quick Quiz

1

	Focus	Means	Aims
Marketing concept	(1)	(4)	(6)
Selling concept	(3)	(2)	(5)

2 C

3 (1) expectations, (2) awareness, (3) customers, (4) accountable, (5) standards.

4 C

5 False

6 Choice, cost, convenience, communication, care, corporate competence, consistency

7 1 Product, 2 Sales and promotion activity, 3 After sales activity, 4 Corporate culture

8 C

9 Proactive

10 See paragraph 5.4 for a full list – or use examples relevant to your own culture.

Now try Question 2 from the Question Bank at the end of this Text

Action Programme Review

1 You were invited to reflect on your own awareness of your rights and power as a customer to take your business to a competitor if you aren't satisfied.

- Library: competition from non-book alternatives (eg Internet) as well as other libraries
- Utilities: depending where you live, this could be more difficult: traditionally, virtual monopolies.
- Charities: depend entirely on appealing contact: competition with other charities – and anything else you may do with your money or time!
- TV: competition from other channels – and other uses of your time.
- Business suppliers: may be more difficult to switch, because of negotiated relationship, stability – and perhaps components designed specially for your needs. But for same reasons, supplier wouldn't want to lose your business: power to negotiate improvement.

2 Reaching new customers takes longer and costs more, because you don't have existing contact with them. New customers require more information: free samples, product brochures, sales staff time etc. At the end of the process, a percentage of the potential new customers reached will not be converted into a sale. Existing customers can (ideally) be easily contacted (for example through databased information): they already have the information and predisposition to purchase.

Cares are generally subject to 'pull' switching factors: competitors easily 'win' customers by more attractive features and offers. Banking is said to be more subject to 'push' factors: requiring suppliers to 'lose' customers by mistakes or poor customer relations.

3 You should have ample experience as a customer to formulate your own case studies. If you are stuck for ideas, think through para 3.3. Customer 'delight' may be harder to identify. In customer relations, you may have experienced examples such as receiving personalised offers which were particularly timely or on-target (anticipating needs), or surprising gestures such as a birthday card from a retailer. Such experiences create positive rapport with a firm or brand. However, as Ted Johns points out, even 'delighting' features and services become taken for granted: marketers have to constantly stay ahead of customer expectations.

4 Notes: PLAY YOUR CARDS RIGHT

- Changes to terms and conditions = necessary. But HOW COMMUNICATED TO CUSTOMERS >> keeps or loses customers!
- State changes clearly: don't be perceived as 'sneaky'

  – Highlight and refer customers to important information strongly

  – Don't 'hide' information in small print
- Don't underestimate customer awareness of promotional style

  – Don't claim 'benefits' if they are really costs: customers see through this!
- See things from the customer's point of view

  - The fact that you need to recoup costs is NOT THE CUSTOMER'S PROBLEM!

5 Some ideas:

Consumers: advertisements and PR (targeting parents) highlighting nutritional value of offering; introduce new 'healthy choice' alternatives; sponsor 'activity/sports days' in schools

Loyal customers: invitation and discount voucher to try 'healthy choice' meals at local outlet; personalised letter reinforcing perceptions ('As you know, we offer healthy, nutritious...')

Employees: inform of ways to challenge customer doubts, Press queries; internal marketing of 'healthy choice' branding

State health authorities: report on nutritional values of offerings etc (if positive!); statement of willingness to co-operate in socially responsible measures to protect children etc.

6 If you can't find an annual report, you may find employer value statements on corporate Web sites. Such statements have multiple target audiences. They market internally to employees: 'selling' cultural values, encouraging identification/loyalty and commitment. They also address other stakeholders: shareholders, media and employer bodies. They project an employer brand in the labour market – and this can contribute to public perception of their offerings. (The positive employee relations policies of organisations like the Body Shop, for example, are part of their brand.)

Part B

Buying behaviour

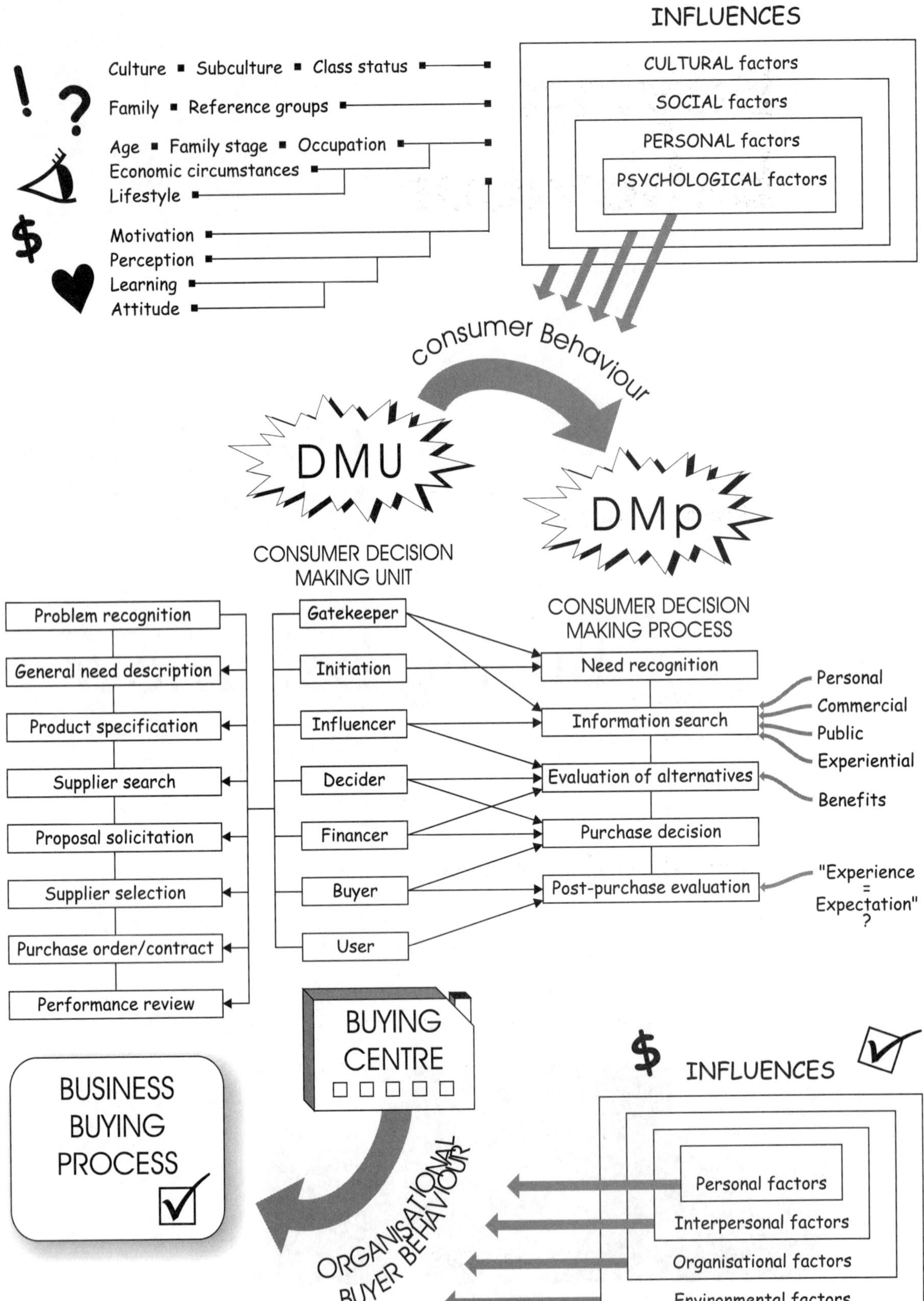
INFLUENCES
Culture ▪ Subculture ▪ Class status
Family ▪ Reference groups
Age ▪ Family stage ▪ Occupation
Economic circumstances
Lifestyle
Motivation
Perception
Learning
Attitude
CULTURAL factors
SOCIAL factors
PERSONAL factors
PSYCHOLOGICAL factors
consumer Behaviour
DMU
DMp
CONSUMER DECISION MAKING UNIT
CONSUMER DECISION MAKING PROCESS
Problem recognition
General need description
Product specification
Supplier search
Proposal solicitation
Supplier selection
Purchase order/contract
Performance review
Gatekeeper
Initiation
Influencer
Decider
Financer
Buyer
User
Need recognition
Information search
Evaluation of alternatives
Purchase decision
Post-purchase evaluation
Personal
Commercial
Public
Experiential
Benefits
"Experience = Expectation" ?
BUYING CENTRE
BUSINESS BUYING PROCESS
ORGANISATIONAL BUYER BEHAVIOUR
INFLUENCES
Personal factors
Interpersonal factors
Organisational factors
Environmental factors

Buying behaviour

3

Chapter Topic List	
1	Setting the scene
2	The decision making unit (DMU)
3	The decision making process (DMP)
4	Influences on consumer buying behaviour
5	Influences on organisational buying behaviour

Learning Outcomes

☑ Appreciate the importance of understanding buyer behaviour and the needs of the target audience

☑ Identify and explain the roles of stakeholders in consumer and organisational purchase decisions (the decision making unit)

☑ Explain the purchase decision making process for consumers and organisations

☑ List the various influences on consumer and organisational buying behaviour

Syllabus References

☑ Explain the difference between consumer buyer behaviour and organisational buyer behaviour (2.1)

☑ Explain the importance of understanding buyer behaviour (2.2)

☑ Describe the decision-making unit (DMU) and the roles of its constituents (2.3)

☑ The decision making process (DMP) for consumers and organisations (2.4)

☑ The impact and effect of the DMU and the DMP on the communications mix (2.5)

Key Concepts Introduced

- Consumer buying behaviour
- Organisational buying behaviour
- Decision making unit (DMU)
- Motivation
- Perception
- Attitude
- Culture

1 Setting the scene

The importance of understanding buyer behaviour

1.1 The main aim of this chapter is to develop an understanding of the various elements that influence how individuals use information to make purchase decisions. From this, you will be able to see how marketing communications can be used to support and reinforce these decisions.

1.2 Dibb *et al* suggest that the study of buying behaviour by an organisation is important for a number of reasons.

(a) The **buyer's reaction** to the organisation's marketing strategy has a major impact on the survival and success of the organisation.

(b) If organisations are truly to implement the marketing concept, they must examine the main influences on **what, where, when and how customers buy**. Only in this way will they be able to devise a marketing mix that satisfies the needs of customers.

(c) By gaining a better understanding of the factors influencing their customers and how their customers will respond, organisations will be better able to **plan effective marketing communications** and activities.

1.3 However, it is important to note that not all consumers behave in the same way. Decision making and purchase patterns vary considerably within markets or product categories, between individuals – and even within individuals according to circumstances and over time! You must begin to recognise this complexity and aim to adapt marketing communications to the needs of different **target audiences**.

Elements of buyer behaviour

1.4 The variables in buying behaviour are wide ranging and complex. However, they can be broadly categorised as:

- **Stakeholders** and **participants** in the buying decision
- The **decision making processes** by which information is used to solve problems, make choices and reach the decision to purchase
- Various **factors and characteristics** which influence buyers' perceptions, judgements, choices and decisions

1.5 We will look at each of these in turn, in relation to both **consumer buying behaviour** and **organisational buyer behaviour**.

Key Concept

Consumer buyer behaviour refers to the buying behaviour of final consumers, those individuals and households who buy goods and services for personal consumption. (Kotler)

Organisational buyer behaviour refers to the buying behaviour of organisations which buy goods and services to use in the production of other products and services that are sold, rented or supplied to others.

1.6 Most large organisations sell, one way or another, to other organisations. Some sell products and services predominantly to other businesses or government bodies. Some supply raw materials, components and machinery to manufacturers of those products. However, even companies that produce consumer goods and services must first sell their products to other businesses (wholesalers and retailers) who serve the consumer market or institutions (such as schools, hospitals, nursing homes and prisons) which pass them on to the end users in their care.

Exam Tip

'Buying behaviour' is a new topic for this module. However, it was previously examined as part of 'Marketing Fundamentals', and recent questions for that paper included topics such as the stages in the consumer buying decision process, influences impacting on it, differences in consumer and organisational decision processes – and the reasons why all the above are important to the marketer.

2 The decision making unit (DMU)

The decision making unit

2.1 Purchase decisions often involve more than one person. This is usually the case in organisations, where specialist purchasing or other decision-making teams ensure that a range of different factors – and the needs of different units and functions within the organisation – are taken into account. Even consumer purchase decisions (which brand of toothpaste will you buy? should you get a DVD player?) may involve input from a number of people who have an influence or interest in the decision: **stakeholders** in the purchase.

Key Concept

The **Decision Making Unit (DMU)** is a group of people who participate in or influence the purchase decision at any stage in the buying process.

2.2 There are a number of different models of the DMU, but most identify the following roles.

Gatekeeper	Accesses and controls the flow of information about the product or service to the others.
Indicator or **initiator**	First draws attention to a particular product, or suggests the idea of buying it. May be influenced by a **trigger** – and identifiable event or item of information which brings the need for the purchase to the fore.
Influencer	Stimulates, informs or persuades at any stage of the buying process. Examples include children who urge their parents to buy, friends who recommend the product – or the 'expert' in a TV advertisement.
Decider	Makes the decision that the product should be bought.
Buyer	Implements the purchase decision by ordering or purchasing the product/service.
Financier	Sets the budget and authorises or provides the funds for the purchase.
User	Uses, consumes or benefits from the product or service.

2.3 An individual may exercise one or more of these roles in a given purchase process: the decider/buyer/financier/user, for example, may be the same person. However, the following examples (from organisational and consumer settings) may help to clarify the various roles.

(a) A secretary receives office equipment catalogues and passes them on to relevant people **(gatekeeper)**. A marketing assistant proposes the purchase of a colour laser printer **(initiator)**. The Marketing Manager supports the idea and asks the Office Manager to recommend various models **(influencers)**. The Purchasing Manager authorises the requisition **(decider)**, the Accounts Manager authorises the expenditure **(financier)** and the marketing assistant sends a purchase order **(buyer)**. The marketing department utilise the new printer **(users)**.

(b) A father browses the 'food' section of the newspaper **(gatekeeper)** and comments that there is a new brand of cereal on the market **(initiator)**. The mother approves of its nutritional content and the younger child begs for the promotional toy that comes with it **(influencers)**. The mother (in charge of grocery buying in this traditional household) decides to try the cereal **(decider)**, determines that it is within the weekly budget **(financier)** and purchases the cereal **(buyer)**. The children eat the cereal **(users)**.

Action Programme 1

Produce a flow chart representing the stages in any major purchase you have recently been involved with at work or at home. Identify all those who were involved in the purchase, their DMU roles and how each step in the purchase decision was made. (In our answer, we chart a family's decision to purchase a holiday for their parents to celebrate a wedding anniversary.)

[Key Skill for Marketers: Presenting information]

The DMU as target audience

2.4 Although the **buyer** may appear to be the 'customer' at the point of sale, the entire decision-making unit can be identified as the target audience for the marketing message.

2.5 The marketing organisation needs to understand the complexity of the DMU in each market and market segment in which it operates. It is clearly relevant to marketers whether, for example, the woman or man in a household is the buyer/decision maker; whether a young or older person is the user; which gender or age group consumes which promotional media. This kind of information determines the product's positioning (masculine/feminine? youthful/mature?), media choices and target audience.

2.6 The communication mix should **leverage** influence on the purchase decision: reaching and persuading the **most influential role** in a given purchase with the **least expenditure** of effort and cost. The decider may be an obvious target, but for price sensitive decisions, for example, it may be important to target the financer (if a separate individual); if deciders are difficult to reach, it may be important to target gatekeepers; and for shared or complex decisions, it may be more cost effective to target influencers (co-opting them to share the work of promotion).

- Identify **gatekeepers** (who is most likely to be open to, or in charge of acquiring, product information?) and the most effective information **media** to reach them (where do they prefer to gather product information and in what format?)
- Identify **indicators/initiators** (who is most likely to notice and draw attention to product information?) and target them with messages that arouse **interest** (how is the product relevant to needs, wants or interests of the DMU?)
- Identify **influencers** (whom will the decider consult or listen to?) and target them with persuasive information to arouse or reinforce **desire** (how does the product solve a problem, meet a need? How can it be endorsed or validated?)
- Identify **deciders** (who will have the final say?) and target them with information to arouse or reinforce **intention** (what are the decisive benefits of the product for meeting needs and wants? How can the perceived risks of decision be lowered – and the benefits of acting quickly be conveyed?)
- Identify **buyers** (who actually makes the purchase?) and target them with messages which facilitate **action** (what does the buyer need to do next? How can it be made easy?)

- Identify **financiers** (who pays or authorises payment?) and target them with information to help them to **justify** expenditure (what benefits can be weighed against the costs?) and to complete the transaction (how can payment be made easy?)
- Identify **users** (who uses, consumes or benefits?) and target them with practical information to enable them to **use** the product safely and satisfyingly (what are possible areas of ignorance or difficulty? What on-going support may be required?)

2.7 The marketing organisation will also seek appropriate forms of **feedback** to fine-tune its marketing mix in satisfying the needs of each of the DMU roles. (Is product packaging effectively attracting the attention of initiators? Are promotional messages effectively persuading influencers and deciders? Is customer service effectively satisfying users?)

Action Programme 2

How might you target your communications in the ways suggested in paragraph 2.6 above if you were marketing

- A new model of family car?
- Professional office cleaning services?

The consumer decision making unit

2.8 The people who make up a DMU will vary according to the context in which the purchase decision is being made and the stakeholders who will be affected by and involved in the decision. Consumers belong to a number of different groups and networks.

(a) The **family** is a primary group for most individuals: family norms and influences are particularly strong. Socio-cultural factors influence customary decision-making roles within the family structure: be aware that such norms vary from culture to culture. In a traditional Western or Latin family model, marketing messages may be targeted at the child (initiator/influencer) in the purchase of a toy; at the wife/mother (decider/buyer) in the case of household items; or at the husband/father (decider/buyer) in the case of the family car. Be aware, however, that gender roles and household structures are becoming more diverse, as discussed in Chapter 2.

(b) The **work group** can be an important influence, especially if colleagues are also part of the individual's social network. Needs to project status, professionalism and image at work also influence decisions: cars, clothes, office furniture and other products are often positioned accordingly.

(c) **Friendship groups** are an important influence on buyer behaviour: the desire to form and maintain social relationships is a basic human need. People often trust friends to advise them: marketers frequently depict product choice, in advertising, in the context of friendly sharing, advice and encouragement – and attempt to capitalise on positive word-of-mouth promotion.

(d) **Interest groups** (action groups, pressure groups, consumer groups and so on) may influence purchase behaviour. Membership of (or advocacy by) groups may lead to supporting or boycotting brands that do or do not conform to the group's values.

Marketing messages may be targeted defensively or positively to address environmental, human rights or consumer concerns.

Marketing at Work

The Advertising Association (www.adassoc.org.uk) has produced a leaflet called *Parent Power* which takes parents through the rigours of saying no to children's repeated requests for new purchases. It also describes how to explain the process of advertising to children, has guidelines for advertising to children and describes how to lodge a complaint.

The industrial decision making unit

2.9 The DMU of a buying organisation is called its **buying centre**. This is not to be confused with a purchasing function or team: it is a set of buying roles exercised by different individuals and units that participate in the business decision making process. As Kotler notes, 'the buying centre concept present a major marketing challenge. The business marketer must learn who participates in the decision, each participant's relative influence and what evaluation criteria each decision participant uses.'

2.10 The buying centre will involve those formally involved in purchase decisions, such as department managers, purchasing managers and accountants. It may also involve less obvious, informal participants who may initiate or influence the buying process.

Action Programme 3

List five people (or positions) who might influence a buying decision in an organisation.

2.11 As in consumer marketing, it is helpful to consider the information needs of different roles (and individuals, if known) within a corporate buying centre.

(a) **Users** may be targeted with information on the technical characteristics, reliability, performance and service contracts pertaining to a product, since this will be relevant to their desired outcomes from the purchase – and they may have influence in this area.

(b) **Influencers** may have technical expertise, or may be concerned with rational criteria such as cost/benefit analysis and competitor comparison. Influencers are a particularly useful contact where the purchase relies on technical knowledge: the sales person can be a respected technical adviser, especially in markets where (due to competitive pressures and security constraints) knowledge is not widely shared. Trade journals, professional bodies and consultants are also used as a source of influential information, so trade/public/media relations will be an important component of the promotional mix.

(c) **Deciders/buyers/financiers** are likely to be powerful individuals or teams: the marketer may need to take into account a variety of personal, organisational and task objectives. Buying centres may be politically complex: there may, for example, be conflict between the interests of influencers/deciders and financiers (who control expenditure).

Marketers may need to facilitate decision-making in such situations, offering a cost/benefit analysis that will satisfy all parties.

(d) Even junior personnel may be **gatekeepers** for marketing information: a lesson to the marketing communicator to use his or her relationship-building, public relations and persuasive skills at **every** contact with the customer...

3 The decision making process (DMP)

3.1 A number of complex or 'comprehensive' models have been developed in the attempt to describe or explain the dynamics of consumer behaviour: the Nicosia model (1996), the Engel-Kollat-Blackwell model (1968) and the Howard-Sheth model (1969) are the main 'grand' models.

3.2 At its simplest level, however, decision-making can be seen as a linear process with a number of steps. Not every decision will involve an orderly progression through all the steps, but such a model provides a useful framework for considering systematic decision-making activities by consumers – and how marketing communications can be used to influence them.

3.3 The decision-making process (DMP) for consumers may be illustrated as follows (Figure 3.1). (We have added the DMU roles to suggest how the process may be shared by different stakeholders.)

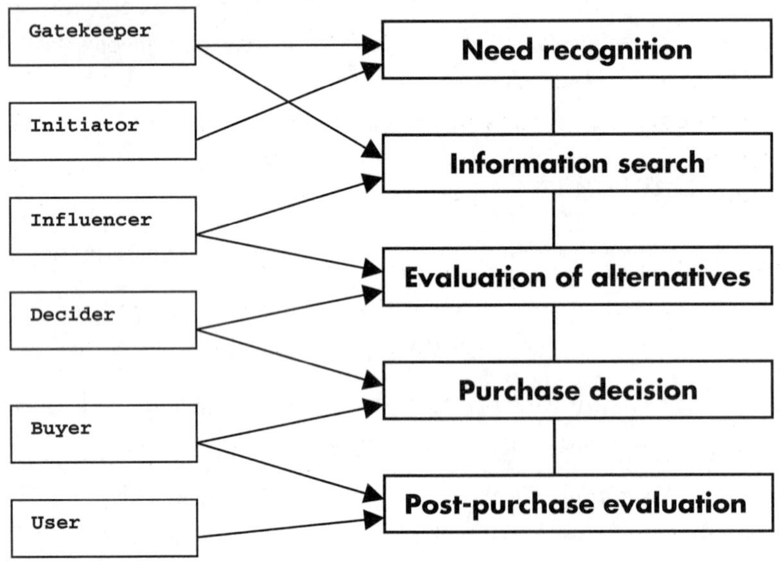

Figure 3.1 The decision-making process

Action Programme 4

Before reading on, think about a recent purchase of a fairly major item that you have made. Did you go through the stages listed above? Explain what the **need** was, how you searched for **information** and so on.

Need recognition

3.4 The process begins when the consumer recognises a need or problem: the difference between a **desired state** and the **actual state** (s)he is experiencing. This sense of need can be triggered by **internal** stimuli in the consumer, such as thirst or a desire for status – or **external** stimuli such as the smell of coffee brewing, or a TV ad showing someone being admired and respected (for having chosen an up-market brand, say).

3.5 The marketer's task will be to identify (through consumer research):

- What kind of needs and problems their target audience experiences (in order to develop products and marketing messages offering satisfaction)
- What stimuli trigger the target audience's awareness of the need or problem (in order to stimulate the sense of need through marketing messages)

Information search

3.6 Once aroused, the consumer may have accustomed ways of satisfying the need (products that have worked for them in the past) or the need may be so strong that the consumer simply buys the nearest satisfying product to hand. If the need is not immediate, or the 'best' product not obvious, the consumer may:

- Develop **heightened attention**: become more receptive to information about the product category that might satisfy the need, from advertising, conversations or point of sale, and/or
- Actively **search for information**. If additional information is relatively easy (or even satisfying) to locate and the consumer believes that it will materially improve the quality of the decision, this may be an extensive process.

3.7 The marketer's task will be to determine which information sources will be most consulted and most influential: for example, by researching consumer information-seeking behaviour and asking where existing customers 'first heard about the product'. Kotler identifies four major sources of product information:

Source	Description	Supporting marketing activity
Personal	Family, friends, neighbours, work colleagues	Product samples/trials, customer satisfaction and creating 'virtual communities' of users
Commercial	Advertising, selling, packaging, point of sale display, promotions, Web sites, exhibitions	(By definition, all marketing activities)
Public	Mass media, consumer rating and watchdog organisations	Positive public and media relations
Experiential	Handling, examining and using the product	Product demonstrations, sampling and trial promotions

3.8 Consumers generally receive most information from **commercial** sources (initiated by the marketer) which **inform** them about the product. However, **personal** sources have been shown to be more effective – particularly in service markets – because they **endorse** the product, pre-evaluating it for the potential buyer. (Some of this effect can be harnessed by the use of expert, celebrity or distributor recommendations in marketing.)

Evaluation of alternatives

3.9 There is no universal model of how consumers process information to arrive at the choice of a particular brand. It may involve the rational calculation and weighing up of benefits and costs; comparisons of competing brands; recommendation by friends, sales people or consumer guides; and so on. In other cases, it may involve purchase on impulse, instinct or emotion, with little or no logical evaluation. The task of the marketer is thus to find out **how** buyers evaluate brand alternatives, so that they can support the process appropriately.

3.10 Kotler suggests that, as the consumer is trying to satisfy some need with the buying process, (s)he will be looking for certain **benefits** from the product chosen: each product will be seen as a 'bundle of attributes' with varying capabilities of delivering the benefits sought. The composition and the relative importance of the components of this bundle of attributes/benefits will differ between brands – and also between consumers. The task of the marketer is thus to determine:

- What attributes/benefits the consumers desire of a particular product
- The importance they attach to each benefit and
- The extent to which they believe a given brand will deliver the most valued benefits.

Marketing messages can then be targeted at promoting the most valued benefits.

Action Programme 5

What do you think are the key benefits sought by the target audience in the following consumer markets?

- Domestic white goods (refrigerators, washing machines)
- Pharmaceuticals
- Education
- Snack foods
- Cars
- Financial services

If convenient, you may like to discuss this question with fellow students, friends or family: an informal 'market research' exercise into consumer needs and perceptions. *[Key Skills for Marketers: presenting information]*

Purchase decision

3.11 As a result of evaluation, the consumer forms the **intention to purchase** the brand which most readily promises to satisfy the need. The task of the marketer is primarily to ensure that the purchase decision is easy to put into effect, through availability, stockist information, effective customer service and so on.

Post-purchase evaluation

3.12 Having purchased the product, the consumer will either be satisfied or dissatisfied/disappointed with it, depending on how his **experience** matches up to his **expectations**. The task of the marketer will be:

- To **manage consumer expectations**, by making accurate and realistic claims for the product or service
- To **manage consumer experience** of the product to ensure satisfaction – or, if possible, delight (experience exceeding expectation) through offering added value
- To manage the **post-purchase relationship**. This may involve dealing with **dissatisfied** customers, to minimise damage: for example, by accepting the return of products that do not give full satisfaction; swift acknowledgement and adjustment of complaints; encouraging feedback and responding constructively. It may also involve proactive follow-up of **satisfied** customers, to further the relationship: offering after-sales service or advice, checking that everything is OK and so on.

3.13 As we will see in Part E of this Text, dealing with customer dissatisfaction and complaints is particularly important, as **negative** word-of-mouth about a product travels faster – and further – than **positive** word-of-mouth!

The business buying process

3.14 A similar process to the consumer DMP will apply in organisational buying, but steps may be added to reflect the **formal requirements** of buying policies and criteria: organisational buying decisions are generally more formal and more rationally motivated than consumer decisions, with a range of financial and managerial objectives to be met.

3.15 A systematic business buying process is shown on the next page (Figure 3.2.)

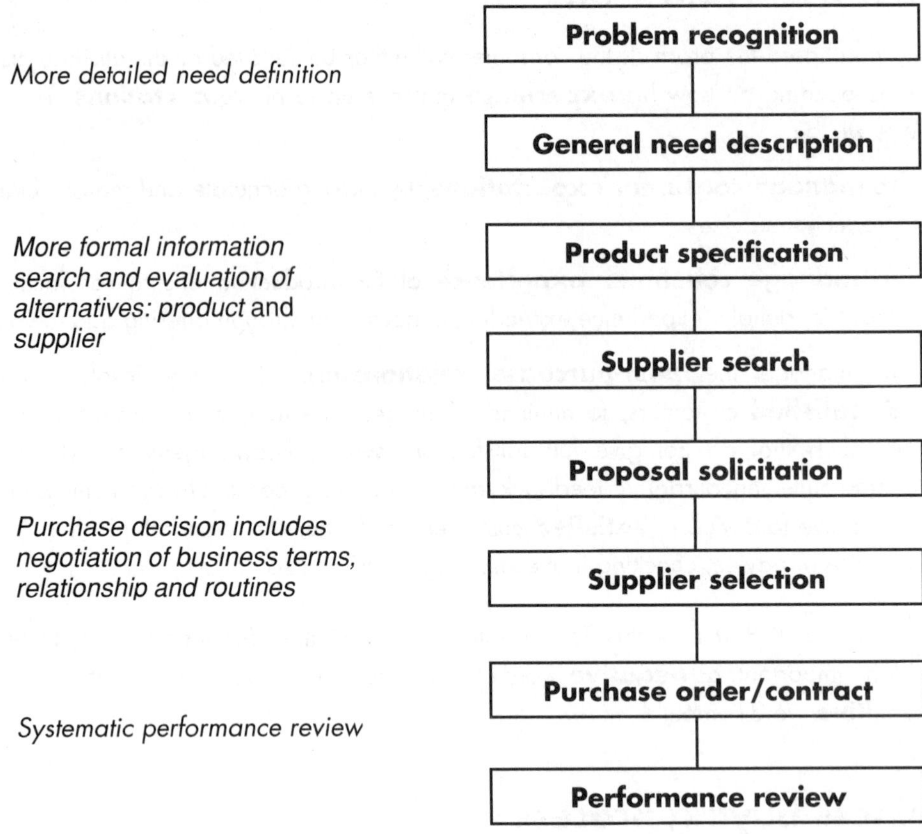

Figure 3.2: the business buying process

3.16 Whether the organisation will go through all these stages in a given case will depend on the nature of the buying situation.

(a) Some purchases will be a **straight rebuy** or the routine topping up of stocks without changing supplier or product specifications: for example, the re-ordering of stationery supplies. (This may be done on an automatic re-ordering system by the purchasing department or even the supplier, requiring only post-purchase review to ensure satisfaction.)

(b) Some purchases will be a **modified rebuy**: the organisation wants to change product specifications, prices, terms or suppliers (which should stimulate competitive offerings from existing and alternative suppliers). Any or all stages of the buying decision may be revisited.

(c) Some purchases will be a **new task** situation: the organisation is buying a product or service for the first time. In such circumstances, an extensive and systematic decision-making process may take place. This is an opportunity for the marketer to reach key members of the buying centre and to offer support and information in making the decision.

4 Influences on consumer buying behaviour

4.1 The basic process of consumer decision making described above will be influenced by a wide number of internal and external variables. These may broadly be classified as follows (Figure 3.3).

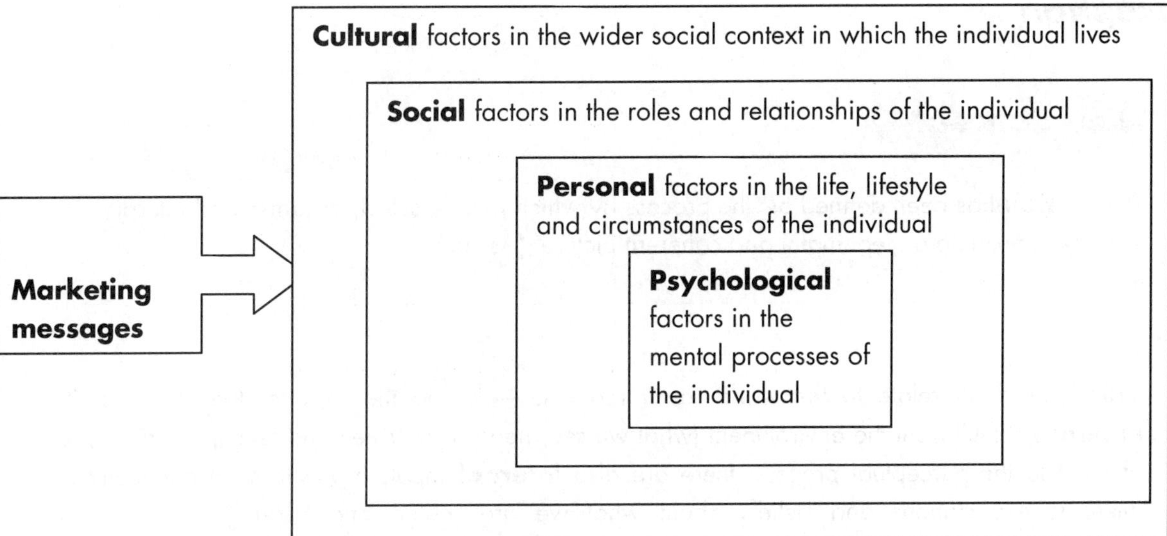

Figure 3.3: Influences on consumer behaviour

Psychological influences

Motivation

Key Concept

Motivation has been defined as 'an inner state that energises, activates or moves, that directs or channels behaviour towards goals' (Assael)

4.2 There are various complex theories of what motivation is and how it works. 'Need' theories are perhaps the most immediately helpful: they propose that human beings have certain innate needs and will choose to behave in ways that satisfy those needs.

4.3 People have a range of needs at any given time. Abraham Maslow, in his influential needs theory, classified and arranged these in a hierarchy of importance or urgency as follows.

- Physiological needs (hunger, thirst, sex drive)
- Safety needs (shelter, safety, security)
- Social needs (love, friendship, belonging)
- Esteem needs (self-esteem, status, recognition)
- Self actualisation needs (growth, fulfilment, realisation of one's potential).

4.4 While the hierarchy is not precise, nor observed across all cultures, it does propose some useful ideas for the marketer. People occupied with more urgent needs (such as hunger or insecurity) will not be motivated by the offer of higher satisfactions (such as status or fulfilment). All these needs are, however, universal and basic to human beings, and can be used as the basis for emotionally engaging and powerful marketing communications.

Perception

Key Concept

Perception has been defined as 'the process by which people select, organise and interpret sensory stimuli into a meaningful and coherent picture' (Assael)

4.5 Individuals don't relate to the world 'as it really is' – but to the 'picture' they have of it. **External** stimuli from the environment (what we see, hear, taste, smell and touch) are one type of input to the perceptual process: there are also **internal** inputs in the form of our motives, interests, expectations and beliefs about what we are seeing and hearing. This is why perception is so personal: each individual's world picture is unique!

4.6 Three aspects of perception are important for the marketer.

Selective attention	People do not (and could not) give their attention to all the messages they come into contact with: they filter out messages which are less powerful or less relevant to their needs and interests. Repetition, colour, size, volume of sound, standing out from the context and so on can increase a message's impact. Relevance to the target audience's needs will be most effective, especially if they are at the 'heightened attention' stage of the DMP.
Selective retention	People do not (and cannot) retain all the messages they receive in their short term memory. They tend to retain information that confirms their expectations, attitudes or beliefs. Repetition, relevance and positive first impressions will all help recall of promotional messages.
Selective distortion	People really do 'see what they want to see' and 'hear what they expect to hear'. Past experience, expectations, needs and interests, attitudes and beliefs influence how we interpret information. Marketers need to find out what expectations, prejudices and images (positive or negative) consumers have about their products or brands which might how marketing messages are perceived.

Learning

4.7 Learning is the process whereby an individual's behaviour is changed as a result of experience. There are various different theories about how this works, but essentially it involves:

- **Stimulus**: something we perceive or experience (for example an advertisement or product) which arouses a need or want
- **Response**: how we behave in order to satisfy that need or want (for example, buying the product)
- **Feedback**: how far we are satisfied by the results of the experience
- **Reinforcement**: whether our experience is an incentive (positive reinforcement) or a deterrent (negative reinforcement) to our giving the same response next time we encounter the same stimulus

4.8 A bad or disappointing experience makes customers less likely to buy that product again, or shop at that store, or call the helpline, or trust an advertising claim. A positive experience encourages repeat business. Learning theory also confirms the benefits for marketers of identifying needs and making stimuli impactful and relevant to those needs.

Attitudes

Key Concept

Attitudesare an enduring mixture of thoughts, feelings and tendencies which pre-dispose the individual to respond in a certain way to objects to which they relate.

4.9 Attitudes lead people to behave in a fairly consistent way towards people, things, ideas and situations that are familiar to them. Attitudes are a kind of 'short-cut' in our responses: we do not have to interpret, evaluate and respond to things each time we encounter them, because we already have a 'standpoint' (positive or negative) towards them.

4.10 Attitudes are stable and difficult to change. They can, however, be shifted by:

- Powerful contrary information, especially from sources we respect: it is less uncomfortable to change the attitude than revise our opinion of the source
- Changing our behaviour, for example by being asked to trial products we 'dislike' or to explain their benefits as part of a promotional competition: it is less uncomfortable to change the attitude than admit that our behaviour is inconsistent

Marketing at Work

HEA Drugs Education

Advertising can successfully educate consumers, getting them to reappraise attitudes and moderate behaviour. The HEA Drugs Education campaign shows that even in seemingly intractable circumstances advertising can persuade consumers to change their behaviour.

Drug usage, fuelled by the 'love drug' Ecstasy, had exploded by 1995, becoming mainstream and accepted within youth culture. Attempts by the adult world, including politicians, teachers and parents, had failed to stem the growth. The campaign's aim was to reduce demand for drugs, and it had to communicate to users and non-users, across a range of recreation drugs and the entire 11-25 age range.

A unifying strategic insight gave a clear campaign direction. Young people are not pressured into taking drugs. They actively choose to take them, weighing up the pros and cons. The one things that would deter them from taking drugs was the one thing that they knew little about – health risks carried by drug usage. But the messages still have to be accepted by this cynical audience.

Source: Reproduced with kind permission of IPA

Action Programme 6

Identify and describe your own experiences of how:

- Motivation affects your response to marketing messages
- Selective distortion affects your perception of a brand
- You 'learn' to be a loyal customer
- Marketing messages can change your attitudes

Personal factors

4.11 Personal influences on behaviour include the following.

(a) **Age**. Individuals consume different products and services, and respond to different marketing messages, according to their age. This is particularly relevant to lifestyle products such as clothes, furniture and recreational pursuits. It also impacts on the kinds of media which will be effective in reaching the target audience.

(b) **Stage in the family life cycle**, through which families pass as they mature over time. Traditional stages are identified as:

Young singles: few financial burdens; recreation/fashion led.
Young married couples: strong financial position; focus on home
'Full nest' stages: *Young couple, child under 6:* peak financial burdens; reliance on credit; child focus *Young couple, child over 6:* better financial position (wife return to work); child focus Older couple, dependent child: *better financial position (more wives work); school focus*
'Empty nest' stages: *Children left, head of family working:* strong financial position; focus on travel, leisure *Children left, head of family retired:* cut in income; focus on health
Solitary survivor: reduced spending; focus on health, hobbies, care, companionship

However, new markets are emerging with non-traditional households: single parents, childless couples and so on.

(c) **Occupation**: influencing income, status, interests and attitudes. Marketers may target occupational groups with particular interest in their products or services.

(d) **Economic circumstances**: level and stability of disposable income, savings and assets, borrowing power – and attitudes towards spending and saving.

(e) **Lifestyle**, an individual's mode of living as identified on key AIO dimensions: *Activities* (work, shopping, hobbies, sports, events attended), *Interests* (family, recreation, fashion, computers, food and drink, travel) and *Opinions* (about products, issues, events, people). Marketers will seek to identify how their products/services 'fit' different lifestyle groups or profiles (of which there are many researched classifications).

Marketing at Work

Chris Watt (in Australian marketing and advertising magazine *B & T Weekly*, 5/7/02) draws the following portrait of the **youth market**.

- The youth market is extremely media-savvy and immediately dismissive of those who employ the standard tricks of the trade. Promoting a product as "cool" in this market, is definitely not. They are cynical and untrusting of advertising and marketing promises.
- The fear of not belonging and the desire to be accepted are the key to understanding youth consumer behaviour. The flow-on effects of having a sense of belonging and control are the feelings of empowerment, confidence and independence – emotions highly sought by young people. Marketers must emphasise the elements within their product that evoke these emotions when communicating with this market.
- In the youth market more than any other, being seen to be 'on the cutting edge' has a major impact on the attention that a brand, product or service receives. SMS (mobile phone text messaging) and the Internet are essential media of cutting edge communication, enabling the marketer to get closer to its market – and to fulfil their desires for instant interaction, gratification and belonging.

Social factors

4.12 The immediate social environment in which the individual has an important influence on behaviour, because of the basic human needs for belonging and esteem. We have already mentioned the **family** as a primary group (see paragraph 2.8), together with various other **small groups** with whom the individual may have interactions and relationships.

4.13 **Reference groups** is the term given to groups 'with which an individual identifies so much that he or she takes on many of the values, attitudes or behaviours of groups members' (Dibbs et al). These include:

- **Primary membership groups**: generally informal groups, to which individuals belong and within which they interact (family, friends, work groups, neighbours).
- **Secondary membership groups**: generally more formal, allowing less involvement and interaction (trade unions, professional bodies)
- **Aspirational groups**, to which an individual would like to belong. (This is an important factor in 'aspirational' buyer behaviour: people buying products to create an image of status, income, job position or lifestyle above what they currently enjoy. It also accounts for many fashions, through which consumers seek to identify with celebrity or 'in' groups.)

4.14 The task of marketers is to identify the reference groups of targets audiences and:

- Offer products (and associated images) that help them to identify with the group
- Use images and values associated with the group to arouse interest and need
- Use members of aspirational groups (such as celebrities, successful business figures) to endorse products

Action Programme 7

If you are using this Text, the CIM – or the marketing profession – is probably one of your 'aspirational' groups. What other groups do you aspire to belong to or be like? How does this affect the kinds of products/services you buy – and the kind of marketing you respond to?

Cultural factors

Key Concept

Culture comprises 'the values, attitudes, beliefs, ideas, artefacts and other meaningful symbols represented in the pattern of life adopted by people that help them interpret, evaluate and communicate as members of society' (Rice)

4.15 Culture is the most basic underlying influence on an individual's behaviour, values and perceptions, as it is absorbed through upbringing, education and 'socialisation', the process by which a person is taught to conform to the norms of a group.

4.16 Culture operates on many levels. It distinguishes the members of one category of people from another, but that "category of people" may be a nation, regional or ethnic group, religious group, women versus men (gender culture), old versus young (generation culture), a social class, a profession or occupation (occupational culture), a type of business, or a work organisation or part of it (organisational culture). These may be identified as **sub-cultures** within the wider 'society'.

4.17 Each of these sub-cultures transmits its values, perceptions, norms (desirable behaviours) and taboos (forbidden behaviours), artefacts (including clothing, furniture, art works, books, music and so on) to its members as they learn to belong within the group.

4.18 There are particularly wide variations in cultural values and norms between **countries** – and even regions (northern and southern Italy, for example). This is a key understanding for marketers operating in international or global markets, and a vast area of study. There may be differences in consumer wants and needs, different media, different buyer behaviours, different environmental factors. There are invariably different communication norms: the meaning of body language, values about formality/respect, acceptable levels of proximity or eye contact and so on – let alone different languages used! (Imagine launching Vauxhall Nova cars in South America – and then discovering that 'no va' means 'doesn't work' in Spanish... This may be an urban advertising myth, but it makes a good point: do your cultural homework!)

Marketing at Work

Domino's Pizza

'In the US, Domino's Pizza stresses its delivery system as a way to differentiate itself from other pizza companies, but abroad it is not so easy. In Britain, customers don't like the idea of the

delivery man knocking on their doors – they think it's rude. In Japan, houses aren't numbered sequentially, so finding an address means searching among rows of houses numbered willy-nilly. In Kuwait, pizza is more likely to be delivered to a waiting limousine than to someone's front door. And in Iceland, where much of the population doesn't have telephone service, Domino's has teamed with a drive-in movie theatre chain to gain access to consumers. Customers craving a reindeer-sausage pizza – one of the most popular flavours – flash their turn signals, and a theatre employee brings them a cellular phone to order a pizza that is delivered to the car.'

Adapted by Cateora & Graham (International Marketing) *from an article in* The Wall Street Journal*: "The Most Successful Companies Have to Realise a Simple Truth: All Consumers Aren't Alike"*

For reflection
What are the most important cultural values and/or infrastructure factors in your own country that impact on marketing practices and trends?

---

5 Influences on organisational buying behaviour

Distinctive features of organisational buying

5.1 Organisational buying behaviour is different from consumer buying behaviour in several respects. Its distinctive features – and their implications for marketing – can be summarised as follows.

(a) There are generally far **fewer customers** placing orders of far **higher value** than in consumer markets. Suppliers often need to maintain a constant flow of orders to keep production and other business processes running efficiently. They may need to ascertain and meet the needs of individual customers: buyers and sellers often work closely together to build in on-going **partnership relationships**.

(b) There is generally greater **inertia**, created by loyalty to existing suppliers, than in the consumer market because of the importance of reliable (trusted) supply, established networks of contacts, and negotiated relationships. The key customer communication task will be to maintain existing relationships.

(c) Industrial buyers are much more **rationally motivated** than consumers: they tend to buy according to specific financial and managerial objectives. (They are using company money – not their own, as consumers do.) Suppliers' sales policies tend to be more influential than promotional messages. The focus of marketing effort should be on product quality and availability, price, credit arrangements, prompt quotation and timely delivery, after-sales service and so on.

(d) Organisations are more likely to buy a **complex total offering**, with added value from technical support, staff training, delivery scheduling, financing arrangements and so on. (Integrated marketing effort and communications will be important.)

(e) The need to optimise decisions tends to encourage the **participation of more buyers**, to integrate a range of stakeholder objectives, and more **professional purchasing effort**, giving technical and buying expertise. The process tends to be **lengthier and more formal**, requiring written documentation, authorisation, feasibility studies and so on – perhaps subject to detailed purchasing policies (as in the UK public sector requirement for competitive tendering).

Action Programme 8

Whenever you have the chance – when visiting clients, looking in Newsagents, or sitting in waiting rooms – browse through any trade or B2B (business to business) magazines and journals you find: from *Campaign* and *Advertising Weekly* to *Farmer's World, Banking World, Engineering Today* and so on.

What do you notice about the way products and services are marketed in such media? Is more technical language used? Are the ads less 'glossy'? What do you learn about the importance of price and other factors in the marketing mix?

Influences on organisational buyers

5.2 Webster and Wind *(Organisational Buying Behaviour)* identify four main groups of influences on business buyers.

Environmental factors	▪ Health and prospects of the economy and market sector in which the business operates (affecting ability to invest in stocks) ▪ Scarcity of materials (affecting importance of secure supply) ▪ Cultural factors (business ethics and customs) ▪ Legal/political influences (for example obligation to seek tenders)
Organisational factors	▪ Objectives of the organisation (requiring cost efficiency, long-term supply continuity, risk management, quality) ▪ Policies, procedures and systems (buying policies, quality assurance, authorisation requirements) ▪ Structure (purchasing responsibilities, communication and decision-making channels)
Interpersonal factors	▪ Nature and distribution of influence within the buying centre: (influence based on authority, status, expertise, control of resources? Who 'really' makes the decision?) ▪ Flow of information into and within the buying centre (who are the gatekeepers?) ▪ Interpersonal skills of buyers (negotiating, persuading, conflict resolution, networking)
Personal factors	▪ Personal needs, preferences and perceptions of the buyer (authority, expertise, values, professionalism, attitudes to risk/quality/cost etc)

5.3 The American Marketing Association (AMA) model suggests that these influences can be classified in a different way, according to whether they come from within or outside the purchasing department and within or outside the organisation. This can be depicted in a cruciform chart as follows (Figure 3.4)

Figure 3.4 The AMA Model

5.4 The four quadrants represent the following spheres of influence on the buying process.

(a) Within the purchasing department in the organisation, the **purchasing agent** will bring to bear personal preferences and perceptions, as well as purchasing policies and technical concerns such as price, cost, risk and supply continuity.

(b) Outside the purchasing department, but within the organisation, there are other members of the **buying centre**. They will exercise mainly interpersonal influences through power, persuasion, political alliances and conflicts, and control of information through gatekeeping.

(c) Within the purchasing department **outside** the organisation, there is **professionalism** in purchasing (membership of the Chartered Institute of Purchasing and Supply, access to specialist journals and conferences etc), which brings to bear influences such as professional education, standards and ethics, information about industry best practice, network contacts and relationships.

(d) Outside the purchasing department **and** the organisation, there is the **organisational environment**, bring to bear all the influences listed earlier.

5.5 The precise criteria which determine the choice of supplier will thus depend on a number of factors, over and above need recognition and product specification.

Action Programme 9

If possible, arrange to conduct an informal interview or discussion with someone you know who is responsible for purchasing in a business or institution at any level. Find out what sort of things (s)he personally looks for when selecting a supplier, and what criteria (if any) are set out in the organisation's buying policies.

Chapter Roundup

- In order to reach and influence members of the target audience it is crucial to understand how customers receive, understand and utilise marketing messages to make buying decisions.
- The Decision Making Unit (DMU) comprises all stakeholders in a decision. This may involve a number of roles: gatekeeper, initiator, influencer, decider, financer, buyer and user.
- Marketers need to identify, reach and target the needs of the most influential member of the DMU for a given product purchase. A business DMU is called the buying centre.
- The Decision Making Process (DMP) can be summarised as: Recognition of problem/need; Information search; Evaluation of alternatives; Purchase decision; Post-purchase evaluation. The business buying process is similar, allowing for more extensive product definition and supplier selection.
- A range of influences impacts on consumer buying behaviour:
  - Psychological factors (motivation, perception, learning, attitudes)
  - Personal factors (age, family lifecycle, occupation, economic circumstances, lifestyle)
  - Social factors (family and other reference groups) and
  - Cultural factors (the values and norms of 'society' and sub-cultures based on region, ethnic group, religion and other distinctives).
- Organisational buying differs from consumer buying primarily through being a longer, more formal, more professional process; involving more people and more collaborative between buyer and seller. Industrial markets are usually subject to greater loyalty and inertia than consumer markets, with fewer but higher-value customers.
- Personal, interpersonal, organisational and environmental factors influence business buying decisions. The AMA model shows how influences may come from various sources within and outside the purchasing function and organisation: the purchasing agent, the buying centre, professionalism in purchasing and the organisational environment.

Quick Quiz

1 Understanding buyer behaviour is important for marketers to anticipate:

A How consumers will respond to advertising and promotions
B How consumers will respond to product/brand features
C How consumers will respond to different elements of the marketing mix
D All of the above

2 The term 'DMU' describes:

A Factors and characteristics which influence purchase decisions
B How information is used to solve problems and reach purchase decisions
C How database marketing is used to analyse actual purchase decisions
D Stakeholders in purchase decisions

3 Allocate the following roles to the appropriate cells in the table below.

■ Gatekeeper ■ Indicator ■ Decider ■ Buyer

(1)	Authorises a purchase requisition
(2)	Recognises the need for a particular product
(3)	Sorts the mail
(4)	Signs a contract for service

4 Identify the five stages of the consumer DMP.

5 Allocate the following product information sources to the appropriate category in the box below.

(1) Mass media (2) Product trial (3) Neighbour
(4) Sales person (5) ISO or British Standards mark (6) Work colleague
(7) Product packaging (8) Product purchase

Personal	*Commercial*	*Public*	*Experiential*

6 Which of the following is *not* included in Maslow's hierachy of needs.

A Safety
B Social
C Satisfaction
D Self-actualisation

7 What does AIO (dimensions of lifestyle) stand for?

8 Groups that serve as direct or indirect points of comparison in forming a person's attitudes are called 'reference groups'.

☐ True ☐ False

9 Fill in the gaps using the words given in the box below.

'Organisations are more likely to be a (1)......... (2)......... offering. They are generally more (3).........motivated than consumers, and tend to involve (4)........ people in the buying process, together with (5).........expertise. Industrial markets have (6)......... customers of (7).........value than consumer markets, but with a (8)......... tendency to switch suppliers.'

■ lower	■ higher	■ more	■ less
■ professional	■ total	■ rationally	■ complex

10 Label the four quadrants of the AMA model.

Within the organisation

Within purchasing department | **(1)** | **(2)** | Outside purchasing department

(3) | **(4)**

Outside the organisation

Answers to Quick Quiz

1 D

2 D

3 (1) decider, (2) indicator, (3) gatekeeper, (4) buyer

4 Need recognition; information search; evaluation of alternatives; purchase decision; post-purchase evaluation

5 Personal: 3, 6. Commercial: 4, 7. Public: 1, 5. Experiential: 2, 8.

6 C

7 Attitudes, interests, opinions

8 True

9 (1) complex, (2) total, (3) rationally, (4) more, (5) professional, (6) fewer, (7) higher, (8) lower.

10 (1) Purchasing agent, (2) Buying Centre, (3) Professionalism, (4) Organisation environment.

Now try Question 3 from the Question Bank at the end of this Text

Action Programme Review

1

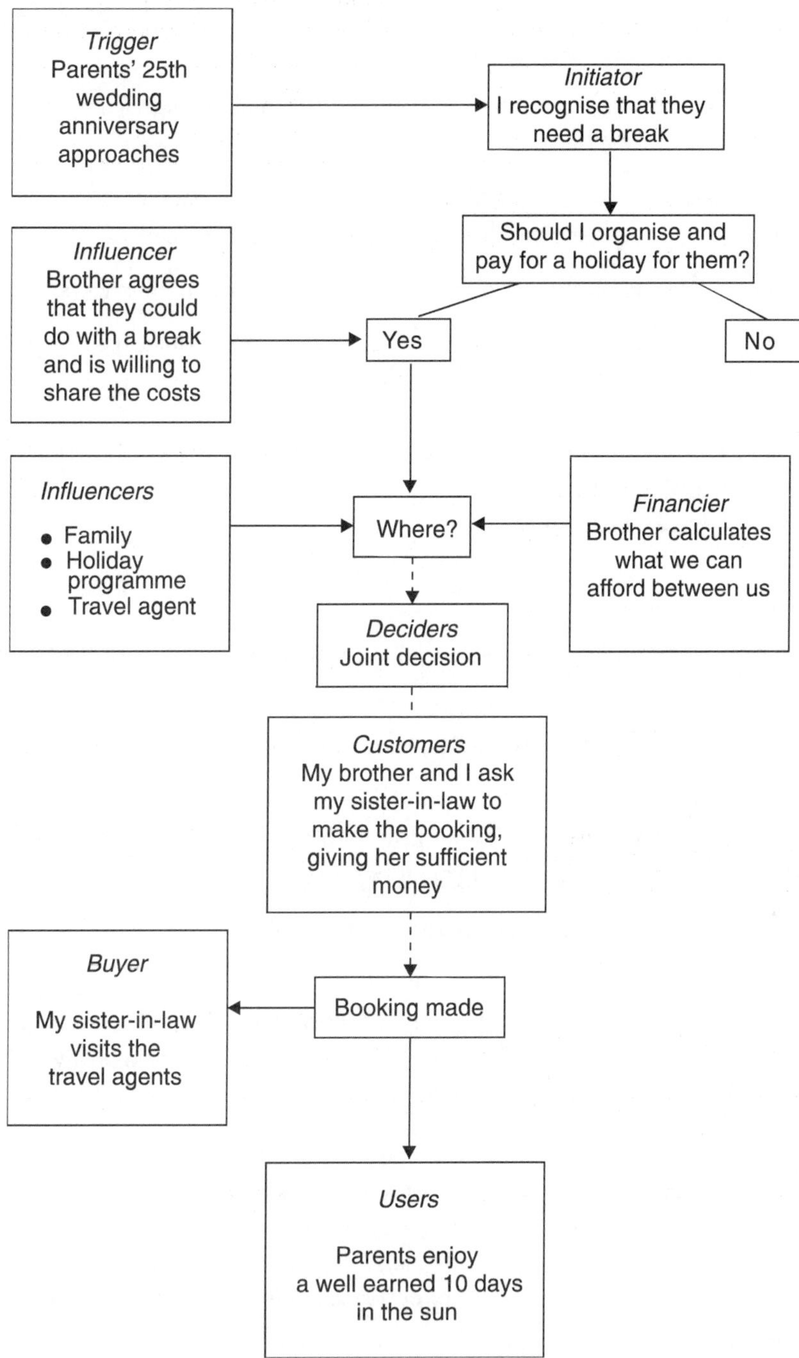

2 *Family car.* Gatekeepers/initiators/deciders/buyers traditionally the male head of household: other members of family influencers/users. So wide reach: TV advertising. Also a high-value, well-researched purchase: target specialist media ('What Car?', Auto section of newspaper, Motor Show). Message focus on family: spacious, good fuel economy, family fun outings and/or school transport.

Office cleaning. Business market: may be dealing with more individuals. Target officer/premises managers as gatekeepers/initiators: if large, advertise in specialist journals, business directories; if small, brochure and personal letter, with follow-up call. Supply information to help persuade senior management (decider/buyer/financer): brochure or sales presentation (depending on communication channels) emphasising professionalism, benefits of clean offices (image, health and safety), convenience, cost.

3 Purchasing decisions may be influenced by:

- Employers or managers in operational departments: requisition or recommend purchase of supplies/equipment/services (initiators, influencers)
- Purchasing or buying managers: recommending, authorising or implementing purchases (influencers, deciders, buyers)
- Engineers and other technical staff: providing technical specifications or recommendations for component/equipment purchases (gatekeepers, influencers)
- Accounts: set a limit on the price the organisation will pay (influencers, financiers)
- The Board of Directors and perhaps also shareholders: authorise large items of capital expenditure (deciders)

4 Give some additional thought to whether you performed this process independently, or whether others were involved: what DMU roles did they perform, and how did they contribute to each stage of your decision-making process?

5 Some ideas:

- White goods: durability, energy efficiency, simplicity to operate, effectiveness, size, cost, design
- Pharmaceuticals: effectiveness, safety (few side effects), cost, availability (for example, without prescription)
- Education: quality service and support, good results, accreditation/recognition of qualifications, cost, personal and social benefits
- Snack foods: taste, energy/hunger reduction, nutritional 'goodness' (for some consumers), convenience ('eat and go')
- Cars: design, spaciousness (for families), cost, fuel efficiency, size (ease of parking), speed, status/luxury (high-end models), branding (for example, BMW, Porsche), special features (for example, off-road capability)
- Financial services: reliability/trust/expertise, service, low charges/high returns, range/integration of products, tailored products (for example, for small business), convenience (transactions, account management)

6 You were asked to reflect on your own experiences, but here are some examples to stimulate your thinking.

- *Motivation*: If your needs are for esteem and self-actualisation, you might respond positively to marketing by the CIM to undertake their qualification. Advertisements showing smartly dressed, competent young professionals might attract you because your motivation heightens your attention to such images.
- *Perception:* If you have had a bad experience of a product (say, a Microsoft software product), you may focus on and amplify the negative aspects (there are 'always' glitches, they keep 'making' you buy updates). When a sales assistant demonstrates a new improved version, you may notice only the negative things and make negative comparisons with other brands.

- *Learning:* If you win a promotional competition for a brand, you'll be more likely to pay attention to its promotions in future – because of the (reinforcing) reward!
- *Attitudes*: Government TV advertising showing (in graphic terms) the effects of smoking on the lungs may change attitudes because it is less uncomfortable to change pro-smoking attitudes than to explain away the evidence of your eyes.

7 This is very personal to you, and will depend on your age, lifestyle and other personal factors. Do think through the question on what kinds of marketing you respond to: this is the kind of thinking you will need to do as a marketer – and in the exam!

8 Your findings will depend on the media you browsed, and the needs of their target audience. Generally, you may find that substance is more important in industrial markets than style. In scientific and technical markets, for example, product specification will be the main message. However, in some B2B markets – such as consultancy services – sophisticated image may be an important part of the message. In trade journals aimed at selling in consumer products (such as books) to distributors (booksellers, wholesalers, stationers etc) you may find a more consumer-like image used (getting potential stockists excited about the style with which the product will be promoted to 'pull' consumers into their stores). However, the emphasis will still be on the interests of the *target audience:* how energetically the product will be promoted, how great the potential demand, how profitable for the retailer. Get used to asking this question of all marketing communications you encounter or generate: what are the needs and interests of the target audience – and how effectively are they being addressed?

9 Some supplier selection criteria you may have encountered include the following (the results of a survey of purchasing managers.)

- Delivery capability
- Quality
- Price
- Repair and after sales service
- Technical capability
- Performance history
- Production facilities
- Help and advice
- Control systems
- Reputation
- Sound financial position
- Positive attitude towards the buyer
- Compliance with bidding procedures
- Training support
- Communication on order progress
- Good management/organisation
- Convenient packaging
- Legal/ethical dealings
- Convenient location
- Good labour relations

Part C

Implementing elements of the promotional mix

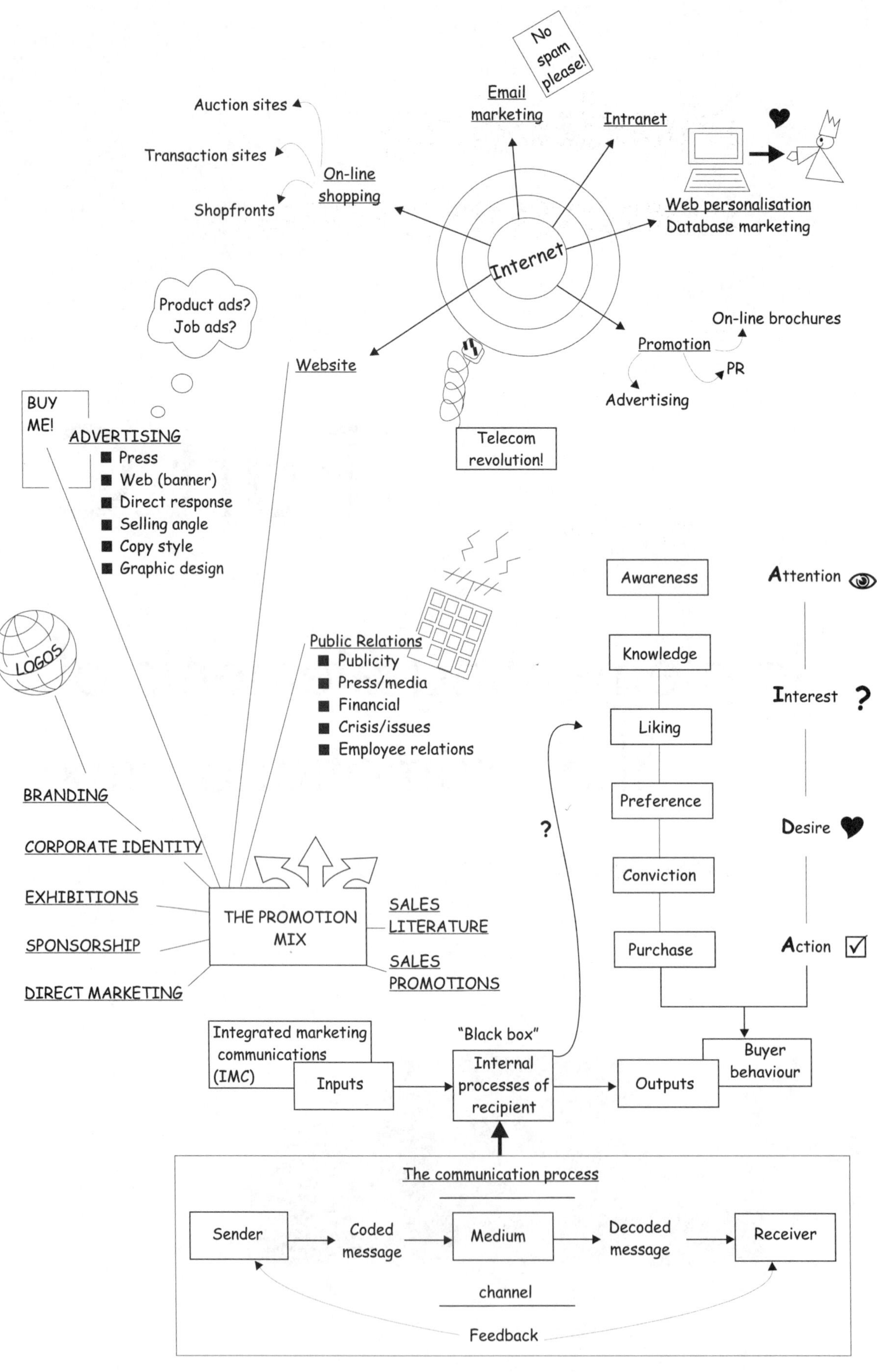
No spam please!
Email marketing
Intranet
Auction sites
Transaction sites
Shopfronts
On-line shopping
Web personalisation
Database marketing
Internet
Product ads? Job ads?
Website
On-line brochures
Promotion
PR
Advertising
Telecom revolution!
BUY ME!
ADVERTISING
Press
Web (banner)
Direct response
Selling angle
Copy style
Graphic design
LOGOS
Public Relations
Publicity
Press/media
Financial
Crisis/issues
Employee relations
Awareness
Knowledge
Liking
Preference
Conviction
Purchase
Attention
Interest
Desire
Action
?
BRANDING
CORPORATE IDENTITY
EXHIBITIONS
SPONSORSHIP
DIRECT MARKETING
THE PROMOTION MIX
SALES LITERATURE
SALES PROMOTIONS
Integrated marketing communications (IMC)
Inputs
"Black box"
Internal processes of recipient
Outputs
Buyer behaviour
The communication process
Sender
Coded message
Medium
Decoded message
Receiver
channel
Feedback

Marketing communications

4

Chapter Topic List	
1	Setting the scene
2	Integrated marketing communications
3	The function of communication
4	The communication process
5	Communication and consumer behaviour

Learning Outcomes

- ☑ Understand the strategic role of marketing communications (promotion)
- ☑ Describe an integrated approach to planning marketing communications
- ☑ Explain the aims of communication, particularly in relation to customer communications
- ☑ Describe the communication process
- ☑ Understand the black box and promotional (AIDA) models of consumer behaviour

Syllabus References

- ☑ Explain the concept of, and need for, an integrated marketing communications approach and the links between communications and marketing planning (3.1)
- ☑ Explain the role and importance of promotion in marketing (3.2)
- ☑ Explain the structure and function of the communication process (3.3)

Key Concepts Introduced

- Marketing communications
- Integrated marketing communications (IMC)
- Feedback

1 Setting the scene

1.1 In this chapter, we introduce some basic theories about the communication process and its effect on customer behaviour, so that you can begin to design effective customer communications at a basic level, as we discuss various promotional tools in the chapters that follow. You will also draw on your knowledge of the various influences on consumer behaviour from Chapter 3.

1.2 However, the emphasis in this element of the Customer Communications module is the **promotional mix**. A range of underpinning practical communication skills are covered in detail in Part D of the Text: how to identify and solve communication problems, how to plan effective messages to target audiences, how to analyse and present data, plus skills in oral, face-to-face and written communication formats. (This is why Part D is longer than the 10% weighting given to Element 4 would suggest: it covers the skills necessary to format **all** your exam answers – and customer communications – on **any** topic area.)

1.3 In the chapters that follow, we will be looking at a wide range of promotional tools. It may be tempting to see them as separate elements, but they are pulled together by the strategic role of communication and promotion and their place in the overall marketing plan. They have one overarching aim: to reach customers with a consistent, effective marketing message. Each element of the communications and promotional mix must contribute to creating the overall picture. So we start this part of the Text by introducing the concept of Integrated Marketing Communications.

Key Concept

Marketing communications is 'a management process through which an organisation enters into a dialogue with its various audiences. To accomplish this the organisation develops, presents and evaluates a series of co-ordinated messages to identified stakeholder groups. The objective of the process is to (re)position the organisation and/or their offerings, in the mind of each member of the target audience in a consistent and likeable way. This seeks to encourage buyers and other stakeholders to perceive and experience the organisation and its offerings as solutions to some of their current and future challenges.' (Fill, 1999)

2 Integrated marketing communications

The strategic role of marketing communications

2.1 For an organisation committed to the marketing concept, we might say that 'Marketing Communications' encompasses **all** forms of an organisation's communications with its external and internal audiences.

2.2 However, marketing communications are part of the overall activity of the organisation towards its business (or other) **objectives**. They are the means to an end: not the end itself.

- **Marketing communications (promotion) strategies** (how elements of the promotional mix will be used to reach the target audience)

  support

- **Marketing strategies** (what target markets and customer needs will be pursued; how elements of the marketing mix – product, place and price as well as promotion – will be used to reach those target markets; what levels of marketing expenditure will be)

  support

- **Organisational strategies** (how the organisation will achieve its market, financial, social and other objectives)

2.3 This can be simply shown as follows (Figure 4.1).

Figure 4.1: the hierarchy of strategic planning

2.4 As a broad example, say an organisation had as one of its strategic objectives the maintenance of ethical and socially responsible business practices.

(a) The organisation would develop its marketing strategies accordingly: pricing its products fairly; ensuring that its products were environmentally friendly and safe for consumers, and manufactured without exploitative employment practices; arranging distribution through channels that allowed fair access to consumers; and differentiating its brands by ethical/responsible values.

(b) The organisation would get these messages across to its target audiences through its promotion strategies: honest advertising and public relations messages; helpful product labelling; communication of ethical values to employees; professional relationships with suppliers and distributors; fair and responsible dealings with customers; sponsorship of community events and causes; and so on. (We will look at the variety of communication tools in Chapters 5 – 8.)

2.5 Different communications strategies will likewise be appropriate to support a range of specific marketing strategies. Here are some of the strategic options (covered in the *Marketing Fundamentals* module) and the communication strategies that may be used to support them.

	Strategic options	Examples of communication strategies
Competitive strategies	■ Cost leadership	■ Communicate price advantage
	■ Differentiation leadership	■ Differentiate; create brand identity/value; reinforce customer loyalty
	■ Focus/Nicheing	■ Target market segments/niches; emphasis niche needs
Growth strategies	■ Market penetration	■ Persuade non-users to use (advertising and promotion); persuade users to use more (relationship marketing and loyalty programmes)
	■ Market development	■ Target new markets/segments with existing products (advertising, launch promotion, exhibitions, public relations, e-commerce)
	■ Product development	■ Research and target new needs of existing market; focus on product benefits; direct mailings and advertising to raise awareness
	■ Diversification	■ Research and target new needs of new markets; gain awareness of brand and business (advertising, direct mailings, public relations, exhibitions)

Action Programme 1

Consider the following organisations.

- Coca Cola Enterprises Inc
- Amnesty International (or a similar organisation you are familiar with)

How do their marketing communications reflect their overall strategic objectives?

For additional insight, you might like to explore the Web site of one or more of these organisations.

Coca Cola has two sites: its corporate Coca Cola Enterprises Inc site (www.cokecce.com) and its consumer-facing site (www.coca-cola.com). Visit both – and consider what the different communication objectives of each site may be and how they support the company's overall objectives.

[Key Skill for Marketers: Using ICT and the Internet]

The marketing plan

2.6 Communications (or promotions) planning is therefore part of the overall **marketing planning** of the organisation. Marketing planning is covered in detail in the *Marketing Fundamentals* module, but we can summarise the process as follows (Figure 4.2).

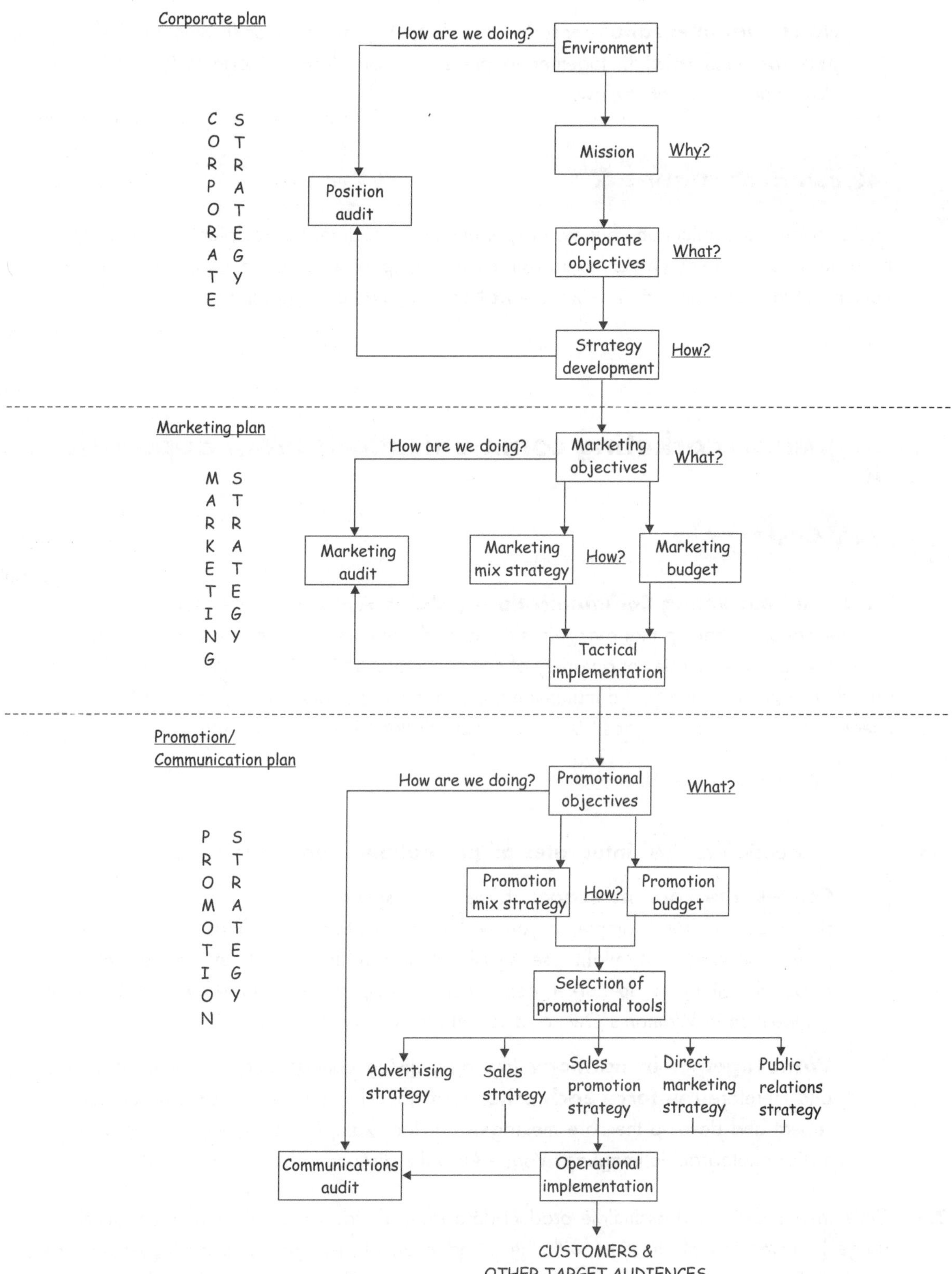

Figure 4.2: Marketing planning and communications

2.7 As you can see from the above diagram, a lot of elements come together at the interface between the organisation and the customer, represented by customer communications! If marketing messages are to be 'co-ordinated', 'consistent' and 'likeable' (as our Key Concept definition at the beginning of this chapter suggests), **integration** is required in two directions.

- **Vertical integration**: ensuring that communication/promotion activities fit with 'higher' marketing and corporate objectives (as discussed above).
- **Horizontal integration**: ensuring that diverse communication/promotion activities (the **promotional mix**) fit together to present a consistent message. We will look more closely at this concept below.

Action Programme 2

Before reading on, reflect on your own experience as a customer or recipient of marketing messages and see if you can come up with some examples of what might happen if different elements of the communications mix were **not** co-ordinated or integrated.

An integrated marketing communications (IMC) approach

Key Concept

Integrated Marketing Communications (IMC) is 'A concept of marketing communications planning that recognises the added value of a comprehensive plan that evaluates the strategic roles of a variety of communications disciplines and combines them to provide clarity, consistency and maximum communications impact through the seamless integration of discrete messages.' (American Association of Advertising Agencies)

2.8 At the most basic level, IMC **integrates all promotional tools** so that they:

(a) **Convey the core message** of the organisation or brand, in line with marketing strategies. So, for example, if you wished to position yourself as an exclusive, luxury perfume house, you might use stylish photographic images in *Vogue* and discreet personal selling in up-market department stores, rather than a 'win a body spray' competition in *Woman's Own* or discount offers at Woolworths.

(b) **Work together in harmony** (avoiding giving contradictory or confusing messages) and therefore **reinforce each other** (cumulatively adding messages which consistently repeat and develop the core message). So, for example, you would not want to use the stylish photographic images in *Vogue* AND the discount offers at Woolworths...

2.9 Consumers receive and assimilate product data from a wide range of sources and media. (This range is increasing all the time with the introduction of new media technologies such as the Internet.) From the **consumer's point of view**, tools such as advertising, public relations and sales promotion aren't experienced as 'separate disciplines' or 'separate functions in the organisation': they comprise a **total experience** of an organisation and its brands and services. The customer doesn't (and shouldn't) care that the person who published a sales promotion leaflet is not in the same department or location as the sales person who doesn't know anything about the special offer: what the customer sees is an organisation whose left hand doesn't know what its right hand is doing!

Exam Tip

Integrated Marketing Communications is a new topic in this syllabus. You may be asked to address it at a content level: describing the concept and importance of IMC. You may also be asked to demonstrate your awareness of IMC principles by considering the vertical and horizontal integration of any promotional tools you recommend for a given scenario.

2.10 Integrating marketing communications offers the following wide-ranging **benefits**.

- Greater direction, efficiency and accountability in marketing management
- Competitive advantage through more co-ordinated brand development
- More effective response to the increasing communications 'literacy' and sophistication of consumers
- More effective response to the increasing fragmentation/proliferation of media and audiences with new media such as the Internet, interactive television, DVD and so on (discussed in Chapter 8)
- More effective response to the increasing information needs (and rights) of customers and other stakeholders – while minimising the tendency to information overload and 'clutter'
- Support for relationship marketing: co-ordinating multiple (consistent) contacts with customers to develop on-going dialogue and relationship
- Support for network marketing: co-ordinating multiple (consistent) contacts with suppliers, distributors, marketing service agencies and other links in the customer value delivery chain
- Increased effectiveness of promotions, through consistency and reinforcement of core messages
- More effective triggers for brand and message recall, and less confusion in brand images

Marketing at Work

Forsyth *(Communicating with Customers)* gives the following examples of mismatched messages creating customer mystification or annoyance. (You might add some from your own experience.)

- *'You know the advertisement you have in "Professional Marketing"?*
  'I'm afraid I haven't seen it yet.'
- *'I see the XM270 has been upgraded!'*
  'Has it?'
- *'Your quotation specifies "optional" installations. What exactly does that mean?"*
  'Well, we don't see the quotes in this department. How was it put again?'

- A 24 hour hotline enquiry number impresses customers – until they find that it takes information literature more than a week to arrive.
- A 'free offer' appeals to customers – until it turns out to be hedged around with terms and conditions in the small print.

Integration and internal communications

2.11 As the above Marketing at Work examples suggest, communication **within the marketing organisation** will be an essential part of an effective IMC approach ensuring that:

- All units of the organisation who deal with customers (directly or indirectly) are aware of the messages being communicated by themselves and others
- All units understand the desired core messages of the organisation/brand, and the need for consistency in getting that core message across
- Promises made by one customer contact are delivered by subsequent customer contacts

Action Programme 3

What items of information would you, as a Marketing manager, want Sales department staff to have on a regular basis? (You may consider this question in the light of a particular product, service or market sector if you wish.) How would you go about disseminating the required information?

An integrated approach to Integrated marketing communications!

The following (Fill, 1999) is a model showing how all the different elements discussed above need to be brought together for IMC to work (Figure 4.3).

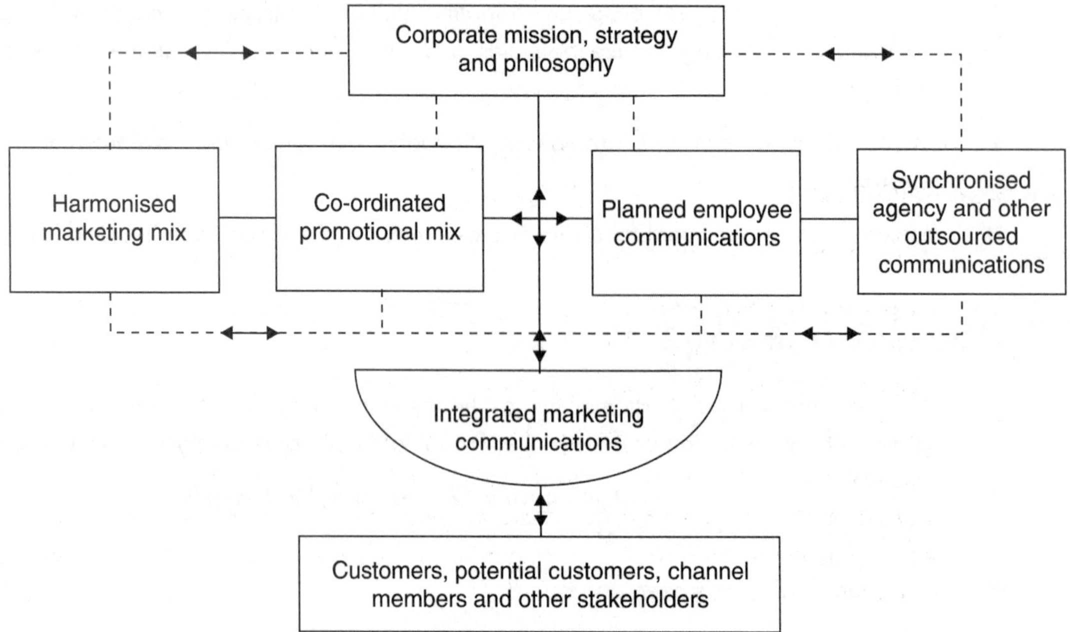

Figure 4.3: Integrated marketing communications

3 The function of communication

3.1 Communications are used in marketing for a range of specific purposes, such as:

(a) **Creating brand awareness**: reaching consumers with brand messages widely and consistently enough to enable recognition and association with the right kind of images (for example through advertising, public relations, brand identity). Like celebrities, brands need to be 'seen in all the right places' and to project their 'personality' in order to be instantly recognisable by the public.

(b) **Motivating purchase**: highlighting product benefits that are relevant to the needs of the target audience (for example through advertising); offering incentives to purchase (for example through sales promotion)

(c) **Facilitating purchase**: direct marketing (for example through mail order advertising or Internet marketing); informing consumers how and where to purchase ('available at...' messages, Web addresses); offering sales service

(d) **Forming and maintaining customer relationships**: customer contacts (for example through personalised mailings, loyalty programmes); personal client contacts (in business markets); after-sales service (for example through carelines and customer service)

(e) **Forming and maintaining network relationships**: networking with suppliers, distributors and marketing service agencies; supplying information to support transaction and decision making.

(f) **Forming and maintaining working relationships**: supplying management and staff in the marketing and other departments with the information they need to integrate their marketing (especially customer-facing activities); fostering a customer-focused organisation culture through 'selling' quality values.

3.2 The functions of the communication process in general can be classified as follows.

- To initiate action
- To exchange information, ideas, attitudes, beliefs or feelings
- To establish, acknowledge or maintain links or relations with other people

It will be helpful to keep these key purposes in mind as you plan any given communication task.

Initiating action

3.3 Initiating action may be achieved by two basic categories of communication.

(a) **Expressing your needs and requirements**. This is the purpose of briefings and instructions, for example, to your team, supplier or advertising agency: to make as clear as possible **what you wish or require them to do**.

(b) **Persuading and motivating others**. Customers (and colleagues) need to be given a **reason** to take the action you want them to take. As a communicator, you will have to **consider the needs and interests of your audience and offer them benefits of importance to them** in order to secure the response you require (purchase, co-operation, payment and so on).

Exchanging information

3.4 **Giving information** is a major part of promotion, and may be aimed at:

(a) **Creating awareness**: for example, promoting a brand image, informing the Press of events, or awakening staff to the need for customer care. Advertisements, press releases, staff notices and reports, for example, focus **on giving the target audience the information it needs in an attention-grabbing, interest-holding way**.

(b) **Creating understanding**: explanations and descriptions, analyses, summaries and illustrations are techniques used in reports, presentations and demonstrations (for example), in order to **enhance the target audience's understanding** of a subject, point of view or product.

(c) **Persuading**: using information and persuasive techniques (interpersonal rapport, logical argument, focus on benefits to your target audience) **to convince your target audience of the benefit to them** of sharing your point of view or doing what you want them to do.

3.5 **Receiving information** is also a major marketing tool: researching the wants, needs, preferences and perceptions of the target market; soliciting and being sensitive to feedback from customers about products and customer service and so on. Customer contacts, exhibitions, personal selling and research/feedback exercises (for example feedback slips with product packaging or direct mailings) are aimed at **facilitating your target audience in telling you what you need to know**.

Managing relationships

3.6 Establishing, acknowledging and maintaining relations with customers, staff, colleagues and business contacts is a vital function of communication. In most social and family contexts, this is taken for granted: communication is designed purely to establish and maintain rapport, or the sense of relationship. Business communication is more constrained by **time**, by the **formality** of organisational structures and roles, and by the size of the **network** within which communication takes place. Business communication therefore tends to be concise, to the point and often formal, even where there are opportunities for it to be otherwise.

3.7 Trust, co-operation and respect, however, are vital to maintain co-ordination and morale within an organisation – just as a favourable impression, credibility, regular contact and even **interpersonal rapport** are a vital ingredient in the organisation's dealings with the outside world of suppliers, customers, potential customers and potential employees. So it will still be important to consider:

(a) **Courtesy and consideration**. This is **never** a waste of time or effort, and should form the basis of all communication!

(b) **'Non-essential' communication**. Supplying unsolicited information to customers, or simply 'touching base' from time to time, not only maintains on-going contact with them, but may remind them of the organisation's services at the right moment to prompt an enquiry or purchase. This is a cornerstone of relationship marketing.

Action Programme 4

A general awareness exercise: start gathering examples of marketing communications from different types of organisations. Ask yourself:

- What they are intended to achieve: what their purpose is
- How well developed the message is to achieve that purpose, given your needs as the target audience

[Key Skill for Marketers: Improving own learning and performance]

4 The communication process

The communication cycle

4.1 Effective communication is a two-way process, perhaps best expressed as a **cycle**. Signals or messages are sent by the communicator and received by the other party, who sends back some form of confirmation that the message has been received and understood ('feedback'). Thus, if you ask the time and get a response, or send an invoice and receive payment, this corresponds to a single cycle of communication.

4.2 A more detailed model of the communication cycle (known as the **'radio signal' model**) can be depicted as follows (Figure 4.4).

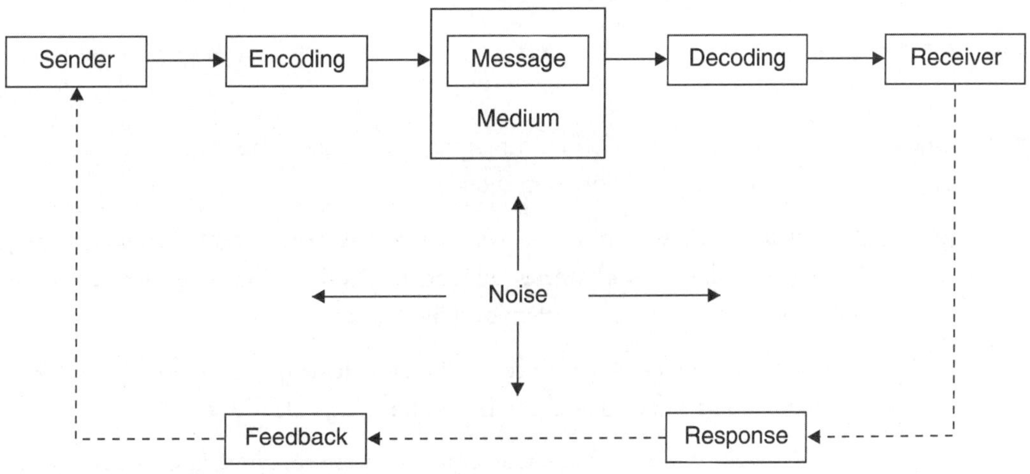

Figure 4.4: The 'radio signal' model of communication

4.3 The **sender** decides to communicate and plans what and how to communicate. In written communications (drafting an advertisement or report, say) you have 'off-line' decision and planning time in which to work out how best to present your ideas to get the desired response from your target audience. In face to face and oral communication (answering a telephone or customer query, say) you may have to plan and formulate messages 'live': this is why oral and face-to-face communication skills (covered in Part D of this Text) are so important.

4.4 **Encoding** is an analogy for how the sender puts his or her intentions into a form which can be transmitted: a form which the sender and receiver must **both** understand, if the sender's message is to be correctly interpreted at the other end by the receiver. This is like a code, because the words, numbers, pictures and gestures we use are only symbols representing our ideas: in communicating we must translate our ideas into a code which we think the receiver will be able to 'decipher' or translate back into the idea.

4.5 It is important to bear in mind that a symbol that we use and understand may be ambiguous (have more than one possible meaning) or mean something different to a person of different age, nationality, experience or beliefs. Just because we understand what we mean, it does not necessarily follow that someone else will: another reason to **consider the needs and capacities of the target audience**. Never mind what you think you'll say: what do you think **they'll hear**?

Action Programme 5

Give three examples of each of the following.

- Words that you use with your friends that other people may not understand. (What are the 'in' expressions in your reference groups?)
- Words that you use in your job or studies that 'lay' people would not understand
- Symbols that are commonly used, of which you have had to learn the meaning. (Think about road signs, for example.)
- Situations where you have been 'accused' of saying something you didn't mean, because of an expression, gesture or tone of voice.

4.6 Once the idea has been encoded as a message, the sender needs to choose how to **transmit** or get it across to the receiver/target audience.

(a) The particular route or path via which the message is sent, connecting the sender and receiver, is called the **channel** of communication: examples include a notice board, postal/telecommunications system and the Internet.

(b) The tool or instrument which is used is the **medium** (plural 'media'). The selected medium will usually come under one of the broad headings of:

- **Visual** (non-verbal) communication: a gesture, chart, graphic poster or Web page
- **Written** (verbal) communication: a letter, memo, report, press-release, e-mail or text advertisement
- **Oral** (verbal) communication ('by mouth'), which includes both face to face media (meetings, presentations) and remote media (telephone, television)

4.7 The choice of medium is an important communication skill: we will discuss it further below.

4.8 If everything has gone well so far, the **receiver** receives the message – and must then **decode** its meaning, using his or her own knowledge, skills and perceptions to interpret its meaning.

(a) The receiver must **grasp the meaning of the words or symbols** used by the sender: the 'key' to the code is, as we have said, not always shared by the receiver. (If you didn't know what the Nike 'tick' logo was, or who the sporting celebrity wearing it was, you might completely miss the significance of a Nike advertisements or sponsorship.)

(b) The receiver must **interpret the message as a whole**. What it 'says' is not necessarily what it 'means', and 'reading between the lines' may be necessary to establish the underlying meaning of the message. (If you know that you are looking at a Nike advertisement, you still need to 'get' the message about challenge, daring, excellence and so on – often just from the associations with various sporting images.)

Key Concept

Feedbackis a response of the receiver which indicates to the sender that the message has (or has not) been successfully received, understood and interpreted.

4.9 Seeking and giving **feedback** (especially in oral and face to face communication) is a key communication skill. Communication is prone to a wide range of factors which interfere with the effective transmission of the message from sender to receiver: these factors are often known by the collective term **'noise'** (illustrated in Figure 4.4) and are discussed in Chapter 9 of this Text. They include technical interference (such as a bad phone line or poorly printed advertisement) and sources of misunderstanding (such as emotion, prejudice and differences in perception) and so on. Only by seeking feedback can the sender trust that the message has been both **received** and **understood**.

4.10 Examples of **positive feedback** include: a staff member accurately reading back your instructions; a presentation audience nodding agreement; a customer sending back the reply form as requested; your target audience buying the advertised product – or, as an example of more systematically gathered feedback, a market research focus group confirming that their response to a brand is as you expected. (You can probably work out what the **negative** equivalents would be.)

Planning effective marketing communications

4.11 We discuss message planning in detail in Chapter 10. In outline, the process includes:

- **Identifying the target audience** (whether in individual, targeted or mass communication). Who are they and what needs, perceptions and attitudes will affect how they respond to the message?
- **Determining the desired response**. What do you want the target audience to do or understand as a result of the message? (Brand awareness? Ad recall? Purchase? Send in the coupon? Pay the invoice? Use the product safely?)
- **Developing an effective message**. What will be the best content, structure and style to elicit the desired response? Will the target audience respond to **rational appeals** (arousing their self interest by offering valued benefits), **emotional appeals** (arousing needs and wants by stirring up emotions) or **moral appeals** (arousing action in response to values)?
- **Selecting appropriate media**. What will be the best way to get the message to the target audience?

Time	The time necessary to prepare and transmit the message, considering its urgency
Complexity	What communication method will enable the message to be most readily understood
Distance	How far the message is required to travel and in what condition it must arrive
Hard copy	Whether a hard copy (printed or written) record is required – for example, to confirm transactions or for legal documents
Interactivity	Whether immediate exchanges of offer/response, question/answer or message/feedback is required
Confidentiality	Whether the message needs to be seen only by selected recipients or disseminated as widely as possible
Personality	Whether the message will be enhanced by being conveyed through personal contact, persuasion or influence
Cost	Considered in relation to all the above, for the best possible result at the least possible expense

- **Gathering feedback**. How effective was the message in achieving the desired outcome?

Action Programme 6

What medium might you choose if your message:

(a) Needed to be delivered to a large number of people, quickly, over a short distance, and with interactive questions and answers?

(b) Contained urgent bad news for just one person whom you know well, over a long distance?

(c) Was to explain a complex process with many stages, which would have to be carried out by a group of people?

(d) Was requesting payment from a large number of people, geographically scattered?

5 Communication and consumer behaviour

5.1 We have already covered some key aspects of consumer behaviour in Chapter 3. Here, we will focus on the **effects of marketing communications** on the decision making process.

Exam Tip

The emphasis on consumer behaviour is new in this syllabus. It may be worthwhile using the models discussed in this section such as the AIDA model to analyse the aims and effectiveness of various promotional communications you encounter – or draft yourself. In this way, you will develop a dual awareness of the models AND the practices they were designed to represent.

The black box model

5.2 A **black box model** of consumer behaviour assumes that only observable behaviour can be studied and talked about with any validity: what goes on in the mind of the subject is basically unknowable, shut up in a 'black box' (Figure 4.5).

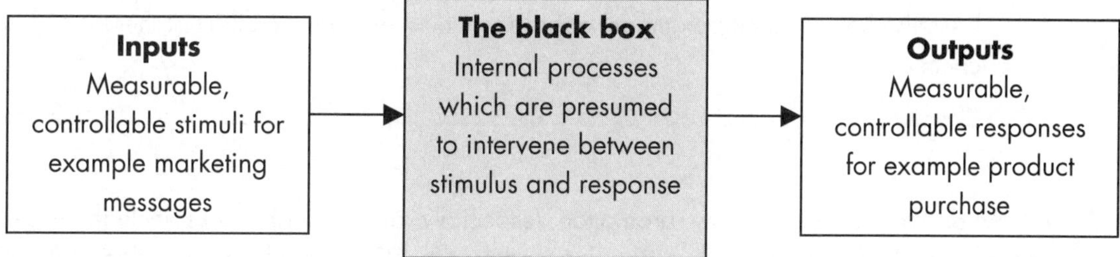

Figure 4.5: black box model of consumer behaviour

5.3 Black box models are useful because they concentrate on a manageable number of measurable input variables on which a communication strategy can be based – without 'analysis paralysis' from speculating about all possible (unobservable) intervening variables.

5.4 Stimulus variables (such as service quality, advertising messages or – at a more detailed level – specific design or content factors like interactivity in a Web site or headline size in a press ad) can be identified for modelling. The effects of each (in terms of brand choice, sales volume, customer retention, ad recollection/recognition and so on) can be set out in a simple, direct way. If a model indicates that pure text advertisements get less response than advertisements with graphic elements in a particular market segment, the marketer can respond accordingly: it does not matter, to an extent, *why* the phenomenon occurs, or what is going on within the black box, as long as that set of inputs reliably creates that set of outputs!

Inside the black box

5.5 A simple psychological framework for what might go on inside the black box suggests that our behaviour is influenced by three attitude components.

- **Cognition**: our awareness, knowledge and thoughts in regard to something
- **Affectivity**: our positive or negative 'feeling' about whether we like it or not
- **Conation**: our intentions to act as a result

5.6 These are often depicted as stages in the decision process (Figure 4.6).

Figure 4.6: A simple three-stage model of how promotion works

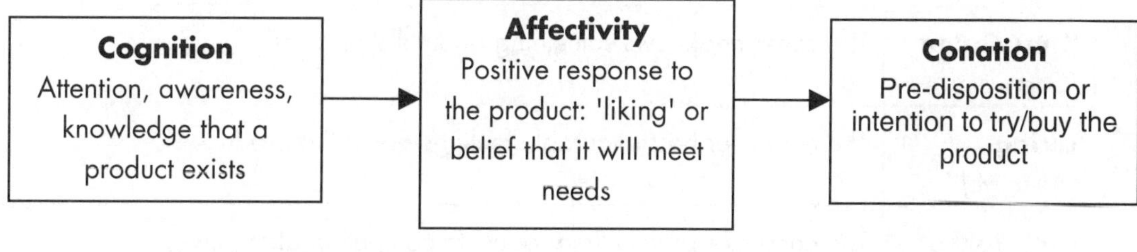

A promotion must be:	A promotion must be:	A promotion must:
■ Seen *and* ■ Noticed	■ Relevant/meaningful to us ■ Appealing(visually, rationally, emotionally)	■ Make us want to act on it ■ Help us to act on it

Action Programme 7

- Give a specific example of marketing communications that could support each stage of a customer's decision process using the DMP discussed in Chapter 3.
- Describe how a black box model approach would explain the effect of these communications.

5.7 All major theories about how promotion (especially advertising) works include these three components. We will discuss two popular models: the AIDA model, and Lavidge and Steiner's 'buyer readiness' model.

The AIDA model

5.8 The AIDA model is a simple framework, which usefully suggests the desirable qualities of an effective promotional message.

Attention *[Cognitive]*	An effective message will **get the attention** of the target audience: it must have sufficient sensory (visual, audible) impact to get noticed
Interest *[Affective]*	An effective message will **hold the interest** of the target audience: it must be sufficiently relevant or intriguing to create engagement
Desire *[Affective]*	An effective message will **arouse desire** in the target audience: it must offer to satisfy a need of want or solve a problem
Action *[Cognitive]*	An effective message will **obtain response** from the target audience: it must describe next steps and helpful contacts to facilitate action

The buyer readiness model

5.9 Lavidge and Steiner developed a more complex model of the process leading to a purchase decision, including six stages:

Awareness *[Cognitive]*	The consumer knows that the product exists.
Knowledge *[Cognitive]*	The consumer knows something about the product.
Liking *[Affective]*	The consumer has favourable feelings about the product.
Preference *[Affective]*	The consumer prefers the product to competing alternatives.
Conviction *[Affective]*	The consumer believes that the product is the best one for his/her needs.
Purchase *[Conative]*	The consumer decides to purchase the product

Marketing at Work

Subaru

When Subaru introduced its four-wheel-drive Forester model in Australasia, it began with an extensive public relations campaign. Motoring journalists were encouraged to write newspaper and magazine articles, to create name familiarity and knowledge of its design and purpose [*awareness*]. Later advertisements showed the car mud-splattered at the back, fresh from the action – but polished at the front, ready for the city [*knowledge*].

Subaru's marketers used a combination of the promotion mix tools to create successively stronger positive feelings about the model [*liking, preference, conviction*]. Advertising extolled its advantages and uniqueness. Press releases, test drives and other public relations activities stressed the car's innovative features, versatility and performance. Dealer salespeople told buyers about options, durability, value for price and after sales service.

Special promotional prices, special showings (by personal invitation from dealers) and other incentives might be used to motivate convinced buyers to take the final step of purchase.

Adapted from Kotler: *Marketing, an introduction* (1999)

Chapter Roundup

- Marketing communications (promotion) strategies must be seen in the context of strategic planning. Promotion mix decisions must be integrated with the tactical objectives of the marketing plan, to ensure that marketing objectives are efficiently pursued and core messages consistently portrayed.
- An Integrated Marketing Communications approach evaluates the strategic roles of a variety of promotional tools (vertical integration) and combines them to provide clarity, consistency and maximum communications impact through the integration of discrete messages (horizontal integration).
- The key functions of all communication are: initiating action; exchanging information and ideas; and to establish, maintain and develop relationships with others. These can be applied to any given *marketing* function, such as: creating brand awareness, motivating or facilitating purchase, or managing customer/network/working relationships.
- The process of communication can be modelled as follows.

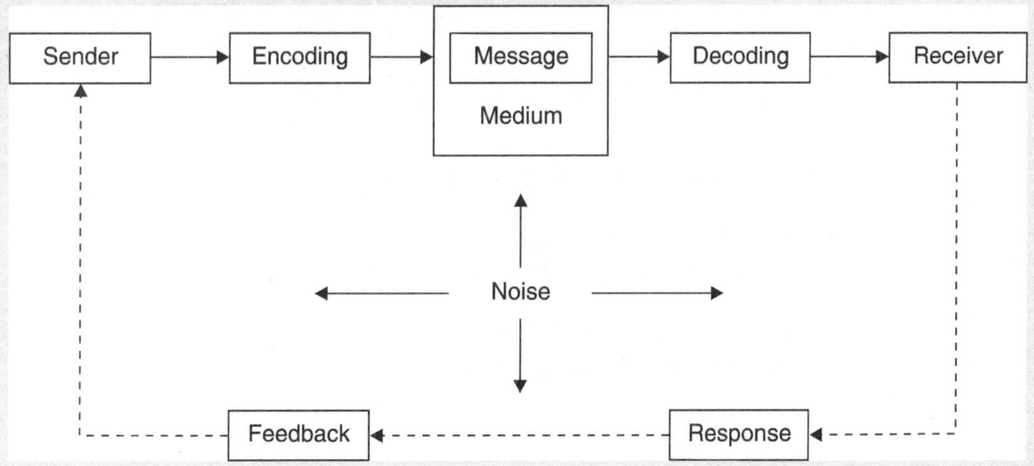

- Black box models are used to show what can and cannot be measured in predicting consumer behaviour. Various models have been developed to suggest what goes on inside the 'black box' of the consumer's mental processes. Popular hierarchy of response models include the AIDA model (Attention, Interest, Desire, Action), and the Lavidge and Steiner (Awareness, Knowledge, Liking, Preference, Conviction, Purchase) model.

Quick Quiz

1 Complete the following sentences, using the words in the box below.

Marketing communications is 'a management process through which an organisation enters into a (1)......... with its various (2).......... To accomplish this the organisation develops, presents and evaluates a series of (3) .... messages to identified (4)......... groups. The objective of the process is to (re)(5)......... the organisation and/or their (6)......... in the mind of each member of the (7).........audience in a (8)......... and (9)......... way.'

target	offerings	likeable	co-ordinated	dialogue
audiences	stakeholder	position	consistent	

2 What sort of integration is represented by the attempt to ensure that diverse promotion activities fit together to present a consistent message?

☐ Horizontal ☐ Vertical

3 Which of the following does *not* describe Integrated Marketing Communications?

A Clear
B Consistency
C Costly
D Co-ordinated

4 An Integrated Marketing Communications approach solely applies primarily communications with consumers and customers.

☐ True ☐ False

5 List the three general functions of communication.

6 Label each box in the diagram below.

7 A notice board is an example of a communication:

message	channel
medium	receiver

8 Which step in the message planning sequence is *missing* from the (randomly ordered) list below?

Develop the message
Gather feedback
Select media
Identify the target audience

9 Intentions or pre-dispositions to act are classified as the psychological process of:

A Cognition
B Conation
C Affectivity
D Attitude

10 What does AIDA stand for?

Answers to Quick Quiz

1 (1) dialogue, (2) audiences, (3) co-ordinated, (4) stakeholder, (5) position, (6) offerings, (7) target (8/9) consistent/likeable.

2 Horizontal

3 C

4 False

5 Initiating action; exchanging information; managing relationships

6 (1) Sender, (2) Encoding, (3) Message, (4) Medium, (5) Decoding, (6) Response, (7) Feedback, (8) Noise

7 Channel

8 Determine the desired response

9 B

10 Attention, Interest, Desire, Action

Now try Question 4 from the Question Bank at the end of this Text

Action Programme Review

1 **Coca Cola**: famous for their brand identity (logo style, bottle shape and 'real thing' slogan). One key strategy objective is to win the 'Cola Wars' against Pepsi: communications pursue this end for example direct competitive advertising, culture-targeted advertising (for example in Australasia, to build local markets), exclusivity deals in stocking school drinks machines (for example in US).

Amnesty International: non-commercial, primarily ethical/political objectives. Communications pursue this end for example responsible (low-cost, non-discriminatory) publications, use of PR/press relations and lobbying; direct contact selling of membership and subscription publications (involving the public rather than 'selling' to them, funds supporting causes, informative on issues)

2 If you are really stuck for ideas (in which case, you have encountered *unusually* well integrated marketing communications!), consult the Marketing at Work feature following. The final effects of mismatched messages, of course, may well be annoyed, disappointed or confused customers.

3 Examples include: information about products and services (especially any changes or updates to the specifications); prices (especially any changes) and terms (for example discount policies); the content of advertising and other promotional activities (press coverage, sponsorship deals, forthcoming exhibitions and so on); feedback from customers (complaints, comments); perhaps technical, industry and competitor developments (in markets where customers may want this sort of information or advice); information about the mission, strategies and policies of the organisation.

Ways of disseminating this information: briefing meetings, corporate newsletter or Intranet, copies of customer information/advertising, team meetings, annual sales conference.

4 As one set of marketing communicators might say: 'Just do it!' This is an excellent discipline to get into, particularly in regard to Element 3.15 of this module: awareness of current promotional trends!

5 This may have been a difficult exercise. Communication is taken for granted: second nature. We need to become aware of the process in order to develop our skills. Note that jargon is often used in a work context – even in marketing!

6 (a) A meeting or presentation or internet 'chat'/video conference – since the short distance does not necessarily mean it will be convenient to get people together.

(b) A telephone call – if privacy could be obtained for the recipient.

(c) Written sets of instructions (ideally with a flowchart or diagram, for reference): perhaps supporting a verbal presentation.

(d) Written statements – for information, checking and economy.

7 **Need recognition/awareness:** for example high-profile 'image/aspiration'-based advertising (and possibly publicity stunts) for example Calvin Klein

Information search: for example customer service at point of sale; price lists; fragrance descriptions in promotional leaflets

Evaluation: for example testers at point of sale, scratch-and-sniff advertisements, promotional samples by direct mail, endorsement by stylish celebrity (for example Kate Moss for CK)

Purchase: for example customer service staff offering aspirational style of service, all information, ease of ordering (on-line? or exclusive to quality department stores/boutiques?)

Post-purchase evaluation: for example desirability of bottle design/packaging, customer offers to reinforce loyalty

It is possible to target the campaign to the status/beauty/desirability/romantic aspirations of the market segment. However, if from trials or industry studies it is known that the use of design-driven TV advertising (or scratch and sniff magazine advertising) increases perfume purchases, it may not be necessary to determine by what process the purchase decision is made: memory associations of images/fragrance, individual responses to specific visual images, beliefs about fragrance and personal desirability etc.

The promotion mix

5

Chapter Topic List
1 Setting the scene
2 The promotion mix
3 Overview of key promotional tools
4 Promotion planning

Learning Outcomes

☑ Understand the role of promotion and promotional tools

☑ Outline an approach to planning promotional activity

☑ Appreciate the range and role of above-the-line and below-the-line promotional tools

Syllabus References

☑ Describe the tools of promotion (the promotion mix) (3.4)

☑ Explain the planning process for developing and implementing promotional strategies and individual elements of the promotional mix (3.5)

☑ Explain how above-the-line and below-the-line activities are used (3.6)

☑ Describe current trends and developments in promotions and their impact on organisations (3.15)

Key Concepts Introduced

- Promotion mix
- Above-the-line promotion
- Below-the-line promotion
- Advertising
- Sales promotion
- Public relations
- Direct marketing
- Push strategy
- Pull strategy

1 Setting the scene

1.1 The aim of this chapter is to make you aware of the very broad range of promotional tools available, and to provide some guidelines for choosing effective combinations of tools (which we call the promotion 'mix').

1.2 We describe the nature, aims and applications of a wide range of promotional tools. You should then be able to consider the strategic issues in selecting a promotion mix for different products, markets and target audiences.

1.3 Having given you this foundation, we will use the following chapters to focus on **implementing** specific elements of the promotional mix highlighted in the syllabus.

- **Advertising** (including direct mail and mail order) and sales promotion (including point of sale display and product packaging) are covered in Chapter 6.
- **Public relations** and **corporate identity** (including sponsorship and exhibitions) are covered in Chapter 7.
- Developments in **information and communications technology** (ICT) – including the Internet – are covered in Chapter 8.

Exam Tip

The syllabus specifically requires you to stay up-to-date with 'current trends and developments in promotion' (Element 3.15). We will be identifying some of these in the context of each of the promotional tools discussed – especially in Chapter 8. However, this is one area in which we strongly recommend that you do some on-going research. Browse regularly through marketing journals (generalist marketing and/or advertising/promotion/PR/direct marketing focused) and the media/marketing sections in the quality press. Explore relevant Web sites. Talk to people. Notice promotional messages on the streets and in your letter box. From influential trends to fashions and fads - if you're interested in marketing, this kind of research should actually be fun!

2 The promotion mix

2.1 **Promotion** is the process of communication by a seller to the market (buyers and potential buyers) for its products and services. As we have seen, this target audience may be:

- A **consumer audience**: purchasers of the product/service
- A **channel audience**: distributors, retailers or agents who pass the product/service on to consumers
- An **all-stakeholder audience**: all the publics who have an interest in the organisation's activities

Key Concept

The **promotion mix** is the total marketing communications programme of the organisation, consisting of a specific combination or blend of promotional tools used to reach the target market for a given product or brand.

2.2 The four major components of the promotion mix have traditionally been recognised as:

- Advertising
- Personal selling
- Sales promotion and
- Public relations.

2.3 However, Figure 5.1 shows the full range of tools that can be used to achieve the aim of promotion: to secure a favourable response from its target audience. (Even then, these are only the tools most obviously identified with 'promotion': as we noted in chapter 1, an organisation cannot **not** communicate – and all elements of the extended marketing mix need to contribute if the organisation is to achieve its marketing objectives.) Direct marketing, in particular, has emerged as a major new component of the promotion mix, and is currently the fastest growing form of marketing.

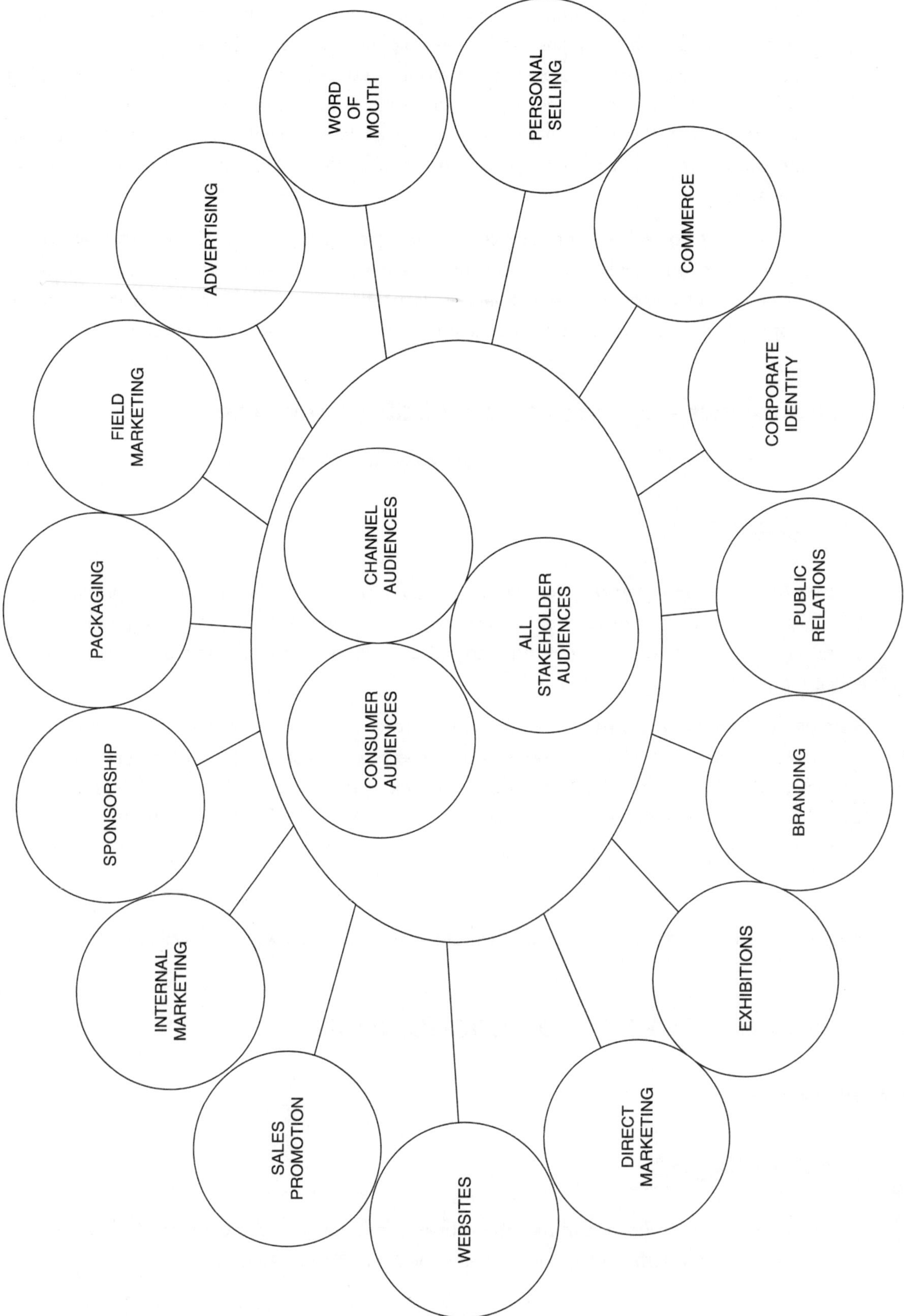

Figure 5.1: the promotion mix

2.4 If the sheer range of tools available seems a bit intimidating, we have bad news – and good news.

(a) **The range of promotional tools and media continues to grow**. The variety of media has increased (or been fragmented) in many ways. There are more print media (publications aimed at more and more highly defined niche segments) and more broadcast media (with developments in satellite, cable and digital TV, DVD, Webcasting and so on). Advertisements are being put on more and more surfaces, from buildings to table-tops to Postit notes to people! Technological developments have created new one-to-one promotion tools such as the Internet, mobile phone text messaging and database marketing.

(b) **There is no 'one best mix'for any given product in any given market**. While some promotional tools may be identified as more or less effective in different contexts, selecting and combining promotional tools is still very much an art – **not** a science, despite the increasing availability of scientific aids to planning and control.

Promotional activity above- and below-the-line

2.5 Promotional activities are often classified as above-the-line and below-the-line.

Key Concept

Above-the-line promotion is advertising placed in paid-for media, such as the press, radio, TV, cinema and outdoor/transport poster sites. The 'line'is one in an advertising agency's accounts, above which are shown its earnings on a commission basis, from the buying of media space for clients.

Below-the-line promotion is a blanket term for a range of non-commissionable marketing communication activities. (Agency earnings on a **fee** basis are shown below the 'line'in their accounts.) More specifically, it refers to activities such as direct mail, sales promotions, sponsorship and exhibitions or trade shows.

2.6 We will discuss the nature and uses of each of these activities as we come to them.

3 Overview of key promotional tools

Advertising

Key Concept

Advertisingis 'any **paid** form of **non-personal** presentation and promotion of ideas, goods or services by an **identifiable** sponsor.'(American Marketing Association)

3.1 Advertising can be effective for a range of purposes.

(a) **To promote sales**

Advertising is particularly good at raising awareness, informing and persuading. It can be used to stimulate both **primary demand** for a product category (as in the introduction of a completely new product) and **selective demand** for a particular brand (as in brand competition). This works in industrial as well as consumer markets, effectively 'introducing' the product in advance of a sales call.

(b) **To create an image or to promote an organisation or idea**

Institutional advertising is used by companies to improve their public image, and by not-for-profit and public sector organisations to promote their programmes (to persuade people not to drink and drive, to support education, to give to a charitable cause and so on).

(c) **To support personal selling**

Advertising can support the sales force by raising consumer awareness of the product/service and motivating/facilitating consumers in contacting sales representatives. (It is also often used for the knock-on effect of motivating the sales force to maximise sales from the leads generated by advertising.)

(d) **To offset competitor advertising**

Companies often attempt to defend market share by responding aggressively to competing campaigns.

(e) **To remind and to reassure**

Advertising reinforces the purchase decision and repeat purchase by reminding consumers that the product continues to be available (and offer benefits) and reassuring them that they made the right choice. In industrial markets, advertising may add credibility to sales visits by demonstrating professionalism and expenditure.

3.2 Major advertising media include television, cinema, radio, newspapers, magazines and outdoor media (poster sites, bus stops, buildings etc). In addition, opportunities are emerging in interactive advertising through the **new media** such as the Internet, Direct Response Television, mobile telephone text messaging, enhanced CD and CD-ROM, Web sites and so on.

3.3 Media are selected according to:

(a) **The size of the audience which regularly uses the medium**. Mass media (such as television, radio and national newspapers) have large exposure. Reader/viewer numbers (newspaper circulation, programme ratings) are closely monitored, helping the media planner to assess the reach of the advertisement.

(b) **The type of people who form the audience of the medium**. There is a trade-off between the size and relevance of the available audience. Segmentation (for example placing an ad in special-interest section of a newspaper) or targeting (in local or regional media, specialist magazines and journals and so on) may be possible.

(c) **The suitability of the medium for the message**. Print ads, for example, allow high volumes of information to be taken in and kept, with response mechanisms (for example coupons) if desired. Television and cinema have a high impact on awareness and retention because of the potential for creativity, and sound/moving image combinations. Radio has a highly personal quality, but as a sound-only medium has limited potential for information retention.

(d) **The cost of the medium in relation to all the above**. Cinema and TV have very high space and production costs. Newspapers and magazines cost by circulation, which may or may not be relevant to the target audience of the advertiser.

Marketing at Work

3M Postit Notes

3M's 'Postit'(self-stick notes) brand has been re-positioned – as an advertising medium!

Copies of Advertising Weekly, in Australia, recently featured the prominent yellow note stuck to a page of editorial content, with the headline (large and in red) 'MAKE YOUR MESSAGE STICK!'In handwritten text, it proceeded: 'The world's favourite self-stick note can now be printed with your advertising message and inserted automatically into magazines'.

On the reverse side is a personal contact name and telephone number for Post-It Note Advertising Products, and the catchy tag line: 'All you need to make a great campaign stick!'

Action Programme 1

From the brief account given in Marketing at Work above, appraise the Postit Note advertisement:

- As a piece of advertising, and
- As a potential advertising medium

3.4 Media planning, buying and scheduling, and the origination and production of highly designed and technically demanding advertising formats, are generally undertaken by specialist agencies, who form a multi-billion dollar global industry. The main tasks of the marketer in the client organisation will be to brief the agency and liaise with account executives to monitor, co-ordinate and approve plans at each stage of the process.

Sales promotion

Key Concept

Sales promotion is 'a range of tactical marketing techniques, designed within a strategic marketing framework, to add value to a product or service in order to achieve a specific sales and marketing objective'(Institute of Sales Promotion)

3.5 Sales promotion activity is typically aimed at **increasing short-term sales volume,** by encouraging first time, repeat or multiple purchase within a stated time frame ('offer closes on such-and-such a date'). It seeks to do this by **adding value** to the product or service: consumers are offered something extra – or the chance to obtain something extra – if they purchase, purchase more or purchase again.

Exam Tip

It is worth being aware of the potential for confusion between the terms 'promotion' (used as another way of saying 'marketing communications'in general) and 'sales promotion' (which is a specialist term reserved for the techniques described here). In an exam, especially if you are reading through questions fairly quickly, it is all too easy to answer the 'wrong' question.

3.6 Consumer sales promotion techniques include:

- **Price promotions**: for example discounted selling price or additional product on **current** purchase or coupons (on packs or advertisements) offering discounts on **next** purchase
- '**Gift with purchase**' or '**premium**' promotions: the consumer receives a bonus on purchase or repeat purchase, or on sending in tokens or proofs of multiple purchases
- **Competitions and prizes** for example, entry in prize draws or 'lucky purchase' prizes, often used both to stimulate purchase (more chances to win) and to capture customer data.
- **Frequent user (loyalty) incentives** for example, Air Miles programmes, points-for-prizes cards.

3.7 Sales promotions are also used extensively in trade marketing, to encourage a distributor to stock and/or sell more of a product. Techniques include:

- **Discounts**, **special terms** or occasional promotions such as 'baker's dozen' packs (13 items/packs for the price of 12)
- **Advertising/promotion** support: for example, dealer/stockist listing; financial contribution to stockist advertising that features the product; collaborative campaigns/promotions benefiting the stockist and brand.

Action Programme 2

Select some products that you buy regularly or are interested in and make a point of tracking their advertising and promotion over a period of several months. Note how posters and shop displays back up TV and press campaigns. See whether the campaign attracts any 'free' publicity in the form of press coverage, or references made by public figures (like TV personalities). Is the promotion talked about by your colleagues and friends? Has a slogan 'caught on' and fallen into general usage? How well integrated are all these types of messages: do they convey a consistent core message about the product?

The more you look, the more you will see. In the examination you are frequently asked to illustrate your answers with examples, or to answer from the point of view of 'an organisation/brand of your choice'. Don't rely on the examples in this Text: everyone else may do the same!

Point of sale and packaging

3.8 Two thirds of purchases are estimated to result from in-store decisions: attractive and informative in-store **displays** and **promotional materials** are therefore a key part of sales promotion.

3.9 Point of sale materials include product housing or display casing (such as racks and carousels), posters, leaflet dispensers and so on. Their purpose is to:

- Attract the attention of buyers
- Stimulate purchase in preference to rival brands
- Increase available display and promotion space for the product
- Motivate retailers to stock the product (because they add to store appeal)

Marketing at Work

Creatable Media (Australia)

'Major advertisers have signed up to secure ad space on a medium targeting consumers at the point of purchase – food court table tops.

'Created by Sydney-based company Creatable, the tables will be located in the food courts of major shopping centres... Flight Centre's marketing director said table-top advertising was "an opportunity to drive sales into stores as well as an effective tool for brand building"

'[Creatable executive directors] said the medium was a way to reach a "captive audience for an average of 10-15 minutes" at a time. "We are targeting shoppers at the point of purchase when they are in buying mode with money in their pockets. About 75% of consumer decisions are made in the shopping environment, and 50% are made in the store itself." '

B & T Weekly, 5/7/2002.

3.10 **Product packaging** is also a promotional aid.

- The design can be used to attract attention, convey brand identity and promote brand recognition. (Most people come to recognise their favourite brands on the shelf – even from a distance – by the packing colour and design.)
- Printable surfaces can be used for product labelling and information (some of which is required by law) and also promotional messages, sales promotions and coupons.
- Values integral to the packaging itself (size, environment-friendliness, convenience, attractiveness, protection of product quality) are part of the overall benefit and image bundle of the product

Public relations and publicity

Key Concept

Public relations is 'the planned and sustained effort to establish and maintain **goodwill** and **mutual understanding** between an organisation and its publics'(Institute of Public Relations). The related discipline of **publicity**is defined as any form of **non-paid**, **non-personal** communication.

3.11 This is an important discipline, because although it may not directly stimulate sales, the organisation's **image** is an important factor in whether it attracts and retains **employees**, whether **consumers** buy its products/services, whether the **community** supports or resists its presence and activities and whether the media reports positively on its operations.

3.12 The scope of PR is very broad, including the following activities.

Consumer marketing support	■ Consumer and trade press releases (to secure media coverage) ■ Product/service literature (including videos) ■ Special events (celebrity appearances and endorsement, product launch events) ■ Publicity 'stunts'(attention-grabbing events)
B2B communications	■ Corporate identity ('house style'of communications, logos etc) ■ Corporate and product videos ■ Trade exhibitions and conferences
Corporate and public affairs communications	■ Corporate literature ■ Corporate social responsibility and community involvement programmes: liaison with pressure/interest groups ■ Media relations: networking and image management through trade, local, national (and possibly international) press ■ Lobbying of local/central government and influential bodies ■ Crisis and issues management: minimising the negative impact of problems and bad publicity by managing press/public relations
Financial PR	■ Financial media relations ■ Design of annual and interim reports ■ Facility visits/information for analysts, brokers etc ■ Organising shareholder meetings and communications
Employee relations	■ In-house magazines, newsletters and Intranet pages ■ Recruitment exhibitions/conferences ■ Employee communications

Action Programme 3

Start collecting examples of:

(a) Editorial articles (or radio/TV news segments) which quote representatives of named commercial organisations): what impression is created by the attribution of the quoted statement?

(b) Named or visibly identifiable brands (watches, cars, soft drinks) in movies and TV programmes: this is called 'product placement': how noticeable are they, and what effect does their presence have?

(c) Letters, notices or statements from spokespersons apologising for mistakes or errors (in advertising or customer service, or on larger issues of public relations crisis such as a product recall or damaging revelations): how effectively do they minimise potential negative feelings on the part of customers/consumers?

Sponsorship

3.13 Sponsorship involves supporting an event or activity by providing money (or something else of value, such as product prizes for a competition), usually in return for naming rights, advertising or acknowledgement at the event and in any publicity connected with the event. Sponsorship is often sought for sporting events, artistic events, educational initiatives and charity/community events and initiatives.

Action Programme 4

List some examples of sporting, artistic, educational and community sponsorships that you are aware of in your country (or internationally).

- What image of the sponsoring company or brand does association with that particular event/group/cause create?
- How much promotional coverage (advertising, publicity) does the sponsor get as a result of sponsorship: how much information about the organisation or brand is conveyed?

3.14 Sponsorship is often seen as part of a company's socially responsible and community-friendly public relations profile: it has the benefit of positive associations with the sponsored cause or event. The profile gained (for example in the case of television coverage of a sporting event) can be cost-effective compared to TV advertising, for example. However, it relies heavily on awareness and association: unless additional advertising space or 'air time'is part of the deal, not much information may be conveyed.

3.15 A relatively new promotional technique in the UK (although already established in the US and Australia, for example) is **programme sponsorship**: the sponsorship of commercial television programmes. The sponsor pays for the rights to get front and end credits ('This programme is/was sponsored by…') and spots at the beginning and end of commercial breaks. Credits usually include the brand name, slogan and logo: although it does not allow time for much information, it does secure repeat viewing opportunities at the times of most impact.

Marketing at Work

Sponsorship can bring a known brand to a new section of the market. Sales of the new Lincoln luxury car in the US were increased among younger customers via its sponsorship of the fashionable Cirque du Soleil shows.

Sponsorship has also spread to the Internet, with companies sponsoring pages on sites which attract their target customers. For example, Charles Schwab sponsors content on a site called Senior Net, which attracts adults over 50 interested in hands-on training in computer technology.

Personal selling

3.16 **Personal selling** is the **direct** and **personal** presentation of products and associated persuasive communication to potential clients by sales representatives employed by the supplying organisation.

3.17 Kotler identifies six different activities that a sales person may perform.

Prospecting	Gathering additional prospective customers, in addition to sales leads generated by the company on his or her behalf.
Communicating	Giving information to existing and potential customers about the company's products and services.
Selling	Establishing rapport with customers; persuasively presenting product benefits; answering objections and resistance; urging and facilitating action to close the sale.
Servicing	Providing various services to the customer, such as rendering technical assistance, arranging finance or expediting delivery.
Information gathering	Acting as a key source of marketing intelligence and feedback to the company, as the (often sole) direct link with the customer.
Allocating	Distributing products among customers in times of product shortage.

3.18 If the organisation relies on consumer advertising to draw customers to enquire after its brands, the role of the sales force may primarily be **servicing**: ensuring that retailers carry sufficient stock, negotiating adequate shelf space for display and so on. In high-value consumer goods/services markets (such as car or insurance sales), where personal information and persuasion may be required to close the sale, the **selling** role may be paramount. In business-to-business markets, the relationship to between client and sales representative (or account handler) is more important, and may involve a range of roles.

3.19 Personal selling is part of the integrated promotional strategy of the organisation. Note that it will be supported by a range of other marketing communication activities.

(a) **Product advertising, public relations and sales promotion**, drawing consumer attention and interest to the product and its sources **and** motivating distributors/retailers to stock and sell the product

(b) '**Leads**'(interested prospective customers) generated by contacts and enquiries made through exhibitions, promotional competitions, enquiry coupons in advertising and other methods

(c) **Informational tools** such as brochures and presentation kits. These can add interest and variety to sales presentations, and leave customers with helpful reminders and information

(d) **Sales support information**: customer/segment profiling; competitor intelligence; access to customer contact/transaction histories and product availability and so on. (This is an important aspect of customer relationship management, enabling field sales teams to facilitate immediate response and transactions without time-lags to obtain information.)

Action Programme 5

What do you think are the advantages and disadvantages of personal selling, compared to other promotional tools discussed so far?

Exhibitions

3.20 Exhibitions (such as the Ideal Home Exhibition) and trade fairs (such as the Frankfurt Book Fair) vary in the opportunities they offer for public relations, sales promotion and selling.

- **Public relations**: both to visitors and via media coverage, taking advantage of the interest generated by the exhibition organisers
- **Promoting and selling** products/services to a wide audience of pre-targeted potential customers, particularly where demonstrations (for example of technical innovations) or visual inspection (for example clothes or motor cars) are likely to influence buyers
- **Networking** within the industry and with existing clients; making supply chain contacts.
- **Testing the response** to new products
- **Researching competitors**, their products and promotions

Exam Tip

Just to motivate you to keep reading at this stage, a question in the Specimen Paper for this module asked you to recommend a range of promotional tools you believe would be most effective for an industrial company of your choice. You were also asked to draft a full A4 page recruitment ad for a marketing post, and to write a letter on behalf of a not-for-profit organisation requesting corporate sponsorship: we will be covering these tools in sufficient depth in the following chapters.

Direct Marketing

Key Concept

Direct marketing is:

- 'An **interactive system** of marketing which uses one or more advertising media to effect a **measurable response and/or transaction** at **any location**.'(US Direct Marketing Association)
- 'The planned **recording, analysis** and tracking of customer behaviour to develop **relational marketing strategies**'(UK Institute of Direct Marketing)

3.21 These definitions highlight key aspects of direct marketing.

Interactivity	Direct marketing is a two-way dialogue between the supplier and the customer.
Response	It is about getting people to respond: to send in coupons, or make telephone calls, in response to invitations and offers.
Recording and analysis	Response data are collected and analysed so that customer needs and wants can be more effectively and efficiently targeted.
Relationship marketing	This allows the supplier to make on-going – and appropriately targeted, customised or personalised – offerings to the customer.

3.22 Direct marketing helps create and develop **direct one-to-one relationships** between the company and each of its prospects and customers. This is a form of **direct supply**, because it removes all channel intermediaries apart from the advertising medium and the delivery medium: there are no resellers. This allows the company to retain control over where and how its products are promoted, and to reach and develop business contacts efficiently.

3.23 Postma (*The New Marketing Era*) goes further and defines direct marketing as 'the execution of the marketing process, or parts thereof, using electronic and/or printed information carriers (media) **without human intervention!**'This has been made possible by e-commerce, database marketing and customer relationship management technologies.

3.24 Direct marketing is the fastest growing sector of promotional activity. It now embraces a range of techniques, some traditional – and some new technology based.

(a) **Direct mail** (DM): a personally addressed 'written offering'(letter and/or sales literature) with some form of response mechanism, sent to existing customers from an in-house databased (or commercially obtained) mailing list.

(b) **E-mail**: messages sent via the Internet from an e-mail database of customers. E-mails can offer routine information, updates, information about new products and so on: e-mail addresses can be gathered together via enquiries and contact permissions at the company's Web site.

(c) **Mobile phone text messaging (SMS)**. 'SMS combines mobility, intimacy, immediacy and the ability to push a simple powerful message to a receptive audience. There is nothing else like it. For marketing purposes SMS allows customer services, alerts, CRM, communication – two-way direct response mechanism, brand bonding, event ticketing: the possibilities are still being explored.'(Mullin, *Direct Marketing)*

(d) **Direct response advertising**. This may be traditional advertising in a newspaper or magazine with a cut out (or stuck on) response coupon; loose inserts with response coupons or reply cards; direct-response TV or radio advertisements, giving a call centre number or Web site address to contact. The ultra-modern equivalent is advertising on interactive (digital) TV when a 'pop up' button gives you the option to interact by transferring to a Web site.

(e) **Mail order**. Mail order brochures typically contain a selection of items also available in a shop or trade outlet, which can be ordered via an order form included with the brochure and delivered to the customer. Mail order extends the reach of a retail business to more (and more geographically dispersed) customers.

(f) **Catalogue marketing** is similar to mail order, but involves a complete catalogue of the products of the firm, which typically would not have retail outlets at all. Electronic catalogues can also be downloaded on the Internet, with the option of transferring to the Web site for transaction processing, and on CD ROM.

(g) **Call centres and tele-marketing**. A call centre is a telephone service (in-house or out-sourced by the marketing organisation) responding to or making telephone calls. This is a cost-effective way of providing a professionally trained response to customer callers and enquirers, for the purposes of sales, customer service, customer care or contact point for direct response advertising.

Marketing at Work

Girlfriend Magazine (Australia)

Objectives: To surround *Girlfriend* readers with the brand and reward readers for brand loyalty

Strategy: To create an SMS VIP club.

Results: 200,000 readers registered for VIP membership and 20% of those submitted their mobile phone number.

'When *Girlfriend* magazine wanted to surround its readers with its brand, it looked not only at the Internet as an extension of the magazine, but also to readers'mobile phones. In addition, the SMS promotion aimed to drive traffic to the website and increase stickiness.

'iTouch developed a system for readers to send free SMS messages from *Girlfriend's* website. VIP members could submit their mobile phone number to receive special offers.

'In addition to leveraging the brand and increasing website visits, *Girlfriend* created a community to reward brand loyalty.'

B & T Weekly, 5/7/2002

Note: SMS text messaging is a 'hot'promotional tool! Keep an eye on this trend as it develops!

3.25 Direct marketing raises a key issue of Integrated Marketing Communications. It's all very well allowing customers to respond instantly to successful promotional messages – but if the delivery infrastructure isn't up to the job, and the product or information then takes weeks to reach them – the relational potential of the approach will be wasted.

Web sites

3.26 Web sites are now a key form of corporate communication. Almost every major company has some type of Web presence. Web sites are used for a number of purposes, of increasing complexity.

- **Advertising/information**: Web sites can be used simply as a form of advertising, plus access to product information and/or information databases
- **Customer service/technical support**. Information, e-mailed questions, FAQ (frequently asked question) lists and other techniques can be used for customer service.
- **Transactions**. More and more firms use Web sites as a means of taking sales enquiries, orders and payment, although security concerns have limited the take-up of e-commerce to some extent.
- **Gathering customer data**. Web sites can be used to obtain information from customers, such as contact details, buying history and preferences, web surfing patterns and so on.
- **Advertising revenue**. Some firms sell advertising space on their Web sites, by offering 'banner'space for a particular period of time. (Banner advertising is included in our discussion of advertising in the next chapter.)

3.27 The general benefits of Internet marketing are set out as follows, in *The Unofficial Guide to Marketing Your Business On-line.*

'If you create an entire Web site specifically to promote your company and its products and services, you're not limited by ad space (as you would be using a traditional print ad in a magazine, for example). You're also not forced to convey your message in 15, 30 or 60 seconds as you are when using TV or radio advertising.

'As long as you're offering the web surfer information she or he wants or needs, your web site can potentially capture that person's attention and keep it for second, minutes or even hours as you convey your marketing/advertising and maybe even sell your products and service directly online. This is something a TV ad, print ad or radio ad can't do.'

3.28 The following is an example of a Web site (Microsoft's Home Page) showing opportunities for information search, on-line purchase, stakeholder communication and customer service.

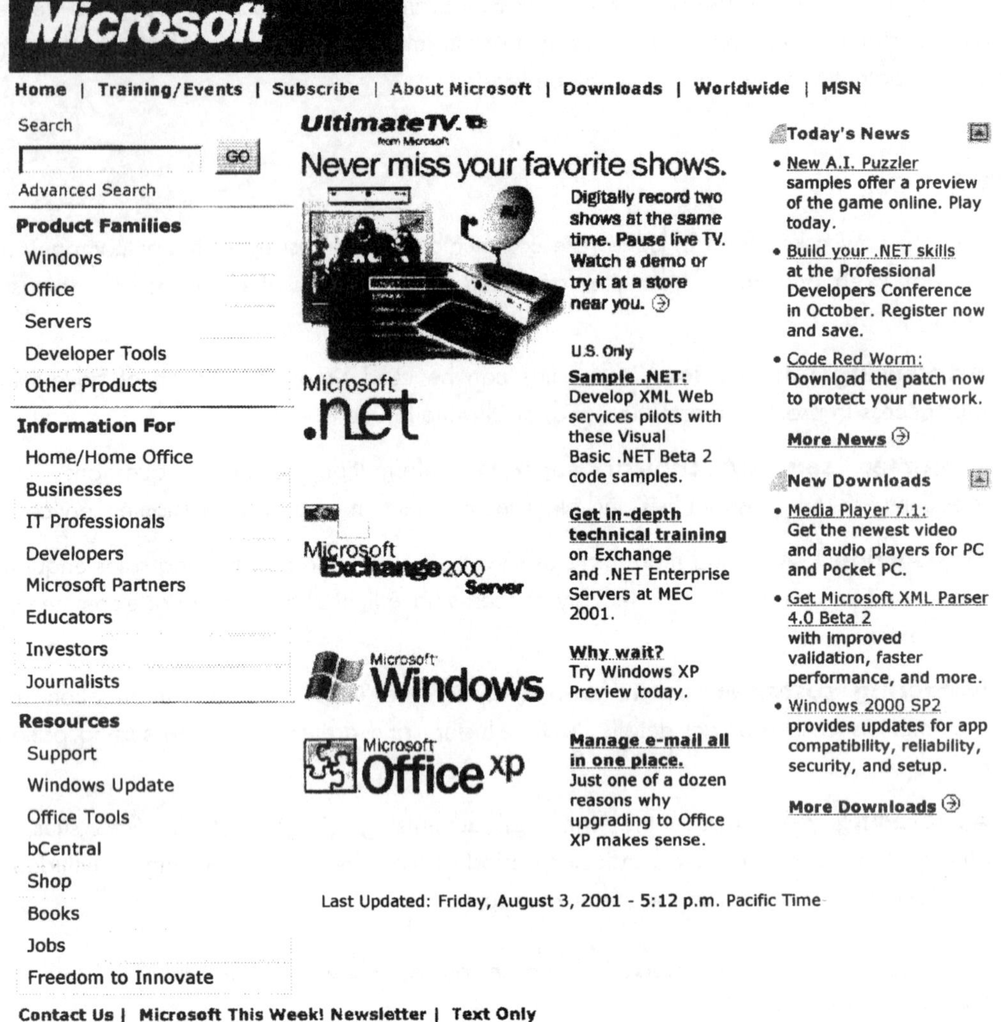

Exam Tip

If you have access to the Internet we highly recommend that you follow through some of the Web site recommendations given at the beginning of this Text and in Marketing at Work examples. This is really the only way to get to grips – and keep up to date – with the potential and constant development of the World Wide Web as a promotional tool.

4 Promotion planning

Promotion mix strategies

4.1 Choosing the correct tools for a particular promotion task is not easy – although new technology is making it somewhat more scientific: computers can match databased consumer and media profiles to formulate an optimal mix, and promotional budgets can be modelled on spreadsheets for a variety of different mixes.

4.2 At a basic level, however, promotion planning can be seen as a typical decision sequence (Figure 5.2).

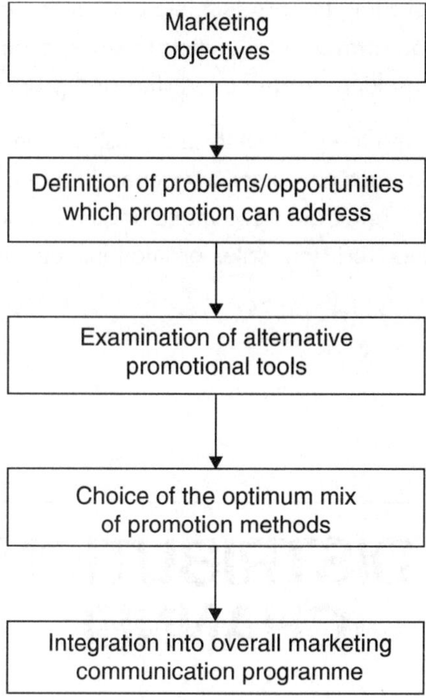

Figure 5.2: the promotion planning process

Action Programme 6

You are the Marketing Manager for a newly-developed software product: home accounting software designed to make home budgeting and finances easy – for non-experts! It's called "e-Z Accounts"

List the different promotional tools you might use to promote this product in its launch months. (Be as creative as you like…)

4.3 The relative emphasis placed on different promotion tools will differ according to:

- Push or pull strategy
- Type of product/market
- Product life cycle stage
- Buyer readiness stage

Push or pull?

4.4 'Push'and 'pull'are two basic promotion strategies, according to whether the target audience of promotional communication is primarily **channel members** (distributors, retail outlets and so on) or **consumers**.

Key Concept

Push strategy involves 'pushing'the product into distribution channels. Marketing activities aim to encourage distribution and/or retail outlets to stock, promote and sell the product. Push techniques include personal selling, trade advertising and promotion, and trade exhibitions.

Pull strategyinvolves 'pulling'the product through distribution channels towards consumers. Marketing activities aim to arouse consumer awareness, interest and desire so that they approach distributors and/or retail outlets to make enquiries and purchases. Pull techniques include television and press advertising, sales promotions, customer loyalty programmes and point of sale display.

Figure 5.3: Push and pull techniques

4.5 In practice, most marketers will use a combination of push and pull techniques. (Remember the Integrated Marketing Communications approach?) Distributors are more likely to stock a product if they can see that their own promotion/sale efforts will be supported by 'pull'promotions for the brand, sending consumers to them. Trade advertising and selling often involves demonstrating how aggressively the product will be promoted to consumers, and what benefits this will create for the distributor (as well as the supplier).

Type of product/market

4.6 As we saw in Chapter 3, consumer and business markets behave differently. In most business markets, there are fewer, higher-value customers, who require a more complex total offering: as professional buyers, they are generally less susceptible to mass communications and prefer to negotiate and develop on-going business terms and relationships with suppliers. While **consumer markets** favour **advertising** (supported by sales promotion), **industrial/business markets** favour **personal selling** (supported by sales promotion).

Product life cycle stage

4.7 Different promotion tools will be most effective at different stages of the product life cycle.

Stage	Aim of promotional activity	Promotion mix
Introduction	■ Produce high awareness ■ Induce early trial ■ Sell in to trade/distributors	■ Advertising, PR ■ Sales promotion ■ Personal selling
Growth	■ Fewer incentives needed?	■ Maintain advertising, PR momentum. Reduce sales promotion?
Maturity	■ Remind buyers of (now well known) brand ■ Maximise sales levels	■ Less aggressive advertising, PR: perhaps sponsorship? ■ Maintain sales promotion, personal selling
Decline	■ Maintain profitability ■ Secure last available sales	■ Reduce all activity ■ Maintain sales promotion

Buyer readiness

4.8 As we saw in Chapter 4, buyers move through different stages from awareness of the product through to readiness to buy, and different promotional tools will be effective at each stage. Note that more labour intensive (and therefore costly) techniques such as personal selling will generally be brought into play where consumers are approaching readiness to buy, and used to 'close'the sale. (In business markets, as noted above, the high value of orders makes them cost-effective for more general use.)

Action Programme 7

Suggest the most effective promotional tools for the stages of the Buyer Readiness Model (a good opportunity for revision, if required!)

Planning individual elements of the promotions mix

4.9 In Chapter 3, we looked briefly at the steps a marketing communicator should take in planning any message, and we will discuss these further (in the context of communication skills) in Chapter 10.

- Identify the target audience
- Determine the desired response
- Develop an effective message
- Select an appropriate medium
- Gather feedback

4.10 The process for developing and implementing plans for individual elements of the promotion mix reflect this sequence.

Identify the target audience	■ *Consumer:* segment characteristics? buying behaviour? media preferences? buyer readiness/brand perceptions? ■ *Business:* sector (or individual client) characteristics? buying centre requirements? media/contact preferences?
Set the promotion budget	■ *Objectives*: criteria for evaluation (exposure, awareness, attitude, sales, profit)? ■ *Expenditure:* estimated (rate card, quote, expenditure history)? target/ceiling (percentage of last period sales, percentage of target sales, percentage of past/target profit)?
Develop the promotional message	■ *Purpose:* attention? knowledge? interest? desire? conviction? action? crisis handling? ■ *Content:* text? still/moving images? sound? less or more? ■ *Style:* informative? persuasive (rational appeal, emotive appeal, moral appeal)? visual/audio impact?
Select and schedule media	■ *Above-the-line (advertising) media:* Select (reach? frequency? targeting? cost?) Purchase and schedule (specialist media planners or advertising agency?) ■ *Below-the-line media:* Select (suitability for purpose? reach? targeting? cost?). Schedule implementation; book (for example exhibition stand, mailing house) where required.
Co-ordinate processes and relationships	■ *Brief agencies and suppliers on requirements:* advertising agency? PR agency? designers/printers? Web site manager? ■ *Co-ordinate processes:* printing? mailing? exhibition set up? ■ *Manage relationships:* agencies and suppliers? sponsored organisations? collaborative promotions?
Evaluate promotion effectiveness	■ *Feedback on results:* (sales/transaction data? consumer surveys? recall/attitude testing?) ■ *Compare to objectives/criteria*

4.11 In chapters that follow, we will see how this sequence works itself out in practice in the case of specific elements of the promotion mix.

Chapter Roundup

- **Promotion** is the process of communication by a seller to the market (buyers and potential buyers) for its products and services.
- The **promotion mix** is the total marketing communications programme of the organisation, consisting of a specific combination or blend of promotional tools used to reach the target market for a given product or brand.
- **Promotional tools** can be classified as:
  - Above-the-line activities: advertising in paid-for media space, and

  - Below-the-line activities. These include: sales promotion, point of sale display and packaging, public relations, publicity, sponsorship, personal selling, direct marketing and Internet marketing.

- The **most effective promotion mix** will be planned according to: whether the organisation has push or pull strategies; the type of product/market (consumer or industrial); the product's stage in the product life cycle (PLC: introduction, growth, maturity or decline); and the stage of buyer readiness (awareness to purchase).
- A systematic **planning sequence** can be used to plan, co-ordinate and evaluate the implementation of individual elements of the mix.

Quick Quiz

1 Name (a) the four major traditional components of the promotion mix and (b) the fastest growing new element of the mix.

2 Promotion of a product using pictures on trains and buses is an example of:

☐ Above the line promotion ☐ Below the line promotion

3 On which of the following criteria would cinema advertising compare most favourably with television, national newspaper and radio advertising?

A Cost
B Targeting
C Impact
D Exposure

4 Sales promotion activity involves adding value to the product or service.

☐ True ☐ False

5 Allocate the following promotional tools to the appropriate boxes below.

(1) 'Gift with purchase'offer (2) Buying naming rights to a local park
(3) A counter-top leaflet dispenser (4) Launch reception for key clients

Public relations	*Sponsorship*	*Point of sale*	*Sales promotion*

6 '........ is any form of non-paid, non-personal communication.'

7 Which of the six activities of a sales person identified by Kotler is missing from the list below?

Allocating
Selling
Prospecting
Information gathering
Servicing

8 Direct marketing is most effective when it achieves:

☐ Mass communication ☐ One-to-one communication

9 Television advertising is an example of:

A Push technique
B Below-the-line promotion
C Direct marketing
D Pull technique

10 What will be the most important form of promotion in the declining stage of a product's life cycle?

Answers to Quick Quiz

1 (a) Advertising, personal selling, sales promotion, public relations (b) Direct marketing.

2 Above the line promotion

3 C

4 True

5 PR: (4); Sponsorship (2); POS (3); Sales promotion (1)

6 Publicity

7 Communicating

8 One-to-one communication

9 D

10 Sales promotion

Now try Question 5 from the Question Bank at the end of this Text

Action Programme Review

1 This is effective as an ad on many levels: (a) it is visually striking; (b) it is placed in a targeted medium (all ad-professionals); (c) it is unavoidable by anyone wanting to read the editorial content; (d) as a self-stick insert, it is easily detachable (to read the reverse and retain for later response) *without* falling out like most loose inserts; (e) it gives a clear direct response mechanism; (f) it *demonstrates* all the qualities of the medium it is promoting; (g) it capitalises on an existing 'friendly'brand, while (h) targeting the branding specifically to the ad audience ('stick'being ad jargon for holding the attention).

It is effective as an advertising medium because of (c), (d) and (g) above, plus the demonstrated ability to print sufficient information to be worthwhile. And it's new!

2 Just do it!

3 Attribution of expert status has an image-building effect, as well as getting the brand/company name mentioned – as long as the nature of the context and the impression given by the spokesperson is positive! Product placement may seem barely noticeable at times, but it builds awareness and positive association (for example with 'cool'characters like James Bond: his brand of watch and car are always keenly anticipated). Problem management is a sensitive area of PR: there is great potential to win customer loyalty by honest and swift response.

4 There are lots of sponsorships to choose from: if you can't think of any, consider what this means for the effectiveness of sponsorship as a promotional tool. Sponsorship suits established brands that want to remind consumers of their existence and emphasise positive associations (such as beers and telecommunications companies with high-profile men's sport, and luxury brands with fine art or opera, say)) or social responsibility values (such as newspapers sponsoring books or computers for schools programmes).

5 Shimp identifies advantages such as: relatively high level of customer attention/focus; ability to customise the message to customer needs and feedback (interactively) at the time; ability to convey larger amounts of technical and complex information (with interactive explanation, demonstration); development of collaborative relationship between buyer/seller. The main disadvantages are the cost of maintaining a sales force and its labour intensive nature (only able to interact with one customer at a time): this may, however, be essential for high-value, relationship- and persuasion-focused sales

6 Bear in mind the needs of your target audience: they are consumers, *not* accountants; they are likely to be household finance managers (male or female?) and they will have some computer literacy. Some ideas for promotion (not all of which require a large budget) include:

- Media advertising in quality family magazines, personal finance sections of newspapers. All ads to give Web site and major stockist contacts ('push'incentive)
- Promotional/information Web site, with opportunities to view (perhaps try?) selected areas of the software
- Free samples of the product to opinion leaders (for example personal finance editors, IT reviewers) and advocates (for example financial counselling organisations) to generate press articles, possible endorsements
- PR campaign to reinforce awareness of problems caused by personal debt and lack of financial planning; quote endorsement by financial planners or financial counsellors. (Consider taped radio PR package: brief 'infomercial'on problems of debt: Publicity manager available for interviews)
- Branding: create a friendly logo and recognisable style for the e-Z brand; slogan 'e-Z DOES IT!'
- Negotiate loading of trial software onto computers in computing/electronics retailers, so consumers can 'try before they buy'(risk-free sampling)
- Attractive point of sale display (dump bins, posters)
- Trade launch promotion: branded 'e-Z DOES IT!'T-shirts for retail staff (extend to consumer merchandise or promotional giveaway if it catches on).

7 Awareness/knowledge: advertising and public relations

Liking/preference/conviction: sales promotion/sampling; exhibitions/demonstrations; personal selling; on-going advertising/PR

Purchase: sales promotion, personal selling, direct marketing

Advertising and sales promotion

6

Chapter Topic List	
1	Setting the scene
2	Developing advertisements
3	Advertising applications
4	Integrated mail media
5	Developing sales promotions
6	Point of sale and packaging

Learning Outcomes

- ☑ Draft basic advertisements and design briefs for various applications
- ☑ Draft formats for integrated mail media
- ☑ Evaluate the effectiveness of Web site advertising and information
- ☑ Develop ideas for effective sales promotions and points of sale displays
- ☑ Appreciate the role of product packaging in the promotion mix

Syllabus References

- ☑ Explain the key stages and considerations when developing and designing advertisements (3.7)
- ☑ Distinguish between the different forms of integrated mail media, such as direct mail leaflets and mail order advertising (3.10)
- ☑ Explain the role of point of sale (POS) material and how it is developing in response to changing customer needs (3.11)
- ☑ Explain the role of packaging in the promotions mix (3.12)

☑ Describe current trends and developments in promotions and their impact on organisations (3.15)

Key Concepts Introduced

- Direct response advertisements
- Banner advertisements
- Direct mail
- Point of sale

1 Setting the scene

1.1 In Chapter 5, we took a broad view of the **role of promotion and promotional tools**, enabling you to determine and plan an effective promotional mix for a given market or brand. This should have consolidated your study of promotion (as an element of the marketing mix) for the *Marketing Fundamentals* module.

1.2 In Chapter 6 and 7 of this Text, we begin to **implement key promotional tools** whose nature and aims were summarised in Chapter 5. Chapter 6 deals with advertising and sales promotion (and related aspects), while Chapter 7 deals with PR and publicity (and related aspects).

1.3 In the *Marketing in Practice* module, you will learn to implement elements of the promotion mix (including advertising and sales promotions) in a role such as that of a **marketing co-ordinator**. This includes evaluating and scheduling advertising media, co-ordinating the production of printed matter, liaising with advertising agencies and budgeting.

1.4 In the *Customer Communications* module, we focus on implementing elements of the promotion mix in your role as a **communicator**. You will learn how to plan, place, develop and evaluate promotional communications in a range of formats and styles.

A planning and implementation framework

1.5 In considering each communication/promotion task, we will apply a simplified framework, based on the planning sequence proposed at the end of Chapter 5 for planning and implementing individual elements of the promotional mix. This will make the material easier to apply – and will, in the process, demonstrate a helpful planning and decision-making framework that you can apply to *any* communication/promotion task you encounter at work or in the exam.

1.6 The framework can be depicted as follows (Figure 6.1). You might like to use the mnemonic POMMIE (Purpose, Objectives, Media/mechanisms, Message, Implement, luate) to remind you.

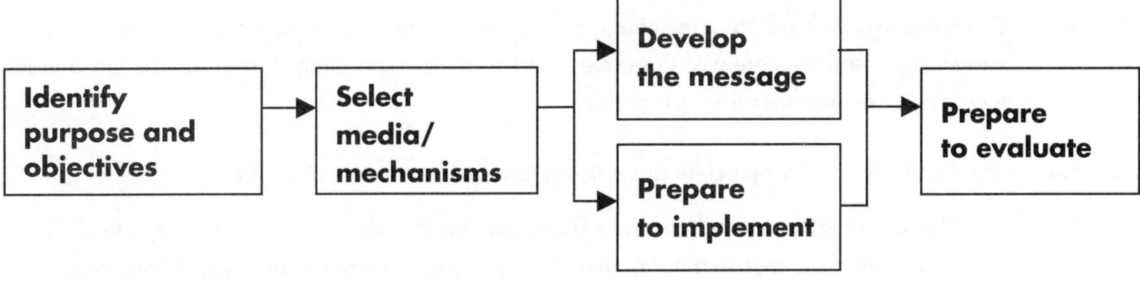

Figure 6.1: A simplified promotion planning framework

1.7 The steps can be outlined as follows.

Identify purpose and objectives	■ Determine what it is you are trying to achieve (general aims or specific performance objectives) ■ Define the needs/characteristics of the target audience
Select media/mechanisms	■ Evaluate alternative advertising media and/or promotional mechanisms (formats, techniques and approaches) and select those most suitable for your objectives
Develop the message	■ Plan the content, structure and style of the communication ■ Draft text (and/or visuals, if relevant)
Prepare to implement	■ Prepare any requests or instructions required for implementation (layout instructions, agency brief, proposals)
Prepare to evaluate	■ Review relevant appraisal criteria: what makes an effective ad, Web site or whatever? ■ Appraise your proposal or draft and adjust if necessary. (This is a useful habit to get into – especially for exams!) ■ Plan a post-implementation evaluation of the communication's effectiveness.

1.8 We will now proceed to apply this framework to some key promotion tasks.

2 Developing advertisements

Objectives of the advertisement

2.1 Kotler sums up the purpose of advertising (as a promotional tool) as follows.

'The purpose of advertising is to enhance potential buyers'responses to the organisation and its offerings. It seeks to do this by providing information, by trying to channelise desires and by supplying reasons for preferring the particular organisation's offerings'.

2.2 Advertising is often classed under one of three purpose-based headings.

- **Informative**: conveying information and raising consumer awareness of the product. (Common in the early stages of the lifecycle, or after modification.)
- **Persuasive**: creating a desire for the product and stimulating actual purchase. (Used for well established products, often in the growth/maturity stage of the product life cycle. The most competitive style of advertising.)
- **Reminding**: reminding consumers about the product or organisation, reinforcing the knowledge held by potential customers and reminding existing consumers of the benefits they are receiving from their purchase.

2.3 The general objectives of a **specific** advertising campaign might include the following.

(a) To **attract attention and arouse interest**: for example, using 'teaser'ads to stimulate consumer curiosity. (For example, Microsoft's 'Xbox is coming'campaign, long before the product was finally identified and described.)

(b) To communicate certain **information** about a product or service: for example what it is, where it is available, changes to price or specification and so on.

(c) To **highlight specific features** of a product, in order to:

- Offer **benefits** which may be desired and important to consumers, to stimulate desire
- Differentiate the product from competitors: the concept of the **unique selling proposition** (or USP) is that emphasising a unique feature, which appeals to a customer need, arouses brand preference and conviction

(c) To build up a **brand image** or **company image** (through corporate advertising)

(d) To **achieve push strategies**: influencing dealers and resellers to stock the items, maximise shelf space or participate in promotions (trade advertising)

(e) To **promote ideas, attitudes or opinions**: for example, in the case of charities and public service organisations.

Action Programme 1

e-Z Accounts

You are Marketing Manager for 'e-Z Accounts', the new home accounts software product. Having brainstormed a selection of ideas for the promotion mix of the product's launch (Action Programme 6 of Chapter 4), you are now ready to plan your consumer advertising programme in detail.

- What will be the main objectives of your advertising campaign?
- How might you use 'teaser ads'?

We will use e-Z Accounts as an **on-going project** in this chapter, to take you through a whole planning sequence. Complete all the Action Programmes, so you can follow the case through.

Selecting advertising media

2.4 Selecting the 'right'medium for your advertisement involves the following steps.

(a) Identify the target group of people you wish to reach and influence.
(b) Identify media which they read/watch/listen to/access frequently and dependably.
(c) Select, from those media, those which give you:

- The **widest coverage of your target group** (that is wide exposure **and** relevant audience profile)
- **With the greatest frequency** (not just frequency of publication or transmission for example daily or weekly newspapers, but frequency of **access/reference** by the target group: magazines, for example, may be referred to several times and be shared with others)
- **With the greatest credibility** (the medium content and style of the medium is congenial, authoritative and relevant to the target group's motives and interests)
- **With the greatest demonstrated/tested ability to yield results** (for example response speed, response volume, response as percentage of audience reached)

- **With the greatest value for money** (for example defined as cost per thousand people reached or cost per response)

2.5 The following shows a comparison of some of the features of the major above-the-line media.

Medium	Advantages	Disadvantages
Newspapers (daily metropolitan/ national)	■ 'Mass' medium: large audience in single exposure ■ Targeted sections (auto, home, computers etc) ■ Reader navigation: seeking news, information ■ Short lead time for production: accept ads 24-48 hours before publication ■ Flexibility of ad size ■ Tangibility of ad (can be torn out and kept) ■ Multiple readers/users ■ Allows detailed information (prices, phone numbers etc) ■ Allows (still) images ■ Allows response mechanisms (eg captions)	■ Circulation does not mean readership: wasted circulation paid for ■ Print/image reproduction of variable quality ■ No exclusivity: ad may be next to competitor's ■ Costs loaded for preferred positions ■ Short life-span of news
Newspapers (local/free)	■ Low cost ■ Geographical targeting ■ High local readership ■ Special sections (especially local real estate, entertainment etc)	■ Circulation of free papers/weeklies not always monitored/audited ■ Variable editorial content ■ Subject to weather and junk mail rejection if letterbox dropped
Magazines	■ High circulation (major titles) ■ Targeted audiences (special) ■ High quality reproduction (colour photography etc) ■ Potential high prestige ■ Reader motivation (selection, subscription) ■ Long shelf life and multiple use/readership ■ Tangibility, detail, images, response mechanisms (see newspapers)	■ High costs of production ■ Hyper-segmentation (by interest and geography, may be insufficient circulation to support local outlets) ■ Long lead times: copy/artwork required 1 – 3 months before publication, can be inflexible

Medium	Advantages	Disadvantages
Television	■ 'Mass' medium: large audience at single exposure, almost universal ownership/access ■ Detailed monitoring of exposure, reach, viewer habits ■ Allows for high degree of creativity ■ Realism: impact of sound + sight + movement ■ High-impact visual images reinforce retention ■ Allows demonstration ■ Flexibility as to scheduling ■ Allows association with desirable products	■ Most expensive of all media costs ■ High production costs ■ Lack of selectivity (except via programming) of audience ■ Lack of opportunity: does not reach commuters/workers ■ Long lead times for booking and production: penalties for withdrawal: inflexibility ■ Passive, unmotivated audience: 'zapping' by video fast-forward and remote controls erodes reach
Radio	■ 'Mass' medium: wide coverage/access ■ Audience selectivity (local/regional) programme style/variety/content) ■ Opportunity: radio is portable – in-home, in-car, on public transport, shops, offices – even jogging ■ Function: high usage for morning news, home 'companionship', background ■ Personal (and potential for participation) ■ Highly competitive costs of air time and production ■ Can be backed by personal DJ promos	■ May be passive 'background' noise: low attention, retention ■ May be 'cluttered' by announcers/DJ promotions ■ Sound only: no tangibility (pressure on retention of message), no shelf-life or 'pass on' circulation, no demonstration, no coupons, limited details
Outdoor media (poster sites bus stops, buildings etc)	■ Flexible: sites, duration of lease ■ Comparatively low cost ■ Opportunity: exposure to commuters, shoppers	■ Difficulty of verification of exposure/response ■ Subject to weather ■ Opportunity: site specific ■ No audience selectivity (except by site)
Cinema	■ Glamorous ■ High impact (large size, highly visual, loud sound, high quality) ■ Captive audience (no TV 'zap' factor) ■ Can segment by local area	■ High cost ■ Opportunity: site/time specific ■ Poor verification of response ■ Limited number of people reached per exposure

Action Programme 2

e-Z Accounts

As the Manager of e-Z Accounts:

(a) Describe some of the interests and media preferences you might identify in your target audience. (If you aren't sure, how might you go about gathering this information?)

(b) Select one specific print medium which you will target with an initial advertisement (bearing in mind your audience and objectives): give brief reasons for your selection.

(c) Specify what size your advertisement will be and whether it will be black and white or colour.

Developing the advertising message

2.6 Developing an effective advertising message will involve:

- Identifying the main selling theme, concept or 'angle'
- Drafting text or copy
- Planning effective design, layout and visuals

2.7 An effective advertisement will have a core **theme, concept or angle**, with which various information and selling points can be integrated. Devising such themes and concepts is often the responsibility of an advertising agency, but it is a useful discipline for marketing communicators: you might use the following procedure to add impact to a range of internal and external customer communications.

Step 1 List the product/service features.

Step 2 Highlight those features which are new and/or differentiate your product from its competitors.

Step 3 Identify those features which are most relevant to your purpose and audience (motives, interests): discard those that are less relevant or have negative connotations ('problems have been ironed out', 'efficient complaints-handling',) that cannot be turned into positives ('even better', 'great customer service').

Step 4 Select the selling point, feature or benefit that will **most effectively** attract attention, hold interest, arouse desire and motivate action. (Price? Quality? Convenience? Prestige?) This will be your **selling proposition** or theme.

2.8 A selling proposition that is *both* **unique** in the market *and* **important** to the audience is an ideal main idea for your advertisement. (Your product may be the only one in a recycled package – but if your consumers are not 'green'conscious, or are cost-conscious and aware that recycled packaging will cost them more, this is not the *best* motivator to offer.)

Action Programme 3

e-Z Accounts

Make a list of product features (you can invent any you wish). Using the method outlined above, come up with the key selling proposition of your ad.

2.9 Having listed the product's features, expressed them as benefits, selected those most relevant to the prospective buyer and identified the main selling them, you have all the ammunition you require to draft the text or advertising **copy**.

Step 1 Draft a few simple statements to outline your selected propositions and benefits.

Step 2 Discard any 'extra'points (however interesting in themselves) that only dilute your argument, or do not fit into your primary theme.

Step 3 Find the words which will express your remaining statements most powerfully.

Step 4 Discard unnecessary words and ideas and uses their 'space'to repeat, enliven and highlight the main ideas.

Marketing at Work

Miele

'Thinking of buying an upright? Think again.

When it comes to vacuum cleaning, we're sure you'll find the Miele Cat and Dog cleaner is the cat's whiskers. It features a powerful turbobrush with rotating brushes – just like an upright – for excellent hair pickup from carpets. Add to that the efficient charcoal filter which eliminates nasty odours and you've got the purrfect cleaner for pet owners. And even if you don't have a four legged friend, you'll appreciate the versatility, manoeuvrability and suction power you get with a cylinder along with some very convenient features such as our height adjustable telescopic tube and useful on-board tools. So, if you're still thinking of buying an upright, you could be barking up the wrong tree!

For further information phone during office hours, or our 24-hour brochure hotline:

www.miele.co.uk'

For reflection: What does the copyrighter see as this product's target audience – and how is this reflected in the (a) selling proposition and (b) style of the ad? Highlight the key words that convey product benefits. Start collecting and evaluating ads you encounter as a consumer. This will provide you with examples to use in the exam *and* practice in evaluating communications.

Ten Commandments for advertising copy

2.10 Carter puts forward a number of rules which he believes are essential to success in all forms of advertising. We have adapted them as 10 Commandments, as follows.

1 Be simple

Avoid technical and exclusive vocabulary.
Use short, easy sentences where possible.
Avoid complex reasoning: keep logical progression and links obvious and simple, so an averagely intelligent person can follow you.

2 Be interesting

Attract attention: make the reader look - then engage.
Use vivid words, enthusiastic tone, congenial images ('cosy home' for 'comfortable house', say).
Arouse curiosity, where possible: use questions and surprises.
Focus on benefits to the consumer; he will rarely be interested in the product features as such.

3 Be brief

Get to the point quickly: be direct.
Small areas of text are easily scanned and so attract the reader.
Leave out unnecessary 'padding' (sentences **and** words).
Prune ruthlessly: retain only what is necessary for sense, style and rhythm.

4 Be positive

Convert warnings and negatives ('Don't miss out on') to positive encouragement ('Take advantage of').
Use positive motivations, generally, rather than negative (eg: desire for success, not fear of failure).

5 Be factual

Keep to the 'real world' of the product and consumer, unless the need for colourful presentation really requires imaginative fantasy.

6 Be honest

The Advertising Standards Authority Code of Practice bans extravagant or misleading claims, indecent copy or illustration, and illegal statements. Besides, dishonest claims get found out (causing disappointment and loss of credibility) and titillating images are generally 'seen through' as the last resort they often are.

7 Be original

Original 'angles' and unusual use of design or words create impact.
Don't be too clever: you may lose the sense or credibility of the message.

8 Be emphatic

Reduce the number of points or themes to a minimum. Then you can repeat, emphasise and illustrate those points, for impact and recall. Use variation, vividness and humour to disguise repetition and avoid boredom.

9 Be instructive

State strongly, frequently and clearly: why, where, when and how to order/ purchase/enquire etc (eg: 'Call us now for details'. 'In all good bookshops now'. 'Send the coupon today: no stamp required'.) Reinforce with incentive if necessary (eg discount for early order, free gift for first order).

10 Be self-contained

Avoid direct comparison with competitors by name; it merely gives them free publicity and implies that you are worried by their product/performance: the reader may investigate.

You may like to remember these rules as a mnemonic.

Interesting	Positive	Factual
Emphatic	Original	Instructive
	Simple	Brief
	Honest	Self-contained

Advertising: IE POSH FIBS!

Action Programme 4

e-Z Accounts

Draft some brief ad copy for the advertisement you have planned.

2.11 As a marketing communicator, you are not expected to be a graphic designer for the purposes of planning advertising **design, layout or visuals**. You would normally get a graphic artist, advertising agency or – say, for simple classified ads – the publication itself to do this for you. (For more complex multi-media formats such as CD ROM, TV, cinema and radio advertising, you will almost certainly get professional creative and production help!)

2.12 However, you might be required to give some general **layout instructions** to:

- Typesetters: specifying page size, type size, the positions of headers and visual elements and so on, or
- Printers: specifying paper and print colours, the position of folds (for leaflets) and perforations (for tear-off coupons) and so on.

2.13 The following guidelines may be helpful.

Unity	▪ Keep it simple: use a small number of visual elements ▪ Have a focal point: one dominant feature to which the reader's eyes will be drawn. (eg a large headline, photo or illustration; a block of text surrounded by white space; one coloured item amid black and white) *Unifying headline*: Experience the Exotic at the Aquarium *Unifying illustration*: Experience the Exotic at the Aquarium

Continuity	▪ Minimise visual interruptions and distractions to the 'flow'of text ▪ Make it clear where text flows to next (especially between columns and around boxes)
Colour	▪ Use colour for impact and interest ▪ Use colour to highlight a particular part of the page. This requires *contrast:* colour only stands out if it is used selectively. ▪ Use different colours for different sections to help structure the text (eg on borders, headlines or tinted boxes) and/or in different segments of charts or diagrams to clarify. ▪ Use colour to reflect or reinforce the message (green for environment friendly) or brand (Campari red, Orange Telecom orange, BP green)
Type	▪ Specify appropriate type style ('typefaces'or 'fonts') for ease of reading, 'personality'or mood (modern, traditional, jazzy, handwritten), and emphasis (bold/dark or light). Explore the options when you use a computer, and note the styles you like. ▪ Specify appropriate type size, for readability (not too small or crowded) and emphasis (bold, italic and so on).
Page layout	▪ Consider whether you want wide or narrow margins (the white space around the edge of your design areas, between columns etc) ▪ Consider using borders, boxes and lines to hold, separate or link elements (eg columns, blocks of text) ▪ Consider using columns (which make it easier to read large bodies of text)
Visual elements	▪ Use diagrams, charts or graphs to explain or clarify information ▪ Use drawings and cartoons to support description in a simplified form ▪ Use photographs to support description and emphasise realism and credibility ▪ Surround elements with sufficient white space for a clean and uncluttered appearance (and to add impact) ▪ Size elements for visibility and legibility (eg for outdoor posters), emphasis (size in relation to surrounding elements) and unity. ▪ Keep images simple and relevant (to the purpose, audience and message)

Marketing at Work

The 'Monet & Japan'Exhibition

Another award-winning ad promoted an exhibition of paintings showing how the painter Monet was inspired by Japanese art. In the centre of a large, otherwise blank page, it simply showed two slender paint brushes positioned so that – at first glance – they looked like Japanese chopsticks. The name Monet & Japan, and location/date details, was placed in the bottom right corner, quite small. A striking visual impression, reflecting the key motif of the product.

For reflection: Start analysing the layout and graphic elements of communications that you receive or see. How effective are they – and how are the best effects achieved? If you were just sending in the *copy* of these ads (as draft text), what kind of instructions and markings might you need to give to the artists in order to help them achieve the finished product that you see?

Briefing for implementation

2.14 Once you have your draft copy and layout (or draft copy and an idea of how you might want the layout to look), you may have to brief a designer or printer as to your requirements. This may take the form of:

(a) A copy of your draft, with a covering **brief**: a letter, setting out clearly what you are trying to achieve, what your requirements are and any other information the recipient may need. (These communications are covered in Chapter 12 of this Text, with other written formats.)

(b) A copy of your draft, **marked up** with layout instructions. Such instructions would normally be handwritten (if the draft is typed: in an exam you might use a different colour) in order to distinguish the instructions clearly from the copy. (There's nothing worse than finding the words 'Insert picture here'in a printed advertisement!) Instructions may be as simple as, for example:

- Specifying the page size of the finished ad: A4 (the size of this page), A5 (half A4), or whatever size space you've bought
- Circling a header and specifying 'large type'or 'red'
- Drawing in lines and boxes to suggest formatting
- Specifying type style (named or described, as in 'modern/high-tech font') and size and layout spacing ('wide left margin required for binding')
- Specifying colours ('please match corporate identity specifications') or tints ('fill box with 10% black tint')
- Noting where a picture or other graphic is placed ('insert photo here')
- And any other items suggested by the table in paragraph 2.13 above.

Action Programme 5

e-Z Accounts

Make a clean copy of your draft advertisement, and add 'marked up'instructions for your designers as to how you want it to look, including any information you think they may need to prepare the ad for the publication.

Evaluating your ad

2.15 We have already suggested the major criteria for evaluating advertising copy and design. In addition, you should consider whether your ad is generally:

- Clear in what it is telling the target audience or asking them to do
- Attention-grabbing and interest-arousing (in content and visual appearance)
- Synergistic in associating the brand with strong, positive and relevant values (for example by the use of celebrity endorsements and lifestyle images)
- Clear in identifying the brand and organisation (unless obscurity is deliberate)
- Helpful in supplying contact details, should the audience wish to respond
- Acceptable to a range of stakeholder audiences (might it be offensive to anyone? might it be perceived as irresponsible by anyone?)

2.16 **Social responsibility** is a key issue in advertising. The advertising of such products as alcohol and tobacco (particularly in mass media such as television where the advertisements might be seen by young people) is a topic of debate, lobbying and industry self-regulation. In addition, there is (in most countries) a legal framework regulating advertising claims, truth in advertising, offensive material, invasion of privacy (for example by sharing customer contact details with other marketing organisations) and so on. You may like to browse the Web site of the Advertising Standards Authority (www.asa.org.uk) or its equivalents in your country.

2.17 Get used to evaluating the effectiveness of the advertisements (in all formats) that you are exposed to: this is a key way of managing your own learning and self-development.

3 Advertisement applications

Direct response advertising

Key Concept

Direct response advertisements are any forms of advertisement that directly invite action: sending in an order, telephoning and enquiry line or call-centre or logging on to a Web site.

3.1 **Purpose and objectives**. To arouse sufficient interest in the target audience that they take action to seek additional information (sales literature, personal consultation, product sample and so on). Or to arouse sufficient desire in the target audience that they take action on impulse to purchase the product immediately.

3.2 **Media/mechanisms**

(a) A magazine or newspaper advertisement with a response coupon or card stuck on or to be cut out. ('Tip ons' are response cards which can be stuck on the advertisement: they are easy to use – without having to cut or tear a coupon.) Added incentives to send in the response may be a free post address (no cost to the sender), a gift offer (if cost-effective) or entry in a Prize Draw, say.

(b) A loose insert: a reply card, leaflet or brochure (with response coupon or fold-and-post in its entirety) which is placed unattached among the pages of the newspaper or magazine. These can be booked for mass or targeted circulation and are usually priced per thousand.

(c) An advertisement (in any medium) which gives a telephone number (leading to a service call-centre) or Web site address. Again, added incentives to call (special offers for first fifty callers and so on) may be used to secure immediate action.

3.3 **Message**. If you expect readers to take positive an immediate action (and especially to buy an unseen product from an unknown organisation) you need to work a bit harder.

(a) Give more factual information (verbal or visual) about the product so that the audience feels they have enough information to order. Or make it clear that more information will gladly be given (by phone or at the Web site) to help them decide.

(b) Use endorsements and styles which will establish the credibility and reputability of the advertiser.

(c) Try harder to arouse interest and desire: use powerful motivators, an easily understood but vivid style, and a simple message strongly emphasised.

(d) Make response easy (especially ordering): emphasise the speed and convenience with which information (or the product) can be obtained.

(e) Encourage immediate, urgent or quick response. (The words 'now'and 'priority'are useful.)

(f) If you are expecting immediate ordering, ensure that you clarify details of any choices available, prices, payment means and so on (to avoid disappointment-causing confusion at the fulfilment stage).

3.4 **Implementation**. Direct response advertisers need to ensure that all measures are in place to handle incoming orders and enquiries: specialist call centres, telemarketers and fulfilment service houses may need to be used where high-volume but occasional take-up is expected. ('Fulfilment'means carrying out the agreed offer made in the direct response ad: sending out brochures, delivering orders and so on.) They will need to be briefed on all aspects of the campaign: when the ad will appear, what response is expected, what service is required and so on.

Banner advertising

Key Concept

Banner advertisements are display ads that are placed on other organisation's or individual's Web pages and act as links to your own Web site.

3.5 Banner advertising is the most common form of Internet advertising. Banner ads are graphic-based ads, usually rectangular, which are positioned at the top or bottom of a Web page. They usually allow the viewer to click on the ad, providing a link to the advertiser's own Web site.

3.6 **Objectives**. To secure:

- **Impressions**: times when people see the ad on a Web page they visit. Impressions are measured by visits to the host site.
- **Ad clicks**: times when people click the ad banner. The 'click-through'(or 'ad-click') rate can be measured to show the percentage of ad views that result in an ad click.

3.7 **Media/mechanisms**. Banner ad space is often used a part of collaborative promotional arrangements, with marketing organisations hosting each other's banner ads on their Web sites. There are also **banner exchange programmes**, allowing Web site operators to swap banner and space without money changing hands: a good way to experiment with on-line advertising at low cost.

Marketing at Work

Here are some examples. check the Internet for many others!

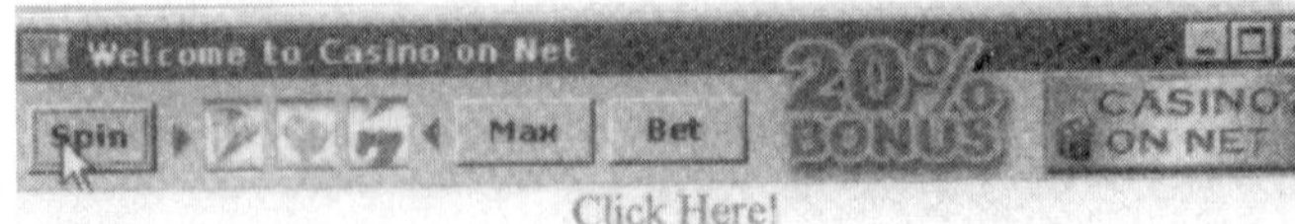

Note the 'click here' tag line. A tag line is a short text-only phrase that can appear below the banner to add impact or remove clutter from the banner itself.

This banner is disguised as part of the search engine (Excite). It is also targeted to likely user interests.

Microsoft Office software ad.

- There are a huge number of sites devoted to on-line advertising. Check out the Banner Ad Museum: www.BannerAdMuseum.com!

3.8 Message. Designing a banner ad is much like designing a print ad: it needs to attract attention, and it needs to motivate 'ad click'to visit the advertiser's Web site – without much space to do it in!

(a) Web sites which take banner ads should have a media kit containing space rates (costs) and guidelines – including **size specifications** (both for dimensions of the ad and the size of the graphic file containing it).

(b) Make the best of the small rectangular space: use colour, type fonts, visuals, animation and other devices.

(c) Research has shown that simpler banners have greater impact and recall.

(d) Target your audience and offer suitable incentives to ad click. For example, promotional offers available at the Web site; pose questions to which the answer is on the Web site; facilitate ad click with instructions ('click here'message, arrow or whatever).

Action Programme 6

e-Z Accounts

Have a go at sketching a banner ad (for submission to your Web site designer) for e-Z Accounts and list some sites that you would like to approach to place the ads (and perhaps agree a banner exchange with).

Job ads

3.9 Objectives

- To attract the **attention** and **interest** of the 'right'people (potentially) for the organisation and for the position advertised: to promote the job and organisation as an employer.
- To **inform** potential applicants of the organisation's requirements: skills, experience and attributes.
- To **inform** potential applicants of the tasks, responsibilities and rewards of the job, so they can decide whether it may be right for them (and vice versa).
- To use all the above (as well as the targeting of the medium) to **target the right people**.

3.10 Media/mechanisms

- **External** job advertisements should be placed in media that will target the right skill groups (for example, *Marketing Business* or the *Media and Advertising* section of a newspaper if you were recruiting marketing professionals). Recruitment for lower-level jobs, however, might more cost-effectively be advertised locally than nationally. Other media may be appropriate, depending on the organisation's needs, such as school or university careers fairs.
- **Internal** advertising of vacancies may take other forms, such as: a memorandum or e-mail informing staff of a vacancy, to which they (or their family or friends) are invited to

reply; a notice on staff noticeboard; an open message sent or posted via an Intranet site; an advertisement in the staff newsletter.

Exam Tip

The Specimen Paper for this module requires you to draft a full A4 page recruitment advertisement for the post of Product Manager for a toy range. A list of items to include is provided, but you are also asked to provide guidance for the magazine's product department with regard to typeface, type sizes, positioning of logos and any other layout details you consider necessary.

3.11 Message. A job advertisement needs to be:

(a) Concise, but comprehensive enough to give an accurate description of the job, its rewards and requirements. (Job ads tend to be fairly small – up to half an A4 page: the information needs usually preclude illustration, but logos and graphic design can still be used effectively to project corporate identity.)

(b) Attractive, conveying a favourable impression of the organisation, but not falsely so: disappointed expectations will be prime source of subsequent employee dissatisfaction. (Even in internal job advertising, where less needs to be said about the organisation, it may take the opportunity to do some internal marketing: congratulating, encouraging and motivating staff: for example by noting that the vacancy has arisen because of the company's success or the promotion of the previous holder.)

(c) Relevant and appropriate to the job and the applicant. Skills, qualifications and special aptitudes required should be prominently set out, along with special features of the job that might attract (or deter) applicants (such as shiftwork or extensive travel).

(d) Non-discriminatory: that is, not excluding or suggesting a preference for a particular gender, race, marital status or (with forthcoming EU measures) age group. (You may wish to state that you are an Equal Opportunities employer, if this is the case.)

Action Programme 7

Browse through the job advertisements in the marketing press and sections of the national press.

- What kinds of images and benefits do they promote in the labour market?
- What items of information do they usually include?

4 Integrated mail media

Mail order advertising

4.1 Mail order is a form of direct response advertising that offers items for sale (via media advertising or brochures mailed direct to prospective customers), with delivery of orders direct to the customer by mail.

4.2 **Objectives**. To sell products direct to customers: especially valuable for retail outlets with restricted geographical coverage, and specialist retail outlets (such as specialist gifts and collectibles). To support on-line shopping with offline catalogues.

Marketing at Work

Roddy Mullin (*Direct Marketing)* offers the following survey of the mail order market in the UK.

'The Next Directory led the mail order revolution in 1988, taking over the Grattan list. Next is a chain of retail clothing shops. The Next initiative helped break the mould that mail order was only for the 'working class'. A plethora of upmarket and specialist mail order products have been launched since, eg Lands End, Orbis, Racing Green, Hawkshead and Boden (who operate in the clothing market), while The White Company brings a niche offering of household lines and goods with the distinguishing feature that they are all white. There are books (Book Club Associates) and CD/video (Britannia) mail order companies. Each book and CD/video mail order company offers a different selection each month to those signed up.

'For business, office stationery companies, such as Viking (now also on the internet), Strakers, Neat Ideas, and others, offer mail order to the business client... For many business-to-business suppliers (serving those in the retail trade, for example) their marketing activities consist of having an exhibition stand at a number of trade exhibitions up and down the country at which orders are taken, which are then topped up through mail order for the rest of the year. Customers then order over the telephone from a brochure/catalogue (with a price list) and receive occasional mail shots with special offers to tempt them to order more. Mail order is becoming a major marketing activity. A number of firms now offer a Web site alternative for placing orders.'

4.3 **Media/mechanisms**. Mail order usually involves a brochure or catalogue, accompanied by an order form and price list: ideally these should be separate, so that the brochure/catalogue (which usually needs to be of expensive colour and quality) does not have to be updated whenever prices change. These may be mailed to recipients, given to them at retail outlets or exhibitions, or downloaded from the Web site.

4.4 **Message**. As well as the qualities of direct response advertising (discussed earlier), mail order is a form of direct supply: it requires detailed attention to issues such as terms and conditions of sale; payment methods; minimum order quantities; volume-scaled postage costs and so on.

4.5 **Implementation**. Mail order is not just a promotional tool: it requires serious commitment to fulfilling customer orders swiftly, correctly and reliably – which in turn requires thorough marketing planning and infrastructure development.

Direct mail promotion

Key Concept

Direct mailis a personally addressed 'written offering'that is creatively presented, usually sent by mail, with some form of response mechanism.

4.6 Objectives

- To raise awareness of new brands/products/services to a target audience (supporting advertising or telemarketing)
- To maintain promotional, service and feedback contacts with existing customers (for relationship marketing)
- To elicit enquiries (by phone, e-mail, Web site visit or reply card) with the added benefit of data capture (building a database for future contacts)
- To follow up call centre and on-line enquiries by supplying requested information or sales literature
- To sell products direct to the target market or general public – if the cost of the exercise per subject reached is at least covered

4.7 Direct mail is often used in the financial, charity, automotive and home shopping sectors. It suits products and services which require some consideration of a complex proposition in writing (for example financial services offers) and do not need to be sampled (although a sample may be included in the mailing if appropriate). A similar operation may also be done by e-mail: inviting the recipient to respond by e-mail or link to the sender's Web site. (We discuss e-mail direct marketing in chapter 8.)

4.8 **Media/mechanisms**. Having defined your target audience, you will need to obtain (or generate, if you have an appropriate database) a targeted mailing list. Databases can segment lists according to a range of criteria: you might choose a list ready-segmented by geographical area, age, profession, interests (as expressed by previous enquiries or purchases) and so on. Mailing lists can be acquired from:

(a) Publications: directories and registers, trade or technical journals

(b) Professional bodies, chambers of commerce, trade associations and so on (although these may handle the mailing themselves, with strict controls)

(c) Specialists in direct mail. Some simply catalogue and sell the lists (as printed labels, on-line or on CD ROM). Others offer a full mailing service.

(d) Your organisation's own database of customers, enquirers, leads or visitors to your Web site (who may have given explicit permission to be contacted by mail or e-mail): this will represent more genuine one-to-one marketing, and will be more likely to be read than unsolicited, unknown-source mail.

4.9 Message

Envelope	■ Appeal and credibility enhanced (especially if organisation unknown) by good quality presentation ■ Add 'return to sender'address: will help update/correct your database ■ Use of organisation name and branding: more likely to be opened if the sender is known (by previous contact or reputation) to the recipient.

Letter	■ Individually addressed (if possible) and written in an informal, personalised style (depending on stage of relationship with the customer) ■ Needs to flow: link points in a 'story': keep the attention going with questions and pointers to relevance. ■ Clearly state what is expected of the recipient: order, request for trial pack, completed questionnaire.
Reply device	■ Response card or (if expecting return of cheques or confidential information such as credit card numbers and personal data) reply/order form and envelope (possibly free of postage) ■ Make all order forms easy to fill out and use (tick boxes, order quantities, prices etc) ■ Add incentives ('free delivery on orders over...')
Other material	■ Brochure, leaflet (or CD ROM) about the product/service; price list (usually separate) ■ Incentives: vouchers, Air Miles, scratch cards, free samples, free entry to Prize draws and so on.
Integration	■ All items in a mailing should be of consistent quality, style, branding and core message.

4.10 Implementation. There are a number of tasks involved in a mailing. Specialist mailing houses may be briefed and used for any or all of the following.

- List building and maintenance
- Envelope and insert (brochure, leaflet, flyer, card) design and production
- Letter printing and folding
- Provision and 'stuffing'(enclosing of items) of envelopes
- Franking or stamp affixing for postage
- Address label printing and/or affixing
- Despatch

Marketing at Work

National Australia Bank

In July 2002, NAB launched a campaign to inform (or remind) its banking customers that they also have a financial planning division. The campaign invited customers to make an appointment to see a Personal Financial Adviser, emphasising that the advisor could come to the customer's home – or anywhere else that might be convenient.

The direct mail campaign featured a simple folded card. On the front, subtly sporting the National's logo and brand colour (red), was three lines of large type:

'A quiet chat over a cup of tea could make you thousands better off'

Inside, the continuation: 'We'll even provide the tea'.

And two Twinings English Breakfast Tea bags (in red sachets) affixed to the card...

The copy (between the headline and the tea bags) was brief, and simply styled in a small, classic type face.

'Arrange to see one of the National's Personal Financial Advisers and, together, we can tailor a financial plan to suit your individual needs. We'll even come to you. To your home if that's convenient. We can discuss your current financial situation and ideally where you'd like to be. Then, we can find the easiest and quickest way to get you there. To set up a meeting just call [freecall telephone number]'

And that was all.

For reflection: What is this message trying to do? What makes it so effective for existing customers? Do you think it would have been effective as unsolicited/unaddressed mail?

Action Programme 8

How do you respond to receiving mailshots (a) from organisations you are aware of, (b) from organisations you have previously purchased from, and (c) from organisations from whom you have **requested** product information? How does this compare to the way you respond to mailings from organisations you don't know? What elements in the style and format of the message makes it more likely that you will (or will not) read and respond?

What kinds of products do you order (or would you consider ordering) by mail order? What makes an effective mail order advertisement. Think about your awareness of mail order advertisements by BPP in *Marketing Business,* for example. Did you order this book from BPP? If so, why?

5 Developing sales promotions

Sales promotion objectives and mechanisms

5.1 Twenty years ago, **promotional incentives** such as gift samples, coupons, prize draws, competitions, on-pack offers and collaborative programmes (get a free X Cola when you buy a Y burger or rent a video from Z store), were considered as short-lived sales boosters. However, it has now been recognised that such campaigns have long-term effects on consumer buying patterns and attitudes, and **promotions marketing** is a discipline in its own right, with agencies capturing a significant proportion of marketing budget.

5.2 Different types of sales promotion **mechanisms** are effective in achieving different **objectives**.

Purpose	Examples
■ Increase short term sales volume	Free gifts or discount coupons with purchase Two-for-one offers
■ Encourage repeat/multiple purchase	Collectible coupons towards more substantial gifts Multiple entries in prize draws/competitions
■ Customer loyalty incentive/reward programmes	Coupons/vouchers for subsequent visits

Purpose	Examples
■ Product launch, encourage new product trial or alternative brand trial (weaning away from competitors)	Money-off coupons Free samples and in-store trials Demonstrations of new products Free gifts with new products (eg magazines)
■ Convey and imbed information	Competitions with questions based on product information
■ Convey a positive brand/corporate image	Purchase incentives linked to charitable donations, equipment for schools.
■ Extend media coverage with 'free' space	Samples/give aways supporting product reviews (press, radio) competitions: space to explain rules, prize (product)
■ Extend database	Coupon returns, competition entries, phone responses giving name/address details (plus high awareness)
■ Motivate supply chain	Consumer promos as 'push' technique to support retailer Gifts/prize draws/competitions to motivate sales force and/or retailers Discount/awards schemes
■ Motivate influencers (journalists, reviewers, style leaders)	Advance sampling/demonstration/showing of new/improved products

5.3 Note that these are not all consumer-focused techniques. **Trade promotions** may be used for 'push'strategies, to motivate retailers, distributors, sales force and trade/industry customers.

- **Monetary incentives** such as increased trade discounts or extended credit
- **Joint advertising** and promotion, sharing costs with the dealer or retailer
- **Point-of-sale support**: supply display materials, information and merchandising
- **Competitions and awards** for salespeople or dealers/distributors
- **Business gifts** linked to sales or purely relational (for example, diaries, calendars and other items traditionally given at Christmas)
- **Consumer promotions** demonstrating aggressive pull strategy

Marketing at Work

Dunlop Olympic (Australia)

Australian tyre manufacturers Dunlop Olympic have produced a free pocket guide booklet called 'Dunlop Olympic Tyre Facts'. It lists tyre sizes and recommended pressures under various conditions for a range of passenger cars and light trucks. It answers questions about tyre performance and maintenance.

The booklet is small and relatively inexpensive to produce and to distribute, since it is perceived as an added-value service by major Australian tyre dealers, who promote it through their network. For Dunlop Olympic, it provides a brand advertising opportunity, PR positioning as 'the tyre experts', added-value sales support to distributors, increasing brand loyalty and creating collaboration marketing opportunities *and* education of customers, which reduces driver related damage to tyres (through under-inflation, hitting kerbs and so on) and so increases customer satisfaction with the product). A good return on promotion investment...

Developing and implementing sales promotion messages

5.4 Various forms of communication may be used to support particular sales promotion mechanisms. In addition to devising the promotion mechanisms themselves, you may need to draft and produce:

- **Advertising** of the sales promotion: announcing that there are price discounts, value packs, gifts and other offers available in-store; cut-out discount coupons
- **Advertising and information** in connection with consumer competitions: publication of the questions or requirements, prizes, entry rules and conditions, how to enter and so on.
- **Product packaging** containing on-pack information and mechanisms for purchase rewards and incentives: tear off coupons; competitions; bonus packs ('10% extra', '12 for the price of 10') and so on.
- **Direct mail** distribution of coupons, vouchers or product samples to stimulate purchase
- **Direct response** advertising: 'write in'schemes to enter prize draws and competitions, apply for free gifts or cash back on proofs of purchase (bar codes or receipts). (The benefit of this approach is the potential for data capture and database building.)

5.5 With any of these messages, the purpose will be to:

(a) Notify and describe the added value offered (extra product; reduced price; free gift; chance to win)

(b) Reinforce brand image through synergy (for example, associations between the product and the free gift, bundled item or merchandise) without losing the focus of the promotion: a free pen with a personal organiser, say, or a honey 'twister'spoon with a jar of honey.

(c) Giving consumers the information they need to respond: instructions for entering draws and competitions, how to be eligible for rewards and so on.

5.6 **Implementation** of sales promotions may be extremely complex, involving not only all the forms of communication mentioned above, but also: negotiation of collaborative promotions with other producers or retailers; negotiation of retailer participation in promotions; production of all the items involved; and the establishing of systems for fulfilment of interactive promotions (competition entries, judging, prize distribution etc)

Action Programme 9

e-Z Accounts

Devise a consumer sales promotion for the e-Z Accounts software launch period. Make notes for the discussion you will need to have with your Promotions Marketing agency, if necessary, or suggest how you might be able to produce and distribute the required elements of the promotion in-house.

6 Point of sale and packaging

Point of sale display

Key Concept

The **point of sale** (POS) is the place (usually in-store) where goods are bought and paid for. By extension 'point of sale'refers to promotional materials displayed in-store to stimulate purchase decisions.

6.1 Objectives

- Attracting buyer attention
- Stimulating purchase in preference to rival brands
- Maximising or augmenting available in-store shelf/display space
- Offering additional product information
- 'Push'incentives for retailers, through offering all the above 'pull'advantages

6.2 Media

- Product housing or display casing for example, metal, plastic or cardboard racks, 'dumpbins'or carousels
- Posters and showcards (self-standing cardboard posters or cut-out images)
- Mobiles (ceiling-hung objects or display cards)
- Shelf-tags and 'wobblers'(attention grabbing messages attached to shelves)
- Counter-standing leaflet dispensers with promotional or informational handouts
- Bookmarks, balloons, branded carriers bags and a range of other devices
- Interactive kiosks with on-line product/store information

6.3 Message

- Attention-grabbing (differentiated from competitors)
- Easy to assemble and use by retailers
- Small enough not to obstruct aisles or take up too much floor/counter space
- Compatible with the retailer's own store design/display plans

- Durable enough at least for the period of the promotion

6.4 **Implementation**. Most point of sale (POS) material is produced by manufacturers/suppliers for use by retailers. You may have to formulate ideas or instructions for an agency, printer or producer. You may also have to formulate trade advertising or information detailing the POS material available, and its intended benefits for retailers in attracting sales.

Action Programme 10

e-Z Accounts

Suggest some ideas for point of sale display and merchandising to support the e-Z Accounts launch.

Product packaging

6.5 Packaging has five key functions.

(a) **Protection**: keeping product contents undamaged, fresh, hygienic and healthy (for example foods) as required. (This in itself will be part of the marketing message and an important contribution to customer care.)

(b) **Distribution**: conveniently bundling products to aid in their transfer from manufacturer to customer. (Goods are usually packaged in more than one layer. Consumer goods might be packaged for sale to consumers, then placed in cartons or similar bulk packages for transport to and storage by resellers.)

(c) **User convenience**: aiding handling, carrying and storing (for example handy packs, family or single-serve packs for diverse household profiles, non-drip bottles, re-sealable packs and so on). This also applies in promoting the product to the trade: packs should allow efficient handling, storage and use of display space, while maximising display ('pull') potential.

(d) **Promotion**: packaging design and labelling further promotional objectives by:

- Carrying product information and benefits
- Carrying information and response mechanisms for sales promotions
- Attracting the attention of first-time impulse buyers to the brand
- Promoting brand recognition by differentiating it from competitors and reinforcing other branding initiatives, making it recognisable to those who may have seen product advertising, or who may already prefer and seek the brand in-store. (Service staff uniforms perform the same function in service markets: the livery of airline, fast food and car hire companies are common examples.)
- Promoting brand values by reflecting customer motivations: projecting value for money, environmental-friendliness (for example, using recycled or bio-degradable materials, less packaging volume)

(e) **Compliance**: conformity with government regulations (for example, by providing a list of ingredients and contents by weight, in food packaging).

Marketing at Work

In the mid-1960s, Heinz held a 95% share of the baby foods market in the UK, selling their food in tins. Gerber then entered the market and secured a wide distribution network, but needed a unique selling point for consumers. The USP they decided on was glass jars instead of tins, in the belief that mothers would consider them to be more hygienic. This campaign was successful and Gerber gained a 10% share of the baby foods market (even though Heinz countered with its own range of foods in glass jars).

Coca Cola has gone to great trouble, in transferring the drink from glass bottles to cans, to preserve some of the global recognition the old (now referred to as 'classic') bottles had established. The cans subtly reflect the shapes of the bottles, as do the plastic bottles now used.

Milk also used to be distributed mainly in glass bottles: now that it is principally marketed in cartons, a range of promotional messages can be printed on their surfaces. However, in keeping with the healthy family profile of dairy products, this space is used in many countries for public service messages (such as 'missing persons'appeals).

For reflection: What products do you instantly recognise in the midst of crowded store displays? What forms of packaging do you find particularly convenient and inconvenient?

Chapter Roundup

- A simple framework for implementing individual elements of the promotional mix is POMMIE: Purpose, Objectives, Media/mechanisms, Message, Implementation and Evaluation.
- The general purposes of advertising may be informative, persuasive or reminding. Specific advertising campaigns may be directed at attracting attention, arousing interest, communicating information, stimulating purchase by highlighting benefits or a unique selling proposition (USP), building up brand or company image, supporting push strategies or promoting ideas.
- An effective advertisement requires:
  - A core theme, concept or angle
  - Copy: simple, interesting, brief, positive, factual, honest, original, emphatic, instructive and self-contained
  - Design/layout: unity, continuity, colour and appropriate type, layout and visual elements
  - Social responsibility and positive images and associations
- Different advertising formats (such as direct response, banner and recruitment advertising) have specific requirements.
- Mail order is a form of direct response advertising that offers items for sale and delivery by mail direct to the customer. Direct mail may be used for a wider range of purposes, including relationship marketing, customer feedback, enquiry follow-up and raising awareness.
- Sales promotions offer added value to consumers (or trade) primarily to stimulate short term sales, but also for longer-term brand awareness and relationship marketing effects.
- Merchandising (including point of sale display and product packaging) is an important part of the marketing mix, and has directly promotional uses in attracting attention, conveying sales

promotion messages, enhancing brand recognition and offering customer convenience/satisfaction.

Quick Quiz

1 What does the mnemonic POMMIE stand for?

2 Fill in the gaps in the following sentence, using the words in the box below.

'The purpose of (1).......... is to enhance potential buyers'(2).......... to the organisation and its (3)............ It seeks to do this by providing (4).........., by trying to channelise (5)........... and by supplying reasons for (6).......... the particular organisation's offerings'.

▪ desires	▪ information	▪ responses
▪ preferring	▪ advertising	▪ offerings

3 Which of the following is *not* one of the Ten Commandments of effective advertising copy?

Be simple	Be brief	Be original
Be honest	Be subtle	Be emphatic

4 'Unity'of layout design means using a large number of visual elements of the same size and style.

☐ True ☐ False

5 An unbound reply card, leaflet or brochure placed among the pages of a newspaper or magazine is called a:

A Response mechanism
B Tip on
C Loose insert
D Direct mail advertisement

6 A mailing to customers asking them to fill out and return a customer survey would be classified as:

Mail order advertising	Direct mail	Direct response advertising	Unaddressed mail

7 Which of the following would be integrated with a sales promotion campaign?

A Advertising
B Direct mail
C Product packaging
D All of the above

8 The .... is the place where goods are bought and paid for.

9 Point of sale material should be large and prominent in order to attract buyer attention.

☐ True ☐ False

10 List the five key functions of product packaging.

Answers to Quick Quiz

1 Purpose; objectives; media/mechanism; message; implementation; evaluation

2 (1) advertising, (2) responses, (3) offerings, (4) information, (5) desires, (6) preferring

3 Be subtle

4 False

5 C

6 Direct mail

7 D

8 Point of sale

9 False

10 Protection, distribution, user convenience, promotion, compliance

Now try Question 6 from the Question Bank at the end of this Text

Action Programme Review

1 Main objectives: raising awareness of target market (because product in launch stage of life cycle), informing target market of product features and benefits (to raise knowledge), 'push'promotion to persuade retailers to stock the product.

Teaser ads might be used to establish the (strong) product name – which all on its own begins to highlight a key product benefit. So, for example, running media (or in-stockist) ads in advance of launch, saying: 'Ever wished things were a bit e-Zer?'or 'Struggling to keep track of your money? Soon it'll be e-Z...'

2 Target audience: middle income (financially responsible), home PC owners/users, household budgeters (NB don't assume male), non-expert in finance. To find out more: survey questionnaire in a 'Personal Finance'or 'Software'magazine? Industry studies; survey of competitor advertising.

(For example): 'Money & You'(monthly national magazine). Read by targeted audience, targeted circulation, frequent reference/sharing, national coverage, opportunity for colour photograph and product information; affordable full page colour ad.

(For example): full page (A4) full colour (allowing photograph and illustrations) ad for maximum impact for launch.

3 Product features (for example): ease of use, specifically designed for non-financial people, includes spreadsheets, tax calculators, annual update, on-line help, tips and instructions, may be endorsed by accountants/financial planners, PC or Mac format

Differentiating features: non-financial targeting, ease of use, on-line help, accompanying booklet

Most relevant of these: ease of use by non-financials (integrates all others)

4 (For example)

WANT TO GET MORE OUT OF YOUR MONEY?

e-Z!

At last, you don't need to be a financial expert to make the most of your money. e-Z Accounts is a brand new way to get to grips with your household budgeting, your financial planning – and even your tax!

e-Z Accounts is a software package specially designed for financial beginners. Load it onto your home computer, and you'll have all the information and tools you need – at your fingertips.

- Easy-to-use budget spreadsheets, to keep track of your cash
- Tax calculator, to take the hassle out of Tax Time
- Helpful tips and instructions – with on-line help if you need it, when you need it.

And at just [price], we think it'll be e-Z on your pocket too.

e-Z Accounts. Available NOW at your nearest electronics store, or check out our website: www.eZaccounts.co.uk.

5 Instructions

Ad specifications: A4 (bleed available), full colour. For technical specifications, please contact the Production Manager at 'Money & You'Magazine (Terry Brady, telephone: xxxxx)

General brief: I'd like to use the full colour photograph of the product (supplied) with the background filling the whole page: the text can be printed against the paler part of the background, below the product itself. I have kept the copy brief to allow the photo to be large (to establish recognition). I would prefer the copy to be in a relatively small type size, with plenty of space around it. Please select a typeface with a simple, friendly, modern feel (match to our house style). I will welcome any recommendations (perhaps I could look at some thumbnail sketches). I have indicated my own ideas as marked up below.

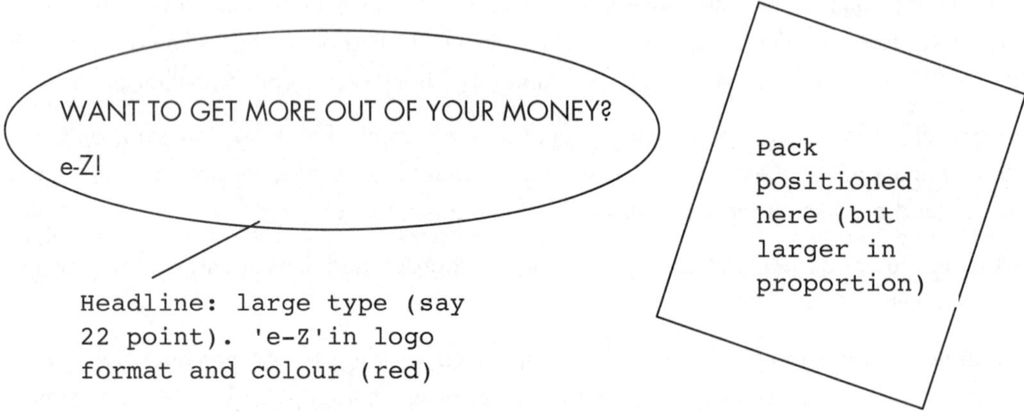

Copy

At last, you don't need to be a financial expert to make the most of your money. e-Z Accounts is a brand new way to get to grips with your household budgeting, your financial planning – and even your tax!

e-Z Accounts is a software package specially designed for financial beginners. Load it onto your home computer, and you'll have all the information and tools you need – at your fingertips.

- Easy-to-use budget spreadsheets, to keep track of your cash
- Tax calculator, to take the hassle out of Tax Time
- Helpful tips and instructions – with on-line help if you need it, when you need it.

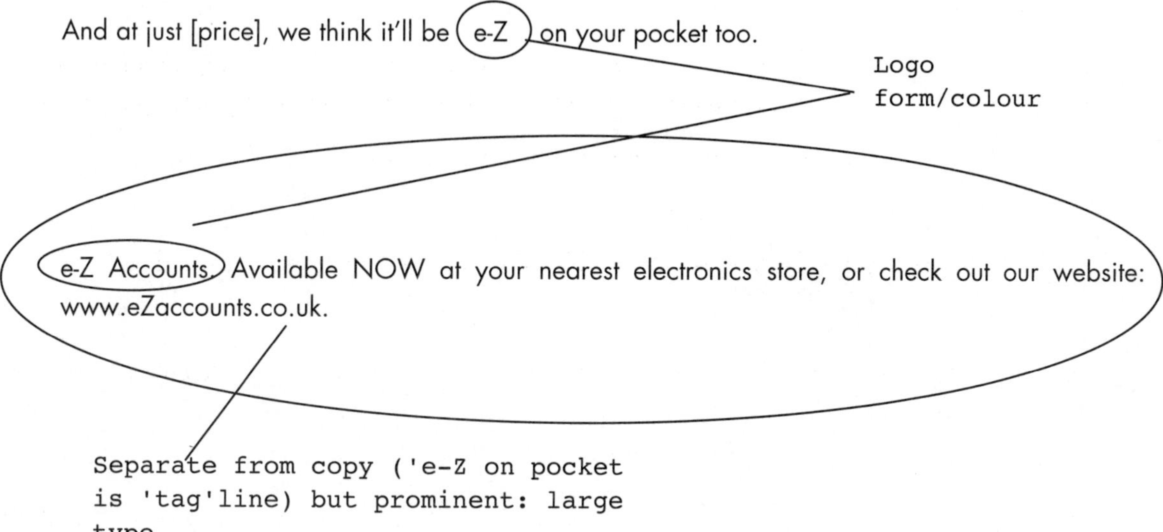
And at just [price], we think it'll be e-Z on your pocket too.
Logo form/colour
e-Z Accounts Available NOW at your nearest electronics store, or check out our website: www.eZaccounts.co.uk.
Separate from copy ('e-Z on pocket is 'tag'line) but prominent: large type.

6

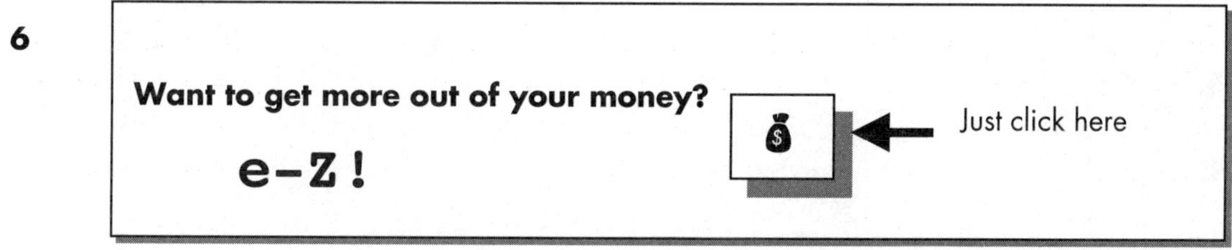
Want to get more out of your money?
e-Z!
Just click here

7 The image will depend on the organisation: they should at least project professionalism, and some will attempt to develop a distinctive employer brand. Information will generally include a summary of the organisation's business; job title, tasks, responsibilities, location; salary; qualities and qualifications considered essential and desirable in the applicant; application instructions.

8 Do take the time to reflect on your experience. As in many areas of customer communications, the best guide to what works – and what's new – will be the communications you receive yourself.

9 (For example): FREE booklet "How to manage your money", placed inside (limited stock of) packs. Sticker on package (to avoid different package printing) promoting: 'Limited edition special offer. FREE "How to manage your money" booklet inside'. Booklet could include advertising and examples from the software (in case read by others). Additional copies could be used as reader giveaways attached to editorial coverage in magazines and newspapers. Discuss with Promotions Marketing agency: sourcing authorship and production of booklet, sourcing offer stickers.

10 (For example): offer stockists a special dump bin (with 'e-Z does it'headboard and branding) to ensure face-out (sticker and product cover visibility) display. Ensure small floor area (footprint) and pre-test idea with stockists first. Consider 'e-Z does it'T-shirts and/or baseball caps to be worn by stockist staff in launch period (negotiate with stockist). Where PCs available in-store, set up demonstration/trial copies – with screen saver scrolling 'Want to get more out of your money? e-Z'.

PR and corporate communications 7

Chapter Topic List	
1	Setting the scene
2	Public relations
3	Drafting press releases and articles
4	Corporate identity and brand image
5	Sponsorship
6	Exhibitions

Learning Outcomes

- ☑ Develop a PR campaign
- ☑ Draft an effective press release
- ☑ Explain the elements of corporate identity and brand image
- ☑ Plan an effective exhibition display

Syllabus References

- ☑ Describe the role and scope of PR and its contribution to the promotional mix (3.8)
- ☑ Explain the role of corporate identity, brand image and logos in corporate communication with customers (3.9)
- ☑ Describe the role of exhibitions as a communications tool and their role in promotions (3.13)
- ☑ Describe current trends and developments in promotions and their impact on organisations (3.15)

Key Concepts Introduced

- Public relations
- Crisis communication
- Issues management
- Sponsorship

1 Setting the scene

1.1 In Chapter 6, we focused on advertising and sales promotion, as key aspects of the promotion mix.

1.2 In Chapter 5, however, we noted that as well as using promotional messages to stimulate and support the sale of products/services, marketing communications activities are used to create a **profile** for the marketing organisation itself, and to maintain positive and mutually-satisfying **contacts** and **relationships** with its various publics.

1.3 The organisation's efforts in these areas will be an important factor in whether or how far:

- It is able to attract and retain **customers**
- It is able to attract and retain **members**, employees, volunteers and **suppliers** to maintain its activities
- Its presence and activities are supported or resisted by **government**, the local **community** and other **stakeholders** (including interest and pressure groups)
- The news/consumer/trade **media** report favourably on its operations
- **Financial media and markets** regard its prospects and earnings potential favourably, in order to maintain dealings in its shares

1.4 Jim McNamara (*Marketing & Promotion Handbook)* argues that 'the total concept of public relations is a part of a company's life whether management of that company wants it to be or not... All contact a company has with its outside world is communication of some sort.' Since an organisation will inevitably project an image in its dealings with the outside world – and the cost of having a *negative* image can be high – it makes sense to **manage the messages** being projected.

1.5 In this chapter, therefore, we focus on developing and implementing public relations and corporate communications.

2 Public relations

Key Concept

Public relationsis 'the planned and sustained effort to establish and maintain goodwill and mutual understanding between an organisation and its publics' (*Institute of Public Relations).*

2.1 In its broadest sense, PR is simply the **interface** of the organisation with the publics listed in paragraph 1.3 above. In terms of corporate activities, this may involve:

- **Publicity**: generating editorial coverage in the press or technical/trade journals
- **Press/media relations**: keeping relevant news/information media informed about organisational activities and offerings; building goodwill in order to secure fair and positive coverage; establishing organisational spokespeople as potential sources of information and comment
- **Public affairs**: lobbying or representations to government and trade bodies
- **Community relations**: contributing to community projects; community sponsorship; dialogue with community and consumer groups.
- **Employee relations**: communicating with employees; managing a range of internal communication mechanisms
- **Customer relations**: consumer marketing support and business-to-business communication for example, through sponsorship, events and exhibitions
- **Financial public relations**: financial media relations and providing information to shareholders and financial markets
- **Issues management**: monitoring potential controversies in relation to the business and initiating communication programmes to manage public perceptions
- **Crisis communication** issuing communications to minimise or counter the negative PR effects of crises (damaging events or revelations)

Purposes and objectives of PR

2.2 Grunig and Hunt *(Managing Public Relations)* suggest that there are four models of public relations practice, according to how the organisation sees its role and what it is trying to achieve.

Model	Role of PR	Comments
Press agency/ publicity	**Propaganda**: spreading the faith of the organisation to the public	■ Communication is one-way from the organisation to its publics: essentially, telling the publics the information the organisation wants them to hear (often through incomplete, half-true or distorted information) ■ For example, sports, theatre, product promotion
Public information	**Information**: reporting objectively information about the organisation to the public	■ Communication is still one-way, but public information specialists (unlike press agency specialists) attempt to present a complete picture ■ For example, government and non-profit organisations

Model	Role of PR	Comments
Two-way asymmetric	**Scientific persuasion**: using behavioural science to change publics' attitudes and behaviour in favour of the organisation	■ Communication is two-way *asymmetric*: feedback from publics is used to improve the effectiveness of further outgoing persuasive communication, rather than to respond to the issues raised. ■ For example, competitive business and PR agencies
Two-way symmetric	**Mediation**: seeking dialogue between the organisation and its publics	■ Information and persuasion works both ways: the organisation adapts to feedback from its publics ■ For example, regulated business agencies

2.3 Grunig and Hunt propose the two-way symmetric model as an ideal to be aspired to by truly customer-focused organisations.

PR mechanisms

2.4 As suggested in Chapter 5, the scope of PR activity is very wide. The most frequently used mechanisms (organised by publics) are as follows.

Consumer (marketing support)

- Consumer/trade press releases and review samples
- Publicity
- Product/service literature
- Product placement (TV, cinema)
- Promotional video/ CD ROM
- Special events (in-store competitions, celebrity store openings)
- Consumer exhibitions and shows
- Magazines or newsletters
- Salesforce/distributor incentive schemes
- Sport, arts sponsorship

Business-to-business communication

- Corporate identity design
- Corporate literature
- Trade/general press relations
- Corporate and product videos
- Trade exhibitions
- Corporate hospitality

Corporate, external and public affairs

- Corporate literature
- Community involvement
- Media relations
- Issues tracking/management
- Local/central government lobbying
- Industrial (trade/profession) lobbying
- Site visits and corporate hospitality
- Community (political?) sponsorship

Financial public relations

- Financial media relations
- Design of annual/interim reports
- Visits by analysts, brokers etc
- Organising shareholder/communication and meetings

Action Programme 1

Suggest similar activities that might be used in **internal/employee communications**.

Publicity

2.5 **Media coverage** in editorial articles, product reviews and news items can be stimulated by:

- Building up a network of **media contacts** (or using a PR or media relations agent)
- Sending **media/press releases** and/or **photos** to relevant journalists/editors, or holding photo calls and press conferences (if something genuinely newsworthy can be revealed: wasting busy journalists' time is *not* good media relations!)
- Sending **product samples** for trial and review (often with added incentives such as supporting competitions or product give-aways, offering added value to the publication/programme's readers/listeners)
- Arranging **publicity 'stunts'** and events to which journalists/editors are invited, or which achieve coverage by being attached to covered events (such as sporting fixtures)
- Offering relevant **spokespeople** and 'experts' for interview, comment, consultation or authorship (for example of technical articles for trade journals).

2.6 Media coverage of this kind is 'free' promotion, but it is only 'promotion' if the coverage is **positive**! Companies make the headlines for all the wrong reasons, and despite the old saying that 'there's no such thing as bad publicity' – there probably is... Bad press can be every bit as creative, attention-grabbing and memorable as the organisation's advertising. When Perrier mineral water was found to contain tiny amounts of a toxic chemical after an accident in the bottling plant, there was an avalanche of headlines based on the brand's own advertising campaign, including: 'Eau dear' and 'What a fiasceau'.

Marketing at Work

A creative, high-impact publicity stunt was recently staged at the Bledisloe Cup rugby union Test Match between the Australian Wallabies and the New Zealand All-Blacks. The following is the main editorial column in Sydney's *Daily Telegraph* (7/8/02)

'A Test of corporate credibility

'The Bledisloe Cup should be remembered for its nail-biting finish... With a crowd of 80,000 at Stadium Australia and a worldwide television audience of millions, the event should have been a triumph for Australian Rugby Union and its principal sponsor, Vodaphone... Instead, it has resulted in a fiasco brought about by the complicity of Vodaphone in a senseless, tasteless stunt that not only disrupted the match but – because of the closeness of the scores – had the potential to impact on its outcome.

'As All Black Andrew Mehrtens prepared to take a penalty kick, two streakers daubed ludicrously with the company's logo ran onto the ground before being apprehended by police.

'The entry of the two into the arena signified a new form of corporate irresponsibility... It was a display of arrogance that leads one to the conclusion that the company believes the end justifies the means – that any ethical questions are secondary to the company gaining a marketing advantage over its rivals. Well, it is wrong...

'From the admissions to the *Daily Telegraph* by Vodaphone managing direct Grahame Maher, he not only knew the two men would attempt a stunt at the game, but he offered to pay any fines incurred...

'The Australian Rugby Union has described the incident as an error of judgement. This must qualify as the understatement of the year. The foolishness of Mr Maher in becoming involved in such a low-grade method of garnering publicity has rebounded on the company. It was only by good fortune that it did not also sully the name of the sport it sponsors. Vodaphone executives should hang their collective heads in shame. Possibly they might now understand that all publicity is *not* good publicity and act more responsibly in future.'

For reflection: How effective was this stunt as (a) public relations and (b) media relations?

2.7 The advantages and disadvantages of publicity may be summarised as follows.

Advantages	Disadvantages
■ Raise awareness of wider audience	■ Can't control editorial content (positive or negative)
■ Generate word-of-mouth	■ Media have their own agenda (circulation/ratings, public information) which may not coincide with positive publicity
■ Greater credibility than advertising, because perceived as third-party view	■ Mistakes and shortcomings are usually more newsworthy than consistent successes or service quality
■ Legitimacy: implies endorsement or recommendation	
■ Supports advertising and promotional campaigns	

Crisis communication and issues management

Key Concept

Crisis communication is public communication in the face of a potential PR disaster, through which the organisation initiates damage control, to minimise or counter the negative PR effects.

Issues managementis an on-going process of being aware of potential controversies and sensitive matters in relation to the business, and initiating communication programmes which can defuse or head off issues before they become crises.

2.8 Examples of **PR crises** include: the withdrawal of a product from the market due to unforeseen safety defects; an ecological disaster such as the running aground of an oil tanker; or the enforced withdrawal of an advertising campaign deemed offensive by complaints to the Advertising Standards Authority.

2.9 Effective **crisis communication** involves the following.

- **Contingency planning**: being aware of areas of risk, identifying audience groups that will need to be communicated with, and preparing a response
- **Recognising** and **responding** to the likely level of public concern when an issue arises
- **Explaining** what has happened: telling the organisation's 'side of the story'; demonstrating openness (not trying to 'cover up' the truth); giving **consistent** messages (which means keeping employees informed)
- **Demonstrating care and concern** about what has happened and its impact on the target audience. (A rule of thumb is: talk about **people** first, the **environment** second, **property** third and **financial** consequences fourth.)
- **Demonstrating action**: steps being taken to resolve the problem
- **Mobilising support**: using independent, credible 'champions' who can speak out in support of the organisation, its steps to resolve the problem and so on.

2.10 Examples of **issues** which require careful handling include: public concerns about carcinogens (cancer causing agents) and food additives; environmental impacts of industry; and ethical investment and business dealings. **Issues management** endeavours not just to fight fires as they arise, but to: initiate dialogue with the public and interest groups; express general responsibility and openness; educate the public in the organisation's position; and establish networks of goodwill and support.

Marketing at Work

Arnott foods (Australia)

Food manufacturer Arnott gave what has been called a 'textbook response' when it was the victim of a blackmail attempt in early 1997. Extortionists sent a letter and a box containing poisoned Arnott biscuits to police and government officials and threatened to place poisoned biscuits in stores throughout two Australian states unless their demands were met by a certain date.

Initially the company kept quiet, allowing police to investigate, but as the deadline approached Arnott went public, removing all of its biscuits from supermarkets and laying off workers producing them. The cost to the company was estimated at $480,000 per day.

PR activity at first focused on reassurance. A customer **call centre** was set up and an **open letter** of regret was placed in **national newspapers**, saying 'Arnotts is the innocent victim of... Your safety is paramount...' A few days later this was reinforced by a **national TV ad campaign** using a well-known TV journalist and emphasising the company's concern, its long history and the plight of its employees – making sure that the public realised Arnotts was as much a victim as its customers. A week after the scare became public, Arnotts went further and announced that it would **proactively** destroy all of the recalled stock: the media were asked to **witness** some of the stock being dumped.

When the scare was over, high profile advertising and in-store promotion made sure that the public knew Arnotts was back – and that all stock was safe to buy.

Evaluating PR effectiveness

2.11 Media coverage can be easily monitored using cuttings or media monitoring agencies, where this is a measure of effectiveness. However, where possible, the achievement of specific objectives should be the criterion: because PR is often perceived as 'free' and its results as invisible 'good will', it is too easy for costs to escalate without detailed justification!

2.12 Some useful measures include the following.

- Define the **key messages** that will fulfil the specific objective of the programme and use media monitoring, feedback, customer/audience research and communication audits to establish whether the programme (a) reaches the target audience and (b) correctly conveys the message, resulting in the desired attitudes and awareness.
- Monitor appropriate **performance measures** for the specific objectives: fall in employee turnover following the introduction of employee communications; focus group awareness raised after a publicity campaign; sales recovery after crisis management. Expect to see some results.

2.13 However, it should be recognised that public relations can be a long-term process of education, attitude change and relationship building. A realistic time-scale for return on investment should be established in the light of the organisation's strategic goals.

3 Drafting press releases and articles

3.1 **Press releases** are brief news items or information sent to journalists for dissemination to their audiences. Releases are most commonly written, but they can also be achieved orally and/or visually (in a press conference, telephone briefing or audio/video-recorded package).

Purpose and objectives of a press release

3.2 A press release (or **media release,** which is sent to radio and television as well as a publication) has two purposes and two audiences.

- **Journalists/editors**. The purpose is to attract their attention and interest, and to persuade and enable them to use the material or to consult its source.
- **The media audience**. The better tailored your release is to the interests of a specific publication's readers, the more likely it is to be used by its journalists/editors. If you are sending a release to a number of different publications, you will simply have to rely on general newsworthiness and journalistic style.

3.3 Journalists, particularly on daily publications, are hungry for material to fill pages: they rely on experts in business, sport, academia and so on to provide them with stories, ideas, background or technical information/confirmation and comment. However:

(a) Your press release may be competing with many others.

(b) News constantly happens: your story will be competing for space in the final copy with a huge volume of other material.

(c) Journalists will not write about a product/organisation just because a PR officer asks them to! They needed to be persuaded that the item is:

- **Newsworthy**: interesting (relevant to readers); local (relevant to the area/region with which readers identify; topical (happening now, has just happened, or is about to happen); important (will make a difference or impact on readers); new or surprising
- **Credible**: usually, verifiable or confirmable
- **Safe**: true, legal, fair, honest, decent and non-defamatory
- **Easy to use**: written in a suitable style, length and format.

3.4 Obviously, you should not fabricate facts: not 'safe'. But if you think around your basic items of information, you should be able to find some perspective which makes them more interesting, local, topical, important or surprising to a particular readership. A human angle, perhaps (Company X greets its one millionth customer) or a touch of controversy ('Recession? What recession?' says Company X).

Action Programme 2

Brainstorm some items of corporate news that might be considered newsworthy, according to the criteria suggested above: interesting, local, topical, important, surprising. Gather some ideas from actual news articles in the press which identify corporations or products/brands by name.

Format and style of the press release

3.5 The structure of a press release has some distinctive features.

- They do not – unlike other written formats – have a beginning, middle and end! Start with a clear **heading** that indicates the overall purpose of the communication, and then your most **important points** which demonstrate the story's newsworthiness. When you have finished your last point, just stop: no conclusion or summary is required. (Newspapers cut copy to length from the bottom upwards. If you leave your best point to last, you may well lose it.) This is called an 'inverted pyramid' style: most information at the top. Insert the word '**ENDS**' at the foot of your body copy.
- Identify your **organisation name** and **location** clearly (to help editors to assess newsworthiness on geographic criteria).
- Include usable and attributable **quotes**, to add human interest and immediacy.
- Press releases are typed on one side of the paper, with **double line-spacing** and wide **margins**, for the journalist's notes or 'subbing marks' (instructions to the printer).
- At the bottom of the release, put a daytime **contact** name, title and telephone/e-mail contact: this identifies the **source** of the information, for immediate queries or future reference.

- The release should be **dated**. If the information is being released before the event, you may not want it published before a certain date. Use an **embargo**: a request to the media to delay publication until the specific date and time stated. An embargo should be printed at the top of the release *and* any accompanying documents (text of a speech, list of people, annual report or whatever). The conventional wording is:

  'Embargo: not for release before [time] hours on [day], [date].'

3.6 The following is an example of a press release which might be sent to local/regional media in an area in which the company concerned is a major employer. (Note that it might also be used for internal promotion.)

STANHOPE AND GRANTLY LTD

S & G House
Victoria Road
WARRINGTON
Cheshire

PRESS RELEASE

FOR IMMEDIATE RELEASE

'The S & G Players' present ... "The 21st Century'"

Newly-formed entertainment group 'The S & G Players' are putting on a sparkling new show called 'THE 21st CENTURY' on Friday 29 and Saturday 30 December 20X6. Performance will begin at 19.30 in Stanhope and Grantly's Staff Association Lounge at the Head Office in Victoria Road, Warrington.

The firm, long established in the area, look forward to welcoming employees, customers and friends to an exciting evening of variety entertainment highlighting some of the changes that have taken place in Warrington this century.

Anthony Bold and John Thorne, of S & G's Marketing Department, thought up the original idea and are the show's co-producers.

'"21st CENTURY" is a witty show with songs, comedy items and poetry as well as a short, humorous play written by members of the cast' explains Bold.

Thorne adds: 'There are over 30 staff taking part - performing or helping behind the scenes - and we have had a lot of help from the management'

Tickets are available now from Stanhope and Grantly Marketing Department. There will be no charge for admission, but a collection will be held in aid of the Red Cross.

— ENDS —

For further information, contact:

Anthony Bold
Marketing Department
S & G House
Victoria Road
Warrington
Cheshire
Telephone: 01925 69358 ext 1527 day
01925 30264 evening
Email: abold@stanhopegrantly.org.uk

18 December 20X6

Action Programme 3

You are the governor of a local school. Draft a press release with the aim of publicising the school's excellent exam results and various sporting successes.

(This is a past exam question set under the old syllabus.)

3.7 Bear in mind that press releases can also be e-mailed to journalists, or posted on-line at the 'media centre' of an organisation/event Web site.

Exam Tip

The requirement to draft a press release has recurred a number of times in exams under the old syllabus. One of the compulsory question parts in the December 2000 exam asked for a press release for the international business press: (a) picking out the key findings of a research report (supplied) and (b) taking the opportunity to promote the research organisation.

Make sure you get to grips with the proper format for a press release. Practise writing in a journalistic style and targeting the likely interests of the publication and its audience.

Editorial articles

3.8 Many of the guidelines on press releases also apply to articles. Many publications (like specialist journals and local newspapers) accept editorial contributions, while others (like national newspapers) do not. You will need to tailor your article to the area of interest, style and length favoured by the publication and its readers, if you are to have any chance of getting published. Editorial articles are also a useful internal communications tool, via staff newsletters, journals and e-zines/Intranet sites.

3.9 Another possibility is that you could be asked to write an **advertorial** or **informercial**. This is an advertisement (the newspaper or magazine space is paid for by the advertiser) but the style and layout imitate that of the editorial content of the magazine or newspaper. Here is the opening of such an ad that appeared recently in national newspapers. See if you can spot the elements of journalistic style that are being used and how it gradually changes from informative to persuasive.

ADVERTISEMENT

Shamed By Your English?

A SIMPLE technique for acquiring a swift mastery of good English has just been announced. It can double your powers of expression. It can pay you real dividends in business and social advancement, and give you added poise, self-confidence and personal effectiveness.

Many people do not realise how much they could influence others simply by speaking and writing with greater power, authority and precision. Whether in business, at social functions, or even in casual conversation with new acquaintances, you can dominate each situation simply by using the right word in the right way.

For example, whether you are presenting a report, training a child, fighting for a cause, making a sale, writing an essay, or asking for a rise ... your success depends upon the words you use.

Never again need you fear those embarrassing mistakes. You can quickly and easily be shown how to ensure that everything you say is crisp, clear, *correct.* What's more, you'll command the respect of people who matter, because you'll learn how to use English accurately, impressively - to cut through many barriers to social, academic, or business success.

3.10 The following are some features of journalistic style (in general) that can be incorporated into your press release or article, including articles for internal publications.

- **Headline**: keep it short, relevant to what follows, and positive, upbeat or challenging
- **First paragraph**: short, direct and simple introduction to the main proposition of the article/release
- **KISS**: keep it short and simple. Cut out superfluous words, keep sentences short.
- **Avoid technical jargon**, esoteric vocabulary and acronyms (like CIM) which the journalist – let alone the reader – may not know.
- **'News not views'**: give facts. *Who* and *what* are you writing about? *How* did it happen and *when*? This is essential information.
- **Comment/opinion**: used for human interest/vividness, put it in quote marks and attribute it to someone (preferably someone congenial or credible in the context)
- **Subheadings**: maintain interest, break up text, give cues to the paragraphs that follow.

Action Programme 4

Look out for articles about corporations. Note how they inject topicality, local and human interest to give the content a 'hook' to attract and hold reader interest.

What kind of hooks might you use in an article for a staff newsletter?

4 Corporate identity and brand image

Corporate identity

4.1 **Corporate image** refers to how a company is perceived by its publics. Public relations activity (as we saw above) seeks to influence the corporate image or profile. **Corporate identity** relates to the logos, 'house style' of communications, preferred colour and palettes and so on, adopted consistently through all external and internal corporate communications.

4.2 **Purpose/objectives**. The aims of a corporate identity exercise may be as follows.

- To maintain a **consistent** style and standard of communications throughout the organisation, and to all customers and other publics, as part of an Integrated Marketing Communication (IMC) approach.
- To **differentiate** the organisation's communications and brands from those of competitors for the recipient's attention.
- To build **recognition** of the organisation's style, so that:
  - (a) Customers will extend the goodwill and interest from existing messages/products to new ones (for example being open to the next in a series of advertisements, or trying a new product from a trusted supplier)
  - (b) Existing messages/products can be identified and located among competing advertisements and point of sale displays
- To **communicate** the values and attributes of the organisation (for example, quality, innovation, service, ethics) to internal and external customers.
- To encourage employees to **identify** with a strong organisational image. 'House style' is one of the major influences in forming, or changing, organisational culture: the organisation's perception of, and attitude to, itself.

4.3 **Mechanism/message**. Corporate identity guidelines may include the following design aspects.

- The use of logotype and logo symbols (discussed further below).
- The use of 'livery': colours (such as Harrods' stores muted green and gold).
- The style, size and position of various design elements (headings, layout, typefaces, paper and so on) for a variety of communications formats.
- The format and content of standard letterheads, memo/message/email stationery.
- Use of the organisation's name or brand name in formal and informal contexts.

4.4 Corporate identity, having been established, is not easy to change. A brand's image may need updating, but if it is changed too much, too quickly, it will lose its familiarity and recognisability: consumers have got used to seeing and looking for a particular ad, package or display style. Marketers therefore tend to make a series of changes over time, each of which is barely noticeable, so that consumers are not aware that they are 'recognising' something different. Think of the logos of Shell and BP and the design of their petrol stations: they have gradually changed over the years to keep pace with design trends, and to combat habituation (people being so used to seeing something that they begin to ignore it): yet at each stage, the general public has found them entirely 'familiar'.

Logos

4.5 Brand symbols ('logos') and name styles ('logotypes') are often designed and adopted by business organisations. The design, adoption and change of a logo or logotype style is so sensitive for the organisation's marketing, and for its internal culture and politics, that it is best left to a first-rate artist or studio, working with in-depth research into perceptions of the organisation's identity. However, you should be aware of the purpose and effect of logos in marketing communications.

4.6 **Purpose/objectives**. A logo symbol or name style may be used in a wide variety of applications: typically on letterheads, memos, press-releases, packaging, merchandise, advertising and sales literature, displays, vans, uniforms and so on. It is therefore a high-profile, consistent and repeated form of marketing communication, designed to:

- Attraction **attention**
- Create an **impression**
- Give **information** (which may or may not include the name of the organisation)
- Stick in the mind, creating **recognition** each time it is seen
- **Integrate** the various outputs of the organisation into a single, recognisable **identity**

4.7 **Mechanism/message**. A logo may be designed to be:

Symbolic	Representing the activity, attributes or name of the organisation	■ The Worldwide Fund for Nature panda ■ The National Trust oak tree ■ The Apple Macintosh apple ■ The Shell Oil shell
Expressive	Creating and impression relevant to the organisation	■ The Nike tick (speed, success) ■ The CIM coat of arms (royal charter)
Recognisable	Creating identification	■ The Coca Cola logotype ■ The BPP logo?

4.8 A logo may use various devices to distinguish it from others.

- **Type style**: for example, Coca Cola, IBM
- **Symbol or picture**: for example, the Lloyds TSB black horse or McDonalds' golden arches
- **Colour**: for example, Barclays Bank blue, BP's green and yellow, ING's orange
- **Slogan or motto**: for example 'Every little helps' (Tesco), 'We'll save you' (Aussie Home Loans)

Action Programme 5

(a) Think of some examples of corporate identity that are bound up in a visual style or logo to the extent that the logo type, colour scheme or slogan is sufficient on its own to recall the brand or organisation. How has this been achieved?

(b) Draft a letterhead and logo for the following organisations:

Books Unlimited Ltd	Chess Appreciation Society	Sudzomatic (UK) Ltd
Central Buildings	2 King Street	(Washing Power that Works)
Ealing Broadway	Pawnbury, nr Rochdale	The Industrial Estate
London W5	Lanc MXX XXX	Frotham-on-Thames

Brand image

4.9 A **brand** is defined as any words, symbols, design or style in any combination that distinguishes a company's offering from competing offerings in the perceptions of the target audience. Brand identity may begin with a product name, such as 'Kleenex' or 'Coca cola', but it extends to a range of features which should assist in attracting attention and reinforcing recognition, including typography, colour, slogans, package design and point of sale display. It may also include people (as, for example, Richard Branson is identified as a visible part of the Virgin brand) – and even animals (such as Dulux dog). Brand identity is a whole bundle of attributes and values associated with the product/service.

4.10 Purpose/objectives. Branding has various promotional uses.

- It aids **product differentiation**, conveying a lot of information very quickly and concisely. This helps customers readily to identify the goods or services, reinforcing customer preference and retention.
- It maximises the impact of **advertising** for product identification and recognition. The more similar a product is to its competitors, the more branding is required to create a separate, recognisable product identity.
- It aids recognition and identification, creating **brand loyalty**. By extension, this may be transferred to new products introduced to the brand range through **brand extension**.
- It is a **push** factor, creating readier acceptance by distributors and retailers.
- It supports **market segmentation**, since different brands of similar products may be developed to meet specific needs of categories of users. (Think of all the different cereal brands – Cornflakes, Special K, All Bran, Sultana Bran – produced by Kelloggs, for example.)

Marketing at Work

Kiwi Fruit Marketing Board (New Zealand)

It used to be called the Chinese gooseberry, but only older people will recall that now. The kiwi fruit was born out of the marketing efforts of a group of farmers who formed the New Zealand Kiwi Fruit Marketing Board in 1988 in order to promote the erstwhile Chinese gooseberry under the cuddlier name thought up a few years earlier by some patriotic NZ horticulturists.

The promotion was spectacularly successful, and the market grew rapidly until markets throughout the world couldn't get enough of the fruit. Rather than becoming an exclusively NZ brand, however, the kiwi turned into a generic name by which the fruit was known. The farmers had not 'branded' the product, but simply given it a new, more acceptable name which anyone could, and did, use. Connections with NZ and the flightless national bird have been forgotten. The incompetent marketers were so successful that American consumers are now unaware of any other meaning for a 'kiwi' than the fruit.

Farmers in other countries – many closer to the high consumption areas such as Germany – simply moved into the market. Orchards planted in the early '80s by farmers in Italy, France and Chile who had seen the growth of NZ kiwi exports by 40-70% per year, matured in the late part of the decade. Today's market is about 800,000 tonnes: NZ has only a quarter of that.

In a desperate attempt to win something back, NZ farmers have done what they should have done in the first place – think of a new name, but this time, register it as a trademark which only they can use. Only time will tell if the kiwi fruit will go the way of the Chinese gooseberry, to be supplanted by the 'Zespri'...

(Adapted from *The Economist*)

---

5 Sponsorship

Key Concept

'**Sponsorship**' is an agreement between a company and an event organiser where the company gives money – or the equivalent in kind – in exchange for rights to associate the company name with the event. This association can include the company name on team shorts, on advertising banners, in press advertisements or whatever is agreed in order to improve the awareness or image of the company.' (www.sportssponsorship.co.uk)

5.1 Marketers may sponsor local area or school groups and events – all the way up to national and international sporting and cultural events and organisations. Sponsorship has offered marketing avenues for organisations which are restricted in their advertising (such as alcohol and tobacco companies) or which wish to widen their awareness base among various target audiences.

- There is wide corporate involvement in mass-support sports such as football and cricket.
- Cultural sponsorship (of galleries, orchestras, theatrical productions and so on) tends be taken up by financial institutions and prestige marketing organisations.
- Community event sponsorship (supporting local environment 'clean-up' days, tree planting days, charity fun-runs, books for schools programmes and so on) is often used to associate companies with particular values (for example, environmental concern, education) or with socially responsible community involvement.

Action Programme 6

Next time you are at an event of any kind, look at the list of sponsors in the programme.

- What kind of sponsors support and identify themselves with different kinds of event – and why? (Does the sponsor and the event identifiably share a common audience?)
- What kinds of amount of sponsorship are cited – and what benefits (in terms of naming rights, advertising, use of facilities) are given to sponsors in return?

For up-to-date advice, publications, news and links, check out:

- www.sports-sponsorship.co.uk/sponsorship.htm
- www.sponsorship.co.uk/intro.htm

[Key Skill for Marketers: Using IT and the Internet]

5.2 The BDS Sponsorship Ltd Web site suggests that 'Sponsorship activities must be fully integrated with other areas of marketing communications in order to capitalise on their potential value.' It also distinguishes sponsorship from:

- **Patronage**, since no commercial advantage is sought or expected in return for the support of a patron (as it is for a sponsor)
- **Signage**, since no link with the event or promotional programme is made by signage, and no brand message or image can be conveyed.

The purpose and objectives of sponsorship

5.3 The objective of the **organisation soliciting sponsorship** is most often financial support – or some other form of contribution, such as prizes for a competition, or a prestige name to be associated with the event. In return, it will need to offer potential sponsors satisfaction of *their* objectives.

5.4 The objectives of the **sponsor** may be:

- **Awareness creation** in the target audience of the sponsored event (where it coincides with the target audience of the sponsor)
- **Media coverage** generated by the sponsored event (especially if direct advertising is regulated, as for tobacco companies)
- Opportunities for **corporate hospitality** at sponsored events
- **Association** with prestigious or popular events or particular values
- Creation of a **positive image** among employees or the wider community by association with worthy causes or community events
- Securing **potential employees** (for example, by sponsoring vocational/tertiary education)
- **Cost-effective** achievement of the above (compared to, say, TV advertising)

Marketing at Work

An article in the Sydney *Daily Telegraph* (July 2002) highlighted a new sponsorship trend.

'The sleek new silver Alfa Romeo 156 doesn't look out of place on the trendy Bondi boulevard – except for the new badge.

'The $65,000 sedan is the latest addition to the police road fleet – but taxpayers didn't fund it. It's part of the new trend in NSW law enforcement – sponsor a cop.

'The car was donated by Alfa Romeo importers ATECO and is a significant upgrade from the standard Holden Commodore and Ford Falcon used by most officers on the beat.

'The police had more than $200,000 in sponsorship last financial year. The last big donation from a car company was during the Olympics when BMW Australia donated 10 security sedans for dignitary and athlete protection. Other donations range from sports bags for the police basketball team to computer equipment and fingerprint gathering material...

"When the community safety officer visits schools in the vehicle he receives a little more attention than he's used to," [said a Superintendent]. "It gives us an extra resource with no cost to the taxpayer."

For reflection: Who gains from this sponsorship (and the press coverage of it)?

5.5 Sponsorship as a promotional technique also has limitations.

- Sponsorship by itself can only communicate a restricted amount of information (unless integrated with advertising and other initiatives).
- Association with a group or event may also attach negative values (such as sports-related violence and alcohol abuse).

Action Programme 7

Quick quiz! The following checklist appears at the Sport-sponsorship Web site. Write 'Yes' or 'No' in response to the question: 'Should you sponsor sport...'

- If your customers or potential customers can be identified as sports participants, spectators or viewers?
- If your company or product will benefit from an association with sport?
- If you want to reach a wide audience with a relatively simple message?
- If you are prepared to integrate sponsorship with other marketing communication such as advertising, point-of-sale, direct mail, corporate hospitality?
- If you are prepared to spend time and effort, as well as money, on sponsorship?
- If you are satisfying a personal interest or ambition to get involved or put something back into sport?
- If you expect putting your logo on a football team, racing car or team bus will bring more sales automatically?

- If you are not prepared to set out clear objectives of what you want to achieve and measure the results afterwards?

Developing a sponsorship programme

5.6 Smith (1993) suggests the following approach to developing and managing a sponsorship programme.

Analyse the current situation	Who else is a present or previous sponsor in the chosen field, and what else competitors are sponsoring?
Define sponsorship objectives	There may be many of these, as discussed above.
Clarify strategy	How does the sponsorship programme contribute to the overall corporate, marketing and communication objectives, and how can it be integrated with other promotions?
Define target audiences	Different sports and events may reach a number of very different audiences.
Develop tactical plans	What events will be sponsored, for how much and in return for what package of benefits (naming rights, advertising, signage, facilities, media rights and so on)?
Budget	What resources are needed to run the programme?
Set criteria	How will you measure the effectiveness of the sponsorship?

5.7 A similar process will be required for the organisation that wishes to **approach potential sponsors**, in order to:

- Describe the event/organisation to be sponsored in terms which are relevant to the potential sponsor's objectives
- Highlight competitor sponsorship or credible current/past sponsors to emphasise the value of sponsorship
- Show how the event/organisation (and its promotion) will reach and appeal to the potential sponsor's target audience, to emphasise potential PR benefits to the sponsor
- Specify what is required of the sponsor (amount of funding or other support) and what package of benefits is available in return
- Emphasise mutual benefits of the relationship.

Exam Tip

A question in the Specimen Paper for this syllabus asked you to draft a letter on behalf of a local dog rescue home to a large petroleum company asking for corporate sponsorship for a newsletter that you send to regular contributors. This is a complex communication task, as you are required to think about the nature of such a newsletter (communicating with your customers), in order to ask the corporation for sponsorship (communicating with an external 'partner') by selling the potential benefits of sponsorship (communicating with its customers)! You will need to think through key details embedded in such scenarios: where might there be a win-win for a local dog rescue home and a large petroleum company (which may not have a great local reputation with animal lovers, for example...)

Corporate hospitality

5.8 Corporate hospitality involves entertaining members of key organisational publics at corporate or public entertainment events. It is used for:

- **Building or cementing relationships** with key clients, media contacts and so on
- **Rewarding and motivating** key suppliers, distributors and/or employees
- **Wooing potential employees** in competitive labour markets
- **Encouraging networking** and informal communication to build relationships
- **Showing a presence** at major sporting or cultural events

5.9 Large scale corporate entertaining at sporting and cultural events is often handled by agencies, who purchase a block of tickets and sell them on to companies as part of a **hospitality package** including a marquee, box or hospitality room, refreshments and even programmes. Larger companies may own – or secure sponsor rights to – a permanent box or block of seats at stadiums and theatres. For a small company with no particular status requirements, ordinary ticket purchase and on-site catering may be sufficient.

5.10 The **return on investment** on such entertaining is not always readily quantifiable, since there are many other factors in client/supplier loyalty – but there may well be industry norms and expectations to live up to.

6 Exhibitions

Purposes and objectives of exhibitions

6.1 Exhibitions and trade fairs offer several promotional opportunities.

- **Public relations** (both to visitors and via media coverage of the event)
- **Promoting and selling** products/services to a wide audience of pre-targeted potential customers, particularly where demonstrations (for example of technical innovations), visual inspection (for example clothes or motor cars) or testing (for example food and wine) are likely to influence buyers.
- **Networking** within the industry and supply chain, and with existing clients.
- **Testing the response** to new products and prototypes.
- **Researching competitor** products and promotions.

6.2 Exhibiting at large shows can be **expensive**, including site fees, stand construction and display (estimated at 66% by the Exhibition Industry Federation); staff costs, including the opportunity cost of staff being withdrawn from their normal sales duties (22%); and promotion and the entertainment of visitors (12%). A **budget** should be drawn up to cover all costs associated with going to the show/exhibition. This should be compared with forecast revenue from the show in order to assess its viability. After the event, the show's **profitability** can be evaluated in the same way.

6.3 However, it should be recognised that your objectives for a particular show may not solely be sales revenue. You may want to find a **distributor** in a new international market, or to **raise awareness** of your brand with the trade press, or to **introduce your product** to a new market. Such achievements may take time to 'ripen' into confirmed sales. In the Exhibition Industry Federation survey, the average time to convert an exhibition lead to a sale was seven months, and in some cases, two years or more.

Planning an exhibition

6.4 Most exhibitions are set up by specialist **exhibition organisers**, who are responsible for: booking and preparing the venue; registering participants and organising seminars and events; issuing catalogues of stand-holders and events; providing stand construction services; organising lounges, amenities and catering facilities, access and parking, power and lighting; and planning event promotion and media coverage.

Action Programme 8

What are the major exhibitions, trade fairs and shows in (a) your industry, and/or (b) your country or city?

Keep an eye on the general and trade press for examples. Do a search on the Internet for any that interest you, and explore the information available for exhibitors, visitors and media on those sites.

6.5 The person responsible for exhibition planning will have to do the following.

- **Research** what fairs/exhibitions are available and relevant to the target audience.
- **Contact** show managers for a 'show pack' with details of facilities, services and costs.
- Make decisions about the **size**, **location**, **design** and **construction** of the exhibition stand, for booking. The size will depend on the number and nature of products you wish to display, whether you want entertainment/meeting space and so on. The location needs to be accessible and in a relevant section of the exhibition space. Design and construction includes your specifications (if you are using the services of the organisers) for shelving, lighting, power and telecom points, floor coverings, furniture, flowers/plants, fire extinguishers and so on. Cleaning services and insurance may also be offered.
- **Book** the stand, and provide relevant **information** for the exhibition catalogue, press pack and signage.
- **Plan staffing**. Trade show networking and selling is hectic, intense and tiring. You will need to arrange for a rotating roster of stand staff, including a Stand Manager to organise the stand and liaise with exhibition organisers, reception staff, sales staff,

technical staff (if the product requires expert demonstration or advice) and multilingual export staff (if relevant).

- **Arrange accommodation and transport for personnel**. A large exhibition can absorb available transport and accommodation even in a major city. If you are outside your home area, ensure that you have arrangements made well in advance.
- **Plan stand displays**. What items will you want displayed or demonstrated? What items (show cards, posters, leaflets) will need to be freshly designed/produced? How will you transport them to the exhibition site? What decorative items will project the desired image of your organisation and be welcoming and attractive to visitors – without taking up too much display or meeting space? What stationery (order books, catalogues and brochures, price lists, visitors books, business cards) will you require to do business on the stand?
- **Prearrange site visits.** Make a 'hit list' of key customers, suppliers and agents (from your database or from a pre-circulated list of exhibitors and attenders).
  (a) Invite them to visit your stand. Give directions, offer incentives (apart from the interest value of your display) such as prize draws or free samples, and (if possible) make definite appointments.
  (b) Supply their stand details to your sales staff, who can arrange to go and visit them.

Marketing at Work

New media is having an impact on the exhibitions industry. The Internet can be used to attract visitors to shows and for post-show marketing via e-mail.

In addition, some exhibitors are using Webcast technology to broadcast their shows live on the Internet. While this is not the same as being there, such facilities are still good for communicating useful information about exhibited products, with on-line visitors able to view just the stands they are interested in.

The director general of the Association of Exhibition Organisers says: 'The growth of exhibitions will go hand in hand with the growth of electronic media.' Visitors can use the Internet to book exhibition tickets, flights, hotel rooms and meetings.

Chapter Roundup

- **Public relations** is the planned and sustained effort to establish and maintain goodwill and mutual understanding between an organisation and its publics. It includes:
  - **Publicity**: generating editorial coverage in the press or technical/trade journals
  - **Press/media relations**: providing press/media with relevant information (in the form of press releases, photos and/or access to a source of expert information/comment)
  - **Public affairs**: lobbying or representations to government and trade bodies
  - **Community relations**: community projects; community sponsorship; dialogue with community and consumer groups

- **Employee relations**: communicating with employees; managing a range of internal communication mechanisms
- **Customer relations**: consumer marketing support and business-to-business communication eg through sponsorship, events and exhibitions
- **Financial public relations**: financial media relations and providing information to shareholders and financial markets
- **Issues management**: monitoring potential controversies in relation to the business and initiating communication programmes to manage public perceptions
- **Crisis communication**: issuing communications to minimise or counter the negative PR effects of crises (damaging events or revelations)
- **Corporate identity**, **logos** and **branding**, in order to create a consistently recognisable and differentiated identity for the company or brand.

Quick Quiz

1 Which of the following are publics of organisational PR?

A Stock market analysts
B Local government
C Local school students
D All of the above

2 Match the models of PR practice on the left with the roles they allocate to PR on the right

(1) Press agency/publicity	(a) Mediation
(2) Public information	(b) Scientific persuasion
(3) Two-way asymmetric	(c) Propaganda
(4) Two-way symmetric	(d) Information

3 Product placement is mainly a technique of business-to-business communication.

☐ True ☐ False

4 The attempt to initiate dialogue with the public and interest groups on the potential environmental impacts of plans to extend a factory site would be:

☐ Crisis communication ☐ Issues management

5 List five criteria of newsworthiness.

6 Fill in the gaps in the following sentences.

'A press release should have a clear (1) .... which indicates the overall purpose of the communication. In the body of the release the most (2)......... points should come first, to demonstrate the story's newsworthiness. This is called an '(3).......... (4)...........' style: most information at the top, less at the bottom. The word (5)'.........' should be inserted at the foot of the body copy. At the bottom of the release, provide a (6)............. telephone number or e-mail address: this identifies the (7).......... of the information, for further queries.'

7 A .... is defined as any words, symbols, design or style in any combination that distinguishes a company's offering from competing offerings in the perceptions of the target audience.

8 Which of the following is not the immediate objective of sponsorship?

A Short-term increase in public awareness
B Short-term increase in sales
C Association with events, causes or values
D Cost-effective media coverage

9 Which of the following might best be used to secure potential employees?

A Educational sponsorship
B Sports sponsorship
C Arts sponsorship
D Programme sponsorship

10 What percentage of exhibition costs is estimated to be spent on staffing the exhibition?

☐ 12% ☐ 22% ☐ 66%

Answers to Quick Quiz

1 D

2 (1) (c), (2) (d), (3) (b), (4) (a)

3 False

4 Issues management

5 Interesting, local, topical, important, new/surprising

6 (1) heading; (2) important; (3) inverted; (4) pyramid; (5) ends; (6) contact; (7) source

7 Brand

8 B

9 A

10 22%

Now try Question 7 from the Question Bank at the end of this Text

Action Programme Review

1 **Internal/employee communications**

- In-house magazines and employee newsletters
- Formal employee communication networks and feedback channels
- Recruitment exhibitions/conferences
- Speech writing and briefings for executives
- Company notice boards, Intranet sites
- Corporate and sales conferences

2 For example:

- Discovered a revolutionary new method/device that will affect audience's lives
- Recruited several hundred new workers in an area of high unemployment
- Won a large export order: good news for the country/region
- Signed up a major celebrity for a promotional campaign
- Decided to save and restore a building of local/historic interest
- Raised money for a local/relevant charity
- Started a programme of recycling/energy saving
- Produced the biggest/fastest/first [whatever!] in the world

3 **Woodton Comprehensive School**

Langport
Somerset
LP1 2RS

7 December 20X8

PRESS RELEASE

WOODTON SCHOOL EXCELS

Woodton Comprehensive has surpassed its previously excellent standards during 1998.

At the school's annual prize-giving the headmaster, Dr A L Hallowes, reported that Woodton had reached new levels in academic and sporting achievement and that the school was receiving national recognition as a result.

Woodton is number one in the region for its General Certificate of Secondary Education (GCSE) results with 80% of pupils passing with Grade 'A' for five subjects. Students taking Advanced ('A') Level examinations did equally well and 70% are taking up places in higher education.

Lisa Proud, headgirl, who is going onto Camford University having gained five straight 'A' grades said in her vote of thanks: 'At Woodton, working and playing to the best of your ability seems to come naturally. Expectations are always high amongst students and staff.'

The school's sporting achievements were acknowledged by Rachel Stone, former England captain of cricket and ex-pupil of the school. She recalled how sport had enabled her to lead a full and interesting life.

'It all began here for me', she said, 'and I am delighted to see that the school is investing even more into a most exciting range of activities.'

Prizes she awarded included:

First XI Football Team – County champions

First XI Hockey Team – Hyatt Cup

Athletics cups Boys – Alex Hunter

Girls – Laetitia Cook

ENDS

For further information call: Valerie Smith, School Secretary, 01625 887766

Editors note

A full listing of all examination and sporting results will be sent to you separately with a selection of photographs.

4 Hooks might include (for example): company successes or heroic failures (celebration, humour); introducing or farewelling members of staff (human interest); profiling key staff members, jobs or departments (relevance to everyone's work); raising issues in the workplace eg discrimination, sexual harassment (challenge); upcoming product launches and promotions (involvement).

5 (a) You may immediately have thought of the Nike tick or the Macdonald's 'Golden Arches' or similar examples. This effect is achieved through high-repetition, high-exposure advertising, sponsorship and consumer exposure to the brand, with gradual removal of supporting names and slogans until only the logo remains.

(b) Have fun!

6 Own research (although we have given some ideas in the text so far).

7 The answers are (in question order) yes, yes, yes, yes, yes, no, no, no.

8 Own research.

New technologies and media

Chapter Topic List	
1	Setting the scene
2	New communication tools
3	New promotion tools
4	The Internet and e-commerce
5	Developing Web sites
6	E-mail marketing
7	The speed of change

Learning Outcomes

☑ Appreciate the range of developments in information and communications technology (ICT) and their impact on the promotion mix

☑ Suggest how the Internet and intranets can be used in external and internal marketing communication

☑ Develop ideas for the effective promotional use of Web sites and e-mail

Syllabus References

☑ Explain the role of information and communications technology (ICT) in communications, including digital TV and interactive marketing (3.14).

Key Concepts Introduced

- ISDN
- Database marketing
- Datamining
- E-commerce

1 Setting the scene

1.1 We have referred to new-technology alternatives to conventional communication media and methods throughout this Study Text. If you have explored the recommended Web sites, you are already well on the way to appreciating the revolution in communication created by the Internet in particular.

1.2 In this chapter, we will describe some of the technical innovations that are facilitating e-commerce and changing the way companies communicate and do business. We will also explore some of their applications for **promotion** and **internal/external customer communication**.

1.3 Many technological developments also have uses in the related field of **customer care** and **customer service**. In Chapter 15, in this context, we will discuss:

- The use of **databases** to pursue and personalise customer contacts
- The use of **Customer Relations Management** (CRM) software to integrate the various contacts between the customer and the organisation and
- Various forms of technology-assisted **telephony** (such as automated call handling and computer-integrated telephony) which streamline or personalise telephone contacts with customers.

1.4 First, we will look at some of the general trends in communication.

Changing communication

1.5 In the last few years, the infrastructure and tools of communication have radically changed. The phone is swiftly being overtaken by e-mail as the most popular method of remote interpersonal communication. The Internet has changed the way people access information. Even 'old' media like the television and telephone are being transformed by new data transmission infrastructures and integration with computer systems.

1.6 Geoff Ebbs (*Living on the Web for Dummies)* sums it up as follows.

'The World Wide Web has truly changed communication. Those of us with a computer at work share jokes and yarns as if we are sitting around a campfire, do the sort of research that five years ago was restricted to major libraries, and write more letters to people than most of the literary giants we grew up studying...'

Action Programme 1

Assess how far Geoff Ebbs' comment is true for you and your work/social networks. Focus on the changes that you have experienced and the way technology is used in the three areas he highlights:

- Networking and 'community-building'
- Data gathering and access (including information about products and services)
- Interpersonal communication

1.7 Broadly, communication has changed in the following ways.

- Higher speed
- Wider access to information
- 24—7 global communication
- Interactivity and multi-media
- Personalisation

1.8 We will look at each of these trends briefly in turn.

Exam Tip

Part of a question in the Specimen Paper for this syllabus asked you to explain (in the format of draft notes for a presentation) how implementing the latest ICT tools can help improve communications and relationships with customers.

You do not need to have detailed technical knowledge of how systems and devices operate – but you are required to have a good awareness of their uses and implications for customer communications. If in doubt, ask yourself: what does it do for the organisation and for its internal and external customers?

Speed of communication

1.9 The development of 'facsimile transfer' (fax) was breakthrough in its day: enabling documents which previously had to be mailed to be transferred down a phone line. Now, messages can be transferred via a local computer network or the Internet almost instantly, to the point where real time conversations can be held using on-line messaging and chat rooms. Recent **infrastructure innovations** such as ISDN (digital communication networks), DSL (Digital Subscriber Lines), satellite transmission (for telephone and television signals), fibre optic cabling and increased 'band width' (allowing more data to pass through networks more swiftly) have supported this process.

Wider access to information

1.10 Krol and Ferguson *(The Whole Internet)* suggest that 'Once you're connected to the Internet, you have instant access to an almost indescribably wealth of information... Through electronic mail and bulletin boards [newsgroups] you can use a different kind of resource: a worldwide supply of **knowledgeable people**, some of whom are bound to share your interests, no matter how obscure... There are also more (and better) resources: there's a whole world of multimedia resources, including museums, exhibitions, art galleries and shopping malls...'

Action Programme 2

How might the marketing organisation exploit the accessibility of the information network? What drawbacks for marketing can you see in the information-richness of the Internet?

24-7 global communication

1.11 ICT has enabled 24-hour 7-day global communication: across working or office hours, time zones and geographical distances. Telex, fax and answer machines were a start in this direction – but they required (possibly delayed) human intervention to initiate a response. The Internet allows users to access information/services and perform transactions at any time of any day. Nor is there any distinction between local and international sites, in terms of speed or cost of access. (Physical delivery of products ordered will, of course, re-erect some of the geographical barriers...)

Interactivity and multi-media

1.12 **Interactivity** is mutual responsiveness. Consumers are increasingly demanding in terms of interactivity in accessing and responding to promotional messages. According to Postma *(The New Marketing Era)*, true interactivity implies:

- Speed of dialogue/response (for example, the immediacy of telephone, e-mail and Internet)
- Up-to-dateness of the information provided at time of contact
- Flexibility and scope of response (for example, access information, get questions answered *and* submit detailed order requirements and payments)

1.13 Consumers are also increasingly demanding in terms of the stimulation provided by promotional messages. **Multi media** communication implies the use of written, visual and audio elements to enhance a message's impact and interest. Postma notes that 'there is nothing the human nervous system desires more than colour video pictures with sound'.

1.14 The Internet and related technologies have habituated people (particularly young media and IT consumers) to multi-media presentations, high-level animated/video-based graphics and interaction with material. Although the impact of such trends may be limited by the power of the individual user's PC and the speed of the modem, printed matter may seem relatively unstimulating in comparison: some of the features of on-line and multi-media presentation are being added to traditional print advertising and information: simulated 'links' and buttons, multi-directional graphics and so on.

Personalisation

1.15 Database, document generation and Web technologies have improved the ease and sophistication of targeting and personalisation of contact between organisations and customers. Examples include:

- Allowing users to customise Web pages for their personal interests and tastes
- Making individually-targeted product offers and recommendations based on browsing/buying behaviour
- Sending personally addressed and targeted-content messages to customers
- Encouraging users/customers to form 'virtual communities' (for example using chat rooms, discussion boards and newsgroups)

Action Programme 3

How might the marketing organisation exploit the 'virtual community' aspects of ICT?

Overview of the hi-tech promotion mix

1.16 These general technological trends can be seen to impact across the promotional mix.

Promotion activity	Impact/opportunity	Examples of supporting technology
Advertising	■ Reach more customers worldwide ■ Target audiences more specifically ■ Increase response via interactivity	■ Web sites and ads ■ Specialist TV channels ■ Direct Response TV, SMS text messaging
Sales promotion	■ Target segment/individual interests and preferences ■ Facilitate/motivate response ■ On-line discounts (lower admin costs)	■ Customer databases, EPOS data ■ On-line entry/'coupons' ■ On-line transaction
Direct marketing	■ Personalised, one-to-one messages ■ Permission-based database/contacts to enhance response rate ■ Speed and interactivity of response ■ Direct response/transaction	■ Database ■ E-mail, Web site, SMS requests for info ■ E-mail + website links ■ E-commerce sites
PR & Publicity	■ Speed of information dissemination and response to crisis/issues	■ E-mail media releases and on-line information
Marketing/ Sales support	■ Publicising sponsorships ■ Publicising exhibition attendance ■ Up-to-date information for sales force & call centre staff	■ Web site ■ Web site/email clients ■ Access to product/stock and customer database
Internal marketing	■ Staff access to information relevant to their jobs ■ Co-ordination/identification of dispersed offices and off-site staff	■ Intranet newsletters, bulletins, policy info ■ E-mail, tele- and video-conferencing
Network marketing	■ Supplier/client access to information relevant to business relationship	■ Extranet: access to selected information

1.17 Consider the following examples.

- What image is conveyed these days by an organisation that does not have a Web presence, or does not cite a Web site or e-mail address for customer contact?
- What competitive edge is gained where an organisation is able to offer e-mail contact, secure on-line transactions (24-7, world-wide), interactive data search and shopping

experiences – as opposed to an organisation which can only be contacted by 'snail' mail or during business hours, and supplies only printed, pre-selected information?

- How does printed promotional matter compare (for impact, usability, interest, memorability) with audio-visual, and/or interactive presentations and/or searchable on-line databases and linked sites?
- How does a poorly designed Web site (hard to navigate; limited in content, interactivity and visual interest) compare to what is possible and visible elsewhere on the Web?
- How does customer research information gathered by focus group or questionnaire ('stated preferences') compare to the monitoring of website usage over time, with the added ability to personalise the organisation-customer interface by name, shopping preferences/history and so on?

1.18 We will now look at some specific developments and tools in more detail.

2 New communication tools

2.1 Some people have referred to the period around the turn of the century as the 'Telecom Revolution' in the same way as the 1980s were regarded as the computer revolution. External applications of ICT revolve around developments in this field.

2.2 In broad outline, the developments can be seen as falling into two areas.

(a) Developments in the **telecommunications infrastructure** (means of connecting A to B). These have generally allowed **more data** to be carried **more swiftly**.

- ISDN (Integrated Systems Digital Network), a faster alternative to existing analogue services
- Fibre optics (instead of copper-based cable)
- Digital mobile phone networks (such as GSM – Group Spécial Mobile – a pan-European digital cellular network)
- Satellite transmission of data (for television and remote telephone connection)

(b) Developments in the **tools** and **media** for sending and receiving messages: fax, video and mobile phones, e-mail and so on.

2.3 We will be discussing developments in telephony (including **voice mail**, **computer telephone integration**, **video-conferencing** and **video telephones**) in Chapter 15, considering internal/external customer communications as part of customer service and relationship marketing.

Exam Tip

Under the old syllabus, questions have been set on the uses and benefits of communication channels including voice mail, e-mail, ISDN and video-conferencing. You need to have a broad appreciation of the impact of technology – but also a good grasp of specific examples.

ISDN

Key Concept

ISDN (Integrated Systems Digital Network) is a digital telecommunication network, allowing users to send data from desktop computers over the telecommunication link without using a modem.

2.4 Key advantages of ISDN

- Data can be transmitted at least twice as fast over ISDN as over normal telecommunication networks
- Shorter connection times offer cost saving
- ISDN supports high-speed home access to the Internet (at 56Kbps or better)
- More than one service can be sent over the link at the same time. (For example, it would be possible for architects to use one telecom link to view building plans on a PC while simultaneously discussing them with the client via a telephone handset.)

Mobile telecommunications

2.5 Radio networks for portable telephone communications (also known as 'cellular phones') started up in the late 1980s and have boomed in developed countries ever since (as you are no doubt aware from the deluge of promotion.) Later **digital networks** are better able to support data transmission than the older analogue networks, with higher transmission speeds and less likelihood of data corruption.

2.6 This means that a salesperson on the road, say, can send or receive a fax simply by plugging a laptop PC into a mobile handset. A combined palmtop computer and cellular phone is already on the market. In theory it is now possible to do any kind of 'office' activity outside the office, on the move – although limitations in battery power (a technology lagging far behind others described in this chapter) impose restrictions.

2.7 However, the mobile phone is no longer just a means of speaking to customers on the way to meetings, or taking client calls when out of the office. The services available to users are increasing all the time, making the mobile phone a tool of **promotion** and **e-commerce** (discussed in sections 3 and 4 below) as well as interpersonal communication. Communication services include:

Messaging	■ Voice mail ■ Short message service (SMS) which allows text messages of up to 160 characters to be transmitted over a standard digital phone ■ Paging services ■ Access to e-mail messages, downloaded from the Internet
Call management	■ Call barring ■ Conference calls ■ Call divert
Corporate services	■ Integrated numbering, so that people have a single contact number for their desk and mobile phones ■ Virtual private networks that incorporate mobile phones as well as conventional desktop phones

Action Programme 4

Suppose that a marketing colleague does not like mobile phones. Write a memo (paper-based or e-mail) stating whether or not you would recommend that (s)he get a mobile phone and why. (Consider your colleague both as a marketer/business person and as a consumer.)

E-mail

2.8 The term 'electronic mail', or e-mail, is used to describe various systems for sending data or messages electronically via a telephone or data network and a central 'server' computer. E-mail has replaced letters, memos, faxes, documents and even telephone calls – combining many of the possibilities of each medium with new advantages of speed, cost and convenience.

2.9 E-mail offers many advantages for internal/external customer communication.

- Messages can be sent and received very **fast** (allowing real time messaging dialogue)
- E-mail is **economical** (estimated 20 times cheaper than fax): often allowing worldwide transmission for the cost of a local telephone call (connecting to the local service point of the Internet Service Provider).
- The recipient gets a '**hard copy**' message, and the sender has documentary evidence of message transmission and retrieval by the recipient (for legal/logistical purposes).
- Messages can be sent **worldwide** at any **time**.
- The user can prepare **complex documents** (spreadsheets, graphics, photos) for sending as 'attachments' to e-mail covering messages. These can be printed out by the recipient, as a convenient alternative to fax.
- E-mail **message** management software (such as Outlook Express) has convenient features such as: message copying (to multiple recipients); integration with an 'address book' (database of contacts); automatic alert messages sent when the target recipient is unable to access his or her e-mail immediately, with alternative contact details; stationery

and template features, allowing corporate identity to be applied; facilities for mail organisation and filing.

2.10 We will discuss the promotional uses of e-mail in section 3 below. Guidance on how to formulate e-mail messages is given in Chapter 12.

Intranet and extranet

2.11 'Inter' means 'between': 'intra' means 'within'; 'extra' means 'outside'. This may be a useful reminder of some of the inter-related terminology in this area.

- The **Internet** is used to disseminate and exchange information among the public at large.
- An **intranet** is used to disseminate and exchange information 'in-house' within an organisation. Only employees are able to access this information.
- An **extranet** is used to communicate with selected people outside the organisation.

2.12 The idea behind an Intranet is that companies set up their own mini versions of the Internet, using a combination of their own networked computers and Internet technology. Each employee has a browser and a server computer distributes corporate information as well as offering access to the global Net.

2.13 Intranet content

- **Performance data**: linked to sales, inventory, job progress and other database and reporting systems, enabling employees to process and analyse data to fulfil their work objectives
- **Employment information**: on-line policy and procedure manuals (health and safety, disciplinary and grievance), training and induction material, internal contacts for help and information
- **Employee support/information**: advice on first aid, healthy working at computer terminals, training courses, offered, resources held in the corporate library and so on.
- **Notice boards** for the posting of message to and from employees: notice of meetings, events, trade union activities
- **Departmental home pages**: information and news about each department's personnel and activities to aid identification and cross-functional understanding
- **Bulletins or newsletters**: details of product launches and marketing campaigns, staff moves, changes in company policy – or whatever might be communicated through the print equivalent, plus links to relevant databases or departmental home pages.
- **E-mail facilities** for the exchange of messages, memos and reports between employees in different locations
- **Upward communication**: suggestion schemes, feedback questionnaires
- **Individual personnel files**, to which employees can download training materials, references, certificates and appraisals.

2.14 Benefits of Intranet

- Cost savings from the elimination of storage, printing and distribution of documents that can instead be exchanged electronically or be made available on-line
- More frequent use made of on-line documents than printed reference resources (eg procedures manuals) and more flexible and efficient interrogation and updating of data
- Wider access to corporate information. This facilitates multi-directional communication and co-ordinating (particularly for multi-site working). It is also a mechanism of corporate culture and esprit de corps. The term '**virtual team**' has been coined to describe how ICT can link people in structures which emulate the dynamics of teamworking (identity, solidarity, shared goals and information) despite the geographical dispersion of team members in different locations or constantly on the move (as, for example, sales representatives).

Marketing at Work

One of the biggest users of intranets is the Swiss Bank Corporation. In fact, it has so many – around 100 – that it has appointed a Head of Intranets to co-ordinate them all. Intranets are used for: corporate accounting and credit information; publishing research internally (and to a select group of 50 external clients); trading information; ordering IT equipment; IT project management; and informing staff of regulatory changes.

The software enables employees to share information by posting it to Web sites. It also enables workflow applications, which control the flow of work between users in a team.

2.15 An **extranet**, like an intranet, excludes access by the general public, but **selected outside users** are given passwords to enable them to access particular areas or levels of the system. Since information will not be available to the public in general, it can be used as part of a relationship marketing strategy. Examples include the member-only pages of professional bodies (and their student equivalents), which make information and downloads available only to registered members. Check out the CIM's site: both Internet and extranet (member/student areas): www.cim.co.uk.

2.16 Extranets are useful tools for **business partners**. They can share data or systems to provide smoother transaction processing and more efficient services for customers. An extranet may be used to:

- Provide a 'pooled' service which a number of business partners can access
- Exchange news which is of use to partner companies and clients
- Share training or development resources
- Publicise loyalty schemes, sponsorships, exhibition attendance information and other promotional tools
- Exchange potentially large volumes of transaction data efficiently
- Provide on-line presentations to business partners and prospects (and not competitors).

Electronic Data Interchange

2.17 **Electronic Data Interchange** (EDI) is a form of computer-to-computer data interchange: another form of electronic mail. Instead of sending each other paper-based documentation in the form of invoices, statements and so on, details of inter-company transactions are sent via telecom links, avoiding the need for output and paper at the sending end, and for re-keying of data at the receiving end.

2.18 Until recently, compatibility was a major problem, and some form of interface between the computers had to be devised to enable data interchange to take place. This is less and less of a problem as businesses adopt common standards and protocols for using the Internet. Joining an EDI network (there are several) is quite expensive, but many smaller companies are encouraged to do so by their suppliers and/or customers: many of Marks and Spencer's suppliers, for example, have been converted to EDI to streamline transactions.

2.19 A variation on the EDI concept is **electronic funds transfer** (EFT), a system by which computers can be used to transfer funds: making payments to a supplier, pay salaries into employees' bank accounts, or transfer funds from one bank account to another by sending electronic data.

Marketing at Work

SWIFT (The Society for Worldwide Interbank Financial Telecommunications) is a system for the electronic transfer of funds internationally between banks. Interbank settlements by the clearing banks within the UK can be made using CHAPS (Clearing House Automated Payments System). Many large companies now pay the salaries of employees using BACS (Bankers' Automated Clearing Services) or BACSTEL: it has been estimated that switching to BACS can save 90% on transaction charges.

3 New promotion tools

3.1 Technology has opened up new ways for organisations to communicate promotional messages. We will discuss the **Internet** as a promotional and commerce tool in section 5 below. Here, we will look at:

(a) The use of **databases** for market segmentation and targeting, and/or the personalisation of customer communications

(b) The availability of new **promotional media** that are:

- Increasingly **targeted** (eg specialist satellite/cable TV channels, e-mail and SMS text messaging)
- Increasingly **interactive** (eg interactive TV, catalogues, newsletters and kiosks)
- Increasingly **multi-media** (eg CD, CD ROM and DVD)

Databases

3.2 Postma *(The New Marketing Era)* highlights two major shifts in the way customer information is used in the new marketing era.

- 'In a traditional market approach, people have all sorts of ideas about the target group, or they think up some obvious target group for a certain product. Without a marketing database, people are able to approach this target group only as a generic whole, by choosing the correct advertising medium and tailoring the creative ideas to the prescribed target group... In the new approach...we no longer calculate the market from within the company, but instead communicate, listen and record. The **database** will teach us what the market has to say...'
- 'In the new marketing era, we are shifting from derivative and self-reported information to **behavioural analysis**... Information technology makes it possible to determine behaviour, even at an individual level, and even in mass markets. This information is by far the most trustworthy when forecasting future behaviour.'

Key Concept

Database marketinghas been defined by Shaw and Stone (1988) as 'an interactive approach to marketing, which uses individually addressable marketing media and channels to extend help to a company's target audience, stimulate their demand and stay close to them by recording and keeping an electronic database memory of customer, prospect and all communication and commercial contacts, to help them improve all future contacts and ensure more realistic planning of all marketing'.

3.3 A database, in marketing terms, is a collection of data that can be organised to give marketing information. The customer database is one example.

3.4 Allen et all suggest the following projects which can be conducted using database marketing techniques.

Identify the best customers	Use RFM analysis (Recency of the latest purchase, Frequency of purchases and Monetary value of all purchases) to determine which customers are most profitable to market to.
Develop new customers	Collect lists of potential customers to incorporate into the database
Tailor messages based on customer usage	Target mail and e-mail based on the types and frequency of purchases indicated by the customer's purchase profile
Recognise customers after purchase	Reinforce the purchase decision by appropriate follow-up

Cross-sell related and complementary products	Use the customer purchase database to identify opportunities to suggest additional products during the buying session.
Personalise customer service	On-line purchase data can prompt customer service representatives to show that the customer is recognised, his needs known and his time (for example, in giving details) valued
Eliminating conflicting or confusing communications	Present a coherent image over time to individual customers – however different the message to different customer groups. (For example, don't keep sending 'dear first-time customer' messages to long-standing customers!) Remember the Integrated Marketing Communications approach.

3.5 In Chapter 15, we will see how customer databases can be used to target, customise and personalise communications with customers to enhance relationship marketing and customer service.

Datamining

3.6 New data management techniques have been developed to provide marketers with better and quicker access to data analysis.

Key Concept

Data miningis a set of statistical techniques that are used to identify trends, patterns and relationships in data.

3.7 Data mining techniques have been available for many years, but they have only recently grown popular, as more data is being created, data processing power (in the form of computers) is becoming more accessible and data mining software tools are becoming available. Most data mining models are either:

- **Predictive**: using known observations to predict future events (for example predicting the probability that a recipient will opt out of an e-mail list)
- **Descriptive**: interrogating the database to identify patterns and relationships (for example profiling the audience of a particular advertising campaign).

Customer specific marketing

3.8 The logical extension of database marketing is referred to by Kotler as **customer specific marketing** and by Peppers and Rogers as **one-to-one marketing**. The company collects data on **individual** customers, their past Web-browsing and purchase habits, demographic and even psychographic characteristics. It is then possible to customise or personalise the organisation-customer interface to suit individual customer profiles: whether on the telephone (using Computer Telegraphy Integration), by mail (using data merged from database files into word-processing programmes), by e-mail (ditto) or by Web site (personalising and customising pages for known 'surfers').

3.9 The **Internet**, and related technologies, allows for the collection and use of such data (in ways that we will discuss in Section 4 below). It is what Rich calls 'the **ultimate niche marketing tool**. Once you really get to know your target audience, it's relatively easy to focus your on-line marketing efforts to reach that specific audience in a way that will get their attention.'

3.10 **Cookies** are a technology that allows a Web site to 'remember' individual visitors' surfing and/or purchase history and preferences. This information is placed on the visitor's hard disk and when he revisits the site, it references the cookie and is able to show the visitor product selections and recommendations, personalised welcomes and streamline ordering (through remembering names, addresses, credit card details).

Marketing at Work

'Newcomers to database marketing have to make a mental leap from viewing the database as a collection of names to seeing it as an engine for driving truly personal marketing, says Melanie Howard, head of direct marketing studies at the Henley Centre. "Companies must understand the database is not a way of marketing, but it facilitates the personal marketing approach. They must be careful. If they think they are doing personal marketing just because they have a name and address they have a problem". They must understand what will win consumer loyalty.

'Analysing the data properly and using it effectively will separate the winners from the lowers, argues Edwina Dunn of Dunn-Humby, the company involved in running Tesco's Clubcard. "Manufacturers have learned that data about purchasing is valuable and if they can link it to names and addresses, that is even more valuable. Not many are grasping the deeper meaning of that. The few that do are forward-thinking and visionary," she says.

'She puts Tesco in that category. Its Clubcard collects purchasing information at the swipe of the card. The card can be used at any store, enabling marketers to build a picture of individual habits. Because the Tesco system is about collecting points, then sending out vouchers, the retailer has a valid reason to write to customers.'

Marketing Business

New media

Digital television

3.11 **Digital television** broadcasting began in the UK in 1998, through two main suppliers: ITV Digital (formerly On Digital) and Digital Sky TV. According to forecasts, digital will be the only signals broadcast in 15 or 20 years time.

3.12 Transmitting programmes by digital signal **increases the number of services** which can be delivered to audiences. As many as ten services can occupy the frequency previously occupied by one conventional 'analogue' service. Digital broadcasting also allows viewers greater choice over **how and when** they watch, allowing them to **interact** with programmes and to **select** their own programme content: another manifestation of the major trend towards customisation.

(a) At present, programmes can only be scheduled in sequence, with the viewer having to watch a specific programme at a set time. Digital broadcasting allows networks many layers and branches: there is much more flexibility to match services to the viewer's personal timetable.

(b) Broadcasters are able to offer additional programmes, information, sound and graphics to complement what is being shown on the main channel. This allows marketers to add viewer-selected information and shopping services, promotional offers and competitions relating to programme content and so on.

(c) The proliferation of TV channels caters for an increasing number of niche audiences: presenting niche advertising opportunities for marketers.

Interactive television

3.13 Several media developments are based on the increasing interactivity of TV. '**Interactive television**' refers to the possibility of controlling and reacting to transmitted programmes.

- **Teletext** is a limited but popular form of interactivity, by which users can search information pages (traffic updates, weather, transport/entertainment schedules, news headlines) using standard remote control devices.

- **Direct Response Television** (DRTV) may also be a relatively low-tech approach: standard television commercials and infomercials urge immediate response via a call centre or Web site. The advertiser has to display the product convincingly, give a clear 'call to action' (with incentives if required), show prominent contact telephone numbers or Web addresses – and arrange large call centre operations (if necessary) to take calls during the advertising period.

- Digital technology is allowing more genuinely **interactive TV** (eg Sky TV's 'Open...' channel). The TV set is coupled to a set top box with communication access through telecom links. 'Pop up' messages on Sky TV, for example, offer the option to interact, by being switched across to the Sky 'Open...' channel and a branded location: here, there are instructions for accessing more information and making orders. Forrester Research forecasts that by 2005 more Europeans will be using interactive TV than going online to use the Internet.

3.14 Mullin *(Direct Marketing)* notes that interactive TV is described as a 'lean back' advertising medium. 'It is accepted as part of the family. A television set is trusted in the home... Interactive TV is put across as allowing people to go out from their homes to obtain information or purchase – it is not promoted as intrusive in any way... The perceived and actual security is greater than the Internet. security comes from the fact that the database holds details of the address and telephone number of the customer and the set top box has its own unique security code... Using a wrong/stolen credit card causes a security alert when the check is made before purchase is sanctioned.'

Interactive catalogues and newsletters

3.15 Product information can be conveyed with added interactivity by various means.

- **Interactive catalogues** can be downloaded or viewed on-line, with Web-based links to more information on specific products; links to 'shopping trolley' and 'checkout' pages for placing orders and so on.

- **Print-based catalogues** sent to customer's homes can be combined with other **interactive technologies**, such as voice-response computers: the client's queries about price, availability and delivery can be communicated and answered by telephone. Postma notes that 'the strong points of each medium are tapped to full potential, while the weaker points of one (minimal interactivity; minimal stimulation of the senses) are offset by the other.'
- **Interactive newsletters** can similarly be e-mailed, downloaded or viewed on-line, to convey information to customers on topics of interest (new products, industry developments, exhibitions, sales promotions and so on), with Web-based links to related pages if customers want to follow up on particular items.

3.16 These approaches allow complex data to be made available to customers, with the element of choice reinforcing their interest and motivation at the follow-up stage. Instant gratification of curiosity/desire to act can be offered through interactivity. Meanwhile, the 'mechanics' of enquiry/ordering can be separated from the sensory stimulation and relationship marketing aspects of product pictures, news/information and so on, so that they retain their full impact.

Marketing at Work

Freemans, the catalogue company, which currently has 10% of the home shopping market in the UK, is keen to make inroads into the interactive catalogue sector. Over 5,000 of its agents are equipped with the hardware and software to make instant buying decisions. Customers are able to view full motion picture presentations and then order via modem.

Hewlett Packard collects individual customer data (via responses to on-pack 'cash back' promotions for its print cartridges, for example), and e-mails customers with a regular 'Your HP newsletter', with helpful tips on using and maintaining equipment, product offers and so on. This contains links to the HP Web site, and other related sites, for follow-up on particular items of interest.

3.17 **Interactive kiosks** are a relatively new development, currently under trial by some banks and travel marketers to provide information about financial services, potential holiday destinations and so on. In bank kiosks, access can be controlled by customer recognition using retinal image ('eye print'), avoiding the need for cards which can be lost or stolen. These kiosks will 'speak' to the customer and understand spoken commands, making a wider range of services available without human intervention.

3.18 Interactive information displays are increasingly being used in museums and art galleries, to allow visitors to explore artefacts and related databases.

SMS text messaging

3.19 Integration of digital mobile phone networks with the Internet has facilitated a range of **m-commerce** (mobile commerce) applications.

(a) The ability to download data from the Internet. As well as general browsing, this can be used to facilitate conventional commerce: for example, locating stockists of desired products near the current location of the user; accessing maps and directions to meeting venues; accessing stock, product or customer databases for information relevant to meetings and sales visits and so on.

(b) The ability to order goods and access services direct. As an example, recent trials have enabled mobile phone users to buy soft drinks from vending machines in a cashless transaction: all order and payment details are punched into the phone (not the machine) – but the machine delivers the ordered beverage at the user's location. Interactive SMS text messaging also allows users to respond to offers for example, by booking event/entertainment tickets.

3.20 SMS (Short Message Service) allows 160-character messages, logos and ring-tones to be sent across the mobile telecom networks. It is low-cast, easy-to-use and highly personal and compelling (especially in the youth market). In the UK, SMS has exploded as an advertising medium, with brands including Cadbury, Smirnoff, Avon, BA, Nestle, Pepsi, Haagen-Daaz and even Liverpool FC using it to offer promotions and motivate responses.

Action Programme 5

Think through the various techniques of promotion covered in Part C of this Text. How might SMS – as a brief, personal, location-sensitive, text-based medium – be used to apply these techniques effectively?

PC-based tools

3.21 Postma notes that PC-based technology has developed towards greater **multi-media** applications, enhancing the sensory impact of promotional messages. Multi-media refers to the addition of moving picture and sound capabilities to a computer's text and graphics capabilities.

- **Multi-media PC** is a broad term for a PC with digital audio and a CD-ROM player, allowing sound, computer-animated and (in more sophisticated versions) full-screen video pictures to be transmitted. This enhances the entertainment and impact value of Web sites and CD-ROM (for example of product catalogues) experiences.
- **Enhanced CD, CD-ROM and DVD** (digital versatile disc) allow both multi-media and interactivity to greater or lesser extent, adding value to information/entertainment products (for example providing background information and games with films and music CDs).
- **Multi-media laptops, notebooks and palmtops** (Personal Digital Assistants) add **mobility** for m-commerce and sales force support functions.

4 The Internet and e-commerce

4.1 The **Internet** (also known as 'the Net', the 'information super-highway' or 'cyberspace') is a vast computer network offering the ability for computers across the world to communicate via telecommunications links. Information can be exchanged either through e-mail or through accessing and entering data via a Web site: a collection of screens providing information in text and graphic form, any of which can be viewed by clicking the appropriate link (shown as a button, word or icon) on the screen.

4.2 The '**World Wide Web**' (or 'Web') is a navigation system within the Internet. It is based on a technology called 'hypertext' which allows documents stored on host computers on the Internet to be linked to one another. When you view a document that contains hypertext links, you can view any of the connected documents or pages simply by clicking on a link. The Web is the most powerful, flexible and fastest growing information and navigation service on the Internet. In order to 'surf' or navigate the Web, users need a **Web client** (called a '**browser**') which interprets and displays hypertext documents and locates documents pointed to by links. Internet Explorer is the browser from Microsoft: alternatives include Netscape Navigator, Mosaic, WebSurfer and others.

4.3 Access to the Internet will become easier and easier. Most new PCs now come pre-loaded with the necessary hardware and software, and cheaper Internet devices are beginning to reach the market: Microsoft and America Online (AOL) – among others – have been exploring inexpensive 'set-top' TV/Internet connections. Developments in telecom networks are already rendering modems unnecessary. **Personal digital assistants** (PDAs) such as the Palm Pilot, **wireless Internet-compatible cellular phones** and **wireless laptop connections** (such as Apple's 'air port') allow users to surf the Web and send and receive e-mail from almost any location, without cords or cables.

The Internet as a promotional tool

4.4 The Internet can be used across the promotion mix.

Advertising	■ Dedicated corporate Web sites, banner/button advertising, ranking on internet search engines (to increase site exposure). ■ The forecast global penetration of the Internet over the next few years would give it a significantly larger audience than any of the television networks, print media outlets or other advertising vehicles. ■ Studies show that brand awareness increases some 5% after using banner advertising.
Direct marketing	■ E-mail messages sent to targeted mailing lists (rented, or developed by the marketing organisation itself) ■ 'Permission marketing' (targeting consumers who have opted to receive commercial mailings)
Direct response advertising	■ Immediate contact (information/transaction facilities) to follow up customer responses to TV/radio/print advertising
Sales promotion	■ On-line prize draws and competitions ■ One-line discounts (offset by lower transaction costs) ■ Downloadable or e-mailed discount vouchers
Customer loyalty programmes	■ Value-added benefits that enhance the Internet buying experience: ■ User home page customisation ■ Virtual communities (chat rooms etc) ■ Free e-cards/SMS messages
Media/press relations	■ On-line media/press kits ■ E-mailed media releases ■ 'About us' and 'contacts' pages

	■ Technical briefings and articles on key issues
Pubic relations	■ 'About us' and 'FAQ' (frequently asked question) features ■ News bulletins (eg for crisis or issues management) ■ Publicity/information for sponsorships, exhibitions and events ■ Sponsorship of popular/ useful information sites
Relationship marketing	■ Customisation of Web pages and targeting of offers/promotions ■ E-mail follow-up contacts ■ **E-zines**: special interest newsletters published on the Web, or distributed by e-mail direct to subscribers and mailing lists.
'Grass roots marketing'	■ Generating word of mouth promotion and recommendation among customers. ■ On-line chat or message board forums and 'introduce a friend' schemes/incentives. ■ **'Viral marketing'** (co-called because it simulates the way a virus works!): giving visitors communication tools which they send to others, requiring them to visit the site: eg electronic postcards, greeting cards and links ('Send this page to a friend')
Direct distribution	■ Of products (through on-line shopping) and services (including access to information databases). ■ Products can be **ordered** via the Net. ■ Some can also be **delivered** via the Net, by downloading direct to the purchaser's PC: examples include music, computer software, Clipart, product catalogues and instruction manuals.
Partnership development	■ Strategic promotional collaborations with synergistic content-specific sites or 'portals' (search engines, Web directories or other high-traffic sites such as Yahoo!, Excite or MSN)
Customer service and **technical support**	■ E-mail contact, ■ FAQs (frequently asked questions), ■ Access to databased information ■ On-line messaging or voice interruption for interactive support.
Market/customer research	■ Gathering information on customers and visitors for the purposes of market segmentation, personalisation/customisation of future contacts. ■ Site monitoring ■ On-line or e-mailed feedback questionnaires and surveys.
Corporate identity	■ Web site and e-mail messages must be designed to create a unified and coherent marketing message alongside all other marketing messages for **marketing synergy**.

Advantages of Internet promotion

4.5 *The Unofficial Guide to Marketing Your Business On-Line* suggests a number of reasons why the Internet is attractive to marketing organisations of all sizes in virtually all industries.

- The **initial costs** for creating a basic Internet presence are relatively low. Even without developing a Web site or e-commerce site (deigned to sell products and services), organisations can market on-line via e-mail.
- The Internet has a potential **reach** of millions of consumers.
- The Internet can also be used for targeted **niche marketing**, since the technology facilitates reaching small (even individual) audiences according to specifically defined criteria, including **actual** contact/purchase behaviours (rather than stated preferences).
- The Internet is active **24-7**.
- The Internet creates a **global market place** and customer base, abolishing geographical barriers to promotion (if not to fulfilment).
- Internet advertising is **highly interactive** and so offers potentially **instant results**. People can respond to an ad instantly by clicking – and are then 'transported' to the relevant Web site for immediate access to information, contacts and (increasingly) transaction processing facilities.
- On-line promotion can be **accurately monitored** and evaluated: who is visiting the site, when, for how long, what information is sought, what products are ordered. This feedback can be used to adjust the marketing message: customising, storing preferences for the next visit and so on.
- Web sites are highly **versatile** (as shown in their promotion mix applications listed above).

Potential barriers to Internet promotion

4.6 Krol and Ferguson *(The Whole Internet)* argue that a key issue in commercial use of the Internet is 'how to do business **in tune with the Internet's culture**. Although the culture is under stress and changing all the time, there is still a lot of sentiment on the Internet against blatant commercialism... The Internet culture isn't necessarily opposed to advertising, but it demands that you view **advertising as an information service**. You can make marketing data available, but you can't force it on people. There would be nothing wrong, in terms of policy or culture, with an auto manufacturer putting up a server with pictures of its cars, technical data sheets and information about options. If an Internet user wanted to buy a car, they could comparison shop from a computer terminal, decide on a prospect and visit one dealer, rather than three, to do a test drive. In the future, you might even be able to do your test drive over the Internet via a virtual-reality simulation. Even so, we're all trying to avoid a situation in which we're deluged with unsolicited e-mail selling everything from vinyl siding to sexy underwear.'

On-line shopping

Key Concept

E-commerceis an abbreviation of 'electronic commerce': it means business transactions carried out on-line via the Internet.

4.7 The Internet is, subject to a few remaining security concerns, a potential means of **direct selling and distribution** to potential customers. A transaction-based Web site is a virtual warehouse (or supermarket, or bookstore – or whatever its creators wish). Customers can take a virtual browsing tour; download catalogues; explore products; put items in 'shopping baskets'; process to 'checkout' and pay by debit or credit card (in some cases with one click of the mouse, enabled by databased customer details); select delivery options; print out accompanying documentation; monitor the progress of their order; receive e-mailed confirmations and notifications and so on.

4.8 The uptake of interactive on-line purchasing was initially slow, mainly due to consumer perceptions about **security**. People appear more reluctant to supply credit card details over the Internet than over the phone or postal system: despite the illogic, this is a genuine market dynamic, which requires education, reassurance and the development of tighter security controls. On-going developments in encryption (coding) software, together with gradual habituation, is likely to overcome consumer inhibitions.

4.9 Although on-line shopping has not lived up to initial (inflated) forecasts, surveys now suggest that it is growing at a steady rate, particularly in the business-to-business market and for products such as niche market/rare items (such as craft supplies and out of print books), books, CD/cassettes, software, transport/travel and groceries. (You will need to monitor the quality press and marketing magazines for up-to-date figures and projections.)

Marketing at Work

Woolworths supermarkets in Australia recently launched its 'Home Shop' programme, with a deliberately user-friendly information brochure.

www.woolworths.com.au

Convenience at your fingertips

- Shop from your home, office, or from anywhere you have internet access.
- Have your supermarket shopping, including liquor, delivered direct to your door.

It's so easy

- Access www.woolworths.com.au
- Fill in a simple electronic form to obtain a secure user ID and password.
- Log in and shop.

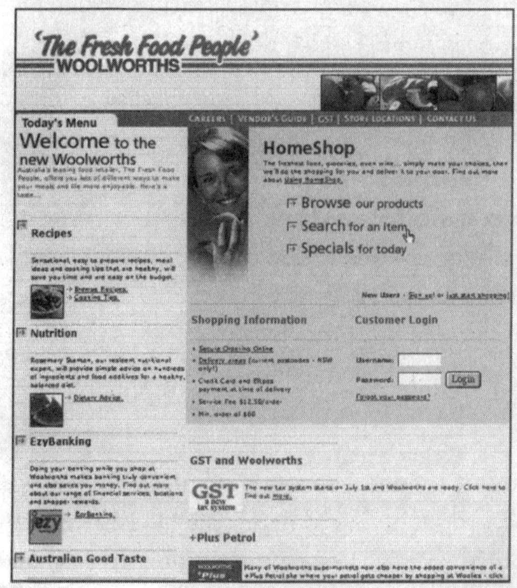

How it works

- Browse and view individual products.
- Create and save your own shopping list/s on-line.
- View on-line recipes and ingredient information.
- View your 'trolley' contents and spend at any time.
- Supermarket specials apply!

Then what?

- Your order is hand-picked by our staff.
- It's delivered to your door in refrigerated vans at a time convenient to you.

Minimum orders and charges

- The minimum order is $60.
- A flat $12.50 service fee covers picking, packing and delivery.

Payment

- Payment is made to your delivery driver using any one of the following methods, through a mobile Eftpos unit: MasterCard, eftpos, VISA

Find out more

- Visit www. woolworths.com.au

4.10 Benefits of on-line shopping for consumers

- Saving time on travel, parking and the location of items
- Greater variety of products to choose from (including worldwide directories of suppliers)
- Ability to browse, watch demonstrations, interrogate databases, get technical advice (etc) from the comfort of one's own computer
- Filling 'shopping trolleys' without physical exertion
- Instant access to services (for example in banking, ticket reservations)
- Less environmental impact (traffic, pollution, construction)

Action Programme 6

What are the benefits of on-line shopping or e-commerce for the marketing organisation?

4.11 Limitations and drawbacks of on-line shopping

- High set-up costs
- Customers may suffer from 'technophobia' or security concerns
- Lack of personal contact, which may be important to customer satisfaction and loyalty (particularly among less technology-accustomed market segments)
- Some products have selling attributes not readily conveyed on-line: smell and taste, for example, are powerful purchase motivators used by supermarkets; tactile values (in toilet tissues, clothing fabrics) may also be a factor in the purchase decision
- The erosion of traditional shopping patterns may have a destabilising effect on communities, through small business failure, downturn in commercial property values, loss of retail jobs and so on.

Action Programme 7

If you have access to the Internet, check out the recommended 'case sites' listed at the beginning of this Study Text (if you haven't done so already). What makes these effective promotional and commercial tools?

There are also on-line 'mega malls' with vast product ranges. These are great if you enjoy browsing and shopping – but rather frustrating if you are trying to find something specific. Having sampled the world of personalised, targeted shopping at an on-line store like Amazon, try the world of one-stop unfocused shopping: www.internet-mall.com.

[Key Skill for Marketers: Using ICT and the Internet]

4.12 Schenk and English suggest the following checklist to decide whether e-commerce is suitable for a business.

- Is the product or service easily explained via written description/photos?
- Is the product easy and affordable to package and ship – to a global market?
- Does the product require only limited after-sales support?
- Is the risk relatively low if a customer makes an ordering mistake?
- It the product or service unique or difficult to find? (If it is readily available in the local shops, added incentives to purchase on-line will be needed)
- Will customers be willing to pay for shipping (or can the organisation afford to absorb shipping costs)?
- Is the organisation ready for the administrative reality of marketing on-line? (Taking credit cards, inputting data, packing and despatch, billing, fraud prevention etc etc – all on a potentially frequent basis...)

4.13 As an alternative to e-commerce through the organisation's own transaction-based Web site, the following options may be considered.

(a) **Storefronts**: getting online stores such as Amazon or Yahoo! to catalogue and sell your products or services on-line through their sites. (In other words, an online distribution channel, with the associated benefits – and the drawbacks of competing with other brands, losing margins and so on.)

(b) **Auction sites**: putting merchandise (surplus products, used products, limited-supply items and so on) up for auction on sites such as eBay. Most auction sites charge a transaction fee, but the marketing organisation has no processing costs: it merely has to set a 'reserve' (lowest acceptable) price, writing a marketing blurb and upload pictures for the auction site, and ship out the product when sold. Products may be put up for auction for promotional purposes, using the blurb, photos and a link to the company's own Web site. Check out: www.ebay.com.

5 Developing Web sites

5.1 Web sites are now a key form of corporate communication. Almost every major company has some type of Web presence. Increasingly, advertisers are using Web sites as key marketing tools – and using their conventional media advertising (especially print) to point consumers to the Web site. (Some print/poster ads now simply feature a prominent Web address.)

Designing and effective Web site

5.2 Web site design is a relatively new skill and the technology is constantly changing. The following, however, are some of the key issues.

Design issue	Comment
■ **House style**	The web-site should be consistent with corporate identity guidelines and other promotional messages.
■ **Interest**	The web site should offer content that is relevant, original or regularly changing/expanding, in order to encourage repeat visits. This may be product information, links, news features, free e-cards or chat communities.
■ **Interactivity** (and/or entertainment)	Colour, graphics, audio, video and movement add impact and entertainment value. Information can be presented as database applications, search tools, notice boards, calculators and other interactive formats.
■ **'Stickiness'**	A web site 'stickiness' refers to (a) how often visitors return to a site and (b) how long they spend there. Stickiness can be improved by continually updated content, and also by promotional techniques such as chat rooms, games and reviews. Keeping visitors longer at the site gives you more time to build up awareness, and gives them more time to take in promotional messages and/or make purchases.

Design issue	Comment
■ **Credibility**	Web sites often contain 'about us' pages to bolster consumer confidence (and public relations) by providing information about the company.
■ **Transaction efficiency**	As well as encouraging 'browsing' with mechanisms such as virtual 'shopping trolleys' and 'wish lists', websites can offer 1-Click or other convenient order mechanisms, automatic e-mail order confirmations and order tracing. A secure site for transactions (using various forms of encryption) is also important.
■ **Personal contact**	People may have questions not answered on the site – or may just wish to talk to a human being for a change. Providing phone, mail and e-mail contact details enhances the 'personalisation' of the site.
■ **Personalisation/ relationship marketing**	As well as page and information customisation (using Cookies), websites can be used to develop two-way relationships by offering e-mailed newsletters, product updates and promotions.
■ **Facilitate navigation**	The structure and signposting of the site (a site 'map', home page, menus, search engines, instructions) help the user to find the information (s)he is looking for.
■ **Facilitate the experience**	The proliferation of technological advancements give the marketer amazing tools for presenting impactful promotional messages. However, these will not be effective if the user does not have the ability to access the format. Site designers need to enable users to download the tools to receive fast-loading visual and audio effects. Common free plug-ins include Macromedia Flash (animated graphics), Real Player (realtime or streaming media) and Adobe Acrobat.
■ **Maintenance**	It is very frustrating (and creates a poor image) to find a site no longer in use, or out of date.

Marketing at Work

Here are some 'snapshots' of various Web pages, to stimulate your thinking as to the different audiences, purposes and styles for which Web sites can cater.

(a) www.ex.ac.uk/flc/germlet

[An extremely user-friendly page for students of all ages. Each of the phrases shown is a hypertext link to the information listed.]

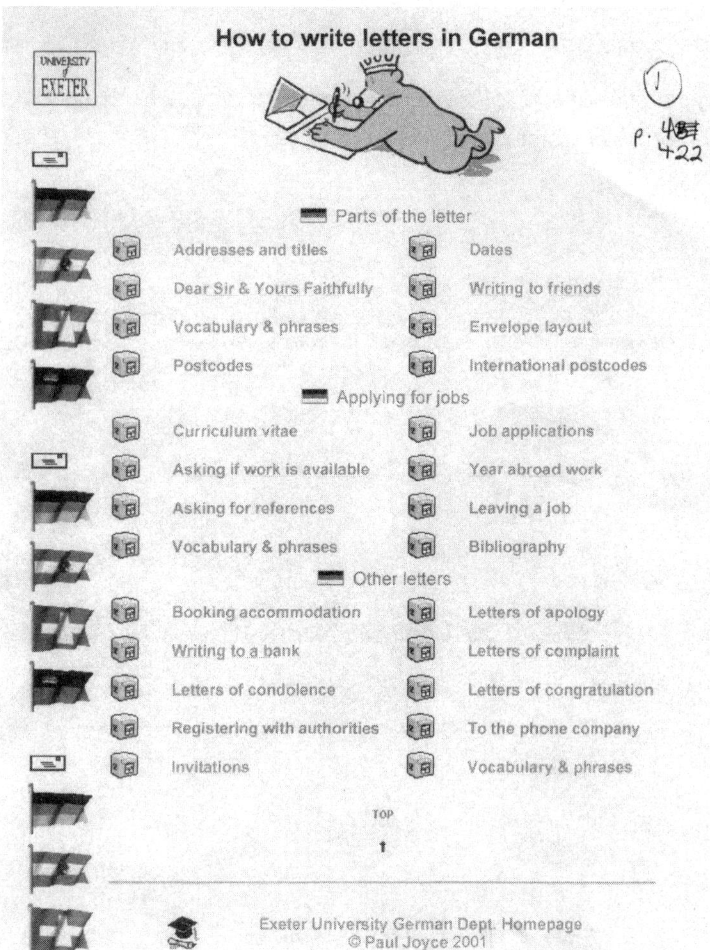
How to write letters in German
UNIVERSITY of EXETER
Parts of the letter
Addresses and titles
Dates
Dear Sir & Yours Faithfully
Writing to friends
Vocabulary & phrases
Envelope layout
Postcodes
International postcodes
Applying for jobs
Curriculum vitae
Job applications
Asking if work is available
Year abroad work
Asking for references
Leaving a job
Vocabulary & phrases
Bibliography
Other letters
Booking accommodation
Letters of apology
Writing to a bank
Letters of complaint
Letters of condolence
Letters of congratulation
Registering with authorities
To the phone company
Invitations
Vocabulary & phrases
TOP
Exeter University German Dept. Homepage
© Paul Joyce 2001

(b) www.fedex.com/gb/

[A highly functional site, allowing customers to access tracking data for parcels: in effect, self-serve customer service]

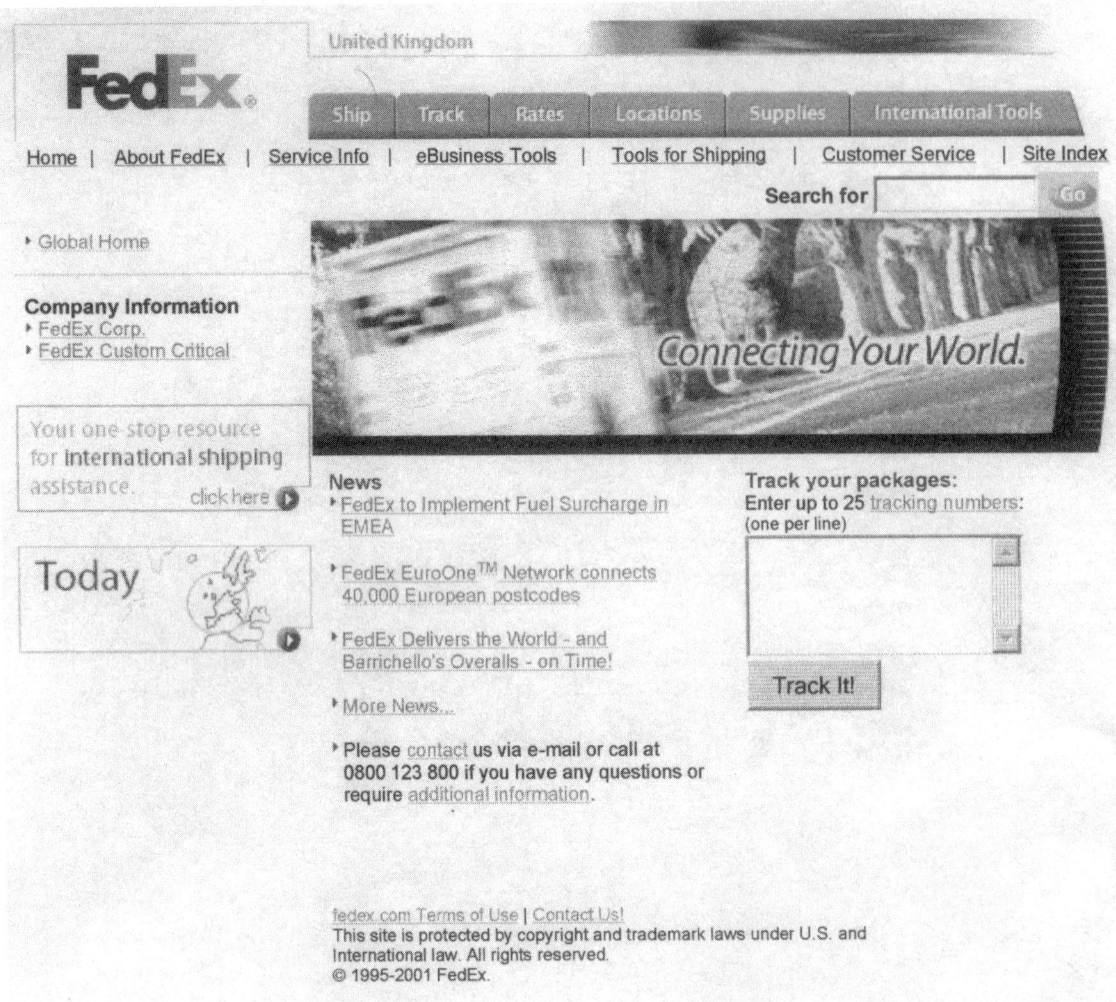

(c) optusnet.excite.com.au/shopping/

[Just one portal into the world of e-commerce...]

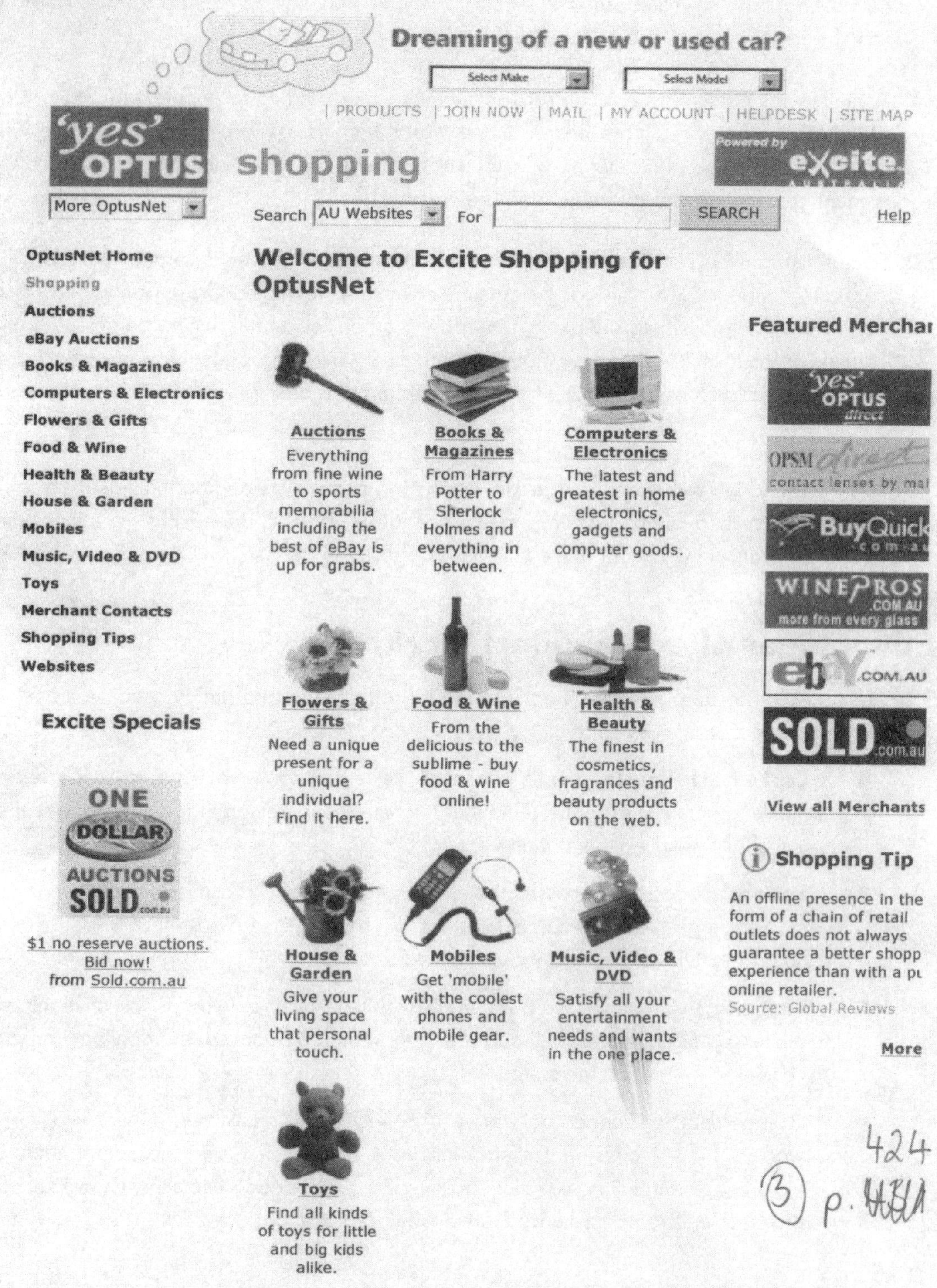

424
③ p.

6 E-mail marketing

6.1 We mentioned e-mail as a communication tool in Section 2 of this Chapter, and will be discussing how to compose and structure e-mail messages in Chapter 12. Here we will emphasise its use as a promotional tool.

6.2 E-mail is one of the most popular uses of the Internet. According to Allen et al *(One to One Web Marketing)*: 'There are more people in the world with access to e-mail than with access to the World Wide Web. This means **e-mail marketing** can grab attention and interest without requiring users to even start their Web browsers.'

6.3 E-mail list can be obtained by buying or renting suitably targeted/segmented lists (of willing subscribers) from list brokers or permission marketing agencies. Organisations can also build their own lists, by inviting people to subscribe to an on-line e-mail list (to participate in two-way discussion or receive one-way announcements) or by inputting customer and contact data from other sources (such as trade exhibitions, sales promotions and so on).

6.4 Various software-based tools exist to enable marketing organisations to maintain and manage e-mail lists and to send **mass mailings** (batched to avoid over-loading individual servers). There are even tools available on-line, free of charge (but supported through the placing of advertisements at the bottom of the e-mail messages).

Advantages of e-mail direct marketing

6.5 Using e-mail as an alternative to (or support for) direct mail and direct response advertising has the following advantages.

- **Cost-effectiveness**. E-mail is one of the least expensive ways to reach people in a highly targeted, personalised manner – whether one person in the office across the hall or millions of people all over the world.
- **Speed of delivery/response**. Apart from instant transmission (unlike postal direct mail packages), most e-mail campaigns are said to elicit 5% of their responses within 24 hours and 15% of their responses within 72 hours.
- **Targeting**. E-mail messages can be written for the interests of a highly targeted audience, using integrated address books and databased information to personalise content for individual recipients.
- **Acceptability**. 'People look forward to receiving e-mail from friends, relatives and co-workers. This means that their attitude is more open and accepting than in more advertising-oriented media, such as advertising-supported Web sites, as well as traditional print and electronic media and direct mail.' (Allen et al)

Action Programme 8

What would be the main marketing purpose of creating personalised ('one-to-one') e-mail campaigns?

Potential barriers to e-mail marketing

6.6 Almost all commentators on e-mail marketing note the fine line that exists between legitimate use of the medium and 'spam': unsolicited, untargeted mass e-mail broadcasts. Much of the controversy comes from companies 'harvesting' e-mail addresses from Web pages, discussion lists, newsgroups and other sources and using them to target users. (It is now illegal in the UK to disclose or sell these addresses to third parties without users' permission.) Spam not only annoys recipients (and the complaint departments of their Internet Service Providers), but frequently causes network traffic problems.

6.7 There are ongoing debates among industry, users and government bodies on setting guidelines for e-mail broadcasting: meanwhile, mail management software offers 'filtering' products – and some cyber-activists have resorted to blocking postings. In fact, a very high percentage of users simply delete spam without reading the message (and a significant percentage actively retaliate against the spammer).

6.8 Allen et al quote the judgement of one senior marketing professional: 'Spam makes you look cheap and sleazy in the eyes of many people online... Regardless of how targeted, relevant or informative you think your message is, unless the recipient specifically agreed to receive the information, you risk alienating a portion of your audience.' Not a recommended marketing communications technique!

Action Programme 9

What steps could you take to ensure that e-mail marketing campaigns overcome consumer resistance to spam? Write a set of guidelines for staff.

7 The speed of change

7.1 Everything in the world of telecommunications and the Internet is changing at the speed of light. New technologies are introduced every day; companies and brands emerge and disappear seemingly overnight in the dot.com marketplace; projections for the penetration of e-commerce (and/or its collapse) vary widely.

7.2 You will be expected to show an awareness of the **dynamic nature of change** in this area – and to keep abreast of developments. You **must** supplement your reading of this Study Text (and other books) with a regular diet of browsing in the quality press, appropriate marketing magazines and their Web equivalents (as well as drawing on your own experience of e-marketing and e-commerce.)

Chapter Roundup

- Communication has changed in recent decades with the development of technologies offering:
  - Higher speed
  - Wider access to information
  - 24-hour, 7-day global communication (and commerce)
  - Greater interactivity and multi-media presentation
  - Greater personalisation/customisation of communication
- These developments impact on marketing across the promotions mix
- Developments in telecommunications include **infrastructure** developments, facilitating the speed, amount and versatility of data transmission (ISDN, digital networks, satellite, increased 'band' width) and **equipment** developments, delivering end-user access (fax, mobile communications, e-mail, e-commerce and electronic data interchange)
- Digital technology has increased the number and variety of media channels and the services they can offer to audiences
- The Internet is used to disseminate and exchange information among the public at large. An Intranet can be used to perform the same function within an organisation, and an extranet within a network of selected customers, prospects, members or business partners.
- The Internet (with related tools such as e-mail and Web-site marketing) is a complex and powerful promotional tool for a wide range of promotional activities.

Quick Quiz

1 Which of the following is not part of the ICT infrastructure?

A ISDN
B Increased 'band width'
C E-mail
D Satellite transmission

2 What three things are implied by the concept of 'interactivity' in the sense in which new technology offers it?

3 The CIM's Virtual Institute Web site is an example of:

Internet	Intranet	Extranet

4 E-mail is cheaper than fax for transmitting hard copy messages to remote locations.

☐ True ☐ False

5 What do the following stand for?

(1) e-mail
(2) v-mail
(3) m-commerce
(4) SMS
(5) EDI
(6) DRTV

6 A set of statistical techniques used to identify trends, patterns and relationships in data is called:

A Database
B Data warehousing
C Datamining
D Data interchange

7 Which of the following qualities (you may select more than one) is enhanced by digital television, compared to analogue television?

- Number of services
- Flexibility of scheduling
- Interactivity
- Targeting of programme content

8 The system of linking documents stored on host computers via 'hypertext' is called:

☐ The Internet ☐ The World Wide Web

9 Giving Web site visitors communication tools which they are encouraged to send to others, requiring the recipient to visit the site in turn, is called .... marketing.

10 Which of the following is likely to be the most effective promotional tool?

A SMS
B SPAM
C SWIFT
D ISDN

Answers to Quick Quiz

1 C

2 Speed of dialogue/response; up-to-dateness of information; flexibility/scope of response

3 Extranet

4 True

5 (1) electronic mail
(2) voice mail
(3) mobile commerce
(4) Short Message Service
(5) Electronic Data Interchange
(6) Direct Response Television

6 C

7 All options

8 The World Wide Web

9 Viral

10 A

Now try Question 8 from the Question Bank at the end of this Text

Action Programme Review

1 Consider yourself a market research subject! Your own experience of how technology impacts on you as an individual, student and consumer/customer will be an important source of relevant and continually up-to-date information on this topic.

2 Marketing organisations can use this accessibility for:

- Their own research requirements (secondary data, market and competitor information)
- Promotion: providing information services to customers and browsers (e-mail, information site sponsorship, information/links on their own Web site)

Challenges. Networking can be used to spread positive – or negative 'word of mouth' publicity about brands and organisations. Information-rich market: may be harder to differentiate own product, and to persuade customers to buy without providing in-depth product information.

3 Virtual communities can be used to:

- Underpin the personalisation of promotional messages/relationship marketing
- Enhance customer relations (and the stickiness of Web sites) by offering opportunities for customers to see shopping/browsing as a social activity (eg free e-cards, chat rooms, discussion boards and so on)
- Facilitate the contracting out of marketing services (especially to overseas facilities), since in cyberspace, it does not mater where the message originated
- Gather customer information by inviting subscription to e-mail discussion lists
- Gather customer feedback through forums (chat rooms, message boards and so on)

4 The content of your answer will depend on the particular system you have chosen to research. For the sake of communication practice, do attempt your answer in the formats requested.

5 Australian SMS marketing service IDStxtra (*SMS: Get the Message*, 2002) suggests the following ways to use SMS as an effective marketing tool.

- *Instant win game of change***.** Product packaging contains unique Instant Win numbers relating to specific prizes. Customers SMS the number to receive automatic responses.
- *Discount coupon distribution.* Product advertising encourages buyers to receive discount coupons by sending SMS messages: discount m-coupons are sent by automatic reply.

- *Ring-tones and logos.* Where brands are connected with cartoon characters, graphics or jingles/tunes, these can be down-loaded for use on the phone, reinforcing brand recognition.
- *Quizzes and games.* Product advertising has fun quiz or game elements: users are encouraged to interact by receiving clues or answering multiple choice questions.
- *Information update service.* Added value for customer care or loyalty programmes: eg SMS used to inform passengers of changes/delays in travel arrangements.
- *Customer Relationship Management (CRM).* Can replace bulk outbound phone calls by call centre agents, when outbound information is simple and instant response is required.
- *Location specific marketing.* Messaging of relevant information based on user address *or* handset location: eg offering discounted tickets of local screenings to members of a cinema loyalty club.
- *Database development.* All mobile numbers can be captured: SMS is an ideal way to build a customer database. (If these are to be used for outbound marketing, this should be clearly stated in advertising, with notes on privacy, to ensure compliance with data security requirements.)

6 Opportunities to gather customer data; opportunities to target (segment or one-to-one(promotional messages; opportunities to establish relationship marketing; opportunities to reach customers with a variety of promotional messages and services; reduced costs of stock holding, staffing, transaction processing and retail outlets.

7 If you want to do a more systematic evaluation of these sites' effectiveness, you might work your way through the checklist in Section 7 of this chapter.

8 According to Allen et al, 'the primary benefits of one-to-one e-mail include its ability to form a lasting relationship with a customer, increase repeat purchases or visits, and provide an inexpensive "push" mechanism in which the information is pushed out to the user, rather than requiring the user to remember to come visit your Web site.'

9 **E-MAIL MARKETING – NOT SPAM!**

(a) Use e-mail sparingly

(b) Develop a message that caters directly to the interests of the intended recipients

(c) Beware campaigns that will be perceived as a scam: if you make an offer, make sure you follow through

(d) Make sure the subject line and introductory sentences are short, catchy and to the point (grabbing interest before the message goes in the recycling bin...)

(e) Be transparent: clearly disclose the sender and consider putting the work 'advertisement' in the subject line of the e-mail

(f) Format your message so that it's easy to read on the computer screen (using different reading programs) and in printout

(g) Either make your message short and to the point, or supply worthwhile editorial content (as in an electronic newsletter or e-zine)

(h) Personalise the e-mail where possible

(i) Don't include attachments: this is one of the most common ways computer viruses are spread, and files with attachments are often blocked

(j) Emphasise that you will not be selling or distributing your e-mail list to other companies – and follow through on all privacy promises

(k) Give recipients the option to have their name deleted from your mailing list (both for their sake and yours) and make the opt-out easy (via a hyperlink or clear instructions)

(l) Pre-test the campaign on a sample list

Part D

Face-to-face communication

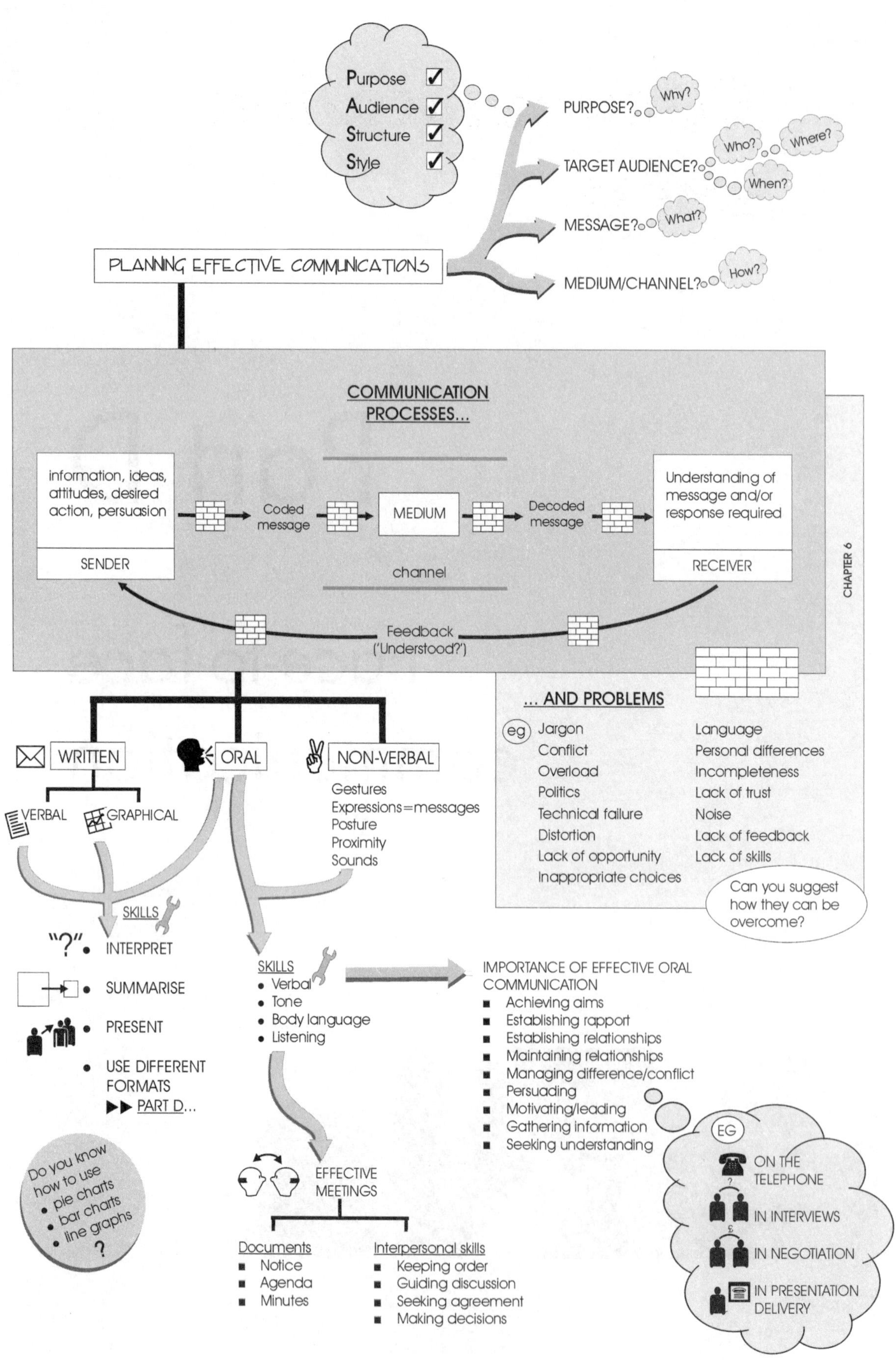

Purpose
Audience
Structure
Style
PURPOSE?
Why?
TARGET AUDIENCE?
Who?
Where?
When?
MESSAGE?
What?
MEDIUM/CHANNEL?
How?
PLANNING EFFECTIVE COMMUNICATIONS
COMMUNICATION PROCESSES...
information, ideas, attitudes, desired action, persuasion
SENDER
Coded message
MEDIUM
channel
Decoded message
Understanding of message and/or response required
RECEIVER
Feedback ('Understood?')
... AND PROBLEMS
eg
Jargon
Conflict
Overload
Politics
Technical failure
Distortion
Lack of opportunity
Inappropriate choices
Language
Personal differences
Incompleteness
Lack of trust
Noise
Lack of feedback
Lack of skills
Can you suggest how they can be overcome?
WRITTEN
ORAL
NON-VERBAL
VERBAL
GRAPHICAL
Gestures
Expressions=messages
Posture
Proximity
Sounds
SKILLS
"?"
INTERPRET
SUMMARISE
PRESENT
USE DIFFERENT FORMATS
▶▶ PART D...
SKILLS
Verbal
Tone
Body language
Listening
IMPORTANCE OF EFFECTIVE ORAL COMMUNICATION
Achieving aims
Establishing rapport
Establishing relationships
Maintaining relationships
Managing difference/conflict
Persuading
Motivating/leading
Gathering information
Seeking understanding
EG
ON THE TELEPHONE
IN INTERVIEWS
IN NEGOTIATION
IN PRESENTATION DELIVERY
Do you know how to use
pie charts
bar charts
line graphs
?
EFFECTIVE MEETINGS
Documents
Notice
Agenda
Minutes
Interpersonal skills
Keeping order
Guiding discussion
Seeking agreement
Making decisions

CHAPTER 6

Communication skills

9

Chapter Topic List	
1	Setting the scene
2	Identifying and overcoming barriers to communication
3	Verbal skills
4	Listening skills
5	Non-verbal communication
6	Improving your skills

Learning Outcomes

☑ Be able to identify and suggest ways of overcoming barriers to effective communication

☑ Understand the skills involved in oral and face-to-face communication

☑ Explain the importance of effective listening and non-verbal skills

☑ Develop strategies to improve your oral and face-to-face communication skills

Syllabus References

☑ Describe the communication process (4.1)

☑ Identify barriers to communication and explain how they can be avoided and overcome (4.2)

☑ Explain the importance of effective body language, tone, verbal and listening skills in communication and strategies for developing and improving verbal, non-verbal and listening skills (4.4)

Key Concepts Introduced

- Distortion
- Noise
- Empathy
- Non-verbal communication

1 Setting the scene

1.1 In Part D of this Text, we turn to some more general communication skills, techniques and formats: not specifically part of the promotional mix, but applicable to a wide range of internal and external communication situations.

1.2 That is why Part D is longer than its 10% syllabus weighting would indicate. The skills, techniques and formats described here will:

- Underpin your the implementation of other, more directly promotional, communications
- Enable you to engage effectively in a wider range of internal and external business relationships and interactions involved in marketing activity
- Enable you to convey the subject matter of your exam answers in the variety of **specific formats required**. (Absolutely essential for exam success!)

1.3 In this chapter, we revisit the communication process introduced in Chapter 4, and discuss a range of face-to-face communication skills.

1.4 In Chapter 10, we revisit the planning process used in Part C to implement elements of the promotional mix, to suggest how **any message** can be planned for maximum effectiveness – advertisements or client presentations, an e-mail to your boss or a discussion with a colleague.

1.5 In Chapters 11, 12 and 13, we look at specific forms, formats and techniques of communication which you might use in a range of marketing activities.

Exam Tip

Most of the questions set for this exam ask you to show that you can do something practical like write a letter in the context of a specific scenario. However, it is not enough just to be able to paraphrase the wording of the question in proper letter format (though proper formats are important). You are also expected to have a broad understanding of the communication process, and of the reasoning behind different aspects and features of business communications.

Practical 'Write a letter ... ' 'Prepare visual aids ... ' 'Analyse the figures ... '	**Theoretical** 'Explain how communication barriers can be overcome ... ' 'Explain the effect of body language ... '
Practical and theoretical 'Write a newspaper **article** on the importance of **logos and letterheads** ... ' 'Provide **guidelines** for the production of **meetings documentation** ... ' 'Write a **memo** about inconsistency in the **appearance and tone** of business letters...'	

As you can see, you not only need to be able to communicate in a variety of ways, but also to explain how and why certain business communications take the form they do.

Back to the communication process

1.6 The following (Figure 9.1) is a recap of the communication process. If none of it looks familiar, we suggest you refresh you memory by referring back to Chapter 4 before proceeding.

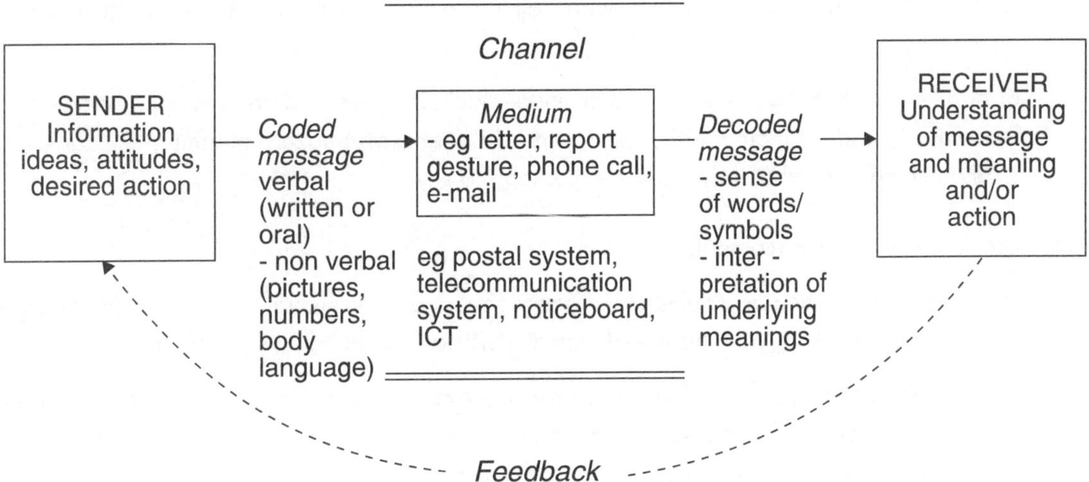

Figure 9.1 The communication process

2 Identifying and overcoming barriers to communication

2.1 Unfortunately, things are rarely so simple. If you've ever been misunderstood, or misunderstood someone else; if you've ever asked someone to do something, and they haven't done it; if you've ever had a bad phone line or Internet connection – you probably realise that there are a number of potential problems in the communication process.

2.2 Two technical terms are used to describe such problems or breakdowns in communication:

- Distortion, and
- Noise

Distortion

Key Concept

Distortion refers to the way in which the **meaning** of a communication is lost in 'handling'

2.3 Distortion occurs largely at the encoding and decoding stages of communication, where:

- The precise **intention** of the sender (what he wants to communicate) is not **translated** accurately into language, so that the 'wrong' message is sent
- The language used is not properly **understood** by the receiver, so that the 'wrong' message is received

2.4 Foreign or regionally-specific language, incorrect use of a word, technical or otherwise obscure terms (jargon), unfamiliar and unexplained pictures or diagrams, or words/pictures with more than one possible interpretation: these can all be sources of distortion, even when both parties are **trying** to understand and make themselves understood. Each party may simply have failed to take into account (a) **who** they were talking to, and (b) the **context or situation** within which they were talking.

In addition, **differing** opinions and attitudes, lack of concentration or co-operation can set up **barriers** to understanding: either party may **deliberately** make a meaning unclear, or choose to understand only what they want the message to say.

2.5 Distortion can be overcome if:

(a) The communicator **chooses** his language and symbols with a view to his **purpose** in communicating, and the **needs and abilities** (or limitations) of the intended recipient

(b) Both communicator and recipient are **aware** of the potential for distortion (intentionally or unintentionally) caused by their limitations: wrong use of vocabulary or technology, unchecked assumptions about the other party, underlying attitudes/ feelings emerging in (or read into) tone of voice, misuse of sarcasm or humour and so on

(c) The communicator seeks, and the recipient gives, constant **feedback**, so that points of misunderstanding can be checked out, assumptions come to light and so on

Noise

Key Concept

Noise refers to distractions and interference in the environment in which communication takes place, obstructing the **process** of communication by affecting the accuracy, clarity or even the arrival of the message.

2.6 Noise can take the following forms.

(a) **Physical noise**, such as other people talking in the room, passing traffic or the clatter of machinery, can prevent a message from being heard, or heard clearly.

(b) **Technical noise** involves a failure in the **channel or medium** of communication while information is being transmitted. A breakdown in a computer printer, a crackle on a telephone line or bad handwriting may prevent an effective exchange of information from taking place.

(c) **Social noise** is interference created by differences in the personality, culture or outlook of the sender and recipient. It includes difficulties in communication experienced by members of different social classes, old and young, male and female, boss and subordinate.

(d) **Psychological noise**, such as excessive emotion (say, anger or fear), prejudice or nervousness, can also interfere with the effective transmission of a message: the meaning may get clouded by irrelevant expressions of emotion or attitude, or the message may reach the recipient in a garbled state (because of a nervous stammer or angry spluttering, perhaps).

2.7 The problem of noise can be reduced by **redundancy**: using more than one channel of communication, so that if a message fails to get through by one channel, it may succeed by another. A spoken comment might be **confirmed** by an appropriate gesture, an agreement or decision made by telephone or at a meeting can be backed up by issuing a letter, or minutes. Communicators must, however, be aware of possible sources of noise in their situation: a bustling office is not the place for a confidential discussion; a computer printer which produces poor quality graphics should not be used for important presentation diagrams; a hot-tempered person with known racial and sexual prejudices should not be appointed to conduct job interviews.

Action Programme 1

Redraw the communication cycle from Figure 9.1 to show noise and distortion. Make your diagram clear enough to use as a presentation slide.

Exam Tip

It is worth learning diagrams such as those of the communications process shown above and it is also worth seeing if you can produce your own variations emphasising different features. For instance questions have asked students to draw diagrams indicating where noise can occur in the communications process or showing what barriers there might be in internal communication in an organisation.

Communication barriers have featured in exam questions very regularly, but different specific contexts: a presentation to overseas visitors, for example, or (December 2000) how distortion might affect an advertising message.

Get used to scanning marketing communications for examples of barriers – and to applying the basic theories discussed here to specific contexts.

Personal differences

2.8 There are many factors in an individual's personality, mentality, experience and environment which make him unique - and can therefore cause distortion or noise in the communication process. Here are just a few of them.

(a) Racial, ethnic or regional **origins**: there are cultural and linguistic implications, but also 'political' implications for the status and perception of 'alien' or minority groups.

(b) **Social class** and socio-economic groupings, with their different values, opportunities and therefore expectations

(c) **Education and training** - to different levels, and in different specialisms

(d) **Age** - with its physiological implications (for hearing, sight, mobility etc) as well as differences in experience, and therefore in values and attitudes, language and culture, skills (eg in new technology) and so on

(e) **Gender** - as well as physiological and psychological differences, there are social factors and customs (such as sexual discrimination and harassment, family rôle expectations and so on)

(f) **Occupation or profession** - offering different opportunities for experience and knowledge, different motivations and different degrees of perceived social standing and value

National/cultural differences

2.9 **Language** itself becomes a serious barrier to communication when people from different countries try to communicate. If you are not based in the UK and/or if English is not your first language, you will be acutely aware of this even as you read this book.

2.10 English is well established as the international business language, but **cultural differences** still interfere with the communication process. For example there are considerable differences between what is regarded as an acceptable degree of politeness in different national cultures, such that what may be normal in Japan, say, might appear, when translated into English, to be far too formal, especially to someone from Australia or America. We discuss these differences further in Chapter 10.

Marketing at Work

A 'smiling school' was recently opened in Japan, to teach Japanese business people and customer service professional how to smile in the Western way. Research had showed that a smile increased sales, but facial expressions in the Far East are different: students are asked to study pictures, grip chopsticks in their teeth, and massage their cheeks and mouth corners upwards in order to learn the Western communication technique.

Other potential problems

2.11 Other potential problems in the communication process include the following.

(a) **Not communicating** (bear in mind that even 'tactful' or 'thoughtful' silences are open to misinterpretation)

(b) Sending the **'wrong' message** - ie one that is meaningless, irrelevant or unsuitable to the purpose, recipient and context of the communication (as discussed in Chapter 10)

(c) **Omission** of information by the sender, which may result in **inaccuracy** (rendering the information useless) or **incompleteness** (rendering the information hard to understand)

(d) **'Overload'** - giving the recipient more information than he can digest in the time available or for his required purpose. (This is often a problem in internal communication, especially from employees who deal with the 'nuts and bolts' of work and managers who deal with the 'bigger picture'. This is why summarising data is an important skill, covered in Chapter 13.)

(e) **Non-verbal signals** (gestures, facial expression, appearance, posture etc) contradicting the verbal message, confusing the recipient (we discuss this later in this chapter).

(f) **Poor listening or reading skills**: inattention, loss of concentration, or passive uncritical reception. (Note that **listening** involves paying attention and attending to the message; without this element it is just **hearing**. We discuss this later in this chapter.)

(g) Failure to seek or offer **feedback**, or ignoring feedback offered

(h) **Lack of credibility** - because of poor preparation or presentation, perhaps

Action Programme 2

Consider how the problems discussed above might be applicable to - or even aggravated in – **internal** customer communications given the typical conditions and relationships within a business organisation

Overcoming barriers

2.12 To an extent, the nature of the barrier suggests the solution. Broadly, however, effective communication requires the following.

(a) **Planning**: taking into account

- The **purpose** or objectives of the communication
- The needs, abilities, limitations and interests of the target **audience** or recipient
- The most appropriate **channel, medium, structure** and **style** of message for the purpose and audience

(b) **Seeking and receiving feedback**, so that potential barriers can be identified and communication strategies adapted accordingly.

(c) **Rapport and trust**: to break down barriers of difference and create co-operation in the process of communication.

(d) **Efficient communication mechanisms and channels**: sufficient lines for customer calls, well designed web site, email facility, databased mailing lists and so on. For internal communications, particular emphasis may need to be placed on creating systems for **upward** communication: team meetings, suggestion schemes or collaborative problem-solving approach to appraisal schemes and so on.

(e) **Communication and interpersonal skills**: staff trained in listening, rapport-building, assertiveness, conflict resolution, persuasion, courteous service, telephone technique, giving presentations, managing discussions and so on. (We will be discussing and practising some of these skills in later chapters.)

2.13 We will now go on to look at some of the key skills in effective face-to-face communication.

Exam Tip

Material in this chapter is not likely to be examined directly. However, it is essentially background for a variety of questions, for instance if you were asked to advise a colleague who has difficulty with oral communication, write an article about talking to customers in a company newsletter; prepare slides for a presentation; or write a telesales call script.

3 Verbal skills

Articulation

3.1 We learn to speak instinctively, and rarely pay attention to our own **articulation** and **pronunciation** until we have encountered a real problem. (You know you have a problem when someone has to ask you to repeat your message several times, and then spell it out.)

Listen to other people speaking. Do they speak clearly, so that you never have trouble understanding them? What judgements do you make about them on the basis of their national, regional or class-associated accents?

Action Programme 3

Dictate the following sentences to someone else, allowing them time to write each sentence down, but speaking at your normal pace, and reading each item only once. (Alternatively, record yourself reading, and come back later and try to transcribe the sentences yourself.)

What a little pop, pet.
Jo gave George a rum for his money.
That stuff isn't it.
You have an aim and a dress.
They are having pea stalks.
He grows great vines.
Why choose 'Glow in the dark'?
You'll hear the waiter speak.
Will we have passed her at dinner?

Write in the alternative ways of hearing these sentences. What did you have to do in the way of articulation, pronunciation and intonation to make yourself clear?

3.2 **Clear articulation** is vital, not because it is associated with a particular region, section of society or level of education, but because you want to be **understood** immediately and unambiguously by any other person, in order to get a response that you require. Similarly, a dialect or accent may be perfectly comprehensible within a certain community, but unless the speaker can make himself readily understood by someone who does not share it (over a long-distance telephone line, say, or in a gathering of people from various countries and regions) it will prevent him from communicating effectively. Be **considerate** to the recipient of your message: don't use or pronounce words in a way that he will not understand, and don't speak too quickly.

Delivery

3.3 If you are **articulating clearly**, you will be much more audible, but you will also have to consider how to **project** your voice. Speaking softly or even at a normal level will be ineffective in a large room with a high ceiling and heavy curtains. You need to pitch your voice to travel to the **furthest** listener, whatever the size of the room.

Look for **feedback** indicating that you are clearly but not painfully audible, and stick to that pitch and volume.

3.4 **Intonation** affects **how** your message reaches its recipient, as much as volume affects **whether** it does. Be aware of how the placing of **emphasis** on different words alters the meaning of a sentence: the stress **implies** something to the listener. Likewise, notice how inflexion and tone alter meaning, when you raise or lower your voice, lift at the end of a question, lift and drop in an exclamation and so on. How do you make your voice sound cheery, gloomy, disapproving, encouraging, affectionate, enthusiastic, indifferent, hostile?

Action Programme 4

Experiment with the simple sentence: 'Nobody is available to see you.'

(a) Try stressing each word in turn, and discuss the implications of each change.

(b) Try each as a statement, and as a question (not all combinations will work).

(c) Try making the statement with each of the emotional overtones mentioned in Paragraph 3.4 above

3.5 **Pace and pauses** are further elements in fluent but clear delivery. Don't garble your words or string together long breathless sentences. If you need time in which to frame your next idea, there are phrases and expressions you can use almost without thought, to preserve the fluency of your message. (Do not resort to stabilisers like 'um', 'sort of', 'like', or 'you know what I mean?'. Credible alternatives include signpost expressions like: 'Of course, that's just one example', 'The next point I'd like to make is ...', or 'on the other hand ...'.)

3.6 You may be interested in the results of a Gallup poll in which American adults were asked how they felt about others' **talking habits**. How many of these habits do you have or do you notice in other people?

Talking habit	*Extremely annoyed* %	*Not annoyed* %	*Don't know* %
Interrupting while others are talking	88	11	1
Swearing	84	15	1
Mumbling or talking too softly	80	20	0
Talking too loudly	73	26	1
Monotonous, boring voice	73	26	1
Using filler words such as 'and um', 'like um' and 'you know'	69	29	2
A nasal whine	67	29	4
Talking too fast	66	34	0
Using poor grammar or mispronouncing words	63	36	1
A high-pitched voice	61	37	2
A foreign accent or a regional dialect	24	75	1

4 Listening skills

4.1 The assumption tends to be that listening is not so much an ability or skill as a physical attribute of human beings: we all have ears, so we can all listen - barring a physical hearing deficiency. Listening is simply equated with **hearing**. However, tests show that the average person remembers only half of what he has heard immediately afterwards. Listening is an **active process**, not a passive one.

Why is it important to listen effectively?

4.2 Larry L Barker reports in *Listening Behaviour* that 70-75% of a person's waking day is spend in communication, of which:

42% is listening
32% is talking
15% is reading
11% is writing

4.3 Many benefits are available from effective listening.

(a) It is a **quick**, **direct** source of information, which you may be interested in, or need in order to make decisions.

(b) It offers the opportunity to use the speaker's **tone** of voice, to help you interpret underlying messages.

(c) It is **interactive** and flexible, so you can:

- Make sure the information is **adapted** to your needs and that you understand it
- **Add** information of your own, to stimulate new ideas and solve problems

(d) It builds **relationships**, encourages understanding of the other person's feelings and point of view, and establishes a personal element to the discussion.

(e) It encourages **further** and more spontaneous communication, which deepens relationships. It also encourages honesty because the speaker has less time to plan ahead, is less likely to withhold information, and will find it more difficult to disguise his feelings.

Action Programme 5

Applying these benefits to the business context, why do you think listening might be particularly useful for a marketer or salesperson?

Ways of listening

4.4 Like reading, listening may have a number of purposes, which should be borne in mind as you listen.

(a) **Listening for content**

If you trust the source of the message to be correct and objective, or you only want to know what the source's viewpoint is (in which case it doesn't matter if it is incorrect or subjective), listening for content will be a straightforward receiving activity - but still requires skilful listening in order to:

- **Receive** physically as much as possible of what is said (ensuring that it is audible, and that your attention doesn't wander)
- **Interpret** as much as possible of what is said, in the way the speaker intends (understanding the message)
- Give appropriate **feedback** to achieve both of the above (asking for repetition or louder delivery, asking questions, encouraging the speaker to continue and so on)

In addition, you may want to make an effort to **remember** the content of the message. The surest way is to write down the important points, but the way you listen - noticing key words, for example, or listening just as hard to repetitions and summaries - will make recall easier.

(b) **Critical listening**

If you require an objective viewpoint or accurate information, and you do not have absolute confidence that the source is able and intending to give it to you, you will need to listen critically.

(i) Be **alert** to things you know to be factually false, and reappraise the source's credibility.

(ii) Appraise the speaker's **vocabulary** and way of speaking for attempts to distract or persuade you. Tone of voice and **body-language** - if you can see the speaker - will be an additional source of guidance in this.

(iii) Question the speaker's **assumptions** and logic (if only to yourself). Consider whether an illogical argument is the product of muddled thinking or an attempt at manipulation - and whether the conclusion is therefore invalid, or may still be true.

(iv) Look for **balance** - or bias - in the argument. It may or may not be conveniently signalled verbally ('On the one hand ... on the other hand ...').

(v) Appraise the **supporting evidence** given, if any.

(vi) Consider the source's **credibility** and purpose in communicating.

(vii) Bear in mind your own biased **perceptions** as you respond critically to the message and to the speaker: don't dismiss the message because you dislike the voice!

Listening to the tone of voice of the speaker adds an extra dimension to the process of interpreting (is he being ironic, for example, or serious?) and evaluating (is he carried away by emotion, or trying to be persuasive?).

(c) **Empathic listening**

Key Concept

'**Empathy**is defined as 'the power of understanding and imaginatively entering into another person's feelings'.

Empathic listening is a supportive form of listening. It enables the listener to interpret both the surface and underlying meanings of the communication and to help the speaker to feel **understood**: this is often very important when people are upset or annoyed. (It is a key skill in dealing with customer complaints, 'difficult' people and when helping customer or colleagues to solve problems sensitively.)

Empathetic listening involves:

- Asking yourself what the person is feeling, and therefore what they are **'really saying'**
- **Reflecting back** to the person what they agree saying in a way that shows you have understood ('You feel disappointed because ...' 'You are annoyed because...')

Active listening

4.5 Here are some brief hints to being a good listener, whether it be in one-to-one discussions, lectures, meetings or telephone conversations.

What to do	How to do it
Be ready	Get your attitude right at the start, and decide to listen. You might even be able to do some background research for the meeting or discussion so that you have established a context for the message you intend to receive.
Be interested	Don't try to soak up a message like a sponge, and then complain that you found it dull. Make it interesting for yourself by asking questions: how is this information relevant to me and how can I use it?
Be patient	Try to hold yourself back from interrupting if you disagree with someone, and don't compete to get your view in before the previous speaker has properly finished. Wait until a suitable opening (while your point is still relevant to the immediate discussion, but not while the speaker is just drawing a breath between phrases). Don't be so preoccupied with how you're going to respond that you forget to listen to what is said in the meantime.
Keep your mind open	Be aware of your negative reactions to the speaker's message, delivery or appearance. Control them, and don't jump to conclusions: you may miss something.
Keep your mind going	Being open-minded does not mean accepting everything blindly. Use your critical faculties: test the speaker's assumptions, logic and evidence. Also test your own interpretation of words and ideas, making sure they make sense in their context.
Keep your mind on the job	Concentrate. It is very easy to switch off as attention wanders or you get tired. Don't be distracted by details of the speaker or the room. Don't get side-tracked by irrelevancies in the message: co-operate with the speaker in getting to the point of what he is trying to say. Listen for main points, and the summary or conclusion.
Give feedback	You can encourage the speaker and ensure your own understanding by sending feedback signals, particularly during pauses in the speech or message. For example, try an interested and attentive look, a nod, a murmur of agreement or query ('Yes... Really?'). If there are opportunities, use some verbal means of checking that you have understood the message correctly. Ask questions, referring to the speaker's words in a way that demonstrates your interpretation of them ('You said earlier that...' 'You implied that..'): the speaker can then correct you if you have missed or misinterpreted something. Reading details back to the speaker is advisable when taking telephone messages. Remember, you're not trying to score points for cleverness or clairvoyancy: co-operate with the speaker, and if you don't understand something, or you think you've got something wrong, say so.
Use non-verbal cues (if available)	Be aware of the messages given by gestures, factual expression, tone of voice and so on.

5 Non-verbal communication

What is non-verbal communication?

Key Concept

Non-verbal communicationis basically anything that conveys a message without using words or symbols.

5.1 Non-verbal communication may be **linked** to words (for example, a tone of voice), or it may be independent of any verbal message. Information is **perceived** by all the senses: tastes and smells convey messages. Movement is highly communicative. Think what you can convey through, for example, frowning or smiling, nodding, scratching your head, putting your head in your hands, slamming a door, turning your back, screaming, being silent, keeping your office door open or closed, slouching or sitting up straight, dressing casually or turning up late to a formal meeting.

5.2 All these examples have aspects in common.

(a) They **convey a message** from or about the person 'doing' them.

(b) They are the kind of things done by everybody all the time: **every** action (or non-action) and every communication (or non-communication) conveys or adds a non-verbal message. (Remember: you cannot NOT communicate.)

(c) The message conveyed is **not consistent from culture to culture**, person to person, or in one person over time. A nod, for example may mean agreement, non-agreement (as in India, where a shake of the head means agreement), a friendly acknowledgement or greeting, an unfriendly acknowledgement or greeting (if you expected a handshake or hug, say), an instruction to sit or move in the direction indicated, the easing of a stiff neck, and so on. We depend on **context**, expectation, **perception** and attitude to interpret the message - and frequently get it wrong! (If someone has her arms folded across her chest, this is not necessarily defensiveness: she may just be cold!)

(d) They may or **may not be conscious or intentional**. In general, we are much more aware of **other** people's gestures and tone of voice, and sensitive to possible meanings in them (even if we misinterpret them), than we are of the things we are doing ourselves, and the signals they convey.

(e) They may **reinforce or contradict** a verbal message. The words 'I'd love to stay for dinner', for example, would be reinforced by a smile, warm tone of voice, or arm around the shoulders: they would be undermined by a worried look, glance at the watch, or getting up and heading for the door. Non-verbal communication which adds meaning over and above what the speaker is saying in the words themselves ('between the lines' of a message) is called **meta-communication** (from the Greek 'meta': beyond, in addition to).

(f) They may convey **information** (pointing out a direction), **emotion** (a jaw dropping in surprise), **relationship** (an intimate closeness), **self-image** (a 'loud' tie and big gestures), or **guidance** to verbal communication (banging a table for emphasis).

Taking control of non-verbal communication

5.3 You can see what a complex and involved process non-verbal communication is, and the extent of misunderstanding or misinterpretation that can occur. What can be done about this? Non-verbal communication can be **controlled** and used fruitfully to:

Provide appropriate **'physical'** feedback to the sender of a message (a yawn, applause, clenched fists, fidgeting)
Create a desired **impression** (smart dress, a smile, punctuality, a firm handshake)
Establish a desired **atmosphere** or conditions (a friendly smile, informal dress, attentive posture, a respectful distance)
Reinforce our spoken messages with appropriate indications of how our interest, seriousness and feelings are engaged (an emphatic gesture, sparkling eyes, a disapproving frown)

5.4 If we can learn to **recognise** non-verbal messages given by others, we can also:

Receive non-verbal feedback from a listener and modify the message accordingly
Recognise people's real **feelings** when their words are constrained by formal courtesies (an excited look, a nervous tic, close affectionate proximity)
Recognise existing or potential **personal problems** (the angry silence, the indifferent shrug, absenteeism or lateness at work, refusal to look someone in the eye)
'Read' situations in order to modify our own communication and response strategy. Is the potential customer convinced? (Go ahead.) Is the boss irritated at having to wait for his tea? (Reassure - and hurry.) Is the complaining customer on the point of hysteria? (Be soothing.)

Body language

5.5 Let's look briefly at some of the **'signals'** we give and receive, and how they may be interpreted.

Facial expression

5.6 The eyebrows, nose, lips and mouth, jaw, musculature, skin colour and movement all contribute to the **expression** on someone's face. Some of these things can be controlled, making facial expression in isolation an unreliable guide to true feelings - especially since different races and cultures have different facial characteristics which make unfamiliar expressions hard to 'read'. Involuntary signals, however, include muscular twitches or tension, and variation in complexion: growing pale or flushed.

Action Programme 6

A Japanese technology company has recently developed a robot which interprets and responds to the mood of a person by reading specific elements of facial expression. How reliably do you think human beings can do this?

Eye contact

5.7 **Eye contact** - the meeting of the other person's gaze - signals interest in the West. Intermittent eye contact is usual in interpersonal communication: less might indicate disinterest or avoidance, while more implies a desire for intimacy (which may or may not be desirable to both parties and is particularly intrusive in Eastern cultures). People also tend to look away if they are thinking, or planning their message: they make contact when communicating directly, or seeking feedback. Excessive eye movement is often interpreted as avoidance, distraction or nervousness.

Gestures

5.8 People make **gestures unconsciously**: jabbing a finger in the air for emphasis, tapping the fingers when impatient. They also make conscious gestures (and not only impolite ones): finger against the lips for silence, jerk of the head to indicate a direction, shrug to indicate indifference. Like any other form of non-verbal communication, there is a wide variety of possible interpretations of any given gesture. Some gestures (the handshake, the handclap, the shrug of the shoulders, the clenched fist, the pointing finger) take on an 'agreed' common meaning within a culture, but you should bear in mind that these meanings can be lost or changed - like words - and that other cultures may not share them. Indeed, some cultures use gestures more or less than others: a level of gesticulation that would seem natural to an Italian, for example, might suggest impending nervous breakdown to a native American.

Posture

5.9 Posture is **positioning**. It includes conscious or unconscious decisions about whether you sit, stand, walk or lie down, and **how**: lounging, hunching and sitting up straight, for example, may convey relaxation, negativity or alertness respectively.

We all have different habitual ways of positioning our bodies. These may be due to physical factors - like developing a curved spine or flat feet. They may reflect psychological factors, like self-confidence or inferiority, sociability or shyness, hostility or attraction.

Action Programme 7

Consider sitting posture. What impression would be created if you sat:

1. With your shoulders hunched forwards, your hands clenched between your knees, and your head hanging?
2. With your back and shoulders straight, hands relaxed on knees, head erect?
3. Leaning right back with your head resting on the back of the chair, hands behind your head, legs straight out in front with ankles crossed?
4. Leaning forward, head up, towards the speaker?
5. Leaning sideways towards the speaker, legs crossed toward them, arm along the back of their chair?

Orientation

5.10 It has been shown that in **co-operative situations** or relationships, people sit or stand next to each other, while in **confrontational or assertive situations** or relationships, they tend to place themselves in opposition - opposite - to each other. Of course, context makes a great difference: sitting opposite an interviewer across a desk (a physical barrier - another non-verbal message) is rather different to sitting across a small candlelit table at dinner. Nevertheless, you might consider the implications for the layout of chairs at meetings and interviews: do you need to establish formality and authority, or informality and a non-threatening, co-operative atmosphere?

Proximity

5.11 Proximity is **'nearness'**: we use the **space** around us to communicate our attitude to other people and objects. You may have heard the expression 'my personal space' (usually 'invaded' by someone else): there is a certain physical **distance** at which we feel **comfortable** with others. This depends on **cultural norms**, personal tastes, the context and our relationship with the other person. In intensely populated countries (like Japan and China) and in socially uninhibited cultures (like Latin cultures), a smaller area of personal space is accepted, even preferred, compared to British society, say, where people feel 'crowded' quite easily.

Personal appearance

5.12 Appearance is a high-profile **visual cue** which tends to form a convenient basis for first impressions, generalisations and attitudes.

(a) Personal **attractiveness** undoubtedly has an effect on people's judgements, often being used as a cue for less obvious attributes (intelligence, personality, capability, trustworthiness and so on): we need to be aware when we are 'reading' more into attractiveness than it really implies.

(b) **Grooming and dress** reflect a person's personality and attitude to a much greater extent than physical attributes. A person's style can be individual, and can indicate self-confidence or insecurity, and taste. In business contexts, it also indicates awareness of what is appropriate for a given situation, and a willingness to adopt social (or organisational) norms in the interests of co-operation and respect for others. Breaking norms or expectations to do with dress, hygiene and grooming are likely to be interpreted as a deliberate challenge, or as insensitivity, in cultures and organisations where 'fitting in' is important.

Action Programme 8

List five further examples of 'norms' or prevailing attitudes, and how breaking those norms might convey a non-verbal message.

6 Improving your skills

6.1 A Study Text (like any other written format) can help you to understand the nature of skilled performance in interpersonal communication skills. It can help you to answer exam questions **about** interpersonal communication skills. What it is not so effective at doing (since you are learning to select the most appropriate communication formats for given tasks) is helping you to develop your skills. That can't be done on paper: only by modelling and practice in interpersonal situations.

6.2 One of the *Key Skills for Marketers* identified by the CIM Syllabus is 'Improving your own learning and performance'. The following are some strategies by which you can plan and manage a programme of learning in this area. Your own circumstances, opportunities and contacts will determine which are the best methods for you.

Learning from others

6.3 Other people are a learning resource.

(a) **Observe skilled communicators** in action and analyse the behaviours they use that make their communication effective. What verbal and non-verbal behaviours by others make **you** feel listened to, or inclined to be persuaded? **Modelling** is the process of selecting the successful behaviours of others, and – by imitation – trying them out yourself to see how they work for you.

(b) **Ask for feedback**. Select someone that you trust to be honest and constructive, and ask him or her to monitor your interpersonal behaviours in day-to-day situations (at work or study) and to tell you afterwards, in private, what you do well and what areas require improvement. **Constructive** feedback is aimed at encouraging and helping you to improve. It needs to be **specific**, **relevant** and targeted at your **behaviours** – not your personality (which is much harder to change!):

eg 'You seem to avoid steady eye contact, which makes me feel as if you are not really listening' – **not** 'You're inattentive!'

Your ability to negotiate a constructive feedback relationship (or study partnership, if the other person wants feedback in return) is in itself useful practice interpersonal skills.

Experiential learning

6.4 Experiential learning is, basically, 'learning by doing'. Honey & Mumford (building on the work of David Kolb) propose a simple approach called the **learning cycle**, which is designed to allow you to learn from your experience (Figure 9.2).

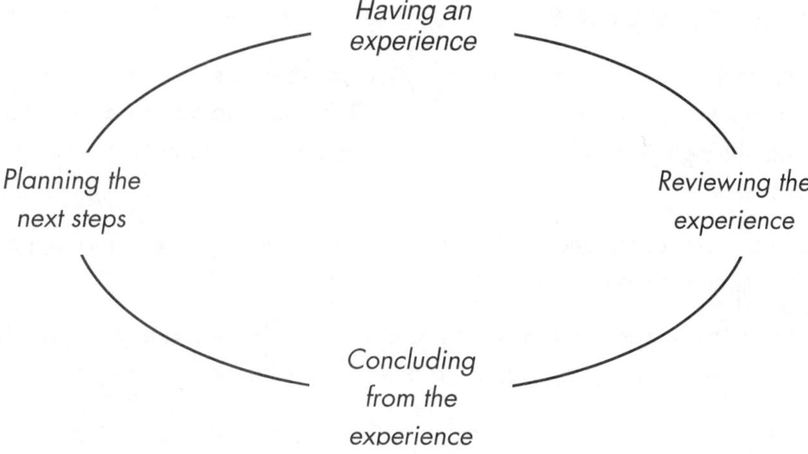

Figure 9.2: The Learning Cycle

6.5 Learning from experience is a process of:

- **Having an experience**: being fully involved in an action or interaction, utilising your current knowledge and skills
- **Reviewing the experience**: looking back at what happened, describing it, reflecting on the causes and effects of your behaviour
- **Concluding from the experience**: forming generalisations, concepts and theories that will enable you to try something different next time in order to achieve different effects
- **Planning the next steps**: planning specific opportunities to apply and test your conclusions in action – which provides a new experience to start the cycle again...

6.6 Say you interview a client (having an experience): you are fully engaged in the activity. Afterwards, however, you are able to think more objectively about the behaviour you observed in the interaction: reflecting on the client's resistance to persuasion, you realise that your responses failed to take into account the client's concerns, which were suggested by her non-verbal behaviours (reviewing the experience). You think that perhaps more empathetic responses may be more persuasive (concluding from the experience). You decide to try out some new empathy behaviours in the next interview you conduct (planning the next steps).

6.7 One strategy for self-development would therefore be to:

- Select an area of interpersonal skills you wish to focus on: perhaps one in which you have experienced unsatisfactory results (as in the example above), or one which has been identified from feedback – or through reading this chapter.
- In an appropriate interpersonal interaction, be aware of your behaviours, their effect on other people and their effectiveness in achieving your aims.

- After the event, reflect on it and ask yourself what happened and why, and what you might try differently next time.
- Make specific plans or identify opportunities to try the new behaviour: monitor, reflect and adjust as required, in an on-going cycle.

Formal training resources

6.8 If you wish to tackle the improvement of your interpersonal communication skills more systematically, there are a number of resources available to help you to do so, some of which may be available through your study or work. It will be up to you to decide whether they will be worth your investment.

- Communication/interpersonal skills training videos are available, offering the advantages of 'virtual' demonstration.
- Communication/interpersonal skills courses and workshops are also widely available: check adult education catalogues, or do a search on the Net.

A general development planning framework

6.9 Whatever method of learning you choose, a systematic approach to planning your own development will include the following steps.

Step 1 Select an area for development: a limitation to overcome or a strength to build on

Step 2 Set a SMART (specific, measurable, attainable, realistic and time-bounded) learning objective: what you want to be able to do or do better. ('To maintain appropriate eye contact in face-to-face discussions, with sensitivity to the response of the other person' – *not* 'To become a better listener'!)

Step 3 Determine how you will move towards your objective. A comprehensive action plan would include:

- The SMART objective
- The learning approaches you will use, described as specific actions: ask a colleague to provide feedback on your presentation skills at a forthcoming team meeting; watch a training video; reflect daily (perhaps keeping a journal) on how you listen. Each action should have a realistic timescale or schedule.
- Monitoring/review plan: how and when will you assess your progress (seek feedback? review results? pass an end-of-course test?)

Step 4 Implement your action plan

Action Programme 9

Think about the communication skills discussed in this chapter, and use the four steps outlined above to develop a draft action plan for improving *one* skill area. (Remember, your learning objective should be SMART. Start small.)

Chapter Roundup

- The main barriers to successful communication are distortion (problems affecting coding and de-coding) and noise (interference in the process of communication). Barriers can be overcome by planning, feedback, rapport and trust, efficient communication systems and effective communication skills.

- *Verbal skills*
  - Clear articulation
  - Audible volume
  - Natural pitch
  - Expressive intonation
  - Appropriate pace
  - Appropriate pauses
  - Fluency

  Listening skills
  - Preparation
  - Activity
  - Patience
  - Objectivity
  - Concentration
  - Feedback

  Non-verbal skills
  - Giving correct cues
  - Reading cues correctly
  - Giving and receiving non-verbal feedback
  - Meta-communication

- Non-verbal cues (body language) include: Facial expression, eye contact, gestures, posture, orientation, proximity and personal appearance.

- A systematic approach to developing your communication skills may include: identifying an area of limitation or strength to work on; setting a SMART learning objective; planning learning methods (including learning from others, learning from reflection on experience and more formal training sources); and monitoring and reviewing progress.

Quick Quiz

1 Interference in the environment in which communication takes place is called:

Noise	Distortion	Redundancy	Proximity

2 A suggestion scheme is primarily a channel for downward communication in an organisation.

☐ True ☐ False

3 Articulation refers to:

A How a person projects his or her voice
B How a person emphasises different words within a sentence
C How clearly a person pronounces words
D How slowly a person speaks

4 Allocate the following activities to the correct boxes, which show the amount of our communicating time we spend doing them.

(1) Speaking (2) Writing (3) Listening (4) Reading

42%	32%	15%	11%

5 If your main aim is to ascertain another person's viewpoint on a subject of interest, the most appropriate style of listening will be:

A Listening for content
B Critical listening

C Empathetic listening
D Passive listening

6 If an important question occurs to you as a person is speaking, the best strategy is to think it through yourself, without stopping the other person.

☐ True ☐ False

7 Sustained direct eye contact is perceived in Eastern cultures as:

A Nervous
B Polite
C Business-like
D Intrusive

8 Body language generally reinforces the message being given verbally.

☐ True ☐ False

9 What does SMART (objective) stand for?

10 Label the stages in the Learning Cycle, as shown in the following diagram.

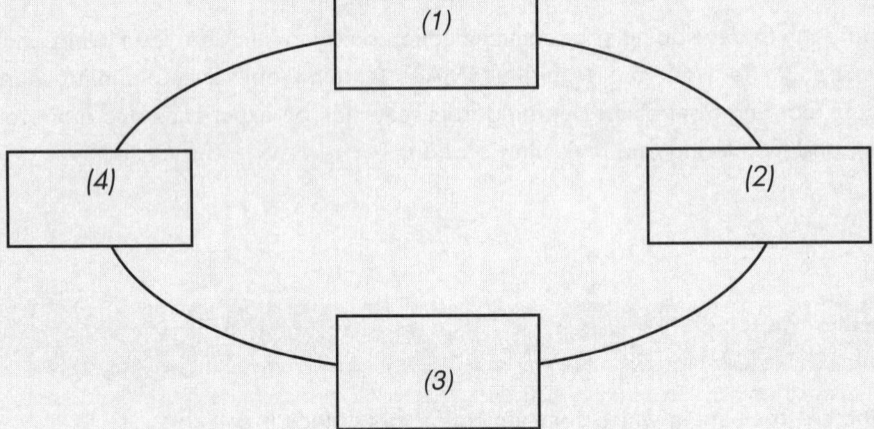

Answers to Quick Quiz

1 Noise

2 False

3 C

4 42% (3); 32% (1); 15% (4); 11% (2)

5 A

6 False

7 D

8 False

9 Specific, measurable, attainable, realistic

10 (1) Having an experience; (2) Reviewing the experience, (3) Concluding from the experience; (4) Planning the next steps

Now try Question 9 from the Question Bank at the end of this Text

Action Programme Review

1

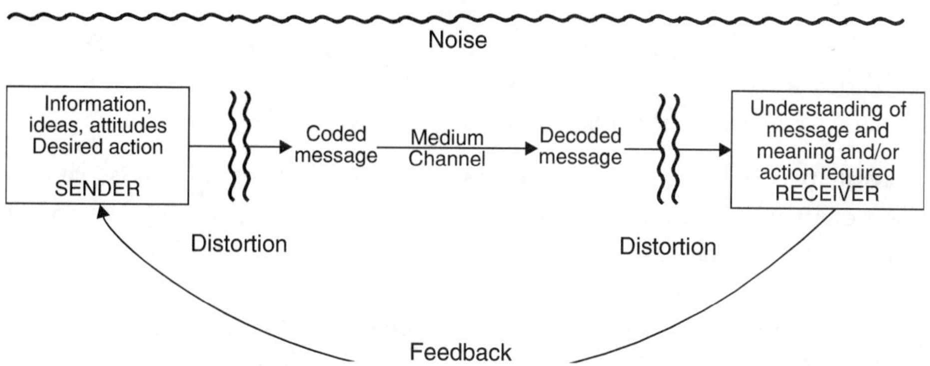

2 Problems may be caused in communication at work between managers and their staff because of the following.

(a) A subordinate fearing or mistrusting a superior and looking for 'hidden meanings' in a message.

(b) Hostility or resentment towards management, resulting in deliberate attempts to 'sabotage' communication.

(c) Subordinates giving superiors incorrect or incomplete information (eg to protect a colleague, or to avoid 'bothering' the superior).

(d) Managers talking 'over the heads' of subordinates, as a means of asserting their authority.

(e) People from different job or specialist backgrounds having difficulty in talking on the same wavelength, for example shop floor workers feeling intimidated by 'men in suits'.

(f) Managers making decisions on a 'hunch', without considering contradictory information from subordinates.

(g) Lack of opportunity, formal or informal, for a subordinate to say what he thinks or feels.

(h) Employees not taking an interest in organisational matters which do not affect them personally.

(i) A manager 'selling' a new work practice to subordinates with little knowledge of how it should be implemented.

3 This programme highlights potential problems in speech and how they can be overcome.

4 Emphasis and intonation can change the meaning of a sentence significantly. This programme highlights that fact.

5
1. **It is a quick, direct source of information** - say, for getting an initial feel for customers' receptivity to a new product.
2. **It is interactive and flexible**. The marketer can ensure that he has got and understood the information he requires. If creative thinking is required, active listening can

stimulate ideas. Active listening is vital for handling and overcoming customers' objections.

3 It contributes to relationships.

(a) A salesperson who listens shows respect for his customers' expertise, experience and opinions in a more direct and personal way than one who asks for written feedback.

(b) Listening also allows the salesperson to use his personality: say, for greater effectiveness in making the customer feel important.

(c) Human relationships are a prime factor in customer satisfaction (or dissatisfaction): customer loyalty may be enhanced by a communication style based on interpersonal communication and a degree of informality.

4 **It encourages communication.** The perception that the salesperson is interested and willing to listen motivates customers to offer information and ideas which may be commercially useful for the organisation. Writing down ideas can be time consuming (or even intimidating for those who are not confident about their writing skills): the opportunity to speak informally to a sales rep is both more convenient and encouraging.

6 From left to right, the faces are *intended* to depict suspicious, indifferent, disappointed and anxious respectively. (You were not meant to be able to identify these easily. The point is, body language is complex: we can only guess what people are feeling and *check out with them* whether we are correct. 'Is this a problem for you?')

7 Much will depend on the context, but the signals in themselves might suggest:

1 Dejection
2 Self-confidence
3 Casual relaxation, or boredom, or contempt (in a formal context)
4 Interest and attention
5 Attraction, the desire for intimacy

8 1 **Attitudes to punctuality, or sense of time.** Conventions, varying from culture to culture, govern the time at which it is acceptable to arrive at, and leave, social gatherings (particularly meals), and how much time should be spent in pleasantries before getting down to business. If you are late for an appointment, or miss a deadline, you signal disregard of the other person or the task in hand.

2 **Eating habits.** 'Table manners' are an important indicator of education and class in Western society. In other cultures, meals can be highly ritualised affairs: trying to hurry a meal may be interpreted as disrespect.

3 **Communication styles**. In any given culture or organisation, people may or may not use first names, formal or colloquial language and so on: use of excessive familiarity or formality may signal disrespect or standoffishness respectively.

4 **Business customs and ethics**. In some cultures (eg in the Middle East and Asia) the giving of gifts in business dealings is an expected courtesy: in others, it is insulting or illegal. There are many similar unwritten rules of conduct in business.

5 **The role of women. In some cultures**, an attempt by a woman to initiate conversation or take the lead in a meeting, say, would be shocking.

9 This is obviously entirely personal. Good luck!

Planning effective messages

10

Chapter Topic List	
1	Setting the scene
2	Purpose
3	Audience
4	Structure
5	Style

Learning Outcomes

☑ Analyse the objectives of any given communication as a guide to planning

☑ Appreciate the factors impacting on your target audience at the point of contact

☑ Structure messages to create intended effects

☑ Develop an appropriate style of communication for the purpose and audience

Syllabus References

☑ Explain the communications planning process to produce effective strategies for improving alternative communication formats (4.3)

Key Concepts Introduced

- PASS
- Five Cs
- Credibility
- Congeniality

1 Setting the scene

1.1 Having covered the processes and problems of communication, including personal and business-related factors, we can now apply that knowledge to the planning of a message. In this chapter, we gather some of the points already raised into a **framework** for decision-making in any communication context.

1.2 In some circumstances, an organisation's policies, procedures and culture – its **'house style'** – will have made many of the decisions for the communicator. There may be standard formats and rules for communications: memo stationery, for example, controls over use of e-mail, or scripted telesales calls. There may even be **standard documents** for a variety of routine communication tasks such as:

- A letter to a customer confirming the opening of a credit account
- Payment-chasing letters
- Acknowledgements of payments, job applications and so on

1.3 Other circumstances, however, require decision-making by the communicator: non-routine communications; communications requiring persuasion, tact or sensitivity; unplanned interpersonal communications like customer queries and complaints; and so on. However strong the influence of house style, there will be decisions to make about what information to put in or emphasise and what to leave out or down-play; what tone and style to adopt; and what vocabulary and medium to use.

1.4 In this Study Text, we can only offer examples of different communication methods and styles. You will need to be alert to:

- The house style that has been established in your organisation (or in an exam question)
- The conventions that pertain to your nation or culture (if you are studying outside the UK) or to **other** nations and cultures with which you may need to communicate in the global market place

A framework for planning messages: PASS

1.5 In this Study Text, we propose a very simple framework, linked to an easy to remember mnemonic (since it should be close to your heart). Think 'PASS'.

Key Concept

Purpose what do you wish or need to achieve as a result of the communication task or event?

Audience what factors in the recipient(s) of the message, or their situation, will affect whether they receive, understand and/or respond to the message in the way you intend?

Structure: what content, emphasis, order and format will be most suitable to achieve your purpose, given the audience factors?

Style what vocabulary, sentence structure, visual elements and 'tone of voice' will be most suitable to achieve your purpose, given the audience factors?

Exam Tip

PASS was included in a Hot Topic discussion on the CIM's Virtual Institute site. It is highly relevant as a framework for every question you will tackle in the exam. If your written answers don't show an understanding of Purpose, Audience, Style and Structure, then there is a good chance that you will not PASS!

2 Purpose

General purposes

2.1 As discussed in Chapter 4, the general purpose of most messages will be as follows.

(a) **To inform**: giving the data and information required in order to initiate or facilitate some action or decision.

(b) **To persuade**: giving information in such a way as to confirm or alter the attitude of the recipient, securing acceptance or compliance, according to the communicator's purposes.

(c) **To request**: giving information about needs or requirements, so as to elicit information or actions.

(d) **To confirm**: giving information that clarifies and crystallises previous communication, ensuring that both parties have the same understanding, and offering an aid to recollection (an **aide-memoir**) and evidence of the communication, should they be required.

(e) **To build the relationship**: giving information in such a way as to acknowledge and maintain the relationship between the sender and receiver – mutual trust, loyalty, respect, benefit and so on.

Specific objectives

2.2 In addition, you may have a specific purpose for communicating. Think in terms of the **outcome** that you want from the communication event: what do you want to happen, and when? This is your **primary objective**.

Here are some examples.

Message	General purpose	Examples of specific outcome desired
Product advertisement	Persuade recipient of benefits of product	Recipient to call/write immediately for more information Recipient to seek free sample pack in retail outlets Recipient to purchase direct from source, by phone or post Recipient to recognise product when seen in retail outlet Recipient to seek and purchase product
Reply to letter of complaint	Placate customer and address complaint	To retain the customer's business To re-establish a positive relationship To cause customer delight

Action Programme 1

Keep going, along the lines of the above. The following are all communication tasks that you may have to tackle in your exam.

Notice of a public meeting

Press release

Payment request

2.3 You will need to take into account the fact that the recipient of the communication will also have purposes and desired outcomes.

(a) A message will be more effective if the desired outcome is (or can be made to seem) **acceptable or congenial** to the recipient as well as the sender. This makes it easier for the recipient to co-operate, to give the required response, because he can achieve his **own** purposes. You may have to compromise so that, instead of **'win-lose'** (where one party gains at the other's expense), the outcome is **mutually beneficial**.

(b) On the other hand, a message may be more effective if it does **not** allow the recipient to take the most congenial course for him, if that would be incompatible with **your** desired outcome.

Action Programme 2

How might the options described in paragraph 2.3 above apply in the case of:

(a) Replying to a letter of complainant?

(b) Responding to a customer whose payment is severely overdue?

Planning a message using objectives

2.4 It is a good idea to **analyse** your objectives **before** you communicate, in order to provide:

(a) A **criterion** against which each element of your message can be assessed for **relevance**, **suitability** to the audience (see Section 3 below) and **effectiveness**

(b) A **guide** for the **content and structure** of the message – a checklist of points to be made, and what order to put them in (see Section 4 below)

(c) A way of determining whether and how far your message is actually **successful** in its outcome

Practical considerations

2.5 The **physical use** to which a message will be put also needs consideration when it comes to deciding on the medium and format of the message.

(a) If it has to be **confirmed** or recalled, a message should be in a precise and concrete form. This will usually mean a **written message**, which can be referred to at need. If it is going to be referred to or handled often, it will have to be fairly durable: on good quality, 'sturdy' paper, perhaps in a protective folder.

(b) If it is going to be referred to in **urgent** or **awkward** circumstances, a message should be particularly brief, clear and neatly presented. Delivery documents, instructions for operation of machinery etc may have to be referred to and grasped at speed, possibly while doing something else. Important details should be quickly identified and located, layout easily readable.

(c) If it is later going to be kept in the organisation's **information storage** system, a message will have to be in an appropriate format. Scraps or vast sheets of paper are not conveniently filed; oral messages will have to be confirmed or summarised in writing; dates and reference details will be helpful.

3 Audience

3.1 In some circumstances, you will be communicating with someone you **know**, or someone you know a bit **about**: if you send a memo to a colleague, for example, or a letter to a customer in response to a query or complaint, or a press release to a journalist who specialises in your area.

3.2 However, if you are writing an advertisement or circular letter say, or designing a web site, you may start off with little idea of who your audience is, what they are like and in what circumstances (or even, in the case of a website, in what part of the world) they will receive your message. In chapter 3, we discussed 'consumer behaviour' in the mass sense: here, we will look at some individual factors that you might take into account in sending a letter/memo, making a phone call and so on.

Who is the audience?

3.3 Some of the **personal factors** and **differences** which you will have to take into account when considering your audience were discussed in Chapter 9. Some of the communication implications are as follows.

Personal factors	Comment
Age	People's attitudes may become less flexible with the years: a young person writing to a senior will have to be respectful and persuasive. From the opposite angle, beware of talking 'over the head' of people younger and less experienced than you, and also of 'talking down' to them in a patronising way.
Work environment	Recognise when you are using technical language or **'jargon'** which your recipient is unlikely to know. An overly simple general vocabulary, however, may be irritating to someone who would understand more specialist terms. In internal communications, bear in mind the position and authority of your recipient: there is usually a well defined hierarchy in any office.
Attitudes, interests and **opinions**	You can target your message to what you know of your recipient's general outlook and interests, arousing their motivation to receive and consider your message. In interpersonal communication (by phone or in person) you might even find some **common ground**, which would help to build up a valuable **rapport**.
Information needs	As we suggested in paragraph 2.3 above, the target audience will have purposes and objectives of its own. What are the intended recipient's abilities and limitations when it comes to receiving or understanding the message? What are his or her needs and expectations? What are his or her information and decision-making priorities?
Market segment	Whatever basis for segmentation is used, the marketing messages media and channels must be tailored to the **target** audience and its known characteristics.

When and where will the message be received?

3.4 Factors in the **context** of the communication (**when** and **where** the message is received, and what the intended recipient is engaged in at the time) include the following.

(a) **Physical conditions**. You need to anticipate and avoid/or compensate for – problems.

- **Physical noise in the 'background'** (people chatting or moving about, traffic or machine noise)
- **Faults in the communication medium** (a bad phone line, or soft voice in a large room without a microphone, or poor quality fax transmission or slide projection)
- **Inappropriate audience size** for the communication medium (too large for the message to be audible or visible, or too small to create the right atmosphere)

- **Distractions** (interruptions, uncomfortable seating/lighting, a room that is too hot/cold/stuffy, hunger or thirst, full bladders)
- **Disablement** (not just impaired hearing or vision but also tiredness, sensory overload, and physical strains including headache or backache): the timing and duration of the message should be planned to catch people when they are fresh and to avoid exhausting them

(b) **Psychological conditions**. You need to anticipate the affect on the recipient's readiness and ability to take in and accept your message of factors such as the following.

- **Pressure and stress**: 'I can't take this right now'
- **Preoccupations** or other matters and concerns competing for the recipient's attention: 'I haven't got time for this right now'
- Whether the message will reach the recipient **directly and privately**, or be **shared** with others

  A private or sensitive message should not be sent via a noticeboard or open letter: the recipient will experience loss of privacy and embarrassment
- The **role** in which the recipient receives the message, and its relationship to the sender in his perceived role

  'Don't call me at work' is a classic example of refusal to receive a message because you're wearing your 'other hat' at the time – in the role of worker rather than family member or friend. 'I'm not saying this as your boss, but as your friend' is another classic example of the adjustment that needs to take place if the sender is **not** communicating in the role that the recipient anticipates.

Action Programme 3

You need to contact Major Philip Braeburn-Smith, Bursar, Porterhouse College, Oxbridge, OB2 1KB, in connection with the supply of cleaning materials for the college.

How will you go about this, taking into account as many of the 'who, when and where' issues described above as you think are appropriate?

An international audience

3.5 A huge number of potential differences arise when considering communication with customers in other countries, or overseas visiting your country (in person or via the World Wide Web).

(a) **Language** is likely to be the most obvious barrier. You may have to communicate with customers for whom English is not a first language. This can be managed by:

(i) Working through an international marketing services agency (eg for promotional campaigns) or a branch of your organisation with representatives in the other country

(ii) Using translation/interpretation services to prepare or mediate communications (or find a colleague who speaks or writes the language in question)

(iii) Using available technology: websites, for example, may offer different language options or translation help features for foreign 'visitors', including **currency exchange** calculators

(b) **Time differences** worldwide impact on the ability of sender and receiver to co-ordinate communication by telephone, for example. The use of fax and e-mail allow for the sending and receipt of messages outside business hours. Low-tech alternatives may include telephone answering machines or message banks (for example, voice mail), or 24-hour call centres. Another time issue in international communication is the length of time taken for postal communications to reach their destination: again, fax and e-mail solve this problem in some contexts – but consider a delivery promise ('orders should arrive within 5-10 working days') that might be read by an Australian customer!

(c) **Local law and customs**. You will need to be aware (or advised) of relevant legislation (product labelling, advertising claims and so on) in the target country. Business and social customs also vary widely. Negotiation and conflict resolution styles vary; age and gender incur differing degrees of respect; body language and eye contact have different connotations; religious and cultural values may reflect the reception of marketing messages (for example, the use of scantily clad models in advertising to traditional Islamic countries) and channels (for example, use of the telephone or television on religious sabbaths); even the layout of standard letters, and preferred colour schemes, are culturally influenced and differ from nation to nation.

Marketing at Work

Job advertising is subject to varying legal provisions – even within the EU. In France, job ads cannot lawfully specify an upper age limit for applicants (a matter currently under voluntary self-regulation in the UK). In Spain, the state employment service is (in theory) supposed to vet all job ads.

3.6 Clearly this is a vast area of study. You will not be expected to 'translate' every customer communication for international contexts, but you need to be **aware** that cultural differences exist and that they impact on communication in many ways (which you may not be able to guess or assume).

3.7 The World Wide Web or Internet has, in particular, globalised the market for small organisations. If you have a website, you need to analyse 'traffic reports' of the hits on the site: by tracking your international exposure, you may identify pockets of international customers and be able to consider their needs (a foreign language page, currency converter and so on).

Action Programme 4

Check out some international websites. What facilities do they offer (if any) to help overseas users? What features of their content and style seem noticeably foreign to you, and what impact does this have on your impression of the site and organisation?

An ICT audience

3.8 the World Wide Web, among other developments, has created new 'audience' issues.

(a) The on-line audience is increasingly **segmenting** itself by gravitating towards specialised on-line communities. All major search engines provide users with personalised news and information services, discussion groups and channels focused on areas of interest: hobbies, media and entertainment, health, travel, business, education and so on.

(b) The on-line audience is used to a high degree of **personalisation**, **interactivity** and proactive, ongoing dialogue in its communication with website content providers. Users want timely answers, product recommendations based on their tastes and preferences, and personalised interaction.

(c) The on-line audience is used to **high-quality content and presentation**: full colour graphics, audio-visual effects, instant links and navigation amongst information, instant response mechanisms (both contact, eg by e-mail, and transaction processing).

(d) The on-line audience has access to a vast array of **information, products and services** to choose from. Messages need to be differentiated to a greater extent than ever before, and they need to be focused on acquiring and **retaining** customers.

(e) Computer technology has turned uninformed customers into **informed customers**, according to McKenna (*Relationship Marketing*).

'Customer technology literacy presents a challenge to [marketers]. Customers are no longer pushovers. They want to understand more about the products they buy. They are sceptical and critical, and more often dissatisfied ... companies must become more sensitive to customer needs.'

4 Structure

4.1 Having identified your purpose and relevant audience factors, you are in a position to make decisions about **what** you are going to say in your message, and **how**.

4.2 **Structure** involves decisions about:

The **volume** of material to be communicated
The **selection** of material, according to: • **Relevance** • **Importance**
The **classification** or **grouping** of ideas into logical chunks
The **ordering** of the 'chunks' so as to achieve desired effects
The **shape** or **pattern** of the argument as a whole

Volume of information

4.3 More information is not necessarily better information. Think about the purpose of your communication. Think about what the recipient will be able and willing to take in.

4.4 Providing the **right** volume of information means:

(a) Not **overloading** recipients with information they will not be able to get through or take in, in the time available.

(b) Not giving recipients more information than is **relevant** to either your purpose in communicating or theirs in receiving.

(c) Not giving recipients **less** information than you need to give them, or they need to receive, in order to fulfil the purpose of communication.

(d) Giving the required degree of **accuracy**. All information should be accurate in the sense of 'correct' – without falsehood or error – but need not be minutely detailed: an approximation or average figure is often all that is needed. (If you asked: 'Is it hot in Brighton in August?' because you were planning a holiday, you would be happy to hear that it 'averaged 78°F': you would waste time and effort poring through daily temperature readings for a five year period...).

4.5 In practice, it is advisable to offer only three or four main points in a single communication, if you expect the recipient to absorb your message. (**'KISS'** is a useful mnemonic: **Keep It Short & Simple**.)

Offer a short form of the information, enabling the recipient to get an **overview** in a short time and without undue effort. An abstract or summary of the content might be added to a report, say, or an introductory paragraph to a long letter.
Keep the main body of the message as short and to-the-point as possible. Supporting data, examples and digressions could, for example, be separated from the body of a report and put into appendices (singular: appendix), appropriately cross-referenced. Definitions and references could be put in footnotes.
Break the main body of the message up into logical units, to aid concentration and offer natural 'breathers'. Headings, subheadings and numbered points have this effect on the page: similar pauses and signals can be given orally in a speech.
Reinforce important elements of the message at each stage. Summaries, recapitulation of key points, conclusions, diagrams and examples can be used to help the recipient digest each stage of the argument before moving on to the next.

Ordering your ideas

4.6 Once you have selected your main ideas, or clusters of ideas, you need to decide what order to put them in, so as to:

- Get the message across clearly
- Convey the **logical progression** or **links** between the ideas, which are an important part of the message as a whole, particularly in persuasion

- Achieve a **balance** between the ideas so that the audience notices and remembers the ideas you most wish to emphasise – again, particularly in persuasion

4.7 A 'natural' logical order may suggest itself for some categories of information. Here are some of the most common options.

(a) **Chronological order**: sequence according to time/date. This is useful for describing events, correspondence, procedures and so on, which may have no other links between them. In a reply to a complaint letter, for example, you might describe the sequence of events which caused the problem, and the steps taken to resolve it, in order as they have been taken. In a set of instructions, similarly, you would outline the sequence of actions as they occur.

(b) **Order of importance**

(i) **Descending** order – starting with the most important point, and following with those less important. This has the effect of grabbing the audience's attention, motivating them to continue. (This is often used in writing press releases and editorial articles which get 'cut' by editors.)

(ii) **Ascending** order – starting with less important matters and building to the important point. You have to be sure of your audience's motivation and attention to risk this method – although it does have the advantages of building suspense, giving the major point last (where it will be most easily recalled) and preparing the ground for a major point which may be controversial or unpleasant (and therefore rejected if brought out without preparation). This order is most often used in persuasive communication.

(c) **Order of complexity**. Complexity usually works best in **ascending** order: presenting simple ideas first, to build understanding and confidence, and progressing to increasingly difficult ideas. It is suitable for conveying technical information or concepts, in education and training of staff, say, or in product description and demonstration to customers. A similar idea is the **descending** order of **familiarity**, starting with what is known, to establish credibility and confidence, and progressing to the unknown.

(d) **Order of specificity**

(i) You can start with a **general** topic or statement and follow up with **specifics**. This gives an overview, before explaining or demonstrating particular areas. It can also be used to create curiosity (which is then satisfied) or doubt (which is then resolved). For example:

- **Statement + illustration or example**

  'Bad telephone technique can lose you business. If a customer rings to place an order, and you ...'

- **Statement + definition or explanation**

  'Your first problem is bad telephone technique. In other words, the way in which you respond to customers who call ...'

- **Statement + elaboration or enumeration**

  There are three good reasons to improve your telephone technique. First... Second... Third...'

(ii) Alternatively you can present the specifics first and move to the general – by drawing a conclusion, say, or making a generalisation – demonstrating what the

specific items have in common. This can be used to build evidence and suspense, preparing the ground for conclusion: it is a persuasive method.

- Imagine if you were the customer faced with all these responses. They are all symptoms of bad telephone technique. And bad telephone technique can lose you business.

(e) **Balance**. The appearance of objectivity – giving 'both sides of the story' – enhances the message's **credibility**. There a number of ways of achieving a clearly balanced structure. Some immediately suggest themselves from the content of the message or topic.

- An argument often has two sides or viewpoints.
- A problem has two possible solutions, each of which has merit.
- A proposal or product often has advantages ('pros') and disadvantages ('cons').
- Two things or people can be similar (compared) or different (contrasted).
- You can ask a question – and then answer it.

Such topics lend themselves to formats such as 'split' lists (to show the two aspects side by side), or sets (to show the unique qualities of one thing, the unique qualities of another thing, the shared qualities of both). If you were planning a talk or report on these lines, you could 'pattern' your notes appropriately.

Action Programme 5

Credit cards: good or bad? Cards are accepted at a wide range of outlets, although you need to have a good credit record, and to be over 18, to get one. Credit allows you to buy now and pay later – and encourages people to do just that, even beyond their ability to pay: with interest charged on later payment, this can be a problem. However, cards offer convenience, with no cheques required, and often 'perks' such as gift schemes. They also offer the security of carrying no cash, although there is still a risk of fraud.

Washing powder X is effective at 40°C, compared to powder Y: 60°C. It has a biological agent – compared to Y's non-bio. X is recommended for washing machines, and Y for hand washing. X gives much brighter whites than Y. However both powders preserve colour well and both have recyclable packaging, at low cost.

Required

Format notes to show the 'shape' of these two discussions.

4.8 In general, you should consider the following 'order effects'.

- If attention needs to be attracted, the most important point/product benefit should be first.
- If curiosity and interest are already obtained, the message can afford to build up to the most important point at the end. This has the greatest persuasive impact and encourages recall.
- If you have 'good news and bad news', start with the positive: a negative beginning will lose you the audience's support. Once you have established your credibility or congeniality, a negative message might be more readily accepted.

5 Style

5.1 Style, like structure, will be determined by the **purpose** of communication, and the motives, expectations and requirements of the **audience**.

Even more than content, style will be instrumental in establishing the **credibility** and **congeniality** of the source and message, and so how it is received: style is the verbal communication equivalent of personal appearance in face-to-face communication, creating an **impression** that can distort (favourably or unfavourably) the recipient's perception of all other factors.

In some of its aspects, such as the choice of vocabulary, style will also be a deciding factor in whether or not the receiver will understand the message at all.

Key Concept

Sir Ernest Gowers formulated the **five Cs**of good communication.

- CONCISE
- CLEAR
- COURTEOUS
- CORRECT
- COMPLETE

Credibility and congeniality

5.2 A message is more likely to be attended to and accepted if it has **credibility** and **congeniality**.

Key Concept

Credibilitythe message inspires trust and belief in the receiver

Congeniality the message appeals to the recipient's need for satisfaction or confirmation, and desire to avoid unpleasantness, difficulty or dissatisfaction

Credibility

5.3 Factors in the **credibility** of the source include the following.

(a) **Perceived authority**. We are more likely to accept information or opinions from someone who is seen to have a **'right'** to impart them, on the basis of:

- **Prestige and reputation**
- **Knowledge, expertise or experience** in the topic in question

If a known or reputed **expert** gives or endorses a message, people tend to believe it: someone who was only **implied** to be an expert (an actor, say, wearing a white lab coat and carrying a clipboard) can also command credibility, because people tend to associate visual symbols or **'cues'** with particular values (in our actor's case, scientific knowledge). This is why advertisers use celebrity endorsements.

(b) **Perceived intentions**. People may attribute ulterior – say, commercial – motives to the communicator: the source is perceived to have something to gain from moulding or changing the receiver's attitude, and is therefore distrusted. Greater credibility is achieved where the source:

- Appears **honest and straightforward** – giving both sides of the argument
- Appears to be an **objective and unbiased** expert
- Appears to be **acting against** his own best interests

The element of **'disinterestedness'** (not 'lack of interest', but 'having nothing to gain') makes a source highly credible: it is presumed to have the receiver's best interests at heart.

Congeniality

5.4 If things or people are **congenial**, they are:

- Friendly, pleasant or agreeable
- Compatible – having a similar disposition, tastes, attitudes and so on

Congeniality in communication therefore implies the **acceptability** of the message, based on its appeal to values, attitudes, beliefs and expectations the receiver already holds or finds attractive.

5.5 The experience of being confirmed in one's own beliefs is a **psychologically satisfying** or pleasing experience. The same could be said of being informed by an expert, or being talked to socially by an attractive or compatible personality, being told of something that will be to your advantage, or hearing something that appeals to **good** cultural values you accept – like love or peace. Congeniality, in effect, creates **bias**: the receiver has a vested psychological interest in accepting a congenial message or source over an uncongenial one.

Action Programme 6

How credible and congenial do you find the following A5 flyer, which was posted through the door of the editor of this book?

DECORWISE

SERVICES
Est. 1968
999 Upper Richmond Road, Putney, London, SW39 6TH
0181 777 6621

Dear *Householder,*

My name is Jim Smith.

I decorate houses for a living.

I came from Australia in 1966 and have been in the business in this area since then.

I won't go into a big sales talk beyond this:

- A business is as good as its owner
- I'm a straight guy
- I was raised on hard work and honest dealings
- You'll get pretty solid service from me at a moderate price

Please ring for a free quotation.

Jim Smith

Jim Smith
MANAGER

PS We do all aspects of property maintenance and small construction, to supplement the decorating.

THE GUILD OF MASTER CRAFTSMEN

QUALITY PAINT FINISHES • PAPER AND VINYL HANGING • INTERIORS AND EXTERIORS
COMMERCIAL AND DOMESTIC. ASSOCIATED REPAIR WORK - CARPENTRY + PLASTERING.

BPP PUBLISHING

Tone

5.6 Non-verbal messages can be conveyed by **'tone'** of voice in speaking. However, the same effect can be achieved in writing. The total effect on the reader of your use of vocabulary and sentence structure, as well as the content of your message, may be called 'tone'. Writers must aim consciously for a warm, friendly, firm or honest tone, if they are to elicit a positive response.

5.7 There are various ways in which writers display their own **attitudes** to what they are expressing, whether they consciously intend to or not. Some points to look out for include the following.

(a) **Positive and negative sentence constructions**. You can always express things in a positive or in a negative way: people respond more favourably to the positive. 'I haven't finished my assignment today.' 'I will finish my assignment tomorrow.'

(b) **Mood**. There are three moods in English: the indicative (for statements and questions); the imperative (for commands and requests); and the subjunctive (for wishes, doubts, probabilities and possibilities). For example, the imperative 'Shut that door' or even 'Shut that door, please' may not be suitable in situations where courtesy and respect are necessary. The indicative question 'Will you shut that door, please?' would be preferable, as would the even more polite subjunctive 'Would you shut that door, please?'

(c) **Personal and impersonal**. Note the distancing effect of the impersonal construction: 'It + passive verb'. This might be appropriate in a formal report, or where the writer deliberately wants to distance himself from his message, but in a more personal context the air of indifference might be offensive. 'It was considered by the Board that closure of the works may be necessary.' 'It was agreed that you should be made redundant.'

5.8 Be particularly aware of tone when writing e-mails. Because of their brevity and mediation through a computer screen, they can come across much more abruptly than intended. Humour, in particular, can fall flat: what works as irony or sarcasm in spoken words may be taken literally in type.

Emphasis

5.9 **Emphasis** can take the form of a significant stress on **key words**, or the vigour and decisiveness with which an idea is expressed. You can emphasise points which you consider particularly important, or want the other person to remember, by the following.

(a) **Accenting** spoken words, perhaps adding an appropriate gesture or look to signal 'Important. Get this'.

(b) Using **visual techniques** in written messages, such as italicising, emboldening or underlining words, attracting the eye by spacing and so on.

(c) **Repetition** (without becoming irritating or boring). Words or expressions may be repeated: 'It's ridiculous. Absolutely ridiculous.' Another alternative is the use of parallel sentence structures: 'Look at the way absenteeism has risen. Look at the way industrial disputes have increased. Look at the way morale has plummeted. Now look me in the eye and tell me this is an efficient firm.'

Interest

5.10 Style also embraces the methods you use to put across your ideas in a way that is interesting, impactful, persuasive – or whatever is required. There are a wide variety of methods, including the following.

Analogy – comparing one thing to something else that is more familiar or interesting
Anecdote – a story or reminiscence that invites identification, or illustrates a point
Anticlimax – setting up expectation, and then deflating it. (If the expectation was negative, this can be a relief.) Often humorous
Curiosity – setting up an intriguing or mysterious proposition
Definition – making sure all terms are understood in the same way by everyone
Description – using 'picture' language to aid imagination
Emotion – using, or appealing to, warmth, anger, fear, pride, loyalty and so on
Exaggeration – for shock value, humour or (rather dishonestly) persuasion
Example – to illustrate a concept
Explanation – to help the recipient to understand causes or reasons
Facts – to support an argument, building credibility
Humour – a variable and subjective quality: to be used with caution
Metaphor – describing something in terms of something else ('the minefield of industrial relations')
Narrative – telling a 'story', building curiosity as to what happens next
Opinion – challenging the audience, or inviting identification with the communicator
Questions – inviting response, or setting up anticipation (eg 'rhetorical' questions: ones you ask and answer yourself)
Quotations – adding credibility by appealing to other sources
Repetition – reinforcing and emphasising
Statistics – reinforcing credibility, offering supporting evidence
Understatement – inviting the audience to imagine that it is **really** bigger/better etc

Chapter Roundup

- This has been an important chapter, offering practical advice on formulating a business message: you should refer back to it, as required, and apply these principles to each of the communication media and tasks discussed in the rest of this *Study Text.*
- Since all of the material in this chapter is likely to be useful to you in detail, it is not possible to summarise its content, except to reinforce the framework it sets up for your use.
  - **P**urpose: general (inform, persuade, confirm etc) and specific (outcome desired)
  - **A**udience: who are they and what will they want/expect to hear, what will they resist hearing?
  - **S**tructure: volume and selection of material, grouping of ideas, order or shape of argument
  - **S**tyle: vocabulary, syntax, tone, emphasis, interest

Quick Quiz

1 What does PASS stand for?

2 Which of the following might be a problem when communicating with someone when they are at work?

A Preoccupation
B Role conflict
C Privacy
D All of the above

3 Fill in the gaps in the following sentences, using the words provided.

'The (1)......... audience is increasingly (2)........... itself by gravitating towards specialised on-line (3)........... Users want (4)......... answers, product (5)......... based on their tastes and (6)......... and (7)......... interaction. Computer technology has turned (8).......... customers into (9).......... customers.'

- personalised
- recommendations
- on-line
- communities
- informed
- segmenting
- timely
- preferences
- uninformed

4 A report opening with an executive summary and then going through each point in turn is structured in:

Descending order of specificity	Descending order of importance	Ascending order of specificity	Ascending order of complexity

5 .... is the quality that appeals to the audience's need for satisfaction or confirmation.

6 People respond more favourably to positive sentence constructions than negative ones.

☐ True ☐ False

7 Which of the following style elements would *not* be used primarily to enhance the audience's understanding of a complex subject?

A Explanation
B Definition
C Example
D Quotation

Answers to Quick Quiz

1 Purpose, audience, structure, style

2 D

3 (1) on-line, (2) segmenting, (3) communities, (4) timely, (5) recommendations, (6) preferences, (7) personalised, (8) uninformed, (9) informed.

4 Ascending order of specificity

5 Congeniality

6 True

7 D

Now try Question 10 from the Question Bank at the end of this Text

Action Programme Review

1 You may think of other communication tasks as you go through the *Study Text*. It is important to establish the **primary objective** in each case.

2 (a) It would be unrealistic to offer excessive compensation, or the dismissal of all the staff responsible in response to a minor defect on a vacuum cleaner: the perceived gain for the recipient would far outweigh the benefit of keeping their future goodwill and custom. If you offered more moderate redress and emphasised the fact that the complaint was being taken seriously and the matter was being addressed, the communication is much more likely to be successful.

(b) You may wish to air your grievance and to seek immediate payment. If you only attempt the first, the recipient will be able to further stall payment (soothing you at least possible cost to himself) by way of a simple apology. Once you attempt the second, however, the recipient has to address the issue of payment and possible court action: you have left no easy way around your desired outcome.

3 Your response will be affected as much by who you are and what position you occupy in an organisation as that of the recipient. Among factors you should consider are: the Major's age (he is a Bursar); the relative importance of cleaning materials to him (it is more appropriate to contact his secretary, at least in the first instance); and the fact that you are contacting an educational establishment.

4 This is a useful exercise in appreciating international cultural variations.

5

1 *[Split list]*

CREDIT CARDS

Pro	*Con*
1 Wide range of outlets	1 Need good credit record
2 Buy now, pay later	2 Interest charged on late repayment
3 Convenience – no cheques	3 Minimum age 18
4 Security – no cash	4 Encourages spending beyond ability to pay
5 'Perks' – eg gift schemes	5 Risk of fraud

2 *[Set]*

Effective at 40ºC Biological agent Recommended for washing machine Brighter whites	Powder X
Recyclable packaging Low cost	*similarities*
Preserves colours Effective at 60ºC Non-biological agent Recommended for hand wash Poor whiteness	Powder Y

6 Decorwise's letter may be considered credible because of its:

(a) Imposing letterhead and long-established business
(b) Link to the Guild of Master Craftsmen
(c) Modest tone: not trying to raise inflated expectations
(d) Offer of a free quotation

It may be considered congenial because of its:

(a) Simple design and straightforward content
(b) No-nonsense, colloquial style and informality
(c) Personal communication from Jim
(d) Appeal to solid working class values

Oral and face-to-face communication

11

Chapter Topic List	
1	Setting the scene
2	Using the telephone
3	Preparing effective presentations
4	Giving effective presentations
5	Running effective meetings
6	Negotiations

Learning Outcomes

- ☑ Appreciate the advantages and disadvantages of oral and face-to-face communication
- ☑ Make and receive telephone calls in a professional and effective manner
- ☑ Plan, prepare and deliver effective presentations, using appropriate visual aids
- ☑ Arrange and conduct effective meetings, using appropriate documentation
- ☑ Identify the purpose, audience, structure and style (PASS) requirements of a variety of oral and face-to-face communication situations

Syllabus References

- ☑ Explain the importance and the advantages and disadvantages of different types of communication in a variety of face-to-face situations (4.1)
- ☑ Explain key communication factors to consider in meetings, including arranging and convening a meeting, documentation involved and strategies for conducting a meeting (4.6)

- ☑ Plan, prepare and deliver a presentation using appropriate and effective visual aids and media (4.7)
- ☑ Use a variety of formats to communicate with internal and external customers, including the telephone (4.8)

Key Concepts Introduced

- Telemarketing
- Visual aids
- Agenda
- Negotiation

1 Setting the scene

1.1 This is a long chapter, but don't panic! Take it topic by topic, and complete the Action Programmes as you go. It is all highly practical material.

Oral communication

1.2 Oral communication means, simply, communication by speech, or 'word of mouth'. Face to face oral media include conversations, meetings, interviews, negotiations and public addresses, presentations or briefings. Interactive oral communication can also take place when the sender and receiver are not physically face-to-face, through telephone calls, video conferencing or Webcasting.

1.3 The advantages and disadvantages of such communication may be summarised as follows.

Advantages	Disadvantages
Speed/directness: little or no time lapse between sending and receiving	**Less planning time** to formulate and check message and responses
Interactivity: real-time exchange of ideas, opinions, questions. Ability to respond directly to questions, make decisions.	**Ephemeral** (passes with time): does not allow for reception at audience's own pace, repeated reference etc (as writing does)
Feedback: immediate and versatile (non-verbal messages). Ability to clarify, check, reinforce messages.	**Ambiguity**: people's perceptions and memory of what was said may differ. (May need written checking, confirmation.)
Influence: interactivity (plus use of non-verbal messages) supports ability to persuade, motivate	**Influence**: strong personalities/voices can prevent others being heard
Sensitivity: interactivity and personal nature (voice, non-verbals) allows for sensitive handling of difficult messages	**Technical noise**: potential for interference (for example, from noise, bad phone lines)

Face-to-face communication

1.4 Face-to-face communication is particularly effective in:

- Allowing **non-verbal cues**, both **audible** (for example, tone of voice) and **visual** (body language), to be used to enhance understanding and persuasion
- Allowing immediate **exchange and feedback**
- Humanising the **context** of communication by opening the parties to each other's direct scrutiny and to personal factors

1.5 The advantages and their applications can be summarised as follows.

Advantages	Examples of application
Encourages **ideas generation**: participants encouraging and prompting each other	**Brainstorming meeting** for promotion planning or customer care improvement
Encourages **problem solving** and **conflict resolution**: allows exchange and supportive communication, sensitivity to personal factors	**Customer complaint handling**, or **employee counselling**
Improves **decision-making**: adds different viewpoints and information in real time	**Team meetings** to decide strategies or allocate roles
Facilitates **persuasion**: use of personal charisma, logic, adjustment to feedback	**Sales negotiations**, **pitching** ideas to internal/external clients
Encourages **cooperation**: information sharing, participation	**Team meetings**
Shows the **human face** of an organisation, and encourages identification with it	**Personal customer service**

Action Programme 1

What disadvantages can you see in the use of face-to-face communication? (Think about the meetings and interviews you have participated in...)

1.6 We will now look at a number of specific oral and face-to-face formats.

2 Using the telephone

2.1 The range of telecommunication services available to businesses is **constantly expanding**. Developments in satellite communications, cellular radio, video link-ups and even the video-telephone are matched by improvements in the transmission and handling of telephone messages, with computerised telephone networks and switchboards. The telephone is fast, one-to-one, interactive and personal – and it allows communication from different locations – whether offices or continents! this makes it the most widely-used tool for communicating within the office environment. (Its only rival now is e-mail, but the telephone has the advantages of oral communication, where required, and almost universal acceptance and availability.)

Exam Tip

As with oral skills generally, it is clearly difficult to test your competence at using the telephone in the context of a written exam. Questions (under the old syllabus) have, however, asked you to draft out a telephone conversation that might take place in a particular scenario (re-arranging a meeting or apologising to a customer)

A number of past questions have asked you to write a memo or to prepare a presentation on good telephone technique. Others have asked about the advantages of the telephone compared with other media

Preparation

2.2 Firstly you will have to learn how to work the apparatus in use in your organisation, and any rules and procedures applied to its use. The next thing to remember is that telephone technique works on the same principles as any other communication. You should **still** make it **Concise, Clear, Courteous, Correct** and **Complete**. Another useful C in telephone usage is **Control**: prepare, as far as possible, for any call you are going to make, and ensure that you **concentrate** n the conversation with your whole attention.

Making calls

2.3 You can prepare quite extensively before you make a telephone call.

(a) **Know why** you are making the call. What information do you wish to convey or obtain? What do you wish to persuade the other person of? What confirmation or assistance do you seek?

(b) **Know what** result you are aiming at. What action or information will satisfy you, and where and when must you get them? You might **say** 'I was just wondering...' to sound tactful, but make sure that you have done all your 'wondering' before you pick up the receiver.

(c) **Know to whom** you should be talking. Find out names and extension numbers whenever possible, and keep them handy in a personal directory.

(d) **Know what** you want to say, and the order and manner in which you want to say it.

- A **checklist of points**, in logical/persuasive/tactful order, will be an invaluable reminder.
- You might like to give yourself brief **prompts** as to tone and approach, eg 'NB: Sensitive point. Careful.' or 'Agreed at last meeting. Remind.'.
- Have all relevant documents and **reference material** to hand.

(e) Make sure you will not be **interrupted**, distracted or disturbed once you have dialled.

Tactics and techniques

2.4 When you get through to the dialled number, wait for a greeting and identification from the answering party. **Seek** the identification if necessary. ('Good morning. To whom am I speaking?') It is time-wasting and embarrassing to launch into the subject of your call, only to be interrupted two minutes later by: 'I'm sorry. You need to speak to ... ' or even 'Thank you. I'll put you through.'

2.5 If the target recipient of your call is out or otherwise unavailable, carry out your 'Plan B', which may be any one of the following.

(a) Ask to speak to **someone else** who might be knowledgeable enough to help you.

(b) Leave a **message** with the secretary, or switchboard operator. Make it a brief one, but dictate clearly all essential details of who you are, where you can be contacted, and what the main subject of your call was to be. State whether you wish to be called back.

(c) Arrange to **call back** at a convenient time, when it is anticipated that the target will be available.

NEVER BE IN TOO MUCH OF A HURRY TO SAY 'PLEASE' AND 'THANK YOU'

2.6 Once through to the appropriate person, the business of the call should be covered as **succinctly** as possible (consistent with rapport-building and courtesy).

Greet the other person by **name**: if you do not already know it – find out first!
Prepare the ground by briefly explaining the context of your call, what it is about, any relevant details.
Remember that the other person **cannot see you** to lip-read, judge your facial expression, or see you nod your head. Speak clearly, spell out proper names and figures; use your tone of voice to reinforce your message.
Pace your message so that the other person can refer to files or take notes.
Check your own notes as you speak and make fresh ones of any information you receive.
You may easily be **misheard** or misinterpreted over the telephone line, so you will have to seek constant feedback. If you are not receiving any signals, ask for some ('Have you got that?', 'Can you read that back?', 'Am I going too fast for you?', 'OK?')
Close the call effectively. Emphasise any action you require, and check that the other person has understood your expectations.

Action Programme 2

You work in the Marketing Department of Satchel & Satchel Ltd. You have had trouble with the electric sockets in the department, to the point where several of the wordprocessors have 'gone down' without warning and several hours' work lost. You are also worried about the fire hazard involved.

You called Sparx Ltd, the electricians you always use, last Friday (5th August). They immediately sent round an engineer called Boris Jones, who has apparently just joined the company. He kept up a stream of suggestive remarks to the female office staff, and was surly almost to the point of rudeness when you asked him how the work was coming. He worked for four hours, produced a proforma invoice charging you for those hours plus travelling time, and left. On Monday morning, your desk lamp suffers a small explosion, and another wordprocessor bites the dust. Chaos ensues.

You are going to telephone your old contact at Sparx Ltd, Mrs Wilkinson (0171 740 1111 extension 334) who is Boris' supervisor. You are extremely annoyed but you resolve not to take it out on Mrs Wilkinson (who, after all, did send someone promptly). Still, you want to inform her about Boris, you want action, and you do not want to have to pay for Boris' work.

(a) Make full preparatory notes, such as you could conveniently refer to in the course of the conversation.

(b) Mrs Wilkinson is in fact out. You urgently need another engineer sent round, but you want to speak **only** to Mrs Wilkinson about Boris and the invoice. What do you decide to do? If you speak to someone else, mark on your first notes which points you will now be able to use. If you leave a message with the operator, write out what you would dictate.

(Key skill for marketers: working with others)

Taking calls

2.7 It is very important that those who **answer** the telephones in an organisation should be **efficient, courteous and helpful**. A voice on the telephone may be the **first** or only **impression** of the organisation that an outsider receives: remember that you will have to create the impression you make with your voice and responsiveness alone.

Give a **courteous greeting** and **identify yourself** in whatever way is appropriate (name, department, organisation): there may be 'house rules' about this.
Identify and **note** the caller's name and organisation as soon as possible
Listen carefully to the message: it may require instant action or response.
Check your understanding. If the other person speaks too fast, or you do not catch something, are not sure that you have heard it right, or simply do not understand, say so: a courteous interruption to ask for a repetition or spelling is helpful to the caller.
Never leave callers hanging. If you have to transfer them to another extension or put them on hold, tell them what you intend to do.

Speak clearly and with a certain **formality**, and keep your **tone** appropriately helpful, courteous and alert. (It is easy to sound brusque when you intend to sound efficient).

Take **concise notes** of any details you may require in order to follow up the conversation. If you are giving information, pace it so that the caller can also take notes.

Co-operate with the caller. If you can resolve the matter in the course of the call, for example, by providing information, do so. If there are still matters to be resolved – further action to be taken or information to be sent to the caller by post – make sure that you are both clear as to what is required, and within what timeframe.

Marketing at Work

Here is an example of a conversation in which all parties are efficient telephone users.

Operator	Investment Services. Can I help you?
Caller	Can I speak to Mrs Brenda Brown, please. Extension 456.
Operator	I am trying to connect you... . The line is engaged. Will you hold?
Caller	Can I leave a message with someone?
Operator	One moment, please.
	...
Secretary	Mrs Brown's secretary. Can I help you?
Caller	My name is Mrs Elsie Taylor. Will you take a message for Mrs Brown, please?
Secretary	Yes, Mrs Taylor. What is the message?
Caller	I am sorry I have to cancel my lunch engagement with her on Tuesday. Would she please ring me within the next hour to arrange another date. Telephone 68-4956.
Secretary	(Repeats message.)
Caller	That is correct.
Secretary	Thank you, Mrs Taylor. I will pass the message to Mrs Brown **quickly**.
Caller	Thank you. Goodbye.

Action Programme 3

The following is a telephone conversation between a job candidate and the prospective employer.

Lines		
1	Operator:	Can I help you?
2	Caller:	This is Joanne Doe. Can I speak to Mr Armstrong in personnel please?
3	[Silence: clicking and buzzing noises]	
4	Secretary:	I'm sorry, Ms Doe. Mr Armstrong is not available. Can I help?
5	Caller:	I have an appointment with Mr Armstrong at 3 pm today. Can I change it to tomorrow?
6	Secretary:	One moment, please. [Short pause.] I think Mr Armstrong might be able to manage 3 pm tomorrow. Will that suit you?

7	Caller:	Yes. Unless my husband has something else planned.
8	Secretary:	Right Ms Doe. Mr Armstrong will see you then. Goodbye.
9	Caller:	Thank you. Goodbye.

Using the line numbers on the left-hand side, list 7 ways in which this call is inefficiently handled

Telemarketing

Key Concept

Telemarketing can be defined as a marketing communication system using trained personnel to conduct planned, measurable marketing activities by phone which are directed at targeted groups of customers.

2.8 The telephone provides the marketer with a number of positive advantages.

(a) **Quick response**

- Prospective customers receive immediate information about your product/ service.
- Sellers get immediate response (feedback) from consumers and *vice versa*.

(b) **Interaction**

- Although both parties (buyer and seller) do not see each other, telephone provides the fastest person-to-person contact, with two way traffic of information and instant personal reaction.
- A successful telephone conversation can result in a sales appointment, direct sale or customer relationship building (for example, a follow-up service call).

(c) **Accessibility**

- It is often possible to gain access to individuals who would never agree to an appointment.
- Little preparation is needed to access your target audience.
- It enables access to large number of potential customers in a very short time period.

(d) **Easy assessment**

The telephone allows the seller the opportunity to assess the individual's willingness or readiness to buy and focus selling effort and time on prospects with the greatest potential.

(e) **Cost**

- Although telephone contact is still labour intensive, it allows personal contact to be made without physical travel.
- Used in preparation of personal visits, it can ensure the most effective use of personal selling time.

2.9 The telephone does have its limitations and it needs to be used with care to avoid problems.

(a) Unsolicited calls can cause annoyance, particularly amongst householders when calls can be intrusive or received at an inconvenient time.

(b) Calls may be disguised as research or other information-generating activities, and so are misleading.

(c) Sales calls leave no tangible record. Without support literature, the buyer or seller may misunderstand the communication, and verbal contracts negotiated by phone are difficult to prove. In the business sector, however, the increased availability of fax and machines to be used in conjunction with, or instead of, direct telephone selling, offers email the chance for instant tangibility of messages.

(d) There is no chance to demonstrate or show samples, increasing the buyer's risk (unless the seller or brand is already known).

Action Programme 4

The Office of Fair Trading has published guidelines for the use of telephones in selling. Look up a copy of these in your residential phone book, or at OFT's website.

3 Preparing effective presentations

3.1 You may associate **presentations** with a particular context – possibly not one relevant to you personally. However, consider the following situations.

(a) Consultants and advertising agencies make presentations to senior management, to **sell** their conclusions and **recommendations**.

(b) Sales people make presentations or 'pitches' **to clients** or potential clients, discussing and demonstrating the benefits of a product, service or brand.

(c) Specialists make **technical presentations** to management or staff, briefing them on **findings** or facts relevant to their work. A market researcher might brief the sales force on findings with regard to buyer motivation, for example.

(d) A member of staff who has researched and written a **report** may be asked to present it orally to a group of interested parties who may **not have time** to read its contents, or who may require the opportunity to challenge its findings, ask **questions**, or be persuaded further.

3.2 As you can see, presentations may vary widely in a number of aspects.

- **The size of the audience**
- **The composition, knowledge, interests and motivations of the audience**
- **The purpose and approach of the presentation** (information/briefing, persuasion/pitch, demonstration/explanation, entertainment/welcome and so on).
- **The length and complexity of the content**
- **The formality of the situation**

Don't forget to take all these factors into account when planning to **target your presentation** to the purpose and audience.

Action Programme 5

What presentations, conferences, or speech-making occasions have you attended recently? For each, note:

- The style of speech (formal/informal etc)
- The length of the speech
- Any visual aids used

How effective was the speaker in **targeting** each of these elements to

(a) The **purpose** of the speech and
(b) The needs of the **audience**

Purpose

3.3 If your **objectives** are going to help you plan your presentation, and enable you to measure how far you have been successful in achieving them, they need to be:

- **Specific**
- **Measurable**

Your objectives should therefore be stated in active and dynamic terms, in terms of what the **audience** will do, or how they will be changed, at the end of the presentation: they will believe, be persuaded, agree, be motivated, do, understand, be able to ... .

Action Programme 6

Rephrase the following objectives so that they are more helpful, and measurable.

1 To explain to new staff how the fax machine works
2 To tell customers about the new product
3 To contrast Brand X and Brand Y
4 To recommend flexi-time working to management
5 To help students write effective reports

Audience

3.4 Taking into account any **specific** audience needs and expectations, your message needs to have the following qualities.

(a) **Interest**. It should be lively/entertaining/varied or relevant to the audience's needs and interests, or preferably both.

(b) **Congeniality**. This usually means positive, supportive or helpful in some way (eg in making a difficult decision easier, or satisfying a need).

(c) **Credibility**. It should be **consistent** in itself, and with known **facts**; apparently **objective**; and from a source perceived to be **trustworthy**.

(d) **Accessibility**. This means both:

- **Audible/visible**. (Do you need to be closer to the audience? Do you need a microphone? Enlarged visual aids? Clearer articulation and projection?)
- **Understandable**. (What is the audience's level of knowledge/education/ experience in general? and of the topic at hand? What technical terms or **jargon** will need to be avoided or explained? What concepts or ideas will need to be explained?)

Structure

3.5 Armed with your clearly-stated objectives and audience profile, you can plan the **content** of your presentation. Michael Stevens *(Improving Your Presentation Skills)* notes that:

> 'Even if you feel you have a good grasp of all aspects of a subject, trying to put them on paper in their finished form can be a slow, frustrating, ineffective way of writing a presentation. You are asking your brain to do three things at once, each requiring different thinking skills. Trying to recall the information, put it in a logical order, and state it clearly all in one step can cloud your thinking.'

3.6 One approach which may help to clarify your thinking is as follows.

Brainstorm	Write down all the thoughts and points that come to you on the subject in hand, without stopping to analyse them.
Prioritise	Select the **key points** of the subject, and a **storyline** or theme that gives your argument a unified sense of 'direction'. The **fewer** points you make (with the most emphasis) and the clearer the **direction** in which your thoughts are heading, the easier it will be for the audience to grasp and retain your message.
Structure	Make notes for your presentation which **illustrate** simply the **logical order** or **pattern** of the key points of your speech.
Outline	Following your structured notes, **flesh out** your message. ■ **Introduction** ■ **Supporting evidence**, **examples and illustrations** ■ **Notes** where **visual aids** will be used ■ **Conclusion**
Practise	Rehearsals should indicate difficult logical leaps, dull patches, unexplained terms and other problems: adjust your outline or style. They will also help you gauge and adjust the **length** of your presentation.
Cue	Your outline may be too detailed to act as a cue or **aide-memoire** for the talk itself. **Small cards**, which fit into the palm of the hand may be used to give you: ■ **Key words** for each topic, and the logical links between them ■ Reminders for when to use **visual aids** ■ The **full text** of any detailed information you need to quote

Action Programme 7

You have been asked by your manager to give a brief talk to the junior staff on the subject of: 'The tidy office: efficiency, safety and image'.

You know this issue is a bit sensitive at the moment, having recently had to tell people off about the state of the Sales Administration Department offices. The staff are on the defensive, and have been complaining loudly about the cleaning lady. However, several files have been mislaid, others turning up in wastepaper bins or marked by rings from the bottom of coffee cups. It seems as if, every time a visitor is due in the Department, you have to make people interrupt their duties to have a swift 'spring clean': they sulk. Unfortunately you do not always get enough warning of visits – and morale suffers again, because the staff are as aware of the mess as you are. Most recently, you have lost two of your assistants through illness, one suffering asthmatic attacks caused by dust (which you know is the cleaning lady's fault), and another having strained his back picking up a stack of loose files which he had accidentally knocked off the edge of his desk.

You are going to have to do something about the tidiness problem. The staff's habits will have to be corrected firmly – but tactfully, because of the atmosphere of hostility that is creeping into the issue. Stress positive aspects of a tidy office, in line with the title of your talk. Make helpful notes for your talk.

Exam Tip

Presentations have featured often in exams. Typical requirements are to advise others on how to give presentations (in the specimen Paper for this syllabus), to prepare notes for a presentation on a specific topic (also in the Specimen paper), to prepare slides that might be used during the presentation, or to describe visual aids (such as flipcharts) that you might use (see later in this chapter).

3.7 An effective presentation requires two key structural elements.

(a) An **introduction** which:

- Establishes your credibility
- Establishes rapport with the audience
- Gains the audience's attention and interest (sets up the problem to be solved, uses curiosity or surprise)
- Gives the audience an overview of the **shape** of your presentation, to guide them through it: a bit like the scanning process in reading.

(b) A **conclusion** which:

- **Clarifies and draws together** the points you have made into one main idea (using an example, anecdote, review, summary)
- **States or implies what you want/expect your audience to do** following your presentation
- Reinforces the audience's **recall** (using repetition, a joke, quotation or surprising statistic to make your main message **memorable**).

3.8 Your structured notes and outline should contain cues which clarify the **logical order**, shape or progression of your information or argument. This will help the audience to **follow you** at each stage of your argument, so that they arrive with you at the conclusion. You can signal these logical links to the audience as follows.

(a) **Linking words or phrases**

Therefore ... As a result ...	[conclusion, result or effect, arising from previous point]
However ... On the other hand ...	[contradiction or alternative to previous point]
Similarly ... Again ...	[confirmation or additional example of previous point]
Moreover ...	[building on the previous point]

(b) **Framework**: setting up the structure

'Of course, this isn't a perfect solution: There are advantages and disadvantages to it. It has the advantages of ... . But there are also disadvantages, in that ... '

'You might like to think of communication in terms of the 5 C's. That's: concise, clear, correct, complete, courteous. Let's look at each of these in turn'.

3.9 **Visual aids** will also be an important aspect of content used to signal the structure and clarify the meaning of your message. We discuss them specifically in Section 4 below.

Style

3.10 The style of your presentation text delivery should be used to add

- Clarity
- Emphasis
- Interest

to messages. Refer back to Chapter 10 for the elements of style if you need to.

Action Programme 8

You are trying to persuade management to adopt flexitime hours in the marketing department. Suggest six approaches, using different themes and techniques which you might use to build and enhance your argument.

4 Giving effective presentations

Delivery

4.1 **Delivery** of a presentation is equivalent to 'style' and 'presentation' in writing. In Chapter 9, we talked about verbal and non-verbal skills: all these skills will be involved in presenting material effectively to an audience.

Controlling nerves

4.2 **Stage-fright** can be experienced before making a phone call, going into an interview or meeting, or even writing a letter, but it is considerably more acute, for most people, before standing up to talk in front of a group or crowd of people. Common fears are to do with **making a fool of oneself**, forgetting one's **lines**, being unable to answer **questions**, or being faced by blank incomprehension or **lack of response**. Fear can make vocal delivery hesitant or stilted and **body language** stiff and unconvincing.

4.3 A **controlled amount of fear**, or stress, is actually **good for you**: it stimulates the production of **adrenaline**, which can contribute to alertness and dynamic action. Only at excessive levels is stress harmful, degenerating into **strain**. If you can **manage your stress** or stage-fright, it will help you to be **alert** to feedback from your audience, to think 'on your feet' in response to questions, and to project vitality and enthusiasm.

(a) **Reduce uncertainty and risk**. This means:

- **Preparing thoroughly** for your talk, including rehearsal, and anticipating questions
- **Checking** the venue and facilities meet your expectations
- **Preparing** whatever is necessary for your own confidence and comfort (hayfever medication, glass of water, handkerchief, note cards etc)
- **Keeping your notes to hand**, and in order, during your presentation.

(b) **Have confidence in your message**. Concentrate on the desired outcome: that is why you are there. Believe in what you are saying. It will also make it easier to project enthusiasm and energy.

(c) **Control physical symptoms.** Breathe deeply and evenly. Control your gestures and body movements. Put down a piece of paper that is visibly shaking in your hand. Pause to collect your thoughts if necessary. Smile, and maintain eye contact with members of the audience. If you **act** as if you are calm, the calm will **follow**.

Non-verbal messages

4.4 Any number of factors may contribute to a speaker **looking confident and relaxed**, or nervous, shifty and uncertain. **Cues** which indicate confidence – without arrogance – may be as follows.

(a) An upright – but not stiff – **posture**: slouching gives an impression of shyness or carelessness.

(b) **Movement** that is purposeful and dynamic, used sparingly: not constant or aimless pacing, which looks nervous.

(c) **Gestures** that are relevant, purposeful and flowing: not indecisive, aggressive, incomplete or compulsive. Use gestures **deliberately** to reinforce your message, and if possible keep your hands up so that gestures do not distract the audience from watching your face. In a large venue, gestures will have to be exaggerated – but practise making them look **natural**. Watch out for habitual, irrelevant gestures you may tend to make.

(d) **Eye-contact** with the audience maintains credibility, maintains the involvement of the audience and allows you to gather audience feedback as to how well you are getting you message across. Eye-contact should be **established immediately**, and **re-established** after periods when you have had to look away, to consult notes or use visual aids.

The most effective technique is to let our gaze wander (purposefully) across the whole audience, **involving** them all, without intimidating anybody: establish eye-contact long enough for it to be registered, to accompany a point you are making, and then move on.

Visual aids

Key Concept

The term **visual aids**covers a wide variety of forms which share two characteristics.

(a) **They use a visual image**.

(b) **They act as an aid to communication.** This may seem obvious, but it is important to remember that visual aids are not supposed to be impressive or clever for their own sake, but to support the message and speaker in achieving their purpose.

4.5 Michael Stevens (*Improving Your Presentation Skills*) notes:

> 'The proper use of aids is to achieve something in your presentation that you cannot do as effectively with words alone. They are only *a means to an end*, for instance to clarify an idea, or prove a point. A good aid is one which does this efficiently.'

4.6 A number of media and devices are available for using visual aids. They may be summarised as follows.

Equipment/medium	Advantages	Disadvantages
Slides: photographs, text or diagrams projected onto a screen or other surface	■ Allow colour photos: good for mood, impact and realism ■ Pre-prepared: no speaker 'down time' during talk ■ Controllable sequence/ timing: pace content/audience needs	■ Require a darkened room: may hinder note-taking ■ Malfunction and/or incompetent use: frustration and distraction
Film/video shown on a screen or TV monitor	■ Moving images: realism, impact: can enhance credibility (eye witness effect)	■ Less flexible in allowing interruption, pause or speeding up to pace audience needs
Overheads: films or acetates (hand drawn or printed) projected by light box onto a screen behind/above the presenter	■ Versatility of content and presentation ■ Low cost (for example, if hand written) ■ Clear sheets: can be used to build up images as points added	■ Require physical handling: can be distracting ■ Risk of technical breakdown: not readily adaptable to other means of projection
Presentation software: for example, Microsoft PowerPoint. PC-generated slide show (with animation, sound) projected from PC to screen via data projector	■ Versatility of multi-media: impact, interest ■ Professional design and functioning (smooth transitions) ■ Use of animation to build, link and emphasise as points added	■ Requires PC, data projector: expensive, may not be available ■ Risk of technical breakdown: not readily adaptable to other means of projection ■ Temptation to over-complexity and over-use: distraction
Flip charts: large paper pad mounted on frame – sheets are 'flipped' to the back when finished with	■ Low cost, low-risk ■ Allows use during session (for example, to 'map' audience views, ideas) ■ Can be pre-prepared (for example, advertising 'story boards') ■ Easy to refer back	■ Smaller, still, paper-based image: less impact ■ Hand-prepared: may lack perceived quality (compared to more sophisticated methods)
Handouts: supporting notes handed out for reference during or after the session	■ Pre-prepared ■ Audience doesn't need to take as many notes: reminder provided	■ Audience doesn't need to take as many notes: may encourage passive listening.
Props and demonstrations: objects or processes referred to are themselves shown to the audience	■ Enhances credibility (eye witness effect) ■ Enhances impact (sensory solidity)	■ May not be available ■ Risk of self-defeating 'hitches'

4.7 The following (Figures 11.1 and 11.2) show two of the media discussed above, demonstrating some of their key features – and how a picture can be a helpful 'break' from reading or hearing lots of verbal content!

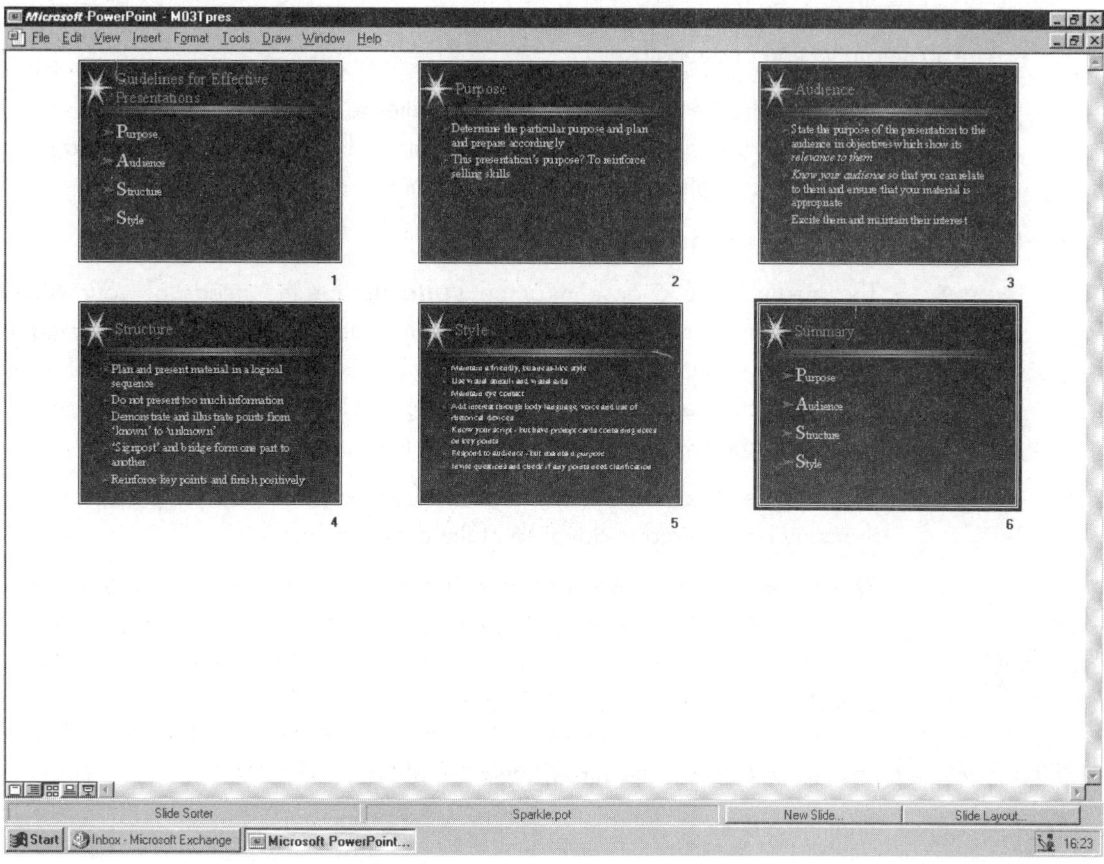

Figure 11.1: A PowerPoint slide planner

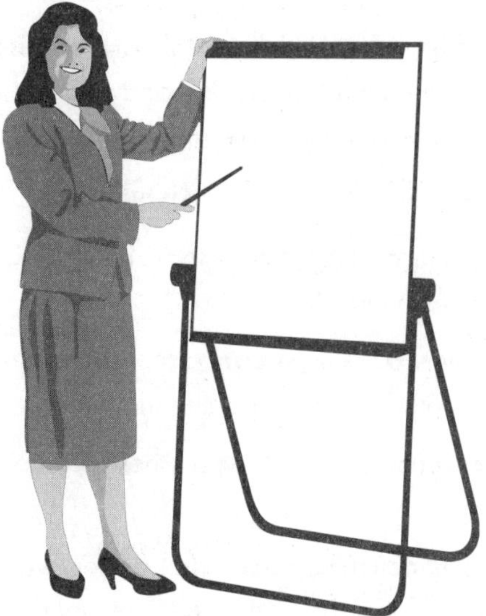

Figure 11.2: A flip chart

4.8 Whatever medium or device you are using, visual aids are **versatile** with regard to **content**: maps, diagrams, flowcharts, verbal notes, drawings, photographs and so on.

4.9 When planning and using visual aids, consider the following points.

(a) Visual aids are **simplified and concrete**: they are easier to grasp than the spoken word, allowing the audience to absorb complex relationships and information.

(b) Visual aids are **stimulating** to the imagination and emotions, and therefore useful in gaining attention and recall.

(c) Visual aids can also be **distracting** for the audience – and for the presenter, who has to draw/write/organise/operate them. They can add complexity and ambiguity to the presentation if not carefully designed for relevance and clarity.

(d) Visual aids impose **practical requirements**.

- The medium you choose must be **suitable** for the needs of your **audience**. Demonstrations, or handing round a small number of samples, is not going to work for a large audience. A flipchart will not be visible at the back of a large room; a slide projector can be overwhelming in a small room. A darkened room, to show video or slides, will not allow the audience to take notes.
- **Skill, time and resources** must be available for any pre-preparation of aids that may be required in advance of the presentation.
- **The equipment, materials and facilities** you require must be available in the venue, and you must **know** how to **use** them. (No good turning up with a slide projector if there is no power source, or film when there is no overhead projector, or without proper pens for a particular type of board.)

4.10 The following are some **guidelines** for effective use of visual aids.

(a) Ensure that the aid is:

- **Appropriate** to your message, in content and style or mood
- **Easy to see** and understand
- Only used when there is **support** to be gained from it

(b) Ensure that all **equipment** and materials are **available and working** and that you can (and do) operate them efficiently and confidently. This includes having all your slides/acetates/notes with you, in the right order, the right way up and so on.

(c) Ensure that the aid does not become a **distraction**.

- Show each image **long enough** to be absorbed and noted, but not so long as to merge with following idea.
- Maintain **voice and eye contact** with your audience, so they know that it is you who are the communicator, not the machine.
- **Introduce** your aids and what they are for, placing the focus on the verbal presentation.
- Hand out **supporting material** either well before the presentation (to allow reading beforehand) or at the relevant point: if you hand it out just before, it will distract or daunt the audience with information they do not yet understand.
- **Write or draw**, if you need to do so during the presentation, as quickly and efficiently as possible (given the need for legibility and neatness).

4.11 The **look of presentation slides** (or other visual aids) is very important. Make sure that they are:

- Simple: not too many points
- Visually appealing: use graphics and type styles to create an effect
- Neat: especially if you are preparing them by hand

Action Programme 9

Look back at your answer to Action Programme 7: your notes for a presentation on the tidy office.

Design a visual aid for each section of your presentation.

5 Running effective meetings

5.1 **Meetings** play an important part in the life of any organisation.

(a) **Formal meetings** required by government legislation or the Articles of a company, and governed by strict rules and conventions laid down in the organisation's formal constitution.

(b) **Discussions** held **formally** for information exchange, problem-solving and decision-making, such as negotiations with suppliers, meeting to give or receive product/idea presentations or 'pitches', or employee interviews as part of formal selection, disciplinary, grievance or appraisal procedures.

(c) **Informal discussions** called together regularly or on an *ad hoc* basis for communication and consultation on matters of interest or concern: informal briefings and marketing team meetings, for example.

(d) **Internal meetings** of any of the above types, involving different members of the team or organisation.

(e) **External meetings** of any of the above types, involving members of the organisation in discussion with suppliers, customers or any other of the external stakeholders discussed in Chapter 1.

5.2 Whatever the purpose and level of formality of a given meeting, its effectiveness will broadly depend on the following.

- There is usually a discussion leader, **chairperson**, or at least an organiser, who guides the proceedings of the meeting and aims to maintain order.

- There is often a **sequence of business** or at least a list of items to be covered: topics of discussion or decisions to be reached. It is not essential to formalise this point with an **agenda**, but meetings usually do have one.

- The purpose of the meeting is achieved by reaching some **decision or expression of opinion** at the end of the discussion. In some circumstances this may lead to taking a vote to determine what is the majority view. In other circumstances, the discussion may just be **summarised** by the leader and written confirmation of the decisions reached provided later for perusal by the various parties.

5.3 An **informal meeting**, such as might be called from time to time by a department head or working party, may take the form of a **group discussion** chaired by a leader, and **informally documented**: notes handed round or taken during the meeting, a summary of arguments and decisions reached provided afterwards.

5.4 **Formal meetings**, however, are governed by strict rules and conventions (and generate formal documentation) for the announcement, planning, conduct and recording of the proceedings. The principal documents for formal meetings are as follows.

- **Notice**: the announcement of and 'invitation' to the meeting.
- **Agenda**: the list of items of business to be discussed at the meeting.
- **Minutes**: the written record of a meeting, approved by those present.

Planning the meeting

5.5 Meetings planning will mainly involve sending out notices and agenda, but it may also be necessary to make provisions for:

- **Meeting space** of appropriate accessibility and privacy for all participants.
- **Seating layout**. Most team meetings will be fairly informal, and will be designed to involve all members: a circular or square table may facilitate this better than a long oblong which focuses attention on the 'head', or than rows of seating facing the 'front'. Sight lines should also be considered so that all members can see flip charts and so on.
- **Facilities**: visual aids, refreshments and so on, as required.

Roles and responsibilities

5.6 Key roles and responsibilities in the meeting will include:

(a) A **leader** (in formal meetings, called a meeting **chair**) or **facilitator**.

Responsible for ensuring that: the meeting follows the agenda; discussion is conducted in a way that permits equitable participation by all members and decisions are reached in appropriate ways. (In formal meetings, there may be additional responsibilities such as ensuring that correct procedures are followed, and signing the minutes of the previous meeting.)

(b) A **scribe** (in formal meetings, called a **secretary**)

Responsible for taking notes of what is discussed and agreed, what actions will be taken and by what deadlines. Team meetings may or may not require formal minutes, but it will help if someone is concentrating on recording the proceedings. (For formal meetings, the secretary is also the one who issues the various documents before and after the meeting.)

Convening a meeting

5.7 A formal meeting must be convened in accordance with any regulations laid down, otherwise it is not a proper meeting and its proceedings may be invalid. Even informal meetings must be 'called together' somehow.

(a) **Automatic**. If a meeting is one of a series of similar gatherings, it may simply be held at pre-arranged dates, times and places: the marketing team, for example, may meet in the Board Room at 10am every Monday.

(b) **Notice**. Formal and non-routine meetings require a notice (of meeting) to be issued. Notice of a formal meeting usually takes the form of a card, personal letter or (for internal meetings) a memo, containing details of when and where the meeting will be held. The **agenda** for the meeting (if already drawn up) is often included, to give participants a guide to the business to be discussed and the preparations they will need to make. The **minutes** of the last meeting may also be attached so that any objections or queries can be discussed at the beginning of the meeting.

WALKER & WATSON

Imperial House
Grand Parade
Midtown MT23 H47

NOTICE OF MARKETING MEETING

To all Section Heads in the Sales and Marketing Departments (Imperial House & Dalton Building)

The next Marketing meeting will be held at Imperial House on Thursday, 23 June 20X1 at 8.00pm

I hope it will be convenient for you to attend. Items for inclusion on the agenda should reach me by Thursday 16 June.

Signed:

K. Bruce (Secretary)

Action Programme 10

Show how the above notice would look in memorandum format.

Agenda

5.8 A meeting should have a list of matters for discussion and decision: this should be prepared and distributed before each meeting so that everyone knows what will be discussed and what information to bring with them.

Key Concept

An **agenda** (Latin for 'things to be done') is a list of the various items of business of a meeting.

5.9 The meeting agenda should reflect its priorities, both in the **sequencing** of the items of business (so that the meeting focuses its 'best' time on the most important or difficult items) and by allotting **target times** for the discussion of each item (to stop it rambling). A 'bell curve' is often used to suggest the sequencing of agenda items (Figure 11.3).

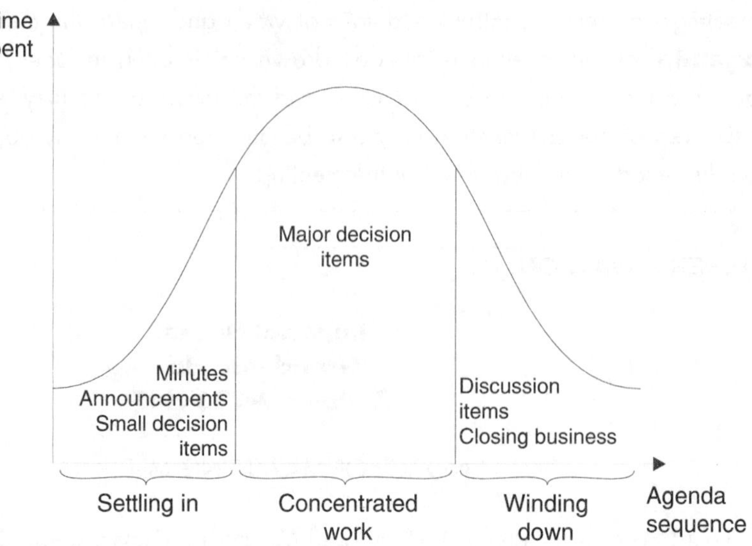

Figure 11.3 A bell curve agenda format

5.10 A **formal agenda** will usually contain the following elements.

Membership	(Optional) The chair introduces new members or announces retirements or resignations.
Apologies for absence	Apologies sent to the secretary by members unable to attend are read out.
Minutes of the last meeting	The previous minutes are approved, if considered **accurate** and a **true record** of the meeting, or amended.
Matters arising	If a situation has developed, or action been taken in response to the previous meeting, the fact should be reported.
Correspondence	Letters received by the secretary from outside parties relevant to the meeting may be reported.
Fresh business	This includes items for reporting, discussion and decision.
Any other business (AoB)	If a topic has been overlooked or has arisen between the drafting of the agenda and the meeting, it may be dealt with at this point.
Date of next meeting	The meeting is then formally declared closed.

5.11 A combined notice and agenda might look like this.

> **WALKER & WATSON**
> **Imperial House**
> **Grand Parade**
> **Midtown MT23 HJ7**
>
> MARKETING MEETING
>
> The next Marketing Meeting will be held at Imperial House on Thursday 23 June at 8.00pm
>
> AGENDA
> 1 Membership
> 2 Apologies for absence
> 3 Minutes of the last meeting
> 4 Matters arising
> 5 Proposal to take a stand at the 2003 Trade Exhibition
> 6 Report on customer research into the effectiveness of the new promotional campaign for Product [x]
> 7 Proposal to implement a Customer Care Programme
> 8 Any other business
> 9 Date of next meeting

Action Programme 11

You work in the Marketing Department of Wright Bros. Travel Ltd, 13 Daffyd Rd, Cardiff CD3 7WR.

Mrs Ann Wun (the Marketing Director) calls you into her office one day and says that since Esther Zee (her secretary) is away on sick leave, you will have to organise the monthly meeting of regional sales managers. She hopes you won't mind, and that you know the format of all the documentation – nothing too formal, she says, but she likes things to 'look right'. The meeting is scheduled for Tuesday evening, 13 February at 5.30 in the Board room. 'There are a few things we'll have to discuss,' says Mrs Wun. 'I'll give a progress report as usual. Then of course there's Dee Day's proposal to have carphones installed in all company vehicles. Oh – and we have to decide where we want to go for the sales conference in March: we'd better get that sorted out good and early. What else? Yes, I think we'd better make some noises of appreciation to Ms Zee for re-organising the customer database so efficiently. That's about it, I think – but don't forget all the usual stuff at the beginning and end.' You go away and draft a notice and agenda (attaching the minutes of the last meeting). You know that Ms Zee usually draws up a Chair's Agenda for Mrs Wun, who is otherwise not a very good leader of meetings: she would be lost without background information and hints as to the views of the people involved.

You do some work and find that:

(a) Arising from Item 5 of the **last** minutes, the new customer database has been put into operation in the department and is currently on trial.

(b) The staff have been a bit worried by rumours that there will be redundancies in the company: Mrs Wun will have to say something about this in her progress report, being as encouraging as possible.

(c) The proposal of Dee Day to have carphones installed in company cars. The idea was discussed at an earlier meeting with some heat, and defeated by a vote of 4-2.

(d) The sales conference will be during the weekend beginning on Friday March 14. Chris Sikh has expressed a very strong preference for an event linked to the Rugby International at Cardiff Arms Park on the next day.

(e) Ms Zee will not be at the meeting, but a vote of thanks may be relayed to her. She has been seriously ill, so perhaps flowers might be sent?

Draft an agenda for the meeting.

Exam Tip

A question in the Specimen Paper for the new syllabus asked you to draft an agenda for a team meeting. When answering such questions, look for clues in the scenario as to (a) how formal the meeting is and (b) what kind of meeting it is. (If it a 'first meeting', say, remember not to put 'minutes of the previous meeting' in the agenda!)

Conducting the meeting

5.12 Formal meetings may have particular rules and conventions, governing such matters as the following.

(a) **Constitution**: whether the meeting is properly 'made up'. This usually includes having a **chair**, and a minimum number of persons present (a **quorum**).

(b) How matters are put to the meeting. **Proposals** define matters for discussion or points to be decided ('To receive the report of the Marketing Director', 'To approve the purchase of...'). A proposal put to the meeting is called a **motion**: 'That x should be done'. A motion that is '**carried**' (approved by the meeting) is called a **resolution** (decision).

(c) **Conduct**: how debate and discussion is to be managed. A formal meeting may, for example, require all participants to address their comments to the chair, rather than to each other. There may also be rules about when and how often people can speak in regard to a given motion.

(d) **Decision-making**. A formal meeting will usually use **voting** to reach decisions on given motions. The regulations will determine whether this is done by show of hands, voice vote ('Aye' or 'No'), or a poll or ballot (written vote, which may be secret). Once the chair declares the result (which is entered in the minutes), the item of business is closed and cannot be re-opened in the same meeting.

5.13 Informal meetings will also need structure and leadership, but this will generally come from the leader or facilitator.

- Ensuring that all parties have had a chance to speak and that they have been fairly heard. Reluctant contributors may have to be encouraged by supportive questions.
- Controlling over-contribution, disruption, interruption and simultaneous or splinter discussions, so that each contribution is heard by the entire meeting in sequence.

- Keeping the discussion to the agenda or point and hand, and determining when discussion should be brought to a close or postponed to another occasion.
- Monitoring the physical, mental and emotional comfort levels of the participants, to suggest adjournments or breaks for refreshment, 'cooling off', further information-seeking and so on.
- Directing the secretary or other assistants of the meeting to process any information required by or arising from the meeting.
- Summarising the feeling or 'consensus' of the meeting at the end of each passage of discussion. (This may take the place of a vote, if the decision of the meeting is clear. The leader may simply look round the table, saying something like: 'Well, I think we are all agreed that...' and, if there is no dissent, the discussion will close at that point.)

Minutes of the meeting

5.14 The minutes are a written record of the discussion and/or decisions of a meeting. They act as a source of **reference**, so that details of oral decisions will not be disputed, distorted or forgotten afterwards. (They also help to discourage ill-considered contributions in the meeting, since everyone knows their comments may be minuted.)

5.15 Minutes may take three forms.

(a) **Resolution minutes** record only the resolutions (decisions taken), without describing the debate.

'IT WAS RESOLVED that the Christmas party should be held at the Midtown Art Gallery on 20 December 20XX.'

(b) **Narrative minutes** give a concise summary of the main points of the discussion leading up to the resolution. This enables individuals to go on record with their views.

'The Chairman referred the meeting to Mr Patels' proposal on the matter of staff shortage in the Marketing Department. Mrs Gomez expressed some doubt as to the seriousness of the situation, but Ms Hardwick was able to cite several occasions on which delays in providing information to team meetings had been caused. Details of salary levels were discussed. In summarising, the Chairman reminded the meeting that in engaging the staff recommended by Mr Patel, only one new post would be created. By a majority of 6-2, IT WAS RESOLVED that two research assistants be engaged from 1 September.'

(c) **Action minutes** use a right hand column to note the name of the person who has undertaken or been asked to perform specific actions as a result of the decisions taken. Action minutes for a formal committee meeting are shown below.

MINUTES OF THE FUNDRAISING COMMITTEE MEETING

Held at the Blue Room of the White Hart Hotel on Thursday 23 June at 8.00pm

Present: A. Lyne (in the Chair); B. Sting (Hon Secretary); C. Schell (Hon. Treasurer); D. Mobb; E. Tipe; F. R. Vessent; G. Wyz.

		Action
364	APOLOGIES FOR ABSENCE Apologies for absence were received from H. Bomm and I. Reis.	
365	MINUTES OF THE LAST MEETING The minutes of the last meeting were read and signed as a true and fair record.	
366	MATTERS ARISING FROM THE MINUTES There were no matters arising.	
367	POSTERS FOR BENEFIT CONCERT 10 AUGUST It was resolved that J Walker Ltd. be approached by Mr Schell to design and print posters to be circulated on the 20 July.	C Schell (Treasurer)
368	EDITORIAL COVERAGE It was resolved to circulate a Press Release emphasising the relevance of the charity to the local area and the concert details to all local newspapers and magazines.	D Mobb
369	CHARITY WEBSITE It was resolved to request the presence of a representative of Ace Media Ltd at the next meeting of the committee, to present a feasibility report on the setting up of a website to promote the charity	B Sting (Sec)
370	DATE OF NEXT MEETING The date of the next meeting of the committee was scheduled for 25 July at 8pm The meeting closed at 9.00pm	

Signed: A Lyne (Chair)

Action Programme 12

Look back at Action Programme 11: the meeting of the Marketing Department at Wright Bros, for which you drew up a notice and agenda.

Everyone turns up at the meeting, except Ms Zee who sends apologies for absence due to illness.

The minutes of the last meeting are taken as read and signed. You (as acting Secretary) inform the meeting about the new database, arising from the resolution in the last minutes (Item 5) to implement such a change. The meeting progresses, while you take notes. The various items are discussed, with the following results.

(a) Mrs Wun's report is accepted.

(b) Mrs Day's proposal is defeated: carphones will not be installed, for reasons of cost, safety and potential for abuse.

(c) The sales conference will be held on 14 March and will involve the Rugby, if tickets are available.

(d) Thanks and flowers are to be sent to Ms Zee by you.

(e) The next meeting is scheduled for Tuesday 17 March.

Under 'any other business' you draw the meeting's attention to the library of magazines and journals on Marketing, which you heartily recommend. The meeting ends at 7.30pm.

Write out full resolution minutes for the meeting.

6 Negotiations

Key Concept

Negotiationis a process of coming to an agreement with another person on some issue.

6.1 Negotiating is essentially, a **bargaining process**, through which commitments and compromises are reached, using the relative influence of both parties.

6.2 The aim of negotiating is not to get the best position for yourself or your organisation at the expense of the other party (a **win-lose outcome**). This can cause resentment, under-motivated performance by the 'losing' collaborator, or even the breaking of the relationship.

6.3 A basic '**win-win' approach** to negotiating is as follows.

(a) Map out, in advance, what the needs and fears of both parties are. This outlines the psychological and practical territory.

(b) **Define your desired outcome** and estimate the worst, realistic and best case scenarios. ('If I can pay £500, it would be ideal, but I'd settle for £600. Above £700, it's just not worth my while.') Start with the best case and leave room to fall back to the realistic case. Keep your goal in sight.

(c) **Look for mutual or trade-off benefits**. How might you both gain (for example, by getting a higher discount in return for longer or pre-booked series of ads or providing camera ready copy). What might be cheap for you to give that would be valuable for the other party to receive or *vice versa*.

(d) **Spell out the positive benefits** to the other party and support them in saying 'yes' to your proposals by making it as easy as possible. (Offer to supply information or help with follow-up tasks, for example.) Emphasise areas of agreement and common ground.

(e) **Overcome negativity** by asking questions such as:

- 'What will make it work for you?'
- 'What would it take to make this possible?'

(f) **Overcome side-tracks** by asking questions such as: 'How is this going to get us where we need/want to go?'

(g) **Be hard on the issue/problem but soft on the person**. This is not personal competition or antagonism: work **together** on problem solving (eg by using flip chart or paper to make shared notes). Show that you have heard the other person (by summarising their argument) before responding with your counter argument.

(h) **Be flexible**. A 'take it or leave it' approach breaks relationships. (However, saying 'no' repeatedly to sales people is a good way of finding out just how far below the list price they are prepared to go!) Make and invite, reasonable counter offers.

(i) **Be culturally sensitive**. Some markets thrive on 'haggling'. Some cultures engage in a lot of movement up and down the bargaining scale (eg Asian and Middle Eastern), while others do their homework and fix their prices (eg German). In the former cultures, much emphasis is placed on building relationships and extending hospitality before getting down to terms.

(j) **Take notes**, so the accuracy of everyone's recollection of what was proposed and agreed can be checked.

(k) Summarise and **confirm the details** of your agreements to both parties (by memo, letter, contract) and acknowledge a mutually positive outcome.

Chapter Roundup

- Oral and face-to-face communication have specific advantages and disadvantages which make them particularly effective (or limited) in different communication situations.
- Elements of effective telephone technique include: greetings and identification, seeking and giving verbal feedback; being aware of the other person's needs; brevity; confirmation of details/action agreed.
- A systematic approach to preparing a presentation is Brainstorm, Prioritise, Structure, Outline, Practise and Cue.
- Visual aids for presentations, in any format, should be appropriate, functioning and not distracting.
- The main documents associated with meetings are the: notices, agenda and minutes (narrative, resolution or action)
- The way a meeting is conducted should facilitate equitable participation and efficiency.
- Negotiating is a bargaining process through which compromises are reached, using the relative influence of both parties. Effective negotiating may involve a 'win-win' approach.

Quick Quiz

1 Which of the following (you may select more than one) may be an advantage *and* a disadvantage of oral communication?

Interactivity	Speed of response	Influence	Feedback

2 It is easier to be misunderstood on the telephone than in face-to-face conversation.

☐ True ☐ False

3 Which step is missing from the recommended framework for planning presentations as listed below (in random order).

Brainstorm
Outline
Practise
Structure
Cue

4 Which of the following is *not* one of the key purposes of the introduction of a presentation

A Establish credibility with the audience
B State what you expect the audience to do at the end
C Attract the audience's attention and interest
D Give the audience an idea of the shape of your talk

5 The most effective use of eye contact to appear confidence when giving a presentation is:

A Sustained eye contact with particular individuals
B Avoiding the eyes of the audience
C Making brief eye contact with each person or area of the audience in turn
D Scanning quickly and constantly over the whole audience

6 If you wanted to get the audience to participate actively in a presentation by incorporating their views in your content, the most effective visual aids (choose one or more of the options given) would be:

Slides	PowerPoint slides	Overhead acetates
Handouts	Flip chart	Video

7 If a proposal has arisen between the drafting of the agenda and the meeting itself, it should be introduced into the agenda as:

A Matters arising
B Fresh business
C Minutes of the last meeting
D Any other business

8 Fill in the gaps in the following sentences, using the meetings terminology given below.

'A meeting may not be properly (1).......... unless due (2).........has been issued. It may not be properly (3)......... if it does not have a (4).......... or (5).........of members. In the process of discussion, a (6) .... that has been put to a meeting is called a (7)............ Once (8)............ by the meeting, it is called a (9).........'

- quorum
- proposal
- resolution
- notice
- chair
- convened
- motion
- constituted
- carried

9 Minutes of a meeting which summarise the discussion or debate are termed .... minutes.

10 Win-win negotiation means using your influence and negotiating skills to get the best terms for yourself and your organisation.

☐ True ☐ False

Answers to Quick Quiz

1 Speed of response, influence

2 True

3 Prioritise

4 B

5 C

6 Overhead acetates, flip chart

7 D

8 (1) convened, (2) notice, (3) constituted, (4) chair, (5) quorum, (6) proposal, (7) motion, (8) carried, (9) resolution

9 Narrative

10 False

Now try Question 11 from the Question Bank at the end of this Text

Action Programme Review

1 Disadvantages include:

- Slowing down the process of decision-making (where face to face discussion is involved). Meetings are often felt to be a 'waste of time'.
- Allowing the personal charisma of one or more participants to dominate others (an advantage in persuasion, but not in collaborative problem-solving or view-sharing)
- Making it difficult to conceal or distort information (a disadvantage if you are the person who wishes to do so: eg if you are in a weak negotiating position, or wish to put a positive 'spin' on a PR problem)
- Not allowing preparation and polishing of the message (verbal and non-verbal) prior to communication.
- Lacking concreteness: 'just talk' unless something is done or put in writing.

2 This programme will help you to consider the points made about telephone calls and how best to ensure you are effective on the 'phone.

3 Line 1: The operator does not give the name of the organisation.

Line 2: The operator does not reply to the caller's request: it sounds as if she has been cut off.

Line 3: The secretary is not announced by the operator and does not identify herself

Line 5: The caller does not identify the nature of her interview, which may be relevant.

Line 6: 'Might' is not definite enough for an appointment.

Line 7: The caller does not give a definite answer (perhaps expecting to be given an alternative).

Line 8: The secretary summarily ends the call without resolving the appointment, or offering alternatives.

4 If you do not live in the UK, find out what the guidelines are in your own country!

5 The point is that there are many different approaches to presentations, but they must be targeted at the Purpose and Audience of the communication. The PASS framework (proposed in Chapter 10) is a good guide to presentation planning.

6
1. Staff should be able to operate the fax machine.
2. Customers should be able to describe the features of the new product.
3. Audience should be able to distinguish between Brand X and Brand Y [or show preference for whichever you wish].
4. Management should be persuaded to investigate flexi-time implementation.
5. Students should be able to write an effective report.

7

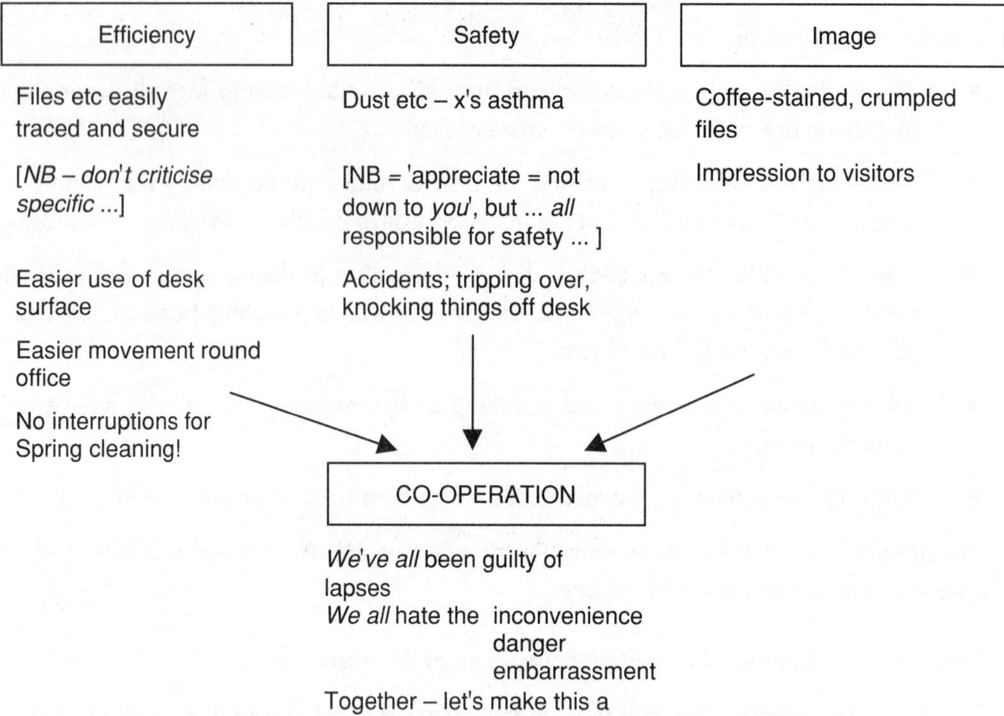
TIDY OFFICE
Efficiency
Safety
Image
Files etc easily traced and secure
[NB – don't criticise specific ...]
Easier use of desk surface
Easier movement round office
No interruptions for Spring cleaning!
Dust etc – x's asthma
[NB = 'appreciate = not down to you', but ... all responsible for safety ...]
Accidents; tripping over, knocking things off desk
Coffee-stained, crumpled files
Impression to visitors
CO-OPERATION
We've all been guilty of lapses
We all hate the inconvenience
danger
embarrassment
Together – let's make this a
TIDY OFFICE: FOR EFFICIENCY, SAFETY + IMAGE

8

1. Explain the working and theoretical benefits of the scheme.
2. Quote statistics on absenteeism and labour turnover, showing reduction where flexitime is in operation.
3. Offer a case study of another organisation which introduced flexitime to their benefit.
4. Present quotes and opinions of staff who are working 9-5, and others in a flexitime scheme.
5. Present a series of scenarios (from the organisation's and employees' points of view) in which a problem – seasonal demand, dentist's appointment, travel delays etc – would be solved by flexitime.
6. Compare flexitime, in an analogy, with a school day of fixed hours, with the freedom to do homework outside those hours, at the pupil's discretion.

9 Here are just some suggestions to go with our notes (Action Programme Review 8). We've assumed that the content will be easy enough to follow: we've used the slides to attract attention and 'sweeten the pill' of criticism.

Slide 1

TIDY = EFFICIENT

simple picture/cartoon of a person looking perplexed (ideally surrounded by mess – piles of paper?)

Now, where did I put that file?

Slide 2

TIDY = SAFE

picture of (same) person, with black eye, arm in sling etc

Oh, *that's* where I put that file ...

Slide 3

TIDY = GOOD PR

picture as slide 2, with mess surrounding

They're here to see *me*? *Now*? *Here*?

Slide 4

TIDY = EVERYONE'S BUSINESS

10

MEMORANDUM

To:	Section Heads, Sales & Marketing Departments	Ref: KB/ff
From:	K. Bruce, Secretary	Date: 20 June 20X1
Subject:	Notice of committee meeting	

The next meeting of the Committee will be held at Imperial House on Thursday 23 June 20X1 at 8.00pm.

I enclose a copy of the minutes of the last meeting and an agenda. I would be grateful if you would bring with you to the meeting any relevant documentation.

K Bruce

11 The main business will be:

1. The Chair's progress report
2. The proposal to install carphones
3. The sales conference
4. Vote of thanks to Ms Zee.

12 This is a good opportunity to put into practice what you have been reading in this section.

12

Written communication

Chapter Topic List	
1	Setting the scene
2	Letters
3	E-mails
4	Memoranda
5	Briefs
6	Notices
7	Reports

Learning Outcomes

☑ Draft various types and formats of business letter

☑ Draft effective e-mail messages

☑ Draft memos, briefs and notices as required by a range of business contexts

☑ Draft reports in formal and informal formats and styles

Syllabus References

☑ Use a variety of formats to communicate with internal and external customers including letters, memoranda, notices, reports and e-mails (4.8)

1 Setting the scene

1.1 In this chapter we look at some of the key written formats you might use in everyday communication with customers (internal and external) and other stakeholders.

1.2 As discussed in previous chapters, the **context** of the communications activity will determine the way in which the various written formats described here are used. We will be giving general guidelines, but you will need – both at work and in the exam – to bear in mind the following.

- The 'house style' of your organisation and cultural context
- The specific **purpose** for which you are writing and
- The specific **audience** for whom you are writing.

1.3 In other words, bear in mind what you learned in Chapters 9 and 10 about the communication process and message planning. We will try not to repeat ourselves in this section, but to confine ourselves to the distinctive features of these communication formats.

Exam Tip

Letters, memoranda, notices, reports and emails are always (always!) set in <u>Customer Communications</u> exams. Whatever the specific knowledge content of exam questions (Customer care, consumer behaviour or the role of PR, say) you will be required to present your answers – not in an 'essay' form – but in an specific business format and your answer will be assessed on how well you <u>demonstrate</u> your communication <u>skills</u> in drafting an effective and properly structured report, letter, memo or email) as well as how well you know the factual content of the syllabus.

2 Letters

2.1 A **letter** is a written (or printed) communication addressed **to** a person or organisation **by** a person or organisation and usually sent through the post.

- As you can see, this definition allows a great deal of scope for variations: the letter is an extremely versatile medium and format, which can be adapted to almost any purpose. At the same time, its direct person-to-person nature makes it particularly well suited to private, confidential or 'sensitive' communications.
- The letter is a 'high profile' medium of communication. It is in many cases the first or only contact between organisations or the individuals who represent them.
- A letter is the main method of written business-to-business communication, although email is swiftly replacing it.

Purpose

2.2 Purposes of letters in the marketing context

- Requesting information – or providing it (asked or unasked)

- Ordering goods or services – or acknowledging the order (or information request)
- Confirming information or arrangements
- Expressing thanks or congratulations
- Complaining about a product or service – or answering ('adjusting') a complaint
- Introducing or explaining the contents of a package (a 'covering' letter)
- Conveying the benefits of a product or service (or offering a direct opportunity to purchase – ie direct marketing)
- Providing information or news as part of a customer care or relationship marketing programme
- Giving instructions to suppliers

Whatever the specific purpose of a business letter, there is also the general purpose of **creating a positive image**, if only to help get the letter read.

Audience

2.3 A letter is more **likely to be read** (as you may know from your own experience in handling your mail) if:

It is one that you have requested, or expect, and is readily identifiable as such.
It is clearly relevant to your needs, wants or interests.
It is clearly and attractively presented, or looks 'professional' (in business letters).
It is reasonably brief and well structured. Even if you have no particular motivation to read the contents of the letter, you may do so, for interest – but you will probably not read all the way through, or attentively, if the letter is (or looks) lengthy, or loses your attention and interest by rambling, repeating itself and so on.
The letter is written in an appropriate or congenial style. Again, unless you are given a good reason for doing so, you are unlikely to read through a letter that comes across as patronising, pompous, grovelling, unsuitably 'chummy' or otherwise contrary to you taste or expectations.

Format

2.4 A business letter contains various **standard elements**. Use the following as a checklist.

- Letterhead
- Reference
- Date
- Recipient name and address
- Greeting/salutation
- Subject
- Main body
- Complimentary close
- Signature
- Author name and designation
- Enclosure/copy reference

You can see these elements laid out on the following page, with an example of what they should contain following the 'template' version.

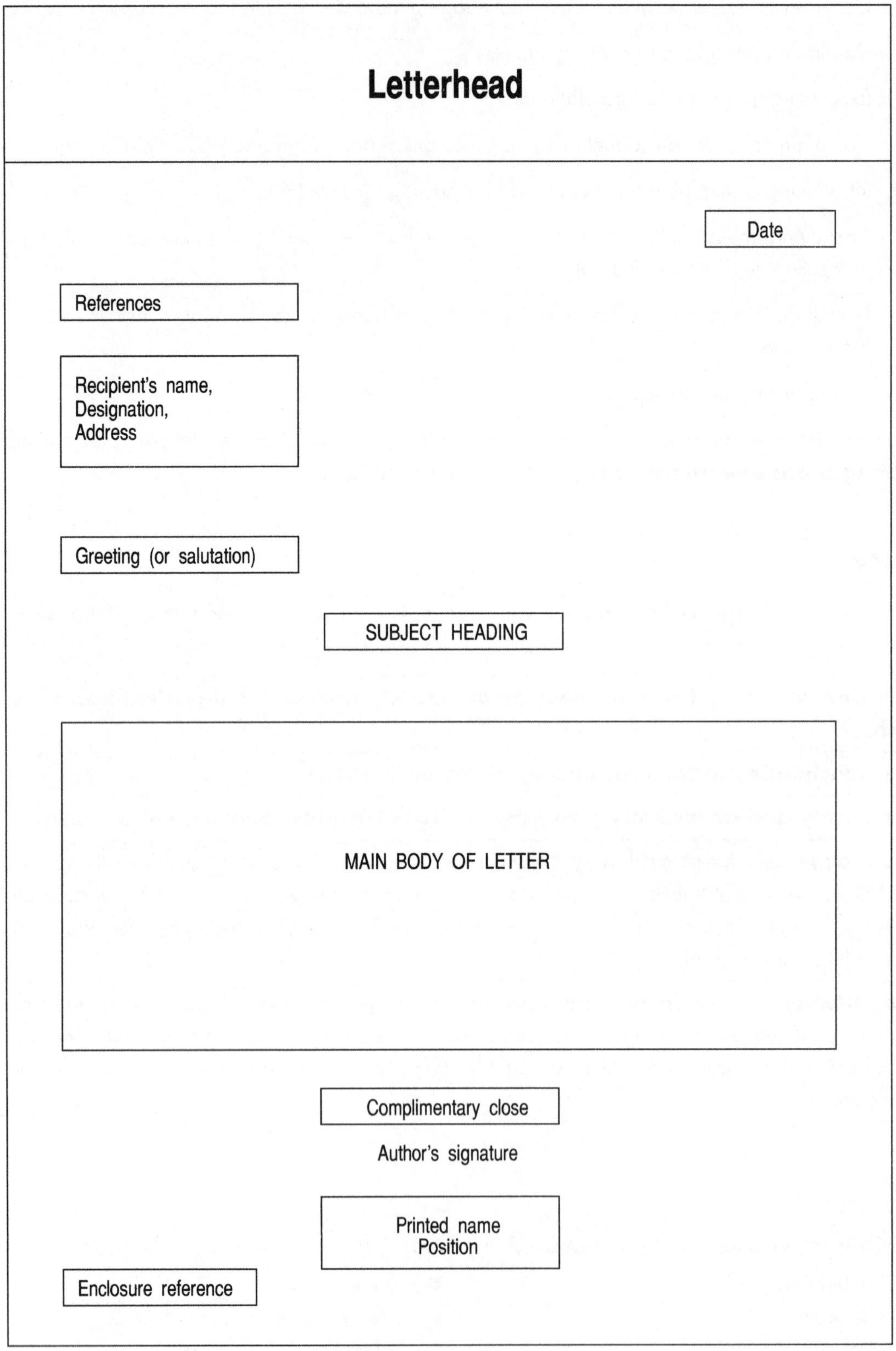

Letterhead

Date

References

Recipient's name,
Designation,
Address

Greeting (or salutation)

SUBJECT HEADING

MAIN BODY OF LETTER

Complimentary close

Author's signature

Printed name
Position

Enclosure reference

Hi-Tech Office Equipment Ltd

Micro House, High St, Newtown, Middlesex NT3 0PN

Telephone: Newtown (01789) 1234 Fax: (01789) 5678

Directors:
I. Teck (Managing)
M. Ployer
D. Rechtor
N. Other

Registered Office:
Micro House, High St, Newtown
Middx NT3 0PN
Registered No 123 4 56 789
Registered in England

7th June 20X1

Your Ref: JB/nn
Our Ref: IW/cw

J M Bloggs, Esq
Adminstrator
Toubai Forze Timber Yard
Wood Lane Industrial Estate
SUSSEX SX1 4PW

Dear Mr. Bloggs

WORD PROCESSING EQUIPMENT

Thank you for your letter of 3rd June, 20X1, in which you request further details of Hi-Tech's range of personal computers with wordprocessing software packages. I am delighted to hear that our earlier discussions were of some help to you.

Please find enclosed our list of hardware and software with current prices. I have also included our leaflet entitled 'Desktop', which outlines some of the options for word-processing on personal computers: I trust this will answer your questions and give you an idea of the exciting possibilities.

I would also take this opportunity to remind you that two of your old electric typewriters are currently under maintenance contract with us, and that both of them become due for routine servicing within the next month. Perhaps you would contact my secretary to arrange a convenient date for our engineer to call at your offices.

I look forward to hearing from you, when you have thought about the word processing option. If you have any queries or need further information on printers or accessories do not hesitate to let me know.

Yours sincerely

I M Wright

I M Wright
SALES MANAGER

Enc.

Notes

- 'Our ref.' or simply 'Ref.' signals the reference given to the current letter, the one being written and sent (and duplicated for the organisation's own files).
- 'Your ref.' tells the recipient the reference number of **his** letter to **you**, which you are now acknowledging, or referring to. This will enable him to retrieve and refer to his copy of the letter, so that he will appreciate the details of your response.
- Various date forms are currently in use, so this may be a question of house (and national) style. The date can be located in various places on the letter – different layouts will be demonstrated later.
- Above or below the recipient's name/address, you may insert a clear warning as to the status of the letter, if its contents are confidential. This should also appear on the envelope.

  CONFIDENTIAL **or** Private and confidential
- The salutation (or opening greeting) is conventionally paired with an appropriate **complimentary close** (the 'signing off'), to end the letter in similar tone and formality.

Greeting	Close	Context
Dear Sir/Madam/Sirs (Name not used)	Yours faithfully	Formal situations Recipient not personally known Recipient senior in years, position
Dear Dr/Mr/Mrs/Miss Bloggs (Name used) Dear colleague Dear customer	Yours sincerely	Established relationships Implied relationships
Dear Joe/Josephine etc	Kinds regards Best wishes	Close informal relationships (More various, because more personal)

- The subject heading gives a one- or two-word indication of the main subject of the letter. It directs the reader's thoughts to the matter in hand, and provides a convenient signal for those scanning for contents when sorting mail or retrieving material from files.
- If an assistant or secretary is signing a letter on behalf of the writer, the writer's name is preceded by 'For' (or its equivalent from legal terminology 'p.p.' which stands for *per procurationem)*.

  Jane Bloggs

  For I. Wrightwell,
  Sales Manager
- **Enclosure reference** ('Enc') signals an 'enclosure'. You are drawing the reader's attention to something else in the same envelope, such as a cheque, price list or leaflet.
- **Copy reference** ('cc') signals that a duplicate of a letter has been sent to an interested third party (who should be named: 'cc. Franz Hals').

2.5 Peculiarities of layout and presentation do tend to vary from organisation to organisation, so you should be prepared to adapt to accept the practice of your workplace. This is known as **housestyle**. Keep an eye out for varaitions of particular details in any correspondence you receive at work or at home. (Please note that we have used a variety of styles in this book because that is what you will encounter in practice.)

2.6 In addition, you should be aware that letter-writing conventions vary from nation to nation:

- The positioning of standard elements on the page
- The phrases used in greeting or to close
- The way titles and addresses are written (including on envelopes)
- Styles indicating formality and informality

Marketing at Work

Check out the University of Exeter Germen Department's extremely user-friendly site 'How to write letters in German' as an example of international differences:
http://www.ex.ac.uk/flc/germlet

Alternative layouts

2.7 The overall impact of a business letter depends on how it first meets the reader's eye – not just the designer letterhead and good quality print, but the clarity and elegance of the layout of text on the page. **Simplicity** and **attractiveness** are general guidelines to good layout. There are two main styles currently in use in the UK, but **flexibility** is more important: house style varies between organisations, and each case may have its own requirements for complexity, speed of typing, grabbing attention and so on. Conventions are not meant to be a straightjacket for creative letter-writing. The two commonly-used outlines appear on the next page (Figure 1.2).

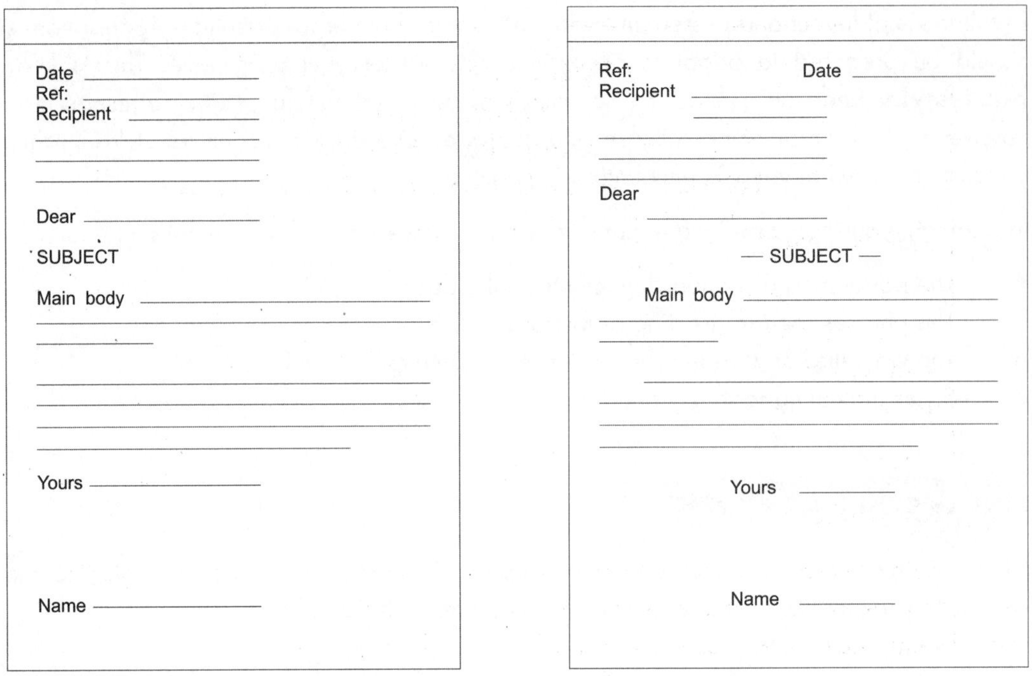

Date
Ref:
Recipient

Dear

SUBJECT

Main body

Yours

Name

FULLY BLOCKED style is the easiest to type and therefore increases the typist's productivity. Everything starts at the left-hand margin. This style is becoming increasingly common.

Ref: Date
Recipient

Dear

— SUBJECT —

Main body

Yours

Name

SEMI-BLOCKED style is much like fully blocked, but selected elements are moved over for balance. The *date* is against the right hand margin: the *complimentary close* starts from the centre: the *subject header* may be centralised.

Figure 12.1 Letter Layouts

Action Programme 1

Look at the letter below.

(a) What term is given to this type of layout?

(b) Name *another* type of layout. What elements of the letter below would have to be moved (and to where) in order to set it out in the way you have chosen?

(c) What useful element(s) are *missing* from the layout of the letter below? *Add* any element(s) you have identified, using appropriate details.

(d) Read the letter carefully and *correct* any errors of convention, structure and usage that you find.

TRUBB, LATT, TAMIL Ltd
Quality Drive
Birmingham B3 4NU
Tel: 0121 – xxx xxxx Fax: 0121 – xxx xxxx

Our Ref: IMB/tp

Mr Stan Duppenby-Counthead Esq
2 Comp Lane
Birmingham
B6 9DP

Dear sir

Quality Complaint

With reference to your letter of yesterday. We have thoroughly investigated your complaint regarding the quality of the items despatched to you on the 3rd January, and their does seem to have been a temporary problem in our Inspection Department on that day.

I would appreciate further details of the defects found, the particular product effected and it's batch number. I enclose our Defects Report Form, and would be grateful if you could complete and return it to me as soon as possible. I will then be happy to immediately replace the relevant items.

Meanwhile please except my apologies for any inconvenience caused.

Yours sincerely

N Competant

N Competant

Sales Director

Structure

2.8 A letter should have a **beginning**, a **middle** and an **end**. The reader will have a very general idea of the letter's contents already, from the letterhead, subject heading and the signature, name and designation at the foot of the letter. However, you can 'lose' your reader very quickly if you do not at each stage make it clear why you are writing, what it is that you are trying to say, and what you think he or she can do for you.

The opening paragraph

2.9 The reader will not be as familiar with the **context of the message** as you are. Describe it briefly: it may be a response to a previous communication from the reader, or you may be making initial contact (if you are introducing yourself or advertising goods). You would usually put the following in your opening.

- A straightforward (brief) explanation of why you are writing. ('Thank you for your letter of 3rd March, in which you requested information about conference bookings'.)
- An acknowledgement of any relevant correspondence received, noting its date and nature. ('As requested [or agreed] in our telephone conversation [or meeting] of 4 September, I am sending you ... .)
- Important details of the circumstances leading to the letter. ('I have been asked by my colleague, George Brown, it contact you in regard to... .')

Development of the message

2.10 The middle paragraph(s) should then be used to set out the letter's message, which will elaborate on or move forward from the introductory paragraph. This section will contain the substance of your response to a previous message, details of the matter in hand, or the information you wish to communicate. If you are making several points, start a new paragraph with each, so that the reader can digest each part of your message in turn.

The closing paragraph

2.11 Your letter will not be effective unless it has the desired result of creating understanding or initiating action. It is a good idea to summarise your points briefly or **make clear exactly what response is required**. Here are some examples.

- I look forward to meeting you to discuss the matter in more detail.
- Thank you again for your order. I trust our service will be to your satisfaction.
- If you require any further information, please [do not hesitate to] call me.
- I will be contacting you in the next few days to arrange a meeting.

Style

2.12 Letters add to the writer's stylistic decisions only because:

- They are often used for interpersonal communications of a confidential and/or sensitive nature – requiring **tact**.
- They are so commonly used, that stale conventions and **clichés** abound.
- **Formal** or semi-formal letters require skills – including judging 'tone' and correct English usage – that many individuals have not been taught.

Action Programme 2

You are the Personnel Manager of Locktite Security Systems Ltd, 51 Boult Street, Edinburgh ED9 3BB. You have recently been receiving applications for the post of Head Clerk in the Accounts Office. Having looked over the CVs of the 60 applicants, you called 30 for interview. From these, a shortlist of 10 was drawn up, and each candidate re-interviewed. You believe you have chosen the most suitable person for the job, and it only remains for you to tell the remaining nine of your decision. One of these is Mr J Wiekowski, currently employed at W D Smith & Son Ltd (16 St Stephen Street, Edinburgh ED8 1DM) which is the only address you have for him. Write to inform him that his application has failed.

2.13 We will now look at some structure and style issues which apply to different types of customer letters, as an example of the planning process in action.

Exam Tip

You may be asked to write letters for a wide variety of specific applications: be flexible, and keep the general format and structure guidelines in mind.

Adjustment (replying to a complaint) letters

2.14 Purpose: To show you have considered the complaint seriously
To soothe the complainant's anger, disappointment etc
To offer redress that will be acceptable to both parties
To keep a positive relationship

Audience: Will want to have been taken seriously
Will be resistant to avoidance of responsibility
May be cynical about 'sincere' apologies
Will have to be motivated to accept what you feel able to offer

Structure and style

Context. Acknowledgement of receipt and understanding of the complaint. Expression of regret.	Briefly reconfirm the details. Apologise gracefully but simply: overdo it and you will only sound insincere.
■ Explanation. Results of an investigation into why the problem occurred.	Don't make **excuses**, or try to blame other people. Explain why the error occurred. Show that you were concerned to find out.
■ Indication of what is being done to put things right.	Don't sound grudging. You are making amends gladly, and swiftly.
Restatement of apology. Assurance of non-recurrence. Hope that good relations not damaged (especially with client, customer, employee).	You want to be conciliatory, as you do **not** want to lose customers. Smooth things over, but again, don't go over the top and grovel.

Action Programme 3

A customer has written to complain that she was refused entry to the bank you work for (The Listening Bank, Thread Needle Street, Megalopolis, EC1 4U) as the doors were closing. She says she only had to make a short transaction. The customer's name is Ms Anne Grie, Notta Mews, Megalopolis W8 8U). You are the branch manager: write her an appropriate letter of adjustment.

Covering letters

2.15 Purpose: To introduce other enclosed items (goods, documents)
To highlight helpful aspects of the items (important points, instructions)

Audience: They may or may not be expecting items (may be perplexed or resistant)
They may or may not need guidance or motivation to use/read items

Structure and style

Context. What you have sent (a CV, Brochure, a press release, a delivery etc) and why, with relevant details.	A letter may be sent to accompany items not expected by the recipient, so putting it clearly in context will be important.
Explanatory notes, if required, or Comments drawing the recipient's attention to particular features of the accompanying item.	If your enclosure is something you need to 'sell', a summary of its most attractive and relevant features may be appropriate. If it is being delivered late, explanation and apology may be required.
What is to be done next: you will follow-up with a phone call? Recipient to act or respond?	If no follow-up action is required, a courteous word of thanks for the reader's attention may be offered – especially if the item sent was unsolicited in the first place.

Information or 'report' letter

2.16 Purpose: To motivate and enable the recipient to read the information (instructions, briefing, report, news, product details)
To convey the information clearly and concisely

Audience: May or may not need, want or be interested in information
May or may not have prior knowledge
May or may not understand technical vocabulary/subject
May or may not want high level of detail/accuracy or lengthy content
May be positive or hostile towards contents

Structure and style

Context. The purpose of the letter with relevant details of when, why and by whom it was requested. Where the information comes from and how it was obtained.	The purpose and source of the information given will be important to confirm or limit its credibility.
The information requested/offered.	Logically grouped and sequenced for ease of 'digestion': controlled volume (or a full-scale report may be preferable).
Further action required (if any). Trust that information relevant and sufficient for the user's needs.	Confirm your willingness to be co-operative in providing information, while being firm if you expect action in return.

Action Programme 4

Draft a letter to be sent to a number of local employment agencies informing them about your company's one-day courses and self-help training packs on business communication skills. The following extracts from newspaper articles may be helpful. Make up any further details you need.

'Recent school-leavers are worse at spelling than any age group educated since the war, according to a survey published yesterday.

Tests of 1,000 people between the ages of 16 and 60 showed that only the simplest words, such as 'have' and 'my', were spelt correctly by everyone. One in 12 could do little more than fill in their name and address when given a straightforward form.

In the first such large-scale comparison, the Basic Skills Agency said many young people were ruling themselves out of the labour market through their poor spelling. The unemployed were 50 per cent more likely to make mistakes than those in work.' *Times*

'A campaign to improve the quality of young people's written and spoken English was launched yesterday by Trevor McDonald, the ITN newscaster.

Under the slogan "Language is Power", the Better English campaign, inspired and modestly funded by Gillian Shepherd, the Education and Employment Secretary, aims to eliminate "communications by grunt" by emphasising the link between communication skills and job prospects.

Mr McDonald, the campaign chairman, contrasted the international zeal to learn English with domestic neglect of the language.

Campaign literature advises young people to go back to college to take a language course and calls on businesses to become Better English employers by giving constructive feedback to unsuccessful job applicants whose English let them down.' *Telegraph*

Letter of request

2.17 Purpose: To elicit relevant information (or order goods)

Audience: Need to know **what** is relevant
May or may not be keen to offer information: motivation required?
Probably overloaded with requests: brevity

Structure and style

Context. How you know about organisation/product etc. Why you are writing: for brochure, meeting, telephone response etc	If you are asking someone to write, call or visit you, you may need to persuade them it is worth their doing so: you are considering buying/writing an article about ... etc.
Information required. Nature of problem or investigation. Relevant details, as required.	Brief, but helpful. Give parameters for what you do and do not wish to know, plus any **particular** interests you have. Add timescale within which you require the information.
Reinforce action desired. Express gratitude in advance.	A formula such as 'I look forward to hearing from you' is all that may be required

Marketing at Work

The plain English campaign has a very useful website, including free downloads of guides on how to write letters, reports, website text and other information (in plain English).

http@//www.plainenglish.co.uk/freepub.html

Marketing letters

2.18 Marketing letters have three distinguishing features.

(a) Most are, in effect, circular letters for mass communication. They **may** be composed for, and addressed to, a specific individual in specific circumstances – but quite frequently are not. There is, however, a trend towards disguising the mass nature of communication. This can be done by personalisation, or even by genuine 'one-to-one' marketing, facilitated by technology such as the merging of personal details from databases into correspondence proformas.

(b) Even if their specific or apparent purpose is to **inform**, they have an underlying purpose to **persuade,** in the interest of customer relations and relationship marketing.

(c) Because of the need to persuade and overcome the impersonality of mass communication **marketing letters tend to simulate semi-formal, or even informal, interpersonal communication in their style**. They use more colloquial language and a simpler prose style.

2.19 A **'circular letter'** is exactly the same in function and format as a specific business letter, except that it is designed to be read by a **larger number of different people**. The circular may be used to give information to a group of known individuals (for example, informing customers of price changes or new products). It may also be used to send out in bulk information that is **'unsolicited'** or unasked-for by its recipient (for example, advertising or sales letters).

2.20 A **standard letter** or reply is one where the **message is standard for a whole category of communications**, saving the necessity of planning and composing the same type of message afresh for each specific requirement. Examples include payment reminders (without mentioning specific account numbers or outstanding amounts), and acknowledgements of orders, complaints or requests for information.

2.21 In **direct mail** contexts, you may wish to encourage the reader to reply with a '**response mechanism'**. This may take a number of forms.

- **Telephone number**

  If you are interested in taking advantage of this fabulous offer please call *Jane Visconti* on *0208 000 0101* and ask for the Product X Information Pack.

- **Tear off slips/returnable enclosures**

> Please send me your *Product X Information Pack*
>
> Name:...
>
> Position: ....
>
> Company: ....
>
> Address: ....
>
> ....
>
> ....
>
> Post code:..
>
> Telephone number:.......................................
>
> *Return to:*
>
> J Visconti, Product X Department, A Ltd, Dogg House, Rat Road, Mouseley, MO1 7UP (Fax: 0198 765432)

3 E-mails

3.1 Many organisations now conduct both internal and external communications via e-mail systems. E-mail can be used for a wide variety of communication purposes, in place of letters, circulars, internal memos, notes and other brief messages. Lengthier messages (such as briefs and reports) and graphic messages (such as diagrams and maps) can be attached as file attachments.

3.2 Most organisations have guidelines for the use of e-mail.

(a) E-mail messages have a legal effect. Firms can be sued for libellous, offensive or misleading remarks made in e-mail, and e-mail messages can be cited as evidence in court.

(b) E-mail can be used excessively, to the exclusion of other forms of communication which might be more appropriate. Excessive personal use (or abuse) is also an issue for many organisations (as it has been with the telephone).

(c) E-mail is not private, and remains on the server. There are thus dangers in using it to send confidential messages.

3.3 The most common e-mail software is Microsoft Outlook. In Outlook, depending on which version you use, a new (empty) mail message looks something like this (Figure 12.2).

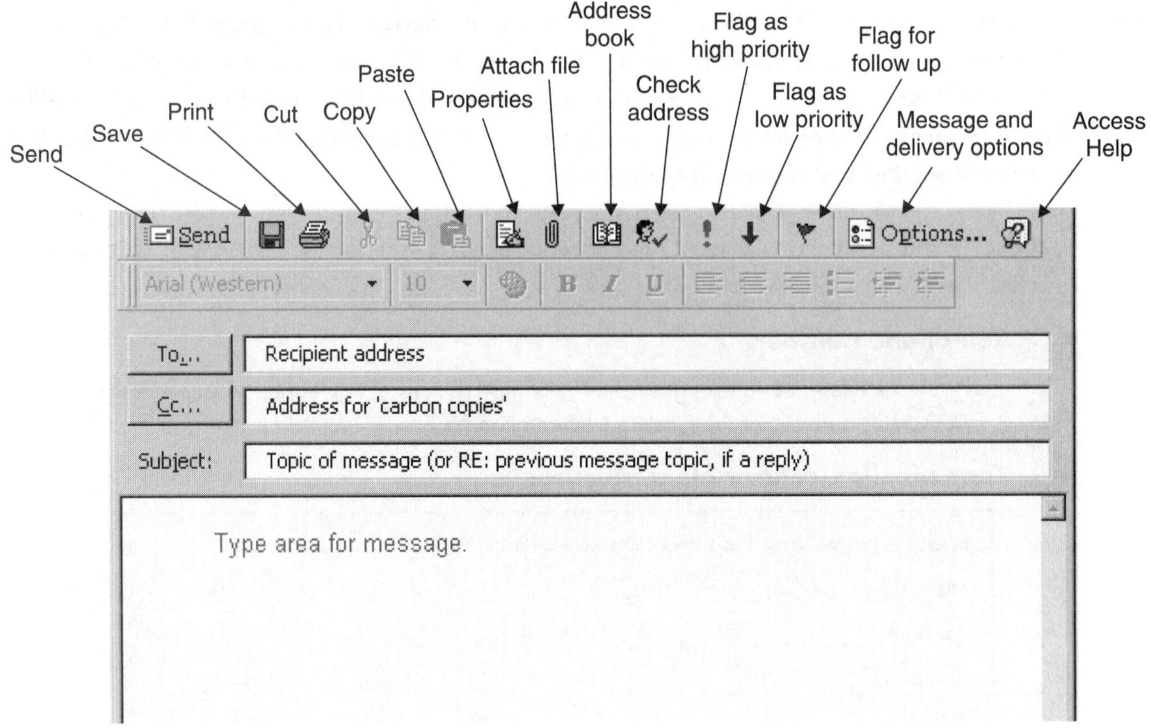

Figures 12.2 Email 'page'.

3.4 You will need to become familiar with the functions and capabilities of whatever software your organisation uses.

3.5 The following are general hints on composing e-mail messages.

Do not commit to e-mail any message that is private or confidential. As mentioned above, it is not a secure medium in general: a co-worker may cover someone's e-mail while (s)he is absent, the system administrator may access messages and companies may monitor e-mail.
Do not send illegal or offensive messages. (This should not be on your agenda anyway – especially for marketing purposes – but abusive, discriminatory and harassing messages do get sent.) E-mails can be traced to their source, and systems administrators can be liable for the misdeeds of users.
Beware of informality. Writers of e-mails may dash off a friendly note, but the recipients may (quite rightly) regard it as a written (and legally valid) response which may imply contract terms.
Beware of 'tone of voice'. Sarcasm and irony do not come across well in brief, typed, computer-mediated messages. If you wish to be humorous (in an informal context), there are conventions: adding 'emoticons' such as 'smiley faces' (☺) or the typed equivalent :).
Use mixed case letters. All uppercase (ie capitals) IS INTERPRETED AS SHOUTING!
Keep the line-length reasonably short, to ensure that it displays effectively on most recipient terminals.

Ensure that you give the recipient's address correctly and that you state a subject. The first will avoid getting the message returned to you (remember that computers are very literal) and the second will avoid getting the message deleted by the recipient as possible junk or virus mail.
Remember that sending e-mail is instant and that you cannot usually re-call a message. Check your message carefully before you click on 'send'.

3.6 Because e-mail messages can be easily personalised and sent to mass mailing lists (as well as instantly, cheaply and conveniently sent to individual recipients), they have particular advantages for marketing communications. The use of e-mail for **transaction processing** and **relationship marketing** can be extremely effective: e-mailed newsletters, product information and order confirmation from known senders is likely to be welcomed – or at least not filtered out by bulk mail avoidance tools.

Action Programme 5

You are CL Wright, Purchasing Assistant of Widget Co, 8 Snale Myall Rd, Post Town PT6 7QH, Telephone 370 8849 2983. You have recently seen press advertisements launching a new product line (Product X) by the SuchNsuch company. The ads give few details, but appear interesting. They cite an e-mail address for enquiries: mail@SuchNsuch.co.uk.

Your company e-mail package has the following input spaces in its new message window:

From:
To:
Sent (date/time):
Subject:
Cc:
Attachments:
Message:
(Digital signature)
(Name and contact details of company)

Draft an e-mail request for more information to SuchNsuch.

4 Memoranda

Purpose

4.1 The memorandum or 'memo' is a very flexible form used within an organisation for communication at all levels and for many different reasons.

(a) It performs **internally** the same function as a letter does in **external** communication by an organisation, but can in effect be used for reports, briefings or instructions, brief messages or 'notes' and any kind of internal communication that is more easily or clearly conveyed in writing (rather than face-to-face or on the telephone).

(b) A memorandum may be sent upwards, downwards or sideways in the organisation. It may be sent from one individual to another, from one department to another or from one individual to a department or larger body of staff. The **channel** will be the internal mail system of the organisation.

(c) Nowadays, internal e-mail (using networked computers) often substitutes for hard-copy memoranda.

Format

4.2 A memorandum may be typed onto blank sheets but many companies which generate a large volume of memoranda streamline the system and have 'memo pads' with appropriate headings already printed or memo styles set up in word processing or e-mail software.

4.3 Memorandum format will vary slightly according to the degree of formality required and the organisation's policy on matters like filing and authorisation of memoranda by their writer. Follow the conventions of **'house style'** in your own organisation. A typical format, including all the required elements, is illustrated below. (You may note the similarity to e-mail message windows.)

Organisation's name (optional)
'MEMORANDUM' heading

To: (recipient's name or designation) Ref: (for filing)

From: (author's name or designation) Date: (in full)

Subject: (main theme of message)

The message of the memorandum is set out like that of a letter: good English in spaced paragraphs. Note, however, that *no* inside address, salutation or complimentary close are required.

Copies to: (recipient(s) of copies) Signed: (optional) author signs/initials

Enc.: to indicate accompanying material

Forrest Fire Extinguishers Ltd

MEMORANDUM

To: All Staff Ref: ID/mp
From: I. Drant, Managing Director Date: 13 October 20XX

Subject: Overtime arrangements for October/November

I would like to remind you that thanks to Guy Fawkes celebrations on and around the 5th November, we can expect the usual increased demand for small extinguishers. I am afraid this will involve substantial overtime hours for everyone.

In order to make this as easy as possible, the works canteen will be open all evening for snacks and hot drinks. The works van will also be available in case of transport difficulties late at night.

I realise that this period puts pressure on production and administrative staff alike, but I would appreciate your co-operation in working as many hours of overtime as you feel able.

Copies to: All staff Signed: I. Drant

Structure

4.4 The structure and style of the message will vary according to its nature, the number of people it is addressed to, who those people are and what position they occupy. The flexibility of the medium means that some memos can be less formal than others**. The same guidelines apply as with a letter**.

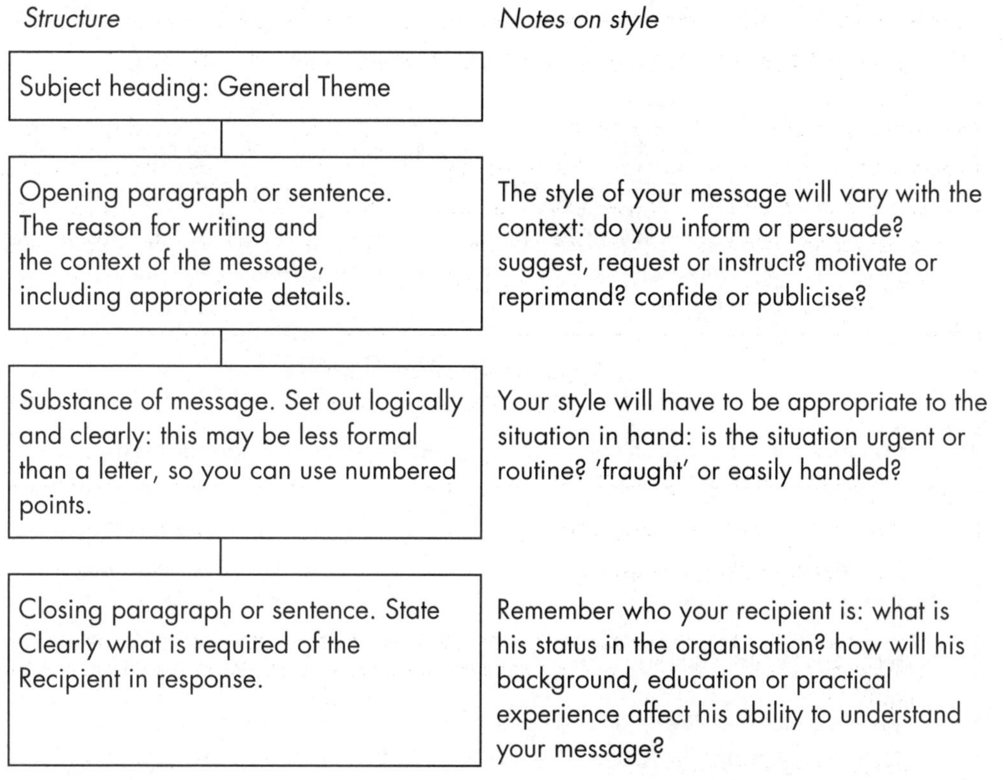

Structure
Notes on style
Subject heading: General Theme
Opening paragraph or sentence. The reason for writing and the context of the message, including appropriate details.
The style of your message will vary with the context: do you inform or persuade? suggest, request or instruct? motivate or reprimand? confide or publicise?
Substance of message. Set out logically and clearly: this may be less formal than a letter, so you can use numbered points.
Your style will have to be appropriate to the situation in hand: is the situation urgent or routine? 'fraught' or easily handled?
Closing paragraph or sentence. State Clearly what is required of the Recipient in response.
Remember who your recipient is: what is his status in the organisation? how will his background, education or practical experience affect his ability to understand your message?

Style

4.5 The **audience** of a memo will be people **within your organisation** or business network.

- You may be writing to a fellow-specialist, and so be able to use technical language and complex ideas. Think first, however: a memo to all staff might cover a vast range of fields and abilities, from tea lady to accountant to engineer.
- If you are reporting to, or making a suggestion to, someone **higher in the hierarchy** than yourself, your tone will have to be appropriately formal, businesslike and tactful.
- If you are dashing off a handwritten note on a memo pad to a **colleague** with whom you enjoy an informal working relationship, you can be as direct, familiar and friendly as you like.
- If you are instructing or disciplining **junior personnel**, you will have to retain a certain formality for the sake of authority; a more persuasive and less formal tone might be appropriate if you are congratulating, motivating or making a request.

4.6 Here is an example with a persuasive (though formal) style – reflecting the authority relationship between the writer (a staff selection specialist but only an assistant) and recipient (a senior line manager).

RETAIL DIVISION

MEMORANDUM

TO: S Clifford, Side Street Branch Manager — DATE: 13 July 20XX
FROM: M Arrigoni, Personnel (Central Branch) — REF: MA/ 13.34/B

P M WRIGHT – JOB APPLICATION

This is to confirm our conversation on the phone this morning regarding Mr Wright's application for the post of Marketing Assistant.

In his preliminary interview, I found Mr Wright a personable and articulate candidate. I enclose my notes and his CV, which is outstanding and includes three years' marketing experience.

I do recommend that you see him at the branch for a further and more technical interview. Please let me know if his CV interests you, and if so, when it would be convenient for you to meet Mr Wright and show him around the branch.

Encs. Signed: M. Arrigoni

4.7 Here is an example of a larger memorandum used to make an informal **report**.

MEMORANDUM

To: M. Ployer, Office Manager — Date: 17 September 20XX
From: M. Ployee, Supervisor — Ref: MP/XX/913

Subject: ABUSE OF TELEPHONE PROCEDURES

As you requested, in view of the rising costs of maintaining current telephone equipment and procedures, I have investigated the possible causes of the rise in costs over the last quarter. I have identified three main causes.

(a) There are more telephones in the office than are necessary for efficient communication.
(b) Staff have become accustomed to making personal calls on office apparatus.
(c) Many calls are made at expensive charge rates and unnecessary length.

I outline below a number of courses of action which could be taken to prevent further increases.

(a) *Remove superfluous equipment.* Several extensions are unallocated or little used for business purposes, and are therefore not only unnecessary but open to abuse. These could be disconnected immediately.

(b) *Circularise all staff and Department Heads.* This might discourage personal and unnecessarily lengthy calls on office apparatus, and encourage staff to be more conscious of economy.

(c) *Monitor the length and cost of calls.* A variety of devices are currently available at a reasonable cost, capable of displaying the value of units used on calls and logging long-distance calls.

(d) *Route all calls through the central switchboard.* This would provide control over use of the apparatus, each call having to be verified. The risk of congestion at the switchboard and the inconvenience to the operator, however, make this an unacceptable long-term option.

(e) *Provide alternative telephone facilities to staff.* The installation of pay telephones at generally accessible locations within the building would allow staff to continue to make personal calls, thereby preserving good working relations in the office.

If you wish to discuss these suggestions, I would be more than happy to supply further details, at your convenience.

Action Programme 6

Write a memo from M Ployer, responding to M Ployee's report (given in the example above). Ployer wishes to set up a meeting with Ployee to discuss his suggestions, and would like Ployee to come prepared with relevant information: including a draft circular.

5 Briefs

5.1 The main points about an **instruction brief** (such as you might use to explain the requirements of a job to an advertising agency or designer) is that it should be:

- Clear
- Sufficient for the recipient to be able to carry out the instructions to your satisfaction
- Highly structured and 'indexed' by headers, numbered lists and so on

5.2 A complete and detailed brief may include the following elements.

Desired outcomes or results, including:
■ The standard to which they should be achieved ■ The criteria on which successful performance will be judged ■ The time-scale within which the task or project must be completed ■ Resources available; financial targets and budgets set; payments agreed.
Definition of all relevant terms, to minimise misunderstanding.
A breakdown of the task or project into logical components, and their: ■ Context ■ Requirements ■ Resource budgets (if relevant) ■ Methods (if required) – don't try to teach the experts their job ■ Relevant background.
Information required to understand and carry out the task ('briefing' in the other sense).

5.3 The following shows the structure of an artist/designer brief.

	Notes
Purpose/objectives of task ■ What task needs to achieve ■ Media with size/colour requirements ■ Deadlines ■ Budget	■ Purpose, method of campaign. Place of task in campaign (if only one element) ■ eg A5 6 pp brochure in 4 colours, or A4 black and white ad ■ Including artist's fee + printing costs: a constraint on the artist's imagination
Information about the market and medium ■ Audience composition and tastes ■ Media style and constraints	■ Verbally/visually inclined? What images? etc ■ Glossy magazine, or tabloid. Paper quality, colours, space size etc.
Information about the product and message ■ Priorities ■ Features ■ Content	■ Which are the important items that need emphasising in the design. ■ What features should be reflected in the design style? ■ Are there photographs/drawings/text to be incorporated: if so, of what type, how big? etc.
Information about the client ■ House 'style' ■ Culture	■ Logotypes, house style for design or layout etc. Does this task need to match other output? ■ Is the organisation design-oriented? Modern or old-fashioned? etc.

Action Programme 7

You are the Marketing Manager for Gateways, a firm that manufactures high-quality gates for the consumer market. You decide to update the current catalogue to promote an extended product range.

Produce a brief which indicates your print requirements, such as the number of catalogues needed, the quality of paper required and any other information that you think is relevant, so that an advertising/design consultancy could provide you with an approximate price for undertaking the work. (This was a question in the 12/99 exam under the old syllabus.)

6 Notices

6.1 A **notice** is basically, as it sounds, a way of bringing a matter to people's attention. It may be used for warnings, reminders, notice of meetings, invitations to events and so on.

6.2 A notice is often used as a back-up to the circulation of a memorandum to members of staff, reinforcing and confirming the message. Its aim is to provide:

- Impact and emphasis in the presentation of the message
- Longer-term display of the message, as a continual reminder and record
- Ease and speed of reading

Marketing at Work

Look around you in your home, work, shopping and study environments: begin to notice notices! If possible, collect examples (once they have passed their 'post until...' date) that you find helpful as positive or negative models.

6.3 The format and appearance, content and style of a notice are extremely flexible: use your imagination, but keep firm hold of the PASS framework.

(a) **Purpose**. Are you simply conveying information or do you want to elicit a particular action or response from your audience? Are you announcing good news or bad news? Are you introducing changes that you want your audience to get excited about and remember? Are you delivering a warning or reprimand that you want them to take to heart? Are you trying to persuade them of the value of some practice or attitude? Are you encouraging or motivating them to greater effort?

(b) **Audience**. People of various abilities, backgrounds, and attitudes may be reading your notice.

(c) **Structure and style**. Not many people go around looking for notices to read. If they see one, they will not necessarily read it. If they read it they will not necessarily pay any attention to its message. You have to create a notice that is **clear** and **eye-catching** and content that is **brief** and **appropriately expressed** – even **interestingly** if possible.

Staff noticeboard: permanent display

STOP!

HAVE *YOU:*

* **Backed up your day's work?**
* **Put away your floppy disks where they will be safe from damage, fire or theft?**

Thank you

PROTECT YOUR WORK

Action Programme 8

There have been a number of thefts from guests at the hotel where you are manager. Design a notice to warn guests to be careful with their belongings, but ensure that it does not give the impression that the hotel is an unsafe place to be.

7 Reports

7.1 'Report' is a general term and one that may suggest a wide range of formats. If you give someone a verbal account, or write them a message in a letter, memo or e-mail informing them of facts, events, actions you have taken, suggestions you wish to make as a result of an investigation and so on, you are reporting. In this sense the word means simply 'telling' or 'relating': we have seen reports of this kind in memorandum form, in the visual presentation of statistics, and in the minutes of meetings.

7.2 There will be variety in the format and style of a report, according to the context.

- **Formal or informal**. You may think of reports as huge documents with sections, subsections, paragraphs, subparagraphs, indexes, appendixes and so on. There **are** extensive, complex reports like this, but a single-sheet ordinary memorandum may be sufficient in many contexts.
- Special reports may be commissioned for **one-off** planning and decision-making, such as a market research report, or reports on a proposed project or particular issue.
- **Routine** reports are produced at regular intervals. Examples of routine reports are budgetary control reports, sales reports or progress reports. **Occasional** reports include an accident report or a disciplinary report.

Purpose

7.3 A business report is usually written on the **instructions** (or at the request) of a superior. Whether the report is one-off or routine, there is an obligation on the part of the manager calling for it to state the use to which it will be put.

(a) In the case of **routine reports**, the purpose of each and how it should be used ought to be specified in a procedures manual.

(b) One-offs will require **terms of reference**, explaining the purpose of the report and any restrictions on its scope. For example, the terms of reference of a sales report might be to investigate the viability of the discounts offered to **small** customers, that is, not large ones, with a view to recommending either the withdrawal of the discount or its continuation (recommendations required).

Be aware of this in your exam. You don't have time to write about irrelevancies.

Audience

7.4 The reader needs to be able to trust and **use** report information.

- It should be concise, clear and helpfully structured (especially if large volumes of information are involved).
- Any assumptions, evaluations and recommendations by the report writer should be clearly 'signalled' as such.
- Facts and findings should be balanced against each other, clearly cross-referenced in the main report.
- The extent to which technical language should be used depends on the needs of the user – **not** the expertise of the writer.

Marketing at Work

The *Financial Times* and the Management Consultancies Association started a Business Jargon Competition (FT, 11/97). The three principal criteria used in judging a piece of writing are as follows.

'First, it took an astoundingly long time to say astonishingly little. Second, it used big words and grand phrases preferably infused with malapropisms, mixed metaphors and muddled grammar or syntax – to conceal banal, platitudinous thoughts. Third, and most important, it had to be utterly incomprehensible – to a point where its obscurity deepened with each reading.'

Here is one of the runners up.

'By Secretary-General's bulletin ST/SGB/1997/1 of 28 May 1997, I introduced a new system for the promulgation of administrative issuances. In this context I have also issued a separate bulletin on information circulars (ST/SGB/1997/2, of the same date).'

'A scrutiny of the current indexes of these issuances (ST/A1/218/Rev.18 and Add.1) shows that many issuances that appear in the indexes are obsolete. At the same time it is obvious that the Organisation is in need of deregulation. I have therefore decided to reform the system, and the first steps were taken through the two Secretary General's bulletins mentioned above.'

'The reform will now continue. The promulgation of administrative issuances is the responsibility of the Department of Administration and Management, which will review all administrative issuances for substantive provisions.'

Action Programme 9

Your manager would like your views on the use of flexible working hours in your company. You are to write him a report considering the advantages and disadvantages to all concerned, and give your conclusions. Compose a *plan* for this report.

Style

7.5 There are certain stylistic requirements in the writing of reports, formal or informal.

(a) **Objectivity and impersonality**. Even in a report designed to persuade as well as inform, subjective value judgements and emotions should be kept out of the content and style as far as possible: the bias, if recognised, can undermine the credibility of the report and its recommendations.

(b) **Ease of understanding**.

- (i) Avoid technical language and complex sentence structures for non-technical users.
- (ii) The material will have to be logically organised, especially if it is leading up to a conclusion or recommendation.
- (iii) Relevant themes should be signalled by appropriate headings, or highlighted for easy scanning.

(iv) The layout of the report should display data clearly and attractively. Figures and diagrams should be used with discretion, and it might be helpful to highlight key figures which appear within large tables of numbers.

(v) Background or supporting information may be removed 'appendices' at the end of the report, in order to keep its main body concise and relevant at the appropriate level of detail.

(c) **Precision**

(i) Do not use vague language. 'This option is likely to be very expensive' is far superior to 'it would cost an awful lot of money'.

(ii) Recommendations should be specific and firm. 'I feel more could be done...' is too vague to be helpful. Say precisely what should be done: 'customers should receive a verbal explanation in layman's terms...'.

Exam Tip

The compulsory mini-case question in the exam invariably includes a requirement to write a report, and reports have been asked for as the response format for shorter questions, too.

Getting the structure right is the key to earning the marks that are available for report format, but make sure that you can apply the formats flexibly in an exam.

Structure: Formal report

7.6 A formal report is laid out according to certain basic guidelines. It will be split into logical sections, each referenced and headed appropriately.

TITLE	*Ask yourself....*
I TERMS OF REFERENCE (or INTRODUCTION)	*What was I asked to do?*
II PROCEDURE (or METHOD)	*How did I go about it?*
III FINDINGS	*What did I discover?*
1 Section heading	
2 Section heading	
(a) sub heading	
(i) sub point	
IV CONCLUSIONS	*What is the general 'thrust' of the result?*
V RECOMMENDATIONS	*What particular recommendations do I wish to make?*

SHORT FORMAL REPORT

TITLE At the top of every report (or on a title page, for lengthy ones) should be the *title* of the report (its subject), *who* has prepared it, for *whom* it is intended, the *date* of completion, and the *status* of the report ('Confidential' or 'Urgent').

I TERMS OF REFERENCE

Here is laid out the scope and purpose of the report: what is to be investigated, what kind of information is required, whether recommendations are to be made etc. This section may more simply be called *'Introduction'*, and may include the details set above under *'Title'*. The title itself would then give only the subject of the report.

II PROCEDURE or METHOD

This outlines the steps taken to make an investigation, collect data, put events in motion etc. Telephone calls or visits made, documents or computer files consulted, computations or analyses made etc. should be briefly described, with the names of other people involved.

III FINDINGS

In this section, if it is required, the information itself is set out, with appropriate headings and sub-headings, if the report covers more than one topic. The content should be complete, but concise, and clearly structured in chronological order, order of importance, or any other *logical* relationship.

IV CONCLUSIONS

This section allows for a summary of main findings (if the report is complex and lengthy). For a simpler report it may include *action taken* or decisions reached (if any) as a result of the investigation, or an expression of the overall 'message' of the report.

V RECOMMENDATIONS

Here, if asked to do so in the terms of reference, the writer of the report may suggest the solution to the problem investigated so that the recipient will be able to make a decision if necessary.

7.7 EXAMPLE: A SHORT FORMAL REPORT

REPORT ON FLOPPY DISK STORAGE SAFETY AND SECURITY

To: Mr M Ployer, Personnel Department Manager
From: M Ployee, Supervisor
Date: 3 October 20XX

I INTRODUCTION

This report details the findings of an investigation into methods of computer disk storage currently employed at the Head Office of the bank. The report includes recommendations for the improvement of current procedure

II METHOD

In order to evaluate the present procedures and to identify specific shortcomings, the following investigatory procedures were adopted:

1 Interview of all staff using floppy disks
2 Storage and indexing system inspected
3 Computer accessory firm consulted by telephone and catalogues obtained (see Appendix I)

III FINDINGS

1 *Current system*

(a) Floppy disks are 'backed up' or duplicated irregularly and infrequently.

(b) Back-up disks if they exist are stored in plastic containers in the personnel office, the same room as the disks currently in use.

(c) Disks are frequently left on desk tops during the day and even overnight.

2 *Safety and security risks*

(a) There is no systematic provision for making copies, in the event of loss or damage of disks in use.

(b) There is no provision for separate storage of copies in the event of fire in the personnel office, and no adequate security against fire or damage in the containers used.

(c) There appears to be no awareness of the confidential nature of information on disk, nor of the ease with which disks may be damaged by handling, the spilling of beverages, dust etc.

IV CONCLUSIONS

The principal conclusions drawn from the investigation were that there was insufficient awareness of safety and security among non-specialist staff, that there was insufficient formal provision for safety and security procedure, and that there was serious cause for concern.

V RECOMMENDATIONS

In order to rectify the unsatisfactory situation summarised above, the author of the report recommends that consideration be given as a matter of urgency to the following measures.

1 Immediate backing up of all existing disks;

2 Drafting of procedures for backing up disks at the end of each day.

3 Acquisition of a fire-proof safe to be kept in separate office accommodation.

4 Communication to all staff of the serious risk of loss, theft and damage arising from careless handling of computer disks.

Action Programme 10

Having seen a full example, expand your report *plan* of Acton Programme 9 (or ours, but do attempt the exercise, if you have not already done so) into a short formal report for your manager.

Structure: Informal report

7.8 An informal report is used for less complex and lower-level information. Its structure is less developed: it will not require elaborate referencing and layout. There will be three main sections, each of which may be headed **in any way appropriate to the context** in which the report is written.

SHORT INFORMAL REPORT

TITLE Again, the subject title, 'to', 'from', 'date' and 'reference' (if necessary) should be provided, perhaps in the same style as memorandum headings.

1 *Background* or *Introduction* or *Situation*
This sets the context of the report. Include anything that will help the reader to understand the rest of the report: the reason why it was requested, the current situation, and any other background information on people and things that will be mentioned in the following detailed section. This section may also contain the equivalent of 'terms of reference' and 'procedure'/'method'.

2 *Findings* or *Analysis of the situation* or *Information*
Here is set out the detailed information gathered, narrative of events or other substance of the report as required by the user. This section may or may not require subheadings: concise prose paragraphs may be sufficient.

3 *Action* or *Solution* or *Conclusion* or *Recommendations*
The main thrust of the findings may be summarised in this section and conclusions drawn, together with a note of the outcome of events, or action required, or recommendations as to how a problem might be solved.

7.9 EXAMPLE: A SHORT INFORMAL REPORT

REPORT ON CUSTOMER COMPLAINT BY F R VESSENT

Confidential

To: M Ployer, Sales Manager Date: 13 June 20 - -
From: M Ployee, Sales Assistant

1 *Background*

The substance of Mr Vessent's complaint was that he had paid in an amount of £1,306.70 to the Dibbin & Dobbs account on April 4. On receiving his statement, he noted that the payment had not appeared. Mr Vessent is Accounts Clerk for Dibbin & Dobbs Ltd. who have had an account with us since June 20–: account number ______.

I have questioned our Junior Sales Assistant concerning the Dibbin & Dobbs account, and we have together consulted the records. In addition I looked at the recent transactions of our client Doobey & Sons to check for possible misallocation of the payments.

2 *Findings*

Our records show no credit in April to the Dibbin & Dobbs account. However, an amount of £1,306.70 was credited to the account of Doobey & Sons on April 4. Doobey & Sons when consulted admitted to having been puzzled by the inclusion on their statement of this amount.

The Junior Sales Assistant was absent through illness that week, and a temporary Assistant employed.

It would appear that the temp credited the payment to the wrong account.

3 *Action and recommendations*

The entries have been duly corrected.

I am writing appropriate letters of apology and explanation to Mr Vessent and to Doobey & Sons.

Obviously this is a matter of some concern in terms of customer relations. I suggest that all sales assistants be reminded of the need for due care and attention, and that temporary staff in particular be briefed on this matter in the future.

7.10 In informal reporting situations within an organisation, the 'short informal report' may well be presented in A4 memorandum format, which incorporates title headings and can thereafter be laid out at the writer's discretion. (See paragraph 4.8 earlier.)

Action Programme 11

You mentioned in conversation with your manager that you considered facilities for staff recreation and refreshment were either non-existent or inadequate. 'Is that really important?', she asked, 'and is it really that bad?' She thinks for a moment, then says: 'OK, why don't you put something in writing for me – and make some recommendations. I might want to show it to the others at the management meeting, though, so put it into some sort of order for me. Thanks.'

This is your brief. Write the report.

Form reports

7.11 Some commonly prepared reports have certain standard content requirements, and can therefore be preprinted with appropriate format and headings and filled in when the need arises: an **accident report form**, for example, or a **damaged goods report** (for incoming orders found to be faulty). Pre-printed forms allow the details of the report to be presented under the relevant headings, and in the space available.

7.12 A pre-printed form will specify each detail to be provided, use tick boxes for yes/no answers, or '*delete as appropriate' etc to save the writer from having to make the decision of what is relevant and how to put it across. In the narrative section, in which the reporter is asked to give details of the event itself, the important thing is to be:

(a) **Brief**: space may dictate this in any case.

(b) **Factually accurate**. As the report of an incident may be used for serious purposes, such as compensation claims, it is important that 'the truth, the whole truth and nothing but the truth' should be told, consistent with brevity.

7.13 An example that might be used in a telesales department or a large shop is shown on the next page.

ALLWAYS, WRIGHT
& SOVEREIGN

Report of a major breakdown in customer service

Person reporting the breakdown

Name: ____________________
Department: ____________________
Position: ____________________
Signature: ____________________
Date of report: ____________________

Details of customer

Customer name: ____________________
Customer address: ____________________
____
____
Account number: ____________________
Contact name: ____________________
Customer personnel
involved in the incident: ____________________

Details of incident:

Date: ______________
Time: ______________
Brief description: ____
____
____
____
____

Action taken

Replacement ☐
Refund ☐
Letter of apology ☐
None ☐

Other ☐
(specify) ____________________
____
____

Is the customer likely to take the matter further? Yes/No

Chapter Roundup

- Standard elements of a letter include: Letterhead, references, date, recipient name/address, salutation, subject heading, main body (introduction, development, conclusion), complimentary close, signature, name and designation of sender, enclosure/copy references.
- E-mails can take the role of letters, memos, notes and messages. They are deceptively secure and informal: care must be taken to ensure sensitivity to the recipient's needs, confidentiality and effective tone.
- A memorandum is the internal equivalent of a letter: it can be used for a variety of purposes. Memoranda have highly structured introductory elements, including sender, recipient, subject, date and reference: thereafter there are no formal elements required.
- A brief is a set of instructions and requirements intended to initiate and guide performance. It needs to include all criteria for fulfilment, plus supporting information, in a concise and highly-structured form.
- Notices are written or graphic messages, posted for general attention, which aim to attract attention to information or advice in such a way as to promote speed, ease and memorability.
- Report writing involves particular requirements for objectivity, impersonality, ease of reading, precision and appropriate formality. Reports are highly structured (especially formal reports), with sections covering: context-setting, description of methodology and findings, and conclusion/recommendation (as required).

Quick Quiz

1 In a business letter, what is the appropriate complimentary close for the salutation 'Dear Sirs'?

A Kind regards
B Yours faithfully
C Yours sincerely
D Yours

2 What device is used to signal that something else is in the same envelope as a letter?

3 In an e-mail, the use of all upper case (capital) letters is a helpful use of emphasis.

☐ True ☐ False

4 Which of the headings commonly found in a memo format is missing from the list given below?

To:
From:
Date:
Ref:

5 Which of the following (you may selection more than one option) does a memorandum require?

Complimentary close	Salutation	Date	Signature

6 Which of the following formats would *not* be appropriate to inform staff of health and safety procedures in the workplace?

A Memo
B Notice
C Brief
D E-mail

7 Specifications of the scope and purpose of a report are called ....

8 Which of the key elements of formal report format is missing from the following list?

Conclusions
Recommendations
Findings
Procedure/method
Terms of reference/introduction

Answers to Quick Quiz

1 B

2 Enc.

3 False

4 Subject:

5 Date

6 C

7 Terms of reference

8 Title

Now try Question 12 from the Question Bank at the end of this Text

Action Programme Review

1 (a) Fully blocked

(b) Semi-blocked. Date to right-hand margin, subject-heading to centre, close and signature starting at centre.

(c) Date, enclosure reference (see below).

(d) Open punctuation (see below).

TRUBB, LATT, TAMIL Ltd
Quality Drive
Birmingham B3 4NU
Tel: 0121 – xxx xxxx Fax: 0121 – xxx xxxx

Our Ref: IMB/tp

Mr Stan Duppenby-Counthead Esq
2 Comp Lane
Birmingham
B6 9DP

14 February 200X

Dear Sir

Quality Complaint

Thank you for your letter of yesterday. We have thoroughly investigated your complaint regarding the quality of the items despatched to you on the 3rd January, and there does seem to have been a temporary problem in our Inspection Department on that day.

I would appreciate further details of the defects found, the particular product affected and its batch number. I enclose our Defects Report Form, and would be grateful if you could complete and return it to me as soon as possible. I will then be happy to replace the relevant items immediately.

Meanwhile, please except my apologies for any inconvenience caused.

Yours sincerely

N Competant

N Competant
Sales Director

Enc.

2

Locktite Security Systems Ltd
51 Boult Street Edinburgh ED9 3BB

Our Ref: YN/pb Today's date
Private and confidential

J Wiekowski Esq.
WD Smith & Son Ltd
16 St Stephen St
Edinburgh ED8 1DM

Dear Mr Wiekowski

Position of Head Clerk

Thank you for your application for the post of Head Clerk with our firm. We were all greatly impressed by your curriculum vitae and by your performance in the interviews. It is with some regret, therefore, that I write to inform you that the post has been filled.

The decision was made after much deliberation, as the competition was of a high standard and reflects great credit on the ten individuals short-listed for second interview.

I trust this will be of some encouragement to you, although I realise that you will be disappointed, especially after the time and effort which you clearly put into your application.

May I take this opportunity to wish you every success in your search for a similar position elsewhere.

Yours sincerely

Your name

Your name

Personnel manager

Notes

(a) This letter is in semi-blocked layout.

(b) The letter is 'Private and Confidential', because WD Smith & Son may not know that Mr Wiekowski is looking for another job!

(c) The 'blow' is put into context in the first paragraph, then delivered straightforwardly in the second. The other paragraphs are designed to soothe, to rebuild the failed candidate's confidence: it reflects well on the company's attitude to people.

3

THE LISTENING BANK
Thread Needle Street
Megalopolis EC1 4U

Ms Anne Grie
Notta Mews
Megalopolis
W8 8U

Today's Date

Dear Ms Grie

Thank you for your letter of [yesterday's date]. I was sorry to hear that you were distressed at being refused entry to the bank. I understand your frustration, especially since your transaction was to have been a short one.

I am sure you will appreciate, however, that our staff are obliged to abide by the Bank's rules, which have been formulated after careful consideration and in the interests of orderly conduct of business. Much as we would like to make an exception for short transactions at the end of the day, it would not be fair to other customers and would be contrary to the discipline and reliability which we believe is an important part of our service.

Should you often find it inconvenient to visit us during banking hours, might I draw your attention to our out-of-hours facilities? Our 'through the wall' machines dispense cash twenty-four hours a day and can also be used to request a balance or statement.

Please accept my apologies for yesterday's incident. I trust that you will have no cause to complain of our service in future.

Yours sincerely

Your name

Your Name
Branch Manager

4

Communication Matters Ltd
43 Comma Street
Speke
Cheshire
SP2 4UP
Tel: 01234 567890

Our ref: LIP/0001

Mr E A Gency
Joblots Ltd
Grunt Road
Speke
Cheshire
SP4 2OB

Dear Mr Gency

Communication skills and job prospects

You may have read press reports in recent months highlighting the link between basic communication skills and the success – or failure – of job applications.

For instance, surveys suggest that an unemployed person is 50% more likely to be a poor speller than someone who has managed to get a job.

This has clear implications for your clients – both job candidates and prospective employers – and we should like to share with you a solution backed by the government's 'Better English' campaign.

Communication matters

Our one-day business communication courses cover all of the basic communication skills that people need to develop if they are going to improve their job prospects.

- Spelling
- Punctuation and grammar
- Letter writing
- Memos
- Filling in forms
- Verbal communication

The course is accompanied by a self-help training pack which includes a booklet, a set of exercises and a cassette tape to consolidate matters covered on the course.

I enclose a leaflet giving fuller details about the course and the training pack. We are prepared to offer a 30% discount to anybody who signs up for one of our courses as a result of a recommendation from you.

If you would like us to supply you with more leaflets to give to your clients, please contact Lucy Tunne on 01234 567890.

Yours sincerely,

Mark Letterman
Marketing Manager

5 **From:** C L Wright <clwright(a)widget.co.uk
To: <mail?SuchNsuch.co.uk>
Sent: Wednesday, 4 July 2001 1:10
Subject: Enquiry

Dear Sirs,

I am most interested in your Product X line introduced in recent advertisements. I would like to receive a detailed up-to-date product brochure, if available, including full specifications and prices.

Our postal address in supplied below. Alternatively you can e-mail me the information or an appropriate web-link, if the information is available on-line.

Thank you for your assistance.

CL Wright
Purchasing Assistant

Widget Co
8 Snale Myall Rd
Post Town
PT6 7QH
Tel: 3780 8849 2983

6 We have left the content to you, without suggestions, since so many of the details will be invented. Study our examples, if in doubt – and make sure that you are familiar with the *format* of both media.

7 **Gateways**

Timber Vale
Nonesuch
Nottinghamshire
NT1 4BU
02626 493949

To: Ms G Locks
Operations Director
Winsome Design

Date: 6 December 20XX

Ref: 468/SL

From: Mr A Woods
Marketing Manager

A brief for the production of a new Gateway product catalogue.

Introduction

This brief details Gateway's requirements for an updated product catalogue.

Task

To product an up-dated and more comprehensive company catalogue to promote and stimulate demand for our extended product range.

Production specifications

Size – A4, three page foldover
Paper – glossy, medium weight, accept four colour
Number of catalogues – 20,000

Content specifications

Catalogue content and design is to reflect the following to potential customers.

- Highest quality standards.
- The availability of advisory services and 24 hour responses.
- The existing and increased product range, with selected pictures of wrought iron and timber gates.
- Our highly competitive pricing.

Target audience

We wish to do the following.

(a) Retain our existing customer profile.
(b) Target new potential customers who normally buy top of the range garden products.

Budget

In addition to accepting costings you may budget for a one day, on site photographic session to photograph our products and working environs with a view to using selected photographs in the catalogue.

Conclusion

Please contact me either to indicate an early interest or ask for any further information you may require.

If you are interested in tendering for the work a detailed written response to this brief is required by 10 January 20XY.

A Woods

8

Notice for the Attention of Hotel Guests

(Hotel Logo)

IMPORTANT NOTICE

Protection of Personal Belongings

Dear Guest

Thefts from hotel rooms do occur occasionally – as they regrettably do in many other situations.

We are not, of course, complacent about this and have instituted a number of measures which have had considerable success.

Staff are trained in security as part of our wide ranging customer care programme and are available to advise you if you have any particular concerns or questions. Other services available to you include:

A room safe for your personal use

Hotel safety boxes for larger items

Dedicated cleaning staff for each floor

On behalf of all our staff I can assure you that we are constantly vigilant and ask you to help us make your stay safe as well as enjoyable by using the services available to you.

Ken Lightfoot

K LIGHTFOOT

(Manager)

9 The central section of the report might be structured: *Advantages* – party 1, party 2, party 3. *Disadvantages* – party 1, party 2, party 3. However, we have chosen to take the 'concerned' parties in turn, and consider the advantages and disadvantages for each.

I INTRODUCTION

How flexible working hours operate (briefly), core period and flexible hours. Debit/credit of hours per week or month.

II EFFECTS

1 Staff

(a) *Advantages*

(i) Reduced stress: vagaries of traffic etc no longer a major worry
(ii) Flexibility: fitting in with family patterns, shop hours etc
(iii) Morale enhanced by discretion in own work patterns
(iv) Favourable results for morale, attendance etc in trial schemes

(b) *Disadvantages*

(i) Reduced discipline: some staff may take advantage
(ii) Fluctuating work patterns may be psychologically disruptive
(iii) Friction may result from scheduling to cover non-core periods

2 *Management*

(a) *Advantages*

(i) Morale/attendance (of staff) → help management as well
(ii) Fewer idle staff (wastage) during quieter periods

(b) *Disadvantages*

(i) Planning, administering, controlling scheme
(ii) Cost of mechanical logging in/out devices

3 *Customers*

(a) *Advantages*

(i) High morale of staff hopefully → better service

(b) *Disadvantages*

(ii) Possible bottlenecks of work during flexi-periods: delays
(iii) Possible discontinuity of service: personnel changing through day etc.

III CONCLUSIONS

(a) Disadvantages: few and can be overcome with good management

(b) Advantages: fundamental, shown to be effective elsewhere

(c) Recommend trial scheme of flexi-time with a view to introducing it later in full

10 Report writing is a key skill. A successful structure and style will help you to pass your exams.

11

REPORT
RECREATION AND REFRESHMENT FACILITIES

I INTRODUCTION

This report was compiled by [Your Name] at the request of [Manager's Name], and submitted on the [Date].

II ANALYSIS OF THE SITUATION

(a) *Importance of facilities*

(i) Although it has not been conclusively proven that 'happy' staff are invariably more productive, there is a relationship between job satisfaction and effectiveness. Dissatisfaction can impair performance, engendering a range of negative responses and high labour turnover.

(ii) The provision of recreation/refreshment facilities would not necessarily be an issue *if it were not perceived to be so by staff.* [Your Name] has reason to believe that staff do feel disadvantaged by the lack of facilities, and that morale is suffering.

(iii) Moreover, such facilities impact on staff health: refreshment and recreation are important in the control of fatigue and stress.

(iv) The matter is therefore worthy of the company's consideration, not only for 'humane' but for practical reasons.

(b) *Present inadequacy: refreshment*

(i) Provision for hot drinks is inadequate: the 'kitchen' area is cramped and equipped only with one kettle and insufficient crockery; supplies are ill organised. Facilities for preparing and/or storing foodstuffs are non-existent.

(ii) There are few congenial eating-places or food-providers in the surrounding area. Take-away food is expensive, and Luncheon Vouchers not widely accepted.

(iii) There is nowhere on the premises for staff to take refreshments except at their desks, which is less than satisfactory with potentially messy or highly aromatic foods.

(c) *Present inadequacy: recreation*

(i) There is no venue for informal communication between staff – except the office, where it is discouraged. The company is frustrating a potential team-building and co-ordinating activity.

(ii) There is no organised encouragement of constructive recreation or relationship-building outside work.

(iii) No effort is made to encourage health and fitness through sports, nor to broaden employees' other interests.

III CONCLUSION AND RECOMMENDATIONS

(a) Without wishing to incur unnecessary expenditure, or concentrating unduly on non-work activities, the company should be concerned to review its provisions, in view of II above.

(b) A Committee should be formed to investigate measures including:

(i) Food provision. An independent caterer might be engaged to offer a daily selection of sandwiches and snacks, subsidised via the Luncheon Voucher scheme.

(ii) The setting aside of a rest area, with seating, pleasant décor and extended facilities for the preparation of drinks and simple foods.

(iii) Access to sports facilities and/or tickets to artistic/sporting events, which could be made cheaply available to staff.

(c) A 'Social Club' should be instituted to co-ordinate independent activities and encourage wider socialising among employees.

Signed: *Your name*

Date:

13

Statistical and graphic information

Chapter Topic List	
1	Setting the scene
2	Interpreting statistical information
3	Summarising data
4	Presenting graphic data
5	Graphic illustration of data

Learning Outcomes

- ☑ Classify data and understand the simple use of frequency distributions, averages, correlation and trends
- ☑ Summarise written information
- ☑ Identify the key points of statistical and graphic information
- ☑ Use tables, charts, graphs, diagrams and illustrations to present statistical data

Syllabus References

- ☑ Interpret, summarise and present oral, written and graphical information (4.5)

Key Concepts Introduced

- Frequency distribution
- Average
- Correlation
- Time series
- Trend
- Summary

1 Setting the scene

1.1 This chapter is particularly valuable for the compulsory question in Part A of the *Customer Communications* exam. It discusses:

- How written, graphic and statistical information can be interpreted, analysed and summarised in order to produce concise reports, presentations, press releases and other formats
- How you can use charts, graphs, diagrams and other graphic formats in your report, presentations, advertisements and other formats

2 Interpreting statistical information

2.1 Statistics are raw 'data'. They must be **processed** in some way to create **'information'** which is **meaningful and helpful** for a particular purpose. We will here look very briefly at some of the ways of using statistical data.

Classification

2.2 Classification can be used to add meaning to data by grouping items into helpful categories or classes. For example, consider the following list of customer complaints.

Product X: complaints in July and August 2001			
Date	*Name*	*Account number*	*Complaint*
August			
23	Greenwald, G	2428	Broken sprocket
22	Wharf, C	2991	Wrong colour
19	Walters, P	3367	Delivered late
16	Taylor, H	3623	Delivered late
14	Meadham, S	2476	Faulty sprocket
10	Jones, D	3048	Too big
8	Hoggart, R	2782	Delivered late
4	Lane, A	2987	Wrong colour
July			
31	Lewis, M	3744	Not specified ('does not work')
31	Lord, J	2625	Broken sprocket
31	Chester, B	3109	Delivered late
29	Ryan, C	2989	Delivered late
14	Wood, J	2785	Wrong colour
7	Prior, S	3460	Ten ordered; nine received
2	Tucker, S	2815	Not specified ('quite unsuitable')

2.3 Certain faults seem to recur, and you decide to see if there is a **trend**: you decide to **classify** the complaints according to type.

Mechanical problems:

■ Broken sprockets	(3)
■ Unspecified	(1)

Order processing:

■ Wrong colour supplied	(3)
■ Customer needs (size, 'suitability') not properly identified	(2)

Despatch:

■ Late delivery	(5)
■ Short delivery	(1)

You can now concentrate your efforts in helpful areas.

Frequency distribution

2.4 One type of classification often used in the organisation of large sets of data (and their presentation, as we will see later) is a **frequency distribution**.

Key Concept

A **frequency distribution** is a method of classification in which the data is divided into segments or **classes**, and the number of items of data that fall into (or are observed in) each class is called the class **frequency**.

2.5 Classes might be ranges of: age, or costs/numbers/frequency of products purchased, time spent, errors made and so on. You can compare the relative frequency of one class against another, or against the same class over time, to show trends.

Example

Given below is a set of raw data on the number of minutes in each hour reported spent on the telephone by 40 sales office staff.

19	15	1	24	5	19	27	34	14	23
9	5	4	18	41	17	15	19	23	14
34	11	16	17	28	29	31	11	21	12
8	5	16	6	17	29	7	9	23	18

As a frequency distribution, the data would be organised as follows. For example, count up how many times a number between 0 and 10 occurs.

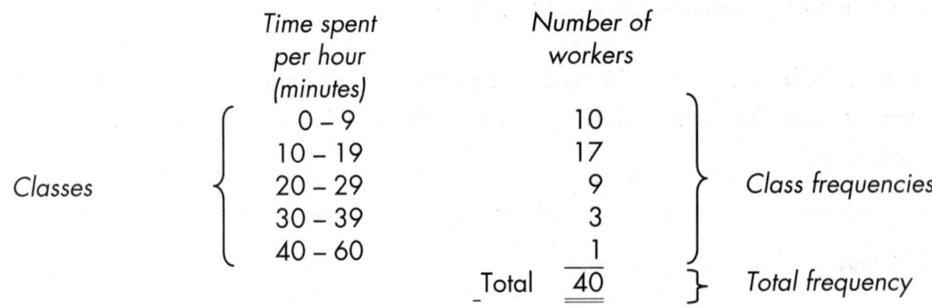

	Time spent per hour (minutes)		*Number of workers*	
Classes	0 – 9		10	*Class frequencies*
	10 – 19		17	
	20 – 29		9	
	30 – 39		3	
	40 – 60		1	
		Total	40	*Total frequency*

2.6 A **cumulative frequency distribution** uses 'ceilings' instead of ranges to define classes: 'under 10, under 20' etc. But the class 'under 20' **includes** 'under 10' as well as '10 to 19': the frequency distribution accumulates. To use our example:

Time spent per hour (minutes)	*Number of workers = cumulative frequency*	
Under 10	10	
Under 20	10 + 17 = 27	
Under 30	10 + 17 + 9 = 36	
Under 40	10 + 17 + 9 + 3 = 39	
Under 60	10 + 17 + 9 + 3 + 1 = 40	(Total sample)

Averages

Key Concept

An **average** is a value which is 'typical' or representative of a set of data, a measure of its '**central tendency**'.

2.7 The main types of average are as follows.

(a) The **arithmetic mean**, often shown by the symbol $\bar{x}$ ('x bar'). This is found by adding up all the items in the set, then dividing by the number of items in the set.

Eg: customer complaints per month over a six month period.

January	*February*	*March*	*April*	*May*	*June*
0	26	0	5	3	2

The average number of complaints is $\frac{0+26+0+5+3+2}{6} = \frac{36}{6} = 6$ per month.

The problem with this is that **extremes** (like the 26) **distort** the average: the actual monthly complaints are not as bad as 6 – which also disguises the fact that you had a real problem in February!

(b) The **median**: the **middle value**, when you arrange the data in ascending order. (If there is an even number of items, the median is mid-way between the middle two. For example, here are our monthly complaints reordered:

0 0 2 3 5 26

↑

Median = 2.5

(c) The **mode**: the **most frequently occurring** value in a set of data. So the mode for our monthly customer complaints is 0!

2.8 You can probably now begin to appreciate why Disraeli said 'There are three kinds of lies: Lies, damned lies and statistics'. It is very easy for the unscrupulous to use averages to disguise the true facts.

Correlation

Key Concept

Correlation is the measurement of the nature and strength of **association** between two **variables**.

2.9 Do price cuts coincide with changes in sales volume? If so, do sales go **up** when prices go down, or do they go **down** (in which case, perhaps the lower price is affecting the perception of our product's quality)? Is there an association (close enough to base decisions on) between hours worked and employee absenteeism?

(a) **Positive correlation** occurs when there is an association between the two variables, in the same direction: one increases as the other increases, or else both decrease at the same time. The longer the working hours (the value for 'working hours' increases), the more absenteeism there is (the value 'days absent' also increases). The more advertisements you transmit, the higher the sales.

(b) **Negative correlation** occurs when there is an association between the two variables, but in opposite directions: as one increases, the other decreases, or vice versa. So the longer the working hours, the fewer the days absent. As volume of production goes up, unit production cost goes down.

Trends

Key Concept

A **time series** is a set of data recorded at intervals over a period of time (eg monthly sales or customer complaint figures for the year).

A **trend**is an underlying movement (upwards or downwards) in a time series over the long term.

2.10 Patterns which can be observed in business time series include the following.

(a) **Trends**. Figures (for example, sales revenue, or number of women in managerial positions) may show a **positive trend** (there is an increase, in **each** successive set of data, or in general over time), or **negative trend** (that is, there is a regular decrease or downward movement).

(b) **Seasonal patterns or variations** that is, observable peaks and troughs at the same times of each successive year. There may be a repeated **seasonal pattern** (peak at Christmas, falling to low during Summer holidays, rising steeply to a peak at Christmas again, say). There may also be a **general trend:** the peaks and troughs get higher (or lower) from one year to the next (Figure 13.1).

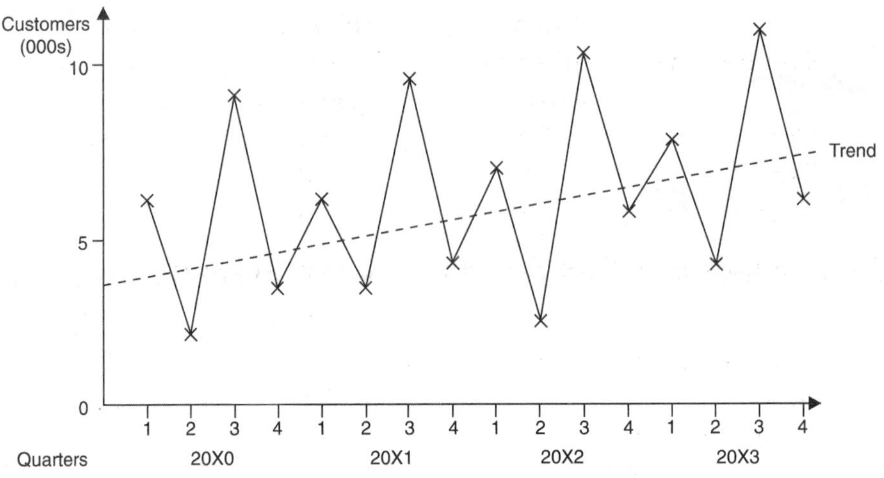

Figure 13.1 General trend

(c) **Cyclical variations**, reflecting the 'larger' pattern of the swing in an economy (usually over many years) from 'boom' to 'bust' and back again.

(d) **Random variations:** irregular ups and downs reflecting all the unpredictable factors that lie behind data gathered over time. The underlying or overall trend or seasonal cyclical pattern need not be altered.

Marketing at Work

'..... a certain charity ..... sent a test mailing to existing donors, asking for an additional contribution for a key project. It presented three boxes for respondents to tick, marked £15, £25 or £50 for this extra donation. The overall results were as follows: mailed 20,000; response rate 2.27 per cent; responders 453; money received £15,025; average gift £33.17.

On this basis, a roll-out to 200,000 was undertaken, with the goal of raising £150,000. But despite a similar response rate, the sum received fell short by more than £25,000. So what happened? Why did the average gift drop so dramatically (from £33.17 to £27.82)? Could this have been predicted?

In fact, the test result proved inaccurately high because of a single exceptional donation of £2,500 – an outlier that distorted the figures badly. This one donation changed the average gift from £22.71 to £33.17.

Marketing Week

Action Programme 1

What do you notice about the following findings?

(a) **Car ownership per home of those owning at least one car**

	Number owned by age of head of household			
Cars per home	*Head of All homes Aged < 45*	*Head of household Aged 45-64*	*Head of household Aged >65*	*Household*
One	70%	65%	58%	80%
Two	25%	30%	30%	18%
Three	5%	5%	12%	2%

(b) **Forecast growth of the US on-line market ($bn)**

	1996	*1997*	*2001*
Business-to-business sales	6	8	183
Travel	0.5	0.6	7.4
Financial services	0.8	1.2	5

Source: *Business Research*

3 Summarising data

Key Concept

A **summary** or **précis**is a concise outline of source materials, with points selected for relevance to a specific purpose.

3.1 You probably use the techniques of summarising every day: telling someone else what happened, or describing the plot of a film. You simply pick out the more important points and communicate them in connected, understandable sentences.

Exam Tip

In the exam you will be given a marketing article or a report to summarise for someone else who wants to get an overview of the material. The Senior Examiner has said:

'Part A [of the exam] forms a mini-case based on an article from the marketing press or a collection of marketing data. The questions may ask for structured notes for a presentation, or a report, letter or memo about some aspect of the data. Your comprehension ability and skill in selecting relevant data are important for the compulsory question. Candidates should be selective in their use of information, and they should use the report to summarise the most important findings.'

3.2 At work, too, you will often want to summarise something, perhaps for a plan or first draft, or for an introductory or concluding paragraph. You may have to give an account of events or discussions to someone who was not present – minutes of a meeting, say, or a telephone message.

Summarising written data

3.3 A summary should be:

- **Clear**: well set out for the user's ease of understanding. If your purpose in transferring information in condensed form is to save the user's time **and** help his comprehension, you can't **just** weed out the excess volume of information: your purpose will be defeated by lack of clarity as well.
- **Complete**. Don't 'prune' **too** much, or you may lose the logical progression from one point to another, or miss out an item of data that is essential to the user's grasp of the material.
- **Correct**. Whether you are passing on data, or representing an argument, make sure you do so faithfully and objectively. Check that you have transferred the facts correctly (numbers and spellings included). Check that you have not added weight to one point, or omitted another, with the result that the 'balance' of the original argument is lost. Have you said – in essence – what the original message-sender wanted to say?

3.4 If you summarise or quote someone else's data (verbal *or* visual, as in a chat or graph), remember to cite your **source.**

Selecting the essentials

3.5 The most vital element of summarising is **purpose**.

(a) Identify the **writer's** or **speaker's** purpose. What is he or she really trying to say that will be helpful to you? Have you understood and noted no more, no less and no other than that?

(b) Identify **your** purpose. What is your summary going to be used for, by whom, and in what circumstances? Will it be legible, understandable and relevant?

3.6 If you are going to be the only one using your notes, you can use any system and any 'short-cuts' that will make sense to you and effectively trigger your memory of the original text or ideas. Do take the trouble to find a system that works: you will find it invaluable for revision, for planning answers in exams, and in practice, for the preparation of 'cue-cards' for yourself for a meeting with a customer, say.

3.7 If you are taking notes as a summary for **someone else**, you will have the added concern of making them logical, easy to follow and easy to understand for someone who has not heard, seen or read the original item. We suggest graphic formats for presentation slides and reports later in this chapter.

Action Programme 2

You work in a marketing consultancy called The Brand Tracker Partnership. As marketing assistant you are involved in a variety of activities, ranging from marketing research on behalf of clients to assisting in the marketing of the Brand Tracker Partnership itself.

The firm has been commissioned to undertake research into the women's fragrance market by Sian Singh, the brand manager of Georgie, a perfume made by the leading cosmetics manufacturer Lanroche.

The raw data was collected by a colleague and is very disorganised. It needs to be analysed and put into an appropriate format for the client to read.

Marketing research data

Annual advertising spend	£'000
Georgie	955
Possession	1,870
Esta Lauda	877
Eternal	1,206
Ana	1,049
Charly Klein	698

Marketing research was conducted during December 200X. A sample of 300 women aged between 16-55, which was representative of the fragrance buying market, was questioned by means of a survey. Following a telephone survey, four focus groups were held in different hotels around the country to obtain further qualitative information.

Desk research, using secondary data sources published by MEAL and SalesMonitor, was analysed to produce advertising expenditure and industry sales figures. In addition, advertising in women's magazines and below the line promotional activity in retail outlets were monitored over a period between October to December 200X.

Reasons for purchase

	% saying
I tried it in the shop	55
It is the one I usually buy or wear	53
I wanted to try something new/different	32
I saw it advertised in a magazine	25
I smelt it on someone else	19
I smelt a scratch-and-sniff ad	16
I saw it advertised on television	14
Advice from the sales assistant	12
There was a money off offer	8
It was cheaper than the others	6

Thirty two fragrances were named as being bought or requested and received as gifts indicating that it is a fragmented market. However, eleven major brands had 73 per cent of total market share.

Of those mentioned, 64 per cent sell for more than £15 per 30 ml. Lady, Carlie and Max Maxa were ranked as the least expensive perfumes. ABC1s are no more likely to buy or receive premium priced fragrances than anyone else, with figures indicating that fragrances generally have a flat class profile. Charly Klein and Carlie draw more than two thirds of buyers from the 16-25 age group, with Cachet concentrated amongst those in their 30s. Ana, Georgie and Eternal appear to have popularity with all age groups. Channelle and Esta Lauda were popular amongst the older market – mainly those in the 40-55 age group.

Fragrances bought

Brand	*% market share*
Channelle	3.7
Max Maxa	2.0
Cachet	2.0
Possession	10.5
Georgie	8.8
Lady	7.2
Ana	13.0
Eternal	11.0
Charly Klein	5.5
Esta Lauda	5.0
Carlie	4.3

Price was not considered to be important except amongst buyers of Carlie. Of these, 34 per cent gave cheapness as the reason for purchase. Brand recognition levels were generally high for many fragrances. Newer entrants into the market such as, Cachet, Georgie and Possession, achieved high recall levels possibly influenced by the impact of point of sale and in-store promotional activity. Advertising expenditure was generally high amongst most brands.

Sampling is very important both on the counter and through scent strips in magazines.

Spontaneous ad recall	%
Ana	22
Possession	18
Eternal	12
Georgie	12
Channelle	9
Charly Klein	8
Max Maxa	7
Cachet	5
Esta Lauda	3
Lady	2
Carlie	2

Required

Write a short formal report for Sian Singh, using the market research data shown here.

Summarising statistical data

3.8 Some essential points to look out for in summarising statistical data include the following.

(a) **What is the 'argument' or 'story' of the data: what point does it make?**

It may help if you think about this as if you were writing a press release – as you may be asked to do? What is newsworthy about the findings revealed by the figures or graph? (Are Italians slow to take up e-commerce compared to the rest of Europe? Are women more likely than men to respond positively to direct mail?) Ask yourself what information the organisation will be able to **use**.

(b) **What comparisons are suggested?**

Mentally translate figures into slices of a pie chart, or bars of a bar chart (covered in the next section of this chapter) to see some possibilities. Is one brand's market share bigger than others'? Is a disproportionate amount spent on one promotional medium compared to others?

(c) **What trends or correlations can be observed?**

These are particularly useful concepts in summarising the importance of data and indicating what (if anything) needs to be done. A trend suggests change (for good or bad). A correlation suggests that if you manipulate one variable, you will get change in another. Mentally translate figures into a line graph or scatter diagram (covered in the next section of this chapter) to see the possibilities. Is e-commerce penetration rising and projected to rise further? Does a reduction in PR spend correlate with rising product returns?

(d) **How reliable and meaningful is the data?**

Are apparent anomalies, surprises or trends accounted for by the age of the data (when was it gathered?), the size and constitution of the research sample (was it large and random enough to represent a genuine cross-section?), the question asked (was it ambiguous or leading?) and so on.

(e) **Are you interpreting the data correctly?**

Are percentages, for example, percentages out of 100% (showing relative proportions of a total sample such as would be portrayed in a pie chart)? Do they add up to more than 100% (showing overlapping or multiple responses, such as would be portrayed in a bar chart)? What are the figures given percentages **of**? Check all titles, labels, notes and keys carefully.

4 Presenting graphic data

4.1 'A picture paints a thousand words'. A simple visual presentation of data has more **impact and immediacy** than a table or block of text that is uniform to the eye and may contain superfluous elements.

You should, however, remember that a visual image is only effective if the assumptions behind it and the 'key' to its use are **shared by sender and receiver alike**. Symbols which you take for granted may be obscure to someone else with different training, knowledge or experience. Graphs and charts can be complex and highly technical, so they should, like any other medium of communication, be **adapted to suit** the understanding and information needs of the intended recipient: they should be simplified and explained as necessary, and include only as much data as can clearly be presented and assimilated.

4.2 Here we will briefly discuss the most common visual methods of presenting data.

Exam Tip

The compulsory question in the Customer Communications exam will almost certainly include charts and graphs which you are expected to be able to interpret and comment on in the form of a report or a memo.

Past compulsory questions have also asked you to prepare line graphs, pie charts and bar charts including multiple bar charts, (December 2000) and component bar charts (Specimen Paper to this syllabus).

You must be able to deal with facts, figures, charts, graphs to stand a reasonable chance in the exam. You cannot avoid such questions. Make sure you take a compass, a ruler, a protractor and pencils into the exam room.

Tables

4.3 **Tables** are a simple way of presenting numerical information. Figures are displayed, and can be compared with each other: relevant totals, subtotals, or percentages can also be presented as a summary for analysis.

A table is **two-dimensional** (rows and columns), so it can only show **two variables**: a sales chart for a year, for example, might have rows for products, and columns for each month of the year. You simply need to enter the appropriate figures in each position.

SALES FIGURES FOR 20 - -

Product	*Jan*	*Feb*	*Mar*	*Apr*	*May*	*Jun*	*Jul*	*Aug*	*Sep*	*Oct*	*Nov*	*Dec*	*Total £'000*
A													
B													
C													
D													
Total													

Source: Marketing Department

4.4 Here are some further guidelines.

- The table should be given a **clear title**.
- All columns and rows should be **clearly labelled**. State the units being used (eg £).
- Where appropriate, there should be **clear sub-totals**. In the example above it might be appropriate, say, to have sub-totals for products A and B together and for C and D together as well as overall totals.
- A **total figure** is usually needed at the bottom of each column of figures and at the far right of each row.
- Tables should **not** be **packed** with so much data that the information presented is difficult to read: round figures up or down if required, and consider grouping minor items into a single 'Other' or 'Miscellaneous' category.
- Add your **source** if relevant.

Action Programme 3

The number of units of product N50 sold by the salesmen of Tifford Ltd in each of the four regions of the United Kingdom during 20X1 were as follows.

Region 1	quarter 1	72,	quarter 2	53,	quarter 3	19,	quarter 4	42
Region 2	quarter 1	16,	quarter 2	10,	quarter 3	25,	quarter 4	21
Region 3	quarter 1	392,	quarter 2	276,	quarter 3	315,	quarter 4	516
Region 4	quarter 1	152,	quarter 2	141,	quarter 3	137,	quarter 4	119

Required

Tabulate this information to show total sales in each quarter of 20X1 and sales in each region in 20X1.

Charts and graphs

4.5 The purpose of a **chart** or **graph** is to convey data in a way that will demonstrate its meaning or significance **more clearly than a table** of data would. Charts are not always more appropriate than tables, and the most suitable way of presenting data will depend on:

- **What the data are intended to show**. Visual displays usually make one or two points quite forcefully, whereas tables usually give more detailed information.
- **Who is going to use the data**. Some individuals might understand visual displays more readily than tabulated data.

Line graphs

4.6 A line **graph** shows, by means of either a **straight line or a curve**, the **relationship** between **two variables**. In particular it shows how the value of one variable changes, according to changes in the value of the other variable. For example, a graph might show:

- **Changes** in sales turnover **over time**
- How the unit cost of printing leaflets vary according to the number printed

More often than not, one variable will be **'dependent'** on the other variable. For example if time did not pass, sales would not occur, so sales is the dependent variable and time the **independent variable**.

4.7 A graph has a **horizontal axis** (the **x** axis) and a **vertical axis** (the **y** axis). The x axis is used to represent the **independent** variable and the y axis is used to represent the **dependent** variable. If it is not known which variable, if any, is the dependent one (for example cups of tea drunk in relation to pairs of socks purchased) then the choice of axes is **arbitrary**.

4.8 The general rules for plotting graphs can be summarised as follows.

(a) The **scales** on each axis should be selected so as to make the graph big enough to be **easily read**. In some cases it is best not to start a scale at zero: this is perfectly acceptable as long as the scale adopted is clearly shown.

(b) Graphs can show **more than one line** (to compare performance over time of two products, say). However, they should not be overcrowded with too many lines. They should give a clear, neat impression.

(c) The **axes** must be **clearly labelled** with descriptions and units.

(d) Don't forget **title** and **source**.

Exam Tip

The Senior Examiner for the new syllabus has issued a warning to tutors that students need to pay attention to detail when presenting information: name the axes of graphs, provide a source and so on. Make yourself a mental checklist – and use it!

4.9 It is easy to see the progression of share prices in the graph below. The **scale** of the vertical axis is large enough for you to tell with reasonable accuracy the price at any given point during the period. Despite peaks and troughs, the **overall trend** is also obvious, in a way that would not be possible in a table of fluctuating figures.

This will be helpful, for example, in demonstrating the success of a product to encourage employees: consider the following example (Figure 13.2).

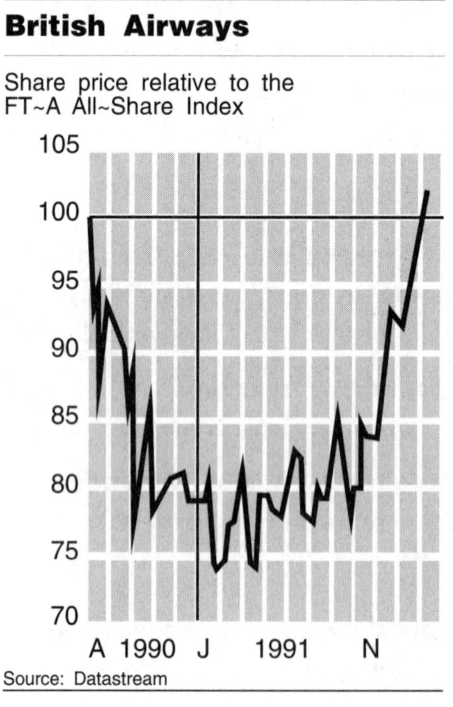

Figure 31.2 Line graph

Bar charts

4.10 The **bar chart** is one of the most common methods of presenting data in a visual display. It is a chart in which data is shown in the form of a bar (two dimensional, or three dimensional for extra impact), and is used to demonstrate and compare amounts or numbers of things. The bars are the **same width** but variable in height and are read off a vertical scale as you would read water levels or a thermometer. A horizontal presentation is also possible.

4.11 The bar chart is very **versatile**. Each block may represent a different (identified) item, for example the annual production cost of a different product (to compare costs of a range of products), or the total sales turnover of a company for a year (to compare success over a period of years), or the number of hours required to produce a product in a particular country (to compare efficiency in a group of industrial nations).

(a) A **simple** bar chart is a visually appealing way of:

- Showing the actual **magnitude** of an item (amount of money, hours, sales or whatever).
- **Comparing magnitudes**, according to the relative lengths of the bars on the chart.

(b) A **component** bar chart divides each bar into **component parts** to show a further breakdown of the information. So, for example, in a bar chart showing numbers of complaints in each month of the year, each bar could be subdivided into type of complaint, as follows (Figure 13.3).

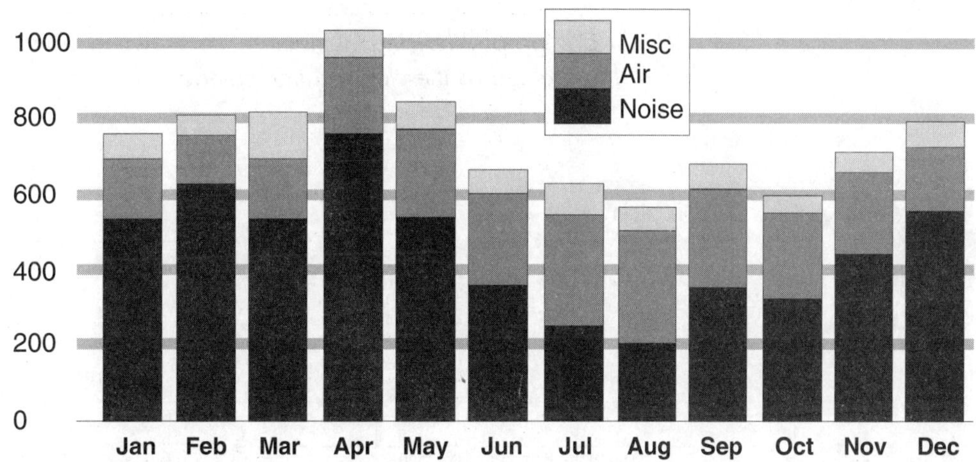

Figure 13.3 Component bar chart
Source: (unknown)

(c) A **multiple** bar chart uses two or more bars (instead of segments of a single bar) to present subdivisions of data, as follows (Figure 13.4). (Note that related bars abut each other, but there needs to be space between the clusters.)

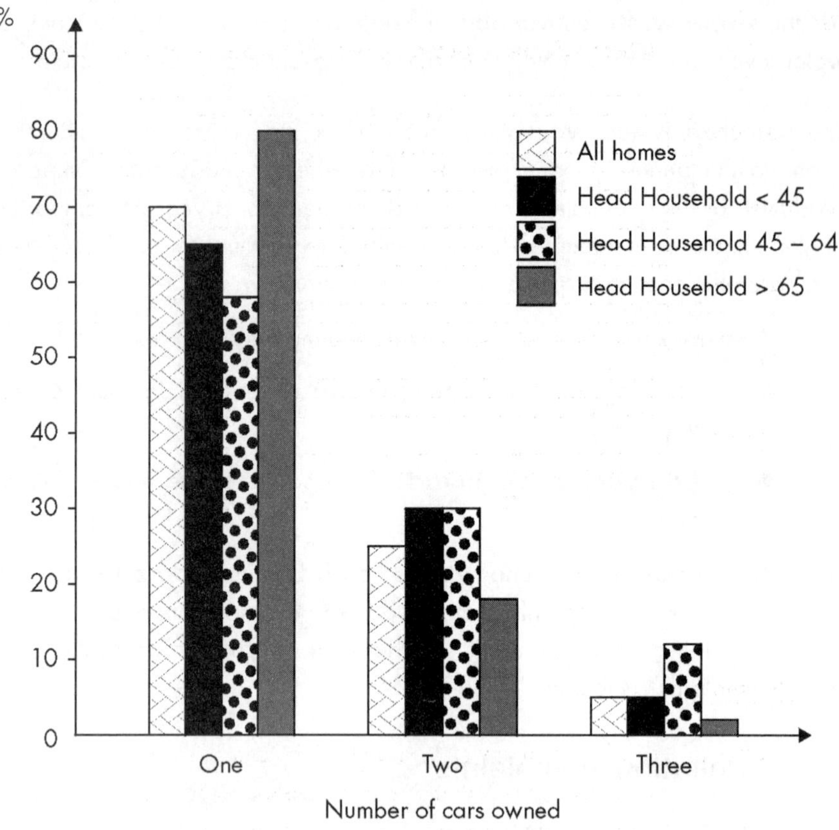

Figure 13.4 Multiple bar graph showing number of cars owned using the age of the head of household as the classification criteria

Action Programme 4

Here are two bar charts. Your task is to explain what they mean.

(a)

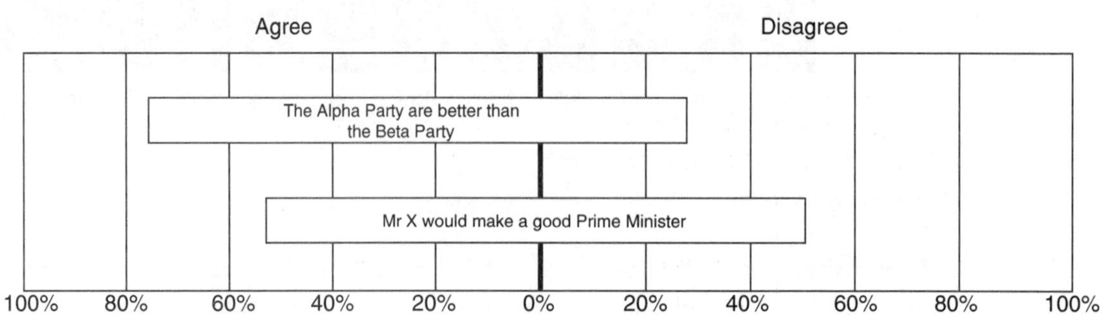

(b)

Which of these players would you like in your team?

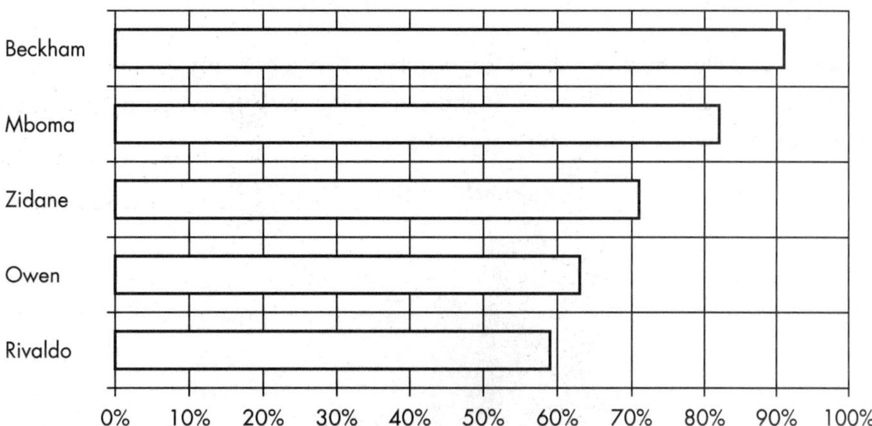

Gantt charts

4.12 Gantt charts are another form of horizontal bar chart. They are used to plan the **time scale** for a project and/or estimate the amount of **resources** required. They can also be used to record planned versus actual **progress** in getting something done. Here are some simple examples.

(a)

	Staff involved in Training Courses								
Staff member	January					February			
	W1	W2	W3	W4	W5	W1	W2	W3	W4
M									
N									
O									
P									
Q									
Number of staff available	3	3	5	5	4	2	3	5	5

(b)

SALES CALLS	Monday	Tuesday	Wednesday	Thursday	Friday
Target	100	125	150	150	150
Actual	75	100	150	180	75

Pie charts

4.13 A **pie chart** is used to show **pictorially** the **relative sizes of component elements** of a total value or amount. It is called a pie chart because it is circular in shape like a pie (from a bird's eye view), which is then cut into 'slices' which represent a component part of the total.

The **whole** 'pie' = 360° (the number of degrees in a circle) = 100% of whatever you are showing. An element which is 50% of your total would therefore occupy a segment of 180°, and so on (360 × 0.5 = 180).

Pie charts are visually effective where the number of components is small enough to keep the chart simple, and where the difference in the size of the components is great enough for the eye to judge without too much supporting information.

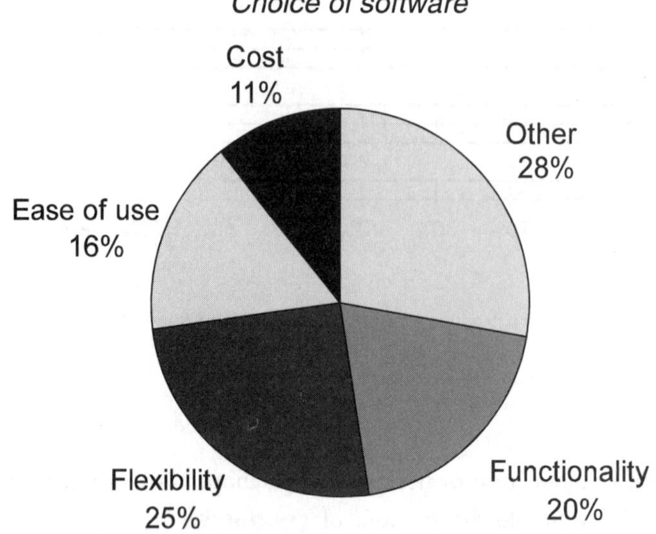

Figure 13.5: Pie chart

Pictograms

4.14 A **pictogram** (or picturegram) is a simple and striking statistical diagram in which the data is represented by a **recognisable picture or symbol**, with a **clear key** to the items and quantities intended. Different pictures can be used on the same pictogram to represent different component elements of the data. For example a pictogram showing the number of visitors to the corporate exhibition stand (Figure 13.6) might use pictures of people:

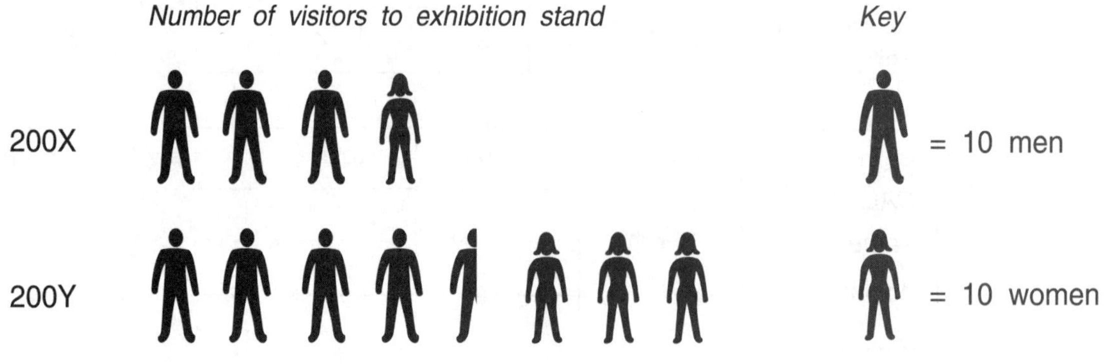

Figure 13.6 Pictogram

You can see at a glance that the visiting rate has grown and that the growth has been greatest among female visitors.

4.15 Guidelines for pictograms are as follows.

- The symbols must be **clear and simple**.
- The quantity of items that each symbol represents ought to be **clearly shown** in a key.
- Bigger quantities are shown by **more** symbols, **not bigger** symbols.

4.16 The advantage of pictograms is that they present data in a simple, attractive and **readily-understood** way. They convey their message **at a glance**, and are consequently often used on television, especially for news items (number of jobs lost, products sold and so on) and in advertisements ('New Sudzo can wash **this** many dishes! **Your** liquid...')

The disadvantage of pictograms is that they can only convey a **limited amount of data**, and they **lack precision**. Each symbol must represent quite a large number of items, otherwise the diagram would be too crowded with symbols.

Action Programme 5

You are marketing assistant of Topper Bowler Ltd (hat and umbrella sellers). You are running a competition in the sales office to see which of your reps can run up the biggest sales total for the week. Just to keep them on their toes, and so they can easily gauge their progress, you put up a bulletin poster in the office, with a 'catchy' pictogram of each rep's sales.

	Hats	*Umbrellas*	
Doe	10	15	
Smith	40	10	
Bloggs	25	20	
Other sales	27	3	
	102	48	Total: 150

(a) Draw the pictogram for the poster.

(b) You have recently been worried about whether umbrellas are pulling their weight in the sales mix. You decide to draw up a pie chart for total sales, which you can show your marketing manager.

(c) What form might have been used to show *all* this information?

Scatter diagrams

4.17 **Scatter diagrams** are used to illustrate **correlations** (see Paragraph 2.10). The x and y axes are the two variables to be investigated in **relation to each other**. Let us take the example of advertising spend and resulting sales.

	Advertising costs	*Sales*
	X	*Y*
	£	£
January	1,000	8,200
February	800	6,700
March	1,100	8,700
April	1,200	9,400
May	700	6,600
June	1,000	7,900
July	1,500	10,200
August	500	5,800
September	900	7,200
October	900	7,600
November	1,400	10,000
December	600	6,400

Plot each point on the graph: 1,000 on the x axis against 8,200 on the y axis and so on (Figure 13.7).

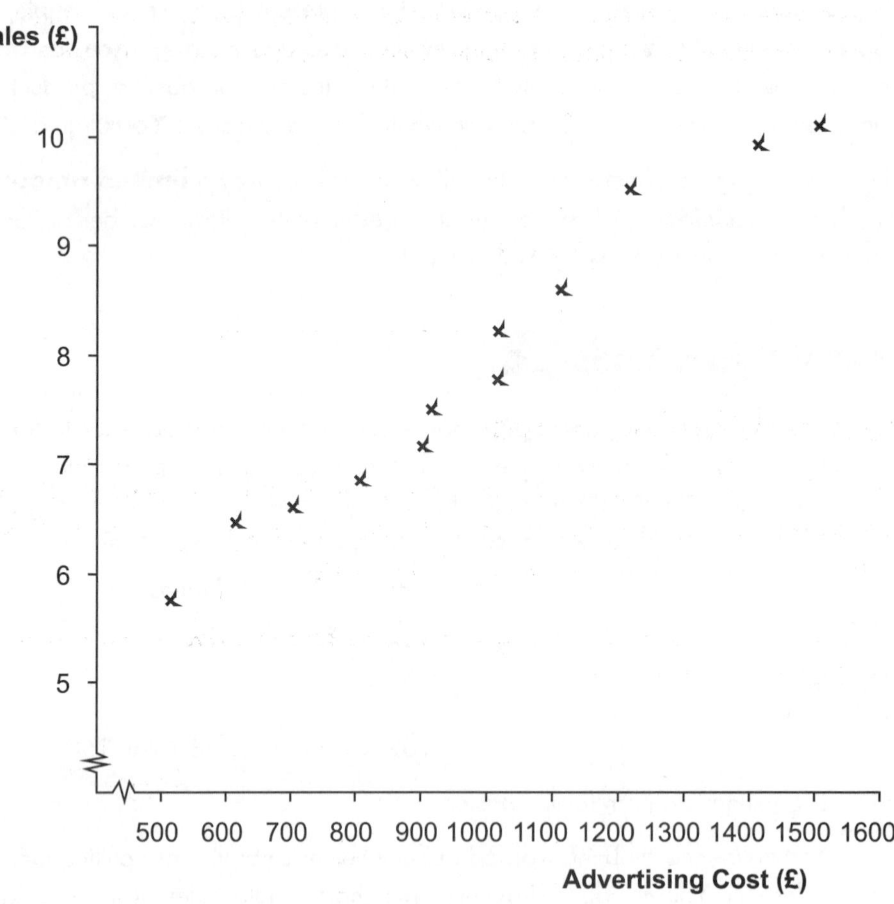

Figure 13.7 Scatter diagram of sales and advertising

4.18 It is clear from the diagram that there is a **strong** relationship between advertising and sales. The strength of the correlation depends on how **closely** the scatter of points approximates to a straight line. In this case the correlation is not perfect but if we were to fit a straight line through the points, none of them would be very far from it. (By 'fitting' a straight line, we mean drawing a line through the middle of the scatter of points, trying to follow the basic slope of the scatter and trying to keep a rough balance of points either side of the line.)

4.19 It is also clear that the correlation is **positive**: ie as advertising spend increases, sales increase. (If the correlation had been negative – sales were high when advertising spend was low, for some reason – the line would have run from top left to bottom right.)

4.20 Our graph of sales and advertising costs shows **partly** correlated variables. This means that there is no exact relationship, but high (or low) values of x tend to be associated with high (or low) values of y.

Perfect correlation would appear as follows: the points lie on a straight line.

(a) *Positive correlation* (b) *Negative correlation*

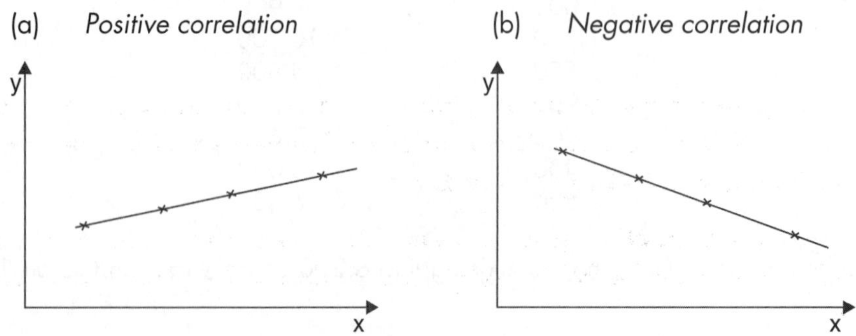

If there were **no** correlation, the scattergraph would appear as follows. There is no clear trend up or down: the two variables are fairly obviously independent of each other.

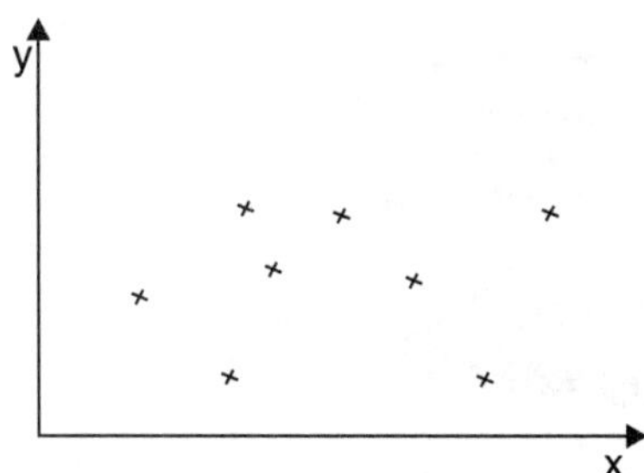

Product positioning maps

4.21 Although they may be called **'maps'** these are really a form of **scatter diagram**. **Two key attributes** of a product are taken and competing products are graded to fit between the extremes of possessing an attribute or not possessing it.

4.22 For example a package delivery service may be **fast** or **slow**, and it may deal with **large** or **small** packages (Figure 13.8).

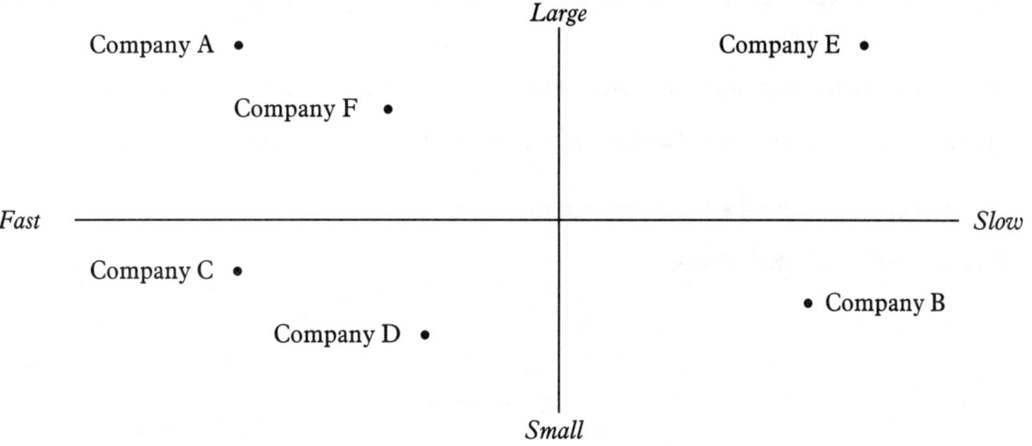

Figure 13.8 Product positioning map

Action Programme 6

Interpret the diagram above.

5 Graphic illustration of data

Drawings

5.1 A **drawing** of a company's product, say, with labels for interesting features, is often a very efficient and effective way of presenting a **lot of information** in a **small space**. It may be either a simple line drawing or something more elaborate.

Photographs have more **impact**, in general, but less clear, for conveying points of detail: a photograph has many elements (foreground, background, shadow, colour etc) competing for the reader's attention.

The essence of a **drawing** is that it can be used to select and highlight basic lines and features,

and **ignore** irrelevancies. Tints and solid colour can be used to fill in areas within the line drawing, to create emphasis, distinguish one type of feature from another and so on.

Diagrams

5.2 A diagram is very useful for presenting a **summary** of fairly complicated information in an **easily digestible form**, and to indicate links and interrelationships between the different components. There are lots of examples throughout this book. The essence of a diagram is to simplify as far as possible:

- The **components** of the object or process being portrayed, and the **relationships** between them
- The **visual representation** of those components and relationships

This is designed to promote **clarity**, without irrelevancy or complexity.

5.3 For example, consider the following (Figure 13.9).

Organisational stakeholders

Figure 13.9 Diagram *Source:* BPP Publishing

Flow charts

5.4 Diagrams are very flexible and versatile. One commonly-used form, however, is the **flowchart or tree chart**. Flow charts are ideal for showing **processes and relationships**. The constants are normally shown in labelled boxes and the processes or relationships indicated by connecting lines and arrows. Flow charts are very good for showing complicated and detailed information in a relatively simple manner. For example they may be used to summarise an organisation's structure and reporting lines, the logistics of how supplies move from source to destination or an electronic communications network.

5.5 An example is given below (Figure 13.10). If you are using this form of presentation remember the following points.

- Take care in **laying out** the diagrams: they can easily end up looking 'lop-sided' if they are not carefully designed.
- Try to keep the number of **connecting lines** to a **minimum**. Avoid lines that have to jump over each other if possible.
- Keep the **narrative** elements brief and **simple**.

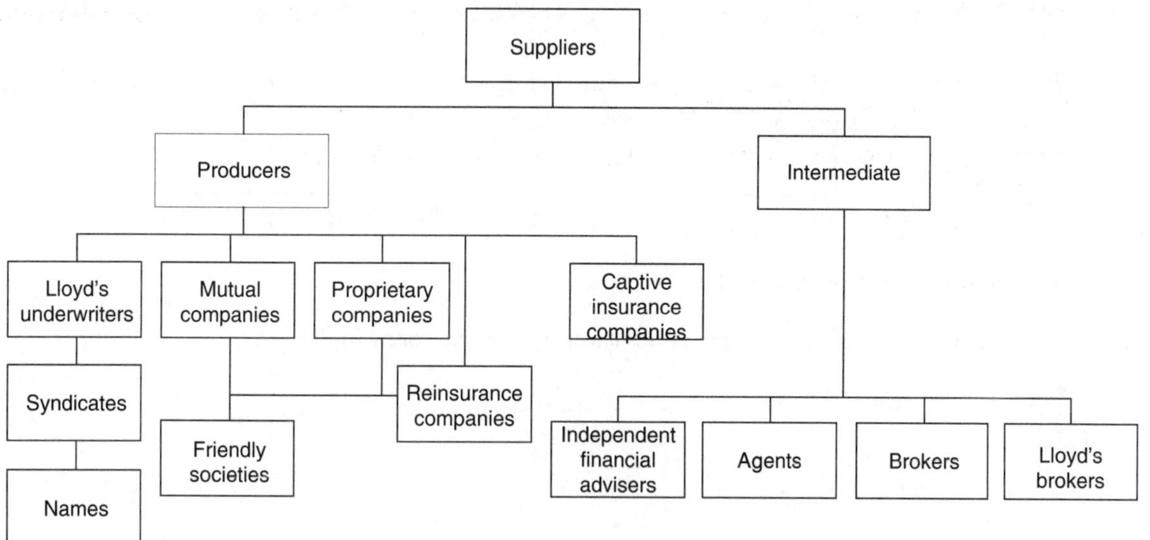

Figure 13.10 Flow chart showing the structure of the insurance market

Chapter Roundup

- Statistical information can be manipulated by classification and calculation to indicate useful characteristics such as frequency, averages, dispersion, correlation and trends.
- Statistical information can be presented in tabular form, or in more accessible visual forms such as graphs, charts and diagrams.
- Common visual forms include:

  Line graphs – which illustrate the relationship between two variables
  Bar charts – which illustrate the magnitudes of a value
  Pie charts – which illustrate percentage components
  Pictograms – which illustrate magnitudes of a value
  Scatter diagrams – which illustrate correlations
- In addition, drawings, photographs, maps and diagrams can be used to show simplified and/or schematic representations of reality.

Quick Quiz

1 If you list the number of users of e-mail under the age of 10, under the age of 20, under the age of 30 and under the age of 40, you are compiling a:

Correlation	Time series
Frequency distribution	Cumulative frequency distribution

2 What is a trend?

3 Which of the options listed below is *not* illustrated by the following?

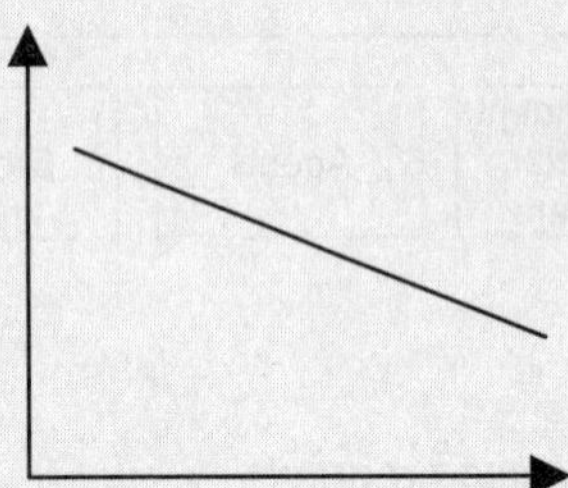

A Line graph
B Positive correlation
C Negative correlation
D Trend

4 The horizontal axis of a graph is known as the (1) .... axis, and is used to represenet the (2) .... variable (if known.)

5 The following is an example of multiple bar chart.

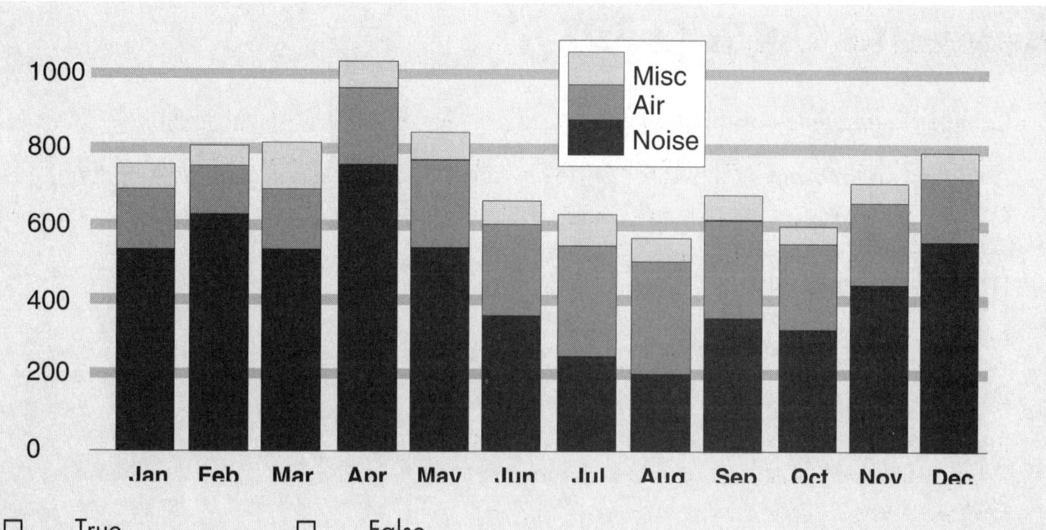

☐ True ☐ False

6 A visual method of showing the relative sizes of component elements of a total value or amount is:

A A pie graph

B A line graph

C A Gantt chart

D A pie chart

7

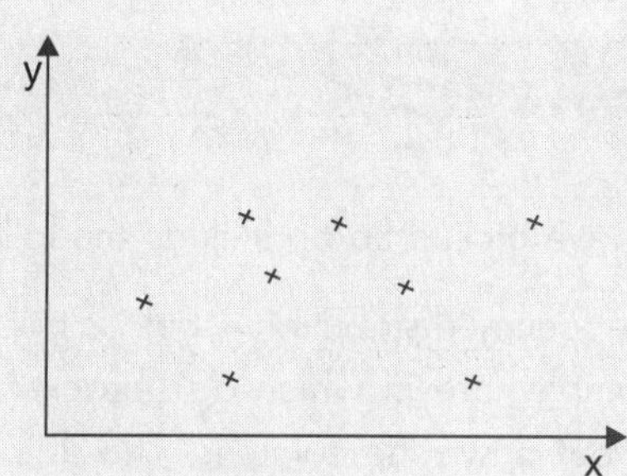

The above graph illustrates:

Strong correlation	Weak correlation
Negative correlation	No correlation

8 A graphic aid used to show processes and relationships is a .... chart.

9 If 💰 represents $15, draw a pictogram for $67.50.

10 The purpose of a summary is to preserve the words of the original text, while removing unnecessary data.

☐ True ☐ False

Answers to Quick Quiz

1 Cumulative frequency distribution

2 An underlying movement (upwards or downwards) in a time series over the long term.

3 B

4 (1) x, (2) independent.

5 False

6 D

7 No correlation

8 Flow

9

10 False

Now try Question 13 from the Question Bank at the end of this Text

Action Programme Review

1 Some of the points you may have picked up on include the following.

(a) This looks a bit like a frequency distribution – but isn't. It doesn't tell us what percentage of one-car owners, for example, are in which age bracket: the percentages don't add up to 100% across the rows, but down the columns. The data tells us what percentage of each age groups owns one, two and three cars. We may note that in any age group, people are most likely to own one car. However, people are more likely to own three cars in the 45-64 age bracket than at any other time, and are least likely to own more than one car in the bracket > (over) 65. You might also suggest that this can be explained by family life cycle factors: at the beginning of family/career launch, income is more likely to be available for one or two cars; at career peak, the family may be more likely to afford a third car; on retirement and post-dependent-family, there is much more likelihood that one car will suffice.

(b) You may note the exponential growth of on-line consumption in all sectors: approx 33%, 20% and 50% respectively in the single year 1996-1997, and a forecast 2,187%, 1,135% and 316% over the 5 years to 2001! If you were in the travel business, for example, you may simply have noted that your forecast growth for 2001 is $7.4bn – more than 12 times the figure of $0.6 bn posted in 1997.

However, you might also note that the 2001 figures are only projections made in 1998: you may want to confirm the findings using actual figures for 2001 and intervening years.

2 FORMAL REPORT ON THE WOMEN'S FRAGRANCE MARKET

For the attention of: Sian Singh
Georgie Brand Manager
Lanroche

Completed by: Wanda Wen
Marketing Assistant

The Brand Tracker Partnership

Date of submission: 10 June 1997

I TERMS OF REFERENCE

'The Brand Tracker Partnership is commissioned by Sian Singh, Lanroche, to research the women's fragrance market and to produce a report on its findings by 30 June 1997.'

II RESEARCH METHODS

The research was conducted during October to December 1996. Secondary data sources were MEAL and Sales/Monitor. These provided industry-wide data and were used to produce advertising expenditure and industry sales figures. In addition women's magazines were analysed for advertising and sales promotion information.

During December primary data was collected by survey from a sample of 300 women aged between 16-55. This is a representative cross-section of the fragrance buying market. From this sample four focus groups were held across the country in order to capture possible regional variations.

III FINDINGS

1. Market size and share

The fragrance market is fragmented (32 fragrances were named). However just 11 brands have 73% of total market share.

Georgie, at fourth place, is one of the leading brands. It has 8.8% market share behind:

Ana – 13%
Eternal – 11%
Possession – 10.5%

The fifth placed brand is Lady with 7.2%.

2. Customer profile

There is no correlation between customers and their socio-economic group. The class profile is flat. ABC1s do not stand out in terms of either buying or receiving premium priced products.

3. Price

Price was only considered important by purchasers of Carlie which, along with Lady and Max Maxa, was at the cheapest end of the market.

64% of fragrances sold were priced at more than £15 per 30ml.

4. Brands and brand recognition

All age groups are attracted to the four leading brands. There is a notable age-based differentiation amongst the others.

16 – 25 years – Charly Klein and Carlie

Thirty-somethings – Cachet
40 – 55 years – Channelle and Esta Lauda

Brand recognition is highest for those brands with the greatest advertising spend (per annum figures).

£1.57m – Possession
£1.2m – Eternal
£1.04m – Ana
£0.955m – Georgie

Note, however, that Esta Lauda with a spend of £0.877m only achieved a 3% spontaneous ad recall.

New entrants to the market may be achieving high recognition figures as a result of point-of-sale and promotional initiatives. Two other forms which these take are: counter samples and scent strips in magazines.

5. **Buyer behaviour**

The key factors for purchase are as follows (in descending order).

55% – 'tried it in the shop'
53% – 'usual one'
32% – 'something new'
25% – 'saw advertisement'

IV **CONCLUSION**

Georgie is well established in the market across the complete age range. It is not discriminated against in terms of price and its advertising strategies are effective.

However, Ana with only a slightly larger spend is the most widely recognised brand (22% against 12% for Georgie). This factor warrants further research.

3 TIFFORD LTD: SALES OF N50 IN THE UK IN 20X1

			Quarters of 20X1		
Region	*1*	*2*	*3*	*4*	*Total*
1	72	53	19	42	186
2	16	10	25	21	72
3	392	276	317	516	1,501
4	152	141	137	119	549
Total	632	480	498	698	2,308

4 (a) People were asked whether they agreed or disagreed with two statements, in other words to choose one option from two.

(i) Nearly 80% of people agreed with the statement that the Alpha party were better than the Beta party.

(ii) However, people were about equally divided on the question of whether Mr X would make a good Prime Minister. Almost 50% of people disagreed with this statement.

(b) The percentages given do not add up to 100%, so people must have been able to nominate more than one player. Once you realise this, the percentages speak for themselves.

5 (a) **REP SALES THIS MONTH**

Doe

Smith

Bloggs

(b) **Umbrella versus hat sales**

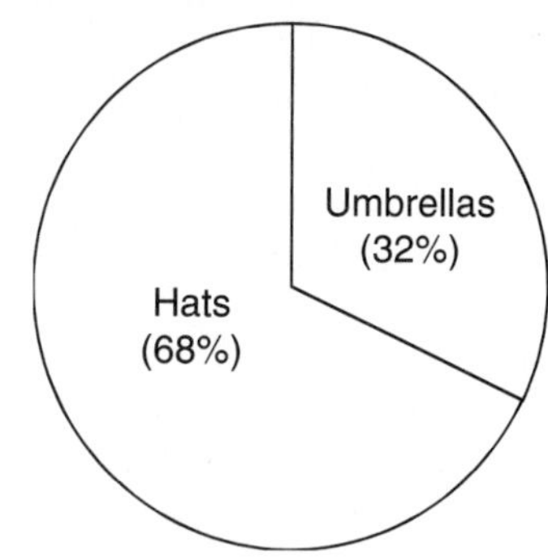

Hats $\frac{102}{150}$ = 68%

Umbrellas $\frac{48}{150}$ = 32%

(c) A component bar chart: one bar for hats, one for umbrellas, each broken into four sections to show individual sales totals.

6 Company A specialises in delivering quite large packages quickly
Company B delivers smaller packages fairly slowly
Company C delivers smaller packages quite quickly
Company D delivers fairly small packages slightly more quickly than average
Company E delivers very large packages very slowly
Company F delivers medium to large packages more quickly than average

Part E

Customer service and customer care

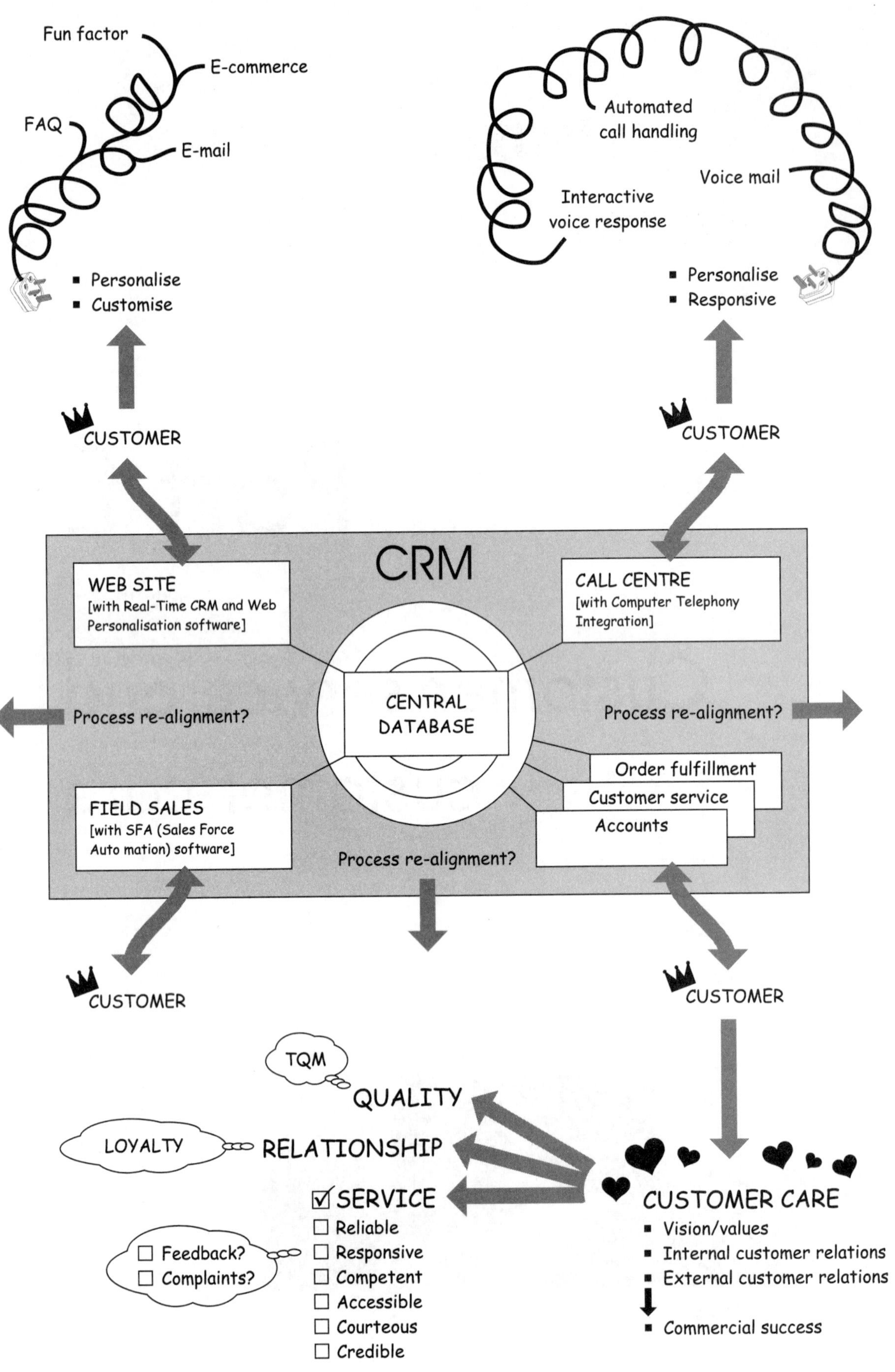

Fun factor
E-commerce
FAQ
E-mail
Personalise
Customise
CUSTOMER
Automated call handling
Voice mail
Interactive voice response
Personalise
Responsive
CUSTOMER
CRM
WEB SITE
[with Real-Time CRM and Web Personalisation software]
CALL CENTRE
[with Computer Telephony Integration]
CENTRAL DATABASE
Process re-alignment?
Process re-alignment?
Order fulfillment
Customer service
Accounts
FIELD SALES
[with SFA (Sales Force Auto mation) software]
Process re-alignment?
CUSTOMER
CUSTOMER
TQM
QUALITY
LOYALTY
RELATIONSHIP
SERVICE
Reliable
Responsive
Competent
Accessible
Courteous
Credible
Feedback?
Complaints?
CUSTOMER CARE
Vision/values
Internal customer relations
External customer relations
Commercial success

Customer care

14

Chapter Topic List	
1	Setting the scene
2	What is customer care?
3	The importance of customer care
4	Aiming for quality
5	Customer service
6	Seeking customer feedback
7	Handling customer complaints
8	Setting up a customer care programme

Learning Outcomes

- ☑ Understand the nature and importance of customer care and relationship marketing
- ☑ Outline methods of achieving product and service quality
- ☑ Explain how customer feedback can be gathered and used to improve service
- ☑ Make contingency plans for handling customer complaints
- ☑ Describe how a customer care programme can be introduced and reinforced

Syllabus References

- ☑ Explain the concept of customer care and its importance in consumer, business-to-business, not-for-profit and public sector organisations (5.1)
- ☑ Explain the importance of quality and customer care and methods of achieving quality (5.2)

☑ Explain the relationship between customer care, customer focus and relationship marketing (5.3)

☑ Explain the importance of obtaining customer feedback and devising contingencies for dealing with customer complaints (5.4)

☑ Describe how to plan and establish a customer care programme (5.5)

Key Concepts Introduced

- Customer care
- Quality
- Total Quality Management (TQM)
- Process alignment

1 Setting the scene

1.1 Part A of this Study Text established the foundations for this chapter by highlighting:

- The increasing **importance of the customer** for organisational survival and competitive advantage
- The nature and importance of **customer focus**: seeing marketing processes and practices from the customer's point of view, in order to meet their needs more appropriately
- The need to retain customers and win their **loyalty**: the key focus of **relationship marketing**.

1.2 We also outlined how customer retention and loyalty can be achieved: by creating customer **satisfaction** and **over-satisfaction** ('delight') and by maintaining on-going, consistent customer **contacts**. These elements are integral to the concept of **customer care**, which embraces both customer service and customer communications.

1.3 In this chapter, we begin by looking at the nature and importance of customer care (Sections 2 and 3), and then focus on approaches to achieving it, through quality management (Section 4) and customer service (Sections 5-7). Finally, we will suggest a systematic approach to implementing a Customer Care programme in an organisation (Section 8).

1.4 This are general principles of customer care and customer care. In Chapter 15, we will look specifically at how they can be facilitated by the use of technology, such as databases, Customer Relationship Management (CRM) software and other methods.

2 What is customer care?

Key Concept

Customer careis 'a fundamental approach to the standards of service quality' which 'covers every aspect of a company's operations from the design of a product or service to how it is packaged, delivered and serviced.' (Clutterbuck). Customer care aims to close the gap between customers' **expectations** and their **experience** in every aspect of the customer/supplier relationship.

2.1 The term '**customer care**' is often used interchangeably with '**customer service**'. The latter term, however, originally had a much narrower focus on order-cycle related activities: it is only comparatively recently, with the recognition of customer focus at the strategic level, that it has been extended to cover activities throughout the organisation at pre-, during– and post-transaction stages. In this chapter, we refer to customer care in this wider sense, and to customer service in the context of direct transaction-based contacts between organisational staff and customers.

2.2 An article in *Customer Service Management* (July 1996) offered a useful overview of the kind of corporate integration required for effective customer care (Figure 14.1).

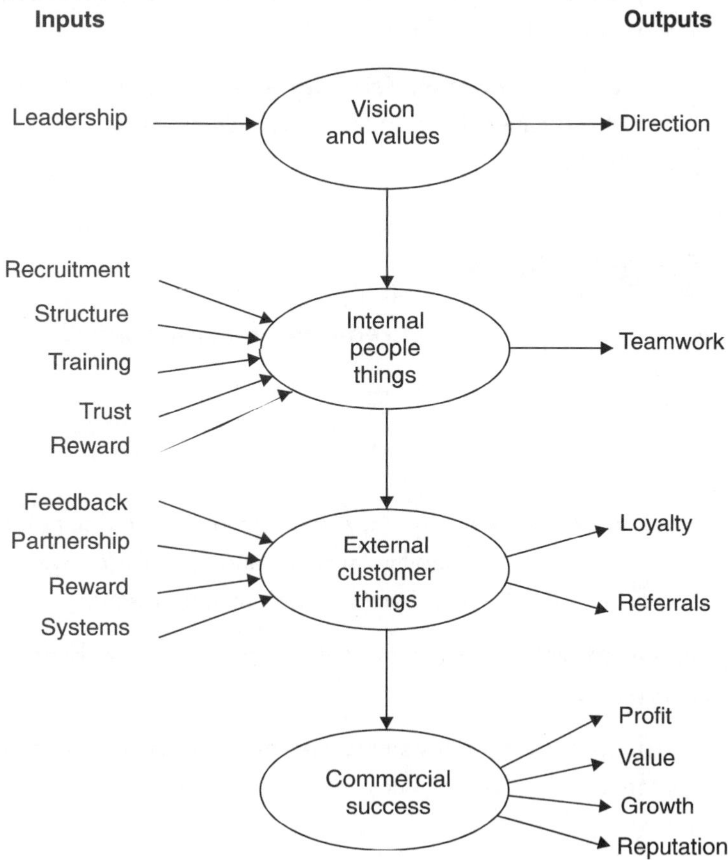

Figure 14.1 Key phases for service delivery

2.3 **Vision and values**. A 'fundamental approach' integrating all aspects of an organisation's activities requires a clear vision, leadership which models customer-focused values, and a culture which reinforces those values through its selection, appraisal and reward systems, and the messages it gives its employees at every level.

2.4 **Internal customer relations**. The satisfaction of **external** customers is the result of a range of satisfying **internal** relationships and transactions between colleagues and departments. Encouraging staff to consider the needs of their internal customers ('the next person to handle your work') will help to foster quality and service at the interface with external customers. Key factors in managing the quality of internal service operations include:

- The recruitment of skilled customer-facing people
- The supply of appropriate (and generous) training
- The empowerment of staff to take decisions which will attract and keep customers
- The reward and recognition of staff who deliver outstanding service

2.5 **External customer relations**. The delivery of customer care depends on:

- Gathering, analysing, communicating and acting upon customer **feedback**. Feedback enables an organisation to remain customer focused and to use the customer's experiences to trigger and drive necessary changes and improvements. (We will discuss this further in section 6 below.)

- Establishing a **partnership** approach to relationships with customers (and suppliers) in order to identify and meet needs more effectively at all links in the value-delivery chain

- Reinforcing customer loyalty with **incentives and rewards**, to show that the organisation values its 'valued customers'.

- Establishing efficient **customer-friendly systems**. It is no good expecting staff to give great service to customers if the systems, procedures, technology and information flows do not support their efforts.

Action Programme 1

What practical ways can you think of to **empower** front line staff to maintain customer care and service?

2.6 **Commercial success**. It must always be remembered that the point of the exercise (at least for commercial organisations) is profitability, survival and (usually) growth. Good customer care is not an end in itself. As we will see in Section 3 below, it represents:

- A **differentiating** competitive advantage: part of the package of benefits that helps to attract customers

- A powerful mechanism for sustaining **customer loyalty** – because retaining customers is more profitable than winning new ones.

Marketing at Work

The Lands End Clothing Company (US)

If you receive a catalogue from this mail-order clothing firm, study the eight principles for doing business which have been developed by the company's founder, Gary Comer. All eight principles can be distilled into the one simple, driving sentence which is internalised by all Lands End employees: 'Don't worry about what's good for the company, worry about what's good for the customer'. That's how 'customer focus' leads to 'customer care'.

Customer care and relationship marketing

2.7 In Chapter 2, we introduced **relationship marketing** as an approach to marketing which aims at keeping customers – rather than merely attracting them: going beyond the stimulation and management of **transactions** to build on-going **customer/supplier** relationships.

2.8 Relationship marketing involves:

- **Customer/supplier partnership**: entering into dialogue with customers to create mutually beneficial (win-win) exchanges
- **Personalisation of contact**: making customer feel that their business is valued and that their individual needs are being recognised and catered for
- **Continual deepening and improving of the relationship**: making sure that every contact with the brand satisfies – or delights – the customer.

2.9 Successful relationship marketing therefore requires the integration of **customer service**, **quality** and **marketing** (Christopher, Payne & Ballantyne, 1992) which is the concept of **customer care**.

2.10 Rosabeth Moss Kanter (1991) describes five challenges for companies that want to develop genuinely close links with their customers.

- Understanding who the customer is
- Making the customer a member of one's own organisation
- Making the customer visible to all employees
- Rewarding faithful customers
- Having the flexibility to handle critical incidents

Action Programme 2

You are the marketing manager of Notown City Football Club, a local professional football club based within the city. It plays in the second division of the Football League and has average home attendances of about 3,000 people per game. Your Chairman, A Richunne, has read Rosabeth Moss Kanter's 'five challenges' in an FT article, and has asked you to 'drop him a memo' making recommendations as to how the club could undertake each. Inventing whatever details you think appropriate, draft the memo.

3 The importance of customer care

3.1 The aim of customer care, as mentioned above, is the survival and success of the organisation. From the organisation's point of view, customer care is:

- Part of the overall package of **purchase benefits** that its product/service offers, and therefore an important part of the marketing mix in attracting customers
- A source of **differentiation** from competing products (particularly where globalisation has diluted the significance of product features and functionality), which may also attract customers
- A mechanism of **customer retention**, by creating 'pull' factors and minimising 'push' factors to make it more likely that customers wi0ll stay with the brand than go elsewhere. It costs between three and seven times more to recruit new customers than to retain existing ones. And 68% of customers who stop doing business with an organisation are said to do so because of poor service.
- A way of creating **customer loyalty**: engaging customers' emotional involvement with the brand, making them feel valued and making on-going contact from the organisation (as part of a relationship marketing strategy) more welcome.
- A way of maximising positive (and minimising negative) '**word of mouth' promotion** by customers on the basis of their experience. The average unhappy customer tells nine other people about the experience. (13% of them tell 20 or more people!) The average happy customer tells five other people – and many of those become customers of the business that was praised.
- A source of vital **feedback information** on customer's expectations and experience, to support more effective and efficient marketing in future. (We discuss this further below.)
- A source of **employee satisfaction** which enhances performance and enables the organisation to retain valuable human resources.
- A source of positive **employer branding** which enhances the organisation's ability to attract high-quality, customer-focused staff.

3.2 In *Raising the standard – A Survey of Manager's Attitudes to Customer Care* (1994) the Institute of Management highlighted the following key benefits of improving customer care.

Benefit	*% of managers citing benefit*
Retention of existing customers	68
Enhanced reputation of the organisation	58
Competitive advantage in the marketplace	53
Attraction of new customers	43
Increased profitability	28
Improved staff morale and loyalty	25
Cost efficiency	11

Action Programme 3

You have been asked to present the information given above to the Board of Directors, in order to justify the implementation of a new customer care programme by the marketing department.

Bearing in mind your aims, and the directors' needs in this situation (as customers of your internal marketing message), prepare a slide (for overhead projector, flipchart or PowerPoint software, as you wish) to show the cited survey results to best effect.

[Key Skill for Marketers: Presenting Information]

3.3 Note that customer care is a source of **internal customer** satisfaction, commitment and retention – as well as external.

(a) A focus on (valued) customers adds value, responsibility and significance to jobs throughout the organisation. Peters and Waterman (*In Search of Excellence)* found that quality and customer-focused values was a key source of employee morale and motivation. Involving employees in the development and implementation of customer care initiatives (for example, through suggestion schemes, or quality/customer care circles or task forces) enhances this effect.

(b) Training and empowerment add to employee's flexibility, competence and employability: enhancing the organisation's human resource.

(c) Supportive customer care initiatives (including managing customer expectations, improving systems and responding to customer feedback) enhances the ability of staff to service customer needs effectively. This minimises the frustration and stress that otherwise leads to high staff turnover in customer service departments.

3.4 These customer care imperatives apply not just to consumer markets (where the advantages of brand differentiation, competition and customer retention are most obvious), but also to:

(a) **Business to business sector**. Customer/supplier relationship and partnership is a feature of industrial buying, as we saw in Chapter 3. The inertia that characterises industrial markets may work in the supplier's favour, but in the face of increasing global competition there is no room for complacency: once lost, a customer will not easily be regained.

(b) **Not-for-profit sector**. Schools, universities, museums and charitable and volunteer organisations still have 'customers' (as we saw in Chapter 1), and operate under more or less competitive conditions. A charity, for example, may be competing for volunteer labour and funding not only with other charitable causes but with a host of other uses for people's time and money. Customer service is integral to the mission and objectives of non-profit organisations, and delivering effective customer care may be essential to their building and maintaining their image, staffing, public funding and ability to attract and retain paying customers (where relevant).

(c) **Public sector**. Despite traditionally operating under monopolistic or near-monopolistic conditions, the public sector is also subject to pressures for better customer care. Some activities will have to compete with the private sector (for example, in the case of local authority leisure and sports centres). They are often subject to external regulation and benchmarking, which impose standards of effectiveness and efficiency. In the UK, the public sector is going through a period of rapid change – from the old-established 'public servant' role to a more dynamic 'competitive' style in line with government policy.

Exam Tip

A question in the Specimen Paper for this syllabus required you to draft a report (in e-mail form) outlining (a) the importance of customer care and relationship marketing, and the role that customer-facing staff (in a Call Centre) play in this process and (b) the key stages involved in developing a Customer Care Programme (for the Call Centre).

4 Aiming for quality

4.1 Customer care is linked to quality – not just of customer service, but of the total offering marketed to and experienced by the customer. A customer care orientation is akin to the quality management orientation which has been called 'total quality management' or TQM.

Key Concept

Quality is 'the degree of excellence' of a thing: how well made or performed it is, how well it serves it purpose, how it measures against rivals or benchmarks and how valuable it is *perceived* to be (for any number of subjective reasons).

TQM is the process of applying quality values and aspirations 'to the management of all resources and relationships within the firm, as a means of developing and sustaining a culture of continuous improvement which focuses on meeting customers' expectations.

4.2 The management of quality is not a new idea. **Control systems** have long been aimed at:

- Establishing **standards** of quality for products/services
- Establishing **systems and procedures** to ensure that quality standards are met, within acceptable tolerance levels
- **Monitoring** output/service quality and **comparing** it against standards
- Taking **control action** to adjust systems and procedures if actual quality fall unacceptably short

Action Programme 4

What would represent 'quality' or 'excellence' in the case of:

- A job application form?
- A corporate Web site?
- A point of sale display?
- A face-to-face interview with an angry customer?

Brainstorm three or four key quality criteria for each example.

What else could customer communications do to promote quality in the organisation's activity?

4.3 TQM, however – like customer care – represents a **radical focus on customer satisfaction** throughout the organisation structure and processes. Three principles guide customer-supplier relationships under TQM:

- Recognition of the strategic importance of customers and suppliers
- Development of win-win relationships with customers and suppliers
- Establishing relationships based on trust

4.4 These principles are translated into practice through customer communications by:

- The constant **collection of information** on customer needs and expectations
- The **dissemination of this information** widely within the organisation, to encourage involvement, learning, problem-solving and ideas generation
- The **use of this information** to deliver and promote the organisation's products and services in such a way as to foster customer satisfaction.

4.5 Key features of a TQM approach (in a handy Mind Map) are as follows (Figure 14.2).

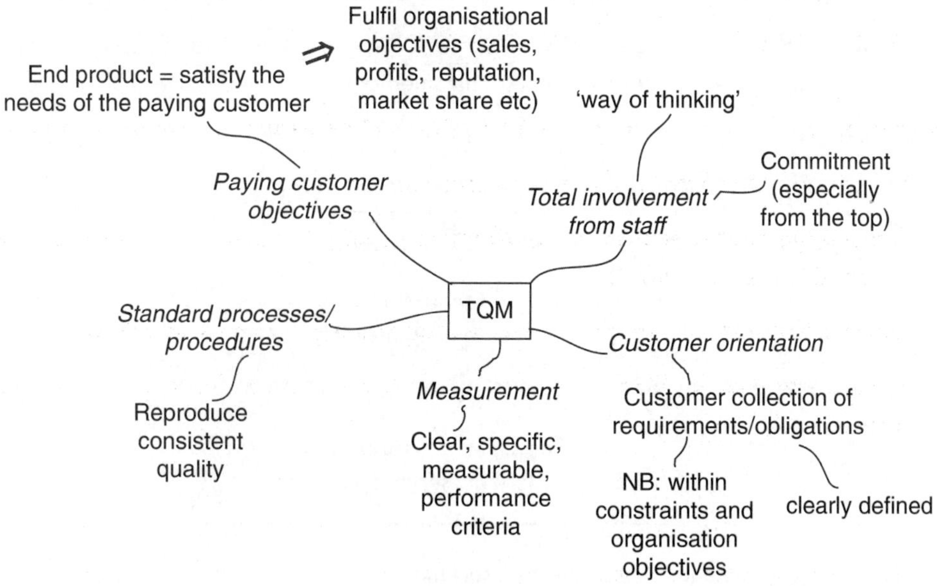

Figure 14.2 TQM Mind Map

Action Programme 5

One of the principles of TQM is that the cost of preventing mistakes is less than the cost of correcting them once they occur: the aim should be to **get it right first time**.

'Every mistake, every delay and misunderstanding, directly costs a company money through wasted time and effort, including the time taken pacifying customers. Whilst this cost is important, the impact of poor customer service in terms of lost potential for future sales has also to be taken into account.' (Bellis-Jones & Hand, *Management Accounting)*

Give an example of how a 'get-it-right-first-time' approach in the area of marketing communications might save costs?

Process alignment

Key Concept

Process alignment is 'deliberately designing and modifying business processes so that every activity is geared to meeting the customer's wants.' (Arthur Anderson)

4.6 A pithy expression of the principle behind process alignment is the suggestion by Jan Carlsen (as Chief Executive of SAS) that: 'If you're not directly serving customers, you need to be serving someone who is.'

4.7 Process engineering typically involves a radical change of organisation structure. Customer-focused organisations, compared to classical models, tend to have the following characteristics.

(a) **Flattened hierarchies**. Daffy *(Once a Customer, Always a Customer)* argues that an organisation structure that is totally customer-focused would have just two layers (Figure 14.3).

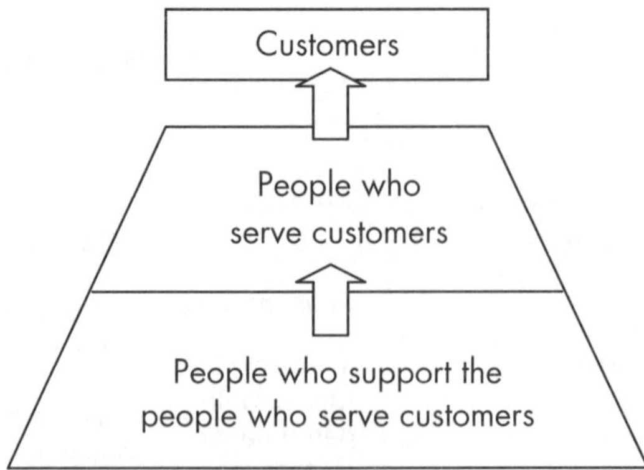

Figure 14.3 Flattened, customer-focused hierarchy

(b) **Horizontal structures.** Customer expectations and experience of an organisation are often horizontal (dealing with one part of the process after another): vertical organisation (such as functions and departments) may get in the way. Tom Peters *(Liberation Management)* quotes a Motorola executive as admitting: 'The traditional job descriptions

were barriers. We needed an organisation soft enough between the organisational disciplines so that... people would run freely across functional barriers with the common goal of getting the job done, rather than just making certain that their specific part of the job was completed.'

What Peters calls 'going horizontal' involves using multi-functional teams and communication mechanisms: equipping customer-facing staff to mobilise resources across departmental boundaries to get customer needs met.

(c) **Chunked structures**: breaking the organisation down into smaller and more flexible units which can respond more readily to customer needs. This has been the approach of many bureaucratic and public-sector organisations, at least in regard to customer-facing functions.

Marketing at Work

Leicester Royal Infirmary

In one area of women's health, the consultation process used to take on average 79 hours of the patient's time: 90 minutes of waiting in the hospital seeing 16 different people, with about 650 yards of walking around the hospital. As a result of customer-focused re-engineering, the process takes just 36 minutes: 8 minutes of waiting, 3 different people to see, and 90 yards of walking around the hospital.

Cigna Services (health insurance)

Cigna now operates almost totally on the basis of multi-functional teams. The customer is assigned to a team and that team, rather than separate functional departments within the organisation, deals with every aspect of that customer's business with Cigna.

Hamilton Acorn (paintbrush manufacturer)

Acorn's customer services department now draws together in a single unit a number of functions that had previously been done separately: warehousing and distribution, customer queries, data input, sales administration and export. The company has also reorganised the factory floor into cells or small teams, each with its own supervisor, and each responsible for a product from start to finish. This manufacturing re-organisation was vital if the improvements demanded by customers were actually going to happen. As the company's Operations Director says: 'You can't just put a sign up and say, "Hooray, now we've got a customer services department, now we're going to be great", because they can't do a damned thing unless they've got the back-up from the manufacturing side all the way through.'

5 Customer service

5.1 **Customer service** is the point of contact between the customer and the organisation at each point of the transaction process (Figure 14.4).

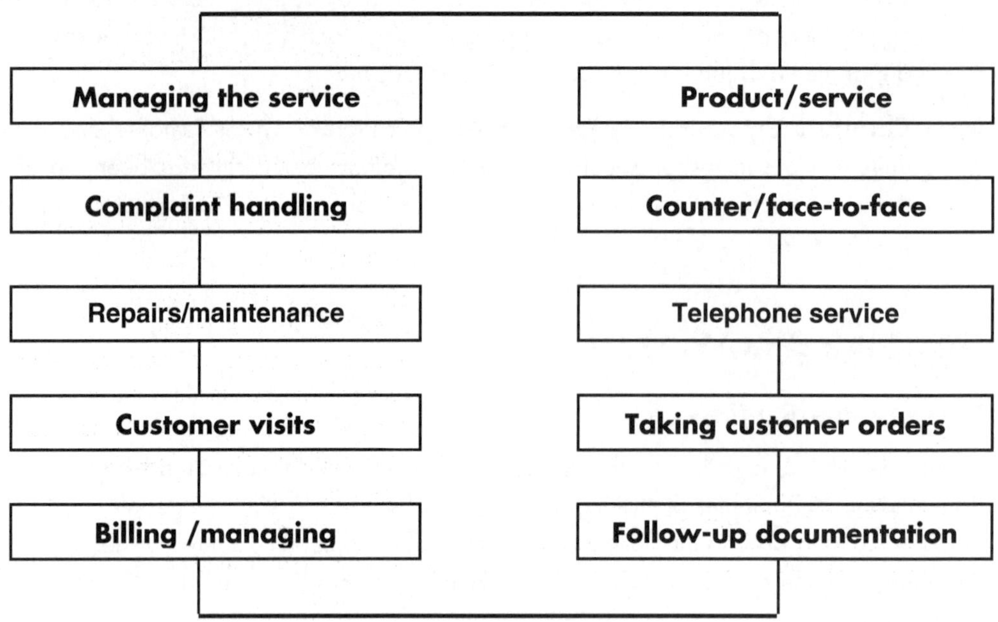

Figure 14.4 Key customer service activities

5.2 Rodney Overton (*Customer Service)* suggests that customer service involves the following key values.

- **Reliability**: being dependable and consistent
- **Responsiveness**: being willing and ready
- **Competence**: skill and knowledge
- **Accessibility**: being easy to approach
- **Courtesy**: being polite, considerate, respectful and friendly
- **Communication**: being understandable, listening
- **Credibility**: being honest, believable, trustworthy
- **Security**: minimising danger, risk or doubt
- **Understanding**: appreciating customers' needs
- **Tangibles**: concrete evidence of the service
- **Focus**: an attitude that puts the customer first
- **TQM**: meeting quality requirements – or planning to meet them

5.3 Then what does 'bad service' look like? A MORI survey in the UK *(Consumer Concerns)* asked people which three or four things dissatisfied them most about the service they receive in retail outlets. The following list includes only those factors mentioned by 3% or more of the sample (about 2,000 people.)

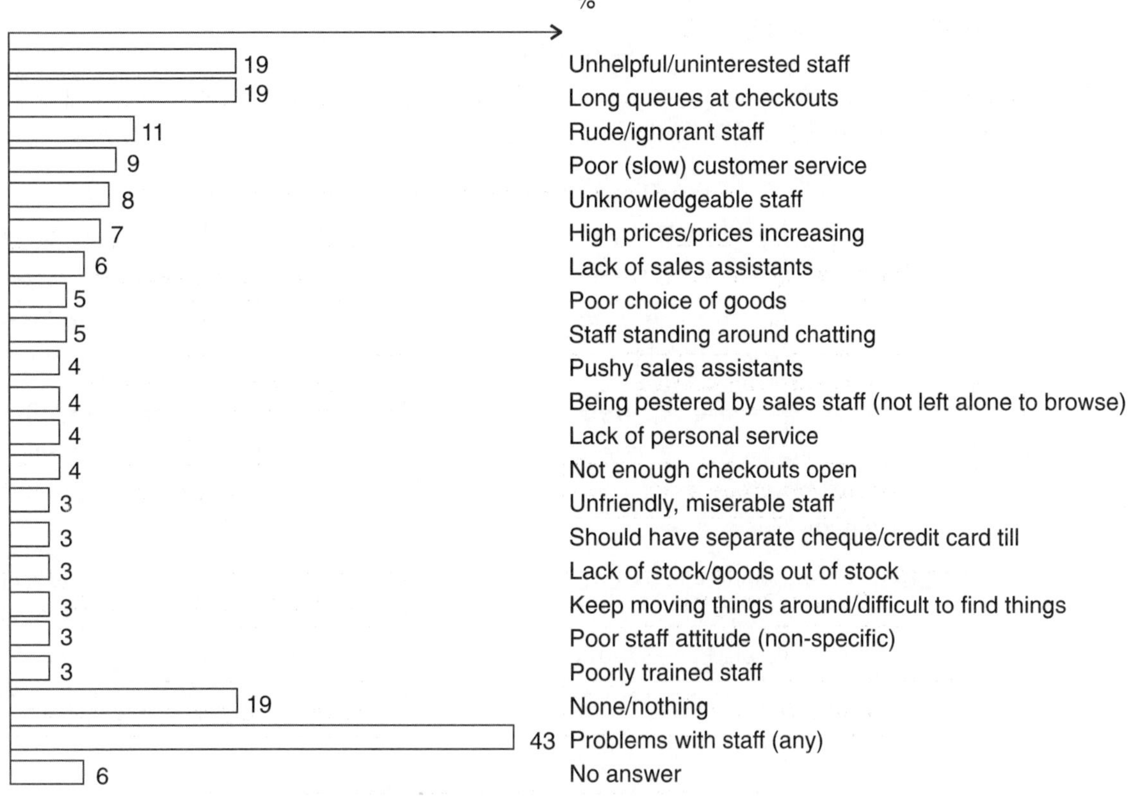

Source: Ros Jay, *The Essential Marketing Sourcebook*

Face-to-face customer service

5.4 Face to face encounters with customers can be easier and more effective than remote oral or written exchanges. As discussed in Chapter 11, face-to-face communication allows for the use of non-verbal signals, more flexible feedback and interactivity in responding to customers. However, it is also more demanding.

- Staff have their appearance and non-verbal signals to think about as well as their verbal messages.
- Lacking the impersonality of the telephone, they may be more exposed to personal factors (for example, if the customer is upset or angry) and the stresses they cause.
- Their exchange with the customer may be audible to others, if not entirely public.

5.5 Staff will be able to **respond effectively** to customers if they follow some simple guidelines.

Ready to serve?

(a) **Familiarise** yourself thoroughly with:

(i) The **range** of products or services offered by the organisation

(ii) The **procedures** that you and the customer each have to complete for these products/services to be supplied

(iii) The products/services **offered by others** in the field, should comparisons be made or advice sought

(b) Be aware of customers as **people**. Look out for signals that suggest stress, distress, perplexity, impatience. Be patient with non-specialists who do not understand what has happened, what our ad or information means, what you are doing, why they need a cheque guarantee card etc.

(c) **Learn**, from experience, ways of dealing with queries and situations that crop up over and over again. You can stay sensitive and responsive to individual cases without having to invent whole new ways of dealing with each one.

Action Programme 6

Draft a similar noticeboard (or staff Web page) notice, with simple guidelines for staff in a bank (or any organisation with which you are familiar) for **dealing with awkward customers**.

Use your own experience and common sense to suggest the content of your guidelines – or check the customer service manual (or similar) of your organisation.

Marketing at Work

Lynne Truss wrote amusingly about customer relations in the *Times*.

'Last week, in a branch of a well-known stationery shop, I had an interesting experience. It went something like this:

Me: Excuse me, I can't see any Amstrad ribbons. Could you ... *(First Assistant points a finger at a low shelf, looks at me as though I am mad, and does not speak.)*

Me: Oh yes, silly me. Thank you very much. *(First Assistant does not react in any way, but then turns to friend and starts discussing lunchbreaks.)*

Me (at till): I'd like to pay for these please. *(Second Assistant silently picks up ribbons and rings up prices on the cash register. He does not announce the total, because of course I can see it quite as well as he can.)*

Me (showing credit card): Can I pay with this? *(Second Assistant wordlessly takes credit card and processes it, so that a bill is printed on the counter).*

Me: Have you got a pen? *(Second Assistant points to biro next to the till: I sign. He fixes his gaze on the middle distance.)*

Me: (gathering up bag from the counter): Well, I'll just take this then. (*Nothing*).

Me: Great. Lovely. Thanks. Byeee'

[Remember: relationship marketing involves dialogue – not monologue!]

5.6 The example given above highlights the importance of the following interpersonal factors.

First contact	■ Immediate focus of attention (even if in the middle of something: an acknowledgement of the customer's presence and a promise to attend to him or her as soon as possible) ■ Greeting ('Good morning') ■ Engagement in the conversation ('Can I help you?')
Attention	■ Concentration (single focus) ■ Eye contact (in cultures where this is a sign of attention and not, as in China – for example – an intrusion)
Information	■ Not leaving the customer mid-contact for any reason, without informing him or her of what you need to do and how long it will take ■ Giving the customer the information (s)he requires, **or** making arrangements to do so, **or** offering other options
Language	■ Avoiding technical jargon ■ Listening for what the problem/request/query really is
Understanding	■ Show willing ■ Offer options, solutions, win-win approaches ■ Look for feedback that suggests satisfaction has not yet been achieved
Responsiveness	■ Treat each customer as a special case: each contact matters ■ Respond to the customer – not the pressure of work problems or distraction (s)he represents ■ Dialogue – not monologue
Finding	■ Confirm, sum-up, repeat back conclusions ■ Close with positive relationship-building ('Thank you')

Action Programme 7

Reflect on your own experience of face-to-face customer service in a retail outlet or other context (college, doctor, transport services and so on). What elements of customer service positively and negatively impressed you – and how did they make you feel about the organisation concerned? What could have been done differently?

Telephone customer service contact

5.7 The use of the telephone in customer communications was discussed in detail in Chapter 11 on effective oral communications. Be aware, however, of the following points.

(a) The telephone may be a customer's first or main point of contact with the organisation. The efficiency of the call answering and routing system, and the words and tone of voice of each person who responds, take on a front-line **ambassadorial role.**

(b) The telephone lacks the visual cues and feedback provided by face-to-face contact. customer service staff will have to be alert to the implications of **oral cues** such as tones of voice, and confirm understanding by seeking and giving **feedback**.

(c) The telephone is not a 'neutral' piece of equipment. Customers may have strong **attitudes** towards being kept on hold, receiving unsolicited calls at home, hearing obviously scripted responses, calling a Care Line and finding an answer machine – and so on.

(d) The telephone costs money: calls should be handled as **efficiently** as possible.

5.8 Using the telephone effectively for customer care involves:

- **Interpersonal skills** in oral communication (discussed in Chapter 11) and
- **Systems development** in order to take advantage of available technologies (discussed in Chapter 15)

5.9 A **care line** is a phone number dedicated to customer care, usually printed on product packaging. Customers are encouraged to call if they have problems, or for further advice or information. Calls may be free or charged at local call rates. Care lines are intended to make customers *feel* looked after – even if they never use them! The purpose of this is theoretically to enhance customer loyalty, but research suggests that care lines actually have comparatively little impact on the purchase decision in the UK. (They are much more popular in the USA.)

Marketing at Work

Cullens (franchise food retailer)

Cullens launched a careline in 1997, enabling customers to call a Freephone hotline displayed throughout the store and on the back of till receipts to give their opinion on the service received. Every call is followed up to find out what action was taken and the caller receives a written report. The caller information is analysed to provide information on branch and staff performance and to highlight where service levels need to be improved at each of the franchises.

6 Seeking customer feedback

The role of feedback in customer care

6.1 **Feedback**, in this context, is part of a control system which reports back the results of a process or action, in order to compare them against the planned or intended outcome.

6.2 The gathering of feedback by customer-facing staff is important primarily so that:

- The organisation will have **customer-generated data** about customer needs and wants, in order to fine-tune the marketing mix, marketing communications (promotion) and customer care.
- Customers will **feel that they have been listened to** – and heard; that their satisfaction or dissatisfaction, and the reasons for it, are taken seriously by the organisation.
- Staff called upon to deal with customers have the ability to **influence** organisational policy (and even strategy) in areas that affect their work
- **Information** keeps flowing into the organisation and through the organisation (particularly in an upward direction), creating opportunities for learning, innovation and adaptation.

6.3 Organisations which do not gather and utilise feedback become rigid, unable to adapt their behaviour to changing environments and customer demands. Michael Crozier (*The Bureaucratic Phenomenon)* suggests that in large, hierarchical, bureaucratic organisations, the control mechanism – whereby feedback on errors is used to initiate corrective action – is hampered: bureaucracies cannot learn from their mistakes! Rigidity is also (according to Ted Johns) a result of bureaucracies' tendency to be inward-looking rather than outward-looking or customer-focused.

6.4 Complacent organisations may measure customer service performance in a vague or misguided fashion. The following are classic examples.

(a) The use of vague, generalised statements like 'quite good', 'getting better', 'world class'

(b) The counting of customer complaints in the belief that the incidence of complaints is a direct measure of customer satisfaction (without realising that, in most cases, only between 10 and 20 per cent of customers actually complain: the rest simply take their business elsewhere).

(c) Reliance on infrequent survey data about customer perceptions – and the selective application of the data thus acquired

(d) So-called 'improvements' which only address front-line 'customer care' features like answering the telephone within three rings – when what really matters is how customers are handled once the telephone has been picked up.

6.5 Organisations must gather systematic, specific and meaningful feedback in order to adapt, learn and grow.

- **Positive feedback** – satisfied responses – is useful to confirm organisational plans and strategies. It is also helpful in encouraging staff and reinforcing positive customer service behaviours through customer recognition and appreciation.

- **Negative feedback** – dissatisfied responses – is, however, even more useful in defining what it is that the organisation needs to do in order to gain and retain customers.

Marketing at Work

Apple Computers

For an example of the gathering of customer feedback, try the Customer Quality Feedback (CQF) Home Page of Apple Computers (www.cqf.apple.com). CQF if an Apple programme that provides end-users with an opportunity to influence the development of Apple products worldwide.

Encouraging customer complaints!

6.6 In other words, **customers should be encouraged to complain!** The following guidelines are given by Ted Johns in *Perfect Customer Care.*

Make it easy for people to complain: eg by establishing free-call or local-call rate telephone numbers or complaint/feedback/review forms.
Ask for feedback by selecting and approaching customers at random.
Use random customer visits to sample the service first hand.
Train staff to listen to complaints positively, as a learning opportunity, without becoming defensive.
Act quickly and with goodwill to solve any problem identified, so complaints will be perceived to be worthwhile and positive. (This may mean replacing products or repeating services.)
Communicate the intention to prevent recurrence of the problem.
Reward customer feedback with appropriate incentives: discount vouchers, entry into Prize Draws and so on. Where feedback leads to change, customers should be thanked for their important contribution.

6.7 In addition, customer-facing staff have extensive opportunities to gather **informal direct and indirect feedback** by observing and talking to customers. They need to listen intentionally for explicit or implied complaints or suggestions for improvement. Returned products, for example, should be interpreted as non-verbal forms of complaint, as should returned mailings – or indeed, customer failure to recall company advertisements when asked.

Action Programme 8

What might be the *internal* customer equivalent of customer-facing staff gathering customer feedback?

6.8 There should be clear reporting lines for staff to convey customer feedback to appropriate decision-makers as swiftly (if necessary to resolve a current complaint) and as regularly as possible. Customer-facing staff are **gatekeepers** of information: they direct in-coming feedback to decision-makers – or do not. They need to know how to pass on feedback and to whom.

6.9 The concept of feedback as a **positive learning tool** should be marketed internally throughout the organisation.

Staff should be trained and resourced to gather feedback (with appropriate forms, questionnaires and interpersonal skills)
Staff should be recognised and rewarded for gathering feedback, especially if it is translated into constructive improvement suggestions.
Suggestions for improvement should be rewarded, whether or not they result in action.
The word 'failure' should be replaced by 'learning opportunity' in the corporate culture. If 'mistakes' are treated harshly, people will avoid gathering or sharing feedback.
Senior management should model positive, feedback-seeking behaviour by welcoming 'upward' feedback from staff.
It should be emphasised that encouraging feedback: ■ Establishes dialogue and relationship with the customer ■ Encourages customers to think about quality and service issues – attracting them to an organisation that demonstrably does the same.
Positive feedback – 'good news' and 'good reviews' – should be generously shared and celebrated.

Action Programme 9

Begin to gather a portfolio of communications from organisations of which you are a customer, which ask you to provide feedback on their product/services. (You might start with the Review Form at the back of this Study Text.) Include communications (such as announcements of product/service changes) that state or imply that customers' feedback has been taken into account by the organisation.

You may like to give your feedback, where requested, and see whether you feel that you have had a genuine 'say' or influence...

7 Handling customer complaints

7.1 The aim of a customer care programme is to minimise the need for customer complaints. Nevertheless, within such a programme, it will be important to develop **contingency plans** for dealing with any complaints that do arise, so that customer service staff can respond:

- Swiftly
- Consistently
- Efficiently
- Effectively and
- Without undue stress

in such a way that:

- The potential for lasting customer **dissatisfaction is minimised**
- Customer **satisfaction is restored** and loyalty (if possible) reinforced
- The **credibility** and **profitability** of the organisation is upheld.

Marketing at Work

A 1997 MORI survey on complaints handling for the UK Citizen's Charter Unit found that customer's **objectives in complaining** were:

(a) Improved service
(b) To get the money/service they were eligible for
(c) To get an explanation
(d) To prevent the same thing happening to others
(e) To get an apology
(f) To 'tell them what I thought of them'
(g) To get compensation
(h) To vent anger/frustration

For reflection: How many of these objectives would be valuable for the customer to receive – yet not too costly for the organisation to give?

7.2 Handling complaints can be an awkward interpersonal interaction. Some customers may follow the rules of assertive communication when they complain: have their facts straight, stay calm, do not take their frustration out on the person answering the complaint and state their needs clearly. Most will not. However, customer service staff are there to **solve problems** (not to add to them), by making it clear that there is no substance to the complaint – or by putting things right if there is. They must *not* take a complaint personally – even if the customer seems to.

7.3 The following guidelines may help.

Handing customer complaints

(a) **Ask for the facts**. Listen carefully and check that you have both got the facts **straight**. There may be some elementary misunderstanding that can be easily cleared up. If you look as if you are trying to get to grips with the substance of the complaint, you will **reassure** the customer that you **intend** to solve the problem and are taking it **seriously**. If you do not even appear willing to listen, you may invite further indignation and the situation may get out of control.

(b) **Empathise**. You may not wish to open yourself or the organisation to liability for an error by making placatory statements which sound like an admission of guilt. However, the customer may be quite overwrought (especially if he is not used to making complaints) and needs to hear that you **appreciate** how he feels, and that you recognise that he is justified in broaching the matter. Apologise for any inconvenience caused. If the customer is simply mistaken or confused about the complaint, explain firmly but politely, and give him time to adjust.

(c) **Be positive**. If a mistake **has** been made, apologise and tell the customer what you intend to do about it. You may be able to put it right immediately: if not, explain what steps will be taken and by whom.

 (i) **Don't grovel**. Apologise for **specific failings**, but do not fall into the trap of getting upset and offering blanket apologies to a customer who is simply angry or looking for something to moan about.

 (ii) **Don't blame**. If there has been a problem, concentrate on **rectifying it**. Don't 'wash the organisation's dirty linen in public' by telling the customer all about its mistakes and short-comings, how inefficient it is etc. Attributing blame to others looks as though you are trying to wriggle out of dealing with the complaint.

(d) Make sure your remedy has actually been **carried out**!

Marketing at Work

Try a website search using the word 'complain' for a selection of resource and feedback sites.

Or check out: www.ecomplaints.com

www.oft.gov.uk/html/consumer/howto.htm

(The Office of Fair Trading: How to Complain Site)

7.4 Customers are generally prepared to wait for a solution to their complaint or problem, provided that:

(a) They are kept informed of proceedings

(b) They are reassured that something is being done

(c) They are not required to contact the supplier repeatedly in order to get action. (With each additional contact, the likelihood of that customer recommending the company to others **halves**.)

7.5 The most important factors in efficient complaint handling, according to the general public (in the MORI survey cited above) were:

- The speed of response
- Being kept informed
- Feeling that the problem was fairly investigated
- Clearly communicated complaints procedures
- Friendliness and helpfulness of handling staff
- Having a named person to deal with
- Receiving written apologies and/or explanations

Marketing at Work

The following press advertisement was released by Target Australia, a popular clothing retailer. Notice the elements of 'positive spin' put on the crisis: the reinforcement of the company's exclusive stock and 'stringent safety standards', vigilance and quick action, and accessibility (via toll free response line). Note also the careful positioning of the apology: following the positive image-reinforcement, yet prominent enough to demonstrate empathy with customers affected by the problem.

Target

Safety recall

Target Australia Pty Ltd wishes to advise that the garments shown below, sold exclusively through Target stores, do not meet our stringent safety standards, and if you have purchased either or both garments, please be advised:

The babies' pink and grey Flowerpot Jacket should be returned to your nearest Target store. The jacket , size 0000-1, was on sale in Target stores between March 1999 and 13 April 1999.

Target has identified that the covered buttons present a potential safety hazard if bitten or sucked.

Please return the jacket to your nearest Target store for a full refund.

New stocks of the jacket are being delivered to Target stores with modified buttons that meet our safety standards. Target staff will be happy to place a raincheck for you on the new stock when you return the jacket.

In the interests of public safety, Target Australia urges customers to return these jackets immediately.

The boys' three-piece set size 1-4, on sale between 21 December 1998 and 16 April 1999 consists of a blue top, tartan cap and tartan pants.

Target has identified that the top has toggles at the end of the drawstring that pose a potential safety hazard if bitten.

Please either:

- Remove the toggles yourself, or
- Return the top to your nearest Target store where our staff will be happy to remove the toggles for you, or
- Return the whole set to your nearest Target store for a full refund.

In the interest of public safety Target urges that you take one of the above actions immediately.

We apologise for any inconvenience caused.

Please direct any queries to the 'Target Customer Relations Department', on our toll free number.

7.6 The key to effective complaint handling is, in the words of *'Small Business Marketing for Dummies'*:

- First fix the customer, then fix the problem.
- Acknowledge the customer's feelings about the problem
- Fix the immediate problem of the customer
- Once the customer has been satisfied, take whatever steps are necessary to prevent the problem from recurring

Action Programme 10

A useful habit to get into when planning customer communications is to consider first the **purpose** of your communication (what you want to achieve) and your **audience** (what the recipient will need or want from your communication and what may cause positive or negative responses to it).

Complete the following grid for a complaint (by letter, phone, email or face to face discussion).

	Complaint	**Adjustment (answer to complaint)**
Purpose	• • • •	• • • •
Audience factors	• • • •	• • • •

---

8 Setting up a customer care programme

8.1 Customer care is an organisation-wide orientation, which requires vision, leadership and cultural reinforcement – not just 'rules for customer service'. Nevertheless, a Customer Care Programme may provide a framework for planning, monitoring and evaluating customer service quality.

8.2 The following is a simple, systematic approach to setting up a customer care programme.

Step 1. **Identify key dimensions of service quality**, both inside and outside the organisation. This process may involve market research to identify existing levels of satisfaction of both customers and service personnel. The research could also be used to identify **expectations** of service quality and identify **gaps between expectation and experience**.

Step 2. **Set standards for service delivery**. These should be specific, measurable and realistic. Common standards specify, for example, a maximum queuing time (or length of queue) or a maximum time before a telephone is answered.

Step 3. **Set up systems for service delivery**. It is pointless setting targets if there is no operating system in place which will support and enable staff in meeting those targets. Attention should be given to organisation structures, information flows, use of technology and so on.

Step 4. **Analyse employee training needs**. Training should be relevant to the needs of staff: the gap between current performance and service standards should be analysed and tested if required.

Step 5. **Develop training programmes** to include (as required):

- Business and product knowledge
- Customer awareness
- Interpersonal skills

Step 6. **Set up systems to measure and monitor success** in terms of achievement of the set targets. Again, systematic research and (internal and external) customer feedback may be required to examine post-implementation (and on-going) levels of:

- Employee performance (and satisfaction with the programme)
- Customer expectations and perceptions of actual current service quality

Step 7. **Set up performance-related pay and recognition systems** for employees. Organisational commitment to service quality should be reinforced via key culture-change mechanisms such as motivation and reward. (Other such mechanisms include making customer care skills the criteria for employee selection, performance appraisal, career development and so on.)

8.3 If the programme is to work, the following conditions will have to be met.

Staff	■ Clear about the programme, its role and their role in it ■ Committed to the programme ■ Well trained in programme needs ■ Sufficiently resourced to carry out their roles ■ Sufficiently skilled to carry out their roles
Management	■ Committed to the programme ■ Committed to empowering staff in customer care roles ■ Provided with regular, relevant feedback to monitor performance

The programme	■ Provide clear benefits/incentives for staff ■ Be perceived as relevant, meaningful and achievable ■ Be reinforced by top management and organisation culture ■ Be clearly communicated to all staff ■ Support marketing objectives

8.4 Potential barriers to effective implementation of customer care include the following.

- **Vertical structures** (specialised functions, departments), which place barriers to cross-functional communication and decision-making. [*Solution:* Introduce horizontal structures in customer facing units, such as multi-functional teams?]
- **Formal role cultures** (bureaucracy), which emphasise positional authority and seniority, placing barriers to the empowerment of customer-facing staff. [*Solution:* Reduce management levels; implement multi-level teams and meetings; promote informal management-staff relations and shared single-status facilities?]
- **Inadequate organisational communication**, which places barriers to the flow of information to customer-facing staff and the flow of feedback back through the organisation. [*Solution:* Implement briefings, meetings and staff newsletters; encourage upward communication through suggestion schemes and feedback sessions; use Customer Care Circles to involve employees from different levels and functions in discussing customer care issues?]
- **Inflexible attitudes** and/or **lack of interpersonal skills**, which may cause resistance to personal and interpersonal change – particularly if the introduction of customer care standards is felt to be critical, blaming and/or unsupported. [*Solution:* Provide full communication, training and resource support; model the change from top management; use cultural reinforcements; ultimately remove those unwilling to change?]

Marketing at Work

TNT Express (delivery and distribution)

Best practice companies have leaders wholly committed to promoting a culture of customer care, an environment in which people are freed and encouraged to service the needs of individual customers. Everyone, from Chief Executive to tea lady, goes through TNT Express's 'Commitment to Customer Care' programme. All employees therefore understand the one core principles of the organisation. Who, then, has ultimate responsibility for providing customer service at TNT Express? 'Everyone,' says Tom Bell, one of the company's directors.

Unisys (computing)

Unisys has carried out research among 100 organisations worldwide that are recognised for the superb quality of their customer service. Unisys defines service excellence as 'everything an organisation does to win, satisfy and retain customers, profitably and more thoroughly than the competitor'. The Unisys research confirms that only organisations which adopt a suitably holistic approach become market leaders in this critical activity.

Chapter Roundup

- Customer care aims to close the gap between customers' expectations and their experience in every aspect of the customer/supplier relationship. It is an important source of product/service differentiation, competitive advantage and customer retention and loyalty.
- Total Quality Management (TQM) is – like customer care – a more radical approach to creating customer satisfaction throughout the organisation. Customer-focused companies are deliberately re-organising in order to empower customer-facing staff to solve customer problems and meet customer demands.
- Key customer service values include: reliability, responsiveness, competence, accessibility, courtesy, communication, credibility, security, understanding, tangibles, focus and TQM. Interpersonal skills, techniques and attitudes, as well as systems, are critical to effect customer service contacts, whether in person or by phone.
- Customer service staff are gatherers of customer feedback, both formally and informally. They can be supported by training; feedback reporting systems; and culture and resources for encouraging feedback (and implementing solutions).
- Complaint handling requires the sensitive use of interpersonal skills to acknowledge and manage the customer's feelings about the problem – and dealing with the problem swiftly, fairly and helpfully.
- Setting up a customer care programme involves standard-setting, systems development, training and control.

Quick Quiz

1 Fill in the gaps in the following definition using the words provided below.

'Customer (1)....... is a fundamental approach to the standards of (2) .... quality which covers every aspect of a company's (3)......... from the design of a (4)......... or service to how it is packaged, (5)......... and (6).......... Customer (1)......... aims to close the gap between the customer's (7)......... and their (8)......... in every aspect of the customer/supplier (9).........

- serviced
- service
- care
- expectations
- delivered
- operations
- relationship
- product
- experience

2 Allocate the following inputs to the appropriate phases of service delivery in the table below.

(1) Partnership (2) Recruitment (3) Leadership
(4) Systems (5) Loyalty incentives (6) Training
(7) Feedback (8) Performance rewards (9) Trust

Vision and values	*Internal customer relations*	*External customer relations*

3 What is most often cited by managers as the key benefit of improving customer care?

4 Which of the following is *not* a key feature of the TQM approach?

A Paying customer objectives
B Customer orientation
C Standard processes/procedures
D Specialisation of quality functions

5 'Horizontal' organisation involves breaking down barriers between departments.

☐ True ☐ False

6 Which three of the tend key customer service activities are missing from the list below?

Managing the service culture
Product/service information
Telephone service
Taking customer orders
Billing/managing payments
Customer visits
Complaint Handling

7 The incidence of customer complaints is a direct measure of customer satisfaction.

☐ True ☐ False

8 *Negative* customer feedback should be:

Avoided	Minimised	Ignored	Sought

9 Which of the following is *not* an effective approach to handling customer complaints.

A Tell the customer that you appreciate how (s)he feels.
B Apologise for specific failings.
C Explain the problems in the organisation's systems.
D Correct any errors of fact in the customer's complaint.

10 List four barriers to effective implementation of a customer care programme.

Answers to Quick Quiz

1 (1) care, (2) service, (3) operations, (4) product, (5) delivered, (6) serviced, (7) expectations, (8) experience, (9) relationship

2 Vision and values: (3), Internal customer relations: (2), (6), (8), (9), External customer relations: (1), (4), (5), (7)

3 Retention of existing customers

4 D

5 True

6 Counter/face-to-face service; Follow-up documentation; Repairs/maintenance

7 False

8 Sought

9 C

10 Vertical structures, formal role cultures, inadequate organisational communication, inflexible attitudes, lack of interpersonal skills

Now try Questions 14 & 15 from the Question Bank at the end of this Text

Action Programme Review

1 Provide front-line staff with information required to serve customers effectively: extension/responsibility, product/service information, briefing on marketing plans etc.

Train staff in interpersonal and communication skills (listening, assertiveness, conflict resolution, persuasion, emotional control etc).

Develop instruments for information-gathering (eg feedback forms, enquiry books) and giving (brochures, newsletters etc).

Facilitate communication flow between departments (eg inter-departmental meetings, breaking down barriers by informal contact).

Communicating, rewarding and recognising positive customer care values and attitudes (and selecting and developing staff who have them).

Giving front-line staff delegated authority (within clear boundaries and objectives) to take action to solve customer problems.

Providing appropriate facilities (private office space, for example) where staff can safely and effectively deal with customers, specially in sensitive situations.

2

NOTOWN CITY FC

Memo

To: A Richunne, Chairman Date: [-]

From: Your Name, Marketing Manager

Re: Recommendations

1. To understand who our customers are we need to carry out marketing research into both our spectators and our commercial sponsors. We would aim to establish what kinds of people come to matches and what their attitudes are towards our current customer care procedures. This could be done through surveys at the stadium and discussion groups. We should also carry out research on a wider canvas to establish attitudes towards the club held by individuals and organisations who are not currently fans or sponsors.

2. To make customers a member of our club, we publish a quarterly 'fanzine' which could emphasise the fact that we welcome them to the club and that their satisfaction is our satisfaction. We could make use of the happy chance that we are a club by making anyone subscribing to the fanzine an associate member of the FC itself – thus literally making the customer a member!

3. To make the customers more visible we should arrange club 'open days' which would allow employees and fans to meet and mingle. This should be made part of the playing staff's contracts and *all* staff should be given simple interpersonal skills training to equip them to better handle such encounters.

4. Rewards could be given to our customers in the form of season tickets with large savings on attendance fees over the whole season. The notion of loyalty could be enhanced by operating a scheme whereby the discounts could be cumulative by having greater discounts the more years an individual has been a season ticket holder. Similarly, loyalty cards for the club merchandise shop should be considered.

5. Stewards and administrative staff should be given extra training to deal with 'critical incidents'. The adverse publicity two months ago when the lad in the wheelchair was 'moved on' by stewards was an example of the damage that can be caused by over-zealous and unthinking application of 'the rules'. We should be using such episodes to create positive public relations messages – we could still learn from that event by improving the facilities for the disabled. The positive message would far outweigh the costs.

Y.N.

3 You wish to present the benefits of customer care: their statistical prevalence is secondary. The directors do not need excessively detailed information in a visual presentation. We suggest the following (a simple horizontal bar chart).

BENEFITS OF CUSTOMER CARE		% of managers who have experienced the benefit
Retention of existing customers	✓	68
Enhanced organisation reputation	✓	58
Competitive advantage in the marketplace	✓	53
Attraction of new customers	✓	43
Increased profitability	✓	28
Improved staff morale and loyalty	✓	25
Cost efficiency	✓	11

Source: Institute of Management, 1994

4 (a) Job application form: conforms to corporate identity guidelines; easy to complete efficiently; content relevant to job selection criteria; presentation professional/effective employer branding; elicits high quality applications.

(b) Website: conforms to corporate identity guidelines; easy of navigation/use; interactivity (with minimal action/waiting required); helpful links; (from organisation's point of view) elicits/captures relevant customer data; (from visitor's point of view) offers personalisation options, confidentiality/security; content true, fair, ethical, relevant to requirements; presentation attractive; intuitive URL for ease of location/recollection etc; attracts target number of 'hits' and on-line transactions. (We'll be discussing this later in the Study Text.)

(c) Point of sale display: projects brand image; allows brand identification; safe, sturdy and convenient to position at point of sale; quality materials to last with time and use without loss of image; effective for purpose (eg to hold sample stock, attract attention, display promotional information); attracts target increase in sales/enquiries.

(d) Interview with angry customer: staff member restraint and appropriate assertiveness (conflict resolution skills); situation offering privacy (but also safety for staff member); relevant information/mechanisms to solve problem at hand without delay: staff member's courtesy and 'can do' problem-solving attitude; elicits customer satisfaction and retention.

Customer communications can also **promote** quality values within the organisation (through employee communications and corporate literature) and to external customers and stakeholders, by expressing and reflecting the organisation's commitment to quality. Customer and employee feedback can also be gathered and used for quality improvements. In addition, communication should be used to minimise or solve problems caused by quality shortfalls or errors.

5 There are many examples you might have thought of. Here is a classic one.

An advertising/informational brochure sent out with a typographical or factual error would lead to customer confusion or complaints; tying up staff answering enquiries; perhaps publication or mailing of corrections and apologies; damage to customer and public relations. Careful checking would have saved these costs. (With discovery of the error prior to printing, only origination costs would be incurred. After printing but prior to delivery, origination and re-print costs may be incurred. After delivery to the customer, retractions, corrections, damaged reputation, complaint handling etc.) Other examples might include the careless leaking of confidential information (leading to law suits and/or competitive disadvantage): The Australian

Tax Office recently had to go into crisis mode when it was discovered that taxpayer information supplied for on-line returns was (due to a website design fault) freely accessible to anyone visiting the site. (And they only found this out when a taxpayer who had downloaded all this confidential information mailed it back to them with an explanatory note of warning ...)

6

The Customer is right – even if (s)he's wrong!

Some customers may simply be **awkward**. They may take up too much of your time with irrelevant chatter; they may be habitual complainers or questioners; they may try to tell you your job; they may get emotional and abusive.

There is **still** no justification for your losing your cool and your courtesy, and entering into a shouting match. **The customer is always right:** you know it is not so, but you must try and act as if it were so, consistent with preserving your own and the bank's dignity.

(a) **Don't respond to rudeness with rudeness.** Be polite but firm.

(b) **Find common ground where possible:**

'I can see how you would have thought that. But....'
'I quite understand your viewpoint. But have you considered....'

These are ways of telling them that they aren't right – without telling them that they're wrong.

(c) **Be honest**. If you don't know an answer, say so – and say you will find out.

(d) **Be patient.** Remember that the customer does not (and should not be expected to) know all about our procedures and policies, and may not understand the technical jargon. He is not stupid: he just is not a banker.

(e) **Be persuasive**. Use your techniques of logical argument, emphasis, appeal to the other person's attitudes and needs and so on.

7 Anecdotal evidence provides powerful illustration. Take the trouble to identify and analyse specific incidents: not 'grumbling', but considering weaknesses and strength in the *behaviours* of customer-facing staff and the systems supporting them.

8 Team leaders informally asking staff opinions; team meetings; suggestion schemes; staff appraisal interviews; staff attitude surveys by questionnaire (perhaps on the company Intranet). The marketing department could ask staff, for example, whether they feel they have enough information about the marketing plan to serve customers effectively, and how the promotional message reflects how they feel about the product/organisation.

9 You may like to give your feedback, where requested – and see whether you feel you have had a 'say' or an influence.

10

	Complaint	**Adjustment**
Purpose	■ Identify problem ■ Express effect of problem on me ■ Notify recipient of my wishes ■ Persuade recipient that wishes should be met	■ Show complaint has been considered seriously ■ Soothe complainant's anger, disappointment etc ■ Offer redress acceptable to both parties ■ Keep relationship/loyalty
Audience factors	■ Will want details to investigate ■ Will weigh cost of leaving me unhappy with cost of satisfying me ■ Will resist implied failure, cost ■ May (or may not) be concerned to retain my goodwill/loyalty	■ Will want to be taken seriously ■ Will be resistant to our avoiding responsibility ■ May be cynical about overly 'sincere' apologies ■ Will have to be motivated to accept redress we are able to offer

15

ICT and customer service

Chapter Topic List	
1	Setting the scene
2	Using databases
3	Web-based customer contact
4	Customer Relationship Management (CRM)
5	Computer-aided telephony
6	Issues in automated customer-handling

Learning Outcomes

- ☑ Understand how databases can be used to improve customer service
- ☑ Explain the customer service opportunities offered by the Internet
- ☑ Appreciate the nature and applications of CRM and e-CRM in customer service
- ☑ Discuss the benefits and drawbacks of various forms of computer-assisted and automated communication for customer service

Syllabus References

- ☑ Demonstrate an understanding of how ICT is used in customer service, for example through the use of databases (5.6)

Key Concepts Introduced

- Database marketing
- Customer Relationship Management (CRM)
- Computer Telephony Integration (CTI)

1 Setting the scene

1.1 In Chapter 8, we discussed the impact of the dynamic Information and Communication Technology (ICT) environment on **marketing communications** (promotions) and **transactions**, in terms of:

- Higher speed communications
- Wider access to information
- 24 hour, 7 day (24-7) global communication
- Greater interactivity and multi-media communication
- Virtual transactions and
- Virtual relationships

1.2 We also discussed some of the developments in the telecommunications infrastructure and equipment which facilitate these trends: ISDN, digital mobile phone networks, the Internet and so on.

1.3 In this chapter, we look specifically at the uses of these technologies in **delivering customer service**.

1.4 Technology can significantly improve customer service performance in such areas as:

- Personalising and streamlining customer contacts
- Responding swiftly to customer-initiated contacts and enquiries
- Soliciting customer feedback on service quality
- Giving customers access to 24-7 service and support

Exam Tip

As we noted in Chapter 8, you are not required to have detailed technical knowledge of how systems and devices operate – but you are required to have a good awareness of their uses and implications for customer communications. If in doubt, ask yourself: what does it do for the organisation and for its internal and external customers?

A part-question in the Specimen Paper for this syllabus asked you to explain (in the format of draft notes for a presentation) how the latest ICT tools can help improve communications and relationships with customers.

2 Using databases

2.1 A database is simply a collection of structured data, which can be interrogated in a variety of ways: in Chapter 1, we suggested a number of items of information that might be collected in a customer database, and how that information could be obtained.

2.2 The sources of information in a customer database and the uses to which these can be put are summarised in the diagram below (Figure 15.1).

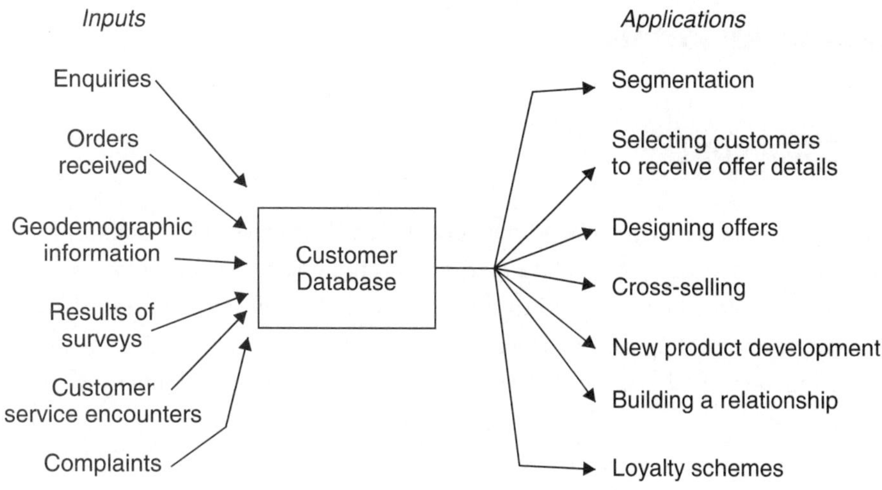

Figure 15.1: Customer database

Gathering customer information

2.3 Internet and database technologies offer some key advantages for gathering customer data.

(a) Market research into customers' 'stated intentions' and perceptions can be replaced or augmented by actual **customer behaviour** and **demonstrated preferences**: Web sites allow the tracking and storage of customer browsing (identifying areas of interest) and transaction/purchase history.

(b) **Market research** and **customer feedback gathering** can be carried out via such methods as:

- On-line or e-mail-distributed questionnaires and feedback forms
- 'Message boards' on the Web site, allowing visitors to communicate with the company (and each other)
- Site monitoring to record hits, browsing and purchase patterns of users
- Inviting e-mailed comments and suggestions

Such methods are more convenient for the customer than face-to-face interviews and writing/mailing: they require less effort and allow 24-7 flexibility. From the company's point of view, they also facilitate the immediate analysis and integration of results, automatic 'thank you' messages and so on.

(c) Companies can also access **external on-line databases** compiled and managed by specialist data providers: market research publishers (for example, Mintel and Keynote), producers of statistical data (for example, the UK Central Statistical Office and Eurostat) and others.

Database marketing

Key Concept

Database marketinghas been defined as 'an interactive approach to marketing which uses individually addressable marketing media and channels to extend help to a company's target audience, stimulate their demand and stay close to them by recording and keeping an electronic database memory of customer, prospect and all communication and commercial contacts, to help them improve all future contacts and ensure more realistic planning of all marketing.

2.4 Customer data held in computerised databases can be interrogated and manipulated in various ways through the process of **datamining** (described in Chapter 8).

Allen et al suggest the following projects which can be conducted using database marketing techniques.

(a) **Identify the best customers**. Use **RFM analysis** (recency of the latest purchase, frequency of purchases and monetary value of all purchases) to determine which customers are most profitable to market to.

(b) **Develop new customers**. Collect lists of potential customers to incorporate in the database.

(c) **Tailor messages based on customer usage**. Target mail and e-mail based on the types and frequency of purchases indicated by the customer's purchase profile.

(d) **Recognise customers after purchase**. Reinforce the purchase decision by appropriate follow-up.

(e) **Cross-sell related and complementary products**. Use the customer purchase database to identify opportunities to suggest additional products during the buying session.

(f) **Personalise customer service**. Online purchase data can prompt customer service representatives to show that the customer is recognised, his needs known, and his time (eg in giving details) valued.

(g) **Eliminate conflicting or confusing communications**. Present a coherent image over time to individual customers – however different the message to different customer groups. (For example, don't keep sending 'dear first-time customer' messages to long-standing customers!)

2.5 The two key points of this for adding value to customer service may be described as follows.

Targeting communications (mailing list management): greater relevance to the customer	■ Targeting customers in a particular geographic areas with information (suppliers, services, events) relevant to their local area ■ Targeting customers with relevant offerings, message content, and style, according to lifestyle, age group and other demographic/personal factors ■ Targeting customers with their preferred communication purposes (new product information, newsletters, special offers) and media (e-mail, phone, mail)
Personalising communications: greater relevance and sense of recognition for the customer	■ Personally addressed mailed/e-mailed communications ■ Individual customer information made available in real time to call centre staff to personalise telephone contacts and streamline transactions (no need for the customer to supply details each time) ■ Contacts and product recommendations based on preferences and contact/transaction history: ('Since you enquired about...', 'As a regular purchaser of...', 'Since we haven't heard from you for some time...') Relational use of personal information (for example, birthday cards)

2.6 Postma (*The New Marketing Era*) suggests that such techniques:

(a) **Build relationship**. 'Reacting to the personal behaviour of customers or prospects by responding to their obvious interests with an electronic message, a latter, a brochure or an offer actually fosters clients' feeling that you are becoming acquainted with their tastes and preferences and are taking them into consideration.'

(b) **Reinforce loyalty**. 'Loyal customers will value being recognised as such and receiving direct communications.'

(c) **Out-perform human beings**! 'An assistant in a fashion store may very well recognise a client's face after half a year, but will not instantly remember the clint's measurements and tastes. A database, on the other hand, has no problem whatsoever retaining these facts or other information about the customer's average expenditure, quality standards or preferred brand. We won't even mention the fact that the employee who served the customer last time has moved on to a different job and been replaced.'

Action Programme 1

Suggest how a database could enable marketing managers to improve their decision-making.

Customer specific marketing

2.7 The logical extension of database marketing is referred to by Kotler as **customer specific marketing**, and by Peppers and Rogers as **'One-to-One' marketing**. The company collects data on individual customers, their past Web-browsing and purchase habits, demographic and even psychographic characteristics. It is then possible to customise or personalise the organisation-customer interface to suit individual customer profiles: whether on the telephone (using Computer Telegraphy Integration), by mail (using data merged from database files into word-processing programmes), by e-mail (ditto), or by Web site (using Cookies to personalise the page for known surfers).

Data security and controls

2.8 **Legislation** and regulations exist in many countries to protect consumers from the misuse of personal details held on computer, unsolicited mail and invasion of privacy. In the UK, these include:

- **The Data Protection Act 1998**, which provided that data users (organisations or individuals who control the contents of files of personal data and the use of personal data) must register with the Data Protection Registrar. They must limit their use of personal data (defined as any information about an identifiable living individual) to the uses registered, and not disclose data to third parties (including e-mail addresses sent in a 'cc' reference) without permission.
- **The Criminal Justice and Public Order Act 1994**, which made it illegal to procure the disclosure of computer-held information, and to sell or offer to sell computer-held information
- **The Mailing Preference Service** which allows customers to state whether they would (and more often would not) be willing to receive direct mail on a range of specific areas. [This is the way to get taken off (or, if you are a Marketing Student, put on) mailing databases.]

Action Programme 2

Find out what the data protection requirements are in your country, if you are based outside the UK.

(*Key Skill for Marketers*: Applying Business Law)

3 Web-based customer contact

3.1 We discussed the World Wide Web and the Internet as promotional and commerce tools in Chapter 8. Note that they are also a medium of customer service delivery. For example:

- **E-commerce** offers 24-7, global customer service at the point of (virtual) sale, payment and followup.
- **E-mail** can be used for fast responses to customer information requests, queries and complaints 24-7 and worldwide. Since it is also 'collected' at the recipient's discretion, it may be less intrusive than telephone service contacts, for example.
- **FAQ** (Frequently Asked Question) features allows the immediate on-line answering of common questions, 24-7.
- **Customisation** techniques allow users to be put in control of Web site content to meet their needs and preferences. For example, most 'my portal' or 'my home page' pages of major search engines and service providers (like Excite or MSN) allow the user to choose the appearance, layout and topic content of pages.
- **Personalisation** techniques put the service provider in control of site content, but tailor it to the preferences of the user. The user does not determine what the programmes or prices will be, but the site 'remembers' the user's selections on subsequent visits and adapts the information accordingly: displaying features and recommendations based on the user's local area or interests, for example. This is where an element of surprise and apparent relationship gives potential for customer delight. (The user does not adapt the content: the content adapts itself, based on the user's profile, to provide something new, different and potentially unexpected.)
- **Documentation**: information, follow-up documentation (order confirmations, payment receipts, event ticketing and so on) can be immediately generated and printed out by the user.
- **Interactivity**: instead of being 'put on hold' while queries and transactions are processed, customers can exchange e-mail with (real or simulated) customer service representatives and/or interrogate information databases: there is no 'passive' waiting time in the same way as telephone service.
- **Fun factor**: using a well-designed Web site – even for transactions and service queries – can be interactive, sociable (with access to user communities) and stimulating (linking with other ideas and sites).

Action Programme 3

Earlier Action Programmes in this Text asked you to collect 'personalised' marketing communications sent to you, as examples of effective and ineffective targeted (or direct) marketing. Compare the best of the print– or telephone-based personalisation techniques with Web-based personalisation.

Again, a great example of what is possible is Amazon.com's personalisation of its service to registered users. Check out www.amazon.co.uk or www.amazon.com if you have not already done so!

4 Customer Relationship Management (CRM)

Key Concept

CRM (Customer Relationship Management) is 'a comprehensive approach that provides seamless co-ordination between sales, customer service, marketing, field support and other customer-touching functions. CRM integrates people, process and technology to maximise relationships with all your customers including eCustomers, distribution channel members, internal customers and suppliers... through the integration of people, process and technology, while taking advantage of the revolutionary impact of the Internet.' *(www.ismguide.com/html/)*

4.1 We discussed the concept of **relationship marketing** in Chapter 14. CRM (Customer Relationship Management) is a process. However, recent media coverage has focused on new technology which as enabled CRM in the dynamic world of the Web.

4.2 Uses of CRM technology

- To increase customer retention, by learning more about what customers value about products, services, customer service, Web experiences
- To predict customer buying behaviour
- To segment customers based on their relative profitability
- To give more consistent customer service across the full range of new communication media and multiple points of contact between the customer and the organisation

4.3 The term '**eCRM**' has been coined to describe a Web-centric approach to **synchronising customer relationships across communication channels, business functions and audiences**. According to Allen et al, 'eCRM represents a shift from having a company's employee take care of customers directly to allowing customers to use self-service tools that allow them to become active players in the purchase and service process. In this environment, the Web is used not just to make it easier to know more about each customer, but to empower the customer to manage and control the process via the Web.'

4.4 Each time a customer contacts a company with an effective CRM system – whether by telephone, in a retail outlet or online – the customer should be recognised and should receive appropriate information and attention. CRM software provides advanced personalisation and customised solutions to customer demands, giving customer care staff a range of key information about each customer which can be applied to the transaction.

4.5 Basically, CRM involves a single **comprehensive database** that can be accessed from any of the points of contact with the customer. Traditional 'vertical' organisation structures have tended to create stand-alone systems developed for distinct functions or departments, which were responsible for the four main types of interaction with the customer: marketing, sales, fulfilment and after sales. These systems need to be integrated into (or replaced by) a central customer database, with facilities for data to be **accessed from** and **fed into** the central system from other departments and applications (including the Web site), so that all customer information can be kept up-to-date and shared (Figure 15.2).

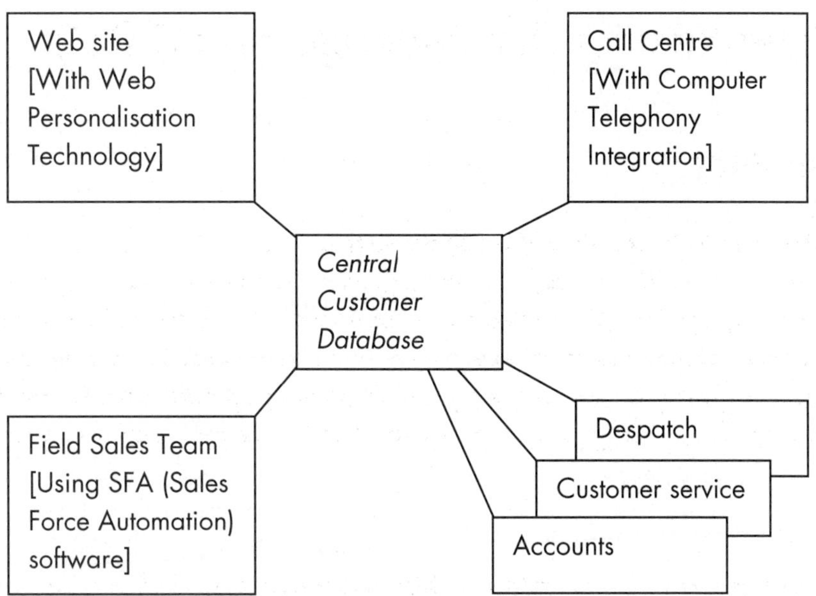

Figure 15.2 CRM system

Marketing at Work

Ticketmaster uses Quintus cContact to sell tickets and provide customers with personalised, consistent service via telephone, Web and e-mail contact. Quintus 'WebCentre' is a customer interaction management software designed exclusively for Web-based transactions.

The largest holiday property site on the Web, Vacationspot.com, uses Talisma to provide e-mail, self-help and chat options for customer care, giving immediate, personalised and consistent responses to high-volume customer enquiries.

4.6 CRM technologies include personalisation, Web traffic analysis, data mining and e-mail systems (discussed elsewhere). Some of the additional facets of CRM systems are as follows.

(a) **E-commerce** and **online customer care.** Real-time CRM software connects the Web server database to the in-house database to ensure that Web visitors are provided with up-to-the minute product and stock information, and so that on-line orders are transmitted immediately to the in-house system for processing. Further technological developments are enabling **real-time multi-media interactions** between customer service representatives and customers over the Web: 'need help' or 'click to talk' buttons give customers access to a live service person in real time, through instant messaging (text-based chat), or talking over the customer's browser (using the computer's microphone and speakers). This kind of multi-channel interactivity can be used for online customer care and the answering of pre-purchase questions.

(b) **Sales Force Automation (SFA)**. Field sales teams use SFA products on laptop computers to enter and update information about prospects and customers and to access up-to-date information on products, prices and stock availability from the central database. They can also share information with others salespeople and sales management. Because laptops are not permanently connected to the Internet, software is used to '**synchronise**' the different versions of the data: any changes in profile data are automatically transmitted to update previous versions, via e-mail, whenever the user is on-line.

4.7 CRM software is produced by a wide variety of providers, including Oracle (which also owns Thinking Machines), Surf Aid (used by IBM and Hilton Hotels), Blue Martini (used by Levis), Netperceptions and NeuralWare.

Marketing at Work

ARE YOU CUSTOMERISED?

1. Do you have as many customers as you want?

☐ **Yes** ☐ **No**

Can a bottom line be too healthy? Of course not. And neither can a growth oriented company have too many customers. They're the engine that generates revenue.

2. Are your customers as loyal as you want?

☐ **Yes** ☐ **No**

It's one thing to gain customers. It's another to keep them. The strength of your business depends largely upon your ability to sustain a relationship with customers.

3. Do you generate as much business from each customer as you want?

☐ **Yes** ☐ **No**

A critical component or business growth is increased sales content. To maximise each business opportunity, you need a way to leverage your entire organisation – to bring it totally to bear at the point of customer contact.

4. Do you really know what your customer? want?

☐ **Yes** ☐ **No**

Are you alert to *every* product your customers could use? *Every* service that might interest them? *Every* transaction they're prepared to make? *Every* sale they'd allow you to follow through? Are you thoroughly plugged into your market?

5. Does your entire organisation know what your customers want?

☐ **Yes** ☐ **No**

A customer orientation has limited value unless it's embedded in the very heart of an enterprise – at all levels and at every place that directly or indirectly involves the customer/

6. Is your information strategy focused on helping you hear what customers and markets are trying to tell you?

☐ **Yes** ☐ **No**

The next best thing to reading your customers' minds is listening to what they're saying. But unless you're constantly tuned in to customers' signals, you're missing messages that could guide you to greater results for your business.

7. Can your organisation respond quickly to what customers and markets are telling you?

☐ **Yes** ☐ **No**

When the flow lines of your information system are not within your customer's reach, you won't always sense when opportunity knocks. But even if you do, getting the message is not enough. If you can't reply rapidly to market signals with information, products and services, revenue opportunities are lost.

8. Does your information strategy enable the – pro active delivery of information to your customers?

☐ **Yes** ☐ **No**

Many business plans underestimate the power of information to build customer relationships. But imagine the advantage of an information technology strategy that transforms information into customer-generating, revenue-generating fuel.

9. Are the full capabilities of your organisation accessible to your customers at all your field locations.

☐ **Yes** ☐ **No**

An office. A branch. A retail site. To a customer, that's your company. One small part of the whole. Which is why you need to leverage your entire organisation by extending its capabilities to each point of customer contact.

10. Does your information strategy reflect the bottom-line importance of customer service?

☐ **Yes** ☐ **No**

Business is built on customers. Without them, there is no bottom line. Government is also built on customers, the public. And whether you're in the business of commerce or the business of government, no objective of an information strategy is more fundamental than enhanced customer service.

The bottom line. *If you answered* No *to any of these questions, you're not yet customerised. But you might well agree that this simple test suggests the enormous advantages of becoming customerised. And as the leader at customerising business and government, Unisys will work with you to provide the answers you need.*

Action Programme 4

Fill out the Unisys questionnaire shown in the Marketing at Work feature above. In this communication exercise you are both (a) a marketer for your own organisation and (b) a customer of Unisys' added-value promotional message in issuing this questionnaire!

Consider how you respond to the questionnaire in each capacity.

Exam Tip

At the time of writing, no question has directly been set on CRM in the 'e-CRM' sense. However, you should be aware that any question on databases, customer feedback, customer care and service, relationship marketing and uses of Web sites (all covered in this module) can be construed as a question on CRM. The point is: do not forget that many of these customer communication techniques can now be partially or wholly automated: show your awareness of current trends by citing automated examples.

5 Computer-aided telephony

5.1 Database, computer and telecommunications technologies have increasingly been applied — and integrated with each other – to offer new customer service methodologies, as part of CRM systems.

Video-conferencing and telephones

5.2 **Video conferencing** was first used commercially in the 1970s and there are now thousands of conferencing studios in use worldwide. ISDN-based technologies, however, mean that there is now no need for dedicated leased lines and studios: 'dial up' video-conferencing systems are available for less than £10,000 (and falling).

5.3 **Video telephones** are still regarded as 'futuristic' by most people, but the spread of ISDN has already made them a reality: video telephones have been on the market in the USA since 1992, and British Telecom have launched a variety of similar products in the UK. These include a terminal with a small camera set into a 9" x 4" screen with a telephone. Users can deny video access if they do not wish to be seen by the other party, and can also use a 'self view' mode to check their appearance before they go live.

5.4 Even more accessible options now include **Web casts** using digital video cameras and microphones linked to computer terminals, which can be connected to one another via the Internet.

5.5 Once initial development and awareness barriers have been overcome, these methods are likely to have a significant impact on contacts with internal (for example, in the case of video-conferencing) and external customers. Given that a high proportion of interpersonal communication is non-verbal, virtual face-to-face communication enhances possibilities for more 'personal' service, better understanding, complaint handling, negotiation and so on.

Voice mail

5.6 Voice mail (or v-mail) systems enable a caller's message to be recorded at the recipient's voice mail box (similar to a mail box in an e-mail system).

5.7 Advantages of v-mail for customer service include the following.

- A 'personal' greeting and invitation to leave a message (as in an answering machine) can be given by a large selection of individual extension-users (not just a central switchboard): maintaining personal contact with the customer/caller.
- Callers can leave messages where the target recipient is unavailable or the office is unattended (due to meetings or different time zones, for example), without the need for waiting or call back. This minimises the risk of 'losing' an unanswered customer call.
- Internal and external customers can contact sales representatives, maintenance teams, consultants and others working 'in the field' or at clients' premises.

Automated call handling (ACH) and interactive voice response (IVR)

5.8 **Automated call handling** is a system whereby computerised or recorded voice asks callers to select from a menu of options by **pressing buttons on their telephone**. This can be used:

- To route calls through a switchboard, by specifying connection choices (nature of call, target department and extension if known) and putting the caller through
- To complete entire transactions (for example, booking cinema tickets and paying bills by credit card) and information searches (for example, transport timetables, cinema film times)
- **Without intervention by a human operator**. (There is usually the option to switch to a human operator in case of difficulties.)

5.9 **Interactive voice response** (IVR) systems involve a similar approach, but selections are made from the menu options by **voice response**: that is, responding verbally by answering questions with selected words ('yes', 'no', numbers and key terminology) which can be recognised by the receiving software. This is now extensively used in the booking of taxis, for example: the caller responds to questions by saying 'yes' or 'no' ('Are we picking you up from this address?' 'Are you ready now?'), numbers ('How many passengers?') and other recognisable words ('What is the destination area?').

5.10 Automated call handling has both advantages and disadvantages for customer care.

Advantages	Disadvantages
■ Customers can leave messages after hours ■ Customers can place orders and perform other transaction (for example, bill paying) 24-7 ■ Customers do not have the frustration of unanswered calls ■ Customers are able to access information (eg transport timetables, cinema times) at any time ■ Customer calls can be swiftly routed to the department they require	■ If not carefully structured, customers can be 'trapped' in a never-ending loop of menus ■ Customers may be frustrated or uncomfortable not being able to talk to a human being (particularly older customers, not used to 'virtual' relationships) ■ Customers may not be able to identify the service or department they require and be put through to the wrong person

Action Programme 5

From your own experience of automated call handling, interactive voice response and call holding systems (which keep you informed when your call has been put on hold waiting for an answer), list some of the features which create a *negative* experience for a customer. How might the effect of such features affect different customers in different circumstances?

Computer Telephony Integration (CTI)

Key Concept

Computer Telephony Integration (CTI) systems link the telephone systems of the organisation or call centre to computerised databases of information about customers (via telephone number recognition) and/or product/market information, so that the receiver of the call has real-time access to information for customer service.

5.11 Information gathered from customers in the course of telephone calls and transactions can be stored in a customer database and can be called up and sent to the screen of the person handling subsequent calls, perhaps before the call has even been put through.

- Sales staff dealing with hundreds of calls every day give the impression of **recognising** individual callers personally and **knowing in advance** what they are likely to order, where the order should be sent and so on. Order forms with key details already entered can be displayed on operators' screens automatically, **saving time** for customer and operator alike.

- A bank customer service person or financial planner might use CTI to call up changes in share prices or details of investment products **relevant** to the customer's enquiry, during the call.

- A busy manager might note that an **unwelcome call** is coming in on the 'screen pop' that appears on her PC and choose to direct it to her voice mail box rather than dealing with it at once.

6 Issues in automated customer-handling

6.1 The automation of customer-handling operations can have a positive impact for the customer and supplier alike.

(a) The organisation is **available for contact** 24 hours, 7 days.

(b) **Ordering** can be conducted 'instantly' and at any time to suit the customer.

(c) Frequently asked questions (FAQs) and e-mail contacts can **reduce waiting time** for answers to customer queries.

(d) Customer information is made available to **personalise** the transaction and build **customer relationships**. This includes recognition of customer telephone numbers, for example, so that call centre staff can address customers by name and do not have to ask repeatedly for address and other details. On a fully automated level, it includes the personalisation of the customer's interface with a web page.

(e) Automation creates significant **cost savings** for the company: reducing the number of customer-service staff required, and enabling other to work from home or in (in house or outsourced) call centres.

(f) Fewer 'missed' calls and better customer service supports customer attraction, retention and loyalty.

6.2 As we discussed above, eCRM can be used to empower customers to control the purchase and service process. Allen et al suggest that 'Many Web users have found that a well-constructed Web site provides better on-demand services than they usually receive through a company's human-based contacts. The Web site lets customers easily obtain product and service information that helps them investigate product features, make purchases and solve problems without help from the more costly sales and support staff.'

6.3 Negative impacts of automation, however, include the following.

- Customers (particularly in certain age or cultural groups) may simply want to talk to a human being.
- Automation leads to the loss of customer service jobs.
- Automated call management systems can frustrate the customer by creating a lengthy 'loop' of menus.

6.4 As mentioned in paragraph 4.6 above, **on-line customer care** is now increasingly concerned with putting live human interaction (by text message or voice-over) **back** into automated transactions. Customers feel reassured by the ability to access 'need help' or 'click to talk' features (not just to send an e-mail and await a reply). These buttons can be programmed to become bigger and more prominent when customers revisit a page several times, visit all FAQs, delete items from their shopping cart or show other signs of having questions or second thoughts.

Action Programme 6

Write a short memorandum report to your manager outlining the benefits (a) to marketers and (b) to customers, of attention to CRM, particularly in the provision of on-line customer care and support.

Problems with the Internet

6.5 Some of the significant issues in Internet usage are as follows.

(a) **Weak infrastructure**, including slow modems in most households. (Clicking slowly through an electronic catalogue, as graphics download, soon becomes tiresome in comparison to print versions.)

(b) **Security fears.** More people are worried about security breaches over the Internet than about orthodox credit card fraud.

(c) **Managing customer expectations.** The convenience of ordering via a computer terminal tends to raise customer expectations which 'real world' delivery systems are incapable of meeting. Except for specific types of product (such as computer software or information), instant electronic ordering is followed up by road, sea or air mail delivery systems: these still take time and can involve inconvenience.

(d) The **Internet customer profile** is still predominantly young male professionals: only a fifth of surfers are women, and just 4% children (although these numbers are rising all the time). Hence, retailers in some sectors are more likely to conduct successful e-commerce that others.

6.6 **Privacy** is a major issue, particularly on the Web. With an increasing number and variety of data collection points, not all of which are visible, permission-seeking or easily understood by customers, concern about the use to which customer data is put by organisations is bound to have a high profile. Allen et al suggest that: 'Marketers have an obligation to tell their customers what they are doing with the information that the customer provides or, as the case may be, what they *intend* to do with it. Honesty is the best policy, and it will be appreciated by your customers, especially as the paranoia continues to rise around the topic of privacy.'

Chapter Roundup

- Database marketing is an interactive approach to marketing, which uses individually addressable marketing media and channels to extend help to a company's target audience, stimulate their demand and stay close to them by recording and keeping an electronic database memory of customer, prospect and all communication and commercial contacts, to help them improve all future contacts and to ensure more realistic planning of all marketing.
- Customer Relationship Marketing (CRM) is a comprehensive approach that provides seamless co-ordination between sales, customer service, marketing, field support and other customer-touching functions... to maximise relationships with all your customer, including e-Customers, distribution channel members, internal customers and suppliers.
- Telephony services can be automated and integrated with database and on-line systems.
- ICT can offer significant advantages in customer service through:
  - Personalising and streamlining customer contacts
  - Responding swiftly to customer-initiated contacts and enquiries
  - Soliciting customer feedback on service quality
  - Giving customers access to 24-7 service and support
- Key issues in the automation of customer handling functions include:
  - The depersonalisation (and re-personalisation) of customer care
  - Overcoming technical fears and infrastructure weaknesses
  - Managing customer expectations of delivery
  - Maintaining privacy in the face of data gathering
  - Maintaining the security of transaction data

Quick Quiz

1 Which of the following (you may select more than one) is a potential customer service benefit of ICT technology?

Speed of response	Feedback gathering	Accessible to all customers
Data security	Cost saving	24-7 access

2 What does 'RFM' analysis stand for?

3 It is illegal in the UK to disclose customer e-mail addresses to third parties (including by entering them in a mass 'copy' reference) without permission.

☐ True ☐ False

4 A Web site that allowed you to post your own photos and specify the items of information you want on your portal/home page is using the technique of:

A Personalisation
B Customisation
C Integration
D Documentation

5 A Web-centric approach to synchronising customer relationships across communication channels. business functions and audiences is called ....

6 Which of the following may be part of a CRM system?

A field sales team	A Call Centre
A Web site	All of these

7 Which of the following is *not* a customer service benefit of voice mail?

A Individually targeted contact
B Message taking
C Co-ordination
D Interactivity

8 A telephone system which allows callers to select options from a computerised menu by answering questions verbally is called:

A Electronic data interchange (EDI)
B Interactive voice response (IVR)
C Automated call handling (ACH)
D Sales force Automation (SFA)

9 Fill in the gaps in the following sentence, using the words provided below.

'Computer (1).......... Integration systems link the telephone systems of the organisation or (2)......... centre to computerised (3).......... of information about (4).......... (via telephone number (5)..........) and/or (6)........./market information, so that the (7)........... of the call has (8).......... access to information for (9).......... service.

■ customer ■ receiver ■ telephony ■ product ■ real-time
■ databases ■ customers ■ recognition ■ call

10 Which of the following is *not* a technique for 're-personalising' automated transactions?

A Instant messaging
B 'Click to talk' button
C FAQ
D Voice interruption

Answers to Quick Quiz

1 Speed of response, feedback gathering, cost saving, 24-7 access

2 Recency of latest purchase, Frequency of purchases and Monetary value of all purchases

3 True

4 B

5 e-CRM

6 All of these

7 D

8 B

9 (1) telephony, (2) call, (3) databases, (4) customers, (5) recognition, (6) product, (7) receiver, (8) real-time, (9) customer

10 C

Now try Question 16 from the Question Bank at the end of this Text

Action Programme Review

1 Linton (1995) indicates the different ways that databases enable marketing managers to improve their decision-making.

- Understanding customers and their preferences
- Managing customer service (helplines, complaints)
- Understanding the market (new products, channels etc)
- Understanding competitors (market share, price comparisons)
- Managing sales operations
- Managing promotional campaigns
- Communicating with customers

2 Own research.

3 You should find good and bad examples of each. 'Spam', for example, has all the attributes of the most intrusive and ill-targeted telesales call or direct mail package. This exercise should help you to distinguish between pseudo-personalisation in the form of 'friendly tone and (often error-filled) personal name and address, and genuine Web-enabled personalisation, which can appear to 'know' the user to a surprising degree. For example, a personal product recommendation (based on past preferences, analysed in such a way as to suggest patterns you may not even have noticed yourself) can be spot on – creating customer delight.

4 No suggested answer. You were invited to use a customer service appraisal tool – as an example of the process – and to consider its relationship marketing potential in a business-to-business setting (ie Unisys supporting business customers in supporting their customers...)

5 A study by the Henley Centre found that only 10% of customers start out feeling 'cheerful and optimistic' when embarking on a telephone call to an organisation – and most of these are rapidly driven to 'anger and fury' as a direct results of their efforts. Complex, slow and unclear menus of options are frustrating feature. The inability of voice recognition to understand your accent, or anything that does not exactly correspond to its menu is another. Hold messages can be particularly annoying. ('Your call has been placed in a queue.' 'Your call is valuable to us...' after 20 minutes on hold, and so on.) Business callers do not have time to waste. Consumer callers may feel *forced* to wait, and resent the fact. Callers wanting to place an order (or give to a charity, or volunteer their services) may well choose not to wait, if their motivation was not very high in the first place. Older callers frequently dislike dealing with machines instead of people.

6 MEMORANDUM

To: X
From: Your Name
Date: –/–/–
Re: Benefits of Customer Relationship Management and Online Customer Support

Benefits to Marketers

- Better customer care and reassurance, leading to customer loyalty. Real-time personal interaction can overcome reluctance to commit to purchase, technophobia and so on.
- Better interactivity, allowing real-time product customisation and pricing negotiation (for customer delight), and the provision of up-to-date availability information (to avoid customer disappointment)
- Access to the customer at the point of willingness to buy. Web-enabled call centres allow customer service staff to answer last-minute questions and give buying guidance (and cross-sell related products) while the customer is still browsing the site. (This solves the common problems of abandoned 'shopping carts', which are not taken to the 'checkout' because of lack of guidance.)
- Reduced costs of service, through 'self service' applications like FAQs, search engines and so on.
- Reduced product returns, because the self-service and support mechanisms increase purchase confidence.

Benefits to Customers

- Customers can access information about orders and products outside business hours
- Purchase confidence is higher, empowering customers to initiate and track transactions themselves
- Customers get faster connection, less waiting and more up to date, targeted information: in short, better service
- Customers in difficulties can speak to live service personnel in real-time, enhancing the personal transaction, minimising the alienating effect of technology
- Customers may be delighted by the recognition and appreciation shown to them on repeat visits

Question bank

1 Micro-environment and stakeholders *32 mins*

In the context of a business of your choice:

(a) Produce a slide defining its microenvironment. **(5 marks)**

(b) State the importance of *three* of its primary stakeholders. **(6 marks)**

(c) Write a brief memorandum on the growing importance of relationship marketing with *one* of these primary stakeholder groups. **(9 marks)**

(20 marks)

2 The importance of the customer *32 mins*

Quotations for question 2

Quotation 1 (from Michael Hammer and James Champy *Re-Engineering the Corporation - a Manifesto for Business Revolution*, London: Nicholas Brearley, 1993).

'Since the early 1980s, in the United States and other developed countries, the dominant force in the seller-customer relationship has shifted. Sellers no longer have the upper hand; customers do. Customers now tell suppliers what they want, when they want it, how they want it, and what they will pay. This new situation is unsettling to companies that have known life only in the mass market.

In reality, a mass market never existed, but for most of this century the *idea* of the mass market provided manufacturers and service providers - from Henry Ford's car company to Thomas Watson's computer company - with the useful fiction that their customers were more or less alike ...

Now that they have choices, though, customers no longer behave as if they are all cast in the same mould. Customers - consumers and corporations alike - demand products and services designed for their unique and particular needs. There is no longer any such notion as *the* customer; there is only *this* customer, the one with whom a seller is dealing at the moment and who now has the capacity to indulge his or her own personal tastes. The mass market has broken into pieces, some as small as a single customer.'

Quotation 2 (from B Joseph Pine II *Mass Customisation - The New Frontier in Business Competition*, Harvard Business School Press, 1993).

'People do not like hard-sell tactics, but they will tolerate them to acquire something they really want. If what they purchase turns out to be not *quite* what they wanted, their dissatisfaction with the product is magnified by the dissatisfaction with the sales tactics.

The basic problem (in years gone by) was that the focus of the marketing function of mass producers was not on *marketing* - it was on *selling*, on 'pushing the product'. Selling is a necessary part of the marketing function, but marketing is so much more, as management guru Peter Drucker observes:

"There will always, one can assume, be need for some selling. But the aim of marketing is to make selling superfluous. The aim of marketing is to know and understand the customer so well that the product or service fits him and sells itself. Ideally, marketing should result in a customer who is ready to buy. All that should be needed then is to make the product or service available."'

Question

To what extent do the arguments advanced in both quotations apply to *any one* of these marketing environments:

(a) The public sector (government departments and authorities responsible for the administration of local/municipal affairs)

(b) The third sector, ie voluntary or charitable organisations

(c) The marketing of services to internal customers within organisations?

Note that you should only write about *any one* of these three options. **(20 marks)**

3 Buyer behaviour *32 mins*

(a) Explain the major stages in the consumer buying decision process. **(10 marks)**

(b) Why might a detailed understanding of the model of consumer behaviour buying decision processes help marketers develop more effective marketing strategies to capture and retain customers? **(10 marks)**

(20 marks)

4 Communication models *32 mins*

You are the Communications Manager of a large retail chain. You have been asked to give a presentation to Marketing staff to help them understand the role and process of marketing communications. Draft an outline for your presentation (using diagrams for visual aids if you wish), describing and evaluating:

(a) The (radio signal) communication model **(10 marks)**
(b) The integrated marketing communication model **(10 marks)**

(20 marks)

5 How to integrate promotion *32 mins*

You are an officer of the Health Education Council, a government supported body and you are charged with a campaign to reduce alcohol consumption among young adults. In a memorandum to your manager state what relative emphasis you would place on each element of the promotion mix. Also set out how you would seek to integrate the campaign.

(20 marks)

6 Recruitment advertisement *32 mins*

For a company of your choice, draft a full A4 page recruitment advertisement for the post of marketing manager to be placed in *The Marketer*. Ensure the advertisement contains the following: the company background; the benefits of the job; information about the role; a brief description of the ideal candidate and any other essential information. Provide guidance for the magazine's production department with regard to the typeface and type sizes to be used, the positioning of logos and any other layout details you consider necessary. **(20 marks)**

7 It's my job *32 mins*

For a company of your choice, assume that you work in the Marketing Department and have responsibility for the staff newsletter. There is a regular feature entitled 'It's our job ...' which provides information about various job roles and departments. To improve internal marketing within the firm, you decide to take this opportunity to explain the relevance of marketing to the company and to describe the work undertaken by staff in your department.

Write a 500 word article for the feature to appear in the next issue and provide production and layout information to enable your article to have both visual and verbal impact on the reader.

(20 marks)

8 DIY website *32 mins*

You are a Brand Manager for a large Do It Yourself retail chain that has developed a web site.

Answer only **one** of the following.

EITHER

(a) Write a press release for the consumer press promoting the launch of the web site and encouraging Internet users to log on in order to take advantage of special discounts. **(20 marks)**

OR

(b) Write a memo to staff explaining how a web site can be used to increase sales, extend the customer database and improve communications with customers. **(20 marks)**

9 Communication barriers *32 mins*

(a) Explain, using business examples, how 'poor listeners' can improve their listening skills. **(10 marks)**

(b) Explain how communication barriers could distort an advertising message. Suggest how this distortion could be avoided. **(10 marks)**

(20 marks)

10 Message planning *32 mins*

You work in the marketing department of a well known charity and have been asked to work with a new member of staff who will be working on the design and copywriting of the next direct marketing campaign. Your colleague is unfamiliar with the terms AIDA which stands for 'Attention, Interest, Desire, Action' and PASS which stands for 'Purpose, Audience, Structure and Style'.

In a memo, advise your colleague how these terms are useful reminders of how to develop effective direct marketing material for your organisation. **(20 marks)**

11 Toy fair *32 mins*

You are the Sales and Marketing Executive for a toy manufacturing company. This year you have decided to take an exhibition stand at an international toy fair.

(a) Draft an agenda for your regular monthly sales meeting. In addition to the usual agenda items, include two additional agenda items relating to the organisation and staffing of the exhibition stand. **(10 marks)**

(b) **EITHER**

(i) Write a memo to staff who will be manning the company's exhibition stand, outlining how they might use appropriate body language to enhance their effectiveness at the trade fair. **(10 marks)**

OR

(ii) Write a memo to staff explaining the importance of exhibitions in achieving company sales objectives and suggest how the value of this type of promotional activity could be measured. **(10 marks)**

(20 marks)

12 It's your letter *32 mins*

(a) You are self employed and run your own marketing consultancy. You have recently completed some consultancy work for a large firm. You were hopeful that this was the beginning of a fruitful business relationship from which you would get repeat business. However, it has been 6 months since you completed the job and you have not yet been paid, in spite of a number of telephone calls which you have made to the accounts department.

Write an appropriate letter to the accounts department of your client. **(10 marks)**

(b) With the introduction of individual work stations in you office you have become concerned about the inconsistency in the appearance and tone of business letters. In particular, the work of a number of junior staff features poor layout and presentation. Write a memo to staff which will highlight good practice. **(10 marks)**

(20 marks)

13 Furry foods *64 mins*

UK pet owners are shunning 'man's best friend' in favour of its feline counterpart. While this nation of animal lovers may be doing away with dogs - especially of the big and vicious variety - they are more likely to have a cat or two.

Adverse publicity over dog attacks and complaints of dog fouling have had some impact, but modern lifestyles increasingly demand 'lazy' pets - with buyers either choosing a cat or a small dog which doesn't require as much care or exercise. The recessionary years may have had a long-term impact as well - a dog is perceived to be more expensive to keep than a cat. At the same time, there is an increased tendency for owners to spoil the pet they have, with concern for health and well-being leading to a trade-up to premium food and pet products.

Pet food and pet products are part of a broader market for products and services, which includes vets, pet insurance, kennels and catteries. The total market was worth about £2.8bn in 1995. The pet food market is the largest sector, with £1.2bn in sales in 1995.

In real terms, the dog food market has expanded by only two per cent since 1991. The continuing decline of the dog population will make market growth of the dog food and accessories market harder to achieve in the run-up to the year 2000.

The outlook for cat and other pet food is more positive, with a continued advance in cat ownership. Although dry food will increase its share at the expense of the moist canned products, it will not seriously challenge the moist sector at the same rate as it has in the dog food market.

The outlook for the pet market is positive. Demographics will work for the benefit of the industry - the number of children in the 10-15 age range, who are most likely to own pets, is likely to grow at a much faster rate than the overall population. As modern lifestyles and working patterns lead to time constraints the trend towards 'lazy' pets is likely to continue.

Figure 1

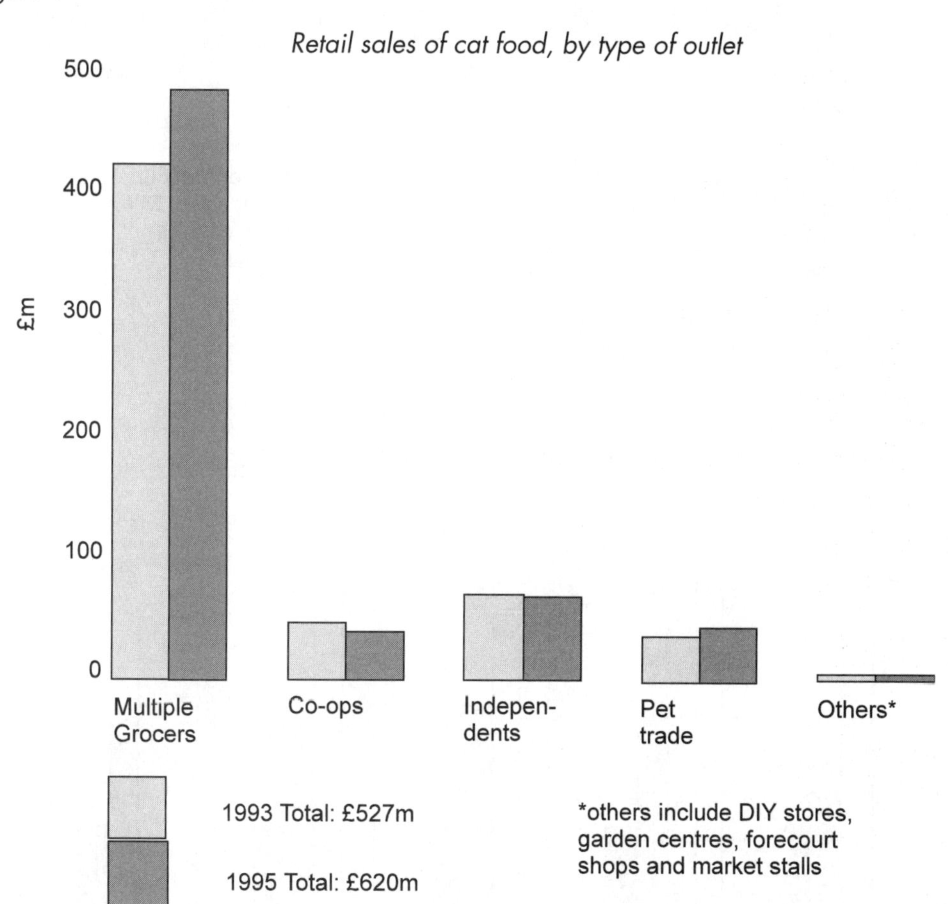

Source: Mintel

Figure 2

Retail sales of dog food, by type of outlet

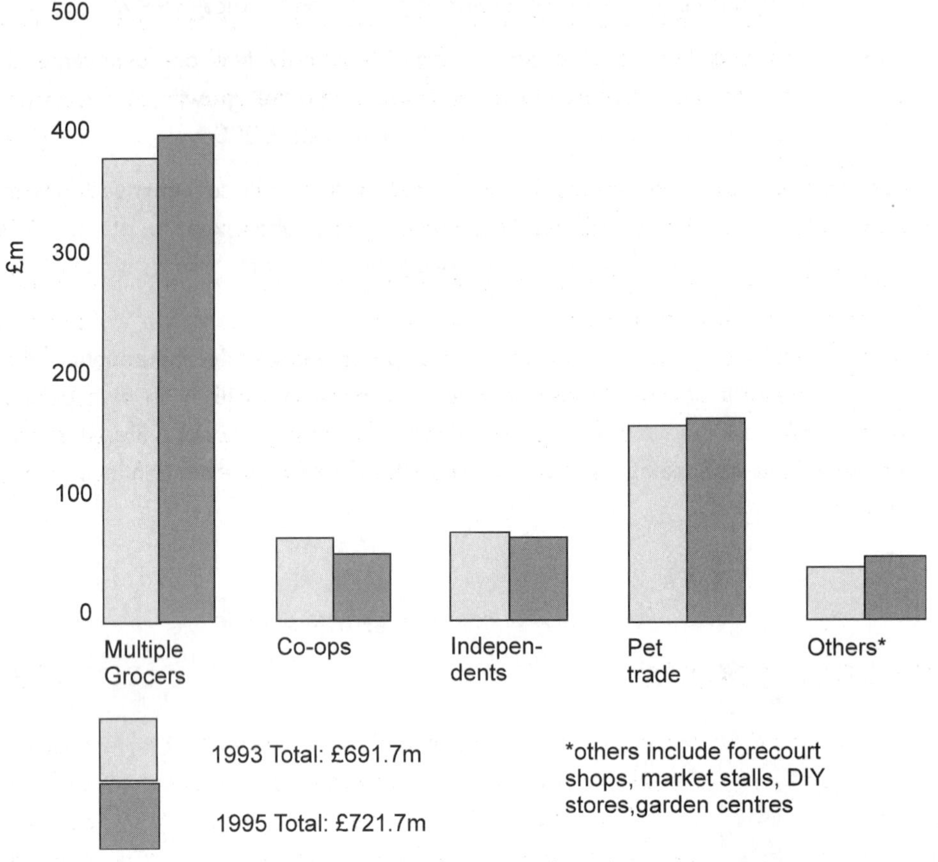

Source: Mintel

Figure 3

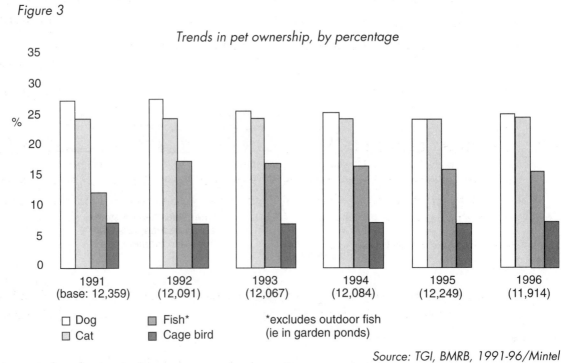

Trends in pet ownership, by percentage

35
30
25
%
20
15
10
5
0

1991 (base: 12,359) | 1992 (12,091) | 1993 (12,067) | 1994 (12,084) | 1995 (12,249) | 1996 (11,914)

□ Dog
□ Cat
■ Fish*
■ Cage bird

*excludes outdoor fish (ie in garden ponds)

Source: TGI, BMRB, 1991-96/Mintel

Material extracted and reproduced with kind permission of Marketing Magazine.

Required

As the marketing assistant at Furry Foods use the data provided to undertake the following tasks.

(a) Summarise the information regarding pet ownership trends onto 3 slides for a presentation to the board of directors. On at least one of the slides include a graph or chart to indicate the size of the pet food sector, within the broader pet product market, for 1995. **(15 marks)**

(b) Use the information in Figures 1 and 2 and write a memo to the distribution manager about retail sales of cat food and dog food by type of outlet. **(15 marks)**

(c) Furry Foods is launching Biskies, a range of dry cat food biscuits in the UK and Europe. The communications task is one of raising awareness that cat food biscuits can be used as a convenient 'complete' alternative to moist tinned food. Many pet owners see them only as a supplement or a treat. There are several specialist magazines aimed at cat owners. Draft a press release for this specialist media outlining the advantages of the product, stating where the product will be on sale and how the product will be launched on the market. **(10 marks)**

(40 marks)

14 Customer care *32 mins*

You work for an airline company and you have just been approached by a business traveller who has a complaint about the level of service which she has just experienced. The customer was delayed by one hour on an outward domestic flight and also by one hour on the return journey later that day. The main emphasis of her complaint was the lack of information about these delays.

(a) What are the practical approaches which could be undertaken by **this** organisation to improve its standard of customer care? **(8 marks)**

(b) Explain the practical steps in establishing an effective customer-care programme. **(12 marks)**

(20 marks)

15 Customer contact *32 mins*

You are the Customer Services manager for a company of your choice. You are keen to develop in-house training on Customer Care. Draft your training notes with illustrative examples to explain the following:

Answer only **one** of the following.

EITHER

How the tone of voice, body language and active listening adopted by a member of staff can affect how customer complaints are handled. **(20 marks)**

OR

How customer feedback is essential to effective customer care, and how this can influence your company's customer communications. **(20 marks)**

16 Databases *32 mins*

Write a report for your Line Manager explaining how it is possible to make the best use of databases in order to develop better customer relationships. Give examples of two different types of organisation that use innovative computer software and systems to do this.

(20 marks)

Pilot paper

Certificate in Marketing

Customer Communications

5.21: Customer Communications

Time:

Date:

3 Hours Duration

This examination is in two sections.

PART A – Is compulsory and worth 40% of total marks.

PART B – Has **SIX** questions; select **THREE**. Each answer will be worth 20% of the total marks.

DO NOT repeat the question in your answer, but show clearly the number of the question attempted on the appropriate pages of the answer book.

Rough workings should be included in the answer book and ruled through after use.

Certificate in Marketing

5.21: Customer Communications – Specimen Paper

PART A

The UK Small Car Market

There is not much to choose between one small car and another in today's market. They are all reliable, offer similar equipment and are similarly priced within their ranges. Yet car manufacturers spent over £120 million on advertising in 1997 to persuade customers that there really is a difference between models such as the Ford Fiesta, Vauxhall Corsa and Nissan Micra.

Advertising plays a crucial role in brand and model choice by building image and promoting real and apparent differences in price and finance. Getting the right image for a model is important but manufacturers also need to carefully target their potential customers using direct marketing techniques.

Based on research undertaken by Lifestyle Research during 1998, car advertisements appear to have more impact on men than women. Men tend to have better recall for the less prominent models. The skew is particularly marked for BMW and Daewoo, men being nearly three times more likely than women to remember these advertisements.

ABC1 drivers are more conscious of car advertising than those in the C2DE social grade groups, perhaps because the first group are twice as likely to be driving new as opposed to second-hand cars. Of the various models with the highest recall levels, only Ford, Nissan and Vauxhall have higher recall levels among C2DE drivers.

Twenty seven per cent of drivers remember receiving a direct mailshot promoting a car during the previous month. For company and new car drivers, this figure rose to 37%.

In the lifestyle research survey, all respondents were asked about activities undertaken in the past six months: 30% had watched a specialist car programme on television; 25% had visited a car dealer; 8% had taken a test drive and 5% had requested a brochure.

Television and newspaper advertising were used extensively, demonstrating that mass media advertising is considered essential to compete effectively in the market, even though the number of buyers in any one year is very small compared with most markets.

A large proportion of Fiestas, the UK's most popular models, are either second-hand cars or form part of company fleets.

Reproduced with the kind permission of Marketing Week.

Figure 1.

Recall of Advertising in Past Month (% Drivers)	
Nissan	33
Vauxhall	38
Rover	17
Ford	44
Renault	27

Source: Car Market, July 1998

Figure 2.

Media Considered to be Informative (% Drivers Intending to Buy New Cars)	
Local press advertisements	40
National press advertisements	27
TV advertisements	18
Direct mailshots	11
Radio	4

Source: Car Market, October 1998

Figure 3.

Top Six Selling Small Cars – 1997						
Model	Rover 200	Renault Clio	Vauxhall Corsa	Peugeot 306	Nissan Micra	Ford Fiesta
Cars sold	40,000	60,000	80,000	50,000	38,000	125,000

Source: Car Market, March 1998

Figure 4.

Car Ownership Per Home of those Owning at Least One Car – Number Owned by Age of Head of Household				
Cars Per Home	All Homes	Head of Household Aged <45	Head of Household Aged 45-64	Head of Household Aged >65
One	70%	65%	58%	80%
Two	25%	30%	30%	18%
Three	5%	5%	12%	2%

Source: Car Market, May 1998

Figure 5.

The Ford Fiesta

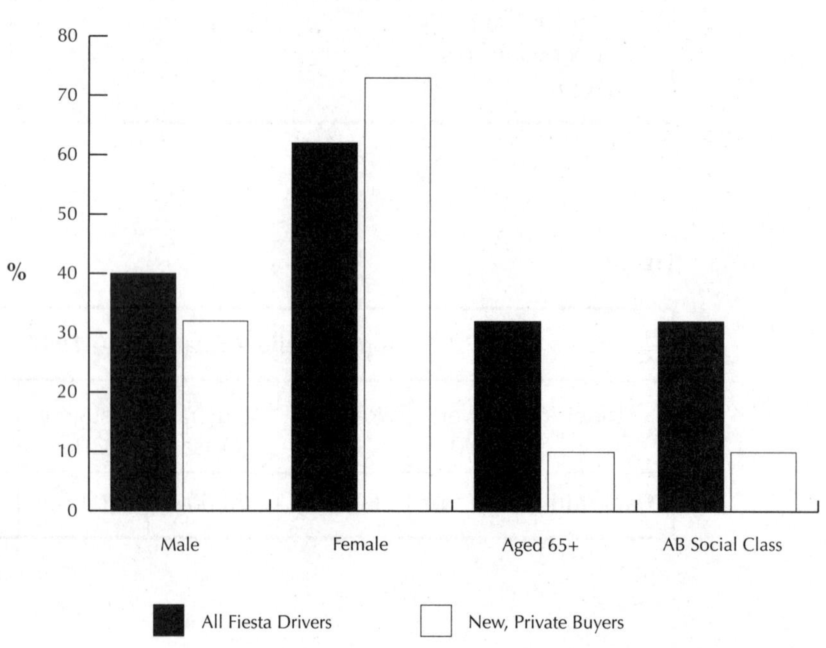

Source: Lifestyle Data, 1998

PART A

Question 1.

As Product Manager for the Ford Fiesta, you are responsible for analysing key data printed in articles in the consumer and trade press. You have extracted the above information from various articles in *Car Market,* the industry's trade paper.

a. In a formal report format addressed to the Marketing Manager for Ford (UK), analyse the data provided and provide reasoned recommendations for how the Fiesta should be marketed in the future. Be selective with the data as appropriate to the case presented in your report.

(25 marks)

b. Add three appendices to your report which should include the following:

i) A line graph to show recall of advertising in the past month.

ii) A component bar chart to show the number of cars owned per home.

iii) A pie chart to show the market share of the top six selling small cars.

(15 marks)
(40 marks in total)

PART B – Answer THREE Questions Only

Question 2.

Your company has recently appointed a new Product Manager to your team who has very little experience in delivering presentations at meetings. To assist your new team member, do the following:

a. Draft an agenda, where one item of business is a presentation from the Product Manager.

(10 marks)

b. Write a memorandum on how to make an effective presentation.

(10 marks)
(20 marks in total)

Question 3.

You work as a Sponsorship Assistant for a local dog rescue home. Draft a letter to a large petroleum company asking for corporate sponsorship for a newsletter that you send to regular contributors. You will need to provide some information about the newsletter in terms of its content, distribution and details about its target audience. You should indicate the amount of sponsorship that is required. Your letter should also explain the potential benefits to the sponsor in communicating with this target audience.

(20 marks)

Question 4.

You work as a Marketing Manager for a large toy manufacturer and you are about to launch a new range of toys aimed at children under 5 years of age. Draft a full A4 page recruitment advertisement for the post of Product Manager for this toy range to be placed in *Marketing Recruitment.* Ensure the advertisement contains the following: the company background; the benefits of the job; information about the role; a brief description of the ideal candidate and any other essential information. Provide guidance for the magazine's production department with regards to the typeface and type sizes to be used, the positioning of logos and any other layout details you consider necessary.

(20 marks)

Question 5.

As Customer Care Manager for a company of your choice, you regularly conduct research on the levels of customer complaints, particularly with regards to the telephone manner of your operatives in your Call Centre. Your recent research highlights an alarming increase in the levels of customer complaints, so you feel the time has come to instigate a new, improved Customer Care Programme. Draft an email to your Line Manager outlining the following:

a. The importance of customer care and relationship marketing and the role that telephone operatives in your Call Centre play in this process.

(10 marks)

b. The key stages which would be involved in developing a Customer Care Programme for your Call Centre.

(10 marks)
(20 marks in total)

Question 6.

You work as a Promotions Assistant for an industrial company of your choice, and it is your job to outline the company's promotions plans for the coming year. Draft an informal report to your Promotions Manager indicating which promotions tools you believe would be most effective, and explain why.

(20 marks)

Question 7.

You have been appointed to the position of Communications Manager for a large airline company.

a. Using illustrations from the airline business, draft notes for a presentation to staff explaining the benefits of using visual methods to convey complex data.

(10 marks)

b. Draft notes for a presentation to your marketing team, explaining how implementing the latest Information and Communications Technology (ICT) tolls can help improve communications and relationships with customers.

(10 marks)
(20 marks in total)

Answer bank

1 Micro-environment and stakeholders

> **Tutorial note**. Make sure you present your slides well. The question reflects the growing importance of relationship marketing. Specify the stakeholder you are referring to in your answer to part (c).

(a) The micro-environment of the car manufacturer Rover

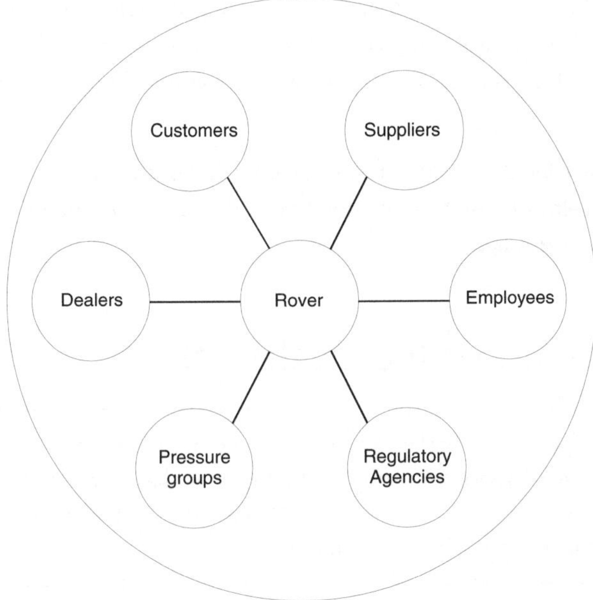

(b) Three primary stakeholders described here are: customers; suppliers and employees.

- Customers are the source of Rover's revenue. Without revenue from this source, it will not be able to satisfy the aspirations of its other stakeholders.
- Suppliers are becoming increasingly important as many firms now entrust considerable responsibility to them for designing component parts and for ensuring availability and timely delivery. The lack of a single critical component form a supplier could prevent Rover satisfying customer demand.
- Employees are essential to the success of Rover. The company requires an adequate supply of trained staff who can add value to the company's output. Poor treatment of staff by the company could result in low motivation which may be reflected in poor product quality.

(c) **MEMORANDUM**

To: Marketing Director
From: Marketing Assistant
Subject: Growing importance of relationship marketing with customers

Relationship marketing has helped to transform the way that individuals buy cars. Traditionally, a private buyer has bought a car and then replaced it after 3 or 4 years, with little contact occurring between the customer and car manufacturer during the intervening period. Relationship marketing methods have brought buyer and seller closer together for a continuous period, using some of the following methods:

- Finance schemes which tie the buyer to a company for three years (typically)

- Maintenance and warranty contracts mean that a customer has to return to the manufacturer's dealers rather than those of the buyer's own choosing
- Many car manufacturers agree to replace a car after a specified mileage or time, thereby extending the relationship with a customer
- Many car manufacturers maintain databases of their customers, which can build up individual profiles. This can be used for targeting of future offers

Of course, relationship marketing is about more than building up databases and locking customers into long-term agreements. To be successful, a company must ensure that it maintains high quality throughout, so that buyers come back as a matter of enthusiastic choice rather than out of inertia. A strong relationship can create great word-of-mouth advocacy.

Finally, it must be noted that many studies have shown that it is more profitable for a company to retain its existing customers, rather than continually recruiting new customers to replace lapsed ones.

2 The importance of the customer

> **Tutorial note**. The question asked you to apply the arguments in the quotations to *any one* of the public sector, the third sector and internal customers. In the answer below we indicate the general ways in which the arguments do and do not hold water in not-for-profit situations. Your answer, however, should focus on *one* of the three areas.

An analysis of the two quotations reveals the following arguments.

(a) Customers know what they want and expect to get it.

(b) Customers have been tricked into buying homogenous goods and services that producers happened to feel like producing.

(c) Because of competition and better information, customers now demand goods and services unique and perfectly adapted to their needs and tastes.

(d) Customers who have been sold a product (by implication against their 'wants') and later experience dissonance are doubly alienated.

(e) The aim should be not to sell but to match products and services so perfectly to customer wants that the product or service sells itself.

(f) Matching to wants necessitates knowing what those wants are.

Broadly, the arguments are suggesting customer supremacy as development of the 1980s and 90s. We shall look now at how each agreement applies to not-for-profit organisations.

(a) Historically it has not been accepted practice to describe the public sector, and the third sector or people within organisations, as customers at all. How far they now have 'wants' which become actions is arguable: taxpayers (a customer of the Inland Revenue?) do not *want* to pay taxes, or at least not at the rate they are required to pay; neglected children (a customer of NCH?) does not *want* to starve before they get food in their mouths. These people are *users* of services, not customers, because they do not pay and they have no choice. With regard to internal customers, they may or may not have conscious wants of another department. Sometimes they may be expressed negatively – 'I wish personnel wouldn't obstruct this recruitment drive!' – and often there is more lip-service then real attention paid to formulating and satisfying internal customers' wants.

(b) This argument appears to hold true for all three sectors. The public sector has been notorious for its self-regarding functional structure; the third sector has administered charity in a way which satisfied its own need to feel charitable as much as other people's need to be helped (charities for drug users, for instance, are not well-supported, while animal charities are 'cute'); internal customers (colleagues in other departments) have often been seen as the enemy, with whom political and financial war is constantly waged.

(c) This seems to be where the argument falls down. There is still not much element of choice available to the 'customers' in question; they are really 'users' who often do not have much clout. In organisations many talk about customer supremacy and pay lip-service to pro-customer sentiments, but in fact there is a great deal of defensiveness and self-delusion because, at the end of the day, perhaps the customers in these contexts are *not* supreme as they are *users*. The paymasters, as ever, pay the money and make the choice. Thus we see public sector organisations acting in a way which aims to please the government or whichever body funds it, rather than the users; charities still help 'cute' concerns to please donors, rather than those in need of help; departments still act politically. It is possible to say, however, that the government donors and bosses are in fact the customers; this still leaves open the problem that different customers have different, and maybe conflicting demands.

(d) 'Customers' of these organisations are not usually 'sold' a product: they are given it. The argument about increased dissonance does not really apply. Since they were not asked what they wanted, they will hardly be surprised nor more alienated when they do not get it.

(e) Having said all that, there is every reason for each organisation to attempt to match delivery to expectations since that is a more efficient way of operating, reducing the amount of confusion and complaints after delivery. How far this will take place depends not so much on the 'customer' but the organisation itself. Often it will need to assume a marketing orientation and possibly restructure according to processes rather than functions.

(f) Assuming that in some cases it is in the interest of the organisation to match the customer's/user's wants, it is obviously important to find out what they are. Many organisations in the public sector and third sector, and some departments with internal customers, do make the effort to identify, investigate and understand their customers/users. Whether this results in the matching of services to wants is another matter. But in many cases there is increased need for change: privatisation, market forces and organised pressure groups and Ombudsmen are encroaching on the public sector; oversupply of charities and the recession means there is a fight for donations and services, and hence a need to be competitive in the third sector. TQM initiatives mean that many organisations require acknowledgement of the internal customer's needs.

3 Buyer behaviour

(a) The major stages in the consumer buying decision process are:

Problem recognition	Information search	Information evaluation	Decision	Post purchase evaluation

(i) **Problem recognition** may be as simple as noticing that a food item needs replacing or petrol tank is near empty through to more complex psychological recognition of a need such as insuring against future illness. It is the recognition of a problem that starts the purchase decision process.

(ii) **Information search** refers to both the consumer's external search for information but also the search of their own memory/knowledge. Information search can be quite complex for certain purchases whereas on others it is virtually non existent, particularly the impulse or routine purchase.

(iii) **Information evaluation** is the stage of the purchase decision when the product is evaluated against certain criteria. This criteria will vary from purchase to purchase and may be quite lengthy or very quick. Information may be evaluated from reading literature, seeing advertisements or other stimuli, endorsements from friends or 'stars' etc. Evaluation may be objective based upon tangible criteria or subjective based more upon emotive criteria.

(iv) **Decisions** may be made consciously based upon a clear evaluation of criteria or subconsciously where no clear evaluation has occurred. The decision time again can range from impulsive to very lengthy. Sometimes it is very hard for individuals to make decisions as no clear choice is favourite or other considerations come to mind to complicate the process.

(v) **Post purchase evaluation** occurs after the purchase. Some consumers suffer doubts immediately after the purchase (Post cognitive dissonance). Others evaluate the product in use against their expectations and this process will have some influence in determining whether they purchase the product again.

(b) Understanding the above process will enable marketers to influence each stage through their marketing strategies. Identifying potential types of problems and making consumers aware of them is a common technique. Radion washing powder advertisements highlighted a mother's concern about the sweaty smell still clinging to the armpits of shirts even after the shirt had been washed. Marketers must be able to come up with solutions to problems and make these solutions available in a form that is acceptable to the consumer.

Making sure that information is available in the right format and place will assist the consumer's information search. Marketers need to know what sources are commonly used or to what extent purchases are based upon experience or endorsement. Information can then be made available to assist the information search. This can be done through advertisements, product literature, sales personnel, publicity or help lines.

Similarly marketers need to be aware of the criteria used to evaluate products and the extent to which this is based on objective or subjective criteria. Closely matching products and service offers around these criteria is likely to assist in capturing or retaining customers.

Providing incentives or communications at point of purchase can influence the consumer's decision to buy the product. The importance of sales people is often crucial at the decision stage to encourage a decision to be made. Where no sales people are involved, factors such as packaging design and displays can also be a powerful means of influencing the decision.

Marketers should also maintain communications and contact with customers after the purchase to monitor satisfaction and minimise post cognitive dissonance. One car distributor offered to replace a new car purchase within one week of it being bought if the customer after using it was not happy with their decision.

The above examples show how marketers through the development of appropriate marketing strategies can play an influential role in capturing new and retaining existing customers throughout the purchase decision process. Close attention to understanding this process is therefore a critical role performed by marketing.

4 Communication models

(a) *(Radio signal) communication model*

The communication process

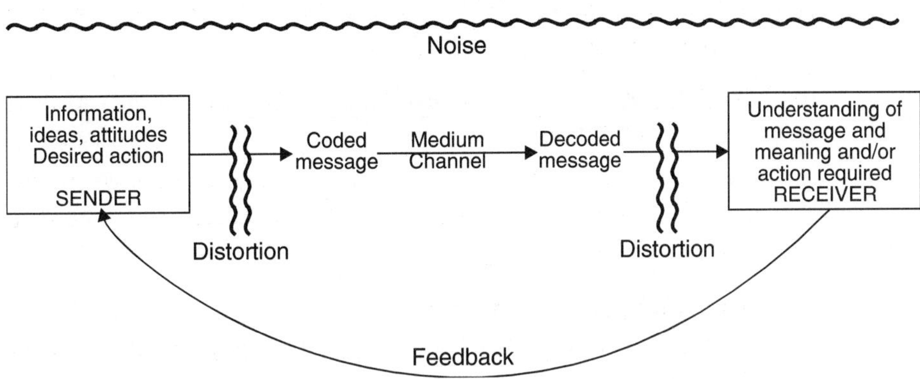

(i) *Description*

This model is clearly based on that of sending a radio or a telephone signal and can be used to emphasise that the communication process is more complex than it appears at first sight. For example, there may be 'noise' in the system. This may equate to the clutter of competing advertisements in the chosen media. The receivers(consumers) may also have to *interpret* what the message means to them. This is the 'decoding' process.

(ii) *Applications*

Increasingly sophisticated advertising is being designed, in which the messages are minimised. They may be coded very cleverly in a colour scheme or by the use of a particular actor representing the product, for example the blonde Rutger Hauer dressed all in black representing Guinness or the puppy representing Andrex toilet tissue. The process of encoding/decoding is obvious in these examples.

(iii) *Limitations*

Like other models, the process of analysis is essentially a qualitative one which does not help with deciding on the absolute amounts of advertising spend. The model is also limited by the many other factors that it does not allow for but which are present in the market place, such as the degree of competitive reaction.

(b) *Integrated marketing communication model*

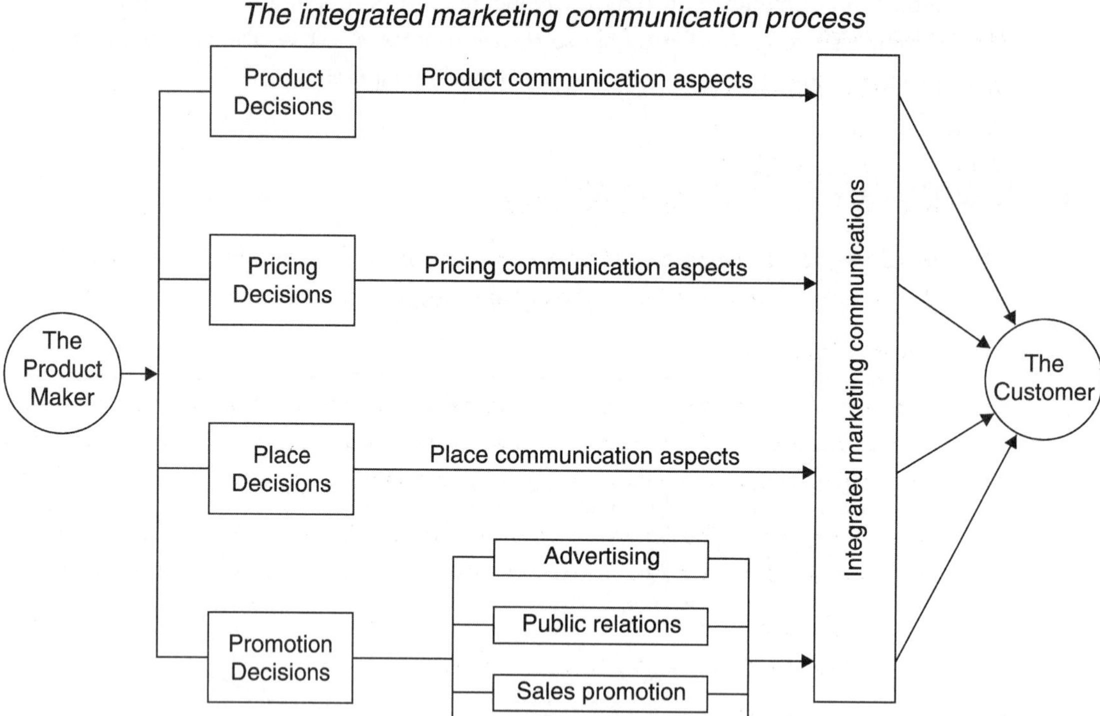

(i) *Description*

This model, apparently comprehensive in nature attempts to depict the whole of the marketing communication process. It demonstrates that each element of the marketing mix can make a contribution to the communication process. It suggests that these elements must be integrated with the elements of the promotional mix. The whole process links the company with its customers in the most effective way.

(ii) *Applications*

Increasingly both agencies and clients recognise the need to integrate campaigns in the method described above. Each element can have a distinct role to play in the overall process. A synergistic combination is possible if the overall result is greater than the sum of the separate parts.

(iii) *Limitations*

Historically major patterns of communication may have been established by a company (for example advertising) and limited knowledge may prevent it from using other techniques such as direct marketing. The above model, though comprehensive, does not show how to make decisions about the relative proportion of each element of the overall mix.

5 How to integrate promotion

Memorandum

To: Chief Executive
From: Information Officer
Date: January 1998
Subject: Reduction in alcohol consumption

In response to your request I set out my recommendations for the relative emphasis to be placed on each element of the marketing communications mix in the first year of our campaign.

(a) *Overall intention*

We should concentrate in the first instance on medium to heavy users. In this way we will avoid a head-on clash with committed users and alcoholics, yet ensure that there is overspill from our work into both the light and heavy user segments.

We should target the influential members of our target audience rather than attempt a widespread campaign that would dissipate our budget and minimise the effect.

The whole campaign should be co-ordinated around a positioning statement so as to ensure that we have consonance throughout.

(b) *Advertising (40% emphasis)*

The role of advertising is to inform, to persuade. It is necessary to target our campaign very carefully so as to hit the target audience, those with influence within the medium to heavy consumers of alcohol.

Trade press should be used to remind vendors of their legal obligations. More profit can be made from certain alternatives to alcohol, and this fact should be stressed.

Media advertising should focus not on the dangers of alcohol, but on the pleasure to be derived from the alternatives.

There should be a strong congratulatory element within the advertising (avoiding smugness) to reinforce the non-users and, in particular, those who have given up, or reduced their consumption.

(c) *Public relations (40% emphasis)*

PR should be our main weapon at this stage. We should endeavour to encourage prominent non-users of alcohol to mention the fact whenever possible without becoming strident nor appearing to preach.

Parliament should be lobbied to introduce legislation similar to that in place for smoking. Both government and opposition parties should be targeted, and individual MPs supportive of the cause recruited and supported.

Public media of regard, and particularly individuals who have an affinity with certain target segments, should be provided with case histories, and pertinent information in easy-to-use press packs.

Evidence of success in similar campaigns across the world should be compiled and used as appropriate in our briefings and press packs.

Non-alcohol events should be encouraged, and sponsorship such as the Milk Race should be supported.

Local pressure groups should be formed, and encouraged to be self-supportive within our overall promotional policy.

(d) *Packaging (Longer term emphasis)*

We cannot use packaging, since this is the province of the manufacturers. It is, however, a major target for our parliamentary lobby since we should endeavour to enforce government health warnings following the pattern established in the tobacco market.

(e) *Sales promotion (10% emphasis)*

We will develop sales promotion and point of purchase materials which will encourage moderation in consumption especially at critical periods such as Christmas and New Year.

(f) *Contingency (10% emphasis)*

We should hold 10% of the budget as reserve to counter the expected reaction from the powerful alcohol industry and their established lobby. This budget should not be committed until six months into our campaign when we have assessed preliminary achievement and can decide where best to focus our effort.

(g) *Integration*

It is vital that we plan the above elements into an integrated campaign. We will use the same creative designs in all elements in a cost-effective manner. We will need to plan each stage so that they reinforce each other in a logical manner.

(h) *Summary*

This will be a prolonged campaign that must be sustained against great odds over a considerable period of time. To judge from the ASH campaign against smoking it may take ten years for the first effects to show in any marked way. However, the ASH curve of success was exponential. This is to be expected as attitude shift gains momentum, but we should not be too optimistic about immediate marked success. There are, after all, more committed users of alcohol than there are smokers, and the secondary effects of alcohol are less pronounced. It is nevertheless a campaign that must be undertaken, and one to which great numbers of the public will subscribe as it gains credibility.

6 Recruitment advertisement

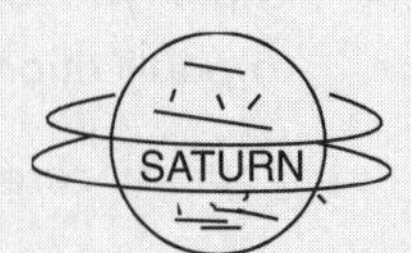

A FIRST CLASS

WORLD CLASS

MARKETING MANAGER

Everyone will recognise Saturn as a global communications company. They may not know that we operate in 130 markets and generate a turnover in excess of £4 billion per annum and have sustained annual growth in excess of 12%, making us a powerful force in the world communications market. We are pursuing a successful growth strategy and are poised to enter new, third world markets which we will provide with communication infra-structures including satellites, the internet and mobile phone networks.

The marketing manager's post is for a capable individual who can market to the world.

You will have experience in marketing management at a senior level. You will impress us with your previous track record and your high-level analytical and creative skills.

You will lead a team which works world-wide. Ideally you are experienced in the international communications field.

If this is you and you would like to hear details of the kind of package we are offering for this well positioned challenging post, then contact Uri Mutch, PO Box 696, World's end, Kent, KT1 3FR, Telephone 01729 62431, or e-mail:UMU@SAT.ac.UK anytime before 31 December 1998.

You are a well educated businessman and an active member of a professional institute.

The Wharf
World's End
Kent
KT1 3FR

Ms Ida Green
Production Manager
The Marketer
Unit 8, Keytown
KE6 9TT

7 December 20XX

Dear Ms Green

I am sending you, for publication, a copy of the text and layout for the marketing manager's post which we discussed earlier today.

Please produce to A4 size with frame and logo as shown.

Type face Arial throughout – sans serif for heading

Text size 10-12 point for main body of text

Header: please use size up to 60 point which uses an appropriate amount of space – given the A4 size.

Thank you for your help. Please fax me a print proof of the advertisement for a final check prior to publication.

Yours sincerely,

Uri Mutch

Marketing Assistant

7 It's my job

> **Examiner's comments**. An extremely unpopular question. It was intended to allow candidates to use their communication skills with an internal audience and describe the value of their department's role.

Copy – deadlines – budgets – clients – customers – quality – events – research – sales – new markets – print – price – promotion – packaging – profit – customers – suppliers – image – profit – briefs – trends – targets – satisfaction – products – advertising – brands – image – analysis – design – sourcing – websites – direct marketing – ethics – standards – customer attitudes – value for money – innovation – tea and coffee – excitement and more – so read on ....

It's our job to market our organisation and its products to the world. In a sense we all do this every day of the week but we have the specific task of satisfying customers by providing excellent levels of service and by building relationships with them.

This article introduces you to your colleagues who are working to do just that.

Gill and Tony lead the Advertising Section. They sell our beauty products, reinforce our brands and enhance our image. Using market research, their experience and expertise they turn advertising strategies into the reality of annual schedules which are the blue prints for Better Body's product advertisement in national magazines and on television. Placing advertisements involves briefings and negotiations with graphic designers and copy specialists-within budget. These activities are based on their knowledge of our company, grasp of the selected themes and audience targets for each campaign and an acute perception of public attitudes. Of course they are required to keep track of their schedules and to evaluate the effectiveness of their work.

Anton, Mark and Lucy are our three marketeers. Using quantitative data based on sociological and economic statistics, combined with qualitative research, they develop existing markets and identify new ones. These activities result finally in the production and sale of new products for Better Body.

Our qualitative research includes consumer surveys, the trade press articles and letters from the public. From this data customer profiles are created and market segments identified, from which we make the demand forecasts which are the basis of what we make, when we make it and how we sell it.

Computers have made a big difference to our work -they've doubled it! Despite what the sceptics may say and although, like a small child, they demand constant attention, they do give us greatly enhanced database management. Our databases include customer details, spend, sales and evaluation of promotions, which becomes subject to further analysis and ultimately leads to assessments and reports for consideration by our directors.

Apart from internal reports, digests, returns etc we are producing copy for and communicating with our customers and potential customers on a daily basis.

We initiate press statements, releases, open-days and visits as well as respond to enquiries and complaints (yes there are a few). Our targeted marketing activities include; direct mail, organising the customer loyalty scheme, promotions, sponsorship, demonstrations, talks and national events. When you see us leaving with our stands, samples and suitcases you may think, "There they are off on another jolly". Well we are ... if you think that working 12-16 hours a day for 2-3 days equals a jolly! Finally we come to Fiona and Patience who work in our production and design section. Many of our leaflets and brochures and much of our packaging is produced in-house over 50 items in all and F and P do it!

Fiona sources paper, card and print materials and together with Patience they propose new designs, layouts and colours. The marketing departments contribution to the company website is sorted out by Patience. She is our cyberspace dude.

Well there you are that's all there is to it (well nearly all). For certain we couldn't do it without you.

Thanks

8 DIY website

(a)

> **Examiner's comments**. A popular question although many candidates did not produce the correct format for a 'press release'. Candidates must consider the targeted audience for the press release – journalists and, through them, the consumer market.
>
> The first paragraph should generate sufficient interest for the journalist to want to read on. It should also contain enough detail for use in a short magazine/newspaper piece.

Di-Y Stores
Head Office
Plane Way
Wallsend

For Immediate Release: 12 June 2000

PRESS RELEASE

Go to .....Di-Y Direct – the first e-stop for DIY

Di-Y is the first retail chain to offer easy access and efficient on-line shopping through the Internet. The new web site www.di-ydirect.com goes 'live' today. This is the address which will do more than open up the complete content of our stores at anytime to anyone.

Paul Jones, MD, says: "We wanted more than a picture gallery of goods with an order form. Uniquely our website offers practical demonstrations of 20 DIY jobs around the house-from fixing a tap to papering a ceiling. For each job there is a complete list of tools and materials required. These can be purchased as a pack or individually. The site also has an interactive, advice facility and a bulletin board where users can post ideas and comments".

Our website offers queue-free shopping, items always in stock and a delivery service.

Advantages of on-line shopping include: a 10% discount on all purchases and for the first three months, a chance to win a prize in our free draw offer. All you need to do is register your name and address, without any obligation to buy, and you have a chance to win one of the store full of prizes which we are offering. Now's your chance to drop in and become the DIY professional in your own home. Go to ..www.di-ydirect.com and let us help you plan your next job.

ENDS

For further details contact Sue Page, Brand Manager by ringing 0208 555 7777.

(b)

> **Examiner's comments**. Weaker candidates did not know how websites can be used to increase sales and improve communications. Good answers were motivational, celebrating the launch of the website and explaining how it could be used as an additional marketing tool.

MEMORANDUM

To: All Staff
From: Sue Page, Brand Manager
Date: 12 June 2000
Subject: Potential of a Website

Now that we have a website it is important that we recognise its potential so that each of us can help to maintain and develop it. If you log on to our site you will see the home page and, from there, may wish to visit the other pages.

The purpose of this memo is to outline three of the ways in which the site can help us in our work.

The site will increase sales because there will be additional customers who cannot access our stores, customers who will choose to use us rather than another store and existing customers who will make additional purchases. The Internet is a bigger market than one we could possibly access any other way. We can also generate sales through our attractive homepage which will interest users and direct them to other pages which will advertise and detail new stock, new offers and new techniques as well as the DIY and financial services which are available.

The site will allow us to add to our customer database in several ways. Site users who become customers can be logged but in addition we will have details of those who enter our free draws and competitions and ask for information about stock items. Advertising literature can also be sent to home addresses and capture the interest of other members of the household.

The website is a new tool in customer communication. E-mails allow a two-way exchange of information between us and our customers and the website itself is an ever present part of the user's Internet resources. Information is current and transmitted instantly. Enquiries and complaints can be quickly dealt with.

9 Communication barriers

> **Examiner's comments**. Good candidates detailed ways of improving listening skills and provided a business/marketing context.
>
> Very few candidates managed to link distortion with an advertising message and show realistically how it could be avoided. Note that noise and distortion are two different things.

(a) Poor listening manifests itself in a variety of ways, which are classified into three broad groups with suggested skill development behaviours for improvement. Although training is recommended there are actions and responses which the individual can practice.

(i) **Passive to active listening** – passivity suggests itself through impatience, lack of interest, little grasp of the key issues. By asking a customer questions, for example, to seek out further information, you show both an interest and a concern for the needs of the individual. Similarly you can challenge a representative or consultant on a point of fact or evidence which will show that you are paying close attention and will not be 'fobbed off''.

(ii) **From poor to effective body language** – who has not been 'served' by someone showing almost total disregard for the customer through his deadpan expression or lack of eye contact – or even his refusal to stop eating? Facial expressions allow us to show a full range of emotions, from pleasure to concern, anger to conciliation. There are occasions in business when each of these emotions is appropriate. They may, for example, all be used in a single interview – and would certainly show both a human and businesslike approach to work and work issues. The effective listening aspect of an interview is well illustrated by appropriate mirroring of a candidate's expression and tone of voice.

(iii) **From closing down to opening up** – a poor listener will try to 'close down' a speaker, give little useful feedback and perhaps ask a lot of unnecessary questions. A good listener will show a quick grasp of the issues, be able to summarise what has been heard and pick up on key words in order to establish the situation.

(b) **The distortion of messages and its avoidance**

An advertising message may be distorted through one or even more of these barriers to effective communication:

(i) **Personal bias/selective hearing** prevents clear communication because the receiver is spending time reflecting on likes, dislikes and preferences triggered by the words or images, which are not themselves central to the advertising message.

(ii) **Information overload** causes receiver 'shut down' which precludes any further information being accepted.

(iii) **Technical language** and abbreviations will lead to lack of understanding in the uninitiated.

(iv) **Inappropriate language** (including body language) for the target audience.

(v) **Technical and physical problems** associated with the technology or environment of either the sender or receiver.

The basis for avoiding most of these distortions is to use the findings of surveys and market research based on the target audience. If this is not possible, the message can be reviewed by small in-company groups primed to comment on any visual image or piece of text which they feel is either unacceptable or capable of being misunderstood. The message should use a communication medium appropriate to its 'weight'. Possible technical and physical problems should have been anticipated and taken into account.

10 Message planning

MEMORANDUM

To: Verity Thomas
From: Saleem Khan
Date: 11 June 2001
Subject: Useful mnemonics for the preparation of effective **direct marketing** materials

1 I am pleased to learn that we will be working together in the preparation of material for our next direct marketing campaign.

2 This memo outlines our organisation's approach to design and copy writing. Basically we use two mnemonics as a check list of what must be in. Responsibility for the power of our words and the outcome of the campaign is ours!

3 **PASS** equals:

Purpose

We must outline and reiterate the purpose of our organisation (environmental conservation) and concentrate on the specific purpose of this campaign (to secure additional funds for footpath protection).

Audience

Our audience is primarily existing members but we can also target those who have written to us or shown an interest in other ways. We may also tap into others who have a particular interest in footpaths. We have to generate excitement and interest in footpaths, access to them and the need for their protection.

Structure

The material must be consistent with existing corporate designs/logos and colours – with limited flexibility. We may use three or five page fold outs (A4 or A5 size). There may be a separate letter and post-back card as an alternative to incorporating them in the fold out. Materials used must be consistent with our 'conservation' role.

Style

As with all copy and design we should aim for:

- Simplicity of message – what we are doing and why
- Interest in the message – the relevance to you, the reader
- Facts about footpaths and the threat to them
- Honesty about ourselves and the issues

As an organisation we are politically neutral, serious but not stuffy, radical about the issues we support, energetic and lively. The style of our material should reflect this.

4 **AIDA** equals:

Attention

This is best secured by originality of text and design (including colours) which makes a dramatic impact. Brevity and small areas of text are the general rule. Define the relationship which exists between you (the reader) and this issue.

Interest

The following facts must be presented in an interesting manner: the choices we face; the impact of losses to date; future scenarios; the benefits of footpath protection. Be emphatic and instructive.

Desire

Generate in the reader a desire to help through positive motivations – concern for the countryside, health benefits, footpaths as testaments to the past and present.

Maintain desire by offering options to contribute and easy ways to do so.

Ensure reader/contributor 'feels good' about proposed action.

Action

Be clear about what we are asking the reader to do. Encourage the quickest possible response by post, e-mail or telephone. Offer thank you.

5 I hope this memo is useful and I look forward to an early meeting with you to begin our research and planning for the campaign.

11 Toy fair

(a)

> **Examiner's comments**. Good answers included the usual agenda items (in correct order) and the two specifically asked for concerning the exhibition. Exceptional candidates included a proposal/motion on one of these topics.

OUTLINE AGENDA

The next monthly sales meeting will take place in the conference room at 8.30am on 12 June.

1. Apologies for Absence
2. Minutes of the last Meeting
3. Matters Arising
4. Sales Report
5. Company Stand at Frankfurt International Toy Fair

6 Carriage of Selected products to the Fair
7 Staffing Requirements for the Fair
8 Any other business
9 Date of next meeting

(b) (i)

> **Examiner's comments**. Better candidates went beyond 'smile at customers' or 'don't yawn' and highlighted reminders by giving examples of 'positive' body language in context.

MEMO

To: Staff Manning the Stand (FITF)
From: Henry House
Date: 12 June 2000
Subject: Body Language at Frankfurt Fair

As this is the first time that any of us has been involved in an international fair I feel that we should consider the implications-one of which is the use of effective body language.

Visitors will, in the main, be Europeans but even so there are cultural differences which we should note. They include a formality of dress and address as well as, more often than not, the shaking of hands when meeting and taking leave of guests.

We should be sensitive also to indications visitors may give of their 'personal space' requirements, or the need for quiet reflection.

There will be a private area for one-to-one conversations and order-taking. There will be chairs and a low table with refreshments available if required. These should be used as you see fit.

Fairs are tiring events but we must be as positive in approach at the end of the day as at the beginning which means that we are welcoming through our expressions, gestures and posture. We can relax in the evening!

(ii)

> **Examiner's comments**. Candidates wrote strong answers on the value of exhibitions, but few could suggest measures in relation to sales, leads or customer feedback.

MEMO

To: All Staff
From: Henry House
Date: 12 June 2000
Subject: **Evaluating the Sales Impact of Exhibitions**

Exhibitions are important due to the following.

- They expose our company to a wider audience of directly interested potential customers.
- They secure repeat and new sales.
- They indicate which of our lines are likely to succeed.

- They maintain company visibility.
- They allow networking.

All of these activities help secure our sales objectives but we must also attempt to measure the value of this type of activity.

I maintain that some benefits are extremely difficult to quantify but in PR terms alone the benefits of a photograph of, for example, royalty visiting our stand is enormous. Our presence reassures existing customers and impresses/attracts new ones.

Measures worth taking include the following.

- Listing all return cards.
- Listing orders taken at the fair.
- Noting results of follow-up letters and calls.
- Noting new ideas gleaned at the fair.

12 It's your letter

> **Examiner's comments**. Many answers to part (a) were deficient because they did not detail the date, invoice number or amount; specify the need for prompt payment.
>
> Weaknesses to answers in part (b) included insufficient content relating to letter layout and a somewhat 'aggressive' tone.

(a)

Taylor Made Consultants
Knot House, Stitch Lane
Rugby 2XP 4PL

Mr R W Short
Manager
Accounts Department
Toobig Services
Fort Knox
Birkenhead

8 December 20X7

Dear Mr Short

Re: Taylor-made invoice 286, 1 June 20X7

As a significant and valued client, I was pleased to complete work for your company in June this year. The work was on behalf of your Marketing Department and was commissioned by the manager, Anna Ford.

Since June I have made several telephone calls to your department to try to determine whether my invoice had been received and when it was likely to be actioned for payment. I appreciate that it may be difficult to follow the progress of an invoice from a new service supplier. I have therefore enclosed a copy invoice with this letter and ask if you would kindly arrange payment as soon as possible (you will note that my normal payment terms are within one calendar month).

Please contact me if you would like to clarify any aspect of this matter.

Yours sincerely

Joy Taylor

(b) **MEMORANDUM**

To: All staff
From: Joy Taylor
Ref: JT/OM16
Date: 9 December 20X7
Subject: Business letters – layout and style

You will recognise the importance of maintaining an excellent standard of written communications with our business associates, suppliers and clients. To that end, I am writing to everyone to ask you to observe the following points regarding layout, tone and style.

1 *Layout.* The layout of a letter conveys the all important first impression and helps the recipient to locate information quickly. You are asked to check that you are following the office standard format for the following.

Letterhead
References, date and headings
Recipient's name and address
Greetings and closure
Subject headings and main body

2 *Tone and style.* The purpose of our letters is to maintain or initiate business relationships, promote understanding and initiate action. Please check that your letters are friendly and positive and contain the following.

An introduction and explanation of the letter's purpose
Acknowledgement of previous correspondence
A logical development of the content
A conclusion which summarises and reiterates the main purpose of the letter

I believe that by following these guidelines we will promote our professional image and the development of the company.

13 Furry foods

Examiner's comments.

(a) Many candidates wrote a report instead of producing the three slides required by the question. Slides frequently contained too many words. Many failed to produce the slide showing the pet food sector as a proportion of the market. Good candidates recognised the design, layout and textual requirements of effective slides.

(b) There was little attempt to analyse or interpret the data.

(c) Press release formats were frequently wrong and written as advertisements – even to the point of including money off vouchers! Candidates should demonstrate their understanding of the PR role in business communications.

(a) *Slide 1*

Pet product market (£bn) 1995

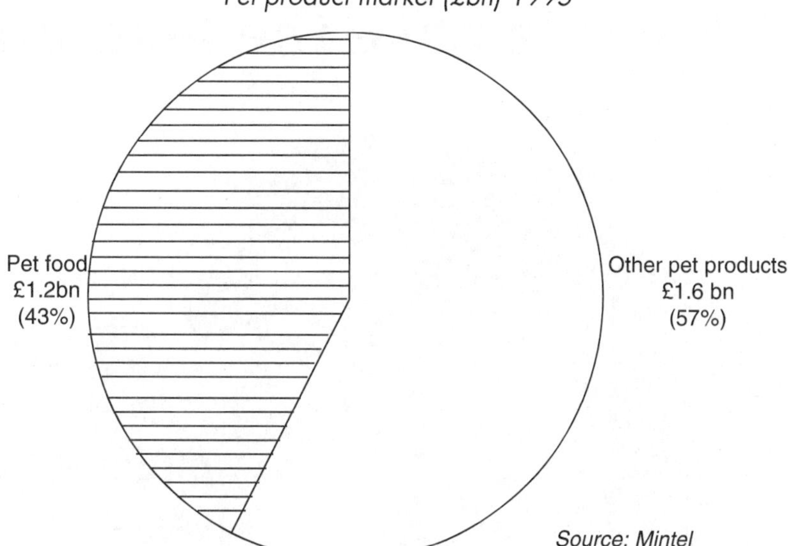

Slide 2

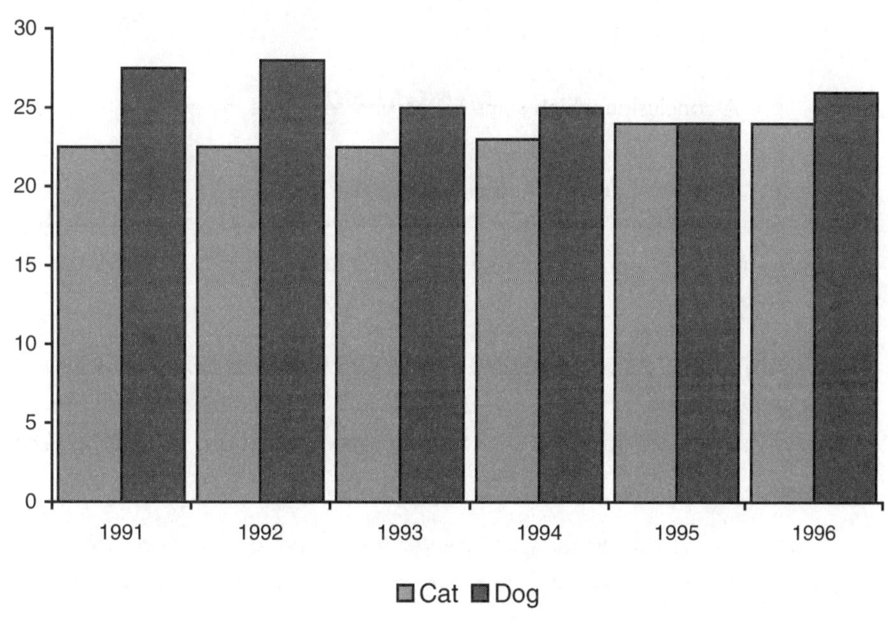

Source: TGI BMRB 1991-96 Mintel

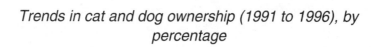

Slide 3

Why cats have the lead on dogs

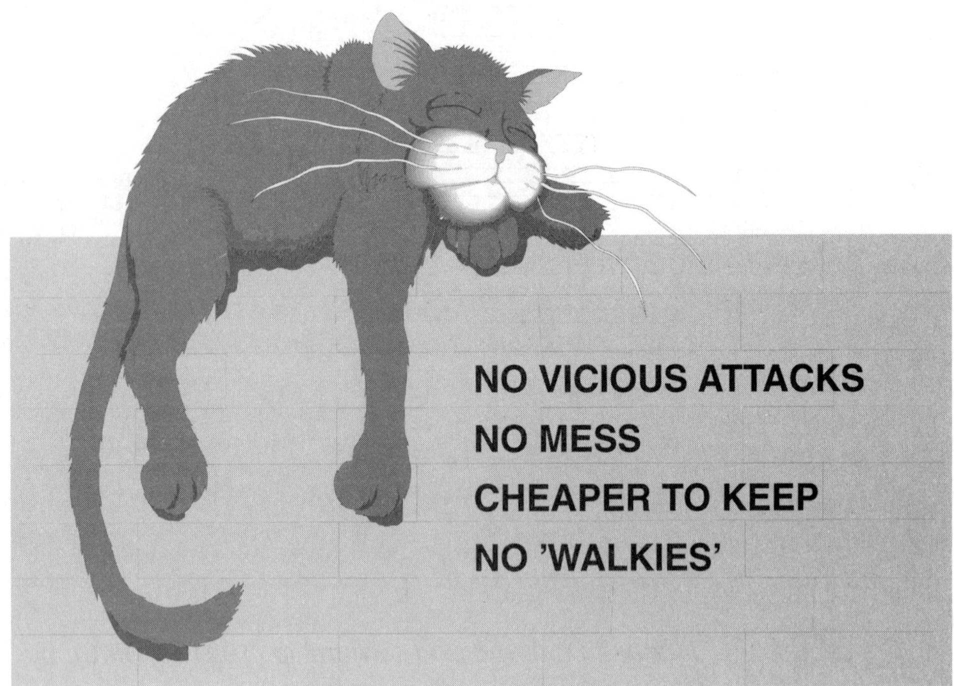

NO VICIOUS ATTACKS
NO MESS
CHEAPER TO KEEP
NO 'WALKIES'

Cats are a more purrfect pet

Source: Marketing Magazine

(b) **MEMORANDUM**

To: Ian Boxer, Distribution Manager
From: Oscar Blacksmith, Marketing Assistant
Date: 8 June 1998
Subject: Retail sales of cat and dog food

Introduction

Using recent data on trends in retail sales of cat and dog food from the different types of outlet which we supply, I have detailed my comments below. Please note that the data is for 1993 and 1995. Even so, I trust that it will be of use for your logistical planning.

Findings

Total sales of dog food were greater than sales of cat food (1995 – £720m compared with £620m for cats). The percentage increase over the two years was 17% for cat food and only 4.5% for dog food.

Multiple grocers dominate both markets increasing their market share over the two years. They alone account for the volume increase in cat food sales between 1993 and 1995 and represent £480m of the 1995 total (77%). Cat food sales to the independents, others and pet trade were virtually static. There was a small decrease in total co-op sales.

Multiple grocers captured most of the increase in dog food sales, the total being £400m in 1995. The pet trade achieved a small increase to approximately £180m. Others also recorded a small increase but their total share was a little less than £40m. The co-ops and independents recorded small decreases.

Please contact me if you require further information.

(c) *Press release*

Furry Foods
Carpet Square
Pawchester
SC1 4PU

8 June 1996

PRESS RELEASE – FOR IMMEDIATE RELEASE

CATS TAKE THE BISCUIT

Trials indicate that Biskies are about to make a significant impact on the dry cat food market in the UK and Europe. 'They are' states Sophie Kate, Marketing Director at Furry Foods, 'an irresistible, nutritionally complete, nugget shaped cat biscuit. Biskies are being launched this month at a time of year when moist food can attract insects. Biskies are hygienic and allow cats to browse'.

Cat owners will welcome this product, which has the flavour of fish without the unpleasant odour. Biskies come in three box sizes which are easy to open and reseal. The contents do not deteriorate.

Stocks will be available from all your usual pet food suppliers from 10 June.

Contact: Isa Cooke, 10697 24 24 24

Ends

Note

Furry Foods, UK's largest cat food supplier has been established for over 30 years. The Biskies product is a result of two years' research and is their first dry food product for cats.

14 Customer care

Tutorial note. This answer has managed to identify some good practical tactics that could be adopted by the airline and has been able to illustrate knowledge about effective customer care well. The answer is also well presented and thus received marks for this.

Examiner's comment: summary/extracts. There was a general tendency to deliver answers in a general context and not in the context of air travel.

(a) **Report on Improving Customer Care**

To: C Broomfield, Marketing Manager
From: D Brindly, Trainee Marketing Executive
Date: 7th December 2000

Introduction

This report will highlight the key practical approaches which our company could undertake to improve the standard of customer care for passengers who have experienced problems within our organisation.

Customer care aims to close the gap between customer expectations and their experience. It is a policy and a set of activities used by a business to bridge this gap.

(i) **Practical Approaches to Customer Care**

To improve customer care it is important to describe the shortfall between expectation and experience. In this case a one hour delay to the journey time occurred in both directions. Our organisation must understand the extent of the problem fully and implement a strategic response within the operating procedures of the business.

We need to ensure that the problem is then corrected. In this case, we need to make sure that effective communication is introduced to inform the customers of any difficulties and also to offer some compensation commensurate with the failure of the service in order to retain customer loyalty. In understanding that some customers will be continuing their journey on connecting flights it would be sensible to provide personal assistance by our staff for these passengers.

This may include complementary meals and drinks, use of the executive lounge as well as accurate, alternative flight details. We also need to provide information and explanation of the cause of delay including likely waiting times and ensure regular updates are provided to the customers. For longer term delays, suitable accommodation would also have to be provided. Particular customer needs would have to be understood as part of the decision making process.

The personal service offered to the delayed passengers should include the collection of personal details to enable correspondence to be undertaken after the event to retail the customer loyalty and make the customer feel appreciated.

The use of IT could be embraced in this process, as the Internet and teletext can be used to provide minute to minute accurate information for customers facing such problems, to make alternative arrangements prior to departing for the airport.

It is important to demonstrate a proactive approach to the solutions being offered to customers to ensure the reputation of the organisation is maintained.

(b) **Steps in Establishing Effective Customer Care**

The practical steps in establishing an effective customer care programme should be as follows:

(i) **Customer Orientation**

Fundamentally, the company must establish a customer-wide orientation. A well-defined mission statement is needed, unifying all members of the company.

(ii) **Customer Requirements**

Customers' needs and requirements must be researched and clearly defined.

(iii) **Management Commitment**

There must be commitment from all staff and most importantly from top management levels.

(iv) **Up-to-date Information**

This must be collected regularly from marketing research, and disseminated throughout the organisation. Customer feedback, for example from surveys, is vitally important to identify changes in the market, the macro-environment and competitors' actions. This information must be used to inform decision making and to design the products and services which we offer.

(v) **Regular progress report**

These should be distributed to keep the staff informed.

(vi) **Customer Care Specifications**

Specifications or plans will aid understanding of the process and improve staff motivation.

(vii) **Measurement and Control**

The measurement and control of the whole cycle of planning, implementation and control is very important. Monitoring our customer service levels and customer satisfaction will enable the company to improve its service – a key to customer care.

(viii) **Conclusion**

Customer care is a crucial company wide method of securing customer loyalty and is key to ensuring long term profitability for the organisation.

15 Customer contact

EITHER

Training Session

Customer Care Programme

Non-verbal Communication and Complaint Handling

Length of session: one hour **Place:** Company Training Room

Training Resources: VCR and monitor, video tape, response and feedback sheets

Notes on Training Session Structure

Introduction: Nature and importance of non verbal communication in context of customer care and complaint handling

Aims: To describe non verbal communication.
To illustrate the impact of good and poor non verbal communication.
To practise non verbal communication.

Structure

Lecture:

(a) What is meant by non verbal communication
- Tone of voice
- Body language
- Active listening

(b) Why excellent non verbal communication is important (include examples of culturally different behaviour)

Demonstration:

(a) Examples of poor non verbal communication
- Video excerpts

1 Assistant becomes exasperated, sarcastic and angry with customer who has, it turns out, a justified complaint but was not good at explaining his situation.

2 Assistant shrugs shoulders and attempts to ignore complaint.

Trainees complete proforma recording examples of poor behaviour in action.

Company example – hand out written case study of poor telephone listening based on a call relevant to the company.

Trainees complete exercise and discuss.

(b) Examples of excellent non verbal communication

- Video excerpts

1 Assistant checks information received from customer and makes suggestions: listens attentively, acknowledges store liability and reduces anger by responses.

2 Discussion and preparation of check list of appropriate responses with trainee participation.

(c) Practise through role play exercises and feedback.

Summary

Review training session and areas covered.

Conclusion

The importance of non verbal communication in working and social life.

OR

Training notes

Training Session

Customer care programme

Customer feedback and its impact on the company's customer communications

Length of session: One hour **Place:** Company Training Room

Training Resources: VCR and monitor, video tape (Tom Peters), response and feedback sheets.

Notes on Training Session Structure

Aims: To establish the importance of customer care.
To show how feedback is essential to customer care.
To show how feedback may influence company's customer communication.

Introduction: Definition of customer care.
The external/internal impact on the company of good/poor customer care.

Lecture: The importance of the feedback loop in the sender/receiver model.
The effects of not having feedback in customer care situations.
(examples will include loss of business, poor reputation, loss of customers)

Video: The effects of having good feedback loops (show Tom Peters (Excellence series) or similar and discuss examples shown (eg assistant who crosses Town to obtain shoes for customer, staff who participate in decision making)

Lecture: Feedback methods currently used by company with methods which might be used (deductions from immediate responses, EPOS systems, market research/soliciting feedback, customer complaints, interactive communication – website, focus group)

Summary

Review the training session and ask trainees to prepare personal action plans based on the issues raised

Conclusion

Note that poor customer care means that customers become ex-customers and that good customer care is the key to building continuing relationships.

16 Databases

> **Examiner's comments**. Not a popular question and those candidates who answered it generally had insufficient knowledge to provide examples of organisations using innovative software to achieve Customer Relationship Management solutions.

REPORT

To: Mr Salim Malik
From: Ms Jane Dell
Date: 16 December 2000
Subject: The use of databases to improve customer relationships

Introduction

This report outlines the merits of using databases to improve customer relationships and shows how this is done in two different types of organisation.

Background

We recognise the increasing use of computerised databases in our daily lives. Our mobile phone accounts, tax returns and vehicle licence renewals provide just three examples of how data is collected, stored and ultimately used to provide us with a timely and accurate service. We acknowledge their efficiency and effectiveness.

Customer relationships

Traditionally, customers have had to access a service themselves and allow sufficient time for the company to respond. They have to complete forms providing personal details such as address, date of birth etc on innumerable occasions. Now, with the help of databases, companies can be proactive and anticipate a customer's needs with the minimum administrative burden to either party. Companies can buy addresses and personal details to help them target and respond to potential customers. It is helpful to the customer, for example, to give only his postcode and then for the company to confirm his address from details already stored in the company's database.

Once a customer purchases goods, the database of these transactions can be used to:

- **Inform** the customer of special events and promotions
- **Remind** the customer of due dates for services or renewals
- **Prompt** the customer to buy into new or additional services

With total **integration** of databases there will be less duplication of the same information, and common up to date information for all departments to share will become the norm.

Examples of databases in use

1 **Building societies**

Building societies, especially those which have remained mutuals, have over the last year or two, recognised the potential uses of the data which they hold about both borrowers and savers. They are adding on banking and loan services as well as stock-broking and life insurance. They know from their databases key information such as impending house moves, retirement and mortgage completion dates and can, through marketing, try to 'piggy back' another service onto this.

2 **Supermarket/retail sector**

This sector was perhaps the first to use databases to improve its levels of service. On the basis of volume sales returns from stores they can optimise the value of their shelf space and provide the goods which customers are wanting to buy. They can also maintain appropriate stock levels at their warehouses – taking into account seasonal and day of the week variations, thus reducing the number of occasions when they are out of stock.

Individual sales can be monitored through till receipts and loyalty cards. This data can be used as the basis for promotions, special offers, and possibly preferred customer status, as well as targeted additional services.

Through the Internet, a completely new stay at home shopping service has become available.

Conclusion

There is every indication that customers welcome the additional level of service – as long as the personal information held is the minimum required and is used confidentially. They appreciate the idea that companies are able to anticipate their needs and give them timely reminders.

I recommend that we should investigate this matter further.

Answers to pilot paper

Part A

1 (a)

Industry Update Report on Small Car Market

For the attention of: Fay Renton, Marketing Manager, Ford (UK)
Written by: Jeremy Barton, Product Manager – Ford Fiesta (UK)
Date: 12 June 2002

1. **Terms of Reference**

This report has been written as part of Ford (UK)'s market intelligence system to identify the key trends in the market in relation to the Ford Fiesta brand.

2. **Methodology**

Key data in the consumer and trade press have been analysed in addition to analysing research undertaken by Lifestyle Research.

3. **Findings**

3.1. *Ford Fiesta Sales*

3.1.1 The Ford Fiesta was the top selling small car in 1997 with sales of 125K out of a total market of 393K. Its nearest competitor was the Vauxhall Corsa with sales of 80K, followed by Renault Clio with 60,000, Peugeot 306 with 50,000 and Rover 200 with 40,000. A large proportion of Fiestas, are either second-hand cars or form part of company fleets.

3.2. *Advertising Spend*

3.2.1. Car manufacturers spent £120M on advertising in the small car market. Advertising clearly plays a crucial role in building image and perception of differences in price and finance. Television and newspaper advertising were used extensively by all players in the market.

3.3. *Advertising Media*

3.3.1. Respondents, who were drivers intending to buy new cars, were asked about the media they considered would be most informative. Local press advertisements were considered to be most informative by 40% of respondents, national press advertisements by 27%, television advertisements by 18%, direct mailshots by 11% and radio by 4%.

3.3.2. Car advertisements appear to have more impact on men than women. Men tend to have better recall for the less prominent models.

3.3.3. 27% of drivers remember receiving a direct mailshot promoting a car during the previous month. For company and new car drivers, this figure rose to 37%.

3.3.4. For drivers who were asked about lifestyle activities in the past six months: 30% had watched a specialist car programme on television; 25% had visited a car dealer; 8% had taken a test drive and 5% had requested a brochure.

3.4. *Advertising Recall*

3.4.1. 44% of drivers surveyed in the last month recalled Ford advertising, while 38% recalled Vauxhall advertising, 33% recalled Nissan, 27% recalled Renault and only 17% recalled advertising for Rover cars.

3.4.2. ABC1 drivers are more aware of car advertising than C2DE groups, this may be down to the fact that ABC1 drivers are twice as likely to be driving new as opposed to second-hand cars. Amongst C2DE drivers, Ford, Nissan and Vauxhall have the highest recall levels.

4. **Conclusions**

4.1. Whilst the Ford Fiesta is the leader in the small car market, the market is very competitive and we must strive to maintain our market share. At present advertising spend is high in this sector but it is necessary to further research competitor levels of activity and spend in relation to ours.

4.2. Ford achieved the highest rate of advertising recall but again there was close competition from the likes of Vauxhall and Nissan. Certain socio-economic groupings and males are more aware of car advertising than others. This information would be even more useful if we were clear exactly which grouping our buyers are in.

4.3. Press advertising is considered to be much more informative than television, radio and mailshots. It may be necessary to look at our promotions mix in the light of this considering that we have put most of our efforts into television advertising in the last year. However, this information must be considered in relation to other survey results which show that brand building is a must in this market and television is the most effective medium to achieve this objective. In addition, it appears that the majority of prospective car buyers watch specialist car programmes and we have successful bought television spots in the breaks in these programmes.

5. **Recommendations**

From the information in the report it is recommended that further research is undertaken. This needs to identify the advertising spend of our competitors and find out more about our core target market. In addition we need to research the effectiveness of our current promotional campaigns with pre and post-campaign research to see how awareness levels have been affected. The research should also investigate the merits of changing the proportion of spend away from television in favour of press advertising.

(b) Appendix (i): Line graph to show advertising recall in the past month.

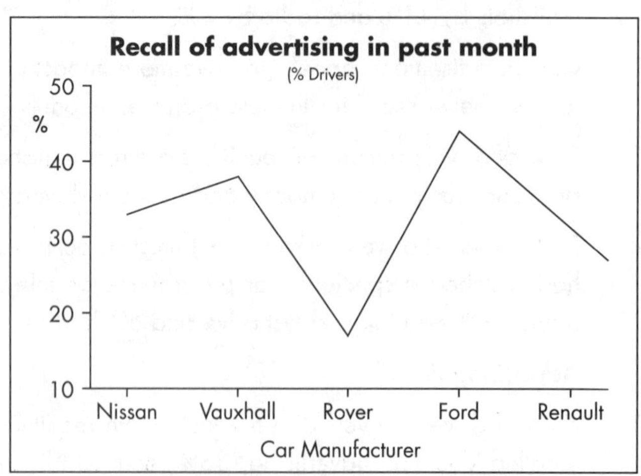

Source: Car Market, July 1998

Appendix (ii): Component bar chart to show number of cars owned per home.

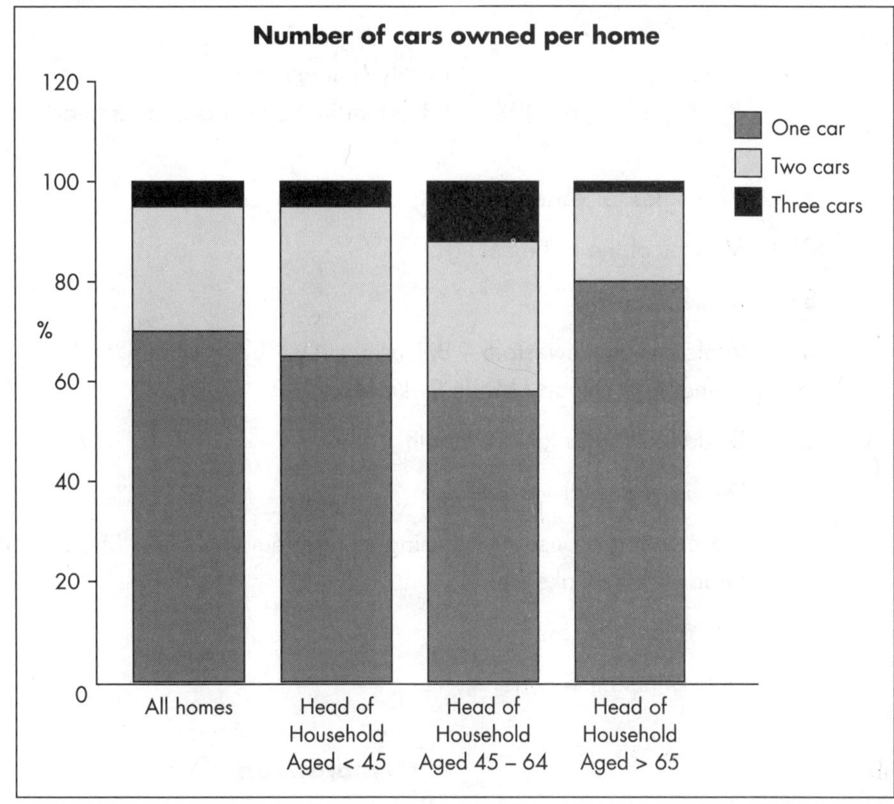

Source: Car Market, May 1998

Appendix (iii): Pie chart to show market share of top six best selling small cars.

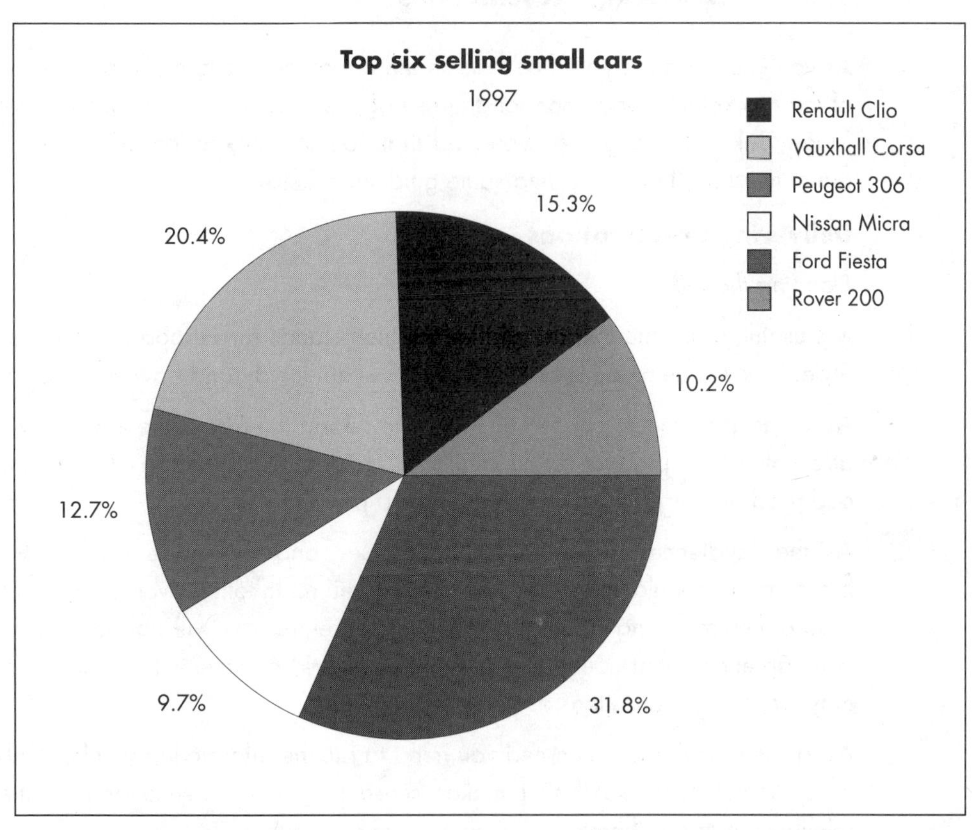

Source: Car Market, March 1998

Part B

2 (a)

Agenda

Monthly Marketing Meeting

12 June 200X – at 3.00pm in the boardroom at head office.

1 Apologies for absence

2 Minutes of the last meeting

3 Matters arising

4 Welcome to new staff – Bill Bright, Database Manager & Lee Shu Fan, Product Manager for Ready Made Cake Mixes

5 Update on sales for last month

6 Discuss plans for website

7 Presentation on use of licensing toy trademarks – Lee Shu Fan, Product Manager, Ready Made Cake Mixes

8 Any other business

9 Date of next meeting

(b)

Memorandum

To: Lee Shu Fan, Product Manager
From: Len Lerer, Marketing Manager
Date: 12 June 2002
Subject: **Delivering Presentations**

As you know, one of your first tasks in the department is to make a presentation to the rest of the Marketing Department on the use of licensing toy trademarks in relation the Ready Made Cake Mix range. As you said that you are inexperienced as far as presentations are concerned, I am providing some guidelines below.

Delivering Presentations

Planning the talk

It is useful to use the PASS framework which stands for Purpose, Audience, Structure and Style. This will help you focus on what you want to say and how you should say it.

As far as 'purpose' is concerned, this is to inform the rest of the team how it is possible to add value to a product range aimed at children, if current toy trademarks are licensed and used on our packaging and used as a product theme.

As the 'audience' will be your colleagues and there are only eight of them, the presentation should be geared to this situation. In other words, you will not be in a lecture theatre facing a large audience. Therefore you will not need a microphone and you can expect that colleagues may casually add comments to what you are saying and may want to ask questions as you proceed.

As far as structure is concerned you need to put the information you have about your topic in a logical order so that it makes sense to your audience and so they know what relevance it has to them and if they need to act upon it.

As the audience is small your style of delivery therefore should be standing up in front of them but you will need to be standing physically close to them (particularly as our meeting room is not very large). Also they all have marketing expertise and knowledge of our product range, so you do not need to provide a long introduction to the product and you can use the jargon that we all use on a daily basis in the department.

You may want to use a PowerPoint presentation on the laptop or use acetates on the Overhead Projector. These visual aids can be very useful when presenting figures and images of trademarks. Speak to my secretary if you need help in preparing them.

With regard to your subject matter, obviously you have a great deal of expertise in this area but you will need to be selective with the material you use as you do not want to overload your audience with information. Obviously you will want to provide some anecdotal examples of how you have used trademarks in other markets.

Delivering the talk

In addition to what you say you also need to think about how you say things. This means considering your body language and your voice.

With regard to voice, you need to speak clearly and project your voice because the acoustics in the meeting room are not very good. In addition the road outside has busy traffic. You will also need to consider your tone of voice. While it is good to sound authoritative, i.e. to sound like you know what you are talking about, you also need to be friendly as the audience will be comprised of your co-workers who you want to get to know better.

Do not rush what you are saying – if you feel that you are doing so – slow the pace down. Don't be afraid to pause to place emphasis on important points. Try to vary the pitch of your voice – allowing it to rise and fall appropriately – as nothing is worse than someone droning on in a monotone voice. If you feel that you are drifting into a monotone remember you are enthusiastic about this topic and want to tell people about it.

In relation to your body language you need to keep eye contact with your audience and avoid reading everything from notes. Stand upright with your shoulders relaxed. This will help you breathe easily and will assist in projecting your voice. Don't fold your arms as this can represent a barrier to your audience.

By all means move around as you don't need to stand rigid in one spot but do not move around too much or use distracting mannerisms such as scratching your head or playing with the change in your trouser pockets.

Logistical Arrangements

You do not need to worry about the physical layout of the room as it will be arranged it the usual round-table arrangement we use. The lighting will be dimmed to accommodate visual aids and refreshments will be served at the end of the meeting.

One thing though, if the windows are open, you may want to close them to avoid the distracting noise of outside traffic.

Hope this helps. If you need any further information please do not hesitate to ask.

Len

3

Dog Day Afternoon Rescue Home
Lowton Rise
Runcorn
Cheshire

Mr T Rowland
Director of Corporate Communications
Shell House
Lowton
Runcorn
Cheshire

12 June 2002

Dear Mr Rowland

As a local resident to the Shell complex, I was greatly heartened yesterday evening after hearing the interview on Granada Reports about how your company has put aside funds for community related projects.

I was also interested to hear that part of Shell's corporate social responsibility policy is to make funds available for animal and wildlife issues. So, on behalf of the Dog Day Afternoon Rescue Home I would be grateful if you would consider our request for newsletter sponsorship.

We send out the newsletter twice a year and each year look for corporate sponsorship of £2,000 to cover printing and distribution costs with amounts left over going towards the running of the home. The newsletter is distributed to 1,000 contributors who either donate money or gifts or offer homes to abandoned dogs. The home is well-known and often gets local press coverage so this year we have decided to expand our distribution to an additional 4,000 residents in the Runcorn area.

The newsletter features the latest news about the home and in last year's issue (please see enclosed) we featured successes we have had in finding homes for dogs, information about how to care for dogs and what to do in the case of finding an abandoned dog.

As you can see from the last edition, the sponsor's name is prominently displayed on the front page and throughout the newsletter. In addition on the back page there is an opportunity to make a statement about your company's support of the charity and anything else that you wish to communicate about your company.

As I know you are concerned that local residents have a good impression about the work that Shell does, and the part it plays in the life of the local community, by sponsoring our newsletter you would have an excellent opportunity to promote a favourable image of the company to the residents of Runcorn.

Yours sincerely

Diana Butler
Sponsorship Assistant

4 Email

To: Jane Jones, Production Department, Marketing Recruitment
From: Gill Driscoll, Marketing Manager, ToyZone
Date: 12 June 2001

As discussed, here is the information for the full-page advert that I require in the July edition of Marketing Recruitment.

Printing and layout instructions

Job title 'Product Manager' to be printed Arial Bold, font size 20, centred. The rest of the copy to be in font size 12 with spacing as indicated below. Please use company logo (you already have our artwork) using correct pantone reference Purple 284.

Copy for advertisement

Product Manager

ToyZone, one of the largest toy manufacturers in the UK, is looking for a Product Manager to be responsible for our new product range aimed at the under-5's age group. We operate in a dynamic and exciting industry and our Marketing team is full of fun – just like our customers.

The job involves researching our market, analysing findings, working with production, commissioning packaging and advertising work and working with our new database system.

The person we are looking for will be:

- Be CIM qualified
- Have experience at brand/product management level
- Not necessary to have experience of the toy sector but an enthusiasm for this area is a must
- Energetic, reliable and looking for more responsibility
- Some knowledge of database management desirable

In return you would receive £27K p.a. plus a competitive benefit package, including company car, BUPA cover, 25 days' holiday and lots of toy samples.

Send your CV, and a covering letter explaining why you are suitable for the job, to Bryan Springings, Human Resource Department, ToyZone, Wigan, Lancashire, LA2 5TY or bspringings@toyzone.co.uk.

5 Email

Ideal Boilers Limited

To: Fabian Petit, Marketing Services Director
From: Andrew Bosson, Customer Care Manager
Date: 12 June 2002

Dear Fabian

Since the restructure of the Customer Care, Marketing and Sales departments, I thought you may want an update on what we do in the Customer Care team and the latest issues that are affecting us.

Currently the Customer Care team's main responsibility has been for the customer care helpline. This helpline deals with both trade enquiries from plumbers wanting parts or who want to reserve places on our training courses and customers who have either bought a boiler from us and have problems with it or wish to extend the warranty.

The help line is run by 10 call centre operatives and is a major part of the business. The role of our telephone operatives is vital because these staff are the first point or only contact most of our customers have with the company. The consequences of poor service or an abrupt attitude can create a negative impression with our customers.

The plumbers who fit our boilers are considered to be a key customer group because they influence householders with regard to the purchase decision of household boilers. The most obvious group of customers are the those who actually buy our boilers but then go on to have a problem with the product. Customers need to be dealt with carefully to avoid them passing on negative word of mouth publicity for the company. In addition we want these customers to feel happy about dealing with our company so that they are keen to purchase an extended service and warranty agreement from us. Consequently the customer care line has the firm's reputation in its hands.

However, in the last piece of research I conducted into customer complaints, I found that there had been a rise of 30% in the number of complaints recorded in the complaints book since last year.

Many complaints are about the harsh tone of voice used by staff and the poor telephone manner that our operatives have. Many customers feel they are an annoying interruption. An overriding comment was that they do not feel that their custom is valued.

Since the call centre was opened three years ago, staffing has reduced from 15 to 10 because the 5 staff who have left, have not been replaced. Staff feel that they have been under increasing pressure recently and they find that customers are angry before they start speaking to them because they have had to wait so long to be connected. In addition since the supervisor has left, staff are unsure of some of the procedures connected with call-out costs and they have made mistakes with ordering wrong parts.

To solve the problems a new Customer Care Programme needs to be introduced to improve standards and morale in the department.

The key stages would be to share the research findings with staff and also the recognition that more staff are needed. An urgent recruitment programme will be necessary to make up the shortfall in staff.

It will then be necessary to embark on a programme of staff training about the role of the help line and the ambassadorial role of operatives in the call centre. It will be essential to set out the required performance levels in terms of when calls should be answered and how they should be answered. It will also be necessary to clarify the procedures for call out costs. We should undertake some sales training to assist staff in selling extended warranties.

It will also be important to explain how performance in future will be monitored and to establish a reward system for staff who exceed standards.

The implementation of this new Customer Care programmes should improve morale and the situation for staff. This in turn should have a positive effect on how customers are treated which will produce good relationships and in the long term create the kind of relationships that lead to repeat purchase and recommendation to others.

I would like to meet to discuss the costings involved with the implementation and running of this customer care programme.

Regards

Andrew B.

6 **Internal report for the attention of Mike Mouseman, Promotions Manager**

Written by Minny Mouseland, Promotions Assistant

12 June 2002

Promotions Plan for ***Mouse Mat Mania***

Background Information

Mouse Mat Mania produces personalised mousemats for companies from a whole range of industry sectors. These companies buy our mousemats because they wish to promote their company name to their clients. From looking at our order book, it seems that the main decision makers in organisations for this sort of purchase decision, is the Marketing Manager, which means we need to target this person within companies. Most of our previous orders have been from SME businesses and although we have a big customer base of computer and software companies, this is not the only sector that we need to aim for.

As a result of the desk research into our customer base which identifies the need to reach marketing managers within SME's in various industry sectors and the need to maintain our profile in the computer industry, this report identifies a number of effective promotion tools for the coming year.

Findings

Advertising

Advertising in the computer trade press needs to be maintained at the same level as last year's advertising. In addition advertising needs to be placed in the marketing trade press such as Marketing, Marketing Week, Campaign and Marketing Business (the CIM members' magazine).

Direct Marketing & Sales Promotion

To use direct marketing as an effective tool, it will be essential to rent a B2B (business to business) list from a company called MarketScan which can identify marketing managers in a number of different market sectors that we may wish to mail to. To ensure that the mailshot is opened and read, it would be good to send an example of one of Mousemat Mania's own mousemats to promote our company name on the desk of Marketing Managers up and down the country.

Exhibitions

It is essential that Mousemat Mania continues to have its stand at the annual Incentives and Sales promotion exhibition at the NEC this year. It will be necessary to update our sales leaflets and backdrop information used on the stand, to include our new 'liquid filled' mat product.

Public Relations

The fact that the company has developed the new liquid filled mat product which has excellent novelty value and also produces a stress-relieving effect computer users, provides an ideal opportunity to gain press coverage in the marketing trade press and the consumer press. This will entail sending press releases to the relevant media and providing a spokesperson who can be interviewed on radio and local news television. This activity will raise our profile considerably.

Conclusion

This outline for our forthcoming promotions activity identifies that Mousemat Mania should concentrate on its current advertising in the computer industry trade press but should also extend it advertising to the marketing trade press .

The company should continue its normal attendance at trade exhibitions. The company should continue to use direct marketing but use it more creatively with the use of free samples to provide more impact for our message.

Finally the company should also consider using PR as it is a relatively inexpensive promotion tool which can work alongside our other efforts to raise our profile.

7 (a) **FLY BY AIRWAYS**

Draft notes for presentation to Marketing Team by Communications Manager

Topic: Benefits of using visual methods to convey complex data

Introduction

The purpose of the presentation – we are increasingly being asked to provide a great deal of complex data for a variety of reasons e.g. internal monthly sales figures and in the production of the annual report.

Findings

- For internal company communications it is much quicker for our colleagues to understand information that has been 'treated' and put into a more understandable and visual format, eg sales figures in bar charts, market share shown in a pie chart.
- Visual data such as line graphs and histograms make it easier for colleagues to make comparisons with previous years and to identify trends in the market. This assists decision-making.
- For external communications such as our annual report the use of visual and graphical information has much more impact than just using narrative/text only information.
- Graphical and visual information that is well produced and uses colour and the benefits of computer software such as 3-D gives a more professional and sophisticated image of the airline and its operations.

Conclusion

There is a need for both our internal and external communications to use visual methods to communicate complex or numerical information to provide both impact and to promote understanding of the information being conveyed.

(b) **FLY BY AIRWAYS**

Draft notes for presentation to Marketing Team by Communications Manager

Topic: How implementing the latest ICT tools can help improve communications and relationships with customers

Introduction

The purpose of this presentation is to update you with the latest ICT tools and to discuss how they can be used to improve customer communication. Fly By is committed to improving its relationships with customers and using ICT in innovative ways.

Findings

- Internal communication between staff at the different sites in Scotland and the East Midlands will be vastly improved once the videoconference link has been installed at the end of the month. In future you should consider whether travel to meetings at another site are necessary when it is possible to use the videoconference link. Bookings to use it can be made through the facilities manager.
- The website has been improved so that customers can not only now check fares and flight times, they can also purchase tickets online and even request particular seat allocations.
- Our new customer database has been improved since the last mailshot we sent to customers asking them to update their details. This information in addition to the new 'Specis' software CRM (Customer Relationship Marketing) system means we can use our customer information to make our communications with them more meaningful. The database means we can categorise our customers into different groups e.g. business class, economy class UK business flights, short haul city break travellers at weekends and long haul flight purchasers. By knowing about our customers' purchase behaviour means that we can build meaningful relationships with them by adding value to the service we offer them and by targeting relevant offers to them.
- Our new automated call handling system has significantly reduced the waiting times for customers during peak call times, as much of the information they want about flight times can be provided without having to speak to a customer service operative.
- WAP (Wireless Application Protocol) means that we can send text messages to customers' mobile telephones about flight offers or other important information.

Conclusion

Fly by is committed to using technological developments in an innovative way that helps us improve our service to customers and the way we communicate with them.

Topic: How implementing the latest ICT tools can help improve communications and relationships with customers

[illegible]

Objective testing bank questions and answers

1 Fill in the blanks in the following quotation.

'In the one-to-one future, it won't be how much you know about (1) ....your customers that's important, but how much you know about (2)......... of your customers.' (Peppers and Rogers.)

2 Which of the following would NOT be classified as a connected stakeholder of an organisation?

A Shareholder
B Retailer
C Bank
D International Standards Organisation

3 List the main sources of the following inputs to the organisation open system.

Input	**Source**
Goods/services	
Skills and time	
Capital	
Revenue	
Market information	

4 The internal customer concept suggests that any unit of the organisation whose task contributes to the task of other units can be regarded as the best available supplier of those services to the organisation.

☐ True ☐ False

5 Complete the following phrases, which describe the key characteristics of relationship marketing.

- Focus on (1)......... customer satisfaction and (2).......... rather than attraction
- Development of two-way (3)......... with customers
- Seeking (4)......... with customers rather than (5)..........

dialogue	retention	long-term	transactions	relationships

6 Relationship marketing means focusing solely on relationships with the customer.

☐ True ☐ False

7 Which of the following is NOT a trend currently affecting consumers in Western societies.

A Erosion of job security
B Challenging traditional gender roles
C More family and leisure time
D Information overload

8 A management orientation which focuses on continuous improvement of product quality is the:

Marketing concept	Selling concept	Production concept	Product concept

9 The term for all the individuals who buy or acquire goods and services for personal consumption is the 'target market'.

☐ True ☐ False

10 Which of the following is *not* a stage in the *consumer* decision-making process?

A Need recognition
B Supplier selection
C Evaluation of alternatives
D Post-purchase evaluation

11 Consumers' recall of advertising messages can be explained by the process of:

Selective attention	Selective retention	Selective distortion	Selective testing

12 .... is the most basic underlying influence on an individual's behaviour and values.

13 What is the name given to the DMU in an organisation?

14 The role of the gatekeeper comes under which of the following categories of influence on organisational purchasing?

A Environmental
B Organisational
C Interpersonal
D Personal

15 The Attention stage of the AIDA model is an example of which kind of psychological process?

Cognitive	Affective	Conative	Behavioural

16 Put the following stages of the 'buyer readiness' model into the correct sequence.

Knowledge Conviction Preference Awareness Liking Purchase

17 The range of data from which consumers assimilate product data is:

☐ Increasing ☐ Decreasing

18 Which of the following is a benefit of an Integrated Marketing Communications approach?

A Greater efficiency and accountability in marketing management
B More effective response to the increasing information needs of stakeholders
C Reduction of information overload and clutter
D All of the above

19 Realising that someone is speaking in a sarcastic tone of voice is an example of which communication activity?

Encoding	Medium	Decoding	Feedback

20 Which of the following would not be a member of a 'channel audience' of promotional communications?

A Distributor
B Sales agent
C Retailer
D Employee

21 The total marketing communications programme of the organisation, consisting of a specific combination or blend of tools used to reach the target market for a given product or brand is called the ....

22 Lobbying local or central government is a public relations activity.

☐ True ☐ False

23 Which of the following is not an example of direct response advertising?

A A magazine advertisement with a cut out response coupon
B A TV advertisement giving a Web site contact address
C A TV advertisement giving list of stockists
D An interactive TV advertisement allowing you to transfer to a Web site

24 What is the most favoured form of promotion in (a) industrial/business markets? (b) consumer markets?

25 Which of the following scenarios would be best suited by 'informative advertising'?

Early stage of the product life cycle	Product modifications have been made
The product is a complex offering	All of these

26 .... ads are display ads placed on another organisation's Web page, acting as a link to your own Web site.

27 Sales promotions are promotional incentives, aimed exclusively at consumers, which seek to stimulate or bring forward purchases.

☐ True ☐ False

28 List the three main elements of a direct mail package.

29 Which of the following is *not* the purpose of Point of Sale promotional materials?

A To attract buyer attention
B To compete for attention with other products' branding
C To compete for attention with the retailer's branding
D To motivate the retailer to carry the brand

30 The way a company is perceived by its publics is:

Corporate image	Corporate identity
Brand image	Employer brand

31 .... is any form of non-paid, non-personal marketing communication.

32 In which model of public relations practice is PR seen as a process of mediating or opening communication channels between the organisation and its publics?

A Press agency/publicity
B Public information
C Two-way asymmetric
D Two-way symmetric

33 The sole purpose of trade exhibitions is to increase sales revenue.

☐ True ☐ False

34 Which of the following electronic media are distinguished by *interactivity*?

A Voice-response kiosks
B Electronic catalogues
C Direct Response Television
D All of the above

35 What do (a) ISDN and (b) EDI stand for?

36. Which of the following (you may select more than one) describes the 'stickiness' of a Web site?

How long visits spend at a site	How much money visitors spend at a site
How many ad clicks the visitor makes	How often visitors return to a site

37 The Internet culture is generally extremely supportive of advertising and direct marketing.

☐ True ☐ False

38 List two e-commerce alternatives to a company's selling products on its own transaction-based Web site.

39 The different use of language by a marketing specialist and a product specialist when communicating, affecting their ability to understand one another, is an example of:

A Physical noise
B Technical noise
C Social noise
D Psychological noise

40 What are the three 'talking habits' which most annoy others (in America)?

41 The skill of 'reflecting back' what another person is saying (including how they feel about it) is a distinctive feature of:

Passive listening	Listening for content	Critical listening	Empathetic listening

42 How you dress is an aspect of non-verbal communication.

☐ True ☐ False

43 List Sir Ernest Gower's five Cs of good communication.

44 Which of the following would not represent a balanced message structure.

A Advantages + disadvantages
B Assertion + illustration
C Similarities + differences
D Option 1 + Option 2 + recommendation

45 Which of the following stylistic devices (you may select more than one), would be used to add credibility to a message?

☐ Statistics ☐ Narrative ☐ Quotations ☐ Anecdote ☐ Description

☐ Facts ☐ Metaphor ☐ Opinion

46 A passive sentence construction is a feature of an informal writing style.

☐ True ☐ False

47 Which of the following (you may choose more than one) are more important in telephone communication than in a face-to-face meeting?

Verbal feedback	Identification of the speaker	Explanations of what you are doing	Courtesy

48 Which of the following qualities of visual aids may *not* contribute to their effectiveness?

A The use of animation
B Pre-prepared sequence, timing and pace of progression
C Do not require the audience to take notes
D All of the above

49 What is a 'quorum' (referring to a meeting)?

50 The person who usually signs the minutes of a meeting is the:

A Proposer
B Seconder
C Secretary
D Chair

51 In a letter or e-mail, what does 'cc. (name)' mean?

52 The purpose of an adjustment letter is to:

A Make a complaint
B Respond to a complaint
C Secure payment of a debt
D Request changes to a previous arrangement

53 A memorandum addressed to a named individual requires the complimentary close 'Yours sincerely'.

☐ True ☐ False

54 Which of the headings usually found in a formal report is missing from the following randomly ordered list?

Terms of reference/Introduction
Recommendations
Findings
Procedure/method

55 The following table shows the customer complaints per month over a six month period.

Jan	*Feb*	*Mar*	*Apr*	*May*	*Jun*
0	26	0	5	3	2

What is the 'average customer complaints per month' using:

(1) the arithmetic mean
(2) the median
(3) the mode

56 If the market share for a product decreases when promotional spending is reduced, this is called a:

☐ Negative correlation ☐ Positive correlation

57 A bar chart which uses two or more bars to present subdivisions of data is a ....bar chart.

58 If an element occupies 20% of a total amount, how many degrees will it occupy in a pie chart?

59 Complete the gaps in the following list of Rosabeth Moss Kanter's five challenges for companies that want to develop close links with their customers.

- Understanding .... the customer is
- Making the customer a .... of one's own organisation
- Making the customer .... to all employees
- .... faithful customers
- Having the .... to handle critical incidents

60 The process of applying quality values and aspirations to the management of all resources and relationships within the firm, as a means of developing and sustaining a culture of continuous improvement which focuses on meeting customers' expectations is called:

A Quality control
B Quality assurance
C Total quality management
D Process realignment

61 Only negative feedback from customers is useful for improving organisational performance.

☐ True ☐ False

62 List the seven steps in setting up a customer care programme.

63 In Customer Relations Management, the synchronisation of field sales team laptops with the central database is called:

A CRM
B SFA
C CTI
D ACH

64 Which of the following is *not* a key customer service benefit of ICT?

A Speed
B Interactivity
C Security
D Integration

65 Complete the following sentence using the words provided.

'(1)......... marketing has been defined as 'an (2).......... approach to marketing which uses individually (3)........... marketing media and channels to extend (4) .... to a company's target audience, stimulate their (5).......... and stay (6)......... to them by recording and keeping an electronic (1).......... memory of customer, (7)........... and all communication and commercial (8)............'

- help
- close
- contacts
- prospect
- demand
- database
- interactive
- addressable

1 (1) All (2) Each

2 D

3

Input	Source
Goods/services	Suppliers
Skills and time	Labour pool
Capital	Financiers
Revenue	Customers
Market information	Customers
	Market research organisations

4 False

5 (1) long-term, (2) retention, (3) dialogue, (4) relationships, (5) transactions

6 False

7 C

8 Product concept

9 False

10 B

11 Selective retention

12 Culture

13 Buying centre

14 C

15 Cognitive

16 Awareness; knowledge; liking; preference; conviction; purchase

17 Increasing

18 D

19 Decoding

20 D

21 The promotion mix

22 True

23 C

24 (a) Personal selling, (b) advertising.

25 All of these

26 Banner

27 False

28 Envelope, letter, reply device

29 C

30 Corporate image

31 Publicity

32 D

33 False

34 D

35 Integrated Systems Digital Network; Electronic Data Interchange

36 How long visitors spend at the site; how frequently they return to the site

37 False

38 Storefronts; auction sites.

39 C

40 Interrupting, swearing, mumbling or talking too softly

41 Empathetic listening

42 True

43 Concise, clear, courteous, correct, complete

44 B

45 Statistics, quotations, facts

46 False

47 Verbal feedback, identification of the speaker, explanations of what you are doing

48 D

49 The minimum number of people required by the regulations to properly constitute the meeting.

50 D

51 A copy of the letter/e-mail has also been sent to the named individual.

52 B

53 False

54 Conclusions

55 (1) 6, (2) 2.5, (3) 0

56 Positive correlation

57 Multiple

58 72%

59 who; member; visible; rewarding; flexibility

60 C

61 False

62 Identify key dimensions of service quality; set standards for service delivery; set sup systems for service delivery; analyse employee training needs; develop training programmes; set up systems to measure and monitor success; set up performance-related pay and recognition systems.

63 B (Sales Force Automation)

64 C

65 (1) database, (2) interactive, (3) addressable, (4) help, (5) demand, (6) close, (7) prospect, (8) contacts

List of key concepts and Index

KEY CONCEPTS

Above-the-line promotion, 110
Advertising, 110
Agenda, 289
Association, 349
Attitudes, 69
Audience, 250
Average, 348

Banner advertisements, 144
Below-the-line promotion, 110

Central tendency, 348
Classes, 347
Computer Telephony Integration, 421
Congeniality, 261
Consumer buyer behaviour, 57
Consumerism, 31
Correlation, 349
Credibility, 261
Crisis communication, 166
CRM (Customer Relationship Management), 416
Culture, 72
Customer, 9
Customer care, 379
Customer relations, 36

Data mining, 200
Database marketing, 199, 412
Decision Making Unit (DMU), 58
Direct mail, 147
Direct marketing, 119
Direct response advertisements, 142
Distortion, 228

E-commerce, 208
Empathy, 236
Experience, 379

Feedback, 97
Five Cs, 261
Formal meetings, 288
Frequency distribution, 347

Integrated Marketing Communications (IMC), 90
Internal customer, 10
ISDN, 194
Issues management, 166

Marketing communications, 86
Marketing concept, 29
Motivation, 67

Negotiation, 295
Noise, 229
Non-verbal communication, 238

Organisational buyer behaviour, 57

Pass, 250
Perception, 68
Point of sale, 153
Précis, 351
Process alignment, 386
Promotion mix, 108
Public relations, 114, 162
Publicity, 114
Pull strategy, 124
Purpose, 250
Push strategy, 124

Quality, 384

Relationship marketing, 39

Sales promotion, 112
Sponsorship, 177
Stakeholders, 12
Structure, 250
Style, 250
Summary, 351

Telemarketing, 276
They act as an aid to communication, 283
They use a visual image, 283
Time series, 349
TQM, 384
Trend, 349

User, 9

Variables, 349
Visual aids, 283

Accuracy, 258
Ace, 34
Adjustment, 313
Advertising, 132, 192
Advertising copy, 137
Advertising design, 139
Advertising media, 111, 133
Advertising Standards Authority, 138
Advertorial, 172
Affectivity, 99
Age, 70, 230
AIDA model, 100
Allen, 40
Allen et al, 199, 412, 422
American Association of Advertising Agencies, 90
American Marketing Association, 110
Appearance, 241, 261
Armstrong, 47
Articles, 172
Articulation, 232
Artist/designer brief, 324
Aspirational groups, 71
Assael, 67, 68
Attention, 63
Attentive listening, 237
Auction sites, 211
Audience, 253, 278
Audience size, 254
Authority, 261
Automated call handling, 420
Averages, 348

Balance, 259, 260
Band width, 190
Banner advertising, 144
Bar charts, 358
Baverstock, 4
Bell curve agenda, 290
Benefits, 64
Bias, 262
Black box model, 99
Body language, 239
Brand, 5, 176
Brand awareness, 93
Brief, 141, 324
Business communication, 94
Business markets, 124
Business to business, 383
Buyer behaviour, 56
Buyer readiness, 100, 125
Buying centre, 61

Call centres, 120
Care line, 392
Catalogue, 324
Catalogue marketing, 120
Chairperson, 287
Chart, 357
Chartered Institute of Marketing, 4
Charts, 357
Christopher, Payne & Ballantyne, 381
Chronological order, 259
Circular letter, 317
Class, 230
Classification, 257, 346
Clichés, 312
Cognition, 99
Collecting statistics, 346
Communication, 5, 190
Communication process, 95, 227
Competition, 30
Complaints, 394, 396
Complimentary close, 308
Conation, 99
Conclusions, 330
Congeniality, 262, 278
Consumer markets, 124
Consumerism, 31
Consumers, 8, 60
Context, 254
Control systems, 384
Cookies, 201
Corporate culture, 35
Corporate hospitality, 181
Corporate identity, 115, 174, 206
Correlation, 349, 355, 363
Credibility, 231, 279
Crisis communication, 163
Critical listening, 236
CRM (Customer Relationship Management), 416
Crozier, 393
Customer, 8
Customer care, 6
Customer care programme, 400
Customer charters, 31
Customer choice, 10
Customer data, 19., 411
Customer expectations, 423
Customer feedback, 411
Customer focus, 30, 34, 378
Customer loyalty, 32, 37, 382
Customer relations, 36, 163
Customer research, 206
Customer retention, 38, 382
Customer reward programmes, 37
Customer satisfaction, 30

Customer service, 189, 206, 379, 388
Customer specific marketing, 200
Customisation, 40, 415

Daffy, 386
Data capture, 18
Data Protection Act, 414
Data security, 414
Databases, 18, 40, 148,199, 410, 416
Decision making process (DMP), 62
Decision making unit, 57
Delivery, 233, 282
Dependent variable, 357
Description, 265
Diagrams, 365, 366
Dibb et al, 56
Differences, 230
Differentiation, 382
Digital television, 201
Direct mail, 119
Direct marketing, 192, 205
Direct response advertising, 119, 205
Direct Response Television, 202
Direct supply, 119
Disinterestedness, 262
Distortion, 228
Distractions, 255
Distributors, 14
Drawings, 365
Drucker, 29

Ebbs, 189
E-commerce, 417
ECRM, 416
Education, 230
Electronic Data Interchange, 198
Electronic funds transfer, 198
E-mail, 119, 195, 216, 317, 415
E-mail marketing, 216
E-mail messages, 318
Embargo, 170
Empathetic listening, 236
Employee communication, 46
Employee relations, 47, 163
Employer branding, 46
EPOS, 19
Ethnic, 230
Evaluating PR, 168
Exhibition planning, 182
Exhibitions, 118, 181
Expectations, 65
Experiential learning, 243
Explanation, 265
Expression, 239
Extranet, 196
E-zines, 206

Face-to-face communication, 271, 389
Family, 60
Family life cycle, 70
FAQ, 415
Feedback, 60, 231 235, 242, 380
File attachments, 317
Fill, 86
Financial public relations, 163
Flow charts, 367
Flyer, 263
Form reports, 333
Formal, 327
Formal meetings, 288, 292
Formal report, 329
Format, 320
Forsyth, 6, 91
Frequency distribution, 347
Friendship groups, 60
Fulfilment, 143
Function of communication, 93

Gantt charts, 361
Government, 163
Graphs, 357
Grass roots marketing, 206
Grunig and Hunt, 163

Hammer and Champy, 20
Hearing, 234
Honey & Mumford, 243

ICT, 190, 410
Impersonal, 264
Impersonality, 328
Importance of the customer, 4, 30
Important to listen, 234
Independent variable, 357
Informal, 327
Informal meetings, 292
Informal report, 331, 332
Informercial, 172
Institute of Public Relations, 114, 162
Institute of Sales Promotion, 112
Intentions, 262
Interactive catalogues, 202
Interactive kiosks, 203
Interactive newsletters, 203
Interactive television, 202
Interactive voice response, 420

Interactivity, 191, 415
Interest, 278
Interest groups, 60
Interface management, 7
Intermediaries, 14
Internal communications, 92
Internal customers, 8, 46, 380, 383
Internal marketing, 11, 192
International audience, 255
Internet, 201, 204
Internet customer profile, 423
Intonation, 233
Intranet, 196
Issues management, 115, 163

Jargon, 228
Job advertisements, 145
Johns, 9, 393, 394

Kanter, 381
Kotler, 4, 17, 28, 61, 63, 102, 117, 132
Krol and Ferguson, 190, 207

Language, 255
Larry L Barker, 234
Lavidge and Steiner, 100
Layout instructions, 141
Layouts, 309
Learning, 68
Learning cycle, 243
Legal environment, 32
Lele and Sheth, 35
Letter, 304
Letter of request, 316
Letter's contents, 311
Lifestyle, 70
Line graphs, 357
Links, 258
Listening, 231
Listening for content, 235
Logical progression, 258
Logo, 175
Loose insert, 143
Loyalty programmes, 205

Mail order, 120, 146
Main points, 258
Market research, 17, 411
Marketing concept, 28
Marketing planning, 89
Marketing strategies, 87
Maslow, 67
Mass marketing, 21
McDonald, 29
McKenna, 257
McNamara, 162
M-commerce, 203
Mean, 348
Media, 96, 97
Media planning, 112
Media relations, 115, 163
Media release, 168
Media/press relations, 205
Median, 348
Medium, 254
Meeting agenda, 290
Meetings, 287
Meetings planning, 288
Memo, 319
Memorandum format, 320
Message planning, 97
Meta-communication, 238
Michael Stevens, 279
Mini-cases, 351
Minutes, 293
Mobile telecommunications, 194
Mode, 349
Modelling, 242
Mood, 264
Mullin, 119, 147, 202
Multi media, 191, 204
Multiple bar chart, 359

Narrative, 265
National differences, 230
Network marketing, 192
Network relationships, 40
Newspapers, 134
Newsworthiness, 169
Nilson, 35
Noise, 97
Non-verbal, 231
Non-verbal communication, 238, 239
Not-for-profit, 383
Notice (of meeting), 289
Notices, 325

Objectivity, 328
Occasional reports, 327
Occupation, 70
One-to-one marketing, 21, 200
On-line customer care, 417, 422
On-line shopping, 208
Open system, 6
Oral communication, 270
Ordering, 257

Organisational buying, 73
Overload, 231
Overton, 388

Pace, 233
Partnership, 380
PASS, 250
Pattern, 257
Peppers and Rogers, 21
Percentages, 355
Personal selling, 111, 117
Personalisation, 191, 415
Persuade, 316
Persuasive, 321
Persuasive style, 265
Peters, 386
Peters and Waterman, 383
Pictograms, 362
Pie charts, 361
Planning messages, 250
Point of sale (POS), 153
Point of sale materials, 113
POMMIE, 131
Postma, 18, 34, 38, 119, 191, 199, 204, 413
Potential problems, 231
PR, 192
Precision, 329
Presentations, 277
Press releases, 115, 165, 168, 186
Privacy, 423
Procedures manual, 327
Product life cycle, 124
Product packaging, 114, 154
Product samples, 165
Programme sponsorship, 116
Promotion, 100
Promotion budget, 126
Promotion mix strategies, 122
Promotion planning, 123
Promotional mix, 192
Promotions marketing, 150
Pubic relations, 206
Public sector, 383
Publicity, 163, 165
Publicity 'stunts', 165
Publics, 163

Questions, 265

Racial, 230
Reading, 231
Recognise non-verbal, 239
Recommendations, 330
Recruitment, 46
Reference groups, 71
Reflecting back, 236
Relationship marketing, 39, 206, 319, 378, 381
Report, 327
Report letter, 314
Research sample, 355
RFM analysis, 412
Role, 255
Routine reports, 327

Sales Force Automation (SFA), 417
Sales promotion, 150, 192, 205
Sales support, 118, 192
Satisfaction, 378
Scatter diagrams, 363
Schenk and English, 210
Selection, 257
Self-development, 243
Selling proposition, 136
Sex, 230
Shaw and Stone, 199
SMART objective, 244
Smith, 180
SMS, 204
SMS text messaging, 203
Social responsibility, 142
Spam, 217
Sponsorship, 116, 163
Sponsorship programme, 180
Stage-fright, 282
Stakeholders, 8
Standard elements, 305
Statistics, 265
Statistics, 346
Storefronts, 211
Strategic planning, 87
Structure, 257, 311, 321
Style, 261, 312, 321
Sub-cultures, 72
Summarising, 351
Suppliers, 14

Tables, 356
Tact, 312
Tactics and techniques, 273
Target audience, 13,17, 59, 96, 97
Target Australia, 398
Target marketing, 21
Taylor, 20
Telecommunications, 193
Tele-marketing, 120

Telephone, 322, 392
Teletext, 202
Terms of reference, 327, 330
Text messaging (SMS), 119
Tip ons, 143
Tone, 264
Total quality management, 384
Trade fairs, 118, 181
Trade promotions, 151
Trends, 349, 355

UK Institute of Direct Marketing, 119
Unique selling proposition, 133
US Direct Marketing Association, 118

Values, 380
Video conferencing, 419
Video telephones, 419
Viral marketing, 206
Virtual team, 197
Visual aids, 281, 283
Voice mail, 420
Volume, 233, 257

Web casts, 419
Web site, 19, 144, 211, 415
Web sites, 120
Webster and Wind, 74
Win-lose outcome, 295
Win-win' approach, 295
Work group, 60
World Wide Web, 205

Youth market, 71

CIM Order

To BPP Publishing Ltd, Aldine Place, London W12 8AA
Tel: 020 8740 2211. Fax: 020 8740 1184
email: publishing@bpp.com
online: www.bpp.com

Mr/Mrs/Ms (Full name)

Daytime delivery address

Postcode

Daytime Tel　　Date of exam (month/year)

		8/02 Texts	9/02 Kits	Success Tapes (old syllabus)
STAGE 1 NEW SYLLABUS				
1	Marketing Fundamentals	£18.95 ☐	£9.95 ☐	£12.95 ☐
2	Marketing Environment	£18.95 ☐	£9.95 ☐	£12.95 ☐
3	Customer Communications	£18.95 ☐	£9.95 ☐	£12.95 ☐
4	Marketing in Practice	£18.95 ☐	£9.95 ☐	£12.95 ☐
ADVANCED CERTIFICATE OLD SYLLABUS *				
5	The Marketing Customer Interface	£18.95 ☐	£9.95 ☐	£12.95 ☐
6	Management Information for Marketing Decisions	£18.95 ☐	£9.95 ☐	£12.95 ☐
7	Effective Management for Marketing	£18.95 ☐	£9.95 ☐	£12.95 ☐
8	Marketing Operations	£18.95 ☐	£9.95 ☐	£12.95 ☐
DIPLOMA OLD SYLLABUS *				
9	Integrated Marketing Communications	£18.95 ☐	£9.95 ☐	£12.95 ☐
10	International Marketing Strategy	£18.95 ☐	£9.95 ☐	£12.95 ☐
11	Strategic Marketing Management: Planning and Control	£18.95 ☐	£9.95 ☐	£12.95 ☐
12	Strategic Marketing Management: Analysis and Decision (9/02)	£25.95 ☐	N/A	N/A

* Texts and kits for remaining new syllabus items will be available in the spring and summer of 2003.

SUBTOTAL £

POSTAGE & PACKING

Study Texts

	First	Each extra	
UK	£3.00	£2.00	£
Europe*	£5.00	£4.00	£
Rest of world	£20.00	£10.00	£

Kits/Success Tapes

	First	Each extra	
UK	£2.00	£1.00	£
Europe*	£2.50	£1.00	£
Rest of world	£15.00	£8.00	£

Grand Total (Cheques to *BPP Publishing*) I enclose a cheque for (incl. Postage) £

Or charge to Access/Visa/Switch

Card Number

Expiry date　　Start Date

Issue Number (Switch Only)

Signature

We aim to deliver to all UK addresses inside 5 working days. A signature will be required. Orders to all EU addresses should be delivered within 6 working days.

All other orders to overseas addresses should be delivered within 8 working days.

* Europe includes the Republic of Ireland and the Channel Islands.

REVIEW FORM & FREE PRIZE DRAW

All original review forms from the entire BPP range, completed with genuine comments, will be entered into one of two draws on 31 January 2003 and 30 July 2003. The names on the first four forms picked out on each occasion will be sent a cheque for £50.

Name: ______________________ **Address:** ______________________

____

____

How have you used this Text?
(Tick one box only)

- ☐ Self study (book only)
- ☐ On a course: college______________
- ☐ With BPP Home Study package
- ☐ Other ______________

Why did you decide to purchase this Text?
(Tick one box only)

- ☐ Have used companion Kit
- ☐ Have used BPP Texts in the past
- ☐ Recommendation by friend/colleague
- ☐ Recommendation by a lecturer at college
- ☐ Saw advertising in journals
- ☐ Saw website
- ☐ Other ______________

During the past six months do you recall seeing/receiving any of the following?
(Tick as many boxes as are relevant)

- ☐ Our advertisement in the *Marketing Success*
- ☐ Our advertisement in *Marketing Business*
- ☐ Our brochure with a letter through the post
- ☐ Our brochure with *Marketing Business*
- ☐ Saw website

Which (if any) aspects of our advertising do you find useful?
(Tick as many boxes as are relevant)

- ☐ Prices and publication dates of new editions
- ☐ Information on product content
- ☐ Facility to order books off-the-page
- ☐ None of the above

Have you used the companion Practice & Revision Kit for this subject? ☐ Yes ☐ No

Have you used the companion Success Tapes for this subject? ☐ Yes ☐ No

Your ratings, comments and suggestions would be appreciated on the following areas.

	Very useful	*Useful*	*Not useful*
Introductory section (How to use this text, study checklist, etc)	☐	☐	☐
Setting the Scene	☐	☐	☐
Syllabus coverage	☐	☐	☐
Action Programmes and Marketing at Work examples	☐	☐	☐
Chapter roundups	☐	☐	☐
Quick quizzes	☐	☐	☐
Illustrative questions	☐	☐	☐
Content of suggested answers	☐	☐	☐
Index	☐	☐	☐
Structure and presentation			

	Excellent	*Good*	*Adequate*	*Poor*
Overall opinion of this Text	☐	☐	☐	☐

Do you intend to continue using BPP Study Texts/Kits/Success Tapes? ☐ Yes ☐ No

Please note any further comments and suggestions/errors on the reverse of this page.

Please return to: Kate Machattie, BPP Publishing Ltd, FREEPOST, London, W12 8BR

REVIEW FORM & FREE PRIZE DRAW (continued)

Please note any further comments and suggestions/errors below.

FREE PRIZE DRAW RULES

1 Closing date for 31 January 2003 draw is 31 December 2002. Closing date for 31 July 2003 draw is 30 June 2003.

2 Restricted to entries with UK and Eire addresses only. BPP employees, their families and business associates are excluded.

3 No purchase necessary. Entry forms are available upon request from BPP Publishing. No more than one entry per title, per person. Draw restricted to persons aged 16 and over.

4 Winners will be notified by post and receive their cheques not later than 6 weeks after the relevant draw date. List of winners will be supplied on request.

5 The decision of the promoter in all matters is final and binding. No correspondence will be entered into.